P9-DOG-900

The Coriolis Group, LLC • 14455 North Hayden Road, Suite 220 • Scottsdale, Arizona 85260

Dear Reader:

Coriolis Technology Press was founded to create a very elite group of books: the ones you keep closest to your machine. Sure, everyone would like to have the Library of Congress at arm's reach, but in the real world, you have to choose the books you rely on every day *very* carefully.

To win a place for our books on that coveted shelf beside your PC, we guarantee several important qualities in every book we publish. These qualities are:

- *Technical accuracy*—It's no good if it doesn't work. Every Coriolis Technology Press book is reviewed by technical experts in the topic field, and is sent through several editing and proofreading passes in order to create the piece of work you now hold in your hands.

- *Innovative editorial design*—We've put years of research and refinement into the ways we present information in our books. Our books' editorial approach is uniquely designed to reflect the way people learn new technologies and search for solutions to technology problems.

- *Practical focus*—We put only pertinent information into our books and avoid any fluff. Every fact included between these two covers must serve the mission of the book as a whole.

- *Accessibility*—The information in a book is worthless unless you can find it quickly when you need it. We put a lot of effort into our indexes, and heavily cross-reference our chapters, to make it easy for you to move right to the information you need.

Here at The Coriolis Group we have been publishing and packaging books, technical journals, and training materials since 1989. We're programmers and authors ourselves, and we take an ongoing active role in defining what we publish and how we publish it. We have put a lot of thought into our books; please write to us at **ctp@coriolis.com** and let us know what you think. We hope that you're happy with the book in your hands, and that in the future, when you reach for software development and networking information, you'll turn to one of our books first.

Keith Weiskamp
President and CEO

Jeff Duntemann
VP and Editorial Director

Look for these related books from The Coriolis Group:

Windows 2000 Systems Programming Black Book
by Al Williams

Windows 2000 Registry Little Black Book
by Nathan Wallace

Windows 2000 Security Little Black Book
by Ian McLean

Windows 2000 Reducing TCO Little Black Book
by Robert E. Simanski

Windows 2000 Mac Support Little Black Book
by Gene Steinberg and Pieter Paulson

Windows 2000 Professional Advanced Configuration and Implementation
by Morten Strunge Nielsen

Windows 2000 Professional Upgrade Little Black Book
by Nathan Wallace

Also recently published by Coriolis Technology Press:

Exchange 2000 Server Black Book
by Marcus Goncalves

HTML Black Book
by Steven Holzner

About the Authors

Stu Sjouwerman is president of Sunbelt Software, an international B2B Internet company specializing in providing system management tools and network utilities to manage eBusinesses running on Windows NT/2000. He is the editor of Sunbelt's W2Knews (the original NTools E-news) that goes to 600,000 subscribers, and also the primary system operator for the MCSE, NTSYSADMIN, Exchange, and MSSQL discussion lists.

Barry Shilmover operates a computer training and consulting company in Calgary, Alberta. He has authored and co-authored several books ranging in topics from Exchange 5.5 to Windows NT to Novell NetWare. He specializes in Windows NT/2000 installation and configuration, network design, and Exchange 5.5/2000 implementations. When not working (rarely), he spends time with his wife Shawna, his son Jory, and his golden retriever (Vicky). Barry, Shawna, Jory, and Vicky are expecting a new addition to their family about the time this book is to be released. You can reach Barry via email at **books@shilmover.com**.

James Michael Stewart is a fulltime writer focusing on Windows NT and Internet topics. Most recently, he has worked on several titles in the Exam Cram and Exam Prep series. Michael has written articles for numerous print and online publications, including C|Net, Computer Currents, InfoWorld, Windows NT Magazine, and Datamation. He is also a regular speaker at Networld+Interop and TISC. Michael has been with LANWrights, Inc., a wholly own subsidiary of LeapIT.com, developing Windows NT and Windows 2000 MCSE-level courseware and training materials for several years. Including both print and online publication, as well as classroom presentation of training materials. He has been an MCSE since 1997. Michael graduated in 1992 from the University of Texas at Austin with a Bachelor's degree in philosophy. Despite his degree, his computer knowledge is self-acquired, based on over 17 years of hands-on experience. He spends his spare time learning to do everything, one hobby at a time. You can reach Michael by email at **michael@lanw.com**, or via the Web at **www.lanw.com/jmsbio.htm**.

Acknowledgments

All three of us would like to thank the team at LANWrights, Inc., for helping us put together a great book. We'd also like to thank the folks at The Coriolis Group: Charlotte Carpentier, Paula Kmetz, Sharon McCarson, and Meg Turecek for their help in geting this book to publication. Finally, thanks to Michelle Stroup, Bart Reed, and Emmett Dulaney for their wonderful attention to detail in their editorial and technical reviews of this book.

A book like this is usually a team effort. In this case, I'd like to thank Barry and Ed for their tireless efforts in making this into a useful resource that is also fun to read.
—*Stuart Sjouwerman*

I would like to extend a special thanks to my wife, Shawna, and my son, Jory. While writing this book, I had moved away to the Seattle area to work on a project. As expected, it was extremely difficult for my 2-year-old son to understand why Daddy did not live with us anymore. All is back to normal now. Shawna, thanks for being there for me when I needed you. While writing this book, my grandfather passed away at the ripe young age of 91. This book is therefore dedicated to him, Dr. S. Shilmover. We miss you. Special thanks also go to Dawn Rader (for keeping me on track) and Ed Tittel (for your constant help).
—*Barry Shilmover*

Thanks to my boss, Ed Tittel, for including me in this book. To my parents, Dave and Sue, thanks for your love and consistent support. To Mark, as best friends go, I couldn't have found better. To HERbert, I hope you adjust well to our new home and all the new roommates. And finally, as always, to Elvis—your strength, your will, and your passion are an inspiration to us all; I just wish we could all grow lamb chops.
—*James Michael Stewart*

Contents at a Glance

Table of Contents

Chapter 6
Windows 2000 Configuration 177

Chapter 9
The Windows 2000 Boot Process 309

Introduction

Welcome to the *Windows 2000 System Administrator's Black Book*. This book is designed to give you all the information you need to successfully manage a Windows 2000 system. Each chapter provides in-depth coverage of the terms and concepts involved in Windows 2000 systems management. Windows 2000 is by far the most advanced operating system released by Microsoft to date. It includes advanced management features that were sorely missing from Windows NT and previous versions of Windows operating systems.

This book provides in-depth detail of all the functions and features of installing, configuring, and maintaining Windows 2000. Each chapter provides hands-on solutions that give you the first-hand experience you'll need to work with Windows 2000 configuration and management.

What this Book Contains

The chapters of this book focus on the following topics:

Chapter 1 discusses the architecture of Windows 2000. This chapter explores how the environment is designed and how each element functions and provides the abilities you know and love.

Chapter 2 examines the differences and similarities between Windows 2000 and Windows NT 4.0.

Chapter 3 looks at the new directory services system of Windows 2000: Active Directory. How to install and work with this new technology is essential to enterprise network management.

Chapter 4 details the steps necessary for migrating from Windows NT 4.0 to Windows 2000. This move can be beneficial but there are some pitfalls to watch out for.

Chapter 5 discusses Windows 2000 installation, which is even more straightforward than ever, but you won't believe how many options or methods of installation are available.

Chapter 6 explores the capabilities of Windows 2000, such as faxing, resource management, file recovery, offline files, drive mount points, and more. This chapter discusses many of these features and how to configure them.

Chapter 7 discusses Windows 2000 file system support, including the FAT, FAT32, and NTFS file systems. With the addition of encryption and new methods of inheritance, you'll need to re-familiarize yourself with the file systems.

Chapter 8 takes a look at the abilities of Windows 2000 to interact with other systems over a network are astonishing. Learn about the new capabilities and new integrated functions.

Chapter 9 discusses the boot process, which is an essential function of Windows 2000. Learn about each step in the boot process and how you can modify booting to meet your needs or even perform troubleshooting and recovery.

Chapter 10 covers Windows 2000's new breed of administration tools made possible by the Microsoft Management Console.

Chapter 11 discusses the Windows 2000 Registry, which contains operating and parameter information for every aspect of the system. Learn about the Registry and how to safely modify it.

Chapter 12 explores data protection. Learn about the fault tolerant and recovery features of Windows 2000.

Chapter 13 explores IntelliMirror, which offers a new level of automated administration designed to grant access to user data anywhere on the network and even offline, deploy software, and enforce environment restrictions. With the integration of Remote Installation Services you can automate the deployment of Windows 2000 Professional and provide a 100% disaster recovery solution.

Chapter 14 discusses automating administrative tasks. Learn about the Windows Scripting Host and how to simplify your repetitive administrative tasks.

Chapter 15 discusses Windows 2000 tuning and performance. You can use System Monitor to watch for performance degradations, locate bottlenecks, and even perform capacity planning analysis.

Chapter 16 explores Windows 2000 application support. Learn how the environmental subsystems function and how you can extract the best capabilities from your applications.

Chapter 17 takes a look at the Windows 2000 print system, which has been enhanced with new features, including Internet printing.

Chapter 18 examines Windows 2000 security. With the addition of Kerberos, encryption, Group Policies and more, maintaining a security environment with Windows 2000 is easier than ever.

Chapter 19 discusses remote access and routing, which have been fully integrated into the networking architecture of Windows 2000. Learn how to configure a system for any inbound, outbound, or internal connection from dial-up to VPN.

Chapter 20 takes a look at some common troubleshooting techniques. When problems occur, use this handy collection of troubleshooting tips, tricks, and resolutions to restore your Windows 2000 system back to normal.

How to Use this Book

If you're a newcomer to Windows 2000, you should read the book from beginning to end because some topics build upon one another to provide complete coverage of Windows 2000 topics. If you are not familiar with some of the more basic tasks covered in earlier chapters, the more detailed, advanced management functions discussed in later chapters might not make much sense. This is particularly true in the areas of networking and Active Directory.

On the other hand, if you're a seasoned Windows veteran and need information on how to perform a certain action, thumb through the index or table of contents and jump right in! The Immediate Solutions sections of each chapter give you step-by-step instruction on how to install, manage, configure, and troubleshoot all areas of Windows 2000.

If you have questions or comments about this book, feel free to contact the authors via email at the following addresses: **w2knews@tampabay.rr.com** (Stu Sjouwerman), **books@shilmover.com** (Barry Shilmover), or **michael@lanw.com** (James Michael Stewart).

Thanks, and enjoy the book!

Chapter 1

Windows 2000 Architecture and Overview

In Depth

Over the past few years, the world has been transformed by the proliferation of computing devices—from networks to handheld assistants—and the explosion of the Internet. Microsoft has endeavored to stay at the forefront of this tidal wave by producing ever more advanced operating systems to take advantage of the new technologies and provide users with the broadest range of resource-access capabilities possible. Microsoft's latest operating system manifestation is Windows 2000, which boasts the strengths of Windows NT and Windows 98, combined with many new technologies and features. This new network operating system offers a solid platform for building communication and information-delivery systems of all sizes.

Windows 2000 Product Family

Microsoft has once again defined the standard against which all other operating systems are judged and all third-party vendors must compete. The Windows 2000 product family has four current members: Windows 2000 Professional, Windows 2000 Server, Windows 2000 Advanced Server, and Windows 2000 Datacenter Server. Although all are based on a common core, each version has specific features and components designed to support its unique purpose. Windows 2000 offers solid solutions for standalone systems and global networks alike.

Although Windows 2000 is the latest release from Microsoft, it is by no means the only or the last. Microsoft has definitive goals to provide full-featured operating systems for every computing device imaginable. Currently, Microsoft offers products for handheld devices to high-end server clusters (see Table 1.1).

NOTE: *Windows ME (Windows Millennium Edition) is the third edition of Windows 98, which is due to be released in the second half of 2000.*

Table 1.1 Microsoft operating systems for computing devices.

Computing Device Types	Operating System
Handheld PCs, PDA (personal digital assistant), and AutoPC	Windows CE (Compact Edition)
Terminals, thin clients, and network PCs	Windows Terminal Server (client software)

(continued)

Table 1.1   Microsoft operating systems for computing devices (continued).

Computing Device Types	Operating System
Notebooks, laptops, and portable computers	Windows 98, Windows 2000 Professional, and Windows ME
Workstation, standalone, and desktop systems	Windows 98, Windows 2000 Professional, and Windows ME
Servers	Windows 2000 Server and Windows 2000 Advanced Server
Server clusters	Windows 2000 Advanced Server and Windows 2000 Datacenter Server

Windows 2000 Professional

Windows 2000 Professional is designed primarily to serve as a client on a Windows 2000 network. However, it can also serve as a client on other networks, including Windows NT and NetWare, or it can function as a standalone system for isolated professional or personal home use. Windows 2000 Professional replaces Windows NT 4.0 Workstation as the network client of choice from Microsoft.

This version of Windows 2000 is tuned to maximize performance for foreground applications and Internet resource access. It offers a platform rich in multimedia support (audio and video), full support for Internet standards, and an intuitive layout and control scheme, all without sacrificing high performance, reliability, and security control.

Windows 2000 Server

Windows 2000 Server is designed to function as a network server in a Windows 2000 domain. It can be deployed as a domain controller or a member server. As a domain controller, the first Windows 2000 Server in a network establishes the domain and its Active Directory. All subsequent Windows 2000 Server domain controllers become peers in supporting the domain and its Active Directory. As a member server, Windows 2000 Server can support a wide range of applications and services, including, but not limited to, file sharing, printer sharing, and Internet Information Services (IIS) hosting (Web, FTP, email, and newsgroups).

This version of Windows 2000 is tuned to maximize the performance of network services for a growing user base. It offers a stable platform for hosting network applications and sharing various resources (such as files, printers, and Internet access).

Windows 2000 Server was designed to create and support a primarily Windows 2000 network; however, it is backward compatible with Windows NT. Therefore, you can create a domain network where a Windows NT Primary Domain Controller (PDC) and Windows 2000 Servers, acting as Backup Domain Controllers (BDCs), coexist. Windows 2000 Server can also be deployed in heterogeneous networks with NetWare and Unix systems. Windows 2000 Server offers sufficient capabilities to support small- to medium-sized networks.

Windows 2000 Advanced Server

Windows 2000 Advanced Server is designed to function as a high-end network server in a Windows 2000 domain. It has all the same base features and capabilities as Windows 2000 Server, but it offers more power and scalability. Advanced Server includes support for eight-way multiprocessing, 8GB of addressable physical RAM, network load balancing, and clustering. Therefore, although it can be deployed as a domain controller or a typical application server in a network, it is designed to offer enhanced performance for e-commerce and line-of-business applications.

Clustering is a computing technology in which two or more computers are connected to share the workload on a common application. Clustering allows more computing power to be leveraged against a single application while offering *fault tolerance* (the ability to continue functioning if a cluster member goes offline).

Windows 2000 Datacenter Server

Windows 2000 Datacenter Server is designed as an even more advanced and powerful network application server than Windows 2000 Advanced Server. It has all the same base features and capabilities as Windows 2000 Advanced Server (including network load balancing and clustering), with added support for up to 32 CPUs (or 64, through special original equipment manufacturer [OEM] versions) and 64GB of addressable physical RAM. Microsoft developed Datacenter Server to provide unparalleled power to support applications such as data warehousing, complex graphics rendering, realtime e-commerce transaction processing, and more. In effect, Microsoft has endeavored to create a server capable of supporting a wider variety of hardware than any previous version of Windows.

System Requirements

The base system requirements for all the Windows 2000 versions are the same. The base hardware requirements for Windows 2000 are:

- 133 MHz Intel Pentium or higher microprocessor(s) or compatible/clone
- VGA or higher resolution monitor and video adapter
- Keyboard
- Microsoft Mouse or compatible pointing device (optional)

TIP: *Pay attention to the need for more RAM and storage space on the more advanced versions.*

Requirements for installing from a CD-ROM:

- A compatible CD-ROM or DVD drive (a bootable drive is preferred)
- A 3.5-inch high-density floppy disk drive is required if the CD-ROM/DVD drive is not bootable

Requirements for installing from a network:

- A compatible network interface card and associated media cable
- Connection/access to a network share containing the setup files (that is, a shared folder or a shared CD-ROM/DVD drive)

Windows 2000 Professional system requirements:

- One or two processors can be present on a single computer
- 32MB of RAM minimum; 64MB RAM recommended; 4GB of RAM maximum
- 650MB of free hard drive space minimum; 2GB or more recommended (if you're installing over a network, more hard drive space is required)

Windows 2000 Server system requirements:

- One to four processors can be present on a single computer
- 128MB of RAM minimum; 256MB RAM recommended; 4GB of RAM maximum
- 1GB of free hard drive space minimum; 4GB or more recommended (if you're installing over a network, more hard drive space is required)

Windows 2000 Advanced Server system requirements:

- One to eight processors can be present on a single computer
- 128MB of RAM minimum; 256MB RAM recommended.; 8GB of RAM maximum
- 1GB of free hard drive space minimum; 4GB or more recommended (if you're installing over a network, more hard drive space is required)

Windows 2000 Datacenter Server system requirements:

- Up to 32 processors can be present on a single computer (or 64 through special OEM versions)
- 128MB of RAM minimum; 256MB RAM recommended; 64GB of RAM maximum
- 1GB of free hard drive space minimum; 4GB or more recommended (if you're installing over a network, more hard drive space is required)

Although Windows 2000 supports a much wider range of hardware devices than Windows NT, you should still verify that all devices present in a computer are fully compatible before performing the installation. You can ensure that your devices are compatible by checking each device against the Hardware Compatibility List (HCL) maintained by Microsoft. This list is available on the Windows 2000 distribution CD and the Microsoft Web site.

The version of the HCL on the CD is only as useful as it is current. Because the information on the CD was finalized in January 2000, any hardware and drivers released afterward are not included on it. Therefore, this version of the HCL should be used with caution, especially after it becomes six months or more out of date. The HCL is stored on the distribution CD in the \Support subdirectory and is contained in the file named hcl.txt.

The version of the HCL on the Microsoft Web site is constantly updated and is the best resource available. The online HCL is located at **www.microsoft.com/ windows2000/upgrade/compat /default.asp/** (this URL is subject to change; if this is no longer valid, you can find it manually by starting from **www.microsoft.com/ windows/**).

A compatible device is a device whose driver is included in the distribution on the Windows 2000 CD or a new/updated driver is available for download from Microsoft or the device's manufacturer. Be sure you have all drivers for all devices on hand before starting the installation. You should also check manufacturers' Web sites and the Microsoft Windows 2000 Web site for special instructions on installing software with drivers not already present on the distribution CD.

Windows 2000 Architecture and Design

Windows 2000 is not a single monolithic program but rather a collection of many small components designed to interact and interface with one another. This modular design has several benefits, which range from versatility of features to ease of upgrade and repair. This structure is evident in the division of user- and kernel-level processes and services. The Windows 2000 operating system environment is separated into two distinct layers: user mode and kernel mode. The user mode layer (or division) is a nonprivileged mode where all user interactive applications and processes are executed. The kernel mode layer is a privileged mode where all kernel- and system-level services and processes are executed. All user mode processes obtain resource access (that is, hardware access) by virtue of proxied (or mediated) service from components in the kernel mode. In other words, user mode processes are completely isolated from hardware. The basic structure of these two modes and their related components is shown in Figure 1.1.

For more detailed information on the Windows 2000 architecture than what's presented in the following sections, see the *Windows 2000 Server Resource Kit*, ISBN: 1-57231-805-8, or search the online version of TechNet at **www.microsoft.com/ TechNet/**.

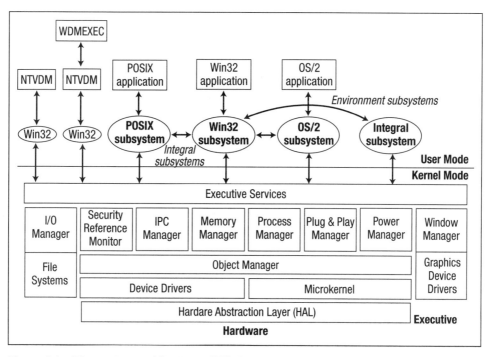

Figure 1.1   The system architecture of Windows 2000.

User Mode

All user operations and initiated processes reside in the user mode. The user mode is completely isolated from hardware, and all resource access is mediated by the Windows 2000 Executive in the kernel mode (see the "Kernel Mode" section later in this chapter). Even the Administration Tools utilities and Control Panel applets are not directly interacting with hardware; instead, they communicate instructions to kernel mode components to perform the necessary operations. If any process within the user mode attempts to access hardware directly, the operating system itself will terminate the process immediately.

Two subsystems reside within the user mode: environment subsystems and integral subsystems. The environment subsystems are the emulation services, or runtime virtual machines, created by Windows 2000 that offer various application-type support. Windows 2000 includes support for the following types of applications:

- Windows 32-bit applications (Win32)
- Windows 16-bit applications (Win16)
- MS-DOS applications
- OS/2 1.x character-mode applications
- POSIX.1 applications

Not all these environment subsystems are actually useful. The OS/2 and POSIX subsystems only support text-only applications and are present only to meet the purchasing requirement minimums for government agencies. Third-party services must be installed to provide true OS/2 and POSIX support.

The Win32 environment subsystem is the key component of the user mode. It provides a common API for all the environment subsystems for interfacing with the Windows 2000 Executive and managing I/O (video, mouse, and keyboard). See Chapter 18 for more information on application support under Windows 2000.

The integral subsystems provide for specialized communication links between certain user mode processes and their kernel mode partners. Examples of integral subsystems include security, Workstation service, and Server service. The security integral subsystem provides a means by which users are authenticated, their shells are launched with a specified access token, and all resource access is controlled based on assigned permissions. The Workstation and Server services integral subsystems provide a means by which user mode processes can access and share resources.

Kernel Mode

All core system and environmental support processes reside in the kernel mode. The kernel mode has complete control over hardware and mediates all resources for user mode processes. This mode protects the stability of the operating system environment and maintains control over hardware resources via three important components: the Windows 2000 Executive, the microkernel, and the Hardware Abstraction Layer (HAL).

Windows 2000 Executive

The collection of resource-management components is known as the *Windows 2000 Executive*. It consists of the following:

- *I/O Manager*—This component manages all I/O channels, including file systems and devices.

- *IPC (Interprocess Communication) Manager*—This component manages all transactions between server and client processes, both within the local computer and with remote computers.

- *Virtual Memory Manager*—This component manages virtual memory.

- *Process Manager*—This component manages the creation, disassembly, and maintenance of processes.

- *Plug and Play Manager*—This component manages all Plug and Play-compliant devices and their associated drivers.

- *Security Reference Monitor*—This component manages the security services, including authentication, resource access, and group memberships.

- *Power Manager*—This component manages the power conservation capabilities of Windows 2000.

- *Window Manager*—This component manages the input (mouse and keyboard) and display of windowing and dialog boxes.

- *Graphics device drivers*—These components manage the graphical rendering of the desktop environment and works with the Graphical Device Interface (GDI).

- *Object Manager*—This component manages all resource objects within the system.

Microkernel

The core of Windows 2000 is the microkernel. This component controls the CPU, handles hardware interrupts, coordinates I/O, and oversees the activities of the Windows 2000 Executive.

Hardware Abstraction Layer (HAL)

The bottom layer of the kernel mode is the HAL, which is a hardware platform-specific component compiled at the time of installation based on the foundational hardware devices of the computer. The HAL must be rebuilt each time a significant change occurs to the system, such as adding a second CPU or upgrading the motherboard.

Memory Architecture

Windows 2000 employs a flat, linear, 32-bit memory scheme that is basically a single contiguous block of memory addresses. This type of memory provides for a robust and reliable environment. Windows 2000 Professional and Windows 2000 Server can both addresses 4GB of memory, whereas Advanced Server can address 8GB, and Datacenter Server can address 64GB. Although modern hardware can support 4GB of physical RAM, the 4GB of addressable memory is actually virtual memory.

Virtual memory is the combination of physical RAM with allocated space from a hard drive. The area of hard drive space used by virtual memory is known as the *paging file*. Windows 2000 creates a paging file 1.5 times as large as the amount of physical RAM present at the time of installation. The Virtual Memory Manager (VMM) manages virtual memory by moving pages (4K chunks) in and out of physical RAM as needed by active processes.

The real job of the VMM is to maintain a mapping between the actual available virtual memory and the address space of each virtual machine active on the system. Every process is executed within a virtual machine. A *virtual machine* is a software construct that fools the process into seeing itself as the only process on the computer. This virtual machine mimics the resources of the computer and is assigned a 4GB address space. Half of this address space is reserved for the kernel, and the remaining 2GB can be used by either the kernel or the process itself. The VMM keeps track of the address pages created and used by each process within their virtual machines and maps those pages to actual locations within the available virtual memory of the computer. This process is depicted in Figure 1.2.

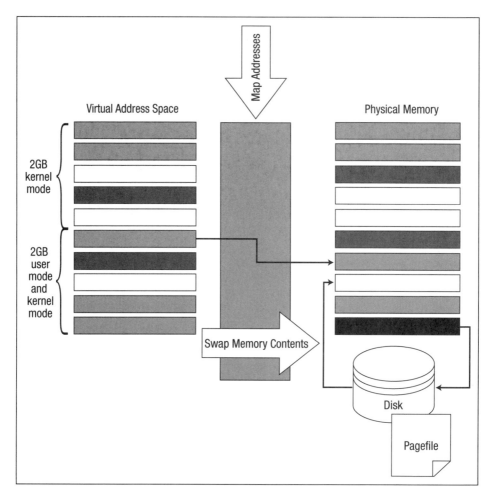

Figure 1.2   The Windows 2000 virtual memory architecture.

Processes and Priorities

Windows 2000 supports multithreading, multitasking, and multiprocessing. Respectively, these features allow a single process to have multiple executable components, a single CPU to juggle multiple processes, and a single computer to have multiple CPUs. Each of these computing advancements adds power and versatility to an operating system. Windows 2000 is a symmetric multiprocessing operating system, as opposed to an asymmetric multiprocessing one. This means that within Windows 2000, processes are not assigned to a specific CPU, but rather are able to execute on any CPU with available execution cycles.

The ability of Windows 2000 to sustain a stable environment is afforded through the use of execution priorities. Each process is assigned a base execution priority that determines its importance for obtaining execution time. Windows 2000 has 32 levels of priority—0 through 31. Levels 0 through 15 are assigned only to user mode processes, and levels 16 through 31 are assigned only to kernel mode processes. Therefore, kernel mode processes always have a higher execution priority than any user mode process.

The Process Manager acts like a traffic cop for the CPU by determining which process gets access and for how long. The Process Manager can raise or lower the execution priority of a process by a maximum of 2 to control traffic flow. Only the system itself has fine-tuning capabilities when it comes to priorities. As a user (or even as an administrator), you are limited to setting one of six priority levels at startup or during execution: low, belownormal, normal, abovenormal, high, and realtime (restricted only to administrators). The priority level names and their associated numbered priorities are shown in Table 1.2.

Table 1.2   Process priority levels, classes, and thread priorities of Windows 2000.

Priority	Priority Class	Thread Priority
0	None executing	Nonexecuting
1	Idle	Idle
2	Idle	Lowest
3	Idle	Below Normal
4	Idle	Normal
5	Idle	Above Normal
6	Idle/Normal	Lowest/Highest
7	Normal	Below Normal
8	Normal	Normal
9	Normal	Above Normal

(continued)

Table 1.2   Process priority levels, classes, and thread priorities of Windows 2000 (continued).

Priority	Priority Class	Thread Priority
10	Normal	Highest
11	High	Lowest
12	High	Below Normal
13	High	Normal
14	High	Above Normal
15	High	Highest
16	Realtime	Idle
17	Realtime	
18	Realtime	
19	Realtime	
20	Realtime	
21	Realtime	
22	Realtime	Lowest
23	Realtime	Below Normal
24	Realtime	Normal
25	Realtime	Above Normal
26	Realtime	Highest
27	Realtime	
28	Realtime	
29	Realtime	
30	Realtime	
31	Realtime	Time Critical

Immediate Solutions

Altering the Size of the Paging File

Windows 2000 creates a paging file automatically when installed. The default initial size is approximately 1.5 times the amount of physical RAM, and the maximum size is set to 2 times the default initial size. Therefore, if you have 128MB of RAM, the initial size will be 192MB and the maximum size will be 384MB. Depending on the applications and services hosted by your computer and the tasks you perform, you may want to alter the size of the paging file. Plus, if you add more RAM to your system, you'll want to increase the paging file size. To alter the size of the paging file, perform the following steps:

1. Click the Start button, select Settings, and then click Control Panel. The Control Panel window will be displayed.

2. Locate and double-click the System applet icon in the Control Panel window. The System applet will open.

3. Select the Advanced tab (see Figure 1.3).

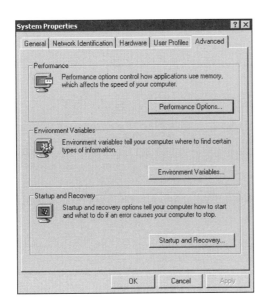

Figure 1.3   The Advanced tab of the System applet.

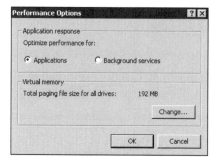

Figure 1.4   The Performance Options dialog box.

4. Click the Performance Options button. The Performance Options dialog box is displayed (see Figure 1.4).

5. Click the Change button in the Virtual Memory section of the Performance Options dialog box. The Virtual Memory dialog box is displayed (see Figure 1.5).

6. Select the drive that currently hosts the paging file—it's the one with the MB range defined under the Paging File Size column. Notice how the initial size and maximum size values appear in the text fields under the Paging File Size For Selected Drive section once you've selected the paging file host drive.

7. Change the initial size to reflect your needs. For example, suppose you added more RAM so your computer now has 256MB. In this case, you would change the initial size to 384 (256 times 1.5) and the maximum size to 768

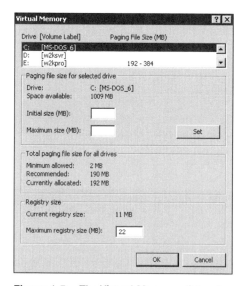

Figure 1.5   The Virtual Memory dialog box.

(384 times 2) and then click the Set button. Notice that new values are
displayed in the Drive/Paging File Size table at the top of the dialog box.

8. Click OK to close the Virtual Memory dialog box.

9. Click OK to close the Performance Options dialog box.

10. Click OK to close the System applet dialog box.

11. Close the Control Panel by clicking the File menu and selecting Close.

A system reboot may be required; if so, you will be prompted.

Moving the Paging File to a New Host Drive

If your boot partition (the partition hosting the main Windows 2000 system files)
does not contain enough free space or if you want to speed system performance
by placing the paging file on a different physical disk, you can move the paging
file from its default location. To move the paging file to a new host drive, perform
the following steps:

1. Click the Start button, select Settings, and then click Control Panel. The
   Control Panel window will be displayed.

2. Locate and double-click the System applet icon in the Control Panel
   window. The System applet will open.

3. Select the Advanced tab (see Figure 1.6).

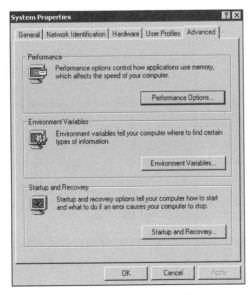

Figure 1.6   The Advanced tab of the System applet.

4. Click the Performance Options button. The Performance Options dialog box is displayed (refer to Figure 1.4).

5. Click the Change button under the Virtual Memory section of the Performance Options dialog box. The Virtual Memory dialog box is displayed (refer to Figure 1.5).

6. Note the initial and maximum size of the current paging file (for example, 192MB and 384MB).

7. Select the drive where you want to place the paging file in the Drive/Paging File Size table at the top of the Virtual Memory dialog box.

8. In the Initial Size field, type the initial size of the current paging file (for example, 192).

9. In the Maximum Size field, type the maximum size of the current paging file (for example, 384).

10. Click Set. Select the drive hosting the original default paging file.

11. Change the initial and maximum sizes of the paging file to 0 and click Set.

12. Click OK to close the Virtual Memory dialog box.

13. You should see a message stating that the computer must reboot for the changes to take effect. Click OK.

14. Click OK to close the Performance Options dialog box.

15. Click OK to close the System applet dialog box.

16. When prompted to reboot your computer, click Yes to allow the system to automatically reboot the system.

17. When the system reboots, you may need to close the Control Panel by clicking the File menu and selecting Close.

Removing Windows Components

Windows 2000 may install components that you do not want installed on your system. By default, the removal tool does not display all the configurable components. To remove Windows components, perform the following steps:

1. Launch Windows Explorer by clicking the Start button, selecting Programs, selecting Accessories, and then clicking Windows Explorer.

2. Locate and select the boot partition in the left pane of Windows Explorer. The boot partition is where the main Windows 2000 system files reside. This is typically drive C or D.

3. Locate the %systemroot%\inf\sysoc.inf file; it is located within the main Windows 2000 directory (which may be named Windows, W2K, Winnt, or something similar). Double-click it. This will open the file in Notepad.

4. Click the Edit menu and select Replace.

5. In the Find What: field type ",hide," (be sure to include the commas).

6. In the Replace With: field type ",," (be sure to include two commas; no space is required).

7. Click the Replace All button. Then click the Cancel button.

8. Click the File menu and select Save.

9. Click the File menu and select Exit to close Notepad.

10. Click the Start button, select Settings, and then click Control Panel. The Control Panel window will be displayed.

11. Locate and double-click the Add/Remove Programs applet icon in the Control Panel window. The Add/Remove Programs applet will open.

12. Click the Add/Remove Windows Components button. The Windows Components portion of the Windows Components Wizard will open (see Figure 1.7).

13. Select the Accessories And Utilities component.

14. Click the Details button (see Figure 1.8).

15. Deselect the checkbox beside Accessibility Wizard.

16. Click OK.

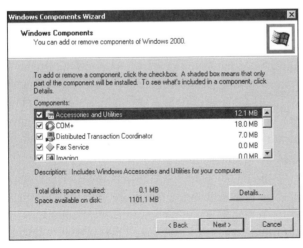

Figure 1.7   The Windows Components portion of the Windows Components Wizard.

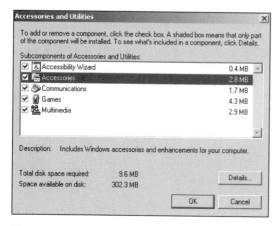

Figure 1.8 The Accessories And Utilities dialog box.

17. Click Next.

18. The Add/Remove service will perform the necessary operations to add or remove the component. Eventually a completed dialog box will be displayed. Click Finish.

19. Click Close on the Add/Remove Programs dialog box.

20. Close the Control Panel and Windows Explorer by clicking the File menu and selecting Close on each window.

Using the Task Manager to View Application Status and Process Details

The Task Manager is a useful tool for gaining quick insight into the current state of the system. To use the Task Manager for viewing system statistics, perform the following steps:

1. Right-click over a blank area of the Taskbar (be sure not to be over the Start button, the icon tray, or any application button). Then highlight and left-click the Task Manager command in the pop-up menu. The Task Manager will open.

2. Click the Applications tab. Notice that this tab displays the currently active applications and their status (that is, Running or Not Responding). See Figure 1.9 for an example.

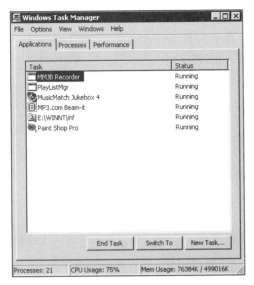

Figure 1.9   The Task Manager's Applications tab.

3. Click the Processes tab. Notice that this tab displays the currently active processes along with several details. The default displayed details are PID (process ID), CPU usage percentage during the last update interval, total CPU usage time, and current amount of virtual memory in use by the process (see Figure 1.10).

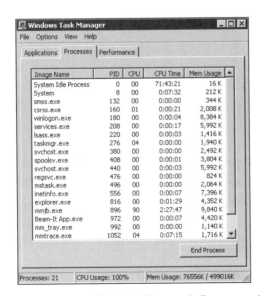

Figure 1.10   The Task Manager's Processes tab.

4. Click the Performance tab. Notice that this tab displays the current and brief historical operational levels of the CPU and memory in graphical format as well as provides numerical details about various memory aspects and system resources (see Figure 1.11).

5. Click the File menu and select the Exit Task Manager command to close the Task Manager.

The Task Manager can also be launched by the following methods:

- Executing **taskmgr** from the **run** command or a command prompt.
- Pressing Ctrl+Alt+Del and then clicking the Task Manager button.
- Pressing Ctrl+Shift+Esc.

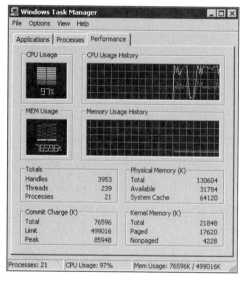

Figure 1.11   The Task Manager's Performance tab.

Launching an Application with a Non-Normal Priority

The default execution priority for user mode applications (that is, anything that a user can launch) is 13 (Normal). Using the **start** command from the command prompt, you can launch applications at other priority levels. To launch an application with a non-normal priority, perform the following steps:

1. Click the Start button, select Programs, select Applications, and then click Command Prompt. The Command Prompt window will be displayed.

2. At the command prompt, type "start /low notepad" and press Enter. The Notepad application will launch.

3. Press Ctrl+Alt+Esc to launch the Task Manager.

4. Select the Processes tab.

5. Locate and select the notepad.exe process.

6. Right-click over the notepad.exe process and then select Set Priority from the pop-up menu. Notice the selected priority is currently Low.

7. Click the Notepad button in the Taskbar.

8. Click the File menu and select Exit to close this instance of Notepad.

9. Click the Command Prompt button in the Taskbar.

10. At the command prompt, type "start /high notepad" and press Enter. The Notepad application will launch.

11. Click the Task Manager button in the Taskbar.

12. Locate and select the notepad.exe process.

13. Right-click over the notepad.exe process and then select Set Priority from the pop-up menu. Notice the selected priority is currently High.

14. Click the Notepad button in the Taskbar.

15. Click the File menu and select Exit to close this instance of Notepad.

16. Repeat Steps 9 through 15 for belownormal, abovenormal, and realtime.

NOTE: *Realtime priority can only be set by administrators.*

---

17. Click the Task Manager button in the Taskbar.

18. Close the Task Manager by clicking its File menu and selecting Exit Task Manager.

19. Click the Command Prompt button in the Taskbar.

20. Close the command prompt by typing "exit" and pressing Enter.

Changing the Priority of an Active Process

After an application is launched, you can still leverage some minor control over its execution priority. To change the priority of an active process, perform the following steps:

1. Click the Start button, select Programs, select Applications, and then click Command Prompt. The Command Prompt window will be displayed.

2. At the command prompt, type "start /low notepad" and press Enter. The Notepad application will launch.

3. Press Ctrl+Alt+Esc to launch the Task Manager.

4. Select the Processes tab.

5. Locate and select the notepad.exe process.

6. Right-click over the notepad.exe process and select Set Priority from the pop-up menu. Notice the selected priority is currently Low.

7. Click the High setting from the list of priorities in the fly-open menu.

8. A warning message may appear stating that changing the priority might cause system instability. Click Yes.

9. Right-click over the notepad.exe process and select Set Priority from the pop-up menu. Notice the selected priority is now High.

10. Click the Notepad button in the Taskbar.

11. Click the File menu and select Exit to close Notepad.

12. Click the Task Manager button in the Taskbar.

13. Close the Task Manager by clicking its File menu and selecting Exit Task Manager.

14. Click the Command Prompt button in the Taskbar.

15. Close the command prompt by typing "exit" and pressing Enter.

Changing the System's Performance Optimization

Windows 2000 can be tuned to provide optimized performance for either applications (that is, foreground user mode processes) or background services (that is, applications and services accessed from the network or required to maintain the local system). Windows 2000 Professional is set to Applications by default, whereas all the Windows 2000 Server variants are set to Background Services. To optimize system performance, perform the following steps:

1. Click the Start button, select Settings, and then click Control Panel. The Control Panel window will be displayed.

2. Locate and double-click the System applet icon in the Control Panel window. The System applet will open.

3. Select the Advanced tab.

4. Click the Performance Options button. The Performance Options dialog box is displayed (refer to Figure 1.4).

5. Select the Applications radio button to optimize performance for applications or select the Background Services radio button to optimize performance for background services.

6. Click OK to close the Performance Options dialog box.

7. Click OK to close the System applet.

8. Click the File menu and select Close to close the Control Panel.

Customizing the Activities of the Start Menu

The default enabled features of the Start menu might not be the best configuration for your method of interacting with Windows 2000. To customize the Start menu, perform the following steps:

1. Right-click over a blank area of the Taskbar. Highlight and click Properties from the pop-up menu.

2. The Taskbar and Start Menu Properties dialog box appears with the General tab selected (see Figure 1.12).

3. If you want the Taskbar to automatically disappear from the desktop when not in use, mark the Auto Hide checkbox. If you want the Taskbar to always appear, unmark the Auto Hide checkbox.

4. To compress the displayed size of the Start menu, mark the Show Small Icons In Start Menu checkbox.

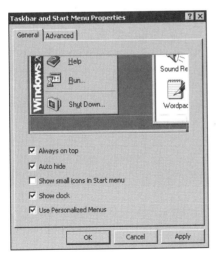

Figure 1.12   The General tab of the Taskbar and Start Menu Properties dialog box.

5. If you want the clock to appear in the Taskbar, mark the Show Clock checkbox.

6. Select the Advanced tab (see Figure 1.13).

7. To display the Administrative Tools menu in the Start menu, mark the Display Administrative Tools checkbox, located in the Start Menu Settings area.

8. To show the Control Panel applets from the Start menu, mark the Expand Control Panel checkbox.

9. To expand the Network and Dial-Up Connections objects from the Start menu, mark the Expand Network and Dial-Up Connections checkbox.

10. To expand the Printers folder from the Start menu, mark the Expand Printers checkbox.

11. Click OK to save these changes and close the Taskbar and Start Menu Properties dialog box.

12. Explore the Start menu and Taskbar to see the changes you just made.

Adding a New Shortcut to the Start Menu

The Start menu is fully customizable. All you need to do is add, remove, or shuffle shortcuts to create the layout you desire. This solution explains how to add new shortcuts. To add a shortcut to the Start menu, perform the following steps:

1. Click the Start menu, select Settings, and then click Taskbar & Start Menu. The Taskbar And Start Menu Properties dialog box appears.

2. Select the Advanced tab.

3. Click the Add button. The Create Shortcut dialog box is displayed.

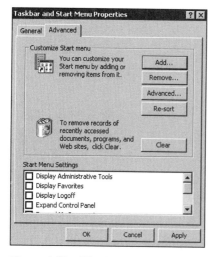

Figure 1.13   The Advanced tab of the Taskbar And Start Menu Properties dialog box.

4. Click the Browse button. The Browse For Folder dialog box appears; it displays all local drive letters.

5. Double-click the drive letter hosting your main Windows 2000 files. The dialog box now displays the top-level contents of this drive.

6. Double-click the main Windows 2000 directory name. The dialog box now displays the contents of the Windows 2000 directory.

7. Locate and select regedit.exe and then click OK. The path and file name of the selected application is now displayed in the Type The Location Of The Item: field of the Create Shortcut dialog box.

8. Click Next. The hierarchy of the Start menu is displayed.

9. Locate and select the Administrative Tools folder located under Programs.

10. Click Next.

11. Type a name for the shortcut, such as 16-bit Registry Editor. Click Finish.

12. Click OK to close the Taskbar And Start Menu Properties dialog box.

13. Click the Start menu, select Properties, and then select Administrative Tools (you must have the Display Administrative Tools setting enabled; see the solution "Customizing the Activities of the Start Menu"). Notice the new shortcut now appears.

Removing a Shortcut from the Start Menu

The Start menu is fully customizable. All you need to do is add, remove, or shuffle shortcuts to create the layout you desire. This solution explains how to remove existing shortcuts. To remove a shortcut form the Start menu, perform the following steps:

1. Click the Start menu, select Settings, and then click Taskbar & Start Menu. The Taskbar and Start Menu Properties dialog box appears.

2. Select the Advanced tab.

3. Click the Remove button. The Remove Shortcuts/Folder dialog box is displayed.

4. This dialog box displays the current Start menu hierarchy. Locate and select the Address Book item in the Accessories subsection. (If you wish to keep the Address Book item, select some other item to delete—otherwise, skip this solution.)

5. Click Remove.

6. Click Yes when prompted to confirm.

7. Click Close to close the Remove Shortcuts/Folder dialog box.

8. Click OK to close the Taskbar And Start Menu Properties dialog box.

9. Click the Start menu, select Properties, and then select Accessories. Notice the shortcut no longer appears.

Customizing the Structure of the Start Menu

The Start menu is fully customizable. All you need to do is add, remove, or shuffle shortcuts to create the layout you desire. This solution explains how to reorganize existing shortcuts. To customize the structure of the Start menu, perform the following steps:

1. Click the Start menu, select Settings, and then click Taskbar & Start Menu. The Taskbar and Start Menu Properties dialog box appears.

2. Select the Advanced tab.

3. Click the Advanced button. A Windows Explorer dialog box is opened with the Start Menu folder selected from the current user's profile (see Figure 1.14).

4. The Start menu is nothing more than a set of folders and subfolders stored in the Start Menu folder within a user's profile.

5. The shortcuts in the subfolders of the Start Menu folder can be edited, added, removed, and rearranged, just like any typical file.

6. The Start menu you see is a combination of the Start Menu folder from your user profile and the contents of the Start Menu folder from the All Users profile. Therefore, be sure to view and edit both these folders to fully customize your Start menu.

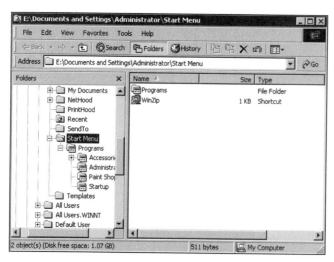

Figure 1.14   Editing the advanced Start menu properties.

Chapter 2

Comparing Windows 2000 to Windows NT

In Depth

The Windows 2000 product line is the result of starting from the foundation of Windows NT and adding features from Windows 98, along with new innovative technologies. The resulting network operating system (NOS) is a flexible and robust Internet-capable computing platform. Microsoft directed the development of Windows 2000 into a multipurpose platform instead of a single- or limited-use system. This adds strength, options, and versatility to an already impressive NOS.

This chapter looks at some of the improvements of Windows 2000 and makes comparisons between the new operating system and its predecessors.

Plug and Play

Through the long-awaited addition of Plug and Play to Windows NT, Windows 2000 now boasts the ease of configuration that only Windows 95 and Windows 98 enjoyed previously. Windows 2000 does not support quite as broad a range of hardware as its desktop predecessors, but it is still significantly broader than that of Windows NT. The benefits of Plug and Play support include:

- Fewer reboots due to configuration changes
- Easier installation of new hardware via automatic detection and driver installation
- On-the-fly reconfiguration, connection, and removal of devices
- Power management capabilities
- Support for hot-swappable and hot-plug-enabled devices
- Better functionality on notebook and portable systems with removable devices and docking stations
- Support for infrared, Universal Serial Bus (USB), and Institute of Electrical and Electronics Engineers (IEEE) 1394 devices

In case you're not already familiar with Plug and Play, it's a technology that enables an operating system (OS) to identify and alter hardware configurations with little or no user intervention. This grants a user the ability to add and remove devices dynamically, without extensive knowledge of the computer's resource structure and state or hardware manipulation.

From an administration perspective, the inclusion of Plug and Play with the Windows 2000 environment simplifies all hardware issues. Basically, adding and removing hardware is actually painless. New Plug and Play devices are detected and their drivers installed automatically, and drivers for removed devices are not loaded into memory. If you need to alter the configuration of one device to accommodate another, just use the Device Manager (accessed on the Hardware tab of the System applet or through the Computer Management utility). Plus, not all configuration changes require a reboot.

For more information on Windows 2000 support for Plug and Play, see the *Windows 2000 Server Resource Kit*, ISBN: 1-57231-805-8.

Security Enhancements

Windows 2000 offers many new security enhancements at nearly every point that users access resources. The new security features include changes to user authentication, networking, remote access/virtual private network (VPN), file access, data storage, encryption, and Internet Information Services (IIS). Most of the improvements to the security system used by Windows 2000 focus on authentication (proving identities) and communications (protecting data transfer). Some of the noteworthy security improvements are:

- Kerberos Authentication Protocol V5
- Public Key Infrastructure (PKI)
- X.509 version 3 Certificate Services
- CryptoAPI version 2
- Secure channel security protocols (SSL 3.0/PCT)
- Private Communications Technology (PCT) 1.0
- Distributed Password Authentication (DPA)
- Transport Layer Security (TLS) Protocol
- IPSec
- Smart card support
- Transitive trusts
- Group policies
- Encrypting File System (EFS)

From a day-to-day administration perspective, the new security features offer subtle improvements to the administrative workload. The presence of encrypted transmissions and a guaranteed source and receiver requires less work in the long run monitoring, testing, and improving communications. In most cases, once you define and configure a security feature within Windows 2000, you can almost just forget about it. The security system is always there; it's always working—verifying identities and restricting access as needed.

That said, you can't simply forget about security. However, once you configure the security of a resource, users are not confronted with the security barriers if a user account meets the requirements to access that resource. The only time security should really be noticed is when it's properly restricting access to a protected resource.

Security is covered in this book in Chapters 6, 7, and 19. For more information on the security improvements of Windows 2000, consult the *Windows 2000 Server Resource Kit*.

Networking Changes

Active Directory is the most significant change brought to Microsoft networking by Windows 2000. Active Directory is a single database of networking resources managed by the domain controllers. It offers a secure, controllable environment for the distribution of information resources. Being fully integrated into the operating system and based on Internet standards, Active Directory revolutionizes how Windows 2000 handles networking. For more details on Active Directory, see Chapter 3.

Other improvements to networking include a simplified networking component-management scheme. The Networking And Dial-Up Connections interface brings all the networking capabilities and features of Windows 2000 into a single, easy-to-use interface. Now, all communication lines from modems to high-speed networks are managed through a single utility.

Virtual private networking (VPN) has been improved with the addition of IPSec (IP Security) and L2TP (a more secure version of the Point-to-Point Tunneling Protocol [PPTP]). The routing has been more thoroughly and natively integrated into both remote access and local networking. This allows Windows 2000 to serve as a remote access server, an Internet connection point for a network, a domain router, or even a gateway between networks. The routing services of Windows 2000, previously only available to Windows NT via the Routing and Remote Access Service (RRAS) add-on, now include enterprise routing features such as Network Address Translation (NAT), Open Shortest Path First (OSPF), and Routing Information Protocol (RIP2) for IP networks, as well as RIP and Service Advertising Protocol (SAP) for Internetwork Packet Exchange (IPX) networks.

Windows 2000 also improves private domain name services through the introduction of Dynamic DNS. This new networking utility simplifies the task of maintaining

2. Comparing Windows 2000 to Windows NT

a Domain Name System (DNS) by automating the addition and removal of systems. See Chapter 9 for more information.

Windows 2000 Advanced Server includes clustering and network load balancing services. *Clustering* is a technology that enables two or more servers to be linked to share a common task. Windows 2000 can leverage several distinct computers against a single application; plus, it provides fail-over capabilities if a member of the cluster goes offline. *Network load balancing* distributes TCP/IP traffic between multiple servers. Network load balancing and clustering display their true capabilities when employed against Internet services, such as high-traffic Web sites, by managing more traffic with excellent performance.

Windows 2000 networking has advanced along with the available networking technologies. Native support for a large assortment of high-speed networking devices, including Asynchronous Transfer Mode (ATM) and Fibre Channel, make Windows 2000 the most advanced network operating system available. Additional information on networking is provided in Chapters 6, 7, and 9. For more information on the networking improvements of Windows 2000, consult the *Windows 2000 Server Resource Kit.*

New Services

Windows 2000 has also introduced several new breeds of services to Windows 2000. These include the following:

- *Recovery Console*—A command-line control system used in system recovery in the event of a failure of a core system component or driver. Through the Recovery Console, simple commands can be used to restore the operating system to a functional state. See Chapter 13 for information on this issue.

- *Windows file protection*—An automated protection measure that prevents in-use system files, such as sys, ddl, ocx, ttf, and exe, from being overwritten by other programs or installation routines.

- *IntelliMirror*—A network desktop-management system that allows administrators to retain control over systems not permanently connected to the network. Each time a portable computer logs back onto the network, the domain's group policies are reinforced, software is added or removed, and user data files are updated. See Chapter 14 for information on this issue.

- *Web-Based Enterprise Management (WBEM)*—The Distributed Management Task Force (DMTF) initiative, included in Windows 2000 via Windows Management Instrumentation (WMI), grants you the ability to remotely manage, configure, and control nearly every aspect of your systems and networks—from software to hardware.

- *Remote Installation Services*—With RIS, clients can be easily installed across the network by booting from a Pre-boot Execution Environment (PXE) ROM NIC or a boot floppy. The installation routine can be fully automated once the destination computer is turned on, or a full or partial user interaction-required installation can be customized. See Chapter 5 for information on this issue.

- *Internet Information Services (IIS) 5.0*—The latest generation of Microsoft Internet Information Server, version 5, is included with Windows 2000. IIS offers a solid platform for building personal Web pages through true distributed, dynamic e-commerce Web sites. IIS integrates with the Windows 2000 system, seamlessly granting Web administrators access to networked resources, security, and management controls.

- *Internet connection sharing*—Built into Windows 2000's routing support is a basic proxy server. This tool can be used to grant Internet access to a small network without requiring additional hardware or applications. Plus, the network clients are automatically configured to use the shared connection. See Chapter 9 for information on this issue.

- *Terminal Services*—Windows 2000 includes native Terminal Services (previously available to Windows NT only as an add-on), which allows thin clients to be employed as network clients. Terminal Services grants remote access to applications and offers limitation controls over application access. See Chapter 20 for information on this issue.

Comparing Windows NT Workstation to Windows 2000 Professional

Windows 2000 Professional is the new desktop client equivalent to Windows NT Workstation. From a basic functional standpoint, these two versions are quite similar. Both provide complete integrated access to a Microsoft domain and all the resources contained there. They offer secured, multiuser environments that can be customized by the user to any extent granted by the system administrator. However, Windows 2000 Professional is definitely a more advanced operating system, offering more reliable application support, more hardware support, and more features throughout the OS.

The Windows 2000 platform includes many significant changes and improvements compared to Windows NT. The client version of Windows 2000 still does not include the network services of Domain Name Service (DNS), Dynamic Host Configuration Protocol (DHCP), and domain controlling. However, this should be a fairly common-sense issue. Windows 2000 Professional is designed to act as a network client, not a network server. To get the tools and services to truly host, manage, and serve resources to a network, you need Windows 2000 Server (or greater).

Both Windows 2000 Professional and Windows NT Workstation take advantage of the Windows 95 desktop environment look and feel. This is primarily identified with the Start menu, Taskbar, and desktop icons, along with common utilities such as Windows Explorer, Control Panel, Printers, Recycle Bin, My Computer, and Network Neighborhood (called *My Network Places* in Windows 2000). The basic methods of navigating the environments are the same. However, Windows 2000 boasts many improvements to these now-familiar interface elements, such as a more advanced Search tools, a user-adaptive Start menu, more intuitively useful dialog boxes (such as Open and Save As), autocomplete dialog boxes, pervasive most-used-recently lists, and more.

With the support for more hardware and the addition of Plug and Play, Windows 2000 offers control over hardware and drivers through the Add/Remove Hardware applet and the Device Manager (via the System applet or the Computer Management tool). Windows 2000 Professional now boasts true support for notebook, portable, and mobile computers, through Plug and Play, power management, versatile hardware profiles, and offline files and synchronization. The offline files feature provides Windows 2000 the capability to cache network resources locally so they can still be used when the computer is not connected to the network. This includes both local network resources and Internet resources. A synchronization tool is integrated with the offline files service that can automatically update the cached content when a network connection is established.

Creating new network connections or managing existing connections is now easier than ever. The Network And Dial-Up Connections interface combines control mechanisms previously located in different utilities under Windows NT. From this interface, you can manage any type of network link, from local NIC connections, to RAS links, to VPNs. Plus, a wizard is used to walk you through the creation of new links, thus eliminating the possibility for gross configuration errors.

Windows 2000 has added support for the FAT32 file system, thus expanding Windows NT's support for only file allocation table (FAT) and New Technology File System (NTFS). FAT32 uses smaller clusters than FAT (FAT16) and supports larger drives (up to 4GB). NTFS has been improved with features such as the Encrypted File System (EFS) and content indexing. Other advances in the storage realm include fault-tolerant drive configuration support on the client. Windows 2000 now offers dynamic storage, which is an alternative method to partitioning. Dynamic storage is not restricted by partitioning rules (that is, only four primary partitions per drive) and allows for on-the-fly reconfiguration of storage devices without rebooting. Windows 2000 also includes a disk defragmenter and a disk cleanup tool. The former increases disk performance due to scattered file storage, and the later removes orphaned and temporary files to regain valuable storage space.

The list of new features in Windows 2000 is seemingly endless. Here are several more you may want to investigate further if they pique your interest:

- *Multiple monitors*—You can configure two to nine monitors to display an expanded desktop.

- *Driver signing*—All drivers from Microsoft and approved vendors are signed. You can configure Windows 2000 to refuse to install any non-signed drivers.

- *Improved graphics*—Support for DirectX 6.0 and OpenGL 1.2 provide a richer graphics rendering environment for productivity and entertainment applications.

- *Microsoft Management Console (MMC)*—This is a new standardized Web-capable management interface. Most of the Windows 2000 administration tasks are accessible through an MMC snap-in.

- *Boot options*—A useful set of optional boot methods can offer an easy out when specific problems occur. Boot options include booting without network support, booting with base VGA support, booting to a command prompt, and booting with the Last Known Good Configuration (LKGC).

- *Windows Scripting Host (WSH)*—Native scripting capabilities of Windows 2000 grant administrators a wider set of automation options. Most tasks can be accomplished through command line utilities. Using WSH, an administrator can automate many redundant tasks.

For more information about Windows 2000 Professional and its new features, visit the Microsoft Web site or consult the *Windows 2000 Professional Resource Kit*.

Comparing Windows NT Server to Windows 2000 Server

Windows 2000 Server includes all the improvements found in Windows 2000 Professional as well as many networking server-specific enhancements. Making a comparison between Windows 2000 Server and Windows NT Server reveals just how advanced the latest NOS from Microsoft truly is.

Both Windows NT and Windows 2000 include solid network capabilities, such TCP/IP networking (routing, DHCP, DNS, and WINS) and remote access (encrypted authentication, callback security, and VPNs). However, Windows 2000 has several new benefits, including the following:

- IPSec (IP Security)
- L2TP (Layer 2 Tunneling Protocol)
- Quality of Service (QoS) control

- Dynamic DNS

- Native ATM and Gigabit Ethernet support

- Improved routing capabilities

- A broader range of native telephony services

In addition, the networking capabilities of Windows 2000 are integrated with Active Directory for better overall control and security.

Both Windows NT and Windows 2000 include solid storage services, such as a 64-bit file system (NTFS) and fault-tolerant drive configurations. However, Windows 2000 boasts hierarchical storage management, dynamic volume management, native disk defragmentation, an encrypted file system, and automated content indexing and searching.

Both Windows NT and Windows 2000 include a solid printing subsystem, which offers features such as priority printing, printer pooling, spooling management, network attached printers, and more. However, Windows 2000 adds Internet printing support, which not only grants access to the printer queues via a Web browser but supports HTTP printing as well.

Both Windows NT and Windows 2000 include centralized management of security and resource access based on a user's network logon and authentication. Windows 2000 has greatly improved on this through the introduction of Active Directory (see Chapter 3 for details). Active Directory offers noncomplex scalability. What's more, it's based on Internet standards, it's flexible and secure, it includes built-in synchronization, and it's supported by a wide range of products from various vendors. In addition to the system policies of Windows NT, Windows 2000 adds group policy control over the entire computing and network environment, thus granting true control over users.

Both Windows NT and Windows 2000 are designed around a virtual memory architecture. The base Server versions of both NOSs support up to 4GB of memory, whereas the Advanced Server and Datacenter Server versions of Windows 2000 can manage 8 and 64GB of memory, respectively.

Both Windows NT and Windows 2000 are multitasking, multithreading, multiprocessor operating systems, with the base Server version supporting up to four CPUs. The Advanced Server and Datacenter Server versions of Windows 2000 can support 8 and 64 CPUs, respectively. Plus, Windows 2000 includes native support for server clustering and network load balancing.

Both Windows NT and Windows 2000 support several application types: Win32, Win16, DOS, OS/2 character mode, and POSIX.1. Both employ Component Object Model (COM) and Win32 APIs to provide a solid applications platform. However,

Windows 2000 has improved on its application support through Distributed COM (DCOM) and native Microsoft Transaction Server (MTS), Active Server Pages (ASP), and Microsoft Message Queuing Server (MSMQ)—all four of which could be added to Windows NT through the Option Pack.

Table 2.1 provides further comparisons between Windows 2000 Server and Windows NT Server.

The content of this table was derived from the Microsoft document "Comparing Windows NT Server and Windows 2000 Server with NetWare 5.0," available from the **www.microsoft.com/windows/** Web area. For more information on any of the items listed in this table, consult this comparison document, the Windows 2000 documentation manuals, the Microsoft Web site, or the *Windows 2000 Server Resource Kit.*

Table 2.1   A comparison of features.

Feature	Windows NT Server 4.0	Windows 2000 Server
Same security model for catalog and native directory	No	Yes
Lightweight Directory Access Protocol (LDAP) support	No	Yes
DNS/directory namespace integration	No	Yes
Autodetection of devices after installation	No	Yes
Hardware configuration as part of OS	No	Yes
Plug and Play support	No	Yes
Power management support	No	Yes
Reboot required for configuration changes	Yes	No
DHCP statistics and analysis reporting	No	Yes
Dynamic DNS	No	Yes
Server-to-server VPN support	No	Yes
Radius server	No	Yes
Connection sharing	No	Yes
ATM routing support	No	Yes
Dynamic bandwidth allocation (admission control service)	No	Yes
DHCP relay agent support	No	Yes

(continued)

2. Comparing Windows 2000 to Windows NT

Table 2.1   A comparison of features (continued).

Feature	Windows NT Server 4.0	Windows 2000 Server
DNS proxy support	No	Yes
Internet Group Management Protocol (IGMP) protocol support (multicast)	No	Yes
Network address translator	No	Yes
Internet printing	No	Yes
Print server clustering	No	Yes
Synchronization between client/server of user data	No	Yes
Desktop application management	No	Yes
Remote operating system installation	No	Yes
Extensible Markup Language (XML) integration	No	Yes
Customized Web error handling	No	Yes
Server scriptlet support	No	Yes
HTTP compression	No	Yes
FTP restart	No	Yes

2. Comparing Windows 2000 to Windows NT

Immediate Solutions

Demonstrating Plug and Play under Windows 2000

The Plug and Play architecture is fully integrated into Windows 2000. It operates seamlessly and automatically. In fact, it's difficult to demonstrate without actually altering your system to force it to function. To view how Plug and Play works, perform the following steps:

> **NOTE:**   *This solution should only be performed if you're using a mouse or pointing device fully compatible with Windows 2000.*

1. Click the Start button, select Settings, and click Control Panel. The Control Panel is displayed.

2. Double-click the System applet. The System applet opens.

3. Select the Hardware tab.

4. Click the Device Manager button. The Device Manager dialog box is displayed.

5. Expand the Mice And Other Pointing Devices section by clicking the boxed plus sign.

6. Select the listed mouse. In Figure 2.1, this is a Microsoft Serial Mouse.

7. Click the Action menu and then select Uninstall.

8. On the Confirm Device Removal dialog box, click OK. Notice your mouse pointer is no longer on the screen.

9. Press Ctrl+Alt+Del. This reveals the Windows Security dialog box.

10. Use the arrow keys to move the selection highlight on the Windows Security dialog box to Shutdown. Then press Enter.

11. Make sure the pull-down list shows Restart and then press Enter. If you need to change the pull-down list, press Tab until the list is highlighted and then use the up- and down-arrow keys to change the selection. The computer will reboot.

12. Upon rebooting your computer, press Ctrl+Alt+Del when prompted by the logon splash screen.

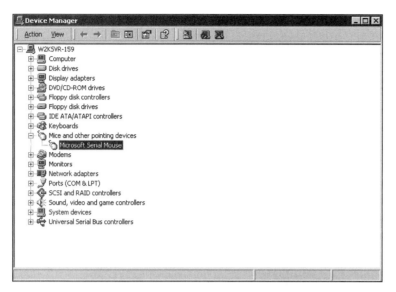

Figure 2.1   The Device Manager with the installed mouse selected.

13. Provide your account credentials and then press Enter.

14. As your desktop loads, you may see a New Hardware dialog box. The system will automatically determine the type of device and will reenable the driver already stored on the hard drive. Your mouse functionality is restored.

Installing a Plug and Play Device

To install a Plug and Play device, perform the following steps:

NOTE: *This solution requires an external Plug and Play device, such as a camera or scanner with USB or infrared capabilities. It also requires that the Windows 2000 computer have the corresponding USB or infrared hardware to support external peripherals.*

1. Boot into Windows 2000.

2. Attach your external peripheral—in this case, an Epson digital camera.

3. Watch as Windows 2000 automatically detects the new device and attempts to install the correct drivers.

4. If drivers are not already stored locally, Windows 2000 will prompt you for drivers. Follow those prompts to provide the drivers for your device.

5. After the system installs the newly discovered hardware, you can view its configuration through either the Device Manager or the Control Panel applet dedicated to its specific type of hardware.

6. If you installed a digital camera or scanner, you can view information about the device through the Scanners And Cameras applet.

7. Click the Start button, select Settings, and click Control Panel. The Control Panel is displayed.

8. Double-click the Scanners And Cameras applet. The Scanners And Cameras applet opens.

9. Your installed device should be displayed, as shown in Figure 2.2.

10. Click OK to close the applet.

11. Click the File menu and then select Close to close the Control Panel.

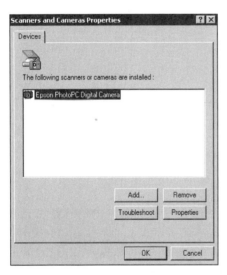

Figure 2.2   The Scanners And Cameras applet.

Changing Display Properties without Rebooting

Windows 2000 no longer requires reboots on nearly 40 system configuration changes that were required under Windows NT. For example, changing the Display properties no longer requires a reboot. To change the Display properties, perform the following steps:

1. Right-click an empty area of the desktop. Click Properties from the pop-up menu that appears.

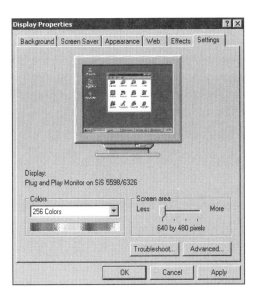

Figure 2.3   The Display Properties dialog box with the Settings tab selected.

2. Select the Settings button, the Display Properties dialog box opens (see Figure 2.3).

3. In the Colors section, take note of the current setting. Change the setting using the pull-down list. For example, change from 256 Colors to High Color (16-bit), or vice versa.

4. In the Screen Area section, take note of the current setting. Change the setting using the slider control. For example, change from 640 by 480 to 800 by 600, or vice versa.

5. Click OK.

6. A Display Properties warning dialog box appears to warn you that the current changes will be applied and if the settings fail, the previous settings will be automatically restored in 15 seconds. Click OK.

7. Once the screen resolves with the new settings, click Yes. Notice that you did not have to reboot to change the display settings.

8. Restore the previous settings using Steps 1 through 7.

Configuring Power Management

Conserving energy is good for the environment and your wallet. If you leave your computers on 24 hours a day, you may want to consider employing the power management capabilities of Windows 2000 to reduce their power drain when they're idle. To configure power management, perform the following steps:

1. Click the Start button, select Settings, and click Control Panel. The Control Panel is displayed.

2. Double-click the Power Options applet. The Power Options Properties dialog box opens (see Figure 2.4).

3. Change the Turn Off Monitor pull-down list to After 10 Minutes.

4. Change the Turn Off Hard Disks pull-down list to After 10 Minutes.

5. Click OK.

6. Wait 11 minutes and watch your monitor turn off and listen to your hard drives power down.

7. Press any key on the keyboard or move the mouse to reawaken your system.

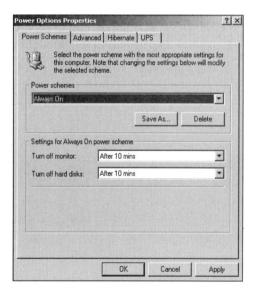

Figure 2.4   The Power Options Properties dialog box.

Seeing the Options for IPSec

The inclusion of IPSec in Windows 2000 offers a more secure communications protocol than standard TCP/IP. To view the options for IPSec, perform the following steps:

1. Click the Start menu, select Settings, and click Network And Dial-Up Connections. The Network And Dial-Up Connections dialog box opens.

2. Select the Local Area Connection option.

3. Click the File menu and select Properties. The Local Area Connections Properties dialog box opens.

4. Select Internet Protocol (TCP/IP).

5. Click Properties. The Internet Protocol (TCP/IP) Properties dialog box opens.

6. Click Advanced. The Advanced TCP/IP Settings dialog box opens.

7. Select the Options tab.

8. Select IP security.

9. Click Properties. The IP Security dialog box opens.

10. Select the Use This IP Security Policy radio button (see Figure 2.5).

11. Read the text in the Selected IP Security Policy Description area.

12. Change the selection in the pull-down list from Client (Respond Only) to Secure Server (Require Security).

13. Read the text in the Selected IP Security Policy Description area.

14. Change the selection in the pull-down list from Secure Server (Require Security) to Server (Request Security).

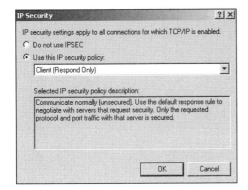

Figure 2.5   The IP Security dialog box.

2. Comparing Windows 2000 to Windows NT

15. Read the text in the Selected IP Security Policy Description area.

16. Click Cancel to close the IP Security dialog box without saving any changes.

17. Click Cancel to close the Advanced TCP/IP Setting dialog box.

18. Click Cancel to close the Internet Protocol (TCP/IP) Properties dialog box.

19. Click Cancel to close the Local Area Connection Properties dialog box.

20. Click the File menu on the Network And Dial-Up Connections dialog box and then select Close.

Viewing the Local Security Policy

The local security policy is the local version of the group security policy, which can apply to an entire domain. It's used to define various aspects of Windows 2000 security. To view a local security policy, perform the following steps:

1. Click the Start menu, select Programs, select Administrative Tools, and then click Local Security Policy. The Local Security Policy dialog box opens.

2. Take your time to review the contents of the Local Security Policy. Expand the Account Polices and Local Policies nodes. Then select each subnode in turn (see Figure 2.6).

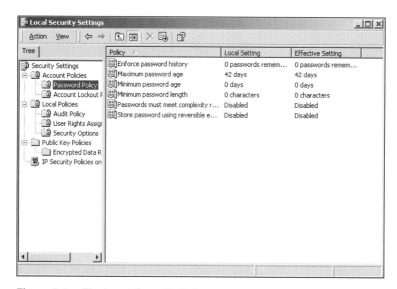

Figure 2.6   The Local Security Policy.

3. As you select a subnode, the policies of that subnode are displayed in the right pane. Read through each listed policy.

4. For more details on any specific policy, highlight the policy and then click the Action menu and select Security. Do not make any changes to the dialog boxes you open and be sure to close them using the Cancel button to discard any accidental changes.

5. Once you've finished exploring, close the Local Security Policy by clicking the close button (the X button) on the title bar.

2. Comparing Windows 2000 to Windows NT

Encrypting a File/Folder

The improved security of Windows 2000 includes the Encrypting File System (EFS). This new capability allows you to encrypt data to prevent prying eyes from discovering its contents. To encrypt a file or folder, perform the following steps:

NOTE: *This solution requires that an encryption recovery agent be defined.*

1. Click the Start menu, select Programs, select Accessories, and then click Windows Explorer.

2. Use Windows Explorer to locate a file or folder to encrypt; select it in the right pane.

3. Click the File menu and then select Properties. The Properties dialog box opens.

4. Click the Advanced button. The Advanced Attributes dialog box opens (see Figure 2.7).

5. Select the Encrypt Contents To Secure Data checkbox.

Figure 2.7   The Advanced Attributes dialog box.

NOTE: *You cannot use both encryption and compression on a file or folder (these are mutually exclusive).*

---

6. Click OK to close the Advanced Attributes dialog box.

7. Click OK to close the Properties dialog box.

8. If you selected a folder, you'll see a dialog box asking you to confirm your selection to encrypt and whether to encrypt only the selected folder or the folder and all its contents. Select the Apply Changes To This Folder, Subfolders, And Files option and then click OK.

   If you selected a file, you'll see a dialog box asking you to confirm your selection to encrypt and whether to encrypt only the selected file or the file and its parent folder. Select the Encrypt The File Only option and then click OK.

9. A warning may appear that states that no valid encryption recovery policy has been configured for this system. If so, click Cancel. This indicates that you do not have an encryption recovery policy properly defined and encryption cannot occur.

10. You'll see a progress dialog box briefly as the system encrypts the selected files.

11. Click the File menu and then select Close to close Windows Explorer.

Related solution:	Found on page:
Installing Encrypting File System	600

Decrypting a File/Folder

If you have encrypted a file or folder and need to grant access to other users, you should remove the encryption. To decrypt a file or folder, perform the following steps:

NOTE: *This solution requires that an encryption recovery agent be defined. It also requires that a file or folder be encrypted.*

---

1. Click the Start menu, select Programs, select Accessories, and then click Windows Explorer.

2. Use Windows Explorer to locate and select the file or folder that's already encrypted; select it in the right pane.

TIP: *The encryption state of a file is not indicated via the default or main Windows Explorer window; instead, you must view the advanced properties of a file or folder to see whether it has been encrypted.*

---

3. Click the File menu and then select Properties. The Properties dialog box opens.

4. Click the Advanced button. The Advanced Attributes dialog box opens.

5. Deselect the Encrypt Contents To Secure Data checkbox.

6. Click OK to close the Advanced Attributes dialog box.

7. Click OK to close the Properties dialog box.

8. If you're decrypting a file, it will be decrypted with further prompts.

   If you're decrypting a folder, you'll be prompted whether to apply the changes to this folder only or to its contents as well (see Figure 2.8). Select the Apply Change To This Folder, Subfolders, And Files option, and click OK.

9. You'll see a progress dialog box briefly as the system encrypts the selected files.

10. Click the File menu and then select Close to close Windows Explorer.

Related solution:	Found on page:
Installing Encrypting File System	600

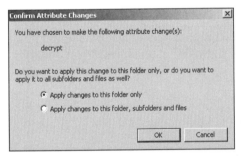

Figure 2.8   The Confirm Attribute Changes dialog box.

Enabling Internet Connection Sharing

If you have a small network and only one computer has a modem or you only have a single ISP account, you can share that precious link to the Internet with your network. To enable Internet connection sharing, perform the following steps:

NOTE: *This solution requires that you have a connection object (modem or other dialing device) predefined for connecting to the Internet.*

1. Click the Start menu, select Settings, and then click Network And Dial-Up Connections. The Network And Dial-Up Connection dialog box opens.

2. Select the connection object used to connect to the Internet.

3. Click the File menu and select Properties. The Properties dialog box for the connection object opens.

4. Select the Sharing tab.

5. Mark the Enable Internet Connection Sharing For This Connection checkbox (see Figure 2.9).

6. Click OK.

7. A message appears stating that your network adapter is being reconfigured to a new NAT-compatible address. Also, all clients on the network that need Internet access should be reconfigured to obtain their IP configurations automatically. Click Yes.

Your Internet connection is now shared, but you must perform two further steps before real access is possible:

1. Reconfigure all clients to obtain their IP configurations automatically.

2. Define the applications (that is, their protocols and ports) that will be proxied by the shared connection.

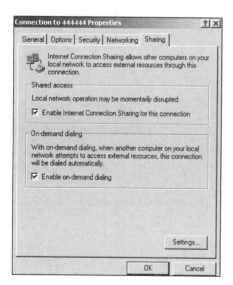

Figure 2.9   The Sharing tab of a connection object's Properties dialog box.

Using Advanced Search Tools

Need to locate a file and you can't remember where you put it, but you remember a bit about its contents? If so, the search tools of Windows 2000 can help. To use the Windows 2000 advanced search tools, perform the following steps:

1. Click the Start menu, select Find, and then click Search For Files And Folders. The Search Results dialog box appears.

2. In the Containing text field, type in your keywords (for example, "1993-1999").

3. Verify that the Look In pull-down list has Local Hard Drives selected.

4. Click Search Now.

5. After a few moments, you should see the hosts file listed in the results (see Figure 2.10). This file happens to contain the string "1993-1999".

6. Click File and then select Close to close the Search Results window.

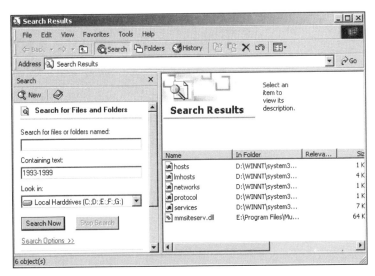

Figure 2.10   The Search Results window after a successful search operation.

Chapter 3

Active Directory

(continued)

In Depth

Before you can install and implement Active Directory, you must understand the purpose of a directory service. You should also understand the role that Active Directory plays in the overall scheme of a Windows 2000 network. In addition, this chapter examines the key features that play a role in the Active Directory design that will help you implement this directory service properly in your Windows 2000 network.

A *directory service* is a network service that's used to store and control all resources on a network, making them available and accessible to all users and applications on the network. These resources include user accounts, group accounts, email addresses, computers, and peripheral devices such as scanners and printers. Ideally, the directory service would be extensible, meaning that an administrator or an application can modify the objects and the object properties stored in the directory service.

Overview

Many people assume that Active Directory is Microsoft's first operating system directory service (not including the directory service that was included in Microsoft Exchange Server). In fact, Windows NT does use a directory service. This directory service, however, used what is known as a *flat file system*. This made the directory service difficult or impossible to modify (or extend). In a flat file system, all information is stored in the directory in a specific order. For example, a flat file directory service might store the following information about a user (in the following order):

- User name
- Full name
- Description
- Password

NOTE: *This example is very simplified and does not coincide with the Windows NT directory service. It is only used to illustrate the limitations of a flat file directory service.*

Similarly, a flat file directory service may store the following information about user groups:

- Group name
- Description
- Member 1
- Member 2
- Member 3

To understand how the data is stored, imagine that you're about to go shopping. You'll be visiting four different stores in four different locations (Store A, B, C, and D). On a piece of paper, you write your shopping list with only one item on a line, as follows:

- Store A: Item 1
- Store A: Item 2
- Store A: Item 3
- Store B: Item 1
- Store B: Item 2
- Store C: Item 1
- Store C: Item 2
- Store C: Item 3
- Store C: Item 4
- Store D: Item 1
- Store D: Item 2
- Store D: Item 3

Now, assume that you cannot write between the lines, place more than one item on a line, or erase any items. What would happen if you forgot to add Item 3 from Store B? You would have to do one of two things—rewrite the list or add the item after the last line of the list. Now, imagine that this list has 5,000 items on it from 2,000 stores. As you can see, this way of making a list becomes extremely difficult to modify and maintain.

Windows NT's directory system operated in a manner similar to this, which limited the Windows NT directory model to how many objects (users, groups, and computers) it could store and maintain. You now know why Windows NT required many domains with trust relationships for organizations with a large number of users, groups, and computers.

Active Directory is a *distributed directory*, which means that all the information within the Active Directory can be placed across multiple computers in multiple locations. Not only does this allow for fault tolerance, but it also enables faster access to the directory information. In a Windows NT environment, if the Primary Domain Controller (PDC) is in company headquarters in New York and your office is in California, all changes to the directory (adding or removing users and groups or changing a user password) must be done on the PDC in New York and then replicated back to the domain controller in your location.

With Active Directory, all the domain controllers maintain a read/write version of the directory. This eliminates the need for the domain controllers to replicate all the information before it appears on the local domain controller. In the previous example, the local domain controller will receive the password changes (making it immediately active locally) and will then replicate the changes to the other domain controllers in the organization.

Another great feature in Windows 2000 that has been a long time in the making is the ability to convert member servers in the network into domain controllers. With Windows NT, once you selected the server's role (domain controller or member server), you had to reinstall the operating system to change that role. As you'll see in the Immediate Solutions section, the utility that allows you to accomplish this is dcpromo.

TIP: *You can also demote a domain controller to a member server using dcpromo.*

Concepts

Active Directory is very different from the directory service used with Windows NT. Before you can implement Active Directory, you need to understand the structure of Active Directory. The Active Directory structure, also known as *logical structure*, consists of the following five components:

- Objects
- Organizational units
- Domains
- Trees
- Forests

With Active Directory, network administrators have the ability to access resources independent of their physical locations. It is the logical structure that makes this possible. The following sections examine the five logical structure components.

Objects

The directory is made up of network resources such as computers, printers, users, groups, and contacts. Each object has attributes associated with it. These can include the following:

- First name
- Last name
- Description
- Alias
- Department
- Phone number
- Manager
- Employee number

As you can see, the amount of information that can be included with an object in Active Directory is vast compared to the Windows NT directory. Microsoft has also designed the Active Directory so that organizations and applications can extend it to add proprietary information, such as date of birth, credit card number, anniversary date, and so on.

Organizational Units

An *organizational unit* (OU) can be defined as a container that's used to organize objects into logical administration groups. Organizational units can contain objects such as users, groups, printers, computers, applications, file shares, and other organizational units. Figure 3.1 illustrates the logical hierarchy of the Active Directory, whereas Figure 3.2 shows the objects as they would appear in the Active Directory.

Domains

The definition of a domain in Windows 2000 is similar to that of a domain in Windows NT. A *domain* is the main structure of Active Directory. By placing objects within one or more domains in an organization, you can duplicate the organization's physical structure. For example, with many different organizations today, each department has its own IT budget and therefore "owns" its part of the network. Although there might be an IT group that oversees the entire network, the department maintains control over daily tasks on its part of the network (creating users, for example). By creating a domain for each department and assigning a delegate from each department to control that domain, a network

3. Active Directory

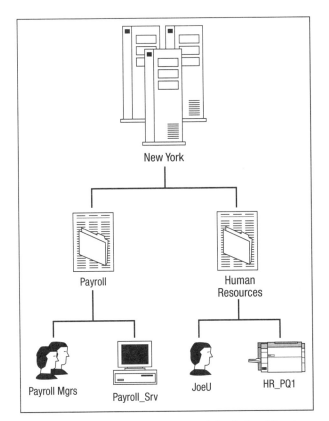

Figure 3.1   The logical hierarchy of the Active Directory.

administrator can allow for the organization to maintain the overall domain, while the department controls its portion of the network, setting policies as they fit that department's criteria.

For example, the information stored on the payroll system is more critical and sensitive than that stored on the marketing system. The payroll department may choose to set the password length to eight characters and have the password changed every 14 days, whereas the marketing department is not worried about password length or its expiration policy. With Windows NT, an administrator would have to create two domains with different policies and create the necessary trust relationships between the two. With Active Directory, an administrator can simply create two new domains in the organization domain, as shown in Figure 3.3, and assign delegate control to the appropriate department.

3. Active Directory

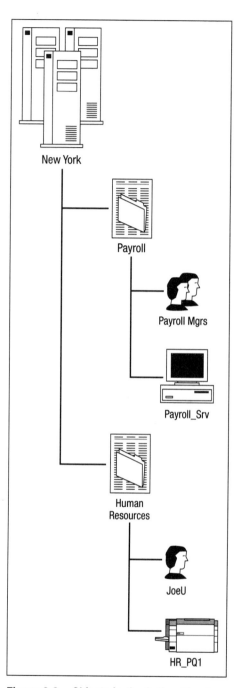

Figure 3.2   Objects in the Active Directory.

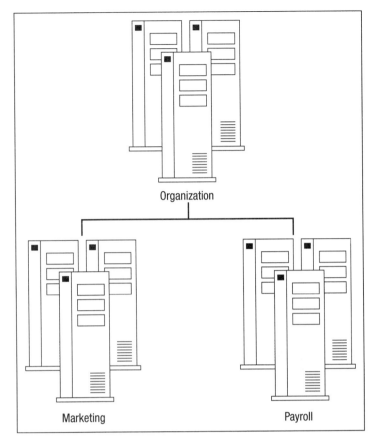

Figure 3.3   The Active Directory domain model.

Trees and Forests

A *tree* is simply a collection or group of one or more Windows 2000 domains. Using the same logic, a *forest* is a collection of one or more trees. Usually only large organizations would implement a forest. Another situation where you might find the need for the implementation of a forest is when organizations merge or acquire one another. Each of the organizational trees must maintain its own security policies but must still be able to communicate between the different organizational domains.

Naming Conventions

Every object in the Active Directory has a name assigned to it. Unfortunately (or fortunately, depending on your point of view), you can have duplicated names within the same organization (as long as they're in different containers and have different logon names). For Active Directory to be able to distinguish one name from another, it uses several different methods. These include the following:

- Distinguished name
- Relative distinguished name
- User principal names
- Globally unique identifier

Distinguished Name

Every object in Active Directory has a distinguished name (DN). Each DN must be unique in the Active Directory. Think of it as a mailing address, such as this:

```
Joe Smith
1234 Center Street N.
Some City, State 12345-6789
USA
```

Using this information, a letter can be delivered to the address from anywhere in the world. An Active Directory DN would be written as follows:

```
/DC=COM/DC=Organization/OU=Payroll/CN=Users/CN=Joe Smith
```

Notice that a DN is written in the opposite direction with respect to a street address. If you were to write the DN information in the address format, it would appear as follows:

```
COM
Organization, Payroll
Users
Joe Smith
```

NOTE: *If you were to compare Active Directory DNs to some of the other directory services out there, such as Novell's NetWare Directory Services (NDS) or Lightweight Directory Access Protocol (LDAP), you would notice that they have a /C option (/C = Country). Microsoft's Active Directory does not support the Country DN field.*

It is important that you understand the different attributes in this example. These attributes are listed in Table 3.1.

Table 3.1   Active Directory distinguished name attributes.

Attribute	Description
DC	DomainComponent
OU	OrganizationUnit
CN	CanonicalName

Usually, the attributes are not included when using the DNs. The previous example will normally be written as follows:

```
/COM/Organization/Payroll/Users/Joe Smith
```

Relative Distinguished Name

A relative distinguished name (RDN) simply makes an assumption as to where in the Active Directory tree a user currently resides. In the previous example, the RDN of the user object is Joe Smith. You can compare the RDN of an object to the working directory when accessing files via the command prompt.

For example, if you're trying to access the C:\Program Files\Application\App.exe application, you can use the full path (C:\Program Files\Application\App.exe) from anywhere in the command prompt and the application will be executed. This would be the same as the DN. If you're in the C:\Program Files\Application directory (that is, you issued a **CD C:\Program Files\Application** command), you can simply type "App.exe" and the application will execute. The operating system will look for App.exe in the current context (C:\Program Files\Application) and run the application if it is found. This would be the RDN.

User Principal Names

Each user account in the Active Directory has a user principle name (UPN) assigned to it. This UPN can be referred to as a friendly name for the user account object. The UPN is a combination of the alias of the user account and the DNS name of the domain. In the previous example, Joe Smith's UPN might be joes@organization.com.

Globally Unique Identifier

Most Windows NT administrators are aware of what security identifiers (SIDs) are. Each object in the Windows NT directory is assigned a unique ID. This is how the operating system recognizes the object. With Active Directory, a SID is still used, but a globally unique identifier (GUID) is also assigned. The GUID is a 128-bit value that not only makes the object unique in the enterprise—it makes the object unique in the world.

Trust Relationships

Much like in Windows NT, a trust relationship is an "understanding" between domains. You can also think of it as a link between two domains, enabling one domain to trust (the domain is known as the *trusting domain*) the users from the other (the trusted domain).

One of the major differences between Windows NT and Windows 2000 trust relationships is that Windows 2000 supports the Kerberos 5 protocol. Kerberos 5 is an industry standard for encrypted authentication across different operating systems.

Windows 2000 supports two types of trust relationships: one-way, nontransitive trusts and two-way, transitive trusts. Each of these trust relationships is covered in the following sections.

One-Way, Nontransitive Trusts

A one-way trust is a trust relationship in which one of the domains trusts the users from the other, but not the inverse. If you refer to Figure 3.4, you'll notice that Domain A trusts Domain B. However, Domain B does not trust Domain A. Any user from Domain A that attempts to access a resource on Domain B will be denied.

With a nontransitive trust relationship, if Domain A trusts Domain B and Domain B trusts Domain C, then Domain A will not automatically trust Domain C (see Figure 3.5). This is the trust relationship model used in Windows NT 4.0. For backward compatibility and the coexistence of Windows NT 4.0 and Windows 2000 systems, Active Directory supports this type of trust relationship.

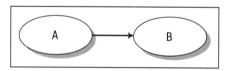

Figure 3.4   A one-way trust relationship.

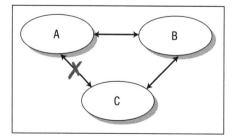

Figure 3.5   A nontransitive trust relationship.

Two-Way, Transitive Trusts

Windows 2000 introduces a new way of creating trust relationships: transitive trusts. In a two-way trust, if Domain A trusts Domain B, then Domain B automatically trusts Domain A, as shown in Figure 3.6. With transitive trusts, if Domain A trusts Domain B and Domain B trusts Domain C, then Domain A trusts Domain C and Domain C trusts Domain A.

This way of creating trust relationships is the default in Windows 2000. When an administrator creates a child domain, a two-way trust is automatically created between the parent and the child domains. With transitive trusts, this means that the new child domain trusts and is trusted by every other domain under its parent domain.

Global Catalog

Active Directory stores all its information about objects in a tree or forest in a repository (or database) known as the *global catalog*. Not all object attributes are stored in the global catalog (this would make replication in a large enterprise impractical). Instead, only the most commonly searched attributes for each object are stored—for example, the first and last names of the user, the logon name, and the group relationships.

When you first install Active Directory, the first domain controller becomes the global catalog server by default. It is this server that's responsible for maintaining the global catalog.

Under normal circumstances, a global catalog server can contain up to a million objects. Once your organization has reached that limit (or is even somewhat close to that number), you have the ability to designate additional domain controllers as global catalog servers.

Schema

The Active Directory *schema* is the structure of the data that's stored with the Active Directory. It can contain all attributes, classes, and class properties. For

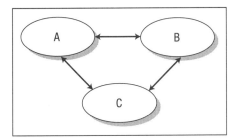

Figure 3.6   A two-way, transitive trust relationship.

example, the schema defines the attributes that a user account can have (such as pager, email, or cellular phone).

Administrators and applications can extend the schema to meet their needs. For example, Microsoft Exchange 2000 extends the schema with Exchange-specific attributes. To modify the schema, an administrator can use either the Active Directory Schema Manager snap-in for MMC or the Active Directory Services Interface (ADSI). Both of these utilities can be found on the CD-ROM that accompanies the *Windows 2000 Server Resource Kit* (Microsoft Press, ISBN: 1-57231-805-8).

Planning

When you finally sit down to plan your Active Directory, you'll quickly notice that you have to decide whether to create domains or organizational units. As previously mentioned, the domain is the core administrative unit of a Windows 2000 network. It outlines the logical boundaries of the network. Every object within a domain falls under its security "umbrella." Organizational units, on the other hand, allow administrators to modify the individual security criterion for each department of an organization without needing multiple domain controllers for each one.

Most organizations fall under the single domain/multiple organizational units model. The first domain that you create in your organization (or Active Directory) becomes the root domain for the entire forest. A forest is simply a collection of domains and organizational units. Therefore, you need to be very careful as to what you name this domain. For example, naming it domain.com will probably come back to haunt you if you ever need to modify the name of the root domain. Most organizations will name their internal forests similarly to their Internet presence. For example, microsoft would use the microsoft.com domain model both externally on the Internet and internally on the network. This is something that you, as an administrator, should strongly consider even if your organization currently does not have an Internet presence.

Organizational units exist below the domain, similar to how subdomains exist below an Internet domain. For example, your organization might have the fully qualified domain name (FQDN) of www.company.com. It might also have multiple locations—www.austin.company.com, www.boston.company.com, and www.seattle.company.com. Figure 3.7 illustrates how this might look.

Similarly, your organization might choose to configure its Active Directory structure as illustrated in Figure 3.8.

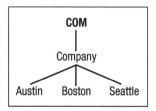

Figure 3.7   A sample Internet domain.

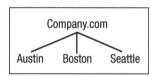

Figure 3.8   A sample Active Directory domain.

Immediate Solutions

Once you decide the infrastructure you'll use in your domain, it is time to implement Active Directory in your organization. To begin, you must install the first domain and domain controller in the organization. Unlike Windows NT, Windows 2000 Servers are never domain controllers at first. They always start up as member servers. To promote them to domain controller status, you simply run a utility (called *dcpromo*) that installs the Active Directory by bringing up the Active Directory Installation Wizard.

As mentioned, the first system in the domain will create the forest root of the domain. You would run dcpromo on the system designated as the first domain controller (see the next section, "Installing Active Directory in a New Domain"). Once the first Active Directory domain is installed, you can simply add new domains (if required) or organizational units to your existing domain.

Installing Active Directory in a New Domain

To install Active Directory, follow these steps:

1. Select Start|Run.

2. In the Open field, type "dcpromo" and click OK.

3. When the Active Directory Installation Wizard appears, click Next.

4. In the Domain Controller Type window, choose the Domain Controller For A New Domain option and click Next (see Figure 3.9).

5. In the Create Tree Or Child Domain window, choose the Create New Domain Tree option and click Next.

6. Choose the Create A New Forest Of Domain Trees in the Create Or Join Forest window, and click Next.

7. Enter the full DNS name of the new domain and click Next. The wizard will verify that this domain name is not duplicated on the network. If it is, click OK and choose a new domain name.

8. Enter the NetBIOS name that's to be assigned to this domain. This name will be used when systems that aren't Active Directory enabled need to

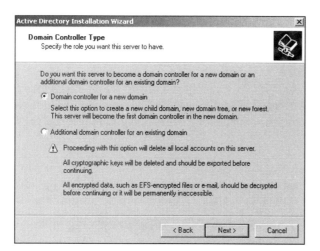

Figure 3.9   The Domain Controller Type window.

communicate with this domain. The wizard will automatically create a
NetBIOS domain name for you; this name will always be uppercase and a
derivative of the DNS name given. You can choose to keep this name or
create a new one. If the NetBIOS domain name exists, the wizard will add a
number to the end of the name. For example, if the NetBIOS domain name
"DOMAIN" exists, the wizard will suggest the name "DOMAIN0". When you
have selected your NetBIOS domain name, click Next.

9. The wizard will now ask you for the location where it should create the
   database and log directories.

TIP: *For best performance, you should place the database and log directories on separate physical hard disks.*

By default, log directories are stored in the %systemroot%\NTDS directory.
You can, however, choose a different location. Once you have selected the
location for these directories, click Next.

NOTE: *The Database directory is used to store the Active Directory information for the new domain, and the
Log directory is used to temporarily store changes made to the Active Directory database before they're
committed to the Active Directory database.*

---

10. Choose the location for the shared system volume. By default, this is stored
    in the %systemroot%\Sysvol directory. The shared system volume directory
    is used to store scripts and Group Policies. Every domain controller in
    Active Directory maintains such a directory. All file replication services use

3. Active Directory

this volume to replicate the scripts and Group Policies information to all domain controllers. Once you have selected the location for this directory, click Next.

WARNING! *For Active Directory to be installed on your system, at least one drive or partition must be formatted with Windows 2000 NTFS (NTFS v5.0). If no such partition exists, you'll be presented with an error message and won't be able to continue the Active Directory installation until you create such a partition.*

11. If the Active Directory Installation Wizard does not detect a DNS server, you'll be notified and must then decide whether you would like the wizard to install and configure DNS.

12. The Windows NT 4.0 RAS Servers window will appear (see Figure 3.10). This window allows you to choose whether Windows 2000 Active Directory will use permissions that are compatible with non-Windows 2000 systems or with native Windows 2000 permissions. Choose your desired option and click Next.

13. In the Directory Services Restore Mode Administrator Password window, choose a password to be used when you need to restore your Active Directory information. Then click Next.

TIP: *For security reasons, do not use your Administrator password as the DS Restore Mode Administrator password.*

---

14. A summary window will appear informing you of all the options you selected. Click Next to start the Active Directory installation.

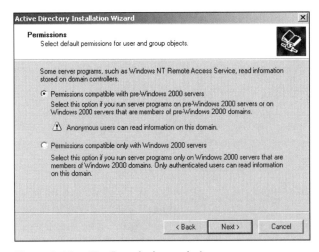

Figure 3.10   The Permissions window.

15. A progress indicator will appear. When the installation is complete, the Complete Active Directory Installation Wizard window will appear. Click Finish.

16. A dialog box will appear notifying you that the system must be rebooted for the changes to take effect. Click Restart Now to complete the installation.

Installing Active Directory in an Existing Domain

To install Active Directory in an existing domain, perform the following steps:

1. Select Start|Run.

2. In the Open field, type "dcpromo" and click OK.

3. When the Active Directory Installation Wizard appears, click Next.

4. In the Domain Controller Type window, choose the Additional Domain Controller For An Existing Domain option and click Next.

5. Enter the full DNS name of the new domain and click Next. The wizard will now verify that this domain name is not duplicated on the network. If it is, click OK and choose a new domain name.

6. Enter the NetBIOS name to be assigned to this domain. This name will be used when systems that aren't Active Directory enabled need to communicate with this domain. The wizard will automatically create a NetBIOS domain name for you. You can choose to keep this name or create a new one. If the NetBIOS domain name exists, the wizard will add a number to the end of the name. For example, if the NetBIOS domain name "DOMAIN" exists, the wizard will suggest the name "DOMAIN0". When you have selected your NetBIOS domain name, click Next.

7. The wizard will now ask you for the location where it should create the database and log directories. By default, these are stored in the %systemroot%\NTDS directory. You can, however, choose a different location. Once you have selected the location for these directories, click Next.

8. Choose the location for the shared system volume. By default, this is stored in the %systemroot%\Sysvol directory. Once you have selected the location for this directory, click Next.

9. If the Active Directory Installation Wizard does not detect a DNS server, you'll be notified and must then decide whether you would like the wizard to install and configure DNS.

10. The Windows NT 4.0 RAS Servers window appears. This window allows you to choose whether Windows 2000 Active Directory will use permissions that are compatible with non-Windows 2000 systems or with native Windows 2000 permissions. Choose your desired option and click Next.

11. In the Directory Services Restore Mode Administrator Password window, choose a password to be used when you need to restore your Active Directory information. Then click Next.

12. A summary window will appear informing you of all the options you selected. Click Next to start the Active Directory installation.

13. A progress indicator will appear. When the installation is complete, the Complete Active Directory Installation Wizard window will appear. Click Finish.

14. A dialog box will appear notifying you that the system must be rebooted for the changes to take effect. Click Restart Now to complete the installation.

Removing Active Directory

To remove Active Directory from your server, follow these steps:

1. Select Start|Run.

2. In the Open field, type "dcpromo" and click OK.

3. When the Active Directory Installation Wizard appears, click Next.

4. The Remove Active Directory window will appear (see Figure 3.11). Make sure that the This Server Is The Last Domain Controller In The Domain option is not selected and click Next.

5. Enter an Administrator's password and confirm it. Click Next.

6. A summary screen will appear. Click Next to begin the domain controller demotion.

7. When the demotion is complete, click Finish.

8. A dialog box will appear notifying you that the system must be rebooted for the changes to take effect. Click Restart Now to complete the installation.

Removing Active Directory from the Last Domain Controller

To remove Active Directory from the last domain controller, perform the following steps:

1. Select Start|Run.

2. In the Open field, type "dcpromo" and click OK.

3. Active Directory

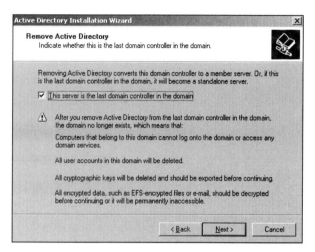

Figure 3.11   The Remove Active Directory window.

3. When the Active Directory Installation Wizard appears, click Next.

4. The Remove Active Directory window will appear. Make sure that the This Server Is the Last Domain Controller in the Domain option is selected and click Next.

5. Enter the username, password, and domain for an account that has the Enterprise Admin rights assigned to it and click Next.

6. Enter an Administrator's password and confirm it. Click Next.

7. A summary screen will appear. Click Next to begin the domain controller demotion.

8. When the demotion is completed, click Finish.

9. A dialog box will appear notifying you that the system must be rebooted for the changes to take effect. Click Restart Now to complete the installation.

Installing the Active Directory Schema Utility

The Active Directory Schema utility is part of the Windows 2000 Administration Tools, which are available on the Windows 2000 Server CD-ROM. To install the Active Directory Schema utility, perform the following steps:

1. Insert the Windows 2000 Server CD-ROM into the CD-ROM drive.

2. Select Start|Run.

3. In the Run dialog box, type "*windows2000CD*\i386\adminpak.msi" (where *windows2000CD* is your CD-ROM drive) and click OK. This will start the Windows 2000 Administration Tools.

4. Once the installer completes the installation, select Start|Run. In the Run dialog box, type "mmc" and click OK.

5. Click Console|Add/Remove Snap-In.

6. Click Add.

7. Choose the Active Directory Schema option and click Add.

8. Click Close.

9. Click OK.

10. The Active Directory Schema utility is now installed. Save the MMC configuration for the next time you need this application.

Identifying the Schema Master

To identify the schema master, perform the following steps:

1. Select Start|Programs|Administrative Tools|Active Directory Schema.

2. Right-click Active Directory Schema and choose the Operations Master option from the pop-up menu.

3. The name that appears in the Current Operations Master field is the schema master.

Modifying the Schema Master Role

To modify the schema master role, perform the following steps:

1. Select Start|Programs|Administrative Tools|Active Directory Schema.

2. Right-click Active Directory Schema and choose the Change Domain Controller option.

3. Click the Any DC option to let Active Directory choose a new schema operations master.

4. Right-click Active Directory Schema and choose the Operations Manager option.

5. Click Change and choose the new schema master.

Creating a User in Active Directory

To create a user in Active Directory, follow these steps:

1. Select Start|Programs|Administrative Tools|Active Directory Users And Computers.

2. Select the container in which you would like the user to be created. Right-click the container and choose New|User.

TIP: *The Active Directory Users and Computers MMC snap-in provides several different ways to a task. For example, you can create a new user in the following ways: right-clicking the container and choosing New|User, clicking Action and choosing New|User, and clicking New User.*

---

3. Enter the desired information (such as first name, middle initial, last name, and user logon name) and click Next. The Create New User Wizard will autofill the Full Name field based on the information entered in the First Name, Initial, and Last Name fields. By default, it will also assume that the non-Windows 2000 name is the same as the Windows 2000 username. If you have multiple domains in your organization, select the desired domain from the drop-down menu.

NOTE: *To create a new user, you must have the User Logon Name and at least one of the following: First Name, Middle Initial, or Last Name. If you do not have at least these selected, Next will be disabled.*

---

4. Enter the user's password and confirm it. Choose any other options for this account (User Must Change Password At Next Logon, User Cannot Change Password, Password Never Expires, or Account Is Disabled). Click Next.

NOTE: *By default, the Domain Security Policy allows you to create a password of zero length (that is, no password).*

---

5. Click Finish to create the user.

Creating a User in Active Directory Using the Command Line without Assigning a Password

To create an account using the command line without assigning it a password, follow these steps:

1. Select Start|Programs|Accessories|Command Prompt.

2. At the command prompt, type the following:

```
Net user Username /add
```

3. Press Enter. The account is now created without a password.

WARNING!   *This operation will fail if your password length policy is set to anything other than zero length.*

Creating a User in Active Directory Using the Command Line and Assigning a Password

To create an account using the command line and assign it a password, follow these steps:

1. Select Start|Programs|Accessories|Command Prompt.

2. At the command prompt, type the following:

```
Net user Username password /add
```

3. Press Enter. The account is now created with the desired password.

TIP: *Instead of typing in the password at the command line, you can substitute the desired password with the asterisk (*) symbol. This will cause Windows 2000 to ask you to enter the password (which is hidden at this point) and then confirm it.*

Working with Users

A number of tasks are involved in managing users in Active Directory. The following solutions address this important issue.

Editing a User in Active Directory

Two methods are used for editing users in Active Directory. One is not necessarily better than the other, but you should be aware of both ways of performing user management.

3. Active Directory

Here is the first method:

1. Select Start|Programs|Administrative Tools|Active Directory Users And Computers.

2. Navigate to the container in which the user you would like to modify resides. Click the user object to select it.

3. Click Action and choose Properties from the drop-down menu.

4. The User Properties window will appear. Make your desired changes and click OK to finish.

Here is the second method:

1. Select Start|Programs|Administrative Tools|Active Directory Users And Computers.

2. Navigate to the container in which the user you would like to modify resides. Click the user object to select it.

3. Right-click the user object and choose Properties from the pop-up menu.

4. The User Properties window will appear. Make your desired changes and click OK to finish.

TIP: You can also access the Properties page of any object by simply double-clicking it.

Deleting a User in Active Directory

Three methods are used for deleting users in Active Directory. One is not necessarily better than another, but you should be aware of the various ways of performing user management.

Here is the first method:

1. Select Start|Programs|Administrative Tools|Active Directory Users And Computers.

2. Navigate to the container in which the user you would like to delete resides. Click the user object to select it.

3. Click Action and choose Delete from the drop-down menu.

4. A dialog box will appear asking you to confirm the deletion of this user. Click OK to delete the user.

Here is the second method:

1. Select Start|Programs|Administrative Tools|Active Directory Users And Computers.

2. Navigate to the container in which the user you would like to delete resides. Click the user object to select it.

3. Right-click the selected user and choose Delete from the pop-up menu.

4. A dialog box will appear asking you to confirm the deletion of this user. Click OK to delete the user.

Here is the third method:

1. Select Start|Programs|Administrative Tools|Active Directory Users And Computers.

2. Navigate to the container in which the user you would like to delete resides. Click the user object to select it.

3. Press the Delete key to delete the user.

4. A dialog box will appear asking you to confirm the deletion of this user. Click OK to delete the user.

Deleting a User in Active Directory Using the Command Prompt

To delete an account from the command line, follow these steps:

1. Select Start|Programs|Accessories|Command Prompt.

2. At the command prompt, type the following:

```
Net user Username /delete
```

WARNING!   Make sure you're deleting the correct account. When using the command line, you are not asked to confirm the deletion.

3. Press Enter. The account is now deleted.

Renaming a User in Active Directory

Three methods are used for renaming users in Active Directory. One is not necessarily better than another, but you should be aware of the various ways of performing user management.

Here is the first method:

1. Select Start|Programs|Administrative Tools|Active Directory Users and Computers.

2. Navigate to the container in which the user you would like to rename resides. Click the user object to select it.

3. Click Action and choose Rename from the drop-down menu.

4. Type the new name for the user and press Enter.

5. The Rename User window will appear. Enter any necessary information (including full name, first and last name, display name, login name and domain, and the pre-Windows 2000 name) and click OK.

Here is the second method:

1. Select Start|Programs|Administrative Tools|Active Directory Users And Computers.

2. Navigate to the container in which the user you would like to rename resides. Click the user object to select it.

3. Right-click the selected user and choose Rename from the pop-up menu.

4. Type the new name for the user and press Enter.

5. The Rename User window will appear. Enter any necessary information (including full name, first and last name, display name, login name and domain, and the pre-Windows 2000 name) and click OK.

Here is the third method:

1. Select Start|Programs|Administrative Tools|Active Directory Users And Computers.

2. Navigate to the container in which the user you would like to rename resides. Click the user object to select it.

3. Press F2.

4. Type the new name for the user and press Enter.

5. A dialog box will appear asking you to confirm renaming this user account. Click OK to rename the user account. The Rename User window will appear. Enter any necessary information (including full name, first and last name, display name, login name and domain, and the pre-Windows 2000 name) and click OK.

Disabling a User in Active Directory

Three methods are used for disabling user accounts in Active Directory. One is not necessarily better than another, but you should be aware of the various ways of performing user management.

Here is the first method:

1. Select Start|Programs|Administrative Tools|Active Directory Users And Computers.

3. Active Directory

2. Navigate to the container in which the user you would like to disable resides. Click the user object to select it.

3. Click Action and choose Disable Account from the drop-down menu.

TIP: *Alternately, you can choose the Disable Account option from the All Tasks submenu.*

---

4. A dialog box notifying you that the account has been disabled will appear. Click OK. Notice that the user icon now has a red "X" on it.

Here is the second method:

1. Select Start|Programs|Administrative Tools|Active Directory Users And Computers.

2. Navigate to the container in which the user you would like to disable resides. Click the user object to select it.

3. Right-click the selected user and choose Disable Account from the pop-up menu.

4. A dialog box notifying you that the account has been disabled will appear. Click OK. Notice that the user icon now has a red "X" on it.

Here is the third method:

1. Select Start|Programs|Administrative Tools|Active Directory Users And Computers.

2. Navigate to the container in which the user you would like to disable resides. Double-click the user object to open its Properties page.

3. Click the Account tab.

4. Under Account Options, select the Account Is Disabled option. Click OK.

5. A dialog box notifying you that the account has been disabled will appear. Click OK. Notice that the user icon now has a red "X" on it.

Enabling a Disabled Account

Three methods are used for enabling disabled user accounts in Active Directory. One is not necessarily better than another, but you should be aware of the various ways of performing user management.

Here is the first method:

1. Select Start|Programs|Administrative Tools|Active Directory Users And Computers.

2. Navigate to the container in which the user you would like to enable resides. Click the user object to select it.

3. Active Directory

3. Click Action and choose Enable Account from the drop-down menu.

TIP: *Alternately, you can choose the Enable Account from the All Tasks submenu.*

---

4. A dialog box notifying you that the account has been enabled will appear. Click OK. Notice that the red "X" disappears.

Here is the second method:

1. Select Start|Programs|Administrative Tools|Active Directory Users And Computers.

2. Navigate to the container in which the user you would like to enable resides. Click the user object to select it.

3. Right-click the selected user and choose Enable Account from the pop-up menu.

4. A dialog box notifying you that the account has been enabled will appear. Click OK. Notice that the red "X" disappears.

Here is the third method:

1. Select Start|Programs|Administrative Tools|Active Directory Users And Computers.

2. Navigate to the container in which the user you would like to enable resides. Double-click the user object to open its Properties page.

3. Click the Account tab.

4. Under Account Options, clear the Account Is Disabled option. Click OK.

5. A dialog box notifying you that the account has been enabled will appear. Click OK. Notice that the red "X" disappears.

Finding a User in Active Directory in a Domain

To find an Active Directory user in the domain, perform the following steps:

1. Select Start|Programs|Administrative Tools|Active Directory Users And Computers.

2. To search the entire domain, right-click the domain node and choose Find from the pop-up menu.

3. In the Name field, type the name of the user you want to find.

4. Click Find Now.

3. Active Directory

Finding a User in Active Directory in an Organizational Unit

To find an Active Directory user in an OU, perform the following steps:

1. Select Start|Programs|Administrative Tools|Active Directory Users And Computers.

2. To search an organizational unit, right-click the Organizational Unit node and choose Find from the pop-up menu.

3. In the Name field, type the name of the user you want to find.

4. Click Find Now.

Copying a User in Active Directory

Two methods are used for copying user accounts in Active Directory. One is not necessarily better than the other, but you should be aware of both ways of performing user management.

Here is the first method:

1. Select Start|Programs|Administrative Tools|Active Directory Users And Computers.

2. Navigate to the container in which the user you would like to copy resides. Click the user object to select it.

3. Click Action and choose Copy from the drop-down menu.

TIP: *Alternately, you can choose the Copy from the All Tasks submenu.*

---

4. The Copy Object - User window appears. Enter the required information and click Next.

5. Enter the password (if any) and confirm it. Select any other desired options and click Next.

6. Click Finish to complete the user account copy.

Here is the second method:

1. Select Start|Programs|Administrative Tools|Active Directory Users And Computers.

2. Navigate to the container in which the user you would like to enable resides. Click the user object to select it.

3. Right-click the selected user and choose Copy from the pop-up menu.

4. The Copy Object - User window appears. Enter the required information and click Next.

5. Enter the password (if any) and confirm it. Select any other desired options and click Next.

6. Click Finish to complete the user account copy.

Changing the User Rights

To change local user rights, perform the following steps:

1. Select Start|Programs|Administrative Tools|Local Security Policy. A screen like the one shown in Figure 3.12 will appear.

2. Expand the Security Settings item.

3. Expand Local Policies.

4. Select the User Rights Assignment item.

5. Choose the desired policy (for example, Access This Computer From The Network), right-click it, and choose the security option from the pop-up menu.

6. Click Add.

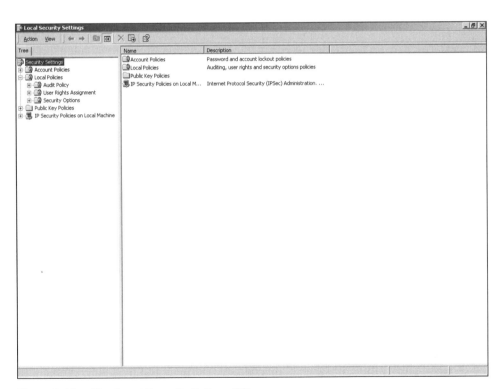

Figure 3.12   The Local Security Policy utility.

7. Choose a group or user to be added to this policy.

8. Click Add.

9. Repeat these steps for any additional users or groups.

10. When finished, click OK.

TIP: *Because you're dealing with both local and domain security settings, an effective policy exists. The effective policy displays the security attribute value that's currently enforced.*

Changing the Domain Rights

To change domain rights, follow these steps:

1. Select Start|Programs|Administrative Tools|Domain Security Settings.

2. Expand the Security Settings item.

3. Expand Local Policies.

4. Select the User Rights Assignment item.

5. Choose the desired policy (for example, Increase Quotas), right-click it, and choose the security option from the pop-up menu.

6. Enable the Define These Policy Settings option.

7. Click Add.

8. Add users and/or groups.

9. Repeat these steps for any additional desired users or groups.

10. Click OK to finish.

Modifying User Account Properties

To modify user account properties, perform the following steps:

1. Select Start|Programs|Administrative Tools|Active Directory Users And Computers.

2. Select the Users container (or any other container in which the desired user resides).

3. Right-click the desired user account and choose Properties from the pop-up menu.

Moving a User Account in Active Directory

To move an Active Directory user account, perform the following steps:

1. Select Start|Programs|Administrative Tools|Active Directory Users And Computers.

2. Select the Users container (or any other container in which the desired user resides).

3. Right-click the desired user account and choose Move from the pop-up menu.

4. In the Move dialog box, click the folder to which you would like the user account moved.

5. Click OK.

Reactivating a Locked Account

To reactivate a locked account, perform the following steps:

1. Select Start|Programs|Administrative Tools|Active Directory Users And Computers.

2. Select the Users container (or any other container in which the desired user resides).

3. Right-click the desired user account and choose Properties from the pop-up menu.

4. Clear the Account Disabled checkbox.

5. Click OK.

Changing Passwords

To change a password, perform the following steps:

1. Select Start|Programs|Administrative Tools|Active Directory Users And Computers.

2. Select the Users container (or any other container in which the desired user resides).

3. Right-click the desired user account and choose Reset Password from the pop-up menu.

4. Enter the desired password and confirm it.

5. If the user is to change the password the next time he or she logs in, select the User Must Change Password At Next Logon checkbox.

Changing a User's Primary Group

To change a user's primary group, perform the following steps:

1. Select Start|Programs|Administrative Tools|Active Directory Users And Computers.

2. Select the Users container (or any other container in which the desired user resides).

3. Right-click the desired user account and choose Properties from the pop-up menu.

4. Click the Members tab.

5. Select the group that you would like to act as the user's primary group and click the Set Primary Group button.

6. Click OK.

Working with Contacts

A number of tasks are involved in managing contacts in Active Directory. The following solutions address this important issue.

Creating a New Contact in Active Directory

To create a new Active Directory contact, perform the following steps:

1. Select Start|Programs|Administrative Tools|Active Directory Users And Computers.

2. Right-click the container where you would like the contact to be created and choose New|Contact.

3. Enter the contact information and click OK.

Modifying a Contact in Active Directory

To modify an Active Directory contact, perform the following steps:

1. Select Start|Programs|Administrative Tools|Active Directory Users And Computers.

2. Choose the contact you would like to modify.

3. Right-click it and choose Properties from the pop-up menu.

4. Modify any desired properties and click OK.

Deleting a Contact in Active Directory

To delete an Active Directory contact, perform the following steps:

1. Select Start|Programs|Administrative Tools|Active Directory Users And Computers.

2. Right-click the contact you would like to delete and choose Delete from the pop-up menu.

3. Click Yes to delete the contact.

Finding a Contact in Active Directory

To search for a contact in the entire domain, follow these steps:

1. Select Start|Programs|Administrative Tools|Active Directory Users And Computers.

2. Right-click the desired domain node and choose the Find option from the pop-up menu. The Find utility will appear.

3. Ensure that Users, Contacts, And Groups is selected in the Find field.

4. Enter the name you would like to search for in the Name field.

5. Click Find Now to begin the search. All matching entries will be displayed in the lower part of the Find window.

TIP: *By clicking on the Advanced tab, you can create extremely powerful search criteria. For example, you can search for all users who do not have a manager assigned to them.*

Adding a Computer in Active Directory

To add an Active Directory computer, perform the following steps:

1. Select Start|Programs|Administrative Tools|Active Directory Users And Computers.

2. Navigate to the Computers container (or any other container where you would like to add the computer) and select it.

3. Right-click the container and choose the New|Computer option from the pop-up menu.

4. Enter the computer name in the Computer Name field. Notice that the system will automatically create a pre-Windows 2000 name for your new computer.

5. By default, the Domains Admins group is allowed to join this new computer to the domain. If you would like to modify this, you can click Change and select a new group or groups.

6. If this new system is a non-Windows 2000 computer, enable the Allow Pre-Windows 2000 Computer To Use This Account option.

7. Click OK to create the account.

Modifying a Computer's Properties

To modify a computer's properties, perform the following steps:

1. Select Start|Programs|Administrative Tools|Active Directory Users And Computers.

2. Navigate to the Computers container (or any other container where the computer you would like to modify resides).

3. Right-click the computer and choose Properties from the pop-up menu (the Properties page will appear, as shown in Figure 3.13).

4. Modify any desired properties and click OK to finish.

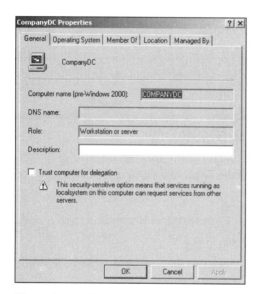

Figure 3.13   The computer's Properties page.

Working with Computer Accounts

A number of tasks are involved in managing user accounts in Active Directory. The following solutions address this important issue.

Adding a Computer Account to a Group

To add computer account to a group, perform the following steps:

1. Select Start|Programs|Administrative Tools|Active Directory Users And Computers.

2. Navigate to the Computers container (or any other container where the computer you would like to modify resides).

3. Right-click the computer and choose Properties from the pop-up menu.

4. On the Member Of tab, click Add.

5. Select the desired group or groups and click Add.

TIP: *If you need to add more than one group, you can select them by holding the Ctrl key down while clicking the groups. You can also select several groups that follow one another in the group list by clicking the first group in the list and then Shift-clicking the last group in the list.*

---

6. Click OK to return the Properties page.

7. Click OK to finish.

Disabling a Computer Account

To disable a computer account, perform the following steps:

1. Select Start|Programs|Administrative Tools|Active Directory Users And Computers.

2. Navigate to the Computers container (or any other container where the computer you would like to disable resides).

3. Right-click the computer and choose Disable Account from the pop-up menu.

4. Click Yes.

5. Click OK to disable the account.

NOTE: *Notice that a red X appears on the computer icon of the disabled account.*

Enabling a Computer Account

To enable a computer account, perform the following steps:

1. Select Start|Programs|Administrative Tools|Active Directory Users And Computers.

2. Navigate to the Computers container (or any other container where the computer you would like to enable resides).

3. Right-click the computer and choose Enable Account from the pop-up menu.

4. Click OK to enable the account.

Finding a Computer Account in Active Directory

To find a computer account in Active Directory, perform the following steps:

1. Select Start|Programs|Administrative Tools|Active Directory Users And Computers.

2. Right-click the domain where you would like to search for the computer and choose Find from the pop-up menu.

3. In the Find list box, select the Computer option.

4. In the Name field, enter the name of the computer you would like to search for.

TIP: *You can customize your search to the role of the computer. By choosing the Domain Controller role, only domain controllers will be displayed. Similarly, by choosing the Workstations and Servers role, only workstations and servers will be displayed.*

---

5. Click Find Now.

To search a specific container, perform the following steps:

1. Select Start|Programs|Administrative Tools|Active Directory Users And Computers.

2. Right-click the container where you would like to search for the computer and choose Find from the pop-up menu.

3. In the Find list box, select the Computer option.

4. In the Name field, enter the name of the computer that you would like to search for.

5. Click Find Now.

Resetting a Computer Account

To reset a computer account, perform the following steps:

1. Select Start|Programs|Administrative Tools|Active Directory Users And Computers.

2. Navigate to the Computers container (or any other container where the computer you would like to reset resides).

3. Right-click the computer and choose Reset Account from the pop-up menu.

4. Click Yes.

5. Click OK to reset the account.

WARNING! *Once you reset the computer account, the computer will have to rejoin the domain. This is very handy when an old computer is removed from the domain and a new system with the same name is taking its place. Because the SID of the computer is different, the domain controllers will think that the account already exists and will not allow the new computer to connect.*

Moving a Computer Account

To move a computer account, perform the following steps:

1. Select Start|Programs|Administrative Tools|Active Directory Users And Computers.

2. Navigate to the Computers container (or any other container where the computer you would like to move resides).

3. Right-click the computer and choose Move from the pop-up menu.

4. Navigate to the destination container where you would like the computer moved to.

5. Click OK to move the computer.

Modifying a Computer Account

To modify a computer account, perform the following steps:

1. Select Start|Programs|Administrative Tools|Active Directory Users And Computers.

2. Navigate to the Computers container (or any other container where the computer you would like to modify resides).

3. Right-click the computer to be modified and choose Properties from the pop-up menu.

4. Make any desired changes and click OK when done.

Managing a Computer Account

To manage a computer account, perform the following steps:

1. Select Start|Programs|Administrative Tools|Active Directory Users And Computers.

2. Navigate to the Computers container (or any other container where the computer you would like to manage resides).

3. Right-click the computer to be modified and choose Manage from the pop-up menu.

4. The Computer Management utility will appear (see Figure 3.14).

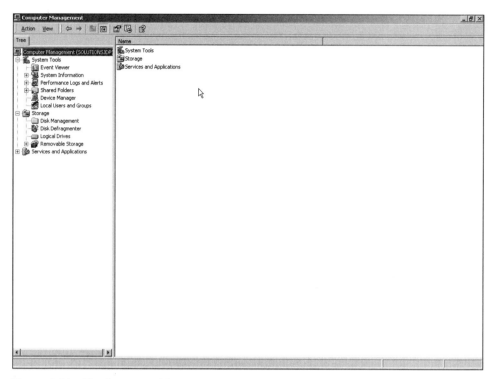

Figure 3.14   The Computer Management utility.

5. You can now manage any component to which you have permissions assigned to you on the remote computer, including system tools, services and applications, and storage.

Deleting a Computer Account

To delete a computer account, perform the following steps:

1. Select Start|Programs|Administrative Tools|Active Directory Users And Computers.

2. Navigate to the Computers container (or any other container where the computer you would like to delete resides).

3. Right-click the computer to be deleted and choose Delete from the pop-up menu.

4. Click Yes to delete the computer account.

Working with Printers

A number of tasks are involved in managing printers in the Active Directory. The following solutions address this important issue.

Creating a New Printer in Active Directory

To create a new Active Directory printer, perform the following steps:

1. Select Start|Programs|Administrative Tools|Active Directory Users And Computers.

2. Navigate to the container in which you would like the printer created.

3. Right-click the container and choose New|Printer from the pop-up menu.

4. Enter the Universal Naming Convention (UNC) name of the printer (for example, \\computer\printer).

5. Click OK to create the printer.

Finding a Printer in Active Directory

To find an Active Directory user in an OU, perform the following steps:

1. Select Start|Programs|Administrative Tools|Active Directory Users And Computers.

2. Navigate to the container in which you would like to search for the printer.

3. Right-click the container and choose Find.

4. In the Find list box, select Printers.

5. Enter the name of the printer in the Name field and click Find Now to search for the printer.

TIP: *You can search for a printer not only by name but also by its capabilities. For example, if you click the Features tab, you can select to search for printers that can print double sided or can staple.*

Deleting a Printer in Active Directory

1. Select Start|Programs|Administrative Tools|Active Directory Users And Computers.

2. Navigate to the container in which you would like the printer deleted.

3. Right-click the desired printer and choose Delete.

4. Click Yes to delete the printer.

Working with Shared Folders

A number of tasks are involved in managing shared folders in Active Directory. The following solutions address this important issue.

Creating a New Shared Folder in Active Directory

1. Select Start|Programs|Administrative Tools|Active Directory Users And Computers.

2. Navigate to the container in which you would like the Shared Folder object created.

3. Right-click the desired folder and choose the New|Shared Folder option.

4. Enter the name and the UNC path to the shared folder.

5. Click OK.

Modifying a Shared Folder in Active Directory

1. Select Start|Programs|Administrative Tools|Active Directory Users And Computers.

2. Navigate to the container in which the shared folder you would like to modify resides.

3. Right-click the shared folder and choose Properties from the pop-up menu.

4. Make any desired changes and click OK when done.

Finding a Shared Folder in Active Directory

1. Select Start|Programs|Administrative Tools|Active Directory Users And Computers.

2. Right-click the domain or container in which you would like to search for the shared folder and choose Find from the pop-up menu.

3. Choose the Shared Folder option from the Find list box.

4. Enter the name of the shared folder in the Name field.

5. Click Find Now to begin the search.

Deleting a Shared Folder in Active Directory

1. Select Start|Programs|Administrative Tools|Active Directory Users And Computers.

2. Navigate to the container that contains the shared folder you would like to delete.

3. Right-click the desired shared folder and choose Delete from the pop-up menu.

4. Click Yes to delete the shared folder.

Working with User Groups

A number of tasks are involved in managing user groups in Active Directory. The following solutions address this important issue.

Creating a User Group in Active Directory

1. Select Start|Programs|Administrative Tools|Active Directory Users And Computers.

2. Navigate to the container in which you would like the group created.

3. Right-click the container and choose New|Group from the pop-up menu.

4. Enter a name for the group.

5. Click OK to create the group.

Removing a User Group in Active Directory

1. Select Start|Programs|Administrative Tools|Active Directory Users And Computers.

2. Navigate to the container that contains the group you would like to delete.

3. Right-click the group and choose Delete from the pop-up menu.

4. Click Yes to delete the group.

Adding Members to a User Group

1. Select Start|Programs|Administrative Tools|Active Directory Users And Computers.

2. Navigate to the container that contains the group you would like to modify the membership for.

3. Right-click the desired group and choose Properties from the pop-up menu.

4. Click the Members tab.

5. Click Add.

6. Choose the user(s) or group(s) you would like to become members of this group.

7. Click OK.

8. Click OK to create the group membership.

Finding a Group in Active Directory

1. Select Start|Programs|Administrative Tools|Active Directory Users And Computers.

2. Right-click the domain or container in which you would like to search for the group.

3. In the Name field, enter the name of the group you would like to search for.

4. Click Find Now.

Finding a User's Group Membership in Active Directory

1. Select Start|Programs|Administrative Tools|Active Directory Users And Computers.

2. Navigate to the container in which the group resides.

3. Right-click the desired group and choose Properties from the pop-up menu.

4. Select the Members tab. The group's members are listed in this window.

5. Click OK to close the membership window.

Removing Members from a User Group

1. Select Start|Programs|Administrative Tools|Active Directory Users And Computers.

2. Navigate to the container in which the desired group exists.

3. Right-click the group and choose Properties from the pop-up menu.

4. Choose the Member tab.

5. Select the user(s) or group(s) you would like to remove and click Remove.

6. Click Yes to remove the selections.

7. Click OK to close the group membership window.

Renaming a User Group in Active Directory

1. Select Start|Programs|Administrative Tools|Active Directory Users And Computers.

2. Right-click the group you would like to rename and choose Rename from the pop-up menu.

3. Enter in a new name for the group and press Enter.

Changing a Group's Scope

1. Select Start|Programs|Administrative Tools|Active Directory Users And Computers.

2. Navigate to the container in which the desired group resides.

3. Right-click the group and choose Properties from the pop-up menu.

4. In the Group Scope section, change the scope to the desired group scope.

5. Click OK to commit the changes.

NOTE: *A Domain Local group cannot be converted to a Global group. Similarly, a Global group cannot be converted to a Domain Local group.*

Converting a Group to Another Group Type

1. Select Start|Programs|Administrative Tools|Active Directory Users And Computers.

2. Navigate to the container in which the desired group resides.

3. Right-click the group and choose Properties from the pop-up menu.

4. In the Group Type section, change the group type to the desired type.

5. Click OK.

Editing a User Group in Active Directory

1. Select Start|Programs|Administrative Tools|Active Directory Users And Computers.

2. Navigate to the container that contains the group you would like to edit.

3. Right-click the group and choose Properties from the pop-up menu.

4. Edit any desired properties for the group and click OK to commit the changes.

Working with Organizational Units

A number of tasks are involved in managing organizational units in Active Directory. The following solutions address this important issue.

Adding an Organizational Unit to Active Directory

1. Select Start|Programs|Administrative Tools|Active Directory Users And Computers.

2. Right-click the domain or container in which you would like to create the organizational unit and choose New|Organizational Unit from the pop-up menu.

3. Enter the name of the new organizational unit.

4. Click OK to create the organizational unit.

Deleting an Organizational Unit

1. Select Start|Programs|Administrative Tools|Active Directory Users And Computers.

2. Navigate to the domain or container in which the organizational unit resides.

3. Right-click the organizational unit and choose Delete from the pop-up menu.

4. Click Yes to delete the organizational unit.

Finding an Organizational Unit

1. Select Start|Programs|Administrative Tools|Active Directory Users And Computers.

2. Navigate to the domain or container in which you would like to search for the organizational unit.

3. Right-click the domain or container and choose Find from the pop-up menu.

4. Choose the Organization Unit option from the Find list box.

5. Enter the name of the organizational unit that you would like to search for.

6. Click Find Now.

Assigning Delegate Control to an Organizational Unit

1. Select Start|Programs|Administrative Tools|Active Directory Users And Computers.

2. Navigate to the domain in which the organizational unit resides.

3. Right-click the organizational unit and choose Delegate Control from the pop-up menu. The Delegation of Control Wizard will appear, as shown in Figure 3.15.

4. Click Next.

5. Click Add.

6. Select the desired users and/or groups and click Add.

Figure 3.15   The Delegation of Control Wizard.

7. Click OK.

8. Click Next.

9. Choose the tasks you would like to grant these users and/or groups permissions for.

10. Click Next.

11. Click Finish.

Modifying an Organizational Unit's Properties

1. Select Start|Programs|Administrative Tools|Active Directory Users And Computers.

2. Navigate to the desired domain or container.

3. Right-click the organizational unit and choose Properties from the pop-up menu.

4. Modify any desired properties and click OK to finish.

Renaming an Organizational Unit

1. Select Start|Programs|Administrative Tools|Active Directory Users And Computers.

2. Navigate to the organizational unit that you would like to rename.

3. Right-click the organizational unit and choose Rename from the pop-up menu.

4. Enter the new name for the organizational unit and press Enter.

Moving an Organizational Unit

1. Select Start|Programs|Administrative Tools|Active Directory Users And Computers.

2. Navigate to the container in which the organizational unit resides.

3. Right-click the organizational unit and choose Move from the pop-up menu.

4. Navigate to the destination container and click OK.

Creating a Server Object

1. Select Start|Programs|Administrative Tools|Active Directory Sites And Services.

2. Navigate to the site where you would like the new Domain Controller Server to be created (see Figure 3.16).

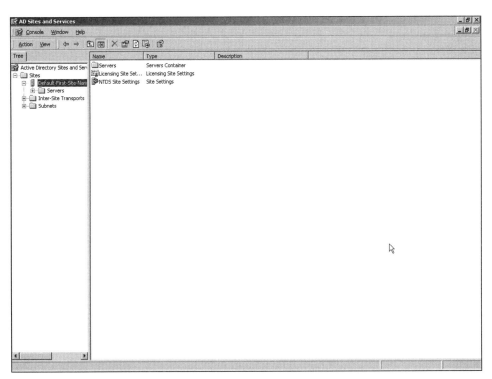

Figure 3.16   The Active Directory Sites And Services utility.

3. Right-click Servers and choose New|Server from the pop-up menu.

4. Enter a new name for the Server object.

5. Click OK to create the Server object

Removing a Server Object from a Site

1. Select Start|Programs|Administrative Tools|Active Directory Sites And Services.

2. Navigate to the server that you would like to remove.

3. Right-click the server and choose Delete from the pop-up menu.

4. Click Yes to confirm the deletion.

Enabling a Global Catalog

1. Select Start|Programs|Administrative Tools|Active Directory Sites And Services.

2. Navigate to the domain controller that's currently hosting a global catalog.

3. Right-click NTDS Settings and choose Properties from the pop-up menu.

4. Ensure that the Global Catalog option is selected.

5. Click OK.

Disabling a Global Catalog

1. Select Start|Programs|Administrative Tools|Active Directory Sites And Services.

2. Navigate to the domain controller that's currently hosting a global catalog.

3. Right-click NTDS Settings and choose Properties from the pop-up menu.

4. Ensure that the Global Catalog option is deselected.

5. Click OK.

3. Active Directory

Moving a Domain Controller between Sites

1. Select Start|Programs|Administrative Tools|Active Directory Sites And Services.

2. Navigate to the domain controller you would like to move.

3. Right-click the domain controller object and choose the Move option from the pop-up menu. The Move Server window will appear, as shown in Figure 3.17.

4. All available sites will appear in the Move Server window. Select the destination site and click OK.

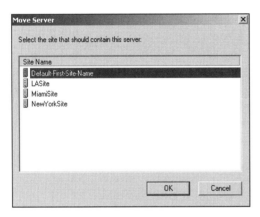

Figure 3.17   The Move Server window.

Connecting to a Forest

1. Select Start|Programs|Administrative Tools|Active Directory Sites And Services.

2. Right-click the Active Directory Sites And Services object and choose the Connect to Forest option.

3. In the Root domain field, enter the root domain of the desired forest.

4. If you would like this setting saved for this session, enable the Save This Domain Setting For The Current Console option.

5. Click OK.

Connecting to a Domain Controller

1. Select Start|Programs|Administrative Tools|Active Directory Sites And Services.

2. Right-click the Active Directory Sites And Services object and choose the Connect To Domain Controller option.

3. You can either manually enter the name of the domain or you can click the Browse button to navigate to the desired domain.

NOTE: *The available domain controllers for the selected domains are listed in the Available Controllers In section of the window (see Figure 3.18).*

4. Click OK to connect to the selected domain controller.

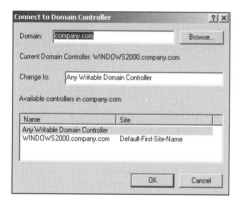

Figure 3.18   The Connect To Domain Controller window.

Working with Trust Relationships

A number of tasks are involved in managing trust relationships in Active Directory. The following solutions address this important issue.

Creating a Trust Relationship

1. Select Start|Programs|Administrative Tools|Active Directory Domains And Trusts.

2. Right-click the domain you would like to administer and choose Properties from the pop-up menu.

3. Select the Trusts tab.

4. If you would like this domain to trust another domain, click Add under the Domains Trusted By This Domain section.

5. If you would like other domains to trust this domain, click Add under the Domains That Trust This Domain section.

6. Enter the domain name to be included in the trust.

TIP: *If you're creating a trust relationship with a Windows NT 4 domain, all you need to enter is the domain name. If, however, you're connecting with a Windows 2000 domain, you'll need to enter the fully qualified domain name.*

---

7. Type and confirm a password for the trust relationship.

8. Complete the trust by configuring the trust relationship on the domain controller in the partner domain.

Deleting a Trust Relationship

1. Select Start|Programs|Administrative Tools|Active Directory Domains And Trusts.

2. Right-click the domain you would like to administer and choose Properties from the pop-up menu.

3. Select the Trusts tab.

4. Select the trust relationship you would like to delete and click Remove.

5. Click Yes to confirm the deletion of the trust relationship.

6. Repeat this process on the other side of the trust relationship.

TIP: *Default two-way transitive trusts cannot be deleted.*

Modifying a Trust Relationship

1. Select Start|Programs|Administrative Tools|Active Directory Domains And Trusts.

2. Right-click the domain you would like to administer and choose Properties from the pop-up menu.

3. Select the Trusts tab.

4. Select the trust relationship that you would like to edit and click Edit.

5. Make any necessary changes to the trust.

6. Click OK.

7. Repeat this process on the other side of the trust relationship.

Verifying a Trust Relationship

1. Select Start|Programs|Administrative Tools|Active Directory Domains And Trusts.

2. Right-click the domain you would like to administer and choose Properties from the pop-up menu.

3. Select the Trusts tab.

4. Select the trust relationship that you would like to verify and click Edit.

5. Click the Verify/Reset button.

6. Click OK.

Adding User Principal Name Suffixes

1. Select Start|Programs|Administrative Tools|Active Directory Domains And Trusts.

2. Right-click the Active Directory Domains And Trusts container and choose Properties from the pop-up menu.

3. In the Alternative UPN Suffix field, enter an alternative UPN suffix for this domain and click Add.

4. Repeat this process for any additional alternative UPN suffixes.

5. Click OK when done.

Changing a Domain Mode

1. Select Start|Programs|Administrative Tools|Active Directory Domains And Trusts.

2. Right-click the domain you would like to administer and choose Properties from the pop-up menu. The domain's Properties window will appear (see Figure 3.19).

3. Click Change Mode.

4. Click Yes to confirm the mode change.

WARNING! *By changing the domain mode, you're changing the mode from mixed mode to native mode. This means that no Windows NT 4.0 domain controllers exist in the domain. This is not reversible.*

5. Click OK.

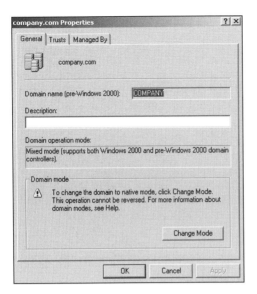

Figure 3.19   Changing the domain mode.

Working with Schemas

A number of tasks are involved in managing schemas in Active Directory. The following solutions address this important issue.

Adding Members to the Schema Admins Group

1. Select Start|Programs|Administrative Tools|Active Directory Users And Computers.
2. Navigate to the user you would like to add to the Schemas Admins group.
3. Right-click the user object and choose Properties.
4. Select the Member Of tab.
5. Click Add.
6. Select the Schemas Admin group and click Add.
7. Click OK.
8. Click OK.

Removing Members from the Schema Admins Group

1. Select Start|Programs|Administrative Tools|Active Directory Users And Computers.

2. Navigate to the user you would like to add to the Schemas Admins group.

3. Right-click the user object and choose Properties.

4. Select the Member Of tab.

5. Select the Schema Admins group and click Remove.

6. Confirm the action by clicking Yes.

7. Click OK.

Modifying Schema Permissions

1. Select Start|Programs|Administrative Tools|Active Directory Schema.

TIP: *If the Active Directory Schema tool is not available, follow the steps outlined in the "Installing the Active Directory Schema Utility" solution earlier in this section.*

---

2. Right-click the Active Directory Schema container and choose Permissions from the pop-up menu.

3. Select the Security tab.

4. Select the group whose permissions you would like to modify.

5. In the Permission section, choose either Allow or Deny for each of the permissions.

6. Click OK to complete the change.

Enabling Schema Extensions

1. Select Start|Programs|Administrative Tools|Active Directory Schema.

2. Right-click the Active Directory Schema container and choose Operations Master from the pop-up menu.

3. Enable the The Schema May Be Modified On This Domain Controller option (see Figure 3.20).

4. Click OK.

Reloading the Schema

1. Select Start|Programs|Administrative Tools|Active Directory Schema.

2. Right-click the Active Directory Schema container and choose Reload The Schema from the pop-up menu.

3. The schema is reloaded.

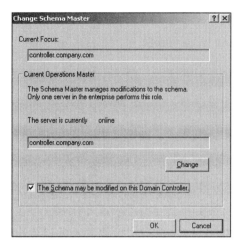

Figure 3.20 Enabling a schema modification.

Working with Classes

A number of tasks are involved in managing classes in Active Directory. The following solutions address this important issue.

Viewing a Class

1. Select Start|Programs|Administrative Tools|Active Directory Schema.
2. Navigate to the Classes container.
3. Right-click the class whose properties you would like to view and choose Properties from the pop-up menu.
4. Click OK.

Adding a Class

1. Select Start|Programs|Administrative Tools|Active Directory Schema.
2. Navigate to the Classes container.
3. Right-click the Classes container and choose New|Class from the pop-up menu.
4. Read the warning informing you that this is a permanent operation and cannot be reversed. Click Continue.
5. Enter the desired information and click OK.
6. Enter the necessary mandatory schema objects and click Finish.

Deleting a Class

1. Select Start|Programs|Administrative Tools|Active Directory Schema.

2. Navigate to the Classes container.

3. Right-click the class you would like to deactivate and choose the Properties option.

4. Enable the Deactivate This Class option.

5. Click OK.

Working with Attributes

A number of tasks are involved in managing attributes in Active Directory. The following solutions address this important issue.

Viewing an Attribute

1. Select Start|Programs|Administrative Tools|Active Directory Schema.

2. Navigate to the Attributes container.

3. Right-click the Attribute whose properties you would like to view and choose Properties from the pop-up menu (see Figure 3.21).

4. Click OK.

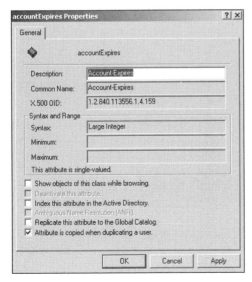

Figure 3.21   Viewing an attribute in Active Directory Schema.

Adding an Attribute

1. Select Start|Programs|Administrative Tools|Active Directory Schema.
2. Navigate to the Attributes container.
3. Right-click the Attributes container and choose New|Class from the pop-up menu.
4. Read the warning informing you that this is a permanent operation and cannot be reversed. Click Continue.
5. Enter the desired information and click OK.

Deactivating an Attribute

1. Select Start|Programs|Administrative Tools|Active Directory Schema.
2. Navigate to the Attributes container.
3. Right-click the attribute you would like to deactivate and choose the Properties option.
4. Enable the Deactivate This Attribute option.
5. Click OK.

Working with Sites

A number of tasks are involved in managing sites in Active Directory. The following solutions address this important issue.

Creating a Site

1. Select Start|Programs|Administrative Tools|Active Directory Sites And Services.
2. Right-click the Sites container and choose the New Site option from the pop-up menu (alternatively, you can choose the New|Site option).
3. In the New Object - Site window, enter the name for the site.
4. Select the link that will be used to communicate with this site.
5. Click OK.

Deleting a Site

1. Select Start|Programs|Administrative Tools|Active Directory Sites And Services.

3. Active Directory

2. Navigate to the site you would like to delete.

3. Right-click the desired site and choose Delete from the pop-up menu.

4. Click Yes to confirm the deletion.

Renaming a Site

1. Select Start|Programs|Administrative Tools|Active Directory Sites And Services.

2. Navigate to the site you would like to rename.

3. Right-click the desired site and choose Rename from the pop-up menu.

4. Enter the new name for the site.

5. Press Enter.

Working with Subnets

A number of tasks are involved in managing subnets in Active Directory. The following solutions address this important issue.

Creating a Subnet

1. Select Start|Programs|Administrative Tools|Active Directory Sites And Services.

2. Navigate to the Subnets container.

3. Right-click the Subnets container and choose New Subnet from the pop-up menu.

4. In the Address field, shown in Figure 3.22, enter the address for the subnet.

5. In the Mask field, enter the subnet mask to be used with this subnet.

6. Select a site to associate with this new subnet.

7. Click OK.

Deleting a Subnet

1. Select Start|Programs|Administrative Tools|Active Directory Sites and Services.

2. Navigate to the Subnets container.

3. Right-click the subnet you would like to delete and choose Delete from the pop-up menu.

4. Click Yes to confirm the deletion.

3. Active Directory

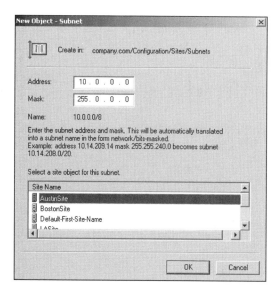

Figure 3.22   Creating a new subnet object.

Associating a Subnet with a Site

1. Select Start|Programs|Administrative Tools|Active Directory Sites And Services.

2. Navigate to the Subnets container.

3. Right-click the subnet you would like to associate with a site and choose Properties from the pop-up menu.

4. Choose the site you would like associated with this subnet from the Site drop-down list and click OK.

Chapter 4

Windows NT 4.0 to Windows 2000 Migration

In Depth

In Chapter 2, you learned of some of the new features in Windows 2000 as they compare to the features in Windows NT 4. Rather than repeat what's covered there, this chapter concentrates on the differences between Windows 2000 and Windows NT 4.0 that might affect how you migrate to Windows 2000.

Remember that Windows 2000 and Windows NT are vastly different operating systems. Also be aware that as far as a Windows NT 4 system can tell, it is the newest server operating system from Microsoft. It was not created to communicate with Windows 2000. Thankfully, however, the developers at Microsoft kept in mind that there are numerous Windows NT installations in the world. Therefore, Windows 2000 can look and feel like Windows NT to a Windows NT system.

When a Windows 2000 system is installed into a network that consists of one or more Windows NT Servers, it runs in what is known as *mixed mode*. With mixed mode, the Windows 2000 Server will use Windows NT authentication to communicate with Windows NT systems and users.

Before you jump right in and upgrade your network to a Windows 2000 network, you should check out all the ramifications this might have. What follows is a recommendation of the steps you should follow when migrating your existing Windows NT network to a Windows 2000 network. Obviously, the more complex your network, the more complex the migration plan.

The migration plan can be divided into several sections:

1. Discover and assess your current network.
2. Optionally, you can cleanse your data.
3. Model and design your Active Directory infrastructure.
4. Run both operating systems in parallel.
5. Test your migration.
6. Switch over to your Windows 2000 network.

Each of these steps is covered in the following sections of this chapter.

Discovering, Assessing, and Cleansing Your Data

If you administer a small network, these tasks should be simple. In fact, if you're the only administrator, you should be able to list out not only all your servers but also what resources they host, the printers that are attached to them, their names, and their assigned TCP/IP addresses. Administrators of medium to large networks, however, might not have this luxury.

In most organizations, servers are added as budgets are approved, needs change, and projects arise. If you administer a medium-to-large network, chances are that you find new servers with new resources occasionally. Because the Microsoft suite of server software is so easy to install, anyone can do so (installing it *properly* is another story, though). To most end users, Windows is Windows is Windows. To most users, Windows 95 is the same as Windows 98, which is the same as Windows NT, which is the same as Windows 2000. Maybe this is a marketing fault of Microsoft, but it is not uncommon to hear "Another version of Windows? No way I am installing Windows 2000 on my home system!" Remember, Windows 2000 is designed for the office environment. Nonetheless, if a user requires Windows installed on his or her system and he or she cannot find you, the user just might grab the first Windows CD-ROM he or she finds and install it.

One of the most important tasks you must perform is to discover your existing domain structure. Again, if you administer a small network, that structure is usually simple—just one domain. Many organizations, however, will have many domains with trust relationships between them. The Windows 2000 networking model (with Active Directory) is usually a single forest with a single domain (although larger organizations might have several domains). With new features in Active Directory, security policies and resource access restrictions are covered in the model.

The following subsections cover what you should consider before you migrate your network to Windows 2000.

Existing Domain Model

The most common domain structure in the Windows NT 4 world is one or more account domains with one or more resource domains. All user and group accounts are stored in the account domains, whereas all the resources (such as printers, fax servers, network scanners, and files) are stored in the resource domains. By knowing your domain structure, you'll ultimately know where all your resources are and, therefore, know of any difficulties during the upgrade process.

Existing Trust Relationships

Two different trust relationship types exist in a Windows NT 4 network: one-way and two-way trusts. Going back to the most common domain model, the account domains trust each other using two-way trusts, whereas the resource domains trust the account domains. This makes sense to you if you have implemented domains and trust relationships before. If not, think of it this way: If two domains exists (account domain A and resource domain B), domain B will trust domain A (in other words, domain B will trust the *accounts* from domain A to use its *resources*).

NOTE: *A two-way trust is actually two one-way trusts flowing in the opposite direction.*

Trust relationships are important. Recall from Chapter 3 that Windows 2000 trust relationships are transitive; therefore, do not include any domains in your forest that you do not want to use resources within your domain.

Domain Controllers

Knowing how many domain controllers you have as well as their geographical and logical locations will help in the migration tremendously. Be extremely careful when upgrading a domain that does not have Backup Domain Controllers (BDCs).

Accounts

Recalling again that Windows 2000 uses transitive trust relationships, you'll want to compose a list of all the user accounts that exist in your domains. When you migrate domains into the Active Directory forest, notice that duplicate accounts are no longer needed. Knowing what accounts are where and what they are used for will speed up the migration process considerably.

Migration Paths

You can follow three different methods when migrating to a Windows 2000 network:

- Domain upgrade
- Upgrade and then restructure
- Restructure and then upgrade

Each of these upgrade processes is covered in the following subsections. You might think that this decision is a no-brainer, but think again. You may not have another opportunity to completely redesign the network again. Anyone who has inherited a network can attest to the fact that not all network installations are efficient or even make sense.

Domain Upgrade

If the current domain structure is sufficient, the domain upgrade process is the way to go. It is also the easiest migration path. By upgrading your Windows NT domains to Windows 2000 domains, no structural changes are made. In essence, the domains look logically the same before the migration as after (except for the fact that Windows 2000 security and Active Directory are controlling the new network).

Upgrade and Then Restructure

If your current domain structure is sufficient but restructuring it would improve efficiency and security, the "upgrade and then restructure" method makes sense. The current domain structure will be migrated to a Windows 2000 domain structure. Then, when the new network is stable, you can start moving resources around to improve performance and security.

Restructure and Then Upgrade

The "restructure and then upgrade" method is reserved for the organizations that's unhappy with its existing domain architecture. This incorrectly or inefficiently designed domain structure could be caused by several factors. The organization may have added domains to its infrastructure by merging or acquiring other organizations. With this method, you would reorganize the domain first and then upgrade the new network. Some organizations may even find that after the restructuring, the upgrade is no longer necessary.

Modeling and Designing Active Directory

Before upgrading any server, you should create an Active Directory design structure. Because most of this information is covered in Chapter 3, this section simply provides an overview of what needs to be done.

Remember that with Windows 2000, you can restructure your domain on the fly. You are no longer presented with the problem of domain controllers being locked into their domains. You can now dynamically move them between domains.

The initial domain structure should mirror your currently installed structure. Your account domains should be the first ones upgraded and will therefore create the forest and the tree for the domain structure.

Running Windows NT and 2000 in Parallel

When it's time to upgrade, the first system that needs to be upgraded is the Windows NT Primary Domain Controller (PDC). The "Immediate Solutions" section shows that this is a relatively easy task because the Windows 2000 setup program does all the work.

The first real step in the upgrade is to ensure that the BDCs have the most up-to-date domain information. If you are upgrading a domain that does not have at least one BDC, you should install one (even if just for the upgrade). Having a BDC on the network ensures that all the user, group, and security information is backed up in case the PDC upgrade fails for any reason. Another reason for having a BDC on the network during the upgrade is to allow users to continue to log into the network. If a BDC does not exist, users will not be able to log into the network while the system is being upgraded.

The Windows 2000 setup program is "smart." It recognizes that the server you are upgrading is a PDC and will automatically launch the Active Directory Installation Wizard (DCPromo.exe) once the core Windows 2000 operating system is installed.

Tables 4.1, 4.2, and 4.3 list all the currently supported upgrade paths from existing Windows operating systems to the Windows 2000 suite of operating systems.

As previously mentioned, when the Windows 2000 setup process is completed, the Windows 2000 domain controller will run in mixed mode. This means that it is fully backward compatible. It does this by masquerading as a Windows NT domain controller using a flat store system, this is commonly referred to as a PDC emulator. A Windows 2000 domain controller appears as follows on the network:

- Other Windows 2000 computers on the network will see the Windows 2000 domain controller as a Windows 2000 system.

- Windows NT systems will see the domain controller as a Windows NT PDC.

- All new accounts in Active Directory will still appear to be part of the Security Accounts Manager (SAM) to Windows NT systems.

- Windows NT and Windows 9x systems will still use the PDC as a logon server.

- If the Windows 2000 domain controller becomes unavailable, an existing Windows NT BDC may be promoted to the role of a PDC.

Table 4.1   Upgrade paths to Windows 2000 Professional.

Installed Operating System	Upgrade Path Support
Windows 3.x	No
Windows NT 3.1	No
Windows NT 3.1 Advanced Server	No
Windows 3.51 Workstation	Yes
Windows NT 3.51 Server	No
Windows 95	Yes
Windows 98	Yes

(continued)

Table 4.1   Upgrade paths to Windows 2000 Professional (continued).

Installed Operating System	Upgrade Path Support
Windows NT 4.0 Workstation	Yes
Windows NT 4.0 Server	No
Windows NT 4.0 Server, Enterprise Edition	No

Table 4.2   Upgrade paths to Windows 2000 Server.

Installed Operating System	Upgrade Path Support
Windows 3.x	No
Windows NT 3.1	No
Windows NT 3.1 Advanced Server	No
Windows 3.51 Workstation	No
Windows NT 3.51 Server	Yes
Windows 95	No
Windows 98	No
Windows NT 4.0 Workstation	Yes
Windows NT 4.0 Server	Yes
Windows NT 4.0 Server, Enterprise Edition	No

Table 4.3   Upgrade paths to Windows 2000 Advanced Server.

Installed Operating System	Upgrade Path Support
Windows 3.x	No
Windows NT 3.1	No
Windows NT 3.1 Advanced Server	No
Windows NT 3.51 Workstation	No
Windows NT 3.51 Server	Yes
Windows 95	No
Windows 98	No
Windows NT 4.0 Workstation	No
Windows NT 4.0 Server	Yes
Windows NT 4.0 Server, Enterprise Edition	Yes

4. Windows NT 4.0 to Windows 2000 Migration

Once the PDC has been upgraded, you can continue with the migration by upgrading each of the BDCs to Windows 2000. Your network will continue to run in mixed mode until you manually set the mode to native. Although native mode provides access to new Windows 2000 features, many organizations decide to run in mixed mode for a while.

One reason for this is the inability to upgrade BDCs. Windows 2000 has higher hardware requirements than Windows NT. For this reason, you may find that some systems that run very efficiently as Windows NT BDCs will cause a bottleneck on your network if upgraded to Windows 2000. Also, if you require the ability to fall back to a Windows NT network, then mixed mode is your solution. In essence, mixed mode gives you a way out of your upgrade. Another reason for not upgrading all your Windows NT Servers to Windows 2000 is software compatibility. Windows 2000 is not 100-percent backward compatible. Given the scores of different applications that currently exist in the Windows NT world, you are likely to find one (or more) that will not function under Windows 2000 (presently). If such applications exist in your organization, you'll need to maintain some Windows NT systems to support them, thus running in mixed mode until such applications can be modified or upgraded.

At this point, all your domain controllers should be running Windows 2000. If the installation went smoothly, none of your users even noticed that anything changed (other than some servers not being available for short periods of time). One thing you should be aware of is that to get the full power of Windows 2000 (both feature based and performance based), you should upgrade all your servers and your clients to Windows 2000 as well.

Once all your domain controllers are upgraded, you should start migrating all your member servers. This allows you to complete the migration by switching to native mode to get all of Windows 2000's functionality and capabilities.

Test, Test, and Test Again

Okay, you have now upgraded all your domain controllers and member servers to Windows 2000 and are happy with the installation. The network has been running smoothly with the new operating system. Many administrators would like to "flip the switch" now and convert to native mode. Honestly, Windows 2000 has so many new "cool" features to make your life easier that you'll want to use them as soon as humanly possible. Take heed, though. Once the switch from mixed mode to native mode is made, you cannot go back without reinstalling your entire network.

Let the network run under the new operating system for as long as possible. Some applications (such as month-end applications) might not be used every day and you won't find out that they failed under Windows 2000 until it is too late.

The best approach to take on your upgrade is to treat it like Microsoft treated Windows 2000. Instead of releasing the application on the original promised date, Microsoft decided to hold the operating system back until all major bugs could be fixed. When Windows 2000 finally shipped, we got a very stable product. This was done with testing. Windows 2000 was tested more than any other application in the history of the computer world. Treat your network in the same way. Test, test, test.

When you are finally ready to convert your network to a native Windows 2000 network, you need to be prepared. Murphy's law exists in the computer world as well. You can be assured that as soon as you switch the mode of your network, some application will appear that cannot run under Windows 2000. Just be prepared.

Cut Over and Continue Optimizing

The process of converting your domain to a native Windows 2000 domain is very simple, but irreversible. If it seems that you're be hounded with this information, it's with good reason. Your job could depend on it.

Once your network is running in native mode, you need to optimize it. As you'll see throughout this book, Windows 2000 has some great new features that will make your network operate better.

Immediate Solutions

Synchronizing a Windows NT Domain

The following steps outline the process of synchronizing a Windows NT domain:

1. Select Start|Programs|Administrative Tools|Server Manager.
2. Select the Primary Domain Controller.
3. From the computer menu, choose the Synchronize Entire Domain option.
4. Click Yes to synchronize the domain.
5. Click OK.

Synchronizing a Single Windows NT Backup Domain Controller

1. Select Start|Programs|Administrative Tools|Server Manager.
2. Select the Backup Domain Controller you would like to synchronize.
3. From the Computer menu, choose the Synchronize With Primary Domain Controller option.
4. Click Yes to begin synchronization.

Upgrading

The following solutions discuss the various ways to upgrade your system.

Upgrading a Standalone Server without Converting the File System

Perform the following steps to upgrade a standalone server without converting the file system:

1. Insert the Windows 2000 Server CD-ROM. The Autorun feature should start the CD automatically. If it does not, double-click My Computer and then double-click CD-ROM drive's icon.

2. A window will appear stating that the CD-ROM contains a newer version of the operating system. Click Yes to begin the upgrade.

NOTE: *Alternately, you can click the Install Windows 2000 option on the Microsoft Windows 2000 CD or run the command-line executable by selecting Start|Run and typing the file name.*

3. Choose the Upgrade to Windows 2000 (Recommended) option and click Next.

4. Once you have read the license agreement, select the I Accept This Agreement radio button and click Next.

5. Enter the 25-digit product key as it appears on your Windows 2000 packaging and click Next.

NOTE: *If the product key is entered incorrectly, you will be informed that it is invalid and will be required to enter it again.*

6. In the Upgrading to the Windows 2000 NTFS File System dialog box, choose to not covert the drive (you can do this at a later date) by selecting the No, Do Not Upgrade My Drive option and clicking Next.

WARNING! **If any other non-Windows 2000 operating systems exist on the system, converting the drive to the New Technology File System (NTFS) will cause them to not be able to read the drive.**

7. Setup will now copy all the necessary setup files.

8. Click Finish (or you can wait; the system will automatically reboot after 30 seconds).

9. When the system reboots, choose the Microsoft Windows 2000 Server setup option from the boot menu and press Enter (or you can wait; the option will be automatically selected after about five seconds).

10. Setup will then examine your disks and copy all necessary files.

11. When setup completes the copy, your system will reboot again.

12. Select the Microsoft Windows 2000 Server option from the boot menu and press Enter (or you can wait; the option will be automatically selected after about 30 seconds).

13. Windows 2000 will start and detect/install devices.

14. Network settings will be set up and configured.

15. Components will be installed.

16. When the setup is done, click Restart Now.

4. Windows NT 4.0 to Windows 2000 Migration

17. Select the Microsoft Windows 2000 Server option from the boot menu and press Enter.

18. When the system starts up, you'll be able to log into the newly converted Windows 2000 system.

Upgrading a Standalone Server and Converting the File System

To upgrade a standalone server and convert the file system, perform the following steps:

1. Insert the Windows 2000 Server CD-ROM. The Autorun feature should start the CD automatically. If it does not, double-click My Computer and then double-click the CD-ROM drive's icon.

2. A window will appear stating that the CD-ROM contains a newer version of the operating system. Click Yes to begin the upgrade.

NOTE: *Alternately, you can click the Install Windows 2000 option on the Microsoft Windows 2000 CD.*

---

3. Choose the Upgrade To Windows 2000 (Recommended) option and click Next.

4. Once you have read the license agreement, select the I Accept This Agreement radio button and click Next.

5. Enter the 25-digit product key as it appears on your Windows 2000 packaging and click Next.

NOTE: *If the product key is entered incorrectly, you will be informed that it is invalid and will be required to enter it again.*

---

6. In the Upgrading To The Windows 2000 NTFS File System dialog box, choose to not covert the drive (you can do this at a later date) by selecting the No, Do Not Upgrade My Drive option and clicking Next.

WARNING!   **If any other non-Windows 2000 operating systems exist on the system, converting the drive to NTFS will cause them to not be able to read the drive.**

7. Setup will now copy all the necessary setup files.

8. Click Finish (or you can wait; the system will automatically reboot after 30 seconds).

9. When the system reboots, choose the Microsoft Windows 2000 Server setup option from the boot menu and press Enter (or you can wait; the option will be automatically selected after about five seconds).

10. Setup will now examine your disks and copy all necessary files.

11. When the setup program completes the copy, your system will reboot again.

12. Select the Microsoft Windows 2000 Server option from the boot menu and press Enter (or you can wait; the option will be automatically selected after about 30 seconds).

13. The setup program will now convert your drive to NTFS. When the conversion is done, the system will reboot.

14. Select the Microsoft Windows 2000 Server option from the boot menu and press Enter.

15. Windows 2000 will start and detect/install devices.

16. Network settings will be set up and configured.

17. Components will be installed.

18. When the setup is done, click Restart Now.

19. Select the Microsoft Windows 2000 Server option from the boot menu and press Enter.

20. When the system starts up, you'll be able to log into the newly converted Windows 2000 system.

Upgrading a Domain Controller Server without Converting the File System

Perform the following steps to upgrade a domain controller without converting the file system:

NOTE: *At least one partition will have to be converted to the NTFS file system for Active Directory to be installed.*

---

1. Insert the Windows 2000 Server CD-ROM. The Autorun feature should start the CD automatically. If it does not, double-click My Computer and then double-click CD-ROM drive's icon.

2. A window will appear stating that the CD-ROM contains a newer version of the operating system. Click Yes to begin the upgrade.

NOTE: *Alternately, you can click the Install Windows 2000 option on the Microsoft Windows 2000 CD.*

---

3. Choose the Upgrade to Windows 2000 (Recommended) option and click Next.

4. Once you have read the license agreement, select the I Accept This Agreement radio button and click Next.

4. Windows NT 4.0 to Windows 2000 Migration

5. Enter the 25-digit product key as it appears on your Windows 2000 packaging and click Next.

NOTE: *If the product key is entered incorrectly, you will be informed that it is invalid and will be required to enter it again.*

---

6. In the Upgrading To The Windows 2000 NTFS File System dialog box, choose to not covert the drive (you can do this at a later date) by selecting the No, Do Not Upgrade My Drive option and clicking Next.

WARNING!   *If any other non-Windows 2000 operating systems exist on the system, converting the drive to NTFS will cause them to not be able to read the drive.*

7. Setup will now copy all the necessary setup files.

8. Click Finish (or you can wait; the system will automatically reboot after 30 seconds).

9. When the system reboots, choose the Microsoft Windows 2000 Server setup option from the boot menu and press Enter (or you can wait; the option will be automatically selected after about five seconds).

10. Setup will examine your disks and copy all necessary files.

11. When the setup program completes the copy, your system will reboot again.

12. Select the Microsoft Windows 2000 Server option from the boot menu and press Enter (or you can wait; the option will be automatically selected after about 30 seconds).

13. Windows 2000 will start and detect/install devices.

14. Network settings will be set up and configured.

15. Components will be installed.

16. When the setup is done, click the Restart Now button.

17. Select the Microsoft Windows 2000 Server option from the boot menu and press Enter.

18. When the system starts up, the setup program will automatically launch the Active Directory Installation Wizard (DCPromo.exe).

19. When the Active Directory Installation Wizard appears, click Next.

20. In the Domain Controller Type window, choose the Domain Controller For A New Domain option and click Next.

21. In the Create Tree Or Child Domain window (see Figure 4.1), choose the Create New Domain Tree option and click Next.

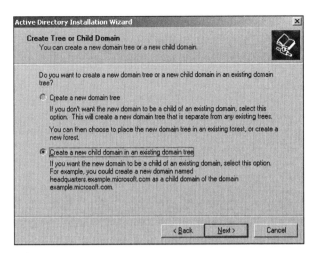

Figure 4.1   The Create Tree Or Child Domain window.

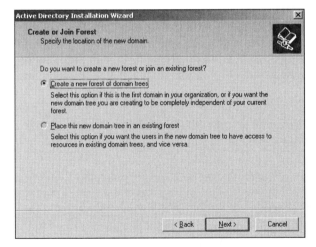

Figure 4.2   The Create Or Join Forest window.

22. Choose the Create A New Forest Of Domain Trees option in the Create Or Join Forest window (see Figure 4.2) and click Next.

23. Enter the full Domain Name System (DNS) name of the new domain and click Next. The wizard will verify whether this domain name is duplicated on the network. If it is, simple click OK and choose a new domain name.

24. Enter the NetBIOS name that is to be assigned to this domain. This name will be used when systems that are not Active Directory-enabled need to communicate with this domain. The wizard will automatically create a NetBIOS domain name for you. You can choose to keep this name or create a new one. If the

NetBIOS domain name exists, the wizard will add a number to the end of the name. For example, if the NetBIOS domain name "DOMAIN" exists, the wizard will suggest the name "DOMAIN0". When you have selected you NetBIOS domain name, click Next.

25. The wizard will ask you for the location where it should create the Database and Log directories. By default, these are stored in the %systemroot%\NTDS directory. You can, however, choose a different location. Once you have selected the location for these directories, click Next.

NOTE: *The Database directory is used to store the Active Directory information for the new domain, and the Log directory is used to temporarily store changes made to the Active Directory database before they are committed. For best performance, you should place the Database and Log directories on separate physical hard disks.*

---

26. Choose the location for the shared system volume. By default, this is stored in the %systemroot%\Sysvol directory. Once you have selected the location for this directory, click Next.

NOTE: *The Shared System Volume directory is used to store scripts and Group Policies. Every domain controller in Active Directory maintains such a directory. All file replication services use this volume to replicate the scripts and Group Policies information to all domain controllers.*

---

27. If the Active Directory Installation Wizard does not detect a DNS server, you'll be notified and must then decide whether you would like the wizard to install and configure DNS.

WARNING!   For Active Directory to be installed on your system, at least one drive or partition must be formatted with Windows 2000 NTFS (NTFS v5.0). If no such partition exists, you will be presented with an error message and will not be able to continue the Active Directory installation until you create such a partition.

28. Next, the Windows NT 4.0 RAS Servers window will appear. This window allows you to choose whether Windows 2000 Active Directory will use permissions that are compatible with non-Windows 2000 systems or with native Windows 2000 permissions. Choose your desired option and click Next.

29. In the Directory Services Restore Mode Administrator Password window, choose a password to be used when you need to restore your Active Directory information. Click Next.

TIP: *For security reasons, do not use your Administrator password as the DS Restore Mode Administrator password.*

---

30. A summary window will appear informing you of all the options you selected. Click Next to start the Active Directory installation.

31. A progress indicator will appear. When the installation is complete, the Complete Active Directory Installation Wizard window will appear. Click Finish.

32. A dialog box will appear notifying you that the system must be rebooted for the changes to take effect. Click Restart Now to complete the installation.

Upgrading a Domain Controller Server and Converting the File System

To upgrade a domain controller and convert the file system, perform the following steps:

1. Insert the Windows 2000 Server CD-ROM. The Autorun feature should start the CD automatically. If it does not, double-click My Computer and then double-click CD-ROM drive's icon.

2. A window will appear stating that the CD-ROM contains a newer version of the operating system. Click Yes to begin the upgrade.

NOTE: *Alternately, you can click the Install Windows 2000 option on the Microsoft Windows 2000 CD.*

---

3. Choose the Upgrade To Windows 2000 (Recommended) option and click Next.

4. Once you have read the license agreement, select the I Accept This Agreement radio button and click Next.

5. Enter the 25-digit product key as it appears on your Windows 2000 packaging and click Next.

NOTE: *If the product key is entered incorrectly, you will be informed that it is invalid and will be required to enter it again.*

---

6. In the Upgrading To The Windows 2000 NTFS File System dialog box, choose to not covert the drive (you can do this at a later date) by selecting the No, Do Not Upgrade My Drive and clicking Next.

WARNING! **If any other non-Windows 2000 operating systems exist on the system, converting the drive to NTFS will cause them to not be able to read the drive.**

7. Setup will now copy all the necessary setup files.

8. Click Finish (or you can wait; the system will automatically reboot after 30 seconds).

9. When the system reboots, choose the Microsoft Windows 2000 Server setup option from the boot menu and press Enter (or you can wait; the option will be automatically selected after about five seconds).

10. Setup will now examine your disks and copy all necessary files.

11. When the setup program completes the copy, your system will reboot again.

12. Select the Microsoft Windows 2000 Server option from the boot menu and press Enter (or you can wait; the option will be automatically selected after about 30 seconds).

13. The setup program will now convert your drive to NTFS. When the conversion is done, the system will reboot.

14. Select the Microsoft Windows 2000 Server option from the boot menu and press Enter.

15. Windows 2000 will start and detect/install devices.

16. Network settings will be set up and configured.

17. Components will be installed.

18. When the setup is done, click Restart Now.

19. Select the Microsoft Windows 2000 Server option from the boot menu and press Enter.

20. When the system starts up, the setup program will automatically launch the Active Directory Installation Wizard (DCPromo.exe).

21. When the Active Directory Installation Wizard appears, click Next.

22. In the Domain Controller Type window, choose the Domain Controller For A New Domain option and click Next.

23. In the Create Tree Or Child Domain window, choose the Create New Domain Tree option and click Next (refer to Figure 4.1).

24. Choose the Create A New Forest Of Domain Trees in the Create Or Join Forest window, as shown in Figure 4.2, and click Next.

25. Enter the full DNS name of the new domain and click Next. The wizard will now verify whether this domain name is duplicated on the network. If it is, click OK and choose a new domain name.

26. Enter the NetBIOS name that is to be assigned to this domain. This name will be used when systems that are not Active Directory-enabled need to communicate with this domain. The wizard will automatically create a NetBIOS domain name for you. You can choose to keep this name or create a new one. If the NetBIOS domain name exists, the wizard will add a number to the end of the name. For example, if the NetBIOS domain name "DOMAIN" exists, the wizard will suggest the name "DOMAIN0". When you have selected you NetBIOS domain name, click Next.

27. The wizard will ask for the location where it should create the Database and Log directories. By default, these are stored in the %systemroot%\NTDS directory. You can, however, choose a different location. Once you have selected the location for these directories, click Next.

NOTE: *The Database directory is used to store the Active Directory information for the new domain, and the Log directory is used to temporarily store changes made to the Active Directory database before they are committed. For best performance, you should place the Database and Log directories on separate physical hard disks.*

---

28. Choose the location for the shared system volume. By default, this is stored in the %systemroot%\Sysvol directory. Once you have selected the location for this directory, click Next.

NOTE: *The Shared System Volume directory is used to store scripts and Group Policies. Every domain controller in Active Directory maintains such a directory. All file replication services use this volume to replicate the scripts and Group Policies information to all domain controllers.*

---

29. If the Active Directory Installation Wizard does not detect a DNS server, you'll be notified and must then decide whether you would like the wizard to install and configure DNS (see Figure 4.3).

WARNING!   **For Active Directory to be installed on your system, at least one drive or partition must be formatted with Windows 2000 NTFS (NTFS v5.0). If no such partition exists, you will be presented with an error message and will not be able to continue the Active Directory installation until you create such a partition.**

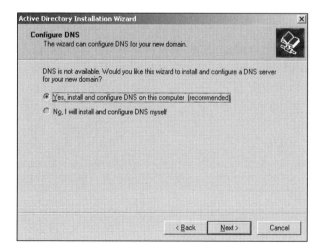

Figure 4.3   The Active Directory Installation Wizard: Configure DNS.

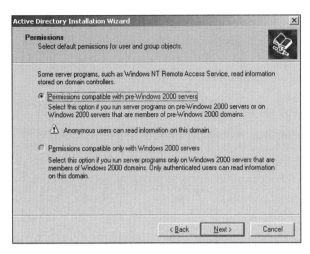

Figure 4.4   The Active Directory Installation Wizard: Permissions window.

30. The Windows NT 4.0 RAS Servers window will appear (see Figure 4.4). This window allows you to choose whether Windows 2000 Active Directory will use permissions that are compatible with non-Windows 2000 systems or with native Windows 2000 permissions. Choose your desired option and click Next.

31. In the Directory Services Restore Mode Administrator Password window, choose a password to be used when you need to restore your Active Directory information. Click Next.

TIP: *For security reasons, do not use your Administrator password as the DS Restore Mode Administrator password.*

---

32. A summary window will appear informing you of all the options you selected. Click Next to start the Active Directory installation.

33. A progress indicator will appear, as shown in Figure 4.5. When the installation is complete, the Complete Active Directory Installation Wizard window appears. Click Finish.

34. A dialog box will appear notifying you that the system must be rebooted for the changes to take effect. Click Restart Now to complete the installation.

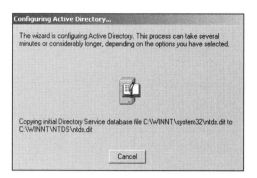

Figure 4.5 The Configuring Active Directory installation progress indicator.

Switching to Native Mode

To switch your system to native mode, perform the following steps:

1. Select Start|Programs|Administrative Tools|Active Directory Domains And Trusts.

2. Select the domain you would like to administer.

3. Choose the Properties option from the drop-down menu.

4. On the General tab, click the Change Mode button.

5. Click the Yes button to change the mode from mixed mode to native mode.

WARNING! Remember that once this is done, it cannot be undone. A Windows 2000 domain controller running in mixed mode will look like a Windows NT domain controller to Windows NT machines.

Chapter 5

Windows 2000 Installation

(continued)

In Depth

Before delving into the Windows 2000 installation process, you'll need to understand the Windows 2000 Setup programs. Although they're still named winnt.exe and winnt32.exe, they have greatly changed. This section will deal with some of the new changes. You'll also look at the system requirements that need to be met before Windows 2000 can be installed successfully.

Two different Setup programs ship with Windows 2000. The first, winnt.exe, is used when installing Windows 2000 when no 32-bit operating systems exist. That is to say that the system is booting from either an MS-DOS floppy or a Windows 9x boot floppy. The second Setup program, winnt32.exe, can be used when installing Windows 2000 on a system that already has a 32-bit operating system installed (Windows 9x, Windows NT, or Windows 2000).

NOTE: *Both of these Setup programs reside in the i386 directory of the Windows 2000 CD-ROM.*

Each of these Setup programs has its own unique set of command-line parameters that you can enter to get it to accomplish different tasks. These command-line parameters are discussed in the following sections.

The Winnt.exe Command-Line Parameters

As mentioned, winnt.exe is the 16-bit version of the Windows 2000 Setup program and can only be used to launch the Setup program from a system booted with an MS-DOS or Windows 9x boot disk.

The winnt.exe Setup program is launched as follows:

```
winnt [/s[:sourcepath]] [/t[:tempdrive] [/u[:answer file]]
[/udf:id[,udf_file]] [/r:folder] [/r[x]:folder] [/e:command]
[/a] [/I:INF_file]
```

Typing **winnt /?** at the command prompt (from the i386 directory) lists and describes all the command-line parameters available.

The Winnt32.exe Command-Line Parameters

Winnt32.exe is the 32-bit version of the Windows 2000 Setup program. It allows for much greater performance by multithreading the setup process. As you'll notice, more preinstallation options are available.

The winnt32.exe Setup program is launched as follows:

```
winnt32 [/s:sourcepath] [/tempdrive:drive_letter]
[/unattend[number]:[answer_file]] [/copydir:folder] [/copysource:folder]
[cmd:command] [/debug[level]:[filename]] [/udf:id[,UDF_file]
[/syspart:drive_letter] [/checkupgradeonly] [cmdcons] [/m:folder_name]
[/makelocalsource] [/noreboot]
```

Typing "winnt32 /?" at the command prompt (from the i386 directory) lists and describes all the command-line parameters available.

System Requirements

Although Windows 2000 is a much more robust and scalable operating system than Windows NT, it does require more hardware resources. For this reason, Table 5.1 lists the recommended minimum requirements for installing Windows 2000 on your system.

NOTE: *Remember, these are minimum requirements. In the computer world, more is generally better.*

Windows 2000 is a fairly new operating system and may not support all existing hardware devices installed on your system. A couple methods can be used to find out whether your system devices are supported. First, you can run the winnt32.exe application with the **/checkupgradeonly** command-line parameter. Results for this program are placed in a file called upgrade.txt for Windows 95/98 systems, or winn32.log for Windows NT systems. Second, you can check the Hardware Compatibility List (HCL). A copy of one exists in the Support directory on the Windows 2000 CD-ROM, but you should check the online version. The online version is updated regularly as new devices get certified to work with Windows 2000. You can find the online HCL at **www.microsoft.com/hcl/default.asp**.

Table 5.1   Minimum requirements for installing Windows 2000.

Hardware	Minimum	Recommended
Processor	Pentium 133	Pentium II (300 MHz or better)
Memory	64MB	128MB or more
Display	VGA	SuperVGA
Hard Drive	650MB free	2GB free

Manual Installation

The following sections examine installing Windows 2000 manually.

Using Boot Floppies

Much like with Windows NT, you can install Windows 2000 using a set of boot floppy disks. Unlike Windows NT, however, these boot floppies do not ship with the product. Instead, two different applications exist. The first, makeboot.exe, is used to create the boot floppies from an MS-DOS prompt or from Windows 9x. The second, makebt32.exe, is similarly used to create the boot floppies from Windows NT or Windows 2000.

To create these floppies, four floppy disks are required. Once the boot disks are created, they can be used to start the Windows 2000 Setup program. In essence, the floppy disks install enough of the Windows 2000 kernel to get the rest of the operating system installed. This includes support for some of the server-based devices and file system drivers.

From a CD-ROM

The Windows 2000 CD-ROM uses the El-Torito standard to boot. What this means to you is that if your system can support this method of booting CD-ROMs, you can bypass the creation of the boot floppies. If your system can support Windows 2000, it should also support the El-Torito standard. This method is faster than using the floppy disks but is not as fast as the hard drive method.

From a Hard Drive

The process of installing Windows 2000 from a hard drive is a simple one. All that needs to be done is to copy the distribution files to the hard drive and launch either the winnt.exe or winnt32.exe Setup program. The setup after that is identical to the other methods.

From a Network Share

Similar to installing from a hard drive, installing Windows 2000 from a network share is also an easy process. All that needs to be done is to copy the distribution files to the server share point, map the client to that share, and launch either the winnt.exe or winnt32.exe Setup program. The setup after that is identical to the other methods.

Automated Installation

The following sections examine the options available for automated Windows 2000 installations.

Using Automated Installation Tools

Several utilities are available from the Windows 2000 CD-ROM and the *Windows 2000 Server Resource Kit* (ISBN: 1-57231-805-8) to automate the installation of Windows 2000. One of these is the Setup Manager Wizard, found in the Deployment section of the *Windows 2000 Server Resource Kit*.

This utility allows you to answer all the questions that the Windows 2000 Setup program may request and store them in a text file. This text file is then used with the **/unattend** command-line parameter to automatically answer these questions.

Another feature is its ability to create a uniqueness database file (UDF). This file, when used in conjunction with the answer file, allows you to install multiple machines using the answer file but modifying machine-specific information (such as the computer name, TCP/IP address, and so on).

Finally, you can create specialized directories in the distribution folder (for example, e:\i386) that will automatically install extra drivers or applications. These directories are outlined in Table 5.2.

Using Remote Installation Services

Another new feature of Windows 2000 is the Remote Installation Service (RIS). This service allows an administrator to create customized images that can then be used to automatically install Windows 2000 Professional on a workstation by

Table 5.2   Folder options under the Distribution folder.

Directory	Purpose
\OEM	Contains all extra files to be copied to the system during the setup process
\$$	Same as %windir% (C:\winnt)
\$$\Help	Installs extra help files into the *%windir%*\help folder during setup
\$$\System32	Installs extra files into the *%windir%*\system32 folder during setup
\$1	Same as the root drive on the hard drive that Windows 2000 is installed on (for example, C:)
\$1*pnpdrivers*	Stores new and updated drivers for Plug and Play devices
\$1\SysPrep	Contains the files used in the SysPrep process
\textmode	Stores extra drivers for mass storage devices and Hardware Abstraction Layers (HALs) to be used during the initial text-based phase of the Setup program
drive_letter	Stores files that are copied to the root of the drive specified
*drive_letter**folder*	Stores files that are copied to the folder specified

simply inserting a boot disk and answering a few simple questions (such as username, password, and computer name). RIS does the rest.

RIS uses a technology known as a *preboot execution environment* (PXE). If you use PXE-compliant network cards in your systems, they can simply boot the images off the network (this is done by pressing F12 during bootup). When the system boots using PXE, it first requests a TCP/IP address from a Dynamic Host Configuration Protocol (DHCP) server. Upon receiving this IP address, it contacts the RIS server (which authenticates its right to be installed in Active Directory) and the image is passed to the client.

Another nice feature of RIS is its ability to reuse files. Instead of creating several images where many of the files are identical, it scans all the images and places links to the files (regardless of which image they exist in). This greatly saves disk space. For example, if you were to create two Windows 2000 Professional images, the first would have a copy of each and every file needed for the installation. The second, however, would only have copies of the files that are different from the first. Any duplicated files are not copied but instead are linked to the real file. This allows you to store a large number of images on a relatively small amount of disk space.

Using Ghosting/Cloning Tools

Many organizations are faced with installing a very large number of systems. Most of these organizations use products such as Norton's Ghost to duplicate their systems. What these applications do is simply duplicate the hard drive from one machine to another.

One of the problems with Windows 2000 is that each system has a unique ID. No two systems may have the same ID on the network and still function properly. To solve this problem, Microsoft released a product called SysPrep on the *Windows 2000 Server Resource Kit*. This utility, when executed after the system has been set up, reverses some of these unique ID settings and allows you to take the "image" of the system. Once this image is restored on a different hard drive and that system is rebooted, the Windows 2000 Setup completes these steps to present you with a Windows 2000 system that's unique on the network.

Immediate Solutions

Creating the Windows 2000 Installation Boot Disks

The following sections explore the various methods of creating boot disks.

From MS-DOS

To create boot disks from MS-DOS, perform the following steps:

1. Boot the system using a boot disk that installs all the necessary CD-ROM drivers.

NOTE: If you need a boot disk, you can use the Windows 98 boot disk.

---

2. Change to the drive assigned to the CD-ROM (for example, D:).
3. Type "cd bootdisk" and press Enter.
4. Type in "makeboot" and press Enter.
5. When prompted, insert a blank, formatted floppy disk and press Enter.
6. Once the first floppy is created, repeat the process for the next three disks.

From Windows 9x

To create boot disks from Windows 95/98, perform the following steps:

1. Select Start|Programs|Accessories|Windows Explorer.
2. Change to the drive assigned to the CD-ROM (for example, D:).
3. Open the Bootdisk folder and double-click makeboot.exe.
4. Enter the drive letter for the floppy drive (A:).
5. When prompted, insert a blank, formatted floppy disk and press Enter.
6. Once the first floppy is created, repeat the process for the next three disks.

From Windows NT or Windows 2000

To create boot disks from Windows NT or 2000, perform the following steps:

1. Select Start|Programs|Accessories|Windows Explorer.
2. Change to the drive assigned to the CD-ROM (for example, D:).

3. Open the Bootdisk folder and double-click makebt32.exe.

4. Enter the drive letter for the floppy drive (A:).

5. When prompted, insert a blank, formatted floppy disk and press Enter.

6. Once the first floppy is created, repeat the process for the next three disks.

Installing Windows 2000 Using Boot Disks

To install Windows 2000 using boot disks, perform the following steps:

1. Insert Windows 2000 Boot Disk 1 into the floppy drive and the Windows 2000 CD-ROM into the CD-ROM drive. Then turn on your system.

2. When prompted, replace Disk 1 with Disk 2.

3. Repeat for the rest of the disks when prompted.

4. When the Welcome To Windows 2000 screen appears, press Enter.

5. Read the licensing agreement. You can use the Page Up and Page Down keys to scroll through it. Press F8 to continue.

6. The Setup program then displays the disks and partitions available on your system. Choose the desired partition (partitions or unpartitioned space).

7. If you want to delete a partition, press D. If you want to create a partition, choose C.

NOTE: *If you choose to create a new partition, Windows 2000 Setup will prompt you to select whether to create an NTFS partition or a FAT partition. If you select the FAT partition option and the partition is less than 2GB, FAT16 will be used. If, however, the partition is greater than 2GB, FAT32 will be automatically used.*

8. When you've created your partition, select it and press Enter.

9. The Windows 2000 Setup program will confirm your partition selection; press Enter when you're ready. If the partition is formatted in a non-NTFSv5 file system, the Setup program will ask you whether you want to convert it.

10. Your hard drives are now checked for errors and all necessary Windows 2000 files are copied to the Windows 2000 folder (\Winnt by default).

11. When the file copy is complete, the Windows 2000 Setup program will ask you to remove the CD-ROM and any floppies. Press Enter to reboot the system.

12. Windows Setup will restart. You'll know that this has occurred when the splash screen appears.

13. The Setup program will now detect and configure the hardware devices installed on your system. If, for some reason, the Setup program cannot detect or install a driver for a particular device, it will prompt you to direct it to the correct drivers.

14. Specify the regional settings for your particular system. You can change your locale and your keyboard settings. Once you've selected these criteria, click Next.

15. Enter the name of the person to which this computer is registered and then enter the company name. Once you've entered this information, click Next.

TIP: *Instead of entering the name of each user, you may want to use a generic name, such as the company name. This will prevent any confusion over the computer name in case a different person inherits the system.*

---

16. Enter the 25-digit product key as it appears on the back of your Windows 2000 CD-ROM jewel case and click Next.

17. Choose the licensing mode that will be used on this system. By default, a Per Server mode is selected. If you keep the Per Server selection, enter the number of Client Access Licenses (CALs) you purchased. Click Next when done.

TIP: *You can complete a one-time conversion from Per Server licensing to Per Seat. This can be done during the setup or at a later date.*

---

18. Enter the name that will be assigned to this computer on the network in the Computer Name field. In this window, you can also choose the password that will be assigned to the Administrator account on this system. This password can be left blank. Click Next.

19. You can now select the components you would like to install on your system. Remember that you can add or remove these components at a later date. Once you've completed your selection, click Next.

20. If Setup detects a modem, it displays the Dialing Location window. Select the country, area code, external line codes, and click Next.

21. Make sure the date, time, and time zone information is correct and click Next.

22. If you chose to install the Windows Terminal Services in the Windows 2000 Components window, choose the mode of operation: Remote Administration Mode (the default) or Application Server Mode. Once you've done so, click Next.

23. The Windows 2000 Setup program will now ask you whether you would like to install the network settings using Typical settings (these include

5. Windows 2000 Installation

Client For Microsoft Networks, File And Printer Sharing For Microsoft Networks, and the TCP/IP protocol configured to use either DHCP or APIPA) or Custom settings. Click Next.

24. If you selected to configure your own network options, enter the desired components and click Next. Again, you can modify the network configuration at a later date.

25. You're now prompted to join either a workgroup or a domain. If you would like to join a workgroup, enter the name of the workgroup in the Workgroup field. To join a domain, select the Yes option and enter the name of the domain in the Workgroup Or Computer Domain field. Click Next.

TIP: *If you want to install a new domain, select the No option and clear the Workgroup Or Computer Domain field.*

26. If you chose to join a domain, the Setup program will prompt you for the username and password of a user with sufficient rights to add your system to the domain. It will then contact the domain controller for the domain and add your computer account. Click Next to attempt to join the domain.

27. The selected components are now installed and configured. Windows 2000 is configured. When this phase is completed, the Setup program deletes any temporary files and prompts you to remove the CD-ROM before it reboots.

28. Windows 2000 is now installed. You can log into it as you would any other Windows 2000 system on your network.

Installing Windows 2000 from a DOS Prompt Using a CD-ROM

To install Windows 2000 from a DOS prompt using a CD-ROM, perform the following steps:

1. Boot into DOS with a boot disk that contains the correct CD-ROM drivers for you drive.

2. At the command prompt, type "*D:*" (where *D* is the drive letter assigned to your CD-ROM drive). Press Enter.

3. Type **cd i386** and press Enter.

4. Type **winnt** and press Enter.

5. Windows 2000 Setup will prompt you to enter the location of the Windows 2000 setup files. The default will be *drive_letter:*\i386.

> **NOTE:**   *You can exit the Windows 2000 Setup program at any point during the text-based phase by pressing F3.*

6. The Windows 2000 Setup program will now copy two sets of files. The first set copies the files necessary for the actual Setup program. These files are the same as those found on the Windows 2000 boot floppies. The second set copies the actual Windows 2000 installation files.

7. When copying is completed, the Setup program will prompt you to remove the floppy disk and CD-ROM from the drives and press Enter to reboot.

8. When the systems boots, the Windows 2000 Setup program will continue.

9. When the Welcome To Windows 2000 screen appears, press Enter.

10. Read the licensing agreement. You can use the Page Up and Page Down keys to scroll through it. Press F8 to continue.

11. The Setup program will now display the disks and partitions available on your system. Choose the desired partition (partitions or unpartitioned space).

12. If you want to delete a partition, press D. If you want to create a partition, press C.

> **NOTE:**   *If you choose to create a new partition, Windows 2000 Setup will prompt you to select whether to create an NTFS partition or a FAT partition. If you select the FAT partition option and the partition is less than 2GB, FAT16 will be used. If, however, the partition is greater than 2GB, FAT32 will be used.*

13. When you've created your partition, select it and press Enter.

14. The Windows 2000 Setup program will confirm your partition selection; press Enter when you're ready. If the partition is formatted in a non-NTFSv5 file system, the Setup program will ask you whether you want to convert it.

15. Your hard drives are now checked for errors and all necessary Windows 2000 files are copied to the Windows 2000 folder (\Winnt by default).

16. When the file copy is complete, the Windows 2000 Setup program will ask you to remove the CD-ROM and any floppies. Press Enter to reboot the system.

17. Windows Setup will restart. You'll know that this has occurred when the splash screen appears.

18. The Setup program will now detect and configure the hardware devices installed on your system. If, for some reason, the Setup program cannot detect or install a driver for a particular device, it will prompt you to direct it to the correct drivers.

19. Specify the regional settings for your particular system. You can change your locale and your keyboard settings. Once you've selected these criteria, click Next.

20. Enter the name of the person to which this computer is registered, followed by the company this system belongs to. Once you've entered this information, click Next.

21. Enter the 25-digit product key as it appears on the back of your Windows 2000 CD-ROM jewel case and click Next.

22. Choose the licensing mode that will be used on this system. By default, a Per Server mode is selected. If you keep the Per Server selection, enter the number of Client Access Licenses (CALs) that you purchased. Click Next when done.

23. Enter the name that will be assigned to this computer on the network in the Computer Name field. In this window, you can also choose the password that will be assigned to the Administrator account on this system. This password can be left blank. Click Next when done.

24. You can now select the components you would like to install on your system. Remember that you can add or remove these components at a later date. Once you've completed your selection, click Next.

25. If Setup detects a modem, it will now display the Dialing Location window. Select the country, area code, and external line codes and click Next.

26. Make sure that the date, time, and time zone information is correct and click Next.

27. If you chose to install the Windows Terminal Services in the Windows 2000 Components window, choose the mode of operation: Remote Administration Mode (the default) or Application Server Mode. Once you have done so, click Next.

28. The Windows 2000 Setup program will now ask you whether you would like to install the network settings using Typical settings (these include Client For Microsoft Networks, File And Printer Sharing For Microsoft Networks, and the TCP/IP protocol configured to use either DHCP or APIPA) or Custom settings. Click Next.

29. If you selected to configure your own network options, enter the desired components and click Next. Again, you can modify the network configuration at a later date.

30. You're now prompted to join either a workgroup or a domain. If you would like to join a workgroup, enter the name of the workgroup in the Workgroup field. To join a domain, select the Yes option and enter the name of the domain in the Workgroup Or Computer Domain field. Click Next.

5. Windows 2000 Installation

31. If you chose to join a domain, the Setup program will prompt you for the username and password of a user with sufficient rights to add your system to the domain. It will then contact the domain controller for the domain and add your computer account. Click Next to attempt to join the domain.

32. The selected components are now installed and configured. Windows 2000 is configured. When this phase is completed, the Setup program deletes any temporary files and prompts you to remove the CD-ROM before it reboots.

33. Windows 2000 is now installed. You can log into it as you would any other Windows 2000 system on your network.

Installing Windows 2000 from Windows 3.x Using a CD-ROM

To install Windows 2000 from Windows 3.x using a CD-ROM, perform the following steps:

1. Boot into Windows 3.x.

2. From File Manager, select the CD-ROM drive.

3. Navigate to the i386 directory.

4. Double-click winnt.exe.

5. The Setup program will copy the necessary files to the hard drive and prompt you to reboot the system.

6. Insert Windows 2000 Boot Disk 1 into the floppy drive and the Windows 2000 CD-ROM into the CD-ROM drive. Then turn on your system.

7. When prompted, replace Disk 1 with Disk 2.

8. Repeat for the rest of the disks when prompted.

9. When the Welcome To Windows 2000 screen appears, press Enter.

10. Read the licensing agreement. You can use the Page Up and Page Down keys to scroll through it. Press F8 to continue.

11. The Setup program will now display the disks and partitions available on your system. Choose the desired partition (partitions or unpartitioned space).

12. If you want to delete a partition, press the D key. If you want to create a partition, choose C.

NOTE: *If you choose to create a new partition, Windows 2000 Setup will prompt you to select whether to create an NTFS partition or a FAT partition. If you select the FAT partition option and the partition is less than 2GB, FAT16 will be used. If, however, the partition is greater than 2GB, FAT32 will be used.*

---

13. When you've created your partition, select it and press Enter.

14. The Windows 2000 Setup program will confirm your partition selection; press Enter when you're ready. If the partition is formatted in a non-NTFSv5 file system, the Setup program will ask you if you want to convert it.

15. Your hard drives are now checked for errors and all necessary Windows 2000 files are copied to the Windows 2000 folder (\Winnt by default).

16. When the file copy is complete, the Windows 2000 Setup program will ask you to remove the CD-ROM and any floppies. Press Enter to reboot the system.

17. Windows Setup will restart. You'll know that this has occurred when the splash screen appears.

18. The Setup program will now detect and configure the hardware devices installed on your system. If, for some reason, the Setup program cannot detect or install a driver for a particular device, it will prompt you to direct it to the correct drivers.

19. Specify the regional settings for your particular system. You can change your locale and your keyboard settings. Once you've selected these criteria, click Next.

20. Enter the name of the person to which this computer is registered, followed by the company this system belongs to. Once you've entered this information, click Next.

21. Enter the 25-digit product key as it appears on the back of your Windows 2000 CD-ROM jewel case and click Next.

22. Choose the licensing mode that will be used on this system. By default, a Per Server mode is selected. If you keep the Per Server selection, enter the number of Client Access Licenses (CALs) that you purchased. Click Next when done.

23. Enter the name that will be assigned to this computer on the network in the Computer Name field. In this window, you can also choose the password that will be assigned to the Administrator account on this system. This password can be left blank. Click Next when done.

24. You can now select the components you would like to install on your system. Remember that you can add or remove these components at a later date. Once you have completed your selection, click Next.

25. If Setup detects a modem, it will now display the Dialing Location window. Select the country, area code, and external line codes and click Next.

26. Make sure that the date, time, and time zone information is correct and click Next.

27. If you chose to install the Windows Terminal Services in the Windows 2000 Components window, choose the mode of operation: Remote Administration Mode (the default) or Application Server Mode. Once you've done so, click Next.

28. The Windows 2000 Setup program will now ask you whether you would like to install the network settings using Typical settings (these include Client For Microsoft Networks, File And Printer Sharing For Microsoft Networks, and the TCP/IP protocol configured to use either DHCP or APIPA) or Custom settings. Click Next.

29. If you selected to configure your own network options, enter the desired components and click Next. Again, you can modify the network configuration at a later date.

30. You're now prompted to join either a workgroup or a domain. If you would like to join a workgroup, enter the name of the workgroup in the Workgroup field. To join a domain, select the Yes option and enter the name of the domain in the Workgroup Or Computer Domain field. Click Next.

31. If you chose to join a domain, the Setup program will prompt you for the username and password of a user with sufficient rights to add your system to the domain. It will then contact the domain controller for the domain and add your computer account. Click Next to attempt to join the domain.

32. The selected components are now installed and configured. Windows 2000 is configured. When this phase is completed, the Setup program deletes any temporary files and prompts you to remove the CD-ROM before it reboots.

33. Windows 2000 is now installed. You can log into it as you would any other Windows 2000 system on your network.

Installing Windows 2000 from Windows 9x, NT, or 2000 Using a CD-ROM

To install Windows 2000 from Windows 95/98, NT, or 2000 using a CD-ROM, perform the following steps:

1. Insert the Windows 2000 CD-ROM. If autorun in enabled, the Windows 2000 Setup Wizard will automatically launch. If not, launch the Windows 2000 Wizard by running the winnt32.exe file in the \i386 directory on the CD-ROM.

2. You can choose to upgrade your existing operating system to Windows 2000 or install a new copy. Make your selection and click Next.

3. Read the license agreement, select the I Agree radio button, and click Next.

4. Enter the 25-digit product key as it appears on the back of the CD-ROM jewel case. Click Next.

5. You can modify your Windows 2000 installations to support multiple languages and accessibility on this screen. If you click the Advanced Options button, you'll be presented with some advanced Windows 2000 installation options. Click Next.

6. The Windows 2000 Setup Wizard will copy the necessary files to the hard drive and reboot your system.

7. The Setup program will now display the disks and partitions available on your system. Choose the desired partition (partitions or unpartitioned space).

8. If you want to delete a partition, press the D key. If you want to create a partition, choose C.

NOTE: *If you choose to create a new partition, Windows 2000 Setup will prompt you to select whether to create an NTFS partition or a FAT partition. If you select the FAT partition option and the partition is less than 2GB, FAT16 will be used. If, however, the partition is greater than 2GB, FAT32 will be used.*

---

9. When you've created your partition, select it and press Enter.

10. The Windows 2000 Setup program will confirm your partition selection; press Enter when you're ready. If the partition is formatted in a non-NTFSv5 file system, the Setup program will ask you if you want to convert it.

11. Your hard drives are now checked for errors and all necessary Windows 2000 files are copied to the Windows 2000 folder (\Winnt by default).

12. When the file copy is complete, the Windows 2000 Setup program will ask you to remove the CD-ROM and any floppies. Press Enter to reboot the system.

13. Windows Setup will restart. You'll know that this has occurred when the splash screen appears.

14. The Setup program will now detect and configure the hardware devices that are installed on your system. If, for some reason, the Setup program cannot detect or install a driver for a particular device, it will prompt you to direct it to the correct drivers.

15. Specify the regional settings for your particular system. You can change your locale and your keyboard settings. Once you've selected these criteria, click Next.

16. Enter the name of the person to which this computer is registered, followed by the company this system belongs to. Once you've entered this information, click Next.

5. Windows 2000 Installation

17. Choose the licensing mode that will be used on this system. By default, a Per Server mode is selected. If you keep the Per Server selection, enter the number of Client Access Licenses (CALs) you purchased. Click Next when done.

18. Enter the name that will be assigned to this computer on the network in the Computer Name field. In this window, you can also choose the password that will be assigned to the Administrator account on this system. This password can be left blank. Click Next when done.

19. You can now select the components you would like to install on your system. Remember that you can add or remove these components at a later date. Once you've completed your selection, click Next.

20. If Setup detects a modem, it will now display the Dialing Location window. Select the country, area code, and external line codes and click Next.

21. Make sure that the date, time, and time zone information is correct and click Next.

22. If you chose to install the Windows Terminal Services in the Windows 2000 Components window, choose the mode of operation: Remote Administration Mode (the default) or Application Server Mode. Once you have done so, click Next.

23. The Windows 2000 Setup program will now ask you whether you would like to install the network settings using Typical settings (these include Client For Microsoft Networks, File And Printer Sharing For Microsoft Networks, and the TCP/IP protocol configured to use either DHCP or APIPA) or Custom settings. Click Next.

24. If you selected to configure your own network options, enter the desired components and click Next. Again, you can modify the network configuration at a later date.

25. You're now prompted to join either a workgroup or a domain. If you would like to join a workgroup, enter the name of the workgroup in the Workgroup field. To join a domain, select the Yes option and enter the name of the domain in the Workgroup Or Computer Domain field. Click Next.

26. If you chose to join a domain, the Setup program will prompt you for the username and password of a user with sufficient rights to add your system to the domain. It will then contact the domain controller for the domain and add your computer account. Click Next to attempt to join the domain.

27. The selected components are now installed and configured. Windows 2000 is configured. When this phase is completed, the Setup program deletes any temporary files and prompts you to remove the CD-ROM before it reboots.

28. Windows 2000 is now installed. You can log into it as you would any other Windows 2000 system on your network.

Installing Windows 2000 from a Bootable CD-ROM

To install Windows 2000 from a bootable CD-ROM, perform the following steps:

1. Set your system's BIOS to boot off the CD-ROM drive prior to attempting to boot from the floppy drive and hard drive.

2. Insert the Windows 2000 CD-ROM into the CD-ROM drive and turn on your system.

3. When the Welcome To Windows 2000 screen appears, press Enter.

4. Read the licensing agreement. You can use the Page Up and Page Down keys to scroll through it. Press F8 to continue.

5. The Setup program will now display the disks and partitions available on your system. Choose the desired partition (partitions or unpartitioned space).

6. If you want to delete a partition, press D. If you want to create a partition, choose C.

NOTE: *If you choose to create a new partition, Windows 2000 Setup will prompt you to select whether to create an NTFS partition or a FAT partition. If you select the FAT partition option and the partition is less than 2GB, FAT16 will be used. If, however, the partition is greater than 2GB, FAT32 will be used.*

---

7. When you've created your partition, select it and press Enter.

8. The Windows 2000 Setup program will confirm your partition selection; press Enter when you're ready. If the partition is formatted in a non-NTFSv5 file system, Setup will ask if you want to convert it.

9. Your hard drives are now checked for errors and all necessary Windows 2000 files are copied to the Windows 2000 folder (\Winnt by default).

10. When the file copy is complete, the Windows 2000 Setup program will ask you to remove the CD-ROM and any floppies. Press Enter to reboot the system.

11. Windows Setup will restart. You'll know that this has occurred when the splash screen appears.

12. The Setup program will now detect and configure the hardware devices installed on your system. If, for some reason, the Setup program cannot detect or install a driver for a particular device, it will prompt you to direct it to the correct drivers.

13. Specify the regional settings for your particular system. You can change your locale and your keyboard settings. Once you've selected these criteria, click Next.

14. Enter the name of the person to which this computer is registered, followed by the company this system belongs to. Once you've entered this information, click Next.

15. Choose the licensing mode that will be used on this system. By default, a Per Server mode is selected. If you keep the Per Server selection, enter the number of Client Access Licenses (CALs) you purchased. Click Next when done.

16. Enter the name that will be assigned to this computer on the network in the Computer Name field. In this window, you can also choose the password that will be assigned to the Administrator account on this system. This password can be left blank. Click Next when done.

17. You can now select the components you would like to install on your system. Remember that you can add or remove these components at a later date. Once you've completed your selection, click Next.

18. If Setup detects a modem, it will now display the Dialing Location window. Select the country, area code, and external line codes and click Next.

19. Make sure that the date, time, and time zone information is correct and click Next.

20. If you chose to install the Windows Terminal Services in the Windows 2000 Components window, choose the mode of operation: Remote Administration Mode (the default) or Application Server Mode. Once you have done so, click Next.

21. The Windows 2000 Setup program will now ask you whether you would like to install the network settings using Typical Settings (these include Client For Microsoft Networks, File And Printer Sharing For Microsoft Networks, and the TCP/IP protocol configured to use either DHCP or APIPA) or Custom settings. Click Next.

22. If you selected to configure your own network options, enter the desired components and click Next. Again, you can modify the network configuration at a later date.

23. You're now prompted to join either a workgroup or a domain. If you would like to join a workgroup, enter the name of the workgroup in the Workgroup field. To join a domain, select the Yes option and enter the name of the domain in the Workgroup Or Computer Domain field. Click Next.

24. If you chose to join a domain, the Setup program will prompt you for the username and password of a user with sufficient rights to add your system to the domain. It will then contact the domain controller for the domain and add your computer account. Click Next to attempt to join the domain.

25. The selected components are now installed and configured. Windows 2000 is configured. When this phase is completed, the Setup program deletes any temporary files and prompts you to remove the CD-ROM before it reboots.

26. Windows 2000 is now installed. You can log into it as you would any other Windows 2000 system on your network.

Installing Windows 2000 from a Hard Drive

To install Windows 2000 from a hard drive, perform the following steps:

1. Insert the Windows 2000 CD-ROM. If autorun in enabled, the Windows 2000 Setup Wizard will automatically launch. If not, launch the Windows 2000 Wizard by running the winnt32.exe file in the \i386 directory on the CD-ROM.

2. You can choose to upgrade your existing operating system to Windows 2000 or install a new copy. Make your selection and click Next.

3. Read the license agreement, select the I Agree radio button, and click Next.

4. Enter the 25-digit product key as it appears on the back of the CD-ROM jewel case, as shown in Figure 5.1. Click Next.

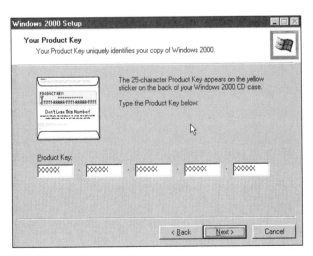

Figure 5.1   Entering the product key.

5. You can modify your Windows 2000 installations to support multiple languages and accessibility on the screen shown in Figure 5.2. If you click the Advanced Options button, you'll be presented with some advanced Windows 2000 installation options (see Figure 5.3). Click Next.

6. The Windows 2000 Setup Wizard will copy the necessary files to the hard drive and reboot your system.

7. The Setup program will now display the disks and partitions available on your system. Choose the desired partition (partitions or unpartitioned space).

8. If you want to delete a partition, press D. If you want to create a partition, choose C.

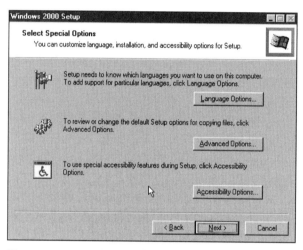

Figure 5.2   The Special Options window.

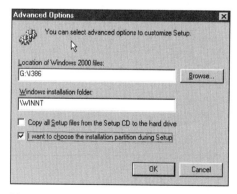

Figure 5.3   The Advanced Options window.

NOTE: *If you choose to create a new partition, Windows 2000 Setup will prompt you to select whether to create an NTFS partition or a FAT partition. If you select the FAT partition option and the partition is less than 2GB, FAT16 will be used. If, however, the partition is greater than 2GB, FAT32 will be used.*

---

9. When you've created your partition, select it and press Enter.

10. The Windows 2000 Setup program will confirm your partition selection; press Enter when you're ready. If the partition is formatted in a non-NTFSv5 file system, the Setup program will ask you if you want to convert it.

11. Your hard drives are now checked for errors and all necessary Windows 2000 files are copied to the Windows 2000 folder (\Winnt by default).

12. When the file copy is complete, the Windows 2000 Setup program will ask you to remove the CD-ROM and any floppies. Press Enter to reboot the system.

13. Windows Setup will restart. You'll know that this has occurred when the splash screen appears.

14. The Setup program will now detect and configure the hardware devices installed on your system. If, for some reason, the Setup program cannot detect or install a driver for a particular device, it will prompt you to direct it to the correct drivers.

15. Specify the regional settings for your particular system. You can change your locale and your keyboard settings. Once you've selected these criteria, click Next.

16. Enter the name of the person to which this computer is registered, followed by the company this system belongs to. Once you've entered this information, click Next.

17. Choose the licensing mode that will be used on this system. By default, a Per Server mode is selected. If you keep the Per Server selection, enter the number of Client Access Licenses (CALs) you purchased. Click Next when done.

18. Enter the name that will be assigned to this computer on the network in the Computer Name field. In this window, you can also choose the password that will be assigned to the Administrator account on this system. This password can be left blank. Click Next when done.

19. You can now select the components you would like to install on your system. Remember that you can add or remove these components at a later date. Once you've completed your selection, click Next.

20. If Setup detects a modem, it will now display the Dialing Location window. Select the country, area code, and external line codes and click Next.

5. Windows 2000 Installation

21. Make sure that the date, time, and time zone information is correct and click Next.

22. If you chose to install the Windows Terminal Services in the Windows 2000 Components window, choose the mode of operation: Remote Administration Mode (the default) or Application Server Mode. Once you've done so, click Next.

23. The Windows 2000 Setup program will now ask you whether you would like to install the network settings using Typical settings (these include Client For Microsoft Networks, File And Printer Sharing For Microsoft Networks, and the TCP/IP protocol configured to use either DHCP or APIPA) or Custom settings. Click Next.

24. If you selected to configure your own network options, enter the desired components and click Next. Again, you can modify the network configuration at a later date.

25. You're now prompted to join either a workgroup or a domain. If you would like to join a workgroup, enter the name of the workgroup in the Workgroup field. To join a domain, select the Yes option and enter the name of the domain in the Workgroup Or Computer Domain field. Click Next.

26. If you chose to join a domain, the Setup program will prompt you for the username and password of a user with sufficient rights to add your system to the domain. It will then contact the domain controller for the domain and add your computer account. Click Next to attempt to join the domain.

27. The selected components are now installed and configured. Windows 2000 is configured. When this phase is completed, the Setup program deletes any temporary files and prompts you to remove the CD-ROM before it reboots.

28. Windows 2000 is now installed. You can log into it as you would any other Windows 2000 system on your network.

Creating a Distribution Folder on the Local Machine

To create a local distribution folder, perform the following steps:

1. Using your favorite method, create a directory on the system and give it a name that will easily identify it (for example, c:\win2000setup).

2. Copy the contents of the i386 directory on the Windows 2000 CD-ROM into this directory.

5. Windows 2000 Installation

3. Create subfolders for any additional drivers or programs that will be installed. The entire contents of this folder will be temporarily copied to the hard drive of the system being installed.

4. Create any special folders that will be used by Setup. These can include \$OEM\$\textmode, \$OEM\$\$\$, \$Oem\$\$1, and \$OEM\$*drive_letter*.

Sharing the Distribution Folder

To share a distribution folder, perform the following steps:

1. Right-click the folder to be shared and choose the Sharing option from the pop-up menu.

2. Select the Share radio button.

3. Enter a name for the shared folder.

4. Click the Permissions button and assign the desired permissions to this folder.

5. Click OK.

TIP: *You'll most likely want to remove the Everyone: Full Control permission and assign the Read permission to the administration group that will complete the Windows 2000 installations.*

Creating a Distribution Folder on a Remote Machine

To create a distribution folder on a remote machine, perform the following steps:

1. Connect to the shared folder on the remote system (make sure you have Write permissions to this share).

2. Copy the contents of the i386 directory on the Windows 2000 CD-ROM to this directory.

3. Create subfolders for any additional drivers or programs that will be installed. The entire contents of this folder will be temporarily copied to the hard drive of the system being installed.

4. Create any special folders that will be used by Setup. These can include \$OEM\$\textmode, \$OEM\$\$\$, \$Oem\$\$1, and \$OEM\$*drive_letter*.

Installing from a Network Share

To install Windows 2000 from a network share, perform the following steps:

1. Connect to the network share and run the winnt32.exe file.

2. You can choose to upgrade your existing operating system to Windows 2000 or install a new copy. Make your selection and click Next.

3. Read the license agreement, select the I Agree radio button, and click Next.

4. Enter the 25-digit product key as it appears on the back of the CD-ROM jewel case. Click Next.

5. You can modify your Windows 2000 installations to support multiple languages and accessibility on this screen. If you click the Advanced Options button, you'll be presented with some advanced Windows 2000 installation options. Click Next.

6. The Windows 2000 Setup Wizard will copy the necessary files to the hard drive and reboot your system.

7. The Setup program will now display the disks and partitions available on your system. Choose the desired partition (partitions or unpartitioned space).

8. If you want to delete a partition, press D. If you want to create a partition, choose C.

NOTE: *If you choose to create a new partition, Windows 2000 Setup will prompt you to select whether to create an NTFS partition or a FAT partition. If you select the FAT partition option and the partition is less than 2GB, FAT16 will be used. If, however, the partition is greater than 2GB, FAT32 will be used.*

---

9. When you've created your partition, select it and press Enter.

10. The Windows 2000 Setup program will confirm your partition selection; press Enter when you're ready. If the partition is formatted in a non-NTFSv5 file system, the Setup program will ask you if you want to convert it.

11. Your hard drives are now checked for errors and all necessary Windows 2000 files are copied to the Windows 2000 folder (\Winnt by default).

12. When the file copy is complete, the Windows 2000 Setup program will ask you to remove the CD-ROM and any floppies. Press Enter to reboot the system.

13. Windows Setup will restart. You'll know that this has occurred when the splash screen appears.

14. The Setup program will now detect and configure the hardware devices that are installed on your system. If, for some reason, the Setup program cannot detect or install a driver for a particular device, it will prompt you to direct it to the correct drivers.

15. Specify the regional settings for your particular system. You can change your locale and your keyboard settings. Once you've selected these criteria, click Next.

16. Enter the name of the person to which this computer is registered, followed by the company this system belongs to. Once you've entered this information, click Next.

17. Choose the licensing mode that will be used on this system. By default, a Per Server mode is selected. If you keep the Per Server selection, enter the number of Client Access Licenses (CALs) you purchased. Click Next when done.

18. Enter the name that will be assigned to this computer on the network in the Computer Name field. In this window, you can also choose the password that will be assigned to the Administrator account on this system. This password can be left blank. Click Next when done.

19. You can now select the components you would like to install on your system. Remember that you can add or remove these components at a later date. Once you've completed your selection, click Next.

20. If Setup detects a modem, it will now display the Dialing Location window. Select the country, area code, and external line codes and click Next.

21. Make sure that the date, time, and time zone information is correct and click Next.

22. If you chose to install the Windows Terminal Services in the Windows 2000 Components window, choose the mode of operation: Remote Administration Mode (the default) or Application Server Mode. Once you've done so, click Next.

23. The Windows 2000 Setup program will now ask you whether you would like to install the network settings using Typical settings (these include Client For Microsoft Networks, File And Printer Sharing For Microsoft Networks, and the TCP/IP protocol configured to use either DHCP or APIPA) or Custom settings. Click Next.

24. If you selected to configure your own network options, enter the desired components and click Next. Again, you can modify the network configuration at a later date.

25. You're now prompted to join either a workgroup or a domain. If you would like to join a workgroup, enter the name of the workgroup in the Workgroup field. To join a domain, select the Yes option and enter the name of the domain in the Workgroup or Computer Domain field. Click Next.

26. If you chose to join a domain, the Setup program will prompt you for the username and password of a user with sufficient rights to add your system to the domain. It will then contact the domain controller for the domain and add your computer account. Click Next to attempt to join the domain.

27. The selected components are now installed and configured. Windows 2000 is configured. When this phase is completed, the Setup program deletes any temporary files and prompts you to remove the CD-ROM before it reboots.

28. Windows 2000 is now installed. You can log into it as you would any other Windows 2000 system on your network.

Installing from Multiple Network Shares

To install Windows 2000 from multiple network shares, perform the following steps:

1. Map a network drive to the first network share. Select Start|Run. Enter "shared_drive:\i386\winnt32.exe /s:shared_drive:\i386 /s:\\server2\share2 / s:\\server3\share3", and so on. Click OK.

2. You can choose to upgrade your existing operating system to Windows 2000 or install a new copy. Make your selection and click Next.

3. Read the license agreement, select the I Agree radio button, and click Next.

4. Enter the 25-digit product key as it appears on the back of the CD-ROM jewel case. Click Next.

5. You can modify your Windows 2000 installations to support multiple languages and accessibility on this screen. If you click the Advanced Options button, you'll be presented with some advanced Windows 2000 installation options. Click Next.

6. The Windows 2000 Setup Wizard will copy the necessary files to the hard drive and reboot your system.

7. The Setup program will now display the disks and partitions available on your system. Choose the desired partition (partitions or unpartitioned space).

8. If you want to delete a partition, press D. If you want to create a partition, choose C.

NOTE: *If you choose to create a new partition, Windows 2000 Setup will prompt you to select whether to create an NTFS partition or a FAT partition. If you select the FAT partition option and the partition is less than 2GB, FAT16 will be used. If, however, the partition is greater than 2GB, FAT32 will be used.*

---

5. Windows 2000 Installation

9. When you've created your partition, select it and press Enter.

10. The Windows 2000 Setup program will confirm your partition selection; press Enter when you're ready. If the partition is formatted in a non-NTFSv5 file system, the Setup program will ask you if you want to convert it.

11. Your hard drives are now checked for errors and all necessary Windows 2000 files are copied to the Windows 2000 folder (\Winnt by default).

12. When the file copy is complete, the Windows 2000 Setup program will ask you to remove the CD-ROM and any floppies. Press Enter to reboot the system.

13. Windows Setup will restart. You'll know that this has occurred when the splash screen appears.

14. The Setup program will now detect and configure the hardware devices installed on your system. If, for some reason, the Setup program cannot detect or install a driver for a particular device, it will prompt you to direct it to the correct drivers.

15. Specify the regional settings for your particular system. You can change your locale and your keyboard settings. Once you've selected these criteria, click Next.

16. Enter the name of the person to which this computer is registered, followed by the company that this system belongs to. Once you've entered this information, click Next.

17. Choose the licensing mode that will be used on this system. By default, a Per Server mode is selected. If you keep the Per Server selection, enter the number of Client Access Licenses (CALs) you purchased. Click Next when done.

18. Enter the name that will be assigned to this computer on the network in the Computer Name field. In this window, you can also choose the password that will be assigned to the Administrator account on this system. This password can be left blank. Click Next when done.

19. You can now select the components you would like to install on your system. Remember that you can add or remove these components at a later date. Once you've completed your selection, click Next.

20. If Setup detects a modem, it will now display the Dialing Location window. Select the country, area code, and external line codes and click Next.

21. Make sure the date, time, and time zone information is correct and click Next.

5. Windows 2000 Installation

22. If you chose to install the Windows Terminal Services in the Windows 2000 Components window, choose the mode of operation: Remote Administration Mode (the default) or Application Server Mode. Once you've done so, click Next.

23. The Windows 2000 Setup program will now ask you whether you would like to install the network settings using Typical settings (these include Client For Microsoft Networks, File And Printer Sharing For Microsoft Networks, and the TCP/IP protocol configured to use either DHCP or APIPA) or Custom settings. Click Next.

24. If you selected to configure your own network options, enter the desired components and click Next. Again, you can modify the network configuration at a later date.

25. You're now prompted to join either a workgroup or a domain. If you would like to join a workgroup, enter the name of the workgroup in the Workgroup field. To join a domain, select the Yes option and enter the name of the domain in the Workgroup or Computer Domain field. Click Next.

26. If you chose to join a domain, the Setup program will prompt you for the username and password of a user with sufficient rights to add your system to the domain. It will then contact the domain controller for the domain and add your computer account. Click Next to attempt to join the domain.

27. The selected components are now installed and configured. Windows 2000 is configured. When this phase is completed, the Setup program deletes any temporary files and prompts you to remove the CD-ROM before it reboots.

28. Windows 2000 is now installed. You can log into it as you would any other Windows 2000 system on your network.

Installing the Setup Manager Wizard

To install the Windows 2000 Setup Manager Wizard, perform the following steps:

1. Insert the *Windows 2000 Server Resource Kit* CD-ROM.

2. Double-click setup.exe from the CD-ROM drive.

3. Click Next to start the installation process.

4. Read through the licensing agreement, select the I Agree option, and click Next.

5. Enter your name and your organization's name and click Next.

6. Choose the Custom option and click Next.

7. Click Next accept the selections.

8. Click Next to begin the file copy.

9. Click Finish to complete the setup.

TIP: *The Setup Manager (as well as the other installation utilities) reside in the Deployment section of the Windows 2000 Server Resource Kit.*

Creating an Answer File

To create an answer file, perform the following steps:

1. Select Start|Run. Enter "Setupmgr" and click OK. The Setup Manager Wizard will appear.

2. Click Next to begin the Setup Manager.

3. Choose the option to create a new answer file and click Next.

4. Choose the type of installation you would like to perform. Click Next.

5. Choose the platform you would like to install—either Windows 2000 Professional or Windows 2000 Server. Click Next.

6. Choose the level of interaction you would like the setup process take. Select the desired level of interaction and click Next.

7. Enter the name and organization you would like to use for the computer and click Next.

8. If you chose to install Windows 2000 Server, select the licensing mode for the server (either Per Server or Per Seat). Click Next when done.

9. At this point, you can choose to enter a single computer name or multiple names. If you choose to enter multiple names, a UDF file will also be created that partners up with the answer file. Click Next after you've added all the different computers.

10. Specify the method for supplying the administrator's password. When done, click Next.

WARNING! *Remember that the answer file is a simple text file. If someone were to gain access to the file, the administrator's password could be discovered. For this reason, if you decide to enter the password into the answer file, make sure you change the password file after the installation.*

5. Windows 2000 Installation

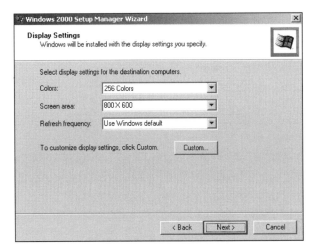

Figure 5.4   Configuring the installation display settings.

11. Choose the display settings for the new system, as shown in Figure 5.4. Three options are available to you: number of colors, screen resolution, and screen refresh rate. Make your desired selections and click Next.

12. Specify your network settings and click Next.

13. Select whether you would like the computer to belong to a workgroup or a domain. If you select a workgroup, enter the name of the workgroup in the Workgroup field. With a domain selection, you can have Setup create a computer account in the domain by supplying a username and password with the correct security credentials to create the account or to create the account ahead of time. When done, click Next.

14. Select the time zone for the system and click Next.

15. At this point, you get to decide whether additional settings are required. If you decide that no additional settings are required, click Next and continue with Step 23. Otherwise, click Next.

16. You can configure what telephony configuration will be set if the Setup Wizard detects any modems. Click Next to continue.

17. Specify the regional settings for the installation systems and click Next.

18. Select any additional required languages for the system. Click Next.

TIP: *To select more than one language, you can Ctrl+click to select items individually or Shift+click to select a list of items.*

---

19. You're now given the option to configure the Internet browser installed on the system and additional Windows 2000 shell settings. Click Next when done.

20. By default, Windows 2000 will be installed in the \winnt folder. You can choose an alternate location in this window. Click Next when done.

21. Any local or network printers can be installed for the new system by configuring them in this window. Click Next to continue.

22. If you would like a specific application or command to be executed once after the installation is complete, enter it here. Click Next to continue.

23. The Windows 2000 Setup Manager gives you the opportunity to have it automatically create a distribution folder for the Windows 2000 files (for example, the i386 folder). If you choose the No option and click Next, you can continue with Step 24. However, if you choose the Yes option and click Next, you'll be given the opportunity to configure the settings for the distribution folder (see Figure 5.5).

24. Enter the name of the answer file. This name will also be used for the UDF file as well as the batch file (BAT). Click Next to continue.

25. Click Finish to create the files and exit the Setup Manager Wizard.

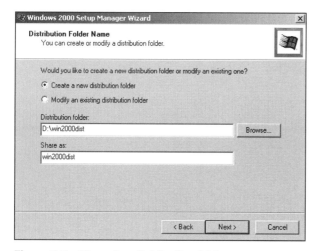

Figure 5.5   The setup distribution folder.

Installing Windows 2000 Using an Answer File

There are two methods to use an answer file. These methods are covered in the following sections.

Using a Batch File

To use an answer file through a batch file, perform the following steps:

1. Copy the files created by the Setup Manager Wizard (assuming that you named these files unattended.bat, unattended.udf, and unattended.txt) to the distribution folder.

2. Navigate to the distribution folder and double-click the batch file (unattend.bat).

Using the Command Line

To use an answer file from the command line, perform the following steps:

1. Copy the files created by the Setup Manager Wizard (assuming that you named these files unattended.udf, and unattended.txt) to the distribution folder.

2. Open a command prompt and navigate to the distribution folder.

3. Type the following:

```
distribution_folder:\i386\winnt32
/s:distribution_folder:\i386 /unattend:.\unattended.txt
```

Creating a Uniqueness Database File

To create a UDF, perform the following steps:

1. Select Start|Run. Enter "Setupmgr" and click OK. The Setup Manager Wizard will appear.

2. Click Next to begin the Setup Manager.

3. Choose the option Create A New Answer File and click Next.

4. Choose the type of installation you would like to perform. Click Next.

5. Choose the platform you would like to install—either Windows 2000 Professional or Windows 2000 Server. Click Next.

6. Choose the level of interaction you would like the setup process to take and click Next.

7. Enter the name and organization you would like to use for the computer and click Next.

8. If you chose to install Windows 2000 Server, select the licensing mode for the server (either Per Server or Per Seat). Click Next when done.

9. At this point, you can choose to enter a single computer name or multiple names. If you choose to enter multiple names, a UDF file will also be created that partners up with the answer file. Click Next after you've added all the different computers.

10. Specify the method for supplying the administrator's password. When done, click Next.

11. Choose the display settings for the new system. Three options are available to you: number of colors, screen resolution, and screen refresh rate. Make your desired selections and click Next.

12. Specify your network settings and click Next.

13. Select whether you would like the computer to belong to a workgroup or a domain. If you select a workgroup, enter the name of the workgroup in the Workgroup field. With a domain selection, you can have Setup create a computer account in the domain by supplying a username and password with the correct security credentials to create the account or to create the account ahead of time. When done, click Next.

14. Select the time zone for the system and click Next.

15. At this point, you get to decide whether additional settings are required. If you decide that no additional settings are required, click Next and continue with Step 23. Otherwise, click Next.

16. You can configure what telephony configuration will be set if the Setup Wizard detects any modems. Click Next to continue.

17. Specify the regional settings for the installation system and click Next.

18. Select any additional required languages for the system. Click Next.

19. You're now given the option to configure the Internet browser installed on the system and additional Windows 2000 shell settings. Click Next when done.

20. By default, Windows 2000 will be installed in the /winnt folder. You can choose an alternate location in this window. Click Next when done.

21. Any local or network printers can be installed for the new system by configuring them in this window. Click Next to continue.

22. If you would like a specific application or command to be executed once after the installation is complete, enter it here. Click Next to continue.

5. Windows 2000 Installation

23. The Windows 2000 Setup Manager gives you the opportunity to have it automatically create a distribution folder for the Windows 2000 files (for example, the i386 folder). If you choose the No option and click Next, you can continue with Step 24. However, if you choose the Yes option and click Next, you'll be given the opportunity to configure the settings for the distribution folder.

24. Enter the name of the answer file. This name will also be used for the UDF file as well as the batch file (BAT). Click Next to continue.

25. Click Finish to create the files and exit the Setup Manager Wizard.

Installing Windows 2000 Using a Uniqueness Database File

To install Windows 2000 using a UDF, perform the following steps:

1. Copy the files created by the Setup Manager Wizard (assuming that you named the filesunattended.udf and unattended.txt) to the distribution folder.

2. Open a command prompt and navigate to the distribution folder.

3. Type "*distribution_folder*:\i386\winnt32 /s:*distribution_folder*:\i386 / unattend:.\unattended.txt /udf:*id*:unattended.udf".

Installing Windows 2000 Using the **/Syspart** Switch

To install Windows 2000 using the **/syspart** switch, perform the following steps:

1. Attach the extra hard drive.

2. Connect to the distribution folder.

3. Select Start|Run and type the following:

```
winnt32 /unattend:unattended.txt /s:distribution_folder
/syspart:second_drive /tempdrive:second_drive
```

4. Shut down the reference computer and remove the hard drive.

5. Install the hard drive in the new system.

6. Turn the new system on.

5. Windows 2000 Installation

Running the SysPrep Application Manually

To run SysPrep manually, perform the following steps:

1. Select Start|Run. Type in **cmd** and click OK.

2. At the command prompt, create a folder to be used by SysPrep at the root (for example, c:\sysprep). Type the following to create a folder called sysprep:

```
mkdir sysprep
```

3. Copy the sysprep.exe and setupcl.exe files from the *Windows 2000 Server Resource Kit* into this folder.

WARNING!   *If you're using the sysprep.inf file, you'll have to copy it to the SysPrep folder as well.*

4. Change to the SysPrep folder.

5. Execute SysPrep with one of the optional parameters.

Running the SysPrep Application Automatically after Setup

To run SysPrep automatically, perform the following steps:

1. Create a folder named \$OEM$\$1\Sysprep and copy the SysPrep files to it.

2. In the [GuiRunOnce] section of the answer file, enter the following command as the last line:

```
%systemdrive%\sysprep\sysprep.exe - quiet
```

3. Run the unattended setup as you normally would.

Installing Remote Installation Services

To install Windows 2000 RIS, perform the following steps:

1. Select Start|Settings|Control Panel.

2. Double-click the Add/Remove Programs applet.

3. Click the Add/Remove Windows Components button from left pane and click the Components button to launch the Windows Components Wizard.

4. Scroll down and select the Remote Installation Services option. Click Next. The Remote Installation Services will be installed.

5. Click Finish and reboot the server if necessary.

6. In the Add/Remove Programs applet, click the Add/Remove Windows Components button in left pane, select Configure Remote Installation Services, and click the Configure button.

7. Click Next.

8. Enter the folder path where you want the root of the Remote Installation Services operating system to reside. Click Next.

WARNING!   The location of the RIS operating system's root must reside on an NTFSv5 partition and cannot be located on the same partition as the system partition.

9. If you want RIS to start immediately, select the Respond To Client Computers Requesting Service checkbox and click Next (see Figure 5.6).

10. Enter the path to the Windows 2000 Professional installation files and click Next.

11. Enter a name for the folder that will be created to store the operating system image and click Next.

12. Enter an explanatory name and a description for this operating system image and click Next.

13. Click Finish to complete the setup. RIS will now create an image of the Windows 2000 Professional operating system and give you a status, as shown in Figure 5.7.

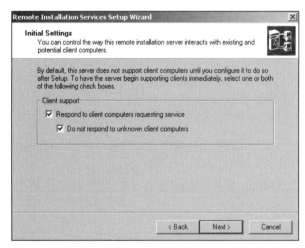

Figure 5.6   Configuring the initial settings for Remote Installation Services.

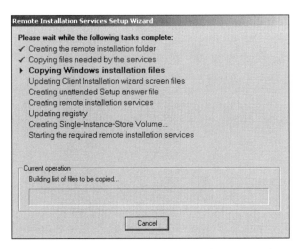

Figure 5.7 Creating the initial operating system image in Remote Installation Services.

Enabling Remote Installation Preparation

To enable remote installation, perform the following steps:

1. Select Start|Programs|Administrative Tools|Active Directory Users And Computers.

2. Navigate to the server where you would like to enable RIS, right-click it, and choose Properties from the pop-up menu.

3. Click the Remote Install tab.

4. Select the Respond To Client Computers Requesting Service checkbox and click OK.

Disabling Remote Installation Preparation

To disable remote installation, perform the following steps:

1. Select Start|Programs|Administrative Tools|Active Directory Users And Computers.

2. Navigate to the server where you would like to disable RIS, right-click it, and choose Properties from the pop-up menu.

3. Click the Remote Install tab.

4. Clear the Respond To Client Computers Requesting Service checkbox and click OK.

Viewing Clients

To view RIS clients, perform the following steps:

1. Select Start|Programs|Administrative Tools|Active Directory Users And Computers.

2. Navigate to the server running RIS, right-click it, and choose Properties from the pop-up menu.

3. Click the Remote Install tab.

4. Click the Show Clients button.

Verifying Server Operation

To verify server operation, perform the following steps:

1. Select Start|Programs|Administrative Tools|Active Directory Users And Computers.

2. Navigate to the server running RIS, right-click it, and choose Properties from the pop-up menu.

3. Click the Remote Install tab.

4. Click the Verify Server button. The Check Server Wizard will appear (see Figure 5.8).

5. Click Next to start the server verification.

6. Click Finish when you're done reading the test result summary generated in Step 5.

Figure 5.8   The Check Server Wizard.

Creating a New Operating System Image

To create a new OS image, perform the following steps:

1. Select Start|Programs|Administrative Tools|Active Directory Users And Computers.

2. Navigate to the server running RIS, right-click it, and choose Properties from the pop-up menu.

3. Click the Remote Install tab.

4. Click the Advanced Settings button.

5. Click the Add button. The Add Wizard will launch.

6. Choose whether a new answer file is being used for an existing image by selecting A New Answer File To An Existing Image option, or create a new image from the Windows 2000 Professional installation files by selecting the Add A New Installation Image option. Click Next.

TIP: *If you choose to use a new answer file with an existing image, you'll save a lot of disk space. Using this method, RIS will only copy the differences between the operating systems rather than the entire installation directory on the Windows 2000 Professional CD.*

7. Follow the wizard to create the new image.

Modifying an Existing Operating System Image

To modify an OS image, perform the following steps:

1. Select Start|Programs|Administrative Tools|Active Directory Users And Computers.

2. Navigate to the server running RIS, right-click it, and choose Properties from the pop-up menu.

3. Click the Remote Install tab.

4. Click the Advanced Settings button.

5. Select the image you would like to modify and click the Properties button.

6. Notice that you may only change the friendly name and the description for this image. Click OK when done.

5. Windows 2000 Installation

Deleting an Operating System Image

To delete an OS image, perform the following steps:

1. Select Start|Programs|Administrative Tools|Active Directory Users And Computers.

2. Navigate to the server running RIS, right-click it, and choose Properties from the pop-up menu.

3. Click the Remote Install tab.

4. Click the Advanced Settings button.

5. Select the image you would like to delete and click Remove.

6. Click the Yes button to confirm the image deletion.

Using Remote Installation Preparation (riprep.exe)

To use riprep.exe, perform the following steps:

1. Install Windows 2000 Professional on a reference system using RIS.

2. Install any desired applications.

3. Configure the system as required.

4. Shut down all services and applications.

5. Run the riprep.exe application from the RemoteInstall\Admin\i386 share on the RIS system. The Remote Installation Preparation Wizard will launch.

6. Click Next.

7. Enter the name of the RIS server you would like to host the newly created image and click Next.

8. Enter the folder name where the image will be stored and click Next.

9. Enter a friendly name and description for the image and click Next.

10. Review the settings and click Next.

11. The image will be created. When you click Next, it will be copied to the RIS server.

Preparing a Client for Remote Installation

To prepare a client for remote installation, perform the following steps:

1. Select Start|Programs|Administrative Tools|Active Directory Users And Computers.

2. Navigate to the container where you would like the new computer created. Right-click the container and select New|Computer from the pop-up menu.

3. In the New Object|Computer window, enter the name of the computer and click Next.

4. Select the This Is A Managed Computer checkbox, enter the ID for the computer, and click Next.

5. Choose whether you would like the client to use the closest and/or fastest RIS server or a specific RIS server. Click Next when done.

6. Click Finish when done.

Creating a Remote Boot Disk

To create a remote boot disk, perform the following steps:

1. Insert a blank, formatted 1.44MB floppy disk, connect to the RIS server's \RemoteInstall\Admin\i386 share, and run the rbfg.exe file.

2. Select the floppy drive you would like to use and click Create Disk.

Completing a Remote Operating System Installation

To complete a remote OS installation, perform the following steps:

1. Insert the remote boot disk and turn on the system.

2. Press F12 to boot from the network.

3. Press Enter to begin the Client Installation Wizard.

4. Enter a username, a password, and the DNS name for the domain and press Enter.

WARNING! *If you did not prepare a client for installation as described in the "Preparing a Client for Remote Installation" section, make sure the username has sufficient privileges to create a computer account in the domain.*

5. Choose the Setup, Custom Setup, Restart A Previous Setup Attempt, or Maintenance And Troubleshooting Tools option and then press Enter.

6. Select the image you would like to use and press Enter.

7. Press Enter to begin the installation.

Chapter 6

Windows 2000 Configuration

In Depth

Windows 2000 offers a wide range of capabilities and features. This chapter takes a brief look at access permissions on files and folders, faxing, the Recycle Bin, Offline Files, compression, encryption, mount points, Disk Cleanup, ScanDisk, Disk Defragmenter, and drive quotas.

Accessing Resources

Controlling access to resources is accomplished through the use of object-level security settings and network shares. Files and folders stored on FAT or FAT32 do not offer file/folder-level security controls, but all other objects (files, folders, drives, printers, and so on) within Windows 2000 do offer security controls. Security controls define which users and groups can access an object and what types of access or functions those users and groups are granted for that object.

Objects accessed over a network are controlled via their network share. The share itself has security controls that define which users and groups can use the share to access resources on other systems.

The mechanisms and interfaces for configuring security controls on files, folders, shares, and printers are very similar. The only difference is that the type of access that can be granted or restricted varies based on the type of object being secured. In every case, each user and group can have one of the following settings: Allow, Deny, or no defined setting for each permission offered for the object.

NOTE: For information on printer shares and printer permissions, see Chapter 18.

Figure 6.1 shows the permissions used to control access to files, folders, and mounted volumes. These permissions are:

- *Full Control (files)*—Allows users to perform any possible actions on a file and access any offered functions for the file.

- *Full Control (folders or mounted volumes)*—Allows users to perform any possible actions on the folder or mounted volume and its contents.

- *List Folder Contents (folders or mounted volumes)*—Allows users to see the names of the contents of the folder or mounted volume.

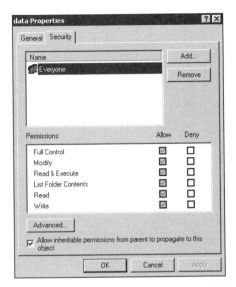

Figure 6.1   The Security tab from a folder's Properties dialog box.

- *Modify (files)*—Allows users to alter files through deletion, change attributes, and overwrite, as well as launch applications and view the files' contents.

- *Modify (folders or mounted volumes)*—Allows users to alter folders and mounted volumes through deletion and changing attributes. This permission also allows users to create new subfolders and files within the container and to view the contents of the objects within the container.

- *Read (files, folders, or mounted volumes)*—Allows users to open the file, folder, or mounted volume.

- *Read & Execute (files)*—Allows users to open files and to launch executables.

- *Read & Execute (folders or mounted volumes)*—Allows users open folders and mounted volumes and grants Read access to the contents of these containers.

- *Write (files)*—Allows users alter existing files through overwriting or changing attributes.

- *Write (folders or mounted volumes)*—Allows users to create new files and folders within the container.

The basic security permissions dialog box offers a checkbox to manage inheritance with the label Allow Inheritable Permissions From Parent To Propagate To This Object. This checkbox is used to enable or disable automatic inheritance from the current object's parent container. When inheritance is disabled, settings can still be forced onto this object from a parent container.

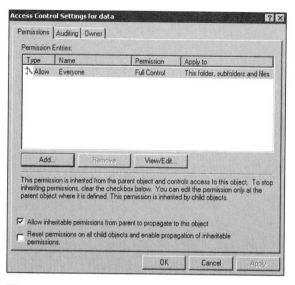

Figure 6.2   The Access Control Settings dialog box.

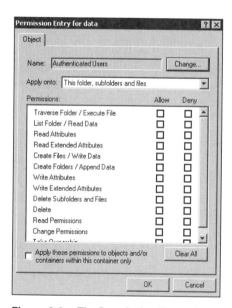

Figure 6.3   The Permission Entry dialog box for setting detailed permissions.

By clicking the Advanced button, you open a dialog box that's used to manage detailed permissions, auditing, and ownership (see Figure 6.2). The detailed permissions, shown in Figure 6.3, that can be individually allowed or denied by user and group are:

- Traverse Folder/Execute File
- List Folder/Read Data

- Read Attributes
- Read Extended Attributes
- Create Files/Write Data
- Create Folders/Append Data
- Write Attributes
- Write Extended Attributes
- Delete Subfolders and Files
- Delete
- Read Permissions
- Change Permissions
- Take Ownership

Two inheritance controls also appear on the Permissions tab:

- Allow Inheritable Permissions From Parent To Propagate To This Object
- Reset Permissions on All Child Objects and Enable Propagation Of Inheritable Permissions

When a new permission entry is defined, you can determine where the new settings will apply via a pull-down list that offers the following selections:

- This Folder Only
- This Folder, Subfolder, And Files
- This Folder And Subfolders
- This Folder And Files
- Subfolders And Files Only
- Subfolders Only
- Files Only

The Auditing tab is used to select which events generate an event detail. Event details are recorded in the Event Viewer. Events are defined by user or group, access or action detail, and success and/or failure (see Figure 6.4). Furthermore, you can determine where the audit setting is defined by selecting This Folder, Subfolder, And Files, This Folder And Subfolders, This Folder And Files, Subfolders And Files Only, Subfolders Only, or Files Only.

The Owner tab, shown in Figure 6.5, is used to view the current ownership of the object and to take ownership. It is only possible to take ownership if you have the Take Ownership permission over this object or the universal user right.

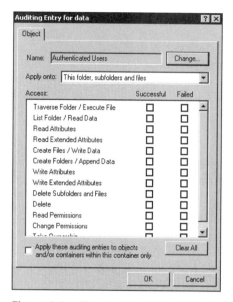

Figure 6.4   The Auditing Entry dialog box.

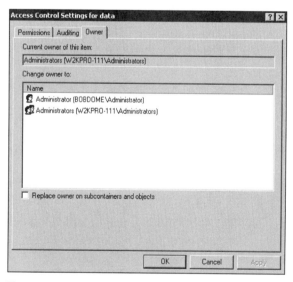

Figure 6.5   The Owner tab of the Access Control Settings dialog box.

When working with the permissions on a share, keep in mind that there are only three types of permissions: Full Control, Change, and Read. Each of these can be set to Allow or Deny for each individual user and group. You should also keep in mind that a resource can be shared multiple times under different share names. Each distinct share can have its own unique permission settings.

Faxing

Windows 2000 includes fax support. This means you can send and receive faxes without additional software if your computer has a supported fax/modem installed. In most cases, Windows 2000 will automatically detect your modem, or when you install your modem, its fax capabilities will be recognized. This causes Windows 2000 to create a fax printer in the Printers folder. In fact, faxing is a similar process to printing. By default, only the ability to send out faxes is enabled.

Faxing is controlled through four interfaces: the Fax applet in the Control Panel, the Fax Service Management tool, the My Faxes folder, and the Fax printer queue. The Fax applet is used to define user information (such as that contained on cover pages), define and create cover pages, and configure received fax notification. The Fax Service Management tool, shown in Figure 6.6, is used to configure fax devices and logging of fax activities. Fax device configuration settings include defining the station identifiers, such as TSID (Transmitting Station Identifier) and CSID (Called Station Identifier), the number of rings before answering, and whether to send received faxes to a printer, folder, or local email box. The My Faxes folder is a container where copies of all faxes handled by Windows 2000 are stored. The Fax printer queue is used in the same manner as any other printer queue to view, manage, and terminate active fax jobs.

To send a fax, just select the Fax object from the list of printers from any application. You'll be prompted for the recipient's name and fax number, whether to use dialing rules, whether to use a cover sheet, and whether to schedule the transmission for a later time. Recipient information can be pulled from an address book, such as Outlook Express. Also, multiple recipients can be defined for a single fax document. The only significant difference between Windows 2000 fax and normal printers is that a native fax device cannot be shared with the network.

File Deletion and Recovery

Windows 2000 offers file deletion protection via the Recycle Bin. This tool is a temporary holding area for objects recently deleted from the desktop, Windows Explorer, or My Computer. The Recycle Bin retains all deleted objects until it is

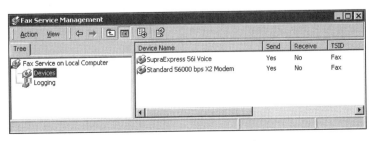

Figure 6.6   The Fax Service Management tool.

manually purged or a newly deleted object's size forces the oldest deleted object to be removed. The Recycle Bin is configured to retain only a specific amount of deleted data as a percentage of total disk space. The Properties dialog box, shown in Figure 6.7, for the Recycle Bin is used to configure the following options:

- Whether a single setting is used for all drives or each drive is configured independently. A single setting is used by default.

- Whether files are removed from the system immediately or are retained in the Recycle Bin when deleted. This is enabled by default.

- The percentage of drive space to be used by the Recycle Bin. This is set to 10 percent by default.

- Whether to display a delete confirmation dialog box whenever a file is manually deleted. This is enabled by default.

- If each drive is configured independently, a tab for each volume is available to configure the Recycle Bin on each.

Opening the Recycle Bin reveals the currently retained deleted objects. Any listed object can be restored to its original location. To do so, select it, then issue the **restore** command from the File menu. If a file does not appear in the Recycle Bin, it cannot be recovered using native Windows 2000 tools.

Using Offline Files

Offline Files is a mechanism within Windows 2000 that can cache network files and folders on a portable system. This allows those files and folders to be accessed when the portable system is not connected to the LAN. Plus, when the

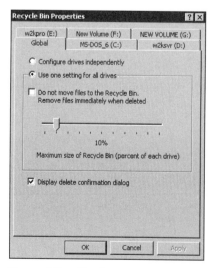

Figure 6.7   The Recycle Bin's Properties dialog box.

portable system is reconnected, updated files can be automatically saved back to the LAN and new files on the LAN are added to the portable system's cache. Items stored in the Offline Files cache are accessed in the exact same manner as they would be when connected to the LAN (that is, through My Network Places).

To mark files to be stored in Offline Files, use My Network Places to locate the files and/or folders. Issue the **make available offline** command from the File menu. This command will appear by default on Windows 2000 Professional systems, but it is not present by default on Windows 2000 Server systems. Offline Files can be enabled or disabled on the Offline Folders tab of the Folder Options dialog box. All such marked files and folders will have a logo added to their icons of two arrows in a circle.

The first time Offline Files is used, a wizard appears to initially configure the system. Even after initial configuration, you can access the settings on the Offline Folders tab of the Folder Options dialog box (which is itself opened from the Folder Options command from the Tools menu or the Folder Options applet in the Control Panel). The configuration settings include:

- Enable/Disable Offline Files

- Synchronize Offline Files Before Logging Off

- Enable Reminders About Working Offline

- Add an Offline Files Shortcut To The Desktop

- Set The Amount Of Space Consumable By Offline Files

- Delete Cached Files

- View Cached Files

- Advanced Settings

Moving and Copying Objects

The processes of copying and moving files and folders can alter the settings on these moved objects in ways you may not expect. In most cases, understanding how copying and moving actually works can help you avoid losing important security and functionality settings. Basically, whenever a new file is created, it inherits the settings of its parent container. This means that a new file created within a directory, a new folder created within an existing folder, or a new file or directory created within the root of a drive will inherit the security settings of the parent container (that is, the directory/folder or drive root).

In all cases, a copy process involves the creation of a new object at the destination location. However, a move process differs depending on whether the source and destinations are within the same or different partitions or volumes. When a move occurs within the same partition or volume, the only change to the file system is an alteration in the directory database pointing to the location of the object. Thus, the original object remains unmoved and just the pointer to its location is changed. In this instance, the object retains all its original settings. However, when a move occurs from one partition or volume to another, the process is now a two-step procedure. First, a new copy of the original object is created at the destination location. Then the original object is deleted. Because this process creates a new object, the new object inherits the settings of its new container.

If you want to move objects from one partition or volume to another without losing the original settings, you must use the **XCOPY** command with the **/O** parameter to copy file ownership and ACL information or the **/X** command to copy auditing settings in addition to file ownership and ACL information. This **XCOPY** command can be used form a command prompt. For complete use information, issue the **XCOPY /?** command.

The proceeding information about copy and move applies mainly when the source and destination locations are formatted with the same file system. When you're copying or moving objects from a partition or volume formatted with one file system to another formatted with a different file system, additional scenarios must be understood. When you're copying from an NTFS volume to a FAT or FAT32 volume, all security settings will be lost. When you're copying from a FAT or FAT32 volume to an NTFS volume, the objects will inherit the settings of the destination container.

Drive Letters and Mount Points

As with all other Microsoft operating systems, Windows 2000 can use the drive letters C through Z to reference various file resources, including network shares, local hard drives, and removable media drives. However, Windows 2000 now adds the ability of using mount points to remove the previous ceiling of 24 accessible volumes.

NOTE: *Drive configurations that are comprised of two or more volumes or partitions are only assigned a single drive letter.*

A *mount point* is a directory on an NTFS volume that's used as an access point to a volume that does not have an assigned drive letter. The process is simple to configure and is invisible to the user and any applications (see Figure 6.8). A mount point can only be created on an NTFS volume, but the mounted volumes can be formatted with FAT, FAT32, or NTFS.

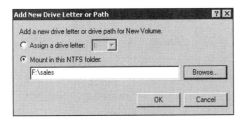

Figure 6.8   The Add New Drive Letter Or Path dialog box.

Disk Cleanup

During a Windows 2000 installation, many useless and forgotten files are created and deposited on the hard drive(s). In some cases, this can consume a significant portion of the drive(s). The Disk Cleanup tool can be used to regain access to hard drive space through deleting temporary, orphaned, or downloaded files, emptying the Recycle Bin, compressing little used files, and condensing index catalog files (see Figure 6.9).

The Disk Cleanup tool can also be used to remove Windows components or installed programs to free space. The tool's More Options tab grants you easy access to the Windows Components Wizard and the Add/Remove Programs applet.

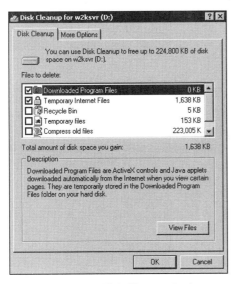

Figure 6.9   The Disk Cleanup tool.

Check Disk

Check Disk is a native tool used to discover and correct problems on hard drives. This tool was previously known as *ScanDisk*. Both physical and logical errors can be detected by Check Disk. When an error cannot be corrected, the area of the drive is marked as *bad* and all other reads and writes to the hard drive will automatically avoid the bad sectors. Any data that is stored in a damaged location or that has become orphaned from its directory listing is copied into text files stored in the root of the drive with incrementing file names, such as FILE0001, FILE0002, and so on.

Check Disk can be launched from the Tools tab of a drive's Properties dialog box by clicking on the Check Now button in the error-checking section. It cannot be launched from a command line as its ScanDisk predecessor could. Windows 2000 can also automatically launch Check Disk if it detects problems or if a nongraceful shutdown occurs. In some cases, Windows 2000 will need to schedule Check Disk to launch upon bootup before the GUI is loaded. Whenever Check Disk runs, you always have the option of aborting the activity of the tool. The GUI interface of Check Disk is very simple (see Figure 6.10). It offers two checkboxes: one to automatically fix errors and one to scan for and attempt recovery of bad sectors. The Start button initiates the scan; the Cancel button terminates the scan.

Only the version of Check Disk included with Windows 2000 should be used on volumes formatted by Windows 2000. Do not use ScanDisk from Windows NT, Windows 98, Windows 95, or MS-DOS on Windows 2000-formatted volumes.

Defragmentation

As objects on a hard drive are written, deleted, changed, and moved, the organization of those objects becomes complex. Files may be broken into sections and stored in nonadjacent sectors of the drive. As free space becomes scattered and insufficient continuous free space is available, the fragmentation of files increases. The more fragmented a drive, the longer it takes for reads and writes

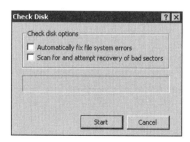

Figure 6.10   The Check Disk tool.

6. Windows 2000 Configuration

to occur. What's more, a highly fragmented drive can lose data through missing directory markers.

Defragmenting a drive reorganizes the files so that they are all stored in a contiguous manner. This improves drive performance. Windows 2000 includes a native defragmentation tool that can be used on any volume on a local drive formatted with FAT, FAT32, or NTFS. The Disk Defragmenter tool, shown in Figure 6.11, is launched from the Tools tab of a drive's Properties dialog box.

Just select one of the volumes listed and click the Defragment button. The progress of the defragmentation process is displayed along side the original analysis of the volume. The process can be paused or stopped at any time. Once the process is completed, you can view a report about the actions performed.

The Disk Defragmenter cannot be scheduled or launched from a batch file. You must obtain a third-party defragmentation tool to obtain scheduling capabilities.

Drive Quotas

Drive quotas grant you the ability to control the amount of disk space a user can consume on both local systems and network shares. This feature is most often used in conjunction with roaming user profiles and network share-based home folders (and redirected folders). Quotas can be defined on a broad basis so the same settings apply to all users, or settings can be defined for individual users.

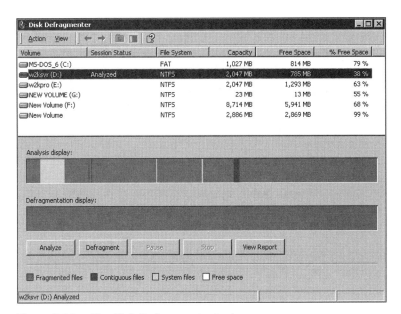

Figure 6.11   The Disk Defragmenter tool.

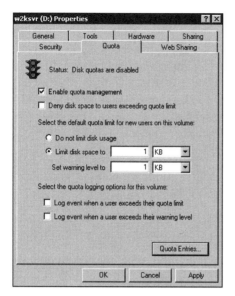

Figure 6.12   The Quota tab of a drive's Properties dialog box.

Quotas are defined on the Quota tab, shown in Figure 6.12, of a drive's Properties dialog box. Quotas are not enabled by default. You have the ability to set both a usage limit and a warning limit. When users exceed their limit, they are unable to log out until they reduce their space consumption.

Task Manager

To gain a quick look at the state of the system, the Task Manager is priceless. This tool allows you to see the standing of applications, the state of processes, and the status of system resources. You'll find yourself employing this utility often, especially when you suspect a problem is occurring. The Task Manager can be launched in several ways:

- Pressing Ctrl+Shift+Esc

- Pressing Ctrl+Alt+Del and then clicking the Task Manager button on the WinLogon Security dialog box

- Right-clicking over an empty area of the Taskbar and then selecting Task Manager from the pop-up menu

The Task Manager has three tabs: Applications, Processes, and Performance. Each of these tabs presents different information and offers content-specific controls or tasks.

The Applications tab, shown in Figure 6.13, displays a list of all currently active applications. This is the same list of applications that's present in the Taskbar.

Figure 6.13   The Task Manager's Applications tab.

Each application's status is included alongside its task name. The status will be Running or Not Responding. A program that has a status of Not Responding may be hung, have performed an illegal operation, or may simply be performing intensive calculations. You should wait 5 to 10 minutes once you notice an application is not responding before terminating the process. This allows the application to return to normal functionality on its own. If you deem an application stagnate and want to terminate it, select its name from the task list and click the End Task button. After you confirm the termination when prompted, the application is removed from memory and the process queue, plus its system resources are returned to the available pool. The Applications tab also offers you the ability to launch new programs using the New Task button. This opens a dialog box that functions exactly like the Run command from the Start menu. The Switch To button is used to bring the selected application to the foreground.

The Processes tab, shown in Figure 6.14, displays a list of all processes currently active on the system. By default, the Processes tab also displays the process ID (PID), CPU utilization (CPU), cumulated execution time (CPU Time), and total consumed virtual memory (Mem Usage).

Through the Select Columns command from the View menu, you can add or remove these four columns of data along with 18 others via the following checkboxes:

- Memory Usage Delta
- Peak Memory Usage
- Page Faults

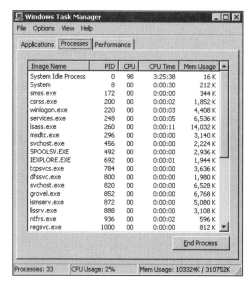

Figure 6.14   The Task Manager's Processes tab.

- USER Objects
- I/O Reads
- I/O Read Bytes
- Page Faults Delta
- Virtual Memory Size
- Paged Pool
- Non-paged Pool
- Base Priority
- Handle Count
- Thread Count
- GDI Objects
- I/O Writes
- I/O Write Bytes
- I/O Other
- I/O Other Bytes

By default, the data displayed on the Processes tab is updated every second. This interval can be increased or decreased through the Update Speed submenu of the View menu. The Update Speed submenu offers the settings of High (twice per second), Normal (once per second), Low (once every four seconds), and Paused.

The Processes tab provides an excellent overview of the state of all processes operating on the system. Every process from both user mode and kernel mode is listed here. You'll also notice a process that doesn't belong to either mode; it's called *System Idle Process*. This is a do-nothing task that the CPU works on when no other process is demanding execution time. If you suspect that a process or a program is consuming too much CPU time, check the Processes tab. If a process is consuming 90 percent or more of the CPU utilization for an extended period of time, you may have a rogue process. It's still recommend that you watch the status for at least 5 to 10 minutes before taking further action. It is not uncommon for intense activities by a single process to consume a significant amount of CPU attention; this does not indicate a problem with the process but rather shows that either your system is underpowered or that some activities require a bit more time on the CPU to complete than most. If you determine that a process really has gone bad, you can select it from the list and click the End Process button. You'll be prompted to confirm the termination; then the process is removed from memory and the process queue, plus its system resources are returned to the available pool. If other processes were dependant on the terminated process, those processes may terminate as well or simply stop functioning until the process is launched again.

This ability to terminate individual processes is an important one to remember, especially if you work with in-house or custom applications, DOS applications, or Win16 applications (that is, those written for Windows 3.x or Windows for Workgroups). Terminating a process is often the only solution to a poorly behaving application short of rebooting. Most Win32 applications that go bad typically attempt to consume the CPU; terminating them restores the system to normal operation. All DOS applications are launched within their own NTVDM. When you are unable to gracefully exit a DOS application, you can terminate the NTVDM hosting the application. All Win16 applications are launched within an environment created by WOWEXEC that itself runs within an NTVDM. Terminating the WOWEXEC, NTVDM, or application process tears down the entire environment. Keep in mind that by default all Win16 applications are launched into the same WOWEXEC environment, so when one application fails and is terminated, often all the other applications are terminated as well.

Another useful feature of the Processes tab is the ability to alter the execution priority of processes. Even though Windows 2000 has 32 levels of execution priority, you are only granted the ability to access the following six levels:

- *Realtime*—Sets the process to an execution priority level of 24. This setting is restricted to administrators.
- *High*—Sets the process to an execution priority level of 13.
- *AboveNormal*—Sets the process to an execution priority level of 10.

- *Normal*—Sets the process to an execution priority level of 8.

- *BelowNormal*—Sets the process to an execution priority level of 6.

- *Low*—Sets the process to an execution priority level of 4.

Changing a process's priority is accomplished by right-clicking a process, selecting the Set Priority submenu from the pop-up menu, and then clicking an execution priority level. You'll be prompted to confirm the priority change. The Realtime priority level is restricted to administrators. Even as an administrator, you can only change the execution priorities of user mode processes. However, it is possible to launch Task Manager (and any other tool) with a system-level privilege context using the **AT** command. AT is the command-line tool used to define automated or scheduled tasks. The command **AT <time> /interactive taskman.exe** launches the Task Manager at the specified time with system-level privileges. Once Task Manager is launched in this manner, you can alter the execution priority of any active process. Be extremely cautious about altering the execution priority of system or kernel processes. The alteration of process priorities is not retained across reboots or even the termination and relaunch of the process during the same boot session.

Defining the execution priority of an application or process upon launching can be performed using the **start** command. The syntax of the command string is **start /<priority> <program>**. Any of the execution priority levels Realtime, AboveNormal, Normal, BelowNormal, and Low can be used. For more details on the **start** command, enter **start /?** at a command prompt. This technique can be used at a command prompt, through the **run** command, or as the target command string of a shortcut.

The Performance tab, shown in Figure 6.15, offers you a brief glimpse into the performance levels of the system. This tab presents performance data focused on CPU, memory, and processes statistics. There is a thermometer bar graph and a history graph for both CPU usage and memory usage. The thermometer bar graph displays the most recent level of activity, whereas the history graph shows the last 20 measurements. Below these graphs are 12 performance metrics:

- *Totals: Handles*—Indicates how many system objects are in use, such as files, Registry keys, and virtual machines

- *Totals: Threads*—Indicates how many execution threads are present from all active processes

- *Totals: Processes*—Indicates the number of active processes

- *Physical Memory (K): Total*—Indicates the size of physical RAM

- *Physical Memory (K): Available*—Indicates the amount of unused physical RAM

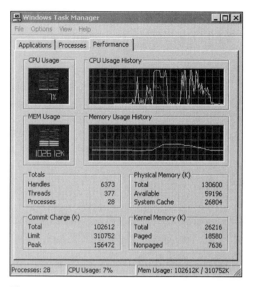

Figure 6.15   The Task Manager's Performance tab.

- *Physical Memory (K): File Cache*—Indicates the amount of physical RAM being used for caching files
- *Commit Charge (K): Total*—Indicates the total amount of virtual memory allocated to processes or the system
- *Commit Charge (K): Limit*—Indicates the maximum amount of virtual memory on this computer
- *Commit Charge (K): Peak*—Indicates the maximum amount of virtual memory used during this boot session
- *Kernel Memory (K): Total*—Indicates the amount of memory used by the kernel
- *Kernel Memory (K): Paged*—Indicates the amount of total kernel memory that can be saved to a swap file
- *Kernel Memory (K): Nonpaged*—Indicates the amount of kernel memory that always remains in physical RAM

The graphs on this tab can be altered using the CPU History submenu and the Show Kernel Times command from the View menu. The CPU History submenu can be used to display a single graph for all CPUs or multiple graphs (one for each CPU). The Show Kernel Times command causes the graphs to display the amount of kernel mode process CPU and memory consumption in red, whereas the remainder used by user mode processes is in green.

This tab can be used to determine in general if your system is overloaded. A consistent level of 90 percent or greater CPU utilization may indicate a rogue process or an underpowered system. Likewise, too little remaining available memory can indicate problems as well—from needing more RAM, to a leaky application (one that consumes too many resources). You'll find Task Manager is the first tool you'll use to diagnose a problem before proceeding to more specialized tools such as System Monitor or Network Monitor (both native to Windows 2000 Server) or even to a third-party tool.

Managing Virtual Memory

Working with virtual memory is simply managing your paging file. That's the only real control over how Windows 2000 uses memory. Windows 2000 uses a flat-linear, 32-bit addressing scheme to manage a contiguous block of memory. Within Windows 2000, memory is actual called *virtual memory* because it's created through combining physical RAM and storage space on a hard drive within one or more paging files. Windows 2000 Professional and Server can both manage 4GB of memory. Windows 2000 Advanced Server boasts support for 8GB of memory, and Windows 2000 Datacenter Server promises support for 16GB of memory. The amount of memory supported by any version of Windows 2000 is the total maximum amount of memory created through the combination of physical RAM and paging file space.

The Virtual Memory Manager (VMM) component of the Windows 2000 Executive is responsible for managing virtual memory. It is responsible for numerous complex activities, including moving pages to and from physical RAM and paging files, maintaining the distinct address spaces for each virtual machine present on the system, managing the correlation between VM address space and virtual memory, and managing the state of memory pages located in both physical RAM and paging files.

By default, a paging file is created in the root directory of the boot partition by Windows 2000 upon installation. This paging file will be the same size as the physical RAM on Windows 2000 Professional systems or 64MB larger than the amount of physical RAM on Windows 2000 Server systems. The paging file can be moved, enlarged, and altered in any manner with only one exception: If the Startup And Recovery options for the system are configured to create a dump file in the event of a STOP error, you must have a 2MB or greater paging file on the boot partition.

Alterations to the paging file are performed through the Virtual Memory dialog box (see Figure 6.16). This dialog box is opened from the System applet by selecting the Advanced tab, clicking the Performance Options button, and then clicking the Change button on the Performance Options dialog box under the Virtual Memory heading.

6. Windows 2000 Configuration

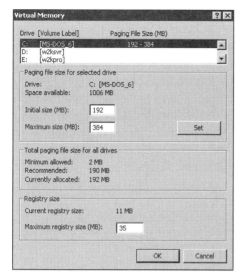

Figure 6.16   The Virtual Memory dialog box.

To alter the size of a paging file, select the drive where the paging file is located in the top list window, alter the initial size and maximum size values, and then click Set. The initial size value determines how much drive space is allocated to the paging file. The maximum size value sets the upper limit for how large the paging file can grow. The value in the initial size is guaranteed, whereas the amount of drive space required to meet the maximum size is not guaranteed and may not be present when requested by the VMM. Notice the middle section labeled Total Paging File Size for All Drives. This area lists some very important numbers. The minimum allowed number indicates the smallest paging file that must exist, and in most cases this minimal paging file must reside on the boot partition. The recommended size is the size of the paging file the system thinks is adequate to perform currently active tasks. The currently allocated value is the total amount of allocated drive space for the paging file across all volumes.

Spreading the paging file across multiple drives simply means adding another paging file to a different volume. This is accomplished by selecting a volume that does not already have a paging file, providing initial and max values, then clicking Set. Removing a paging file is accomplished by setting the initial and max values to zero.

It's a good idea to move the paging file (or all but the minimal required) from the boot partition to some other volume not on the same physical hard drive. When multiple paging files are created, the greatest performance benefit is reaped only when each paging file segment is on a unique physical hard drive. Placing a paging file on two or more partitions or volumes on the same hard drive causes performance degradation.

6. Windows 2000 Configuration

User Profiles

User profiles are employed by Windows 2000 to retain custom user environments across logon sessions even when those sessions occur on different systems on the network. User profiles can also enforce a common or restricted desktop environment when customization is not allowed. Every user has a user profile. By default, these are local, customizable user profiles. A user profile is really little more than the contents of a few user-specific directories, history lists, favorites, and a subsection of the Registry stored in a file named ntuser.dat. A user profile can store Start menu layout, sound schemes, color schemes, desktop icons, mapped network shares, last accessed documents, Web site favorites, and more.

User profiles can be local only or roaming. Plus, user profiles can be customizable or mandatory. A local-only user profile only exists on a single computer. A roaming user profile is available no matter where on the network the user logs on. A customizable user profile records the changes to the environment each time the user logs off; this allows the last saved state of the environment to be returned to him or her at the next logon. A mandatory user profile does not save changes made during a logon session; this means the original mandatory environment will be returned to the user at the next logon. A mandatory profile can be shared by multiple users because no customization is possible.

User profiles from Windows 2000 and Windows NT are compatible, but user profiles from Windows 98 or Windows 95 are not. Therefore, users can move from Windows 2000 clients to Windows NT clients and back while maintaining the same environment throughout. However, once a user moves to a Windows 98/95 system, he or she will not be presented with the normal profile but rather the default local profile for that system. Both Windows 98/95 and Windows 2000/NT user profiles can exist on the same network, and both types support roaming and mandatory configuration. But to keep confusion to a minimum, users should stick with one system type or the other.

The first time a user logs into a computer, the system looks for a roaming profile on a network share for that user. The path to the storage location of a user's roaming profile is defined in his or her domain user account's properties. If no roaming user profile is found, a local user profile is created by duplicating the local default user profile. When a local user profile is created on a Windows 2000 system (whether from a copy of the local default user profile or a copy of the roaming user profile from its network storage location), it is placed in a subfolder of the \Documents and Settings directory, which has the same name as the user account. If a roaming user profile path is defined for a user but no profile is stored there when the system checks, the newly created user profile will be copied to the network share location. The next time the user logs on anywhere, his or her roaming user profile will be found and loaded. If a roaming user profile path is not defined for the user, the

6. Windows 2000 Configuration

newly created user profile will remain a local profile, which will only be available on the one system where it is created. To transform a local user profile into a roaming user profile, just add a user profile path to the user account's properties. The next time the user logs on and then logs off, the user's profile will become a roaming user profile stored on the provided network share path.

NOTE: *By default, all user profiles can be customized by the user. This means that all changes made to the environment during a logon session will be saved when the user logs out. This is true both for local and roaming user profiles.*

The only user account that does not have or cannot have its own unique user profile is the Guest account. Each time the Guest account is used to log on, the Default User profile is given to that user. No changes made by the Guest user are saved and no user profile directory is created.

Each time a user logs onto a system, his or her roaming user profile will be cached locally. This means the next time the user logs onto the same system, only the changed items will be transferred across the network. This also allows users to log on even if the domain controller cannot be contacted to authenticate them. However, if the user profile is a mandatory profile and the domain controller cannot be contacted, the user will not be allowed to log on.

Roaming user profiles are created or defined simply by providing a UNC path statement for the storage location for the profile. This is done on the Profile tab, shown in Figure 6.17, of a user account's Properties dialog box, accessed through the Active Directory Users and Computers utility. A UNC path statement takes the form of \\<servername>\<sharename>\<directoryname>, where *directoryname* is often the user account name.

NOTE: *The directory name can be a folder tree path as well, such as \users\profiles\admins\department1\jsmith.*

If you examine the contents of a user profile's storage folder, you'll see the following subfolders:

- *Application Data*—Contains application-specific data, such as configuration files, custom dictionaries, and file cache for Internet Explorer or Outlook Express
- *Cookies*—Contains the cookies accepted by the user
- *Desktop*—Contains the icons, files, shortcuts, and folders found on the desktop
- *Favorites*—Contains the list of bookmarked URLs from Internet Explorer
- *Local Settings*—Contains user-specific application data, history data, and temporary files

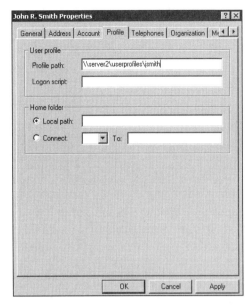

Figure 6.17   The Profile tab of a user account's Properties dialog box, accessed through the Active Directory Users And Computers utility.

- *My Documents*—Contains a user's saved files
- *NetHood*—Contains network mappings and items in Network Places
- *PrintHood*—Contains printer mappings and items in the printer folder
- *Recent*—Contains links to the most recently used resources (documents and folders)
- *SendTo*—Contains items found in the Send To fly-open menu of the right-click pop-up menu
- *Start Menu*—Contains the user-specific portions of the Start menu
- *Templates*—Contains a user's templates

The user profile's storage folder also contains the following items:

- *Ntuser.dat*—A Registry file containing user-specific data
- *Ntuser.dat.log*—A file that logs transactions and changes to a user profile for the purpose of re-creating the profile in the event of a system failure or element corruption.
- *Ntuser.ini*—A configuration file that lists elements of a roaming profile that are not to be uploaded to a network share from a local computer

6. Windows 2000 Configuration

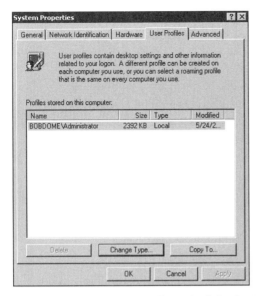

Figure 6.18   The User Profiles tab of the System applet.

The System applet's User Profiles tab, shown in Figure 6.18, offers a few management functions. This tab lists all profiles stored or cached locally. Therefore, only the profiles for users who have logged onto the system locally will appear here. This interface can be used to delete local copies of local user profiles or roaming user profiles from the local hard drive. It can also be used to prevent changes made on the local machine to a roaming user profile from being uploaded back to its network share storage location. This is known as converting a roaming user profile to a local user profile. The Copy To button is used to duplicate an existing profile to a new location. This can be used to create a backup of a profile or to jumpstart a new user's profile with something other than the default user profile.

Any profile can be converted to a mandatory profile simply by renaming the Registry file from ntuser.dat to ntuser.man. This name change must be made in the main storage location of the profile (that is, the network share instead of a local cache in the case of a roaming user profile). Once a profile is set to mandatory, no changes made by the user during a logon session will be saved. To return a profile to a customizable state, just change the name of the Registry file back to ntuser.dat.

Immediate Solutions

Disabling or Enabling Autorun

Autorun is the ability of the operating system (OS) to automatically launch a program or play music from an inserted CD. There isn't a GUI configuration setting to manage this feature. It must be altered via the Registry. To manage Autorun using REGEDIT, perform the following steps:

1. Select Start|Run, type "REGEDIT", and click OK.

2. Locate the HKEY_LOCAL_MACHINE\System\CurrentControlSet\ Services\CDRom key.

3. Select the Autorun value entry.

4. Change the value to 0 to disable Autorun or change the value to 1 to enable Autorun.

5. Close the Registry editor.

Setting Permissions on a File

To set file permissions, perform the following steps:

1. Select Start|Programs|Accessories|Windows Explorer.

2. Locate and select a file to set permissions.

3. Open the Properties dialog box for the object by issuing the **properties** command from the File menu.

4. Select the Security tab (refer to Figure 6.1).

5. Click Add.

6. Select the Authenticated Users group.

7. Click Add.

8. Click OK. Authenticated Users is added to the Name field of the Security tab.

9. While Authenticated Users is selected, mark or unmark the checkboxes under Allow or Deny of each of the listed permissions to set the level of access to grant this group (or user).

10. Repeat Steps 5 through 9 for each user or group desired.

11. Select the Everyone group.

12. Click the Remove button.

13. Click OK to close the Properties dialog box.

Configuring Advanced Permissions

To configure advanced permissions, perform the following steps:

1. Select Start|Programs|Accessories|Windows Explorer.

2. Locate and select a file on which to set permissions.

3. Open the Properties dialog box for the object by issuing the **properties** command from the File menu.

4. Select the Security tab.

5. Click Advanced.

6. On the Permissions tab, click Add.

7. Select the Server Operators group.

8. Click OK.

9. Mark or unmark the checkboxes under Allow or Deny of each of the listed detail permissions to set the level of access to grant this group (or user).

10. Click OK.

11. The Server Operators group now appears in the list of permission entries.

12. Repeat Steps 6 through 10 for each user or group desired.

13. Click OK to return to the Security tab.

14. Click OK to close the Properties dialog box.

Configuring Auditing

To configure auditing, perform the following steps:

1. Select Start|Programs|Accessories|Windows Explorer.

2. Locate a resource object (file or folder) on which to configure auditing.

3. Select File|Properties.

4. Select the Security tab.

5. Click Advanced.

6. Select the Auditing tab.

7. Click Add.

8. Select the user or group to audit.

9. Click OK.

10. Select the access functions to be audited on a success or failure basis by selecting checkboxes.

11. Click OK.

12. The added user/group will appear in the Auditing Entries list.

13. Repeat Steps 7 through 11 for each user and group desired.

14. Click OK to return to the Security tab.

15. Click OK to close the Properties dialog box.

Managing Ownership

If you own an object, you have Full Control over that object. Users with the Take Ownership user right or the specific object permission can recapture ownership of an object. To establish ownership, perform the following steps:

1. Select Start|Programs|Accessories|Windows Explorer.

2. Locate a resource object (file or folder) on which to configure ownership.

3. Open the Properties dialog box for the object by issuing the Properties command from the File menu.

4. Select the Security tab.

5. Click Advanced.

6. Select the Owner tab (refer to Figure 6.5).

7. A list of valid possible owners is displayed.

8. Select the user or group to become the new owner of the object and then click OK.

9. Click OK to close the Properties dialog box.

6. Windows 2000 Configuration

Enabling Fax Receiving

The Windows 2000 Fax system is set to send faxes but not receive faxes by default. To configure fax receiving, follow the following steps:

1. Open the Fax Service Management tool from Start|Programs|Accessories|Communications|Fax|Fax Service Management.

2. Select the Devices node in the left pane (refer to Figure 6.6).

3. Select the fax device in the right pane.

4. Select Action|Properties.

5. Select the Enable Receive checkbox.

6. Set the field for Rings Before Answer to 1.

7. Click OK to close the Properties dialog box.

8. Close the Fax Service Management tool by clicking the close button in the title bar.

Configuring the Recycle Bin

The Recycle Bin stores recently deleted files. To manage Recycle Bin settings, perform the following steps:

1. Select the Recycle Bin icon on the desktop.

2. Right-click the Recycle Bin and select Properties from the pop-up menu. The Recycle Bin Properties dialog box opens (refer to Figure 6.7).

3. Make sure the Use One Setting For All Drives radio button is selected.

4. Make sure the Do Not Move Files To The Recycle Bin. Remove Files Immediately When Deleted checkbox is not marked.

5. Move the slider that determines the amount of drive space to be used by the Recycle Bin to 5%.

6. Make sure the Display Delete Confirmation Dialog checkbox is marked.

7. Click OK.

6. Windows 2000 Configuration

Restoring a File from the Recycle Bin

If a deleted file is still stored in the Recycle Bin, it can be recovered. Here are the steps to follow:

> **NOTE:**   *This solution requires that one or more files be deleted and present in the Recycle Bin.*

1. View the desktop.
2. Select the Recycle Bin icon on the desktop.
3. Right-click the Recycle Bin and then select Open from the pop-up menu.
4. Select the file (or files) to recover.
5. Take note of the path listed in the Original Location column.
6. Select File|Restore.
7. Click Yes in the Confirm File Replace window.
8. Close the Recycle Bin view window by selecting File|Close.
9. Use Windows Explorer or another tool to view the path of the file's original location to access the restored file (or files).

Selecting Files for Storage Offline

To be able to access network files when you're not connected to the network requires that those files be cached locally in Offline Files. Work through the following steps to configure file resources for storage on Offline Files:

> **NOTE:**   *This solution requires Windows 2000 Professional.*

1. Access My Network Places through its desktop icon or via Windows Explorer.
2. Locate and select a file or folder from a network share to make available when not connected to the network.
3. Right-click the select item and select Make Available Offline from the pop-up menu.
4. If a folder was selected, you'll be prompted whether to make just this folder and its nonsubfolder contents available or the folder and all file and subfolder contents available. Select Yes, Make This Folder And All Its Subfolders Available Offline.

6. Windows 2000 Configuration

5. Click OK.

6. A synchronization dialog box will display the progress of the transfer.

Configuring Offline Files

To alter the default configuration and operation of Offline Files, perform the following steps:

NOTE: *This solution requires Windows 2000 Professional.*

---

1. Select Start|Programs|Accessories|Windows Explorer.

2. Issue the Folder Options command from the Tools menu.

3. Select the Offline Files tab.

4. Make sure the checkboxes for Enable Offline Files and Synchronize All Offline Files Before Logging Off are marked.

5. If you want to be reminded when you are using resources cached by Offline Files, mark the Enable Reminders checkbox and set the Repeat Reminder interval.

6. If you want an Offline Files shortcut on the desktop, mark that checkbox.

7. Set the maximum amount of drive space that can be used to host Offline Files to 3% of the drive.

8. Click Delete to delete cached files by shared folder.

9. Click View to see a list of cached files.

10. Click OK to save settings and return to Windows Explorer.

6. Windows 2000 Configuration

Compressing a File or Folder to Save Drive Space

To compress files and folders, perform the following steps:

NOTE: *Only files and folders on NTFS volumes can be compressed. An encrypted file cannot be compressed, and vice versa.*

---

1. Select Start|Programs|Accessories|Windows Explorer.

2. Select a file or folder to compress.

3. Open the Properties dialog box for the selected object.

4. Click the Advanced button.

5. Mark the Compress Contents To Save Disk Space checkbox.

6. Click OK twice.

7. If the object is a folder, you'll be prompted whether to compress just the folder and its contents or the folder, its contents, and any subfolders.

Decompressing a File or Folder

To decompress files and folders, perform the following steps:

> **NOTE:**   *Only files and folders on NTFS volumes can be compressed. Make sure enough free drive space is available to accommodate the uncompressed files.*

1. Select Start|Programs|Accessories|Windows Explorer.

2. Select a compressed file or folder to decompress.

3. Open the Properties dialog box for the selected object.

4. Click the Advanced button.

5. Unmark the Compress Contents To Save Disk Space checkbox.

6. Click OK twice.

7. If the object is a folder, you'll be prompted whether to decompress just the folder and its contents or the folder, its contents, and any subfolders.

Encrypting a File or Folder

To encrypt a file or folder, perform the following steps:

> **NOTE:**   *Only files and folders on NTFS volumes can be encrypted. Only the person who encrypts an object can access it or decrypt it. An encrypted file cannot be compressed, and vice versa.*

1. Select Start|Programs|Accessories|Windows Explorer.

2. Select a file or folder to encrypt.

3. Open the Properties dialog box for the selected object.

4. Click the Advanced button.

5. Mark the Encrypt Contents To Secure Data checkbox.

6. Click OK twice.

7. If the object is a folder, you'll be prompted whether to encrypt just the folder and its contents or the folder, its contents, and any subfolders.

Decrypting a File or Folder

Decrypting a file or folder removes the security protection from the file and makes it accessible to other users. To decrypt a file or folder, follow these steps:

NOTE: *Only files and folders on NTFS volumes can be encrypted. Only the person who encrypts an object can access it or decrypt it.*

1. Select Start|Programs|Accessories|Windows Explorer.

2. Select an encrypted file or folder to decrypt.

3. Open the Properties dialog box for the selected object.

4. Click the Advanced button.

5. Unmark the Encrypt Contents To Secure Data checkbox.

6. Click OK twice.

7. If the object is a folder, you'll be prompted whether to decrypt just the folder and its contents or the folder, its contents, and any subfolders.

Creating a Mount Point

To grant easy access to a volume that does not have an assigned drive letter, create a mount point by performing the following steps:

1. Select Start|Programs|Accessories|Windows Explorer.

2. Create a new directory to be used as the mount point.

3. Select Start|Programs|Computer Management and then select Disk Management.

4. Select the volume to be mounted.

5. Select Action|All Tasks|Change Drive Letter And Path.

6. Click Add.

7. Select the Mount In This NTFS Folder radio button.

8. Use the Browse button locate and select the directory created in Step 2.

9. Click OK.

10. Close the Disk Management/Computer Management interface.

11. The mounted volume is now accessible through the mount point directory.

Cleaning Up a Drive

The Disk Cleanup tool can be used to recover drive space by removing files and compressing others. Here are the steps to follow:

1. Select Start|Programs|Accessories|Windows Explorer.

2. Right-click a drive to clean up and select Properties from the pop-up menu.

3. Click the Disk Cleanup button on the General tab.

4. Wait while the Disk Cleanup tool performs an inspection of your drive.

5. When prompted, mark or unmark the checkboxes beside each of the available means to recover space on your hard drive. When files are to be deleted, a list of those files can be viewed.

6. Click OK to perform the selected space-recovery activities.

7. When completed, close the drive's Properties dialog box.

Testing for Errors on a Drive

To use ScanDisk to test a drive for errors, perform the following steps:

1. Select Start|Programs|Accessories|Windows Explorer.

2. Right-click a drive to test for errors and select Properties from the pop-up menu.

3. Select the Tools tab.

4. Click the Check Now button.

5. Select the Automatically Fix File System Errors checkbox.

6. Select the Scan For And Attempt Recovery Of Bad Sectors checkbox.

7. If ScanDisk is unable to perform its operations while Windows 2000 is booted, you'll be prompted whether to schedule ScanDisk to launch at the next bootup.

8. Once ScanDisk completes, a report of its findings will be displayed.

9. Close ScanDisk.

10. Close the drive's Properties dialog box.

Defragmenting a Drive

The Disk Defragmenter tool is used to improve the organization of files on volumes. If you suspect your drives are highly fragmented, use the following steps to defragment your hard drive:

1. Select Start|Programs|Accessories|Windows Explorer.

2. Right-click a drive to test for errors and select Properties from the pop-up menu.

3. Select the Tools tab.

4. Click the Defragment Now button.

5. Select a volume from the list.

6. Click the Defragment button.

7. Wait while the process is performed.

8. Repeat Steps 6 through 8 until all volumes are defragmented.

9. Close the Disk Defragmenter tool.

10. Close the drive's Properties dialog box.

Configuring Quotas

To use quotas to control user consumption of network shared drives, perform the following steps:

1. Select Start|Programs|Accessories|Windows Explorer.

2. Right-click the drive on which to enable quotas and select Properties from the pop-up menu.

3. Select the Quota tab.

4. Select the Enable Quota Management checkbox.

5. Select the Deny Disk Space To Users Exceeding Quota Limit checkbox.

6. Set Limit Disk Space to 100MB (or other value consistent with your needs).

7. Set the warning level to 90MB (or a similar value for your own limit setting).

8. Mark both Log Event checkboxes.

9. Click Quota Entries.

10. Issue the New Quota Entry command from the Quota menu to add a custom quota setting for the Administrator.

11. Select the Administrator.

12. Click Add.

6. Windows 2000 Configuration

13. Click OK.

14. Select the Do Not Limit Disk Usage radio button.

15. Click OK.

16. Issue the New Quota Entry command from the Quota menu to add a custom quota setting for the Guest account.

17. Select the Guest account.

18. Click Add.

19. Click OK.

20. Select the Limit Disk Space To radio button.

21. Set the limit to 25MB and the warning level to 20MB.

22. Click OK.

23. Issue the Close command from the Quota menu.

24. Click OK to close the drive's Properties dialog box.

Chapter 7

Windows 2000 File Systems

In Depth

It is important that you understand the file systems supported by Windows 2000 to fully use some of its most powerful and useful features. This chapter deals not only with these file systems but with some of the management tasks that go with them. These include old features, such as security, compression, and auditing, as well as new, long-awaited features, such as disk quotas and encryption.

The File Systems

Although many different file systems exist, only the four that Windows 2000 supports are covered in this chapter. These include FAT, FAT32, and NTFS (versions 4 and 5). The benefits and drawbacks of each of these file systems are listed in the sections that follow.

FAT

The File Allocation Table (FAT) file system is the most widely supported file system. Almost all major operating systems support this particular file system, including MS-DOS, Windows 3.x, Windows 9x, Windows NT, Windows 2000, Macintosh OS, and many flavors of Unix.

TIP: *There's another version of FAT known as FAT16. FAT and FAT16 are the same file system. The new name is simply to differentiate it from FAT32, which is described in the next section. Another file system known as Virtual FAT (or VFAT) is an enhanced version of FAT that allows long file names to be used. These three terms (FAT, FAT16, and VFAT) are used interchangeably in most Windows documentation.*

Table 7.1 compares the pros and cons of the FAT file system.

FAT32

Windows 95 Second Edition introduced FAT32. This 32-bit file system is backward-compatible with FAT and has better long file name support, larger partition support, and the ability to change the sector block size. Table 7.2 compares the pros and cons of the FAT32 file system.

TIP: *Use the FAT32 file system when formatting partitions that are 2GB or larger.*

---

7. Windows 2000 File Systems

Table 7.1   The good and bad of FAT.

Pros	Cons
Most widely used file system	No support for local security
Can be supported on small partitions and diskettes	No automatic file recovery
	Uses standard 8.3 file names
	2GB file size limit
	4GB partition size limit
	512 entry limit in root directory
	No quotas
	No compression
	No encryption

Table 7.2   The good and bad of FAT32.

Pros	Cons
Support for long file names	No support for local security
Can be supported on small partitions	No automatic file recovery
4GB file size limit	No compression
Larger than 4GB partition size limit	No quotas
	No encryption

NTFS Version 4

New Technology File System (NTFS) version 4 is the file system used by Windows NT 4.0. It operates much like a relational database rather than a flat file system (as used in FAT and FAT32). It introduced file level security, auditing, and compression to Windows.

NTFS also introduced a technology known as *cluster remapping*. With this technology, when the operating system finds a bad cluster, it automatically moves the data to a new, stable cluster and marks the original cluster as bad. This technology is also known as *self-healing*.

NTFS supports compressions, file- and folder-level security, and auditing. NTFS also supports an extremely large file system: 16 exabytes (or 16EB, which is 16 billion GB). Although this is a theoretical limit (no hardware system currently exists that can support this), the file system will be able to scale to the hardware when it is available.

NOTE: *As an example of the size of this limit: If every man, woman, and child on the planet had a 3,000-page document and each of those pages was 3K in size, and these documents were all placed into a single file system, this would only account for one-sixteenth of 1EB. NTFS supports 16EB!*

Table 7.3 compares the pros and cons of the NTFSv4 file system.

NTFS Version 5

NTFS version 5 (NTFSv5) is the new file system introduced with Windows 2000. This file system has all the features of NTFS version 4 but adds the long-awaited quotas and encryption features.

One of the major downfalls on NTFSv5 is that the only system that supports it "out of the box" is Windows 2000. Windows NT 4.0 supports NTFSv5 only if it is running Service Pack 5 or higher. Table 7.4 compares the pros and cons of the NTFSv5 file system.

TIP: *The only reason to use a file system other than NTFSv5 with Windows 2000 is for dual-boot purposes. If a system is not dual booted, it is a good idea to convert all partitions to NTFSv5. Microsoft does not recommend configuring a server for dual boot.*

Table 7.3   The good and bad of NTFSv4.

Pros	Cons
Support for long file names	No quotas
Local security	No encryption
Very large partition and file size support	Cannot be supported on small partitions or diskettes
Self-healing	No automatic file recovery
Compression support	Only works with Windows NT and 2000

Table 7.4   The good and bad of NTFSv5.

Pros	Cons
Support for long file names	Not supported by non-Windows NT/2000 systems
Local security	Cannot be supported on small partitions or diskettes
Self-healing	No automatic file recovery
Compression support	
Quota support	
Very large partition and file size support	
Encryption support	

7. Windows 2000
File Systems

Choosing and Implementing Windows 2000 File Systems

The simplest way to choose the correct file system is by operating system. Although some would think that the features are more important, if the operating system installed cannot support the file system, it also cannot support the features. Refer to Table 7.5 to decide which file system to use with which operating system.

File System Management

Some very important features have been added to Windows 2000 to assist in managing file systems. These features are covered in the following sections.

Table 7.5   File system support by operating system.

Operating System(s)	File System
MS-DOS	FAT
Windows 3.x	FAT
Windows 3.x or MS-DOS dual booted with Windows 9x/NT/2000	FAT
Windows 95 First Edition	FAT
Windows 95 First Edition dual booted with Windows NT	FAT
Windows 95 Second Edition dual booted with Windows NT	FAT
Windows 95 Second Edition dual booted with Windows 2000	FAT32
Windows 98 dual booted with Windows NT	FAT
Windows 98 dual booted with Windows 2000	FAT32
Windows NT	NTFSv4
Windows NT with pre-SP5 dual booted with Windows 2000	NTFSv4
Windows NT with SP5 dual booted with Windows 2000	NTFSv5
Windows 2000	NTFSv5

7. Windows 2000 File Systems

Windows 2000 Encryption

Windows 2000 and NTFSv5 have finally provided the ability to use encryption to protect files. With Encrypting File System (EFS), files can be protected so that no one but the owner of the files can read and modify them. This takes security beyond NTFS permissions. With EFS, only the person who encrypted the files can decrypt them. Now if someone steals a laptop or other network hardware, the files are secure, even if the administrator password is known.

Compressing Folders and Files

Much like Windows NT, NTFS provides the ability to compress partitions, folders, and individual files. Although compression should not be used on all files all the time, it can be used on files that are not accessed often or if extra disk space is temporally required (for example, while awaiting a hardware maintenance window). This is because the overhead needed to compress and then uncompress the files will slow the system down. Note that compression does not work with encryption.

Defragmenting Drives

Although NTFS is better than FAT, all drives get fragmented. When a file is saved on the hard drive, the operating system will attempt to fill any empty gaps on the disk to use as much of the drive as possible. This, however, slows file access.

NOTE: *Imagine if the first five pages of this chapter started on page 200, the next five on page 250, the next five on page 124, and so on. It would take you longer to read through the chapter than if all the pages were in order.*

Defragmentation of disks simply moves files around so that all the components of an individual file are all placed in the same location. Windows 2000 ships with a basic defragmentation tool. The "Immediate Solutions" section shows you how to defragment a drive using Windows 2000's built-in defragmenter.

Disk Cleanup

Windows 2000 includes a feature for scanning disks for files that can be removed. These include downloaded files, temporary Internet files, Recycle Bin files, and temporary files. The Disk Cleanup utility also scans hard drives for files that have not been accessed in a long period of time and will automatically compress those files if you select the option.

Finally, the disk cleanup utility can also be configured to scan for rarely used Windows 2000 components and rarely used installed applications. These can be automatically uninstalled as well.

Working with Quotas

One of the features that has been missing in the Windows operating system is support for user quotas. Up until now, a user with access to a server could single-handedly bring the server to its knees by filling the server's hard drives with data. Windows 2000 and NTFSv5 can now be configured to support quotas for individual users or global quotas. It is also possible to create different quotas for individual partitions and folders.

Immediate Solutions

Converting a Partition

The three ways to convert NTFS partitions are discussed in the following sections.

Converting to NTFS Version 5

Method 1:

1. Select Start|Programs|Accessories|Command Prompt.

2. Type the following:

```
convert volume /FS:NTFS
```

3. Press Enter. A successful conversion is shown in Figure 7.1.

Method 2:

NOTE: *Method 2 is used if the convert application cannot gain exclusive access to the drive being converted.*

---

1. Select Start|Programs|Accessories|Command Prompt.

```
D:\WINNT.TST\System32\cmd.exe

E:\>convert g: /fs:ntfs
The type of the file system is FAT.
Determining disk space required for file system conversion...
Total disk space:            514080 KB
Free space on volume:        513784 KB
Space required for conversion:   5459 KB
Converting file system
Conversion complete

E:\>
```

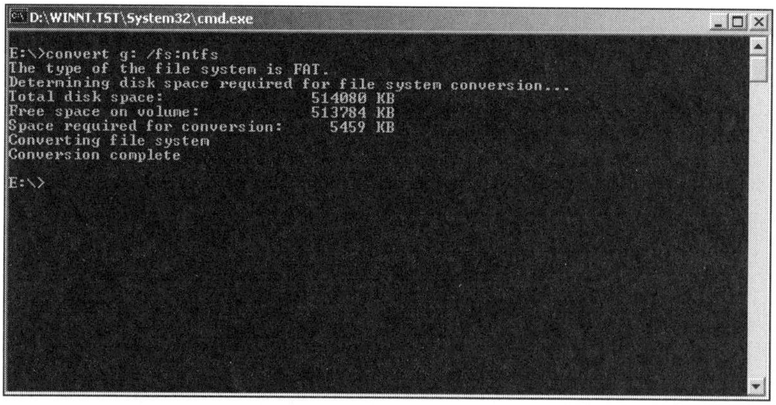

Figure 7.1   A successful conversion.

2. Type the following:

```
convert volume /FS:NTFS
```

3. Type Y and press Enter (see Figure 7.2).

4. Reboot the server. When the server restarts, it converts the file system (see Figure 7.3).

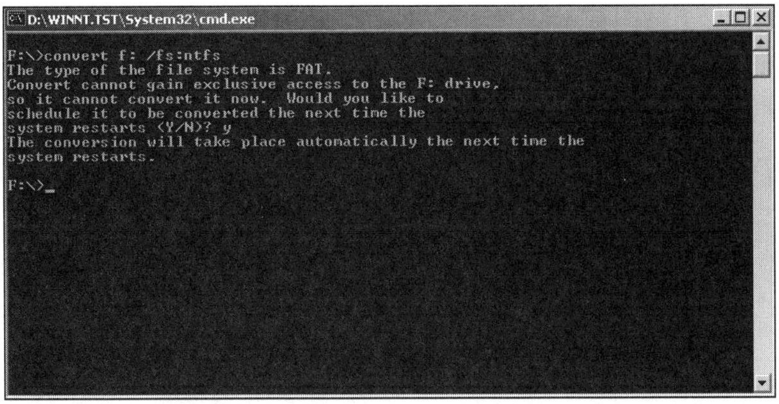

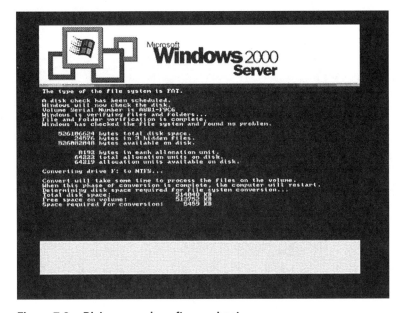

Figure 7.2   Scheduling a volume conversion upon reboot.

Figure 7.3   Disk conversion after a reboot.

Converting to NTFS Version 5 Using Verbose Mode

To convert a volume to NTFS in verbose mode, perform the following steps:

1. Select Start|Programs|Accessories|Command Prompt.

2. Type the following:

```
convert volume /FS:NTFS /v
```

3. Press Enter. A successful verbose conversion is shown in Figure 7.4.

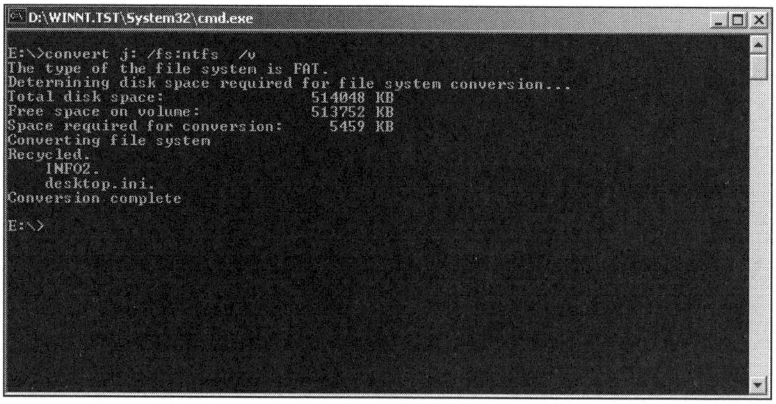

Figure 7.4   A successful verbose conversion.

Working with Compression

A number of management tasks are involved with compressed data. The following sections explore these tasks.

Configuring How Compressed Information Is Displayed

To configure the display of compression information, perform the following steps:

1. Select Start|Programs|Accessories|Windows Explorer.

2. Select Folder Options from the Tools pop-up menu and select the View tab.

3. Select the Display Compressed Files And Folders With Alternate Color option.

4. Click OK. All compressed file and folders will now be shown in blue.

Compressing a File

To compress a file, perform the following steps:

1. Select Start|Programs|Accessories|Windows Explorer.

2. Right-click the file that you would like compressed and choose Properties from the pop-up menu.

3. Click the Advanced button on the General tab.

4. In the Compress Or Encrypt Attributes section of the Advanced Attributes page, check the Compress Contents To Save Disk Space checkbox and click OK.

5. Click OK.

Uncompressing a File

To uncompress a file, perform the following steps:

1. Select Start|Programs|Accessories|Windows Explorer.

2. Right-click the file that you would like uncompressed and choose Properties from the pop-up menu.

3. Click the Advanced button on the General tab.

4. In the Compress Or Encrypt Attributes section of the Advanced Attributes page, clear the Compress Contents To Save Disk Space checkbox and click OK.

5. Click OK.

Compressing a Folder

To compress a folder, perform the following steps:

1. Select Start|Programs|Accessories|Windows Explorer.

2. Right-click the folder that you would like compressed and choose Properties from the pop-up menu.

3. Click the Advanced button on the General tab.

4. In the Compress Or Encrypt Attributes section of the Advanced Attributes page, check the Compress Contents To Save Disk Space checkbox and click OK.

5. If you would like to compress only the folder, choose the Apply Changes To This Folder Only option and click OK.

6. If you would like to compress the folder and its contents, choose the Apply Changes To This Folder, Subfolders, And Files option and click OK.

Uncompressing a Folder

To uncompress a folder, perform the following steps:

1. Select Start|Programs|Accessories|Windows Explorer.

2. Right-click the folder that you would like uncompressed and choose Properties from the pop-up menu.

3. Click the Advanced button on the General tab.

4. In the Compress Or Encrypt Attributes section of the Advanced Attributes page, clear the Compress Contents To Save Disk Space checkbox and click OK.

5. If you would like to uncompress only the folder, choose the Apply Changes To This Folder Only option and click OK.

6. If you would like to uncompress the folder and its contents, choose the Apply Changes To This Folder, Subfolders And Files option and click OK.

Compressing a Volume

To compress a volume, perform the following steps:

1. Select Start|Programs|Accessories|Windows Explorer.

2. Right-click the disk that you would like compressed and choose Properties from the pop-up menu.

3. Check the Compress Drive To Save Disk Space checkbox and click OK.

4. If you would like to compress only the drive but not the files and folders within the drive, choose the Apply Changes To *Drive*:\ Only option and click OK.

5. If you would like to compress the entire drive, including all files and folders, choose the Apply Changes To *Drive*:\, Subfolders, And Files option and click OK.

Uncompressing a Volume

To uncompress a volume, perform the following steps:

1. Select Start|Programs|Accessories|Windows Explorer.

2. Right-click the disk that you would like uncompressed and choose Properties from the pop-up menu.

3. Clear the Compress Drive To Save Disk Space checkbox and click OK.

4. If you would like to uncompress only the drive but not the files and folders within the drive, choose the Apply Changes To *Drive*:\ Only option and click OK.

5. If you would like to uncompress the entire drive, including all files and folders, choose the Apply Changes To *Drive*:\, Subfolders, And Files option and click OK.

File and Folder Management

A number of tasks are involved in managing files and folders. The following sections explore these tasks.

Viewing File and Folder Permissions

To view file and folder permissions, perform the following steps:

1. Select Start|Programs|Accessories|Windows Explorer.

2. Select the file or folder for which you would like to view permissions.

3. Right-click the item and choose Properties from the pop-up menu.

4. Select the Security tab.

5. If you would like to see more advanced properties, click Advanced. Click OK when done.

6. Click OK.

Setting File and Folder Permissions

To set file and folder permissions, perform the following steps:

1. Select Start|Programs|Accessories|Windows Explorer.

2. Select the file or folder for which you would like to view permissions.

3. Right-click the item and choose Properties from the pop-up menu.

4. Select the Security tab and click Add.

5. Select a group or a user and click Add.

6. Assign any desired permissions to the group or user and click OK.

Copying Files and Folders

The four methods for copying files and folders are covered next.

Method 1:

1. Select Start|Programs|Accessories|Windows Explorer.

2. Select the files or folders that you would like to copy.

7. Windows 2000 File Systems

3. Select the Copy option from the Edit pop-up menu.

4. Navigate to where you would like the files copied.

5. Select the Paste option from the Edit pop-up menu.

Method 2:

1. Select Start|Programs|Accessories|Windows Explorer.

2. Select the files or folders that you would like to copy.

3. Press Ctrl+C.

4. Navigate to where you would like the files copied.

5. Press Ctrl+V.

Method 3:

1. Select Start|Programs|Accessories|Windows Explorer.

2. Select the files or folders that you would like to copy.

3. Right-click and drag the files or folders to the destination folder and release the mouse button.

4. Choose the Copy Here option from the pop-up menu.

Method 4:

1. Select Start|Programs|Accessories|Windows Explorer.

2. Select the files or folders that you would like to copy.

3. Select the Copy To option from the Edit pop-up menu.

4. Navigate to where you would like the files copied and click OK.

Moving Files and Folders

The two methods for moving files and folders are covered next.

Method 1:

1. Select Start|Programs|Accessories|Windows Explorer.

2. Select the files or folders that you would like to move.

3. Select the Move To option from the Edit pop-up menu.

4. Navigate to where you would like the files moved and click OK.

Method 2:

1. Select Start|Programs|Accessories|Windows Explorer.

2. Select the files or folders that you would like to move.

3. Right-click and drag the files or folders to the destination folder and release.

4. Choose Move Here from the pop-up menu.

Creating Folders

The two methods for creating files and folders are covered next.

Method 1:

1. Select Start|Programs|Accessories|Windows Explorer.

2. Navigate to the location where you would like the new folder created.

3. Right-click and choose New|Folder from the pop-up menu.

4. Enter a name for the new folder and press Enter.

Method 2:

1. Select Start|Programs|Accessories|Windows Explorer.

2. Navigate to the location where you would like the new folder created.

3. Choose New|Folder from the File pop-up menu.

4. Enter a name for the new folder and press Enter.

Enabling Auditing

To enable auditing, perform the following steps:

1. Select Start|Programs|Administrative Tools|Local Security Policy.

2. Navigate to the Audit Policy container in the Local Policies container.

3. Right-click the Audit Object Access policy in the right pane and choose the Security option from the pop-up menu.

4. To enable auditing of successful object access, check the Success checkbox.

5. To enable auditing of failed object access, check the Failure checkbox.

6. Click OK.

Setting Up Auditing of Files and Folders

To establish file and folder auditing, perform the following steps:

1. Select Start|Programs|Accessories|Windows Explorer.

2. Select the file or folder that you would like to audit.

3. Right-click the file and choose Properties from the pop-up menu.

4. Select the Security tab and click Advanced.

5. Select the Auditing tab.

6. Click Add.

7. Select the group or user to audit and click OK.

8. Choose which components to audit, how to apply them, and click OK.

9. Click OK.

Taking Ownership of Files and Folders

To take ownership of files and folders, perform the following steps:

1. Select Start|Programs|Accessories|Windows Explorer.

2. Select the file or folder for which you would like to take ownership.

3. Right-click it and choose Properties from the pop-up menu.

4. Select the Security tab and click Advanced.

5. Select the Owner tab.

6. Select a new owner and click OK.

7. Click OK.

Restoring Deleted Files from the Recycle Bin

To restore files or folders that have been deleted, perform the following steps:

1. Double-click the Recycle Bin icon on the desktop.

2. Select the item that you would like to recover.

3. Right-click the item and choose Restore from the pop-up menu.

NOTE: *You can recover items from other recycle bins (assuming that you have the correct permissions) by navigating to the Recycler folder in Windows Explorer and choosing the appropriate recycle bin. This folder is hidden by default and you must change the folder view to show hidden files. Refer to Figure 7.5 for an example.*

Customizing the Recycle Bin

To customize Recycle Bin settings, perform the following steps:

1. Right-click the Recycle Bin icon on the desktop and choose Properties from the pop-up menu.

2. Select whether to configure all the drives together by choosing the Use One Setting For All Drives radio button or individually by choosing the Configure Drives Independently radio button (see Figure 7.6).

3. Make any necessary configuration changes and click OK when done.

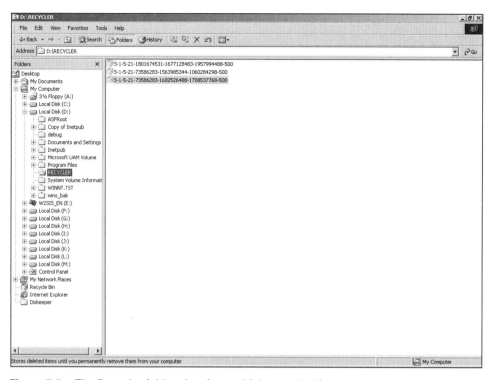

Figure 7.5   The Recycler folder showing multiple recycle bins.

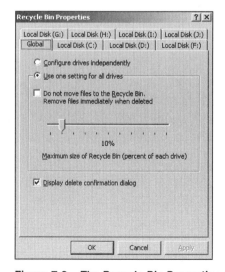

Figure 7.6   The Recycle Bin Properties dialog box.

Working with Quotas

A number of tasks are involved with managing disk quotas; these are discussed next.

Enabling Disk Quotas

To enable disk quotas, perform the following steps:

1. Select Start|Programs|Accessories|Windows Explorer.

2. Right-click the disk for which you would like to establish a quota and choose Properties from the pop-up menu.

3. Select the Quota tab.

4. Check the Enable Quota Management checkbox, as shown in Figure 7.7.

5. Configure any other quota management properties and click OK when done.

Setting Quotas

To set disk quotas, perform the following steps:

1. Select Start|Programs|Accessories|Windows Explorer.

2. Right-click the disk for which you would like to set a quota and choose Properties from the pop-up menu.

3. Select the Quota tab.

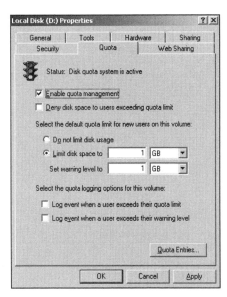

Figure 7.7   Enabling quota management.

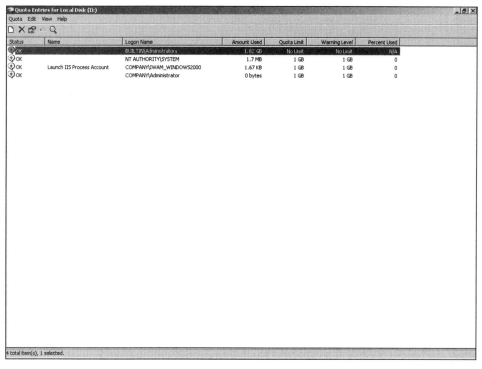

Figure 7.8   The Quota Entries console.

4. Click Quota Entries. The Quota Entries console appears (see Figure 7.8).

5. Select New Quota Entry from the Quota pop-up menu.

6. Select the user or users and click Add. Then click OK.

7. Select the Limit Disk Space To radio button and enter a quota limit amount and an amount for when a warning should be sent to the user.

8. Click OK.

Disabling Quotas

To disable disk quotas, perform the following steps:

1. Select Start|Programs|Accessories|Windows Explorer.

2. Right-click the disk for which you would like to disable a quota and choose Properties from the pop-up menu.

3. Select the Quota tab.

4. Clear the Enable Quota Management checkbox.

5. Click OK when done.

Working with Encryption

A number of tasks are involved in managing encryption. These tasks are discussed in the following sections.

Encrypting a File

To encrypt a file, perform the following steps:

1. Select Start|Programs|Accessories|Windows Explorer.

2. Right-click the file that you would like to encrypt and choose Properties from the pop-up menu.

3. Click Advanced.

4. Check the Encrypt Contents To Secure Data checkbox and click OK.

5. Click OK.

6. If you want to encrypt the file and its parent folder, choose the Encrypt The File And Parent Folder option and click OK.

7. If you want to encrypt only the file, choose the Encrypt The File Only option and click OK.

Decrypting a File

To decrypt a file, perform the following steps:

1. Select Start|Programs|Accessories|Windows Explorer.

2. Right-click the file that you would like to decrypt and choose Properties from the pop-up menu.

3. Click Advanced.

4. Check the Decrypt Contents To Secure Data checkbox and click OK.

5. Click OK.

Encrypting a Folder

To encrypt a folder, perform the following steps:

1. Select Start|Programs|Accessories|Windows Explorer.

2. Right-click the folder that you would like to encrypt and choose Properties from the pop-up menu.

3. Click Advanced.

4. Check the Encrypt Contents To Secure Data checkbox and click OK.

5. Click OK.

7. Windows 2000 File Systems

Decrypting a Folder

To decrypt a folder, perform the following steps:

1. Select Start|Programs|Accessories|Windows Explorer.

2. Right-click the folder that you would like to decrypt and choose Properties from the pop-up menu.

3. Click Advanced.

4. Check the Decrypt Contents To Secure Data checkbox and click OK.

5. Click OK.

Disk Management

The following sections explore the tasks involved with disk management.

Analyzing a Disk

To analyze disk fragmentation, perform the following steps:

1. Select Start|Programs|Accessories|System Tools|Disk Defragmenter.

2. Select the disk that you would like to analyze and click Analyze (see Figure 7.9).

3. When the analysis is complete, click View Report to view what the analysis turned up.

4. Click Defragment to defragment the drive.

Defragmenting a Disk

To defragment a disk, perform the following steps:

1. Select Start|Programs|Accessories|System Tools|Disk Defragmenter.

2. Select the disk that you would like to defragment and click Defragment.

3. Click Close.

Running Cleanup on a Disk

To run Disk Cleanup, perform the following steps:

1. Select Start|Programs|Accessories|Windows Explorer.

2. Right-click the disk that you would like to clean up and choose Properties from the pop-up menu.

3. Click Disk Cleanup. The Disk Cleanup Wizard scans the disk.

7. Windows 2000 File Systems

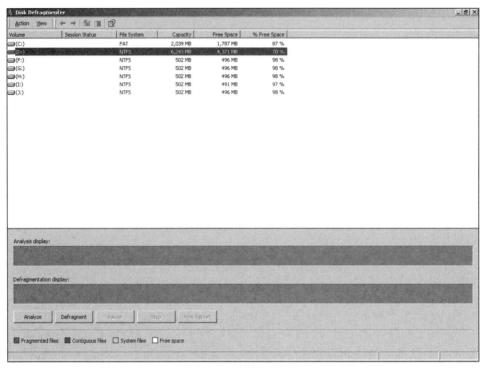

Figure 7.9   The built-in Disk Defragmenter utility.

4. The Disk Cleanup Wizard, shown in Figure 7.10, lists all files that can be deleted to clean up the system. Select any desired files and click OK.

5. You can view the files that are to be deleted by selecting the files to be deleted and clicking View Files.

6. You can also have the wizard check for unused or rarely used Windows components and installed applications by clicking on the More Options tab.

7. Click Yes to confirm the file cleanup.

Figure 7.10   The Disk Cleanup Wizard.

Chapter 8

Windows 2000 Networking

(continued)

In Depth

Entire books have been devoted to the subject of connecting servers to a network and the different protocols that can be used to make these connections. For this reason, this chapter will be more of an overview than a full-blown description.

Meet the Protocols

Although Windows 2000 supports many third-party protocols, four main protocols are supported out of the box. These include the following:

- Internet Protocol (TCP/IP)
- NWLink IPX/SPX/NetBIOS Compatible Transport Protocol
- NetBIOS Enhanced User Interface (NetBEUI)
- AppleTalk
- DLC (Data Link Control) protocol

Each of these protocols is discussed in the following sections.

TCP/IP

The most popular protocol currently used in networks today is TCP/IP. The main reason this protocol is the most used protocol in the world is because of the Internet. The Internet would not be what it is today without TCP/IP.

TCP/IP is the most complex, and therefore the slowest, protocol covered in this chapter. It also is the most complex to configure. As you'll see, some of the services that are available to you with Windows 2000 make this configuration much more simple to configure and manage.

NWLink

Until a few years ago, Novell NetWare was the market leader in network operating systems. The protocol used by NetWare is known as Internetwork Packet Exchange/Sequenced Packet Exchange (IPX/SPX). This protocol, for the most part, is self-addressing and can still be used in large, routed networks. It's also extremely fast.

When Microsoft decided to go against NetWare in the network operating system market, it knew that it had to support the IPX/SPX protocol. Companies are much more likely to convert from one network operating system to another if both can operate together for a time. Not surprisingly, NetWare did not give Microsoft access to the IPX/SPX protocol. Microsoft, therefore, had to come up with its own version of the protocol. This version of the protocol is known as *NWLink* or *NWLink IPX/SPX/NetBIOS Compatible Transport Protocol.*

NetBEUI

Microsoft designed a protocol to work in small network environments with its operating systems. That protocol is NetBEUI. Although this protocol is extremely fast and configures itself automatically, it does have limitations.

For one, it is chatty. Because it is self-configuring, it has to continuously communicate with all other systems on the network. Also, this self-configuration is partially done using broadcasts. Because of these broadcasts, it cannot be used on a wide area network (by default, routers do not route broadcasts from one network to another). If you need to install a network between a small number of computers, all you need to do is connect the computers to the network and install NetBEUI.

Additional Protocols

Several additional protocols ship with Windows 2000. The one covered in this chapter, however, is AppleTalk. AppleTalk is the protocol invented by Apple to work with its Macintosh line of computers.

When Microsoft originally designed File And Print Services For Macintosh, it approached Apple and got Apple's permission to design Windows NT to operate like a Macintosh server. In fact, a Windows NT (or 2000) Server running services for the Macintosh is 100-percent compatible with a Macintosh server.

TCP/IP is Where It's At

Although each network operating system originally had its own protocol, all now rely on TCP/IP (including NetWare and Apple). With the popularization of the Internet, TCP/IP is currently the only protocol used by most operating systems.

Configuration Basics

Before a system can use TCP/IP to communicate with another system on the local network, three pieces of information are required: the IP address, the subnet mask, and the gateway address. These three pieces of information can pinpoint the exact location of the computer anywhere on the network—and anywhere in the world if the computer is connected to the Internet. The IP information can be compared to your home address. The TCP/IP address is like your home and street address. Your house or apartment is the only one with that unique address in your city. The subnet mask defines the boundaries of your city. Defining the default gateway is a little harder. It is more like the local post office.

Domain Name Service

When computers communicate, they use a unique number that's assigned to every networking device made today. This number is known as the *Media Access Control (MAC) address*. It is a unique 48-bit number. The MAC address is usually written in hexadecimal bytes with either colons (:) or dashes (-) separating the bytes. For example, a MAC address might be 1A-34-DC-37-91-AB. The first three bytes are assigned to the company that created the networking device, whereas the last three bytes are a unique serial number for the device. As mentioned, all the major network protocols use this address to communicate (including TCP/IP and NWLink).

With TCP/IP, however, each network host is given a four-byte IP address separated by periods (for example, 192.168.54.145). As you can imagine, most people would have difficulty remembering what the MAC address or IP address of Microsoft's Web site is. Therefore, we use fully qualified domain names (FQDNs) to communicate on the Internet (for example, **www.microsoft.com**).

So we have a bit of a problem. We humans use FQDNs and computers use IP addresses. We need a method to translate between the two. Although several methods exist for the translation between FQDNs and IP addresses, such as HOSTS, LMHOSTS, and WINS, the most common method used today, is known as the *Domain Name Service (DNS)*. Simply put, DNS automatically converts from one format to another. You give a computer the FQDN and it finds the IP address; you give the computer an IP address and it returns the FQDN.

NOTE: *DNS does not perform any IP address-to-MAC address translation. The protocol that accomplishes this is known as Address Resolution Protocol (ARP). This is done in the background automatically. Under normal circumstances, you will not be required to modify any ARP information. The conversion from MAC addresses to IP addresses is performed by Reverse ARP (RARP).*

Dynamic Host Configuration Protocol

If you've ever managed a large network, you'll be one of the first to agree that assigning IP addresses to each workstation can be a tedious task. With IP, every workstation must have a unique IP address assigned to it. If two systems use the same IP address, either one of them will fail or both will cause errors. Also, if the subnet mask is wrong on a single computer on the network, it will not be able to communicate properly with other systems in its network. Finally, if the default gateway address is wrong, the workstation will not be able to communicate with systems on remote networks. Problems can also occur with incorrectly defined domain names, DNS servers, WINS servers, and so on.

When you're configuring a few machines, making such an error in not likely. When you're configuring several hundred or thousand computers, the likelihood of an error becomes increasingly more probable. Fixing errors on such a large network can also be extremely difficult (imagine trying to find the two computers that share the same IP address on your network of several thousand computers).

To allow administrators to automate this task, the *Dynamic Host Configuration Protocol (DHCP)* was created. As the name says, this protocol dynamically assigns IP addresses to any system that asks (assuming that the system is authorized and is asking correctly). Not only will DHCP assign the requesting workstation an IP address, it will also specify the subnet mask, default gateway, DNS servers, and any other servers and services that the administrator configures it to. As shown in the Immediate Solutions section, the configuration of DHCP requires an understanding of scopes and leases. A *scope* is the range (or ranges) of IP addresses that the DHCP server is allowed to assign to computers. A *lease* is also normally assigned when the server assigns the IP address information. This lease is much like that on a car. The address is assigned to the client for the duration of the lease. When the lease expires, the client must either renew the lease or "return it" (at this point, the computer loses its TCP/IP address and will no longer be able to communicate on the network using TCP/IP).

DHCP deals with three types of scopes: regular scopes, superscopes, and multicast scopes. As mentioned, a scope is simply a boundary that is set on the IP addresses that can be assigned by the DHCP server. A *superscope* is a "scope of scopes." It is a scope that is made up of two or more scopes that are in the same network space. Finally, a *multicast scope* is used for multicasting information to systems. Multicasting is the process of sending a single stream of data to multiple machines. Examples of this include streaming audio and video from the Internet and the cloning of multiple machines on the network simultaneously.

Windows Internet Naming Service

Most Windows computers on the network use a NetBIOS name rather than the FQDN. For example, your system might be known as both windows2000 (the NetBIOS name) and Windows2000.company.com (the FQDN). With Windows 2000, NetBIOS is not used as long as you follow this simple rule: There cannot be any non-Windows 2000 systems on the network. Quite a catch!

Normally, when NetBIOS systems come online, they shout their presence on the network. They continue to shout out this information every 12 minutes for the duration of their stay on the network. As you can well imagine, in a network of several thousand computers, this can amount to a lot of shouting.

To fix this problem, Microsoft created the *Windows Internet Naming Service (WINS)*. Simply put, this service converts between NetBIOS names and IP addresses (and the reverse) in much the same way DNS converts between FQDNs and IP addresses. Instead of broadcasting their presence on the network, systems configured with WINS send their information directly to the WINS server. When a computer needs to find another computer on the network, it asks the WINS server for the other computer's IP address.

In much the same way that DNS has a manual method of naming translation (the HOSTS file), WINS has one too. It is known as the LMHOSTS file. The *LMHOSTS* file is used to convert between TCP/IP addresses and NetBIOS names and back.

Internet Information Services

The Internet has become part of everyone's lives; all you have to do is turn on the television or radio and you will hear a reference to the Internet. Most people understand that the Internet is there, but do not know what happens in the background when you enter an address in your Internet browser. Simply enter in the address into your favorite Internet browser and content (text, images, and multimedia) returns to you. The hidden, or server side, of this equation is the Internet Information Services (IIS). This is the component that replies to the request from your browser and sends it the desired information back.

IIS is more complex than that, but when simplified, that's all it really does. IIS also gives you the ability to host multiple Web sites on a single Web server, control how each site is accessed, and specify the security for each.

File Transfer Protocol

Although the Hypertext Transfer Protocol (HTTP) used by the Web servers and browsers has taken the wind out of the File Transfer Protocol's sails, FTP is still a widely used protocol. This protocol is designed for one thing, and one thing only: to transfer files from one location to another over a TCP/IP network.

In the same way that the Internet browser has a server side to it in IIS, the FTP service is the server side of the equation, whereas FTP clients act as the client side. The Microsoft implementation of FTP allows you to configure both private and public FTP sites as well as multiple FTP sites on a single server.

Integrating with NetWare

As mentioned previously, Microsoft designed the Windows operating systems to work with Novell NetWare. Many people are unaware of this, but Novell does not have a desktop operating system. It only builds the server side of the equation. The Novell NetWare operating system runs on top of a secondary operating system, DOS for example. Novell NetWare has used the Microsoft suite of desktop operating systems for almost the entire span of its lifecycle. Microsoft would like you to use its client software to connect to Novell's servers over Novell's version of the client software.

Many arguments can be started by asking this question: Which client is better, the Microsoft one or the Novell one? This question is best answered by your specific needs.

Novell NetWare can be configured to run in one of two modes: bindery and NDS. Windows 2000 allows you to connect to Novell NetWare networks running in one of these two modes. With NetWare versions 3.x and earlier, Novell used a flat directory system (not unlike that of Windows NT). When it introduced NetWare 4.x, it unveiled a new directory service known as *NetWare Directory Services (NDS)*. This directory service is a relational database-type system similar to Active Directory. With the Microsoft Client For NetWare, your system can connect to both these systems.

When connecting a Windows 2000 Professional system to a NetWare network, you'll use the Client Services For NetWare (CSNW). This client allows you to log onto a Novell NetWare network and access files and printers on that network. With Windows 2000 Servers, the client software is known as Gateway (And Client) Services For NetWare (GSNW). GSNW gives you the ability to connect to the Novell NetWare network in the same way as with Windows 2000 Professional, but it also allows your server to act as a gateway into the Novell network, sharing its file and printer resources with non-Novell clients.

Integrating with Apple Networks

Windows 2000 Server includes support for Macintosh systems. When you install the File And Print Services For Macintosh on your Windows 2000 Server, your server effectively becomes a Macintosh server. The Macintosh clients cannot distinguish the Windows 2000 Server from a true Macintosh server.

There are no requirements for sharing Windows 2000 printers with Macintosh systems, other than installing the Print Services For Macintosh. For file sharing, however, at least one partition must be formatted with the New Technology File System (NTFS).

8. Windows 2000 Networking

Immediate Solutions

Installing TCP/IP

Although TCP/IP is installed by default, you can uninstall it (as in the case of Windows 2000 Professional). In this instance, TCP/IP can be installed as outlined in this section.

1. Select Start|Settings|Control Panel.

2. Double-click the Network And Dial-Up Connections applet.

TIP: *You can also access this applet by right-clicking My Network Places and choosing the Properties option from the pop-up menu.*

---

3. Double-click the network connection for which you would like to install TCP/IP.

4. Click Properties. The Local Area Connection window corresponding to the connection selected in Step 3 appears.

5. On the General tab, click Install.

TIP: *The General tab only contains the Install button when you're configuring the Local Area Connection. If you're configuring other types of connections, this option appears on the Networking tab.*

---

6. Select the Protocol option and click Add.

7. In the Select Network Protocol window, select Internet Protocol (TCP/IP) and click OK.

Configuring TCP/IP

The following projects detail the various tasks involved with configuring the TCP/IP protocol suite.

Configuring Static Addresses

To configure static IP addresses, perform the following steps:

1. Select Start|Settings|Control Panel.

2. Double-click the Network And Dial-Up Connections applet.

3. Double-click the network connection for which you would like to configure a static address.

4. Click Properties.

5. On the General tab, select the Internet Protocol (TCP/IP) option and click Properties.

6. Select the Use The Following IP Address radio button.

7. Enter an IP address, a subnet mask, and a default gateway.

8. Enter a preferred DNS server and an alternate DNS server.

9. Click OK.

Configuring Additional TCP/IP Addresses

To configure additional IP addresses, perform the following steps:

1. Select Start|Settings|Control Panel.

2. Double-click the Network And Dial-Up Connections applet.

3. Double-click the network connection for which you would like to configure additional IP addresses.

4. Click Properties.

5. On the General tab, select the Internet Protocol (TCP/IP) option and click Properties.

6. Click Advanced.

7. On the IP Settings tab, click Add in the IP Addresses section of the window.

8. Enter an additional IP address and subnet mask and then click Add.

9. Repeat if desired. Click OK.

10. Click OK.

Configuring Additional Default Gateways

To configure additional default gateways, perform the following steps:

1. Select Start|Settings|Control Panel.

2. Double-click the Network And Dial-Up Connections applet.

3. Double-click the network connection for which you would like to configure additional default gateways.

4. Click Properties.

5. On the General tab, select the Internet Protocol (TCP/IP) option and click Properties.

6. Click Advanced.

7. On the IP Settings tab, click Add in the Default Gateways section of the window.

8. Enter an additional default gateway and metric and then click Add.

NOTE: *The metric is defined as the number of hops between one network to another. For example, if this network is to communicate with a network across three routers, the metric will be 3. One to the first router, a second to the second router, and a third hop to the third router.*

---

9. Repeat if desired. Click OK.

10. Click OK.

Configuring Dynamic Addresses

To configure dynamic IP addresses, perform the following steps:

1. Select Start|Settings|Control Panel.

2. Double-click the Network And Dial-Up Connections applet.

3. Double-click the network connection for which you would like to configure a dynamic address.

4. Click Properties.

5. On the General tab, select the Internet Protocol (TCP/IP) option and click Properties.

6. Select the Obtain An IP Address Automatically radio button.

7. Click OK.

Using Static DNS with TCP/IP

To use static DNS with TCP/IP, perform the following steps:

1. Select Start|Settings|Control Panel.

2. Double-click the Network And Dial-Up Connections applet.

3. Double-click the network connection for which you would like to configure a static DNS entry.

4. Click Properties.

5. On the General tab, select the Internet Protocol (TCP/IP) option and click Properties.

6. Select the Use The Following DNS Server Addresses radio button. Then enter the preferred DNS server and alternate DNS server addresses.

7. Click OK.

8. Windows 2000
Networking

Using Dynamic DNS with TCP/IP

To use dynamic DNS(DDNS) with TCP/IP, perform the following steps:

1. Select Start|Settings|Control Panel.

2. Double-click the Network And Dial-Up Connections applet.

3. Double-click the network connection for which you would like to configure a Dynamic DNS address.

4. Click Properties.

5. On the General tab, select the Internet Protocol (TCP/IP) option and click Properties.

6. Select the Obtain DNS Server Address Automatically radio button.

7. Click OK.

Using WINS with TCP/IP

To use WINS with TCP/IP, perform the following steps:

1. Select Start|Settings|Control Panel.

2. Double-click the Network And Dial-Up Connections applet.

3. Double-click the network connection for which you would like to configure a WINS address.

4. Click Properties.

5. On the General tab, select the Internet Protocol (TCP/IP) option and click Properties.

6. Click Advanced.

7. Select the WINS tab.

8. Click Add.

9. Enter the IP address of the WINS server in the TCP/IP WINS Server section and click Add.

10. Repeat this process for any other WINS servers you want to include. When you're done, click OK.

Enabling the LMHOSTS File to Resolve NetBIOS Names

To configure clients to use an LMHOSTS file for NetBIOS name resolution, perform the following steps:

1. Select Start|Settings|Control Panel.

2. Double-click the Network And Dial-Up Connections applet.

3. Double-click the network connection for which you would like to enable LMHOSTS resolution.

4. Click Properties.

5. On the General tab, select the Internet Protocol (TCP/IP) option and click Properties.

6. Click Advanced.

7. Select the WINS tab.

8. Select the Enable LMHOSTS Lookup checkbox.

9. Click Import LMHOSTS and navigate to its location.

10. Click OK.

Enabling NetBIOS over TCP/IP

To configure NetBIOS for use over TCP/IP, perform the following steps:

1. Select Start|Settings|Control Panel.

2. Double-click the Network And Dial-Up Connections applet.

3. Double-click the network connection for which you would like to enable NetBIOS over TCP/IP.

4. Click Properties.

5. On the General tab, select the Internet Protocol (TCP/IP) option and click Properties.

6. Click Advanced.

7. Select the WINS tab.

8. Select the Enable NetBIOS Over TCP/IP radio button.

9. Click OK.

Disabling NetBIOS over TCP/IP

To disable NetBIOS over TCP/IP, perform the following steps:

1. Select Start|Settings|Control Panel.

2. Double-click the Network And Dial-Up Connections applet.

3. Double-click the network connection for which you would like to disable NetBIOS over TCP/IP.

4. Click Properties.

5. On the General tab, select the Internet Protocol (TCP/IP) option and click Properties.

8. Windows 2000 Networking

6. Click Advanced.

7. Select the WINS tab.

8. Select the Disable NetBIOS Over TCP/IP radio button.

9. Click OK.

Using TCP/IP Filtering

To enable TCP/IP filtering, perform the following steps:

1. Select Start|Settings|Control Panel.

2. Double-click the Network And Dial-Up Connections applet.

3. Double-click the network connection for which you would like to configure TCP/IP filtering.

4. Click Properties.

5. On the General tab, select the Internet Protocol (TCP/IP) option and click Properties.

6. Click Advanced.

7. Select the Options tab.

8. Select the TCP/IP Filtering option and click Properties.

9. Select the desired configuration and click OK.

Using IPSec Security

To enable IPSec security, perform the following steps:

1. Select Start|Settings|Control Panel.

2. Double-click the Network And Dial-Up Connections applet.

3. Double-click the network connection for which you would like to configure IPSec.

4. Click Properties.

5. On the General tab, select the Internet Protocol (TCP/IP) option and click Properties.

6. Click Advanced.

7. Select the Options tab.

8. Select the IP Security option and click Properties.

9. Select the Use This IP Security Policy radio button.

10. Choose the desired security policy from the drop-down list.

11. Click OK.

Installing Simple TCP/IP Services

To install TCP/IP services, perform the following steps:

1. Select Start|Settings|Control Panel.

2. Double-click the Add/Remove Programs applet.

3. Click Add/Remove Windows Components.

4. When the Windows Component Wizard appears, click Next.

5. Select Networking Services and click Details.

6. Select Simple TCP/IP Services in the Subcomponents Of Networking Services window and click OK.

7. Click Next.

8. Click Finish.

Removing TCP/IP

To remove TCP/IP services, perform the following steps:

1. Select Start|Settings|Control Panel.

2. Double-click the Network And Dial-Up Connections applet.

3. Double-click the network connection for which you would like to remove TCP/IP.

4. Click Properties.

5. Click Uninstall.

6. In the Uninstall Internet Protocol (TCP/IP) dialog box, click Yes.

Working with Servers and DNS

The following projects detail configuring DNS.

Installing DNS

To install DNS, perform the following steps:

1. Select Start|Settings|Control Panel.

2. Double-click the Add/Remove Programs applet.

3. Click Add/Remove Windows Components.

4. When the Windows Component Wizard appears, click Next.

5. Select Networking Services and click Details.

6. Select the Domain Name System (DNS) option and click OK.

7. Click Next.

8. Click Finish.

Configuring a DNS Server

To configure a DNS server, perform the following steps:

1. Select Start|Programs|Administrative Tools|DNS. The DNS console appears, as shown in Figure 8.1.

2. Navigate to the server where you would like the DNS server configured, right-click it, and choose the Configure The Server option from the pop-up menu.

3. When the Configure DNS Server Wizard appears, click Next.

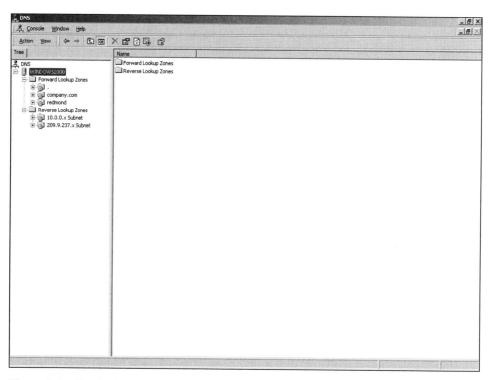

Figure 8.1   The DNS console.

4. Select the zone type (Active Directory-Integrated, Standard Primary, or Standard Secondary) and click Next.

NOTE: *A zone is defined as a domain (for example, company.com). The reason that the word domain is not used is two-fold. First, this is different than Windows NT domains. Second, a reverse-zone is a grouping of IP addresses based on the IP network that they are in (for example, 192.168.1.0 would be a zone).*

---

5. Enter the name for the new zone and click Next.

6. Select the Create A New File With This Name Or Use This Existing File option. Enter the name of the file and click Next.

7. Click Finish.

Configuring a Secondary DNS Server

To configure a secondary DNS server, perform the following steps:

1. Select Start|Programs|Administrative Tools|DNS.

2. Navigate to the server where you would like the secondary DNS server configured, right-click it, and choose the New Zone option from the pop-up menu.

3. When the Configure DNS Server Wizard appears, click Next.

4. Select the zone type (Active Directory-Integrated, Standard Primary, or Standard Secondary) and click Next.

5. Select either the Forward or Reverse Lookup Zone option and click Next.

6. Enter the name for the new zone and click Next.

7. Select the Create A New File With This Name Or Use This Existing File option. Enter the name of the file and click Next.

8. Click Finish.

Configuring a Caching-Only DNS Server

To configure a caching-only DNS server, perform the following steps:

1. Install DNS as described previously.

2. Do not configure any zones.

3. Ensure that the root servers are configured.

Configuring DNS Forwarders

To configure DNS forwarders, perform the following steps:

1. Select Start|Programs|Administrative Tools|DNS.

2. Navigate to the desired DNS server, right-click it, and choose the Properties option from the pop-up menu.

3. Select the Forwarders tab.

4. Select the Enable Forwarders option.

5. Enter the TCP/IP address of any servers that will act as forwarders for this DNS server.

6. Click OK.

TIP: *If you want the DNS server to only use the configured forwarders, select the Do Not Use Recursion checkbox.*

Removing DNS

To remove DNS, perform the following steps:

1. Select Start|Settings|Control Panel.

2. Double-click the Add/Remove Programs applet.

3. Click Add/Remove Windows Components.

4. When the Windows Component Wizard appears, click Next.

5. Select Networking Services and click Details.

6. Clear the Domain Name System (DNS) checkbox and click OK.

7. Click Next.

8. Click Finish.

DNS Server Management

The following projects detail the various tasks involved in managing a DNS server.

Starting a DNS Server

To start a DNS server, perform the following steps:

1. Select Start|Programs|Administrative Tools|DNS.

2. Navigate to the desired DNS server.

3. Right-click the server, navigate to All Tasks, and choose the Start option.

Starting a DNS Server from the Command Prompt

To start DNS from a command prompt, perform the following steps:

1. Select Start|Programs|Accessories|Command Prompt.

8. Windows 2000 Networking

2. Type the following command:

```
net start dns
```

3. Press Enter.

Stopping a DNS Server

1. Select Start|Programs|Administrative Tools|DNS.

2. Navigate to the desired DNS server.

3. Right-click the server, navigate to All Tasks, and choose the Stop option.

Stopping a DNS Server from the Command Prompt

To stop DNS from the command prompt, perform the following steps:

1. Select Start|Programs|Accessories|Command Prompt.

2. Type the following command:

```
net stop dns
```

3. Press Enter.

Restarting a DNS Server

To restart a DNS server, perform the following steps:

1. Select Start|Programs|Administrative Tools|DNS.

2. Navigate to the desired DNS server.

3. Right-click the server, navigate to All Tasks, and choose the Restart option.

Adding a New DNS Server

To add a new DNS server, perform the following steps:

1. Select Start|Programs|Administrative Tools|DNS.

2. From the Action menu, choose the Connect To Computer option.

3. Select the DNS server to add to the DNS console.

4. Select the Connect To The Specified Computer Now checkbox.

5. Click OK.

Deleting an Existing DNS Server

To delete a DNS server, perform the following steps:

1. Select Start|Programs|Administrative Tools|DNS.

2. Navigate to the server you want to delete.

3. From the Action menu, choose the Delete option.

4. Click OK to delete the server.

Modifying the DNS Boot Sequence

To modify the DNS boot sequence, perform the following steps:

1. Select Start|Programs|Administrative Tools|DNS.

2. Navigate to the server you would like to modify the boot sequence for.

3. Right-click the selected server and choose Properties from the pop-up menu.

4. Select the Advanced tab.

5. From the Load Zone Data on Startup drop-down list, choose one of the following:

   - From Registry
   - From File
   - From Active Directory And Registry

6. Click OK.

TIP: *If you select the From File option, the text file must be named "boot" and must be located in the \winnt\system32\dns folder.*

Working with DNS Zones

The following projects detail managing DNS zones.

Adding a Forward Lookup Zone

To add a forward lookup zone, perform the following steps:

1. Select Start|Programs|Administrative Tools|DNS.

2. Navigate to the Forward Lookup Zones container under the desired server.

3. Right-click the container and select the New Zone option.

4. When the New Zone Wizard appears, click Next.

5. Select the zone type (Active Directory-Integrated, Standard Primary, or Standard Secondary) and click Next.

6. Select the Forward Lookup Zone option and click Next.

8. Windows 2000 Networking

7. Enter the name for the new zone and click Next.

8. Select the Create A New File With This Name Or Use This Existing File option. Enter the name of the file and click Next.

9. Click Finish.

Adding a Reverse Lookup Zone

To add a reverse lookup zone, perform the following steps:

1. Select Start|Programs|Administrative Tools|DNS.

2. Navigate to the Reverse Lookup Zones container under the desired server.

3. Right-click the container and select the New Zone option.

4. When the New Zone Wizard appears, click Next.

5. Select the zone type (Active Directory-Integrated, Standard Primary, or Standard Secondary) and click Next.

6. Select the Reverse Lookup Zone option and click Next.

7. Enter the network ID or the name for the new zone and click Next.

8. Select the Create A New File With This Name Or Use This Existing File option. Enter the name of the file and click Next.

9. Click Finish.

Starting a Zone

To start a zone, perform the following steps:

1. Select Start|Programs|Administrative Tools|DNS.

2. Navigate to the zone to start.

3. Right-click the container and select the Properties option.

4. Click Start on the General tab and click OK.

Pausing a Zone

To pause a zone, perform the following steps:

1. Select Start|Programs|Administrative Tools|DNS.

2. Navigate to the zone to pause.

3. Right-click the container and select the Properties option.

4. Click Pause on the General tab and click OK.

Deleting a Zone

To delete a zone, perform the following steps:

1. Select Start|Programs|Administrative Tools|DNS.

2. Navigate to the zone to delete.

3. Right-click the container and select the Delete option.

4. Click OK to confirm the zone deletion.

Modifying the Zone Type

To modify the zone type, perform the following steps:

1. Select Start|Programs|Administrative Tools|DNS.

2. Navigate to the zone to modify.

3. Right-click the container and select the Properties option.

4. Click Change on the General tab.

5. Select the zone type that's opposite the one currently selected zone and click OK.

Using a Notify List for a Zone

To configure a notify list for a zone, perform the following steps:

1. Select Start|Programs|Administrative Tools|DNS.

2. Navigate to the zone for which you would like to create a notify list.

3. Right-click the container and select the Properties option.

4. Select the Zone Transfers tab.

5. Click Notify.

6. Ensure that the Automatically Notify checkbox is selected.

7. Select the method that's to be used for creating the notify list.

8. Click OK.

Specifying Zone Delegation

To configure zone delegation, perform the following steps:

1. Select Start|Programs|Administrative Tools|DNS.

2. Navigate to the zone for which you would like to specify a zone delegation.

3. Right-click the container and select the New Delegation option.

4. When the New Delegation Wizard appears, click Next.

5. Enter the Delegated Domain name and click Next.

6. Click Add.

7. Browse to the server (by clicking on Browse) or enter an IP address and click Add.

8. Click Next.

9. Click Finish.

Configuring Authoritative Servers for a Zone

To configure an authoritative server for a zone, perform the following steps:

1. Select Start|Programs|Administrative Tools|DNS.

2. Navigate to the zone for which you would like to configure authoritative servers.

3. Right-click the container and select the Properties option.

4. Select the Name Server tab.

5. Click Add.

6. Enter the IP addresses of the DNS servers.

7. Click OK.

Configuring DNS to Work with WINS

To configure DNS to work with WINS, perform the following steps:

1. Select Start|Programs|Administrative Tools|DNS.

2. Navigate to the zone for which you would like to configure WINS.

3. Right-click the container and select the Properties option.

4. Select the WINS tab.

NOTE: *For a reverse lookup zone, select the WINS-R tab.*

---

5. Select the Use WINS Forward Lookup option.

NOTE: *For a reverse lookup zone, select the Use WINS-R Lookup option.*

---

6. Enter the IP address of the WINS server.

7. Click Add.

8. Click OK.

Starting a Zone Transfer at a Secondary DNS Site

To start a zone transfer at a secondary DNS site, perform the following steps:

1. Select Start|Programs|Administrative Tools|DNS.

2. Navigate to the zone to transfer.

3. Right-click the zone object and choose the Transfer From Master option from the pop-up menu.

8. Windows 2000 Networking

Permitting Dynamic Updates

To enable dynamic updates, perform the following steps:

1. Select Start|Programs|Administrative Tools|DNS.

2. Navigate to the zone for which you would like to configure dynamic updates.

3. Right-click the container and select the Properties option.

4. Ensure that the zone type is set to either Active Directory-Integrated or Primary. Choose the Yes option from the Allow Dynamic Updates menu.

5. Click OK.

Using Secure Dynamic Updates

To configure secured dynamic updates, perform the following steps:

1. Select Start|Programs|Administrative Tools|DNS.

2. Navigate to the zone for which you would like to configure secure dynamic updates.

3. Right-click the container and select the Properties option.

4. Ensure that the zone type is set to either Active Directory-Integrated or Primary. Choose the Only Secure Updates option from the Allow Dynamic Updates menu.

5. Click OK.

Disabling Dynamic Updates

To disable dynamic updates, perform the following steps:

1. Select Start|Programs|Administrative Tools|DNS.

2. Navigate to the zone for which you would like to disable dynamic updates.

3. Right-click the container and select the Properties option.

4. Ensure that the zone type is set to either Active Directory-Integrated or Primary. Choose the No option from the Allow Dynamic Updates menu.

5. Click OK.

Changing the Refresh Interval

To change the refresh interval, perform the following steps:

1. Select Start|Programs|Administrative Tools|DNS.

2. Navigate to the zone for which you would like to change the refresh interval.

3. Right-click the container and select the Properties option.

8. Windows 2000 Networking

4. Ensure that the zone type is set to either Active Directory-Integrated or Primary. Click the Start Of Authority (SOA) tab.

5. Modify the Refresh Interval setting as needed and click OK.

Changing the Retry Interval

To change the retry interval, perform the following steps:

1. Select Start|Programs|Administrative Tools|DNS.

2. Navigate to the zone for which you would like to change the retry interval.

3. Right-click the container and select the Properties option.

4. Ensure that the zone type is set to either Active Directory-Integrated or Primary. Click the Start Of Authority (SOA) tab.

5. Modify the Retry Interval setting as needed and click OK.

Changing the Expire Interval

To change the expire interval, perform the following steps:

1. Select Start|Programs|Administrative Tools|DNS.

2. Navigate to the zone for which you would like to change the expire interval.

3. Right-click the container and select the Properties option.

4. Ensure that the zone type is set to either Active Directory-Integrated or Primary. Click the Start Of Authority (SOA) tab.

5. Modify the Expires After Interval setting as needed and click OK.

Changing the Default Time-to-Live

To modify the default time-to-live settings, perform the following steps:

1. Select Start|Programs|Administrative Tools|DNS.

2. Navigate to the zone for which you would like to change the default time-to-live (TTL).

3. Right-click the container and select the Properties option.

4. Ensure that the zone type is set to either Active Directory-Integrated or Primary. Click the Start Of Authority (SOA) tab.

5. Modify the Minimum (Default) TTL Interval setting as needed and click OK.

Changing the Time-to-Live for a Record

To change the TTL for a record, perform the following steps:

1. Select Start|Programs|Administrative Tools|DNS.

2. Navigate to the record for which you would like to change the TTL.

3. Right-click the container and select the Properties option.

4. Ensure that the zone type is set to either Active Directory-Integrated or Primary. Click the Start Of Authority (SOA) tab.

5. Modify the TTL for This Record Interval setting as needed and click OK.

Adding a Host (A) Record

To add a host (A) record, perform the following steps:

1. Select Start|Programs|Administrative Tools|DNS.

2. Navigate to the zone where you would like to add the Host record.

3. Right-click the container and choose New Host from the pop-up menu.

4. Enter a name for the new host.

5. Enter the IP address for the new host.

6. If desired, enter the Pointer record for this host by checking the Create Associated Pointer (PTR) Record checkbox.

7. Click Add Host.

WARNING! *The Pointer record will only be created if the corresponding reverse lookup zone was created.*

Adding an Alias (CNAME) Record

To add an alias (CNAME) record, perform the following steps:

1. Select Start|Programs|Administrative Tools|DNS.

2. Navigate to the zone where you would like to add the Alias record.

3. Right-click the container and choose New Alias from the pop-up menu.

4. Enter a name for the alias.

5. Enter the fully qualified name for the target host (or browse to it).

6. Click OK.

Adding a Mail Exchanger (MX) Record

To add a mail exchanger (MX) record, perform the following steps:

1. Select Start|Programs|Administrative Tools|DNS.

2. Navigate to the zone where you would like to add the Mail Exchanger record.

3. Right-click the container and choose New Mail Exchanger from the pop-up menu.

4. Enter a host or domain name.

5. Enter the name of the mail server (or browse to it).

6. Enter the Mail Server Priority setting.

7. Click OK.

Adding a Domain Record

To add a domain record, perform the following steps:

1. Select Start|Programs|Administrative Tools|DNS.

2. Navigate to the zone where you would like to add the Domain record.

3. Right-click the container and choose New Domain from the pop-up menu.

4. Enter the domain name.

5. Click OK.

Adding a Pointer (PTR) Record

To add a pointer (PTR) record, perform the following steps:

1. Select Start|Programs|Administrative Tools|DNS.

2. Navigate to the reverse lookup zone where you would like to add the Pointer record.

3. Right-click the container and choose New Pointer from the pop-up menu.

4. Enter the remaining node numbers in the IP address.

5. Enter the name of the host (or browse to it).

6. Click OK.

Adding Other Records

To add a other records, perform the following steps:

1. Select Start|Programs|Administrative Tools|DNS.

2. Navigate to the zone where you would like to add the other record.

3. Right-click the container and choose Other New Records from the pop-up menu.

4. Select the desired record type from the Select A Resource Record Type list box and click Create Record.

5. When you're done creating the record, click OK.

8. Windows 2000 Networking

Modifying a Record

To modify a record, perform the following steps:

1. Select Start|Programs|Administrative Tools|DNS.

2. Navigate to the record to modify.

3. Right-click the container and choose Properties from the pop-up menu.

4. Make any desired changes and click OK when done.

Deleting a Record

To delete a record, perform the following steps:

1. Select Start|Programs|Administrative Tools|DNS.

2. Navigate to the record to delete.

3. Right-click the container and choose Delete from the pop-up menu.

4. Click OK to confirm the deletion.

Setting the Aging and Scavenging Properties on a DNS Server

To DNS properties, perform the following steps:

1. Select Start|Programs|Administrative Tools|DNS.

2. Navigate to the server to configure aging and scavenging.

3. Right-click the container and choose Set Aging/Scavenging For All Zones from the pop-up menu.

4. Select the Scavenge Stale Resource Records checkbox.

5. Click OK.

6. Click OK.

Setting the Aging and Scavenging Properties on a Zone

To modify zone properties, perform the following steps:

1. Select Start|Programs|Administrative Tools|DNS.

2. Navigate to the zone to configure aging and scavenging.

8. Windows 2000 Networking

264

3. Right-click the container and choose Properties from the pop-up menu.

4. Click Aging on the General tab.

5. Select the Scavenge Stale Resource Records checkbox.

6. Click OK.

7. Click OK.

Scavenging for Stale Resource Records

To find stale resource records, perform the following steps:

1. Select Start|Programs|Administrative Tools|DNS.

2. Navigate to the server where you would like to scavenge for stale resource records.

3. Right-click the container and choose Scavenge Stale Resource Records from the pop-up menu.

4. Click OK to start the scavenging process.

Working with Servers and DHCP

The following projects detail the various tasks involved in working with DHCP.

Installing DHCP

To install DHCP, perform the following steps:

1. Select Start|Settings|Control Panel.

2. Double-click the Add/Remove Programs applet.

3. Click Add/Remove Windows Components.

4. When the Windows Component Wizard appears, click Next.

5. Select Networking Services and click Details.

6. Select the Dynamic Host Configuration Protocol (DHCP) option and click OK.

7. Click Next.

8. Click Finish.

Starting a DHCP Server

To start a DHCP server, perform the following steps:

1. Select Start|Programs|Administrative Tools|DHCP. The DHCP console will appear, as shown in Figure 8.2.

2. Right-click the server to start and choose All Tasks|Start from the pop-up menu.

Starting a DHCP Server Using the Command Prompt

To start a DHCP server from the command prompt, perform the following steps:

1. Select Start|Programs|Accessories|Command Prompt.

2. Type the following command:

```
net start dhcpserver
```

3. Press Enter.

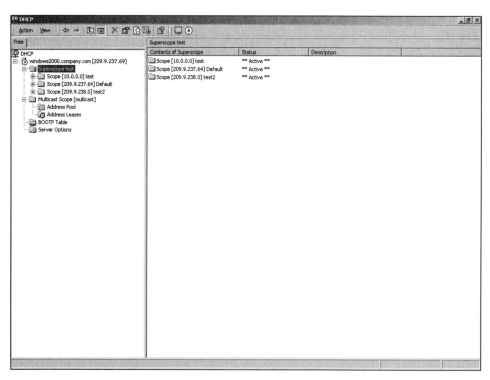

Figure 8.2   The DHCP console.

Stopping a DHCP Server

To stop a DHCP server, perform the following steps:

1. Select Start|Programs|Administrative Tools|DHCP.

2. Right-click the server to stop and choose All Tasks|Stop from the pop-up menu.

Stopping a DHCP Server Using the Command Prompt

To stop a DHCP server from the command line, perform the following steps:

1. Select Start|Programs|Accessories|Command Prompt.

2. Type the following command:

```
net stop dhcpserver
```

3. Press Enter.

Connecting to a DHCP Server

To connect to a DHCP server, perform the following steps:

1. Select Start|Programs|Administrative Tools|DHCP.

2. Navigate to the DHCP container.

3. Right-click the container and choose Add Server from the pop-up menu. The Add Server window appears.

4. Select either this server or another DHCP server that has been authorized.

5. Click OK.

Deleting a DHCP Server

To delete DHCP server, perform the following steps:

1. Select Start|Programs|Administrative Tools|DHCP.

2. Select the server from which to disconnect.

3. Right-click the server and choose Delete from the pop-up menu.

4. Click Yes to confirm the server's deletion.

Repairing the DHCP Database

To repair the DHCP database, perform the following steps:

1. Select Start|Programs|Administrative Tools|DHCP.

2. Navigate to the server whose database you would like to repair.

8. Windows 2000
Networking

3. Right-click the server and choose Reconcile All Scopes from the pop-up menu.

4. Click Verify.

5. If the database checks out properly, click OK.

6. Click Cancel.

Repairing the DHCP Database Manually

To repair the DHCP database manually, perform the following steps:

1. Select Start|Programs|Accessories|Command Prompt.

2. Stop the DHCP server by typing "net stop dhcpserver" and pressing Enter.

3. Type "cd %systemroot%\system32\dhcp" and press Enter.

4. Type "jetpack dhcp.mdb tmp.mdb" and press Enter.

5. Start the DHCP server by typing "net start dhcpserver" and pressing Enter.

Managing DHCP Servers

The following projects detail the various tasks involved in working with DHCP servers.

Authorizing a DHCP Server in Active Directory

To authorize a DHCP server in AD, perform the following steps:

1. Select Start|Programs|Administrative Tools|DHCP.

2. Navigate to the server to authorize in Active Directory.

3. Right-click the server object and choose Authorize from the pop-up menu.

Unauthorizing a DHCP Server in Active Directory

To authorize a DHCP server in AD, perform the following steps:

1. Select Start|Programs|Administrative Tools|DHCP.

2. Right-click the DHCP container and choose Manage Authorized Servers from the pop-up list.

3. Select the server to unauthorize and click Unauthorize.

4. Click Close.

Working with DHCP Scopes

The following projects detail the tasks involved in managing DHCP scopes.

Creating a New Scope

To create a DHCP scope, perform the following steps:

1. Select Start|Programs|Administrative Tools|DHCP.

2. Navigate to the server where you would like the new scope created.

3. Right-click the server and choose the New Scope option. The New Scope Wizard appears.

4. Click Next.

5. Enter a name and an optional description for the scope.

6. Enter the start and end TCP/IP addresses.

7. Enter either the subnet mask or the subnet length and click Next.

8. If you want to exclude any addresses, enter the start and end IP addresses and click Add.

TIP: *If you want to enter a single IP address, enter the same address in both the Start and End fields.*

---

9. Click Next.

10. Set the duration for the DHCP lease and click Next.

11. If you would like to configure any DHCP options, select the Yes, I Want To Configure These Options Now radio button and click Next. Otherwise, select the No, I Will Configure These Options Later radio button and click Next.

12. Click Finish.

Deleting a Scope

To delete a DHCP scope, perform the following steps:

1. Select Start|Programs|Administrative Tools|DHCP.

2. Navigate to the server where you would like the new scope deleted.

3. Right-click the scope and choose Delete from the pop-up menu.

4. Click Yes to confirm the scope deletion.

Activating a Scope

To activate a DHCP scope, perform the following steps:

1. Select Start|Programs|Administrative Tools|DHCP.

8. Windows 2000 Networking

2. Navigate to the scope to activate.

3. Right-click the scope and choose the Activate option from the pop-up menu.

Deactivating a Scope

To deactivate a DHCP scope, perform the following steps:

1. Select Start|Programs|Administrative Tools|DHCP.

2. Navigate to the scope to deactivate.

3. Right-click the scope and choose Deactivate from the pop-up menu.

4. Click Yes to confirm the deactivation.

Modifying a Scope's Properties

To modify DHCP scope properties, perform the following steps:

1. Select Start|Programs|Administrative Tools|DHCP.

2. Navigate to the scope whose properties you would like to modify.

3. Right-click the scope and choose Properties from the pop-up menu.

4. Modify any desired properties and click OK when done.

Excluding TCP/IP Addresses from a Scope

To exclude IP addresses form a scope, perform the following steps:

1. Select Start|Programs|Administrative Tools|DHCP.

2. Navigate to the Address Pool container in the scope from which you would like to exclude IP addresses.

3. Right-click Address Pool and choose New Exclusion Range from the pop-up menu.

4. Click Add.

5. Repeat this process for any other addresses that need to be excluded and click Close when done.

Modifying a Scope's Duration

To modify a DHCP scope's duration, perform the following steps:

1. Select Start|Programs|Administrative Tools|DHCP.

2. Navigate to the scope for which you would like to modify the duration properties.

3. Right-click the scope and choose Properties from the pop-up menu.

4. Modify the Lease Duration for DHCP Clients section of the General tab.

5. Click OK.

Reconciling a Scope

To reconcile a scope, perform the following steps:

1. Select Start|Programs|Administrative Tools|DHCP.

2. Navigate to the scope to reconcile.

3. Right-click the scope and choose Reconcile from the pop-up menu.

4. Click Verify.

5. Click OK.

6. Click Cancel.

Working with DHCP Superscopes

The following projects detail the various tasks involved in working with DHCP superscopes.

Creating a Superscope

To create a superscope, perform the following steps:

1. Select Start|Programs|Administrative Tools|DHCP.

2. Select the server where you would like the superscope to be created.

3. Right-click the server and choose New Superscope from the pop-up menu.

4. When the New Superscope Wizard appears, click Next.

5. Enter the name of the superscope and click Next.

6. Select two or more scopes from the Available Scopes section of the wizard and click Next.

TIP: *Select multiple scopes by either Ctrl + clicking or Shift + clicking.*

7. Click Finish.

Deleting a Superscope

To delete a superscope, perform the following steps:

1. Select Start|Programs|Administrative Tools|DHCP.
2. Select the superscope to delete.
3. Right-click the superscope and choose Delete from the pop-up menu.
4. Click Yes to confirm the deletion.

Activating a Superscope

To activate a superscope, perform the following steps:

1. Select Start|Programs|Administrative Tools|DHCP.
2. Select the superscope you would like to activate.
3. Right-click the superscope and choose Activate from the pop-up menu.

Deactivating a Superscope

To deactivate a superscope, perform the following steps:

1. Select Start|Programs|Administrative Tools|DHCP.
2. Select the superscope you would like to deactivate.
3. Right-click the superscope and choose Deactivate from the pop-up menu.

Adding an Existing Scope to a Superscope

To add an existing scope to a superscope, perform the following steps:

1. Select Start|Programs|Administrative Tools|DHCP.
2. Select the scope to add to the superscope.
3. Right-click the scope and choose the Add To Superscope option.
4. Choose the superscope to which you would like this scope added and click OK.

Working with DHCP Multicast Scopes

The following projects detail the various tasks involved in working with DHCP multicast scopes.

Creating a Multicast Scope

To create a muticast scope, perform the following steps:

1. Select Start|Programs|Administrative Tools|DHCP.

8. Windows 2000 Networking

2. Select the server where you would like the multicast scope to be created.

3. Right-click the server and choose New Multicast from the pop-up menu.

4. The New Multicast Scope Wizard window appears, click Next.

5. Enter a name for the new multicast scope and an optional description and click Next.

6. Enter a starting and ending IP address for the multicast scope and a TTL, and click Next.

NOTE: *A multicast address ranges from 224.0.0.0 to 239.255.255.255.*

---

7. If you want to exclude any addresses, enter the start and end IP addresses and click Add.

8. Click Next.

9. Set the duration for the multicast scope lease and click Next.

10. If you would like to activate the multicast now, select the Yes radio button and click Next. Otherwise, select the No radio button and click Next.

11. Click Finish

Deleting a Multicast Scope

To delete a muticast scope, perform the following steps:

1. Select Start|Programs|Administrative Tools|DHCP.

2. Select the multicast scope to delete.

3. Right-click the multicast scope and choose Delete from the pop-up menu.

4. Click Yes to confirm the deletion.

Setting a Multicast Scope TTL

To set a muticast scope TTL, perform the following steps:

1. Select Start|Programs|Administrative Tools|DHCP.

2. Select the multicast scope for which you would like to modify the TTL.

3. Right-click the multicast scope and choose Properties from the pop-up menu.

4. Select the Lifetime tab.

5. Modify the TTL for the multicast scope and click OK.

8. Windows 2000 Networking

Configuring DHCP Options

The following projects detail the various tasks involved with configuring DHCP.

Configuring a Server-Based Option

To configure a server-based option, perform the following steps:

1. Select Start|Programs|Administrative Tools|DHCP.

2. Navigate to the Server Options container under the server where you would like to configure a new option.

3. Right-click the container and choose the Configure Options option.

4. Select any desired options in the Available Options list.

5. Enter any desired information about the selected options in the Data Entry field.

6. Repeat these steps for any additional server options you desire.

7. Click OK.

Configuring a Scope-Based Option

To configure a scope-based option, perform the following steps:

1. Select Start|Programs|Administrative Tools|DHCP.

2. Navigate to the Scope Options container under the scope for which you would like to configure a new option.

3. Right-click the container and choose the Configure Options option.

4. Select any desired options in the Available Options list.

5. Enter any desired information about the selected options in the Data Entry field.

6. Repeat these steps for any additional scope options you desire.

7. Click OK.

Creating a New Option

To create a new option, perform the following steps:

1. Select Start|Programs|Administrative Tools|DHCP.

2. Navigate to the server where you would like to create the new option.

3. Right-click the server and choose Set Predefined Options from the pop-up menu.

4. When the Predefined Options and Values window appears, click Add.

8. Windows 2000 Networking

5. Enter all the appropriate information in the Option Type window and click OK.

6. Click OK.

Deleting an Option

To delete an option, perform the following steps:

1. Select Start|Programs|Administrative Tools|DHCP.

2. Navigate to the server where you would like to delete an option.

3. Right-click the server and choose Set Predefined Options from the pop-up menu.

4. When the Predefined Options and Values window appears, select the option to delete and click Delete.

5. Click OK.

Modifying an Option

To modify an option, perform the following steps:

1. Select Start|Programs|Administrative Tools|DHCP.

2. Navigate to the server where you would like to modify an option.

3. Right-click the server and choose Set Predefined Options from the pop-up menu.

4. When the Predefined Options and Values window appears, select the option to modify and click Edit.

5. Enter all the appropriate information in the Option Type window and click OK.

6. Click OK.

Working with Leases

The following projects detail the various tasks involved in working with DHCP leases.

Viewing a Client Lease

To view a client lease, perform the following steps:

1. Select Start|Programs|Administrative Tools|DHCP.

2. Navigate to the Address Lease container under the desired server and zone.

3. Double-click the desired client lease in the view pane (the right pane) of the DHCP console.

Verifying a Client Lease

To verify a client lease, perform the following steps:

1. On the client computer, select Start|Programs|Accessories|Command Prompt.

2. Type "ipconfig /all" and press Enter.

3. The lease information will be listed.

Terminating a Client Lease

To terminate a client lease, perform the following steps:

1. On the client computer, select Start|Programs|Accessories|Command Prompt.

2. Type "ipconfig /release" and press Enter.

3. The client lease in now released.

Renewing a Client Lease

To renew a client lease, perform the following steps:

1. On the client computer, select Start|Programs|Accessories|Command Prompt.

2. Type "ipconfig /renew" and press Enter.

3. The client will now terminate the lease and then immediately renew it.

Configuring DHCP Reservations

The following projects detail the various tasks involved in working with DHCP reservations.

Adding a Reservation

To add a reservation, perform the following steps:

1. Select Start|Programs|Administrative Tools|DHCP.

2. Navigate to the Reservations container under the server and zone where you would like to add a reservation.

3. Right-click and choose New Reservation from the pop-up menu.

4. Enter a name for the reservation, the IP address that's to be reserved, the MAC address for the reserved system, and a description.

5. Select the reservation type: Both, DHCP Only, or BOOTP Only.

6. Click Add.

7. Repeat this process for any other reservations you desire. Click Close when done.

Modifying a Reservation

To modify a reservation, perform the following steps:

1. Select Start|Programs|Administrative Tools|DHCP.

2. Navigate to the Reservations container under the server and zone where you would like to modify the reservation.

3. Select the desired reservation.

4. Right-click the reservation and choose Properties from the pop-up menu.

5. Make any desired changes and click OK when done.

Configuring Options for a Reservation

To configure options for a reservation, perform the following steps:

1. Select Start|Programs|Administrative Tools|DHCP.

2. Navigate to the Reservations container under the server and zone where you would like to configure options for the reservation.

3. Select the desired reservation.

4. Right-click the reservation and choose Configure Options from the pop-up menu.

5. Configure any desired options and click OK when done.

Monitoring DHCP

The following projects detail the various tasks involved in monitoring DHCP.

Enabling Logging

To enable logging, perform the following steps:

1. Select Start|Programs|Administrative Tools|DHCP.

2. Navigate to the server where you would like to enable logging.

3. Right-click the server and select Properties from the pop-up menu.

4. Select the Enable DHCP Audit Logging checkbox on the General tab and click OK.

8. Windows 2000 Networking

Viewing Server Statistics

To view server statistics, perform the following steps:

1. Select Start|Programs|Administrative Tools|DHCP.

2. Navigate to the server for which you would like to view statistics.

3. Right-click the server and choose Display Statistics from the pop-up menu.

4. Click Close when done.

Viewing Server Properties

To view server properties, perform the following steps:

1. Select Start|Programs|Administrative Tools|DHCP.

2. Navigate to the server whose properties you would like to view.

3. Right-click the server and choose Properties from the pop-up menu.

4. The server properties will be displayed. Click OK when done.

Enabling Address Conflict Detection

To enable address conflict detection, perform the following steps:

1. Select Start|Programs|Administrative Tools|DHCP.

2. Navigate to the server where you would like to enable address conflict detection.

3. Right-click the server and choose Properties from the pop-up menu.

4. Select the Advanced tab.

5. Increase the Conflict Detection Attempts setting to a number higher than zero and click OK.

Refreshing Server Statistics

To refresh server statistics, perform the following steps:

1. Select Start|Programs|Administrative Tools|DHCP.

2. Navigate to the server where you would like to refresh the server statistics.

3. Right-click the server and choose Display Statistics from the pop-up menu.

4. Click Refresh.

5. Click Close when done.

8. Windows 2000 Networking

Working with WINS Servers

The following projects detail the various tasks involved in working with WINS.

Installing a WINS Server

To install a WINS server, perform the following steps:

1. Select Start|Settings|Control Panel.

2. Double-click the Add/Remove Programs applet.

3. Click Add/Remove Windows Components.

4. When the Windows Component Wizard appears, click Next.

5. Select Networking Services and click Details.

6. Select the Windows Internet Naming System (WINS) option and click OK.

7. Click Next.

8. Click Finish.

Starting a WINS Server

To start a WINS server, perform the following steps:

1. Select Start|Programs|Administrative Tools|WINS. The WINS console will appear, as shown in Figure 8.3.

2. Navigate to the desired WINS server.

3. Right-click the server, navigate to All Tasks, and choose the Start option.

Starting a WINS Server Using the Command Prompt

To start a WINS server from the command prompt, perform the following steps:

1. Select Start|Programs|Accessories|Command Prompt.

2. Type the following command:

```
net start wins
```

3. Press Enter.

Stopping a WINS Server

To stop a WINS server, perform the following steps:

1. Select Start|Programs|Administrative Tools|WINS.

2. Navigate to the desired WINS server.

3. Right-click the server, navigate to All Tasks, and choose the Stop option.

8. Windows 2000
Networking

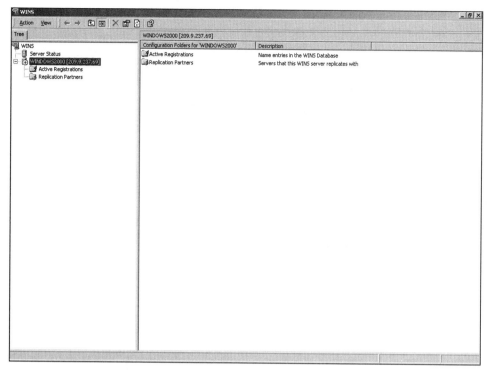

Figure 8.3   The WINS Console.

Stopping a WINS Server Using the Command Prompt

To stop a WINS server from the command prompt, perform the following steps:

1. Select Start|Programs|Accessories|Command Prompt.

2. Type the following command:

```
net stop wins
```

3. Press Enter.

Adding a WINS Server

To add a WINS server, perform the following steps:

1. Select Start|Programs|Administrative Tools|WINS.

2. Right-click the WINS container and choose Add Server from the pop-up menu.

3. Enter the name of the WINS server to add to the console or browse to it and click OK.

Deleting a WINS Server

To delete a WINS server, perform the following steps:

1. Select Start|Programs|Administrative Tools|WINS.

2. Navigate to the server to be deleted.

3. Right-click the server and choose Delete from the pop-up menu.

4. Click Yes to confirm the deletion.

Changing Backup Settings

To change backup settings, perform the following steps:

1. Select Start|Programs|Administrative Tools|WINS.

2. Navigate to the server for which you would like to modify the backup settings.

3. Right-click the server and choose Properties from the pop-up menu.

4. In the Database Backup section, make any necessary changes to the backup configuration and click OK when done.

Changing the Renew Interval

To change the renew interval, perform the following steps:

1. Select Start|Programs|Administrative Tools|WINS.

2. Navigate to the server for which you would like to change the renew interval.

3. Right-click the server and choose Properties from the pop-up menu.

4. Select the Intervals tab.

5. Modify the renew interval as desired.

6. Click OK.

Changing the Extinction Interval

To change the extinction interval, perform the following steps:

1. Select Start|Programs|Administrative Tools|WINS.

2. Navigate to the server for which you would like to change the extinction interval.

3. Right-click the server and choose Properties from the pop-up menu.

4. Select the Intervals tab.

5. Modify the extinction interval as desired.

6. Click OK.

Changing the Extinction Timeout

To change the extinction timeout, perform the following steps:

1. Select Start|Programs|Administrative Tools|WINS.

2. Navigate to the server for which you would like to change the extinction timeout interval.

3. Right-click the server and choose Properties from the pop-up menu.

4. Select the Intervals tab.

5. Modify the extinction timeout as desired.

6. Click OK.

Changing the Verification Interval

To change the verification interval, perform the following steps:

1. Select Start|Programs|Administrative Tools|WINS.

2. Navigate to the server for which you would like to change the verification interval.

3. Right-click the server and choose Properties from the pop-up menu.

4. Select the Intervals tab.

5. Modify the verification interval as desired.

6. Click OK.

Configuring the Logging Properties

To configure logging properties, perform the following steps:

1. Select Start|Programs|Administrative Tools|WINS.

2. Navigate to the server for which you would like to configure logging.

3. Right-click the server and choose Properties from the pop-up menu.

4. Select the Advanced tab.

5. Check the Log Detailed Events To Windows Event Log checkbox.

6. Click OK.

Specifying the WINS Database Path

To specify the WINS database path, perform the following steps:

1. Select Start|Programs|Administrative Tools|WINS.

2. Navigate to the server for which you would like to configure the WINS database.

3. Right-click the server and choose Properties from the pop-up menu.

4. Select the Advanced tab.

5. Enter the desired path in the Database Path field.

TIP: *Instead of entering the drive letter and system directory (for example, C:\WINNT), you can use %windir% instead. This is a variable that maps to whichever system directory is created.*

---

6. Click OK.

Viewing the WINS Server Statistics

To view WINS server statistics, perform the following steps:

1. Select Start|Programs|Administrative Tools|WINS.

2. Navigate to the server for which you would like to view the server statistics.

3. Right-click the server and choose Display Server Statistics from the pop-up menu.

4. Click Close when done.

Refreshing the WINS Server Statistics

To refresh WINS server statistics, perform the following steps:

1. Select Start|Programs|Administrative Tools|WINS.

2. Navigate to the server for which you would like to refresh the server statistics.

3. Right-click the server and choose Display Server Statistics from the pop-up menu.

4. Click Refresh.

5. Click Close when done.

Resetting the WINS Server Statistics

To reset WINS server statistics, perform the following steps:

1. Select Start|Programs|Administrative Tools|WINS.

2. Navigate to the server for which you would like to view the server statistics.

3. Right-click the server and choose Display Server Statistics from the pop-up menu.

4. Click Refresh.

5. Click Close when done.

8. Windows 2000 Networking

Viewing WINS Information

The following projects detail the various tasks involved in viewing WINS information.

Viewing a WINS Record's Properties

To view a WINS record's properties, perform the following steps:

1. Select Start|Programs|Administrative Tools|WINS.
2. Navigate to the Active Registrations container under the server for which you would like to view a record.
3. In the right pane, right-click the desired record and choose Properties from the pop-up menu.
4. Click OK.

Filtering the WINS Database

To filter the WINS database, perform the following steps:

1. Select Start|Programs|Administrative Tools|WINS.
2. Navigate to the server for which you would like to filter records.
3. Right-click the server and choose Find By Owner from the pop-up menu.
4. Select the Record Types tab.
5. Clear the checkbox for any record type you would like to exclude from the view.
6. Click Find Now.

Adding a Filter

To add a filter, perform the following steps:

1. Select Start|Programs|Administrative Tools|WINS.
2. Navigate to the server to add a filter to.
3. Right-click the server and choose Find By Owner from the pop-up menu.
4. Select the Record Types tab.
5. Click Add.
6. Enter the ID and description for the new filter.
7. Click OK.
8. Repeat Steps 4–7 if necessary and click Find Now when done.

Deleting a Filter

To delete a filter, perform the following steps:

1. Select Start|Programs|Administrative Tools|WINS.

2. Navigate to the server from which you would like to delete a filter.

3. Right-click the server and choose Find By Owner from the pop-up menu.

4. Select the Record Types tab.

5. Select the record to delete.

WARNING! *You can only delete records that you have created.*

6. Click Delete.

7. Click Yes to confirm the record deletion.

8. Click Find Now.

Modifying a Filter

To modify a filter, perform the following steps:

1. Select Start|Programs|Administrative Tools|WINS.

2. Navigate to the server for which you would like to modify a filter.

3. Right-click the server and choose Find By Owner from the pop-up menu.

4. Select the Record Types tab.

5. Select the record to modify.

WARNING! *You can only modify records that you have created.*

6. Click Edit.

7. Modify the description of the record.

8. Click OK.

9. Click Find Now.

Clearing the Filters

To clear a filter, perform the following steps:

1. Select Start|Programs|Administrative Tools|WINS.

2. Navigate to the server to which you would like to add a filter.

3. Right-click the server and choose Find By Owner from the pop-up menu.

4. Select the Record Types tab.

5. Click Clear All.

6. Click OK.

Setting Up and Managing WINS Replication

The following projects detail the various tasks involved with setting up and managing WINS replication.

Adding a Replication Partner

To add a replication partner, perform the following steps:

1. Select Start|Programs|Administrative Tools|WINS.
2. Navigate to the Replication Partners container of the server.
3. Right-click the container and choose New Replication Partner from the pop-up menu.
4. Enter the name or IP address of the replication partner computer or browse to it.
5. Click OK.

Deleting a Replication Partner

To delete a replication partner, perform the following steps:

1. Select Start|Programs|Administrative Tools|WINS.
2. Navigate to the Replication Partners container of the server.
3. Select the replication partner to delete from the right pane, right-click it, and choose Delete from the pop-up menu.
4. Click Yes to confirm the deletion.

Configuring a Push Partner

To configure a push partner, perform the following steps:

1. Select Start|Programs|Administrative Tools|WINS.
2. Navigate to the Replication Partners container of the server.
3. Right-click the container and choose Properties from the pop-up menu.
4. Select the Push Replication tab.
5. Make any desired modifications and click OK.

Configuring a Pull Partner

To configure a pull partner, perform the following steps:

1. Select Start|Programs|Administrative Tools|WINS.
2. Navigate to the Replication Partners container of the server.
3. Right-click the container and choose Properties from the pop-up menu.

4. Select the Pull Replication tab.

5. Make any desired modifications and click OK.

Starting Replication

To start replication, perform the following steps:

1. Select Start|Programs|Administrative Tools|WINS.

2. Navigate to the Replication Partners container of the server.

3. Right-click the container and choose Replicate Now from the pop-up menu.

4. Click Yes to confirm the replication.

Adding a Static Mapping

To add static mapping, perform the following steps:

1. Select Start|Programs|Administrative Tools|WINS.

2. Navigate to the Active Registrations container of the server.

3. Right-click the container and select New Static Mapping from the pop-up menu.

4. Enter the computer name, an optional NetBIOS scope, a mapping type (choose from Unique, Group, Domain Name, Internet, or Multihomed), and an IP address.

5. Click OK.

Modifying a Static Mapping

To modify static mapping, perform the following steps:

1. Select Start|Programs|Administrative Tools|WINS.

2. Navigate to the Replication Partners container of the server.

3. Select the static mapping to modify.

4. Right-click it and choose Properties from the pop-up menu.

5. Modify the IP address of the mapping and click OK.

Importing Static Mappings

To import static mappings, perform the following steps:

1. Select Start|Programs|Administrative Tools|WINS.

2. Navigate to the Replication Partners container of the server.

3. Right-click the container and choose Import LMHOSTS File from the pop-up menu.

8. Windows 2000
Networking

4. Navigate to the location of the LMHOSTS file and click Open.

5. Click OK when done.

Backing Up the WINS Database

To back up the WINS database, perform the following steps:

1. Select Start|Programs|Administrative Tools|WINS.

2. Navigate to the server whose database to back up.

3. Right-click the server and choose Backup Database from the pop-up menu.

4. Navigate to the desired backup location and click OK.

5. Click OK.

Restoring the WINS Database

To restore the WINS database, perform the following steps:

1. Select Start|Programs|Administrative Tools|WINS.

2. Navigate to the server whose database to restore.

3. Right-click the server and choose the All Tasks|Stop option. This will stop the WINS service.

4. Right-click the server and choose Restore Database from the pop-up menu.

5. Navigate to the location of the backup and click OK.

6. The database will be restored and WINS will automatically be started. Click OK when done.

Scavenging the WINS Database

To scavenge the WINS database, perform the following steps:

1. Select Start|Programs|Administrative Tools|WINS.

2. Navigate to the server to scavenge.

3. Right-click the server and choose Scavenge Database from the pop-up menu.

4. Click OK.

5. Any errors will be logged in the Event Viewer.

Working with Internet Information Services

The following projects detail the various tasks involved with managing IIS.

Installing the IIS Service

To install IIS, perform the following steps:

1. Select Start|Settings|Control Panel.

2. Double-click the Add/Remove Programs applet.

3. Click Add/Remove Windows Components.

4. When the Windows Component Wizard appears, click Next.

5. Select Internet Information Services (IIS) and click Next.

6. Click Finish.

Starting the IIS Service

To start IIS, perform the following steps:

1. Select Start|Programs|Administrative Tools|Internet Services Manager.

2. The IIS console will appear, as shown in Figure 8.4. Right-click the server where you would like to start the IIS Service and choose the Restart IIS option from the pop-up menu.

3. Select the Start Internet Services on *Servername* option from the drop-down list and click OK.

Starting the IIS Service Using the Command Prompt

To start IIS from the command prompt, perform the following steps:

1. Select Start|Programs|Accessories|Command Prompt.

2. Type the following command:

```
net start w3svc
```

3. Press Enter.

Stopping the IIS Service

To stop IIS, perform the following steps:

1. Select Start|Programs|Administrative Tools|Internet Services Manager.

2. The IIS console will appear. Right-click the server where you would like to stop the IIS Service and choose Restart IIS from the pop-up menu.

8. Windows 2000 Networking

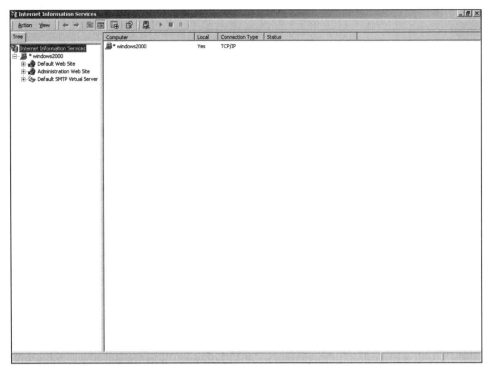

Figure 8.4   The Internet Information Services console.

3. Select the Start Internet Services on *Servername* option from the drop-down list and click OK.

4. The console will wait 30 seconds before shutting the service down. If you would like this done immediately, click End Now.

Stopping the IIS Service Using the Command Prompt

To stop IIS from the command prompt, perform the following steps:

1. Select Start|Programs|Accessories|Command Prompt.

2. Type the following command:

```
net stop w3svc
```

3. Press Enter.

Creating a New Web Site

To create a new Web site, perform the following steps:

1. Select Start|Programs|Administrative Tools|Internet Services Manager.

2. Navigate to the server where you would like a new Web site created.

3. Right-click the server and choose the New|Web Site option from the pop-up menu.

4. When the Web Site Creation Wizard appears, click Next.

5. Enter a description for the new Web site and click Next.

6. Enter the IP address, the port, and the host header for this site and click Next.

7. Select a path for the new Web site.

8. If you would like anonymous access to be allowed for this site, check the Allow Anonymous Access To This Web Site checkbox and click Next.

9. Specify the allowed permissions for this Web site and click Next.

10. Click Finish.

Modifying a Web Site

To modify a new Web site, perform the following steps:

1. Select Start|Programs|Administrative Tools|Internet Services Manager.

2. Navigate to the Web site to modify.

3. Right-click the Web site and choose Properties from the pop-up menu.

4. Make any necessary modifications to the site and click OK when done.

Deleting a Web Site

To delete a Web site, perform the following steps:

1. Select Start|Programs|Administrative Tools|Internet Services Manager.

2. Navigate to the Web site to delete.

3. Right-click the Web site and choose Delete from the pop-up menu.

4. Click Yes to confirm the deletion.

Starting a Web Site

To start a Web site, perform the following steps:

1. Select Start|Programs|Administrative Tools|Internet Services Manager.

2. Navigate to the Web site to start.

3. Right-click the Web site and choose Start from the pop-up menu.

Stopping a Web Site

To stop a Web site, perform the following steps:

1. Select Start|Programs|Administrative Tools|Internet Services Manager.

8. Windows 2000 Networking

2. Navigate to the Web site to stop.

3. Right-click the Web site and choose Stop from the pop-up menu.

Changing the Web Port

To change a Web port, perform the following steps:

1. Select Start|Programs|Administrative Tools|Internet Services Manager.

2. Navigate to the Web site for which you would like to change the port.

3. Right-click the Web site and choose Properties from the pop-up menu.

4. On the Web Site tab, modify the TCP Port value (the default is 80).

5. Click OK.

Using the Administration Web Site

To use the administration Web site, perform the following steps:

1. Select Start|Programs|Administrative Tools|Internet Services Manager.

2. Navigate to the Administration Web Site container.

3. Right-click the container and choose Properties from the pop-up menu.

4. Note the value of the TCP port.

5. Close the IIS console.

6. Start Internet Explorer.

7. In the Address field enter **http://localhost:*portnumber*/** and press Enter

8. The IIS Administration site will appear, as shown in Figure 8.5.

Changing the Administration Web Site Port

To change the administration Web site port, perform the following steps:

1. Select Start|Programs|Administrative Tools|Internet Services Manager.

2. Navigate to the Administration Web Site container.

3. Right-click the container and choose Properties from the pop-up menu.

4. Modify the TCP Port setting and click OK.

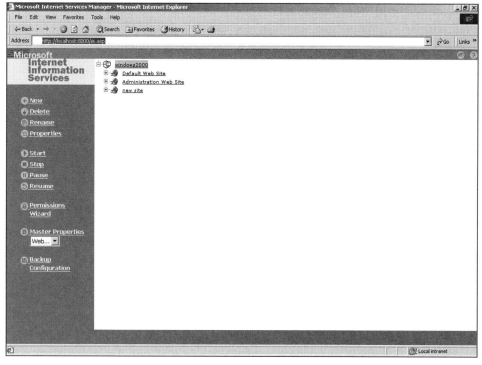

Figure 8.5   The IIS Administration Web site.

Working with the File Transfer Protocol Service

The following projects detail the various tasks involved with managing FTP.

Installing the FTP Service

To install FTP, perform the following steps:

1. Select Start|Settings|Control Panel.
2. Double-click the Add/Remove Programs applet.
3. Click Add/Remove Windows Components.
4. When the Windows Component Wizard appears, click Next.
5. Select Internet Information Server and click Details.
6. Select the File Transfer Protocol (FTP) Server option and click OK.
7. Click Next.
8. Click Finish.

Starting the FTP Service

To start the FTP service, perform the following steps:

1. Select Start|Programs|Administrative Tools|Services.

2. Select the FTP Publishing Service item, right-click it, and choose the Start option.

Starting the FTP Service Using the Command Prompt

To start the FTP service from the command prompt, perform the following steps:

1. Select Start|Programs|Accessories|Command Prompt.

2. Type the following command:

```
net start msftpsvc
```

3. Press Enter.

Stopping the FTP Service

To stop the FTP service, perform the following steps:

1. Select Start|Programs|Administrative Tools|Services.

2. Select the FTP Publishing Service item, right-click it, and choose the Stop option.

Stopping the FTP Service Using the Command Prompt

To stop the FTP service from the command prompt, perform the following steps:

1. Select Start|Programs|Accessories|Command Prompt.

2. Type the following command:

```
net stop msftpsvc
```

3. Press Enter.

Creating a New FTP Site

To create a new FTP site, perform the following steps:

1. Select Start|Programs|Administrative Tools|Internet Services Manager.

2. Navigate to the server where you would like a new FTP site created.

3. Right-click the server and choose the New|FTP Site option from the pop-up menu.

4. When the New FTP Site Creation Wizard appears, click Next.

8. Windows 2000 Networking

5. Enter a description for the new FTP site and click Next.

6. Enter the IP address and the TCP port for this site and click Next.

7. Select a path for the new FTP site.

8. Specify the allowed permissions for this FTP site and click Next.

9. Click Finish.

Modifying an FTP Site

To modify an FTP site, perform the following steps:

1. Select Start|Programs|Administrative Tools|Internet Services Manager.

2. Navigate to the FTP site you would like to modify.

3. Right-click the FTP site and choose Properties from the pop-up menu.

4. Make any necessary modifications to the site and click OK when done.

Deleting an FTP Site

To delete an FTP site, perform the following steps:

1. Select Start|Programs|Administrative Tools|Internet Services Manager.

2. Navigate to the FTP site to delete.

3. Right-click the FTP site and choose Delete from the pop-up menu.

4. Click Yes to confirm the deletion.

Starting an FTP Site

To start an FTP site, perform the following steps:

1. Select Start|Programs|Administrative Tools|Internet Services Manager.

2. Navigate to the FTP site to start.

3. Right-click the FTP site and choose Start from the pop-up menu.

Stopping an FTP Site

To stop an FTP site, perform the following steps:

1. Select Start|Programs|Administrative Tools|Internet Services Manager.

2. Navigate to the FTP site to stop.

3. Right-click the FTP site and choose Stop from the pop-up menu.

Changing the FTP Port

To change the FTP port, perform the following steps:

1. Select Start|Programs|Administrative Tools|Internet Services Manager.

2. Navigate to the FTP site for which you would like to change the port.

8. Windows 2000 Networking

3. Right-click the FTP site and choose Properties from the pop-up menu.

4. On the FTP Site tab, modify the TCP Port value (the default is 21).

5. Click OK.

Working with Routers

The following projects detail the various tasks involved with routes.

Viewing the Routing Table

To view the routing table, perform the following steps:

1. Select Start|Programs|Accessories|Command Prompt.

2. Type the following command:

```
route print
```

3. Press Enter. A screen similar to the one shown in Figure 8.6 appears.

Adding a Static Route

To add a static route, perform the following steps:

1. Select Start|Programs|Accessories|Command Prompt.

2. Type the following command:

```
route add destination mask netmask gateway metric metric IF interface
```

3. Press Enter.

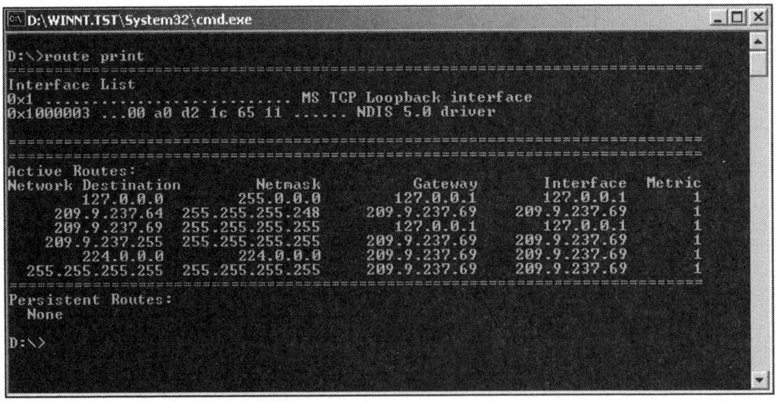

Figure 8.6   The routing table.

8. Windows 2000 Networking

> **NOTE:** *For example, if you wanted to create a static route to the 192.168.0.0 network with a subnet mask of 255.255.0.0, a gateway of 192.168.1.1, and a metric of 1, you can type in the following:*
> **Route add 192.168.0.0 mask 255.255.0.0 192.168.1.1 metric 1**

Deleting a Static Route

To delete a static route, perform the following steps:

1. Select Start|Programs|Accessories|Command Prompt.

2. Type the following command:

   ```
   route add destination mask netmask gateway metric metric IF interface
   ```

3. Press Enter.

> **NOTE:** *If you were to delete the route created in the previous example, you would type in the following command:*
> **Route delete 192.168.0.0**

Working with Routing Protocols

The following projects detail the various tasks involved with managing routing protocols.

Installing the Routing And Remote Access Service

To install RRAS, perform the following steps:

1. Select Start|Programs|Administrative Tools|Routing And Remote Access.

2. In the Routing And Remote Access console, shown in Figure 8.7, right-click the Routing And Remote Access container and choose the Add Server option from the pop-up menu.

3. Right-click the newly added server and choose the Configure And Enable Routing And Remote Access option.

4. When the Routing And Remote Access Server Setup Wizard appears, click Next.

5. Select the desired configuration for the server (this example uses the Manually Configured Server option). Click Next.

6. Click Finish.

7. Click Yes to start the RRAS Service.

8. Windows 2000 Networking

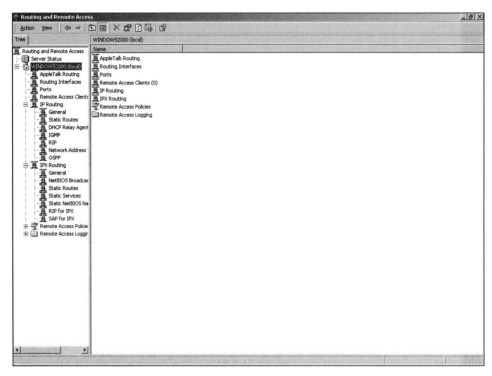

Figure 8.7   The Routing And Remote Access console.

Adding an IP Routing Protocol

To add an IP routing protocol, perform the following steps:

1. Select Start|Programs|Administrative Tools|Routing And Remote Access.

2. Navigate to the General container of the IP Routing Protocol in the desired server container.

3. Right-click the general container and choose the New Routing Protocol option from the pop-up menu.

4. Select the desired Routing Protocol and click OK.

Deleting an IP Routing Protocol

To delete an IP routing protocol, perform the following steps:

1. Select Start|Programs|Administrative Tools|Routing And Remote Access.

2. Navigate to the General container of the IP Routing Protocol in the desired server container.

3. Right-click the routing protocol to delete and choose Delete from the pop-up menu.

4. Click Yes to confirm the deletion.

Adding a Static Route

To add a static route, perform the following steps:

1. Select Start|Programs|Administrative Tools|Routing And Remote Access.

2. Navigate to the General container of the IP Routing Protocol in the desired server container.

3. Right-click the Static Routes container and choose New Static Route from the pop-up menu.

4. Enter the static route information and click OK.

Deleting a Static Route

To delete a static route, perform the following steps:

1. Select Start|Programs|Administrative Tools|Routing And Remote Access.

2. Navigate to the General container of the IP Routing Protocol in the desired server container.

3. Right-click the static route to delete and choose Delete from the pop-up menu.

Configuring Routing Internet Protocol (RIP)

To configure RIP, perform the following steps:

1. Select Start|Programs|Administrative Tools|Routing And Remote Access.

2. Navigate to the General container of the IP Routing Protocol in the desired server container.

3. Right-click the General container and choose New Routing Protocol from the pop-up menu.

4. Select Routing Internet Protocol (RIP) and click OK.

Configuring Open Shortest Path First (OSPF)

To configure OSPF, perform the following steps:

1. Select Start|Programs|Administrative Tools|Routing And Remote Access.

2. Navigate to the General container of the IP Routing Protocol in the desired server container.

3. Right-click the General container and choose New Routing Protocol from the pop-up menu.

4. Select Open Shortest Path First (OSPF) and click OK.

Configuring Network Address Translation (NAT)

To configure NAT, perform the following steps:

1. Select Start|Programs|Administrative Tools|Routing And Remote Access.

2. Navigate to the General container of the IP Routing Protocol in the desired server container.

3. Right-click the General container and choose New Routing Protocol from the pop-up menu.

4. Select Network Address Translation (NAT) and click OK.

Testing TCP/IP

The following projects detail the various tasks involved with testing TCP/IP.

Using the **PING** Command to Test a Connection

To use PING, perform the following steps:

1. Select Start|Programs|Accessories|Command Prompt.

2. Type the following command:

```
PING destination
```

3. Press Enter. If the PING is successful, you'll see a response saying so.

Using the **NET VIEW** Command to Test Connection

To use NET VIEW, perform the following steps:

1. Select Start|Programs|Accessories|Command Prompt.

2. Type the following command:

```
net view \\destination
```

3. Press Enter. If the NET VIEW is successful, you'll see a response that says so.

Using the **TRACERT** Command to Trace a TCP/IP Path

To use TRACERT, perform the following steps:

1. Select Start|Programs|Accessories|Command Prompt.

8. Windows 2000 Networking

2. Type the following command:

```
tracert destination
```

3. Press Enter.

Viewing the NetBIOS Name Table

To view the NetBIOS name table, perform the following steps:

1. Select Start|Programs|Accessories|Command Prompt.

2. Type the following command:

```
nbtstat -n
```

3. Press Enter.

Refreshing the NetBIOS Name Table

To refresh the NetBIOS name table, perform the following steps:

1. Select Start|Programs|Accessories|Command Prompt.

2. Type the following command:

```
nbtstat -R
```

3. Press Enter.

Viewing the Address Resolution Protocol Table

To view the ARP table, perform the following steps:

1. Select Start|Programs|Accessories|Command Prompt.

2. Type the following command:

```
arp -a
```

3. Press Enter.

Adding a Static ARP Entry

To add a static ARP entry, perform the following steps:

1. Select Start|Programs|Accessories|Command Prompt.

8. Windows 2000 Networking

2. Type the following command:

```
arp -s inet_address eth_address
```

3. Press Enter.

NOTE: *For example, to create a static ARP entry for a system with a MAC address of 12-34-56-78-90-AB and an IP address of 192.168.1.2, you would enter the following:*
Arp –s 192.168.1.2 12-34-56-78-90-AB

Working with NetBEUI

The following projects detail the various tasks involved with managing NetBEUI.

Installing NetBEUI

To install NetBEUI, perform the following steps:

1. Select Start|Settings|Control Panel.
2. Double-click the Network And Dial-Up Connections applet.
3. Double-click the network connection for which you would like to install NetBEUI.
4. Click Properties.
5. On the General tab, click Install.
6. Select the Protocol option and click Add.
7. In the Select Network Protocol window, select NetBEUI Protocol and click OK.
8. Click Yes to reboot the server.

Removing NetBEUI

To remove NetBEUI, perform the following steps:

1. Select Start|Settings|Control Panel.
2. Double-click the Network And Dial-Up Connections applet.
3. Double-click the network connection for which you would like to uninstall NetBEUI.
4. Click Properties.
5. On the General tab, select the NetBEUI Option.

8. Windows 2000 Networking

6. Click Uninstall.

7. Click Yes to confirm the deletion.

8. Click Close.

Working with NWLink

The following projects detail the various tasks involved with managing NWLink.

Installing NWLink

To install NWLink, perform the following steps:

1. Select Start|Settings|Control Panel.

2. Double-click the Network And Dial-Up Connections applet.

3. Double-click the network connection for which you would like to install NWLink.

4. Click Properties.

5. On the General tab, click Install.

6. Select the Protocol option and click Add.

7. In the Select Network Protocol window, select NWLink IPX/SPX/NetBIOS Compatible Transport Protocol and click OK.

8. Click Yes to reboot the server.

Removing NWLink

To remove NWLink, perform the following steps:

1. Select Start|Settings|Control Panel.

2. Double-click the Network And Dial-Up Connections applet.

3. Double-click the network connection for which you would like to uninstall NWLink.

4. Click Properties.

5. On the General tab, select the NWLink IPX/SPX/NetBIOS Compatible Transport Protocol option.

6. Click Uninstall.

7. Click Yes to confirm the deletion.

8. Click Close.

8. Windows 2000 Networking

Changing the Internal Network Number

To change the internal network number, perform the following steps:

1. Select Start|Settings|Control Panel.

2. Double-click the Network And Dial-Up Connections applet.

3. Double-click the network connection for which you would like to change the internal network number.

4. Click Properties.

5. On the General tab, select the NWLink IPX/SPX/NetBIOS Compatible Transport Protocol option.

6. Click Properties.

7. Enter a new internal network number.

8. Click OK.

9. Click Close.

Changing the Frame Type

To change frame type settings, perform the following steps:

1. Select Start|Settings|Control Panel.

2. Double-click the Network And Dial-Up Connections applet.

3. Double-click the network connection for which you would like to change the frame type.

4. Click Properties.

5. On the General tab, select the NWLink IPX/SPX/NetBIOS Compatible Transport Protocol option.

6. Click Properties.

7. Select either to automatically detect the frame type (by selecting Auto Frame Type Detection) or manually (by selecting Manual Frame Type Detection).

8. For manual frame type detection, click Add, enter the frame type properties, and click OK.

9. Click Close.

Connecting to a Novell NetWare Server

The following projects detail the various tasks involved with connecting to NetWare computers.

Installing the Gateway Service For NetWare (GSNW)

To install GSNW, perform the following steps:

1. Select Start|Settings|Control Panel.
2. Double-click the Network And Dial-Up Connections applet.
3. Double-click the network connection for which you would like to install Gateway Services For NetWare.
4. Click Properties.
5. On the General tab, click Add.
6. Select the Client option and click Add.
7. Select Gateway (And Client) Services For NetWare and click OK.

Removing the Gateway Service For NetWare

To remove GSNW, perform the following steps:

1. Select Start|Settings|Control Panel.
2. Double-click the Network And Dial-Up Connections applet.
3. Double-click the network connection for which you would like to install Gateway Services For NetWare.
4. Click Properties.
5. Select the Gateway (And Client) Services For NetWare and click Uninstall.
6. Click Yes to confirm the deletion.
7. Click Yes to reboot the server.

Setting a Preferred Server for Bindery Emulation

To set a preferred server for bindery emulation, perform the following steps:

1. Select Start|Settings|Control Panel.
2. Double-click the Network And Dial-Up Connections applet.
3. Double-click the network connection for which you would like to install Gateway Services For NetWare.
4. Click Properties.
5. Select Gateway (And Client) Services For NetWare and click Properties.

6. Select the Preferred Server radio button and enter the name of the preferred server.

7. Click OK.

8. Click Close.

Setting a Default Tree and Context for NDS

To set a default tree and context for NDS, perform the following steps:

1. Select Start|Settings|Control Panel.

2. Double-click the Network And Dial-Up Connections applet.

3. Double-click the network connection for which you would like to install Gateway Services For NetWare.

4. Click Properties.

5. Select Gateway (And Client) Services For NetWare and click Properties.

6. Select the Default Tree and Context radio button and enter the name of the default tree and context.

7. Click OK.

8. Click Close.

Installing Services for the Macintosh

The following projects detail the various tasks involved with configuring Services for Macintosh.

Installing the AppleTalk Protocol

To install AppleTalk, perform the following steps:

1. Select Start|Settings|Control Panel.

2. Double-click the Network And Dial-Up Connections applet.

3. Double-click the network connection for which you would like to install AppleTalk.

4. Click Properties.

5. On the General tab, click Install.

6. Select the Protocol option and click Add.

7. In the Select Network Protocol window, select AppleTalk Protocol and click OK.

8. Click Yes to reboot the server.

8. Windows 2000 Networking

Removing the AppleTalk Protocol

To remove AppleTalk, perform the following steps:

1. Select Start|Settings|Control Panel.

2. Double-click the Network And Dial-Up Connections applet.

3. Double-click the network connection for which you would like to uninstall AppleTalk.

4. Click Properties.

5. On the General tab, select the AppleTalk Protocol option.

6. Click Uninstall.

7. Click Yes to confirm the deletion.

8. Click Close.

Modifying the AppleTalk Zone

To modify the AppleTalk zone, perform the following steps:

1. Select Start|Settings|Control Panel.

2. Double-click the Network And Dial-Up Connections applet.

3. Double-click the network connection for which you would like to modify the AppleTalk zone.

4. Click Properties.

5. On the General tab, select the AppleTalk Protocol option.

6. Click Properties.

7. Select the zone from the drop-down menu and click OK.

8. Click Done.

Chapter 9

The Windows 2000 Boot Process

In Depth

The bootup process of a modern PC is fairly standard. Although some systems (such as Compaq and IBM) go through their own processes, the basic design is the same. Every PC goes through a process known as Power-On Self Test (POST). The "Windows 2000 Bootup—Step by Step" section covers POST in more details.

Important Windows 2000 Boot Files

Before Windows 2000 can start properly, several files need to be present. Many of these files are interchangeable between systems, assuming that the same operating system and service pack are installed on both systems. Some, however, such as boot.ini and bootsect.dos, are specific to the system on which they were installed.

Table 9.1 lists most of the files that might exist on your Windows 2000 installation and their location on the system. Any files that exist on all Windows 2000 systems are marked as default and are listed in the order in which they are loaded.

Windows 2000 Bootup—Step by Step

As outlined in Microsoft's *Windows 2000 Professional Resource Kit* (Microsoft Press, ISBN: 1-57231-808-2), the startup process for Windows 2000 follows these eight steps:

1. Power-On Self Test (POST)

2. Initial startup process

Table 9.1   Windows 2000 Startup Files.

File	Default?	Location
ntldr	Yes	In the active partition (usually C:\)
boot.ini	Yes	In the active partition (usually C:\)
bootsect.dos	No	In the active partition (usually C:\)
ntdetect.com	Yes	In the active partition (usually C:\)
ntbootdd.sys	No	In the active partition (usually C:\)
ntoskrnl.exe	Yes	%systemroot%\System32
hal.dll	Yes	%systemroot%\System32

9. The Windows 2000 Boot Process

3. Bootstrap loader process

4. Operating system selection

5. Hardware detection

6. Hardware configuration selection

7. Kernel loading

8. Operating system logon process

Each of these boot sequences is covered in the following sections.

Power-On Self Test (POST)

Almost every computer made today goes through the same boot process. The order, responses, and what it displays on the screen might be different, but the process is the same nonetheless.

Everything that happens to your computer before the operating system starts up is part of the POST. When you first turn on your computer, your video card will most likely initialize and display a brief message. The system will then check the memory that's installed in the computer and try to detect any errors that might exist.

The hard drives will be detected next, along with some of the installed devices. These devices might include communication ports, parallel ports, Universal Serial Bus (USB) ports, and PS/2 ports.

Initial Startup Process

The last task that the BIOS performs is to scan for the first hard drive that's installed on the system. Once this hard drive is detected, the BIOS will look for a Master Boot Record (MBR). The MBR contains all the information necessary to boot the operating system. The BIOS loads the MBR into memory, launches it, and passes control to it.

Although there's only one MBR, each operating system's MBR is different. Essentially, it knows how to load the operating system. For example, Windows 9x's MBR will look for the io.sys file and pass control to it, whereas Windows NT/ 2000's MBR will look for (and load) the NTLDR file.

Bootstrap Loader Process

The MBR passes control to the NTLDR program. NTLDR is known as the *bootstrap loader* for Windows 2000. Its role is to load the operating system boot files, display the operating system selection menu, and control hardware profiles selection and device detection.

NTLDR will not operate properly unless specific files exist on the system. These files are the boot.ini file and the ntdetect.com file.

NOTE: *If you have a non-Windows NT/2000 operating system installed on your system and are dual-booting the computer, a bootsect.dos file will exist as well. This file maintains a copy of the MBR for the secondary operating system. If that operating system is selected, the MBR from the bootsect.dos file is loaded and control is passed to it. At this point, the Windows 2000 startup process is stopped and the secondary operating system boot process takes over.*

Once NTLDR is loaded and launched, it clears the screen and displays a message such as "OS Loader V5.0." The exact message may vary depending on the version of the operating system installed or the service pack installed.

NTLDR is responsible for performing several tasks. First, it will switch the processor from real mode (the default startup for the system) to 32-bit memory mode. If this step does not occur, NTLDR will fail.

Operating System Selection

Next, the file system drivers are loaded. These include the file allocation table (FAT) and New Technology File System (NTFS) file system drivers. If these drivers are not loaded, the rest of the boot process will fail because the startup programs will not be able to read any information on the hard drives.

At the next phase of NTLDR's execution, the program will search for a boot.ini file. As stated earlier, the boot.ini file is a simple text file that informs NTLDR what operating systems are installed on the system, where they are located, which one to boot by default, and the timeout on the default selection. Once this file is analyzed, NTLDR will display the normal operating system selection screen (see Figure 9.1). Several different switches can be used in the boot.ini files. These switches and their uses are listed in Table 9.2.

From the operating system selection screen, you can either choose the operating system to boot, let NTLDR automatically choose it for you (assuming that a timeout has been set), or use a troubleshooting/advanced setup option (by pressing the F8 key). This troubleshooting/advanced setup menu is shown in Figure 9.2.

Hardware Detection

Once the operating system (including any special startup instructions) is selected, NTLDR will launch an application called *ntdetect.com* whose role it is

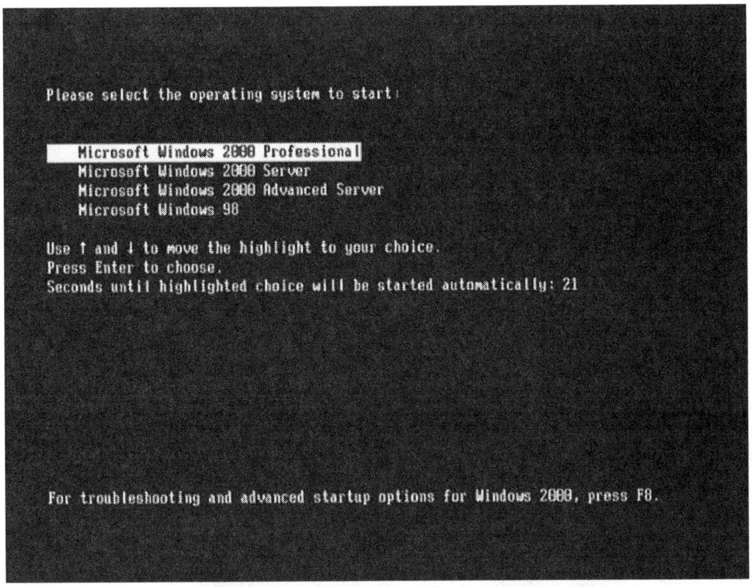

```
Please select the operating system to start:

    Microsoft Windows 2000 Professional
    Microsoft Windows 2000 Server
    Microsoft Windows 2000 Advanced Server
    Microsoft Windows 98

Use ↑ and ↓ to move the highlight to your choice.
Press Enter to choose.
Seconds until highlighted choice will be started automatically: 21




For troubleshooting and advanced startup options for Windows 2000, press F8.
```

Figure 9.1   The operating system selection menu.

Table 9.2   The boot.ini switches.

Switch	Use
/basevideo	Starts the operating system using industry-standard VGA drivers. All video cards support this boot method.
/baudrate=xx	Used for debugging. Sets the baud rate that will be used when the server is debugged. The **/debug** option will be automatically run.
/crashdebug	Loads the debugger but does not launch it until Windows 2000 has a kernel error.
/debug	Loads the debugger so that it can be used when a connection is made to the server via a host PC.
/debugport=comx	Selects the communication port that will be used for the debugging. The **/debug** option will be automatically run.
/fastdetect=comx	Prevents Windows 2000's ntdetect.com from attempting to detect a mouse on the specified communication port. This switch is used when an uninterruptable power supply (UPS) is connected to the serial port.
/maxmem:x	Limits the amount of memory that can be used by Windows 2000. This switch is used if a faulty memory chip is suspected.

(continued)

9. The Windows 2000
Boot Process

Table 9.2   The boot.ini switches (continued).

Switch	Use
/nodebug	Turns off debugging.
numproc=x	Limits the number of processors that a multiprocessor Windows 2000 system will use.
/pae	Enables the Physical Address Extension.
/sos	Displays all device drivers on the screen as they are loaded. Used to find a specific device driver that may be causing a problem on the network.

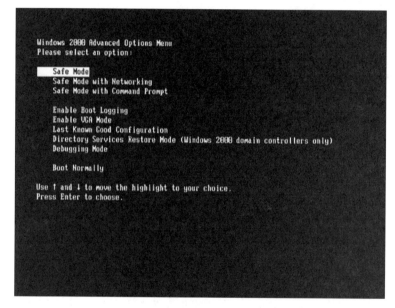

Figure 9.2   The troubleshooting/advanced setup menu.

to detect the hardware devices installed on the system. These hardware devices can include:

- Video
- Keyboard
- Mouse
- Ports (communication, parallel, and USB)
- Floppy drives
- CD-ROM drives

Hardware Profile Selection

While ntdetect.com is running, you have the option to select a different hardware profile if more than one profile has been defined. Hardware profiles are most commonly used with notebook computers. Many of today's notebook computers have docking bays that can greatly enhance functionality.

In fact, many organizations are opting for the notebook/docking bay solution as a desktop replacement. The user has a docking bay that may include fast networking, CD-ROM/DVD drivers, SCSI connectors, and other PC-type peripherals (such as high-end video cards). Also connected to the docking bay is a monitor, keyboard, and mouse. Users now have the ability to take their work with them. When in the office, they "dock" their notebooks and use them like desktop PCs. When they're out, they can take their notebooks with them.

The problem is that the hardware in each of these configurations is different, and although Windows 2000 supports Plug and Play and will detect the changes, the time involved in the detection, installation, and uninstallation process may become too long. For this reason, Windows 2000 gives you the ability to control which drivers are installed for each of these configurations.

You can either configure Windows 2000 to auto-detect the configuration or let you select a hardware profile. The hardware profile screen is shown in Figure 9.3.

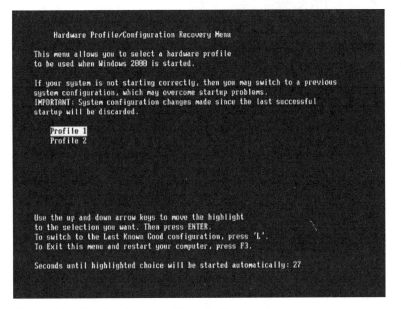

Figure 9.3   The hardware profile selection menu.

Kernel Loading

The last task that NTLDR performs is to load the Windows 2000 kernel (ntoskrnl.exe) and pass control to it. You'll know that this step has occurred when you see the graphical Windows 2000 startup screen.

Ntoskrnl will now load the Hardware Abstraction Layer (HAL) file (hal.dll) and the system configuration from the Registry (HKEY_LOCAL_MACHINE/SYSTEM). It then starts loading the system services and low-level device drivers.

NOTE: *If you select a Last Known Good Configuration, the system configuration information will be read from HKEY_LOCAL_MACHINE/SYSTEM/ControlSetxxx. The value of xxx is read from the LastKnownGood entry in the Select key.*

Logon Process

The final step in the startup process is the launching of the Windows 2000 Logon subsystem. This subsystem (winlogon.exe) will start the Local Security Administration system (lsass.exe). At this point, the Welcome To Windows logon screen appears.

Immediate Solutions

Using the Windows 2000 Boot Menu

To use the Windows 2000 boot menu, perform the following steps:

1. Boot the system.

2. If you would like the countdown stopped, press any key.

3. Select an operating system option by using the up- or down-arrow key.

4. Once you've chosen the operating system to boot, press Enter.

Modifying the Windows 2000 Boot Menu

There are a few ways to customize the Windows 2000 boot menu—these are discussed in the following sections.

Changing the Default Operating System

To change the default operating system using the Control Panel, perform the following steps:

1. Select Start|Settings|Control Panel.

2. Double-click the System applet.

3. Click the Advanced tab.

4. Click Startup And Recovery (see Figure 9.4), the Startup And Recovery dialog box appears.

5. Select the operating system you want booted by default from the Default Operating System drop-down list.

6. Click OK.

Manually Modifying the Default Operating System

To change the default operating system manually, perform the following steps:

1. Double-click My Computer.

2. Navigate to and select the C:\ drive.

3. Right-click the boot.ini file.

9. The Windows 2000 Boot Process

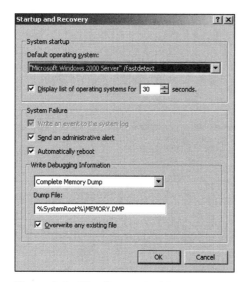

Figure 9.4   The Startup And Recovery dialog box.

TIP: *If the boot.ini file is not visible, follow these steps:*

1. Select Start|Settings|Control Panel.

2. Select Folder Options from the Tools menu.

3. Select the View tab.

4. Select the Show Hidden Files And Folders radio button.

5. Uncheck the Hide Protected Operating System Files checkbox.

6. Uncheck the Hide File Extensions For Known File Types checkbox.

7. Click OK.

The boot.ini file will now appear as a faded icon.

---

4. In the boot.ini Properties window, ensure that the Read-Only checkbox is cleared.

5. Click OK.

6. Double-click the boot.ini file.

7. Find the path from the Operating Systems section of the boot.ini file to the operating system you want to become the default (to the left of the equal sign).

8. Copy the path to the Default parameter of the Boot Loader section of the boot.ini file.

9. Save the file and exit Notepad.

10. Reboot the server.

Manually Modifying the Boot Order

To change the boot order manually, perform the following steps:

1. Double-click My Computer.

2. Navigate to and select the C:\ drive.

3. Right-click the boot.ini file.

TIP: *If the boot.ini file is not visible, follow these steps:*

1. Select Start|Settings|Control Panel.

2. Select Folder Options from the Tools menu.

3. Select the View tab.

4. Select the Show Hidden Files And Folders radio button.

5. Check the Hide File Extensions For Known File Types checkbox.

6. Click OK.

The boot.ini file will now appear as a faded icon.

---

4. In the boot.ini Properties window, ensure that the Read-Only checkbox is cleared.

5. Click OK.

6. Double-click the boot.ini file.

7. Rearrange the items in the Operating Systems section to your liking.

8. Save the file and exit Notepad.

9. Reboot the server.

Disabling and Enabling the Boot Menu Countdown

To enable or disable the boot menu countdown, perform the following steps:

1. Select Start|Settings|Control Panel.

2. Double-click the System applet and click the Advanced tab.

3. Click Startup And Recovery.

4. Clear the Display List Of Operating Systems For X Seconds checkbox to disable the countdown, or you can click this option and set the number of seconds to count down to enable it and click OK.

5. Click OK.

Modifying the Boot Menu Timeout

To change the amount of time before the boot menu times out, perform the following steps:

1. Select Start|Settings|Control Panel.

2. Double-click the System applet.

9. The Windows 2000 Boot Process

3. Click the Advanced tab.

4. Click Startup And Recovery.

5. Check the Display List Of Operating Systems For *X* Seconds checkbox.

6. Enter the amount of time (in seconds) for the boot menu to count down before making a default operating system selection.

7. Click OK two times.

Manually Modifying the Boot Menu Timeout

To change the boot menu timeout manually, perform the following steps:

1. Double-click My Computer.

2. Navigate to and select the C:\ drive.

3. Right-click the boot.ini file.

TIP: *If the boot.ini file is not visible, follow these steps:*

1. Select Start|Settings|Control Panel.

2. Select Folder Options from the Tools menu.

3. Select the View tab.

4. Select the Show Hidden Files and Folders radio button.

5. Check the Hide File Extensions for Known File Types checkbox.

6. Click OK.

The boot.ini file will now appear as a faded icon.

---

4. In the boot.ini Properties window, ensure that the Read-Only checkbox is cleared.

5. Click OK.

6. Double-click the boot.ini file.

7. Modify the Timeout value in the Boot Loader section of the boot.ini file to the desired value.

TIP: *If you do not want the boot menu to wait for a user selection, set the timeout value to 0 (zero).*

---

8. Save the file and exit Notepad.

9. Reboot the server.

9. The Windows 2000 Boot Process

Working with Hardware Profiles

A number of issues are involved in hardware profile management. The following sections explore these tasks.

Adding a Hardware Profile

To add a hardware profile, perform the following steps:

1. Select Start|Settings|Control Panel.

2. Double-click the System applet.

TIP: *You can also access the System applet by right-clicking on My Computer and choosing Properties from the pop-up menu.*

---

3. Select the Hardware tab.

4. Click Hardware Profiles. The Hardware Profiles applet will appear, as shown in Figure 9.5.

5. Select the hardware profile you would like to base the new profile on and click Copy.

6. Enter a name for the new hardware profile in the To field and click OK.

7. Select the newly created profile in the Available Hardware Profiles section and click Properties.

8. If this system is a portable system, you can select whether it has a docking station by selecting The Docking State Is Unknown, The Computer Is

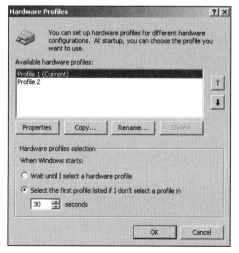

Figure 9.5   The Hardware Profiles applet.

Docked, or The Computer Is Undocked option. This will notify the operating system which hardware components are available in the docked/undocked state.

9. If you would like this hardware profile to always be displayed as an option when Windows 2000 starts, check the Always Include This Profile As An Option When Windows Starts checkbox. This option will display the hardware profile during startup even if Windows 2000 detects that the system is docked or undocked. This allows you to book into a docked configuration even if the workstation is not docked.

10. Click OK when done.

11. Click OK twice.

Deleting a Hardware Profile

To delete a hardware profile, perform the following steps:

1. Select Start|Settings|Control Panel.

2. Double-click the System applet.

3. Select the Hardware tab.

4. Click Hardware Profiles.

5. Select the hardware profile you would like to delete and click Delete.

6. Click Yes to confirm the deletion.

7. Click OK twice.

Renaming a Hardware Profile

To rename a hardware profile, perform the following steps:

1. Select Start|Settings|Control Panel.

2. Double-click the System applet.

3. Select the Hardware tab.

4. Click Hardware Profiles.

5. Select the hardware profile you would like to rename and click Rename.

6. Enter a new name for the hardware profile in the To field and click OK.

7. Click OK twice.

Copying a Hardware Profile

To copy a hardware profile, perform the following steps:

1. Select Start|Settings|Control Panel.

2. Double-click the System applet.

3. Select the Hardware tab.

4. Click Hardware Profiles.

5. Select the hardware profile you would like to copy and click Copy.

6. Enter a name for the new hardware profile in the To field and click OK.

7. Click OK twice.

Booting with a Different Hardware Profile

To boot using a different hardware profile, perform the following steps:

1. Boot the system.

2. Select the operating system you would like to boot.

3. When the Hardware Profile/Configuration Recovery Menu screen appears, select the hardware profile you would like to boot with and press Enter.

Selecting the Hardware Profile Timeout

To specify the amount of time before a hardware profile times out, perform the following steps:

1. Select Start|Settings|Control Panel.

2. Double-click the System applet.

3. Select the Hardware tab.

4. Click Hardware Profiles.

5. In the Hardware Profiles Selection section of the window, select either the Wait Until I Select A Hardware Profile or the Select The Files Profile Listed If I Don't Select A Profile In X Seconds option.

6. If you choose the countdown option, enter a number (in seconds) for the system to wait before automatically making the hardware profile selection for you.

7. Click OK when done.

Working with System Devices

There are a number of items involved in managing system devices. These tasks are discussed in the following sections.

Enabling and Disabling a Device for a Specific Hardware Profile

To enable or disable a device for a hardware profile, perform the following steps:

1. Select Start|Settings|Control Panel.

2. Double-click the System applet.

3. Select the Hardware tab.

4. Click Device Manager. The Device Manager will launch.

5. Select the device you would like to enable in the currently loaded hardware profile.

6. To enable the device, right-click the device and choose Properties from the pop-up menu.

7. In the Device Usage drop-down box, select the Use This Device (Enable) option.

8. Click OK.

9. To disable a device, select the device you would like to disable in all the hardware profiles.

NOTE: *Some devices cannot be disabled because disabling some devices, such as the video display, will render the system inoperative.*

---

10. Right-click the device and choose Properties from the pop-up menu.

11. In the Device Usage drop-down box, select the Do Not Use This Device In Any Hardware Profile (Disable) option.

12. Click OK.

13. Close the Device Manager.

14. Click OK to close the System applet.

Modifying System Services for Hardware Profiles

There are a few issues regarding the management of system services in hardware profiles. The following sections discuss these tasks.

Changing a Service Startup Type to Automatic

To change a service type to automatic, perform the following steps:

1. Select Start|Programs|Administrative Tools|Services.

2. Select the service you would like modified.

3. Right-click the service and choose Properties from the pop-up menu.

4. In the Startup Type drop-down list, choose the Automatic option.

5. Click OK.

Changing a Service Startup Type to Manual

To change a service type to manual, perform the following steps:

1. Select Start|Programs|Administrative Tools|Services.

2. Select the service you would like modified.

3. Right-click the service and choose Properties from the pop-up menu.

4. In the Startup Type drop-down, choose the Manual option.

5. Click OK.

Disabling and Enabling a Service for a Hardware Profile

To enable or disable a service for a hardware profile, perform the following steps:

1. Select Start|Programs|Administrative Tools|Services.

2. Select the service you would like modified.

3. Right-click the service and choose Properties from the pop-up menu.

4. To disable the service, select the Disable option in the Startup Type drop-down list.

5. Click OK.

6. To enable a service, right-click the service and select Properties from the pop-up menu.

7. Select the Log On tab.

8. Select the hardware profile for which you would like to enable this service from the Hardware Profile section and click Enable.

9. Repeat these steps for any other hardware profiles for which a service needs to be enabled or disabled.

10. Click OK.

Managing Services

A number of issues are involved with managing system services. The following sections explore these tasks.

Modifying Service Logon Information

To modify service logon information, perform the following steps:

1. Select Start|Programs|Administrative Tools|Services.

2. Select the service you would like modified.

9. The Windows 2000 Boot Process

3. Right-click the service and choose Properties from the pop-up menu.

4. Select the Log On tab.

5. If you would like the service to use the LocalSystem account, select the Local System Account radio button. If you would like the service to be allowed to interact with the desktop, check the Allow Service To Interact With The Desktop checkbox. Click OK when done.

6. If you would like the service to use a specific user account, select the This Account radio button. Enter the username (or click Browse to list the available users) and password and then confirm the password. Click OK when done.

Configuring a Service to Auto-Restart after a Service Failure

To configure a service to auto-restart after a service failure, perform the following steps:

1. Select Start|Programs|Administrative Tools|Services.

2. Select the service you would like modified.

3. Right-click the service and choose Properties from the pop-up menu.

4. Select the Recovery tab (see Figure 9.6).

5. Select the Restart The Service option from the First Failure drop-down list.

6. Enter an amount of time (in minutes) in the Restart Service After dialog box.

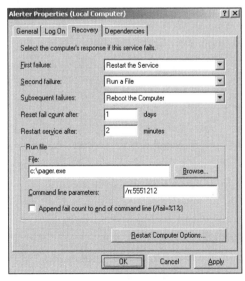

Figure 9.6   The Alerter Properties screen, Recovery tab.

7. Enter a time (in days) for the failure count to be reset in the Reset Fail Count After field.

8. Click OK.

Configuring a Program to Run after a Service Failure

To configure a program to run after a service failure, perform the following steps:

1. Select Start|Programs|Administrative Tools|Services.

2. Select the service you would like modified.

3. Right-click the service and choose Properties from the pop-up menu.

4. Select the Recovery tab.

5. Select the Run A File option from the First Failure drop-down list.

6. Enter the full path to the application or click Browse to navigate to the application.

7. Enter a time (in days) for the failure count to be reset in the Reset Fail Count After field.

8. Enter the required command-line parameters (if any) in the Command Line Parameters dialog box.

9. If you would like to append a fail count to the command line, check the Append Fail Count To End Of Command Line checkbox.

NOTE: *If you select to append a fail count to the command line, the application that's executed must support this feature.*

---

10. Click OK.

Configuring a Server Reboot after a Service Failure

To configure a server reboot after a service failure, perform the following steps:

1. Select Start|Programs|Administrative Tools|Services.

2. Select the service you would like modified.

3. Right-click the service and choose Properties from the pop-up menu.

4. Select the Recovery tab.

5. Select the Reboot The Computer option from the First Failure drop-down list.

6. Enter a time (in days) for the failure count to be reset in the Reset Fail Count After field.

7. Click Restart Computer Options.

8. Enter a time (in minutes) for the system to wait before rebooting in the Restart Computer After.

9. If you would like a message sent to users of the server before the server is rebooted, check the Before Restart, Send This Message To Computers On The Network checkbox and enter the message.

10. Click OK two times.

Dealing with Multiple Service Startup Failure Attempts

To manage multiple service startup failure attempts, perform the following steps:

1. Select Start|Programs|Administrative Tools|Services.

2. Select the service you would like modified.

3. Right-click the service and choose Properties from the pop-up menu.

4. Select the Recovery tab.

5. Select the desired actions from the First Failure drop-down list and configure the parameters (if any).

6. Select the desired actions from the Second Failure drop-down list and configure the parameters (if any).

7. Select the desired actions from the Subsequent Failures drop-down list and configure the parameters (if any).

8. Click OK.

Starting a Service

To start a service, perform the following steps:

1. Select Start|Programs|Administrative Tools|Services.

2. Select the service you would like to start.

3. Right-click the service and choose Start from the pop-up menu.

Starting a Service from the Command Prompt

To start a service from the command prompt, perform the following steps:

1. Select Start|Programs|Accessories|Command Prompt.

2. Type in "net start *ServiceName*".

TIP: *If you do not know the name of the service, you can find it in the Registry key HKEY_LOCAL_MACHINE/SYSTEM/ CurrentControlSet/Services.*

---

3. Press Enter.

Stopping a Service

To stop a service, perform the following steps:

1. Select Start|Programs|Administrative Tools|Services.

2. Select the service you would like to stop.

3. Right-click the service and choose Stop from the pop-up menu.

Stopping a Service from the Command Prompt

To stop a service from the command prompt, perform the following steps:

1. Select Start|Programs|Accessories|Command Prompt.

2. Type in "net stop *ServiceName*".

TIP: *If you do not know the name of the service, you can find it in the Registry key HKEY_LOCAL_MACHINE/SYSTEM/CurrentControlSet/Services.*

---

3. Press Enter.

Pausing a Service

To pause a service, perform the following steps:

1. Select Start|Programs|Administrative Tools|Services.

2. Select the service to pause.

NOTE: *Some services cannot be paused.*

---

3. Right-click the service and choose Pause from the pop-up menu.

Pausing a Service from the Command Prompt

To pause a service from the command prompt, perform the following steps:

1. Select Start|Programs|Accessories|Command Prompt.

2. Type in "net pause *ServiceName*".

TIP: *If you do not know the name of the service, you can find it in the Registry key HKEY_LOCAL_MACHINE/SYSTEM/CurrentControlSet/Services.*

---

3. Press Enter.

Resuming a Paused Service

To resume a paused service, perform the following steps:

1. Select Start|Programs|Administrative Tools|Services.

9. The Windows 2000 Boot Process

2. Select the service to resume.

3. Right-click the service and choose Resume from the pop-up menu.

Resuming a Paused Service from the Command Prompt

To resume a paused service from the command prompt, perform the following steps:

1. Select Start|Programs|Accessories|Command Prompt.

2. Type in "net continue *ServiceName*".

TIP: *If you do not know the name of the service, you can find it in the Registry key HKEY_LOCAL_MACHINE/SYSTEM/ CurrentControlSet/Services.*

---

3. Press Enter.

Restarting a Service

To restart a service, perform the following steps:

1. Select Start|Programs|Administrative Tools|Services.

2. Select the service to restart.

3. Right-click the service and choose Restart from the pop-up menu.

Checking Service Dependencies

To verify service dependencies, perform the following steps:

1. Select Start|Programs|Administrative Tools|Services.

2. Select the service to modify.

3. Right-click the service and choose Properties from the pop-up menu.

4. Select the Dependencies tab.

5. The dependencies for this service (if any) will appear in this tab.

Building a Minimal Boot Disk

To build a boot disk, perform the following steps:

1. Place a blank diskette in the floppy drive.

2. Double-click My Computer.

3. Right-click the A: drive and choose Format from the pop-up menu.

4. Click Start.

5. Copy the following files from the i386 directory of the Windows 2000 CD-ROM: NTLDR, ntdetect.com, and boot.ini.

Manually Shutting Down Windows 2000

There are a couple different methods for shutting down Windows 2000.

The first method for shutting down Windows 2000 is as follows:

1. Select Start|Shut Down.
2. Choose the Shutdown option from the What Do You Want The Computer To Do? drop-down list.
3. Click OK.

The second method for shutting down Windows 2000 is as follows:

1. Press Ctrl+Alt+Del.
2. Click Shut Down.
3. Choose the Shutdown option from the What Do You Want The Computer To Do? drop-down list.
4. Click OK.

Manually Rebooting Windows 2000

There are a couple different methods for rebooting Windows 2000.

The first method for rebooting Windows 2000 is as follows:

1. Select Start|Shut Down.
2. Choose the Restart option from the What Do You Want The Computer To Do? drop-down list.
3. Click OK.

The second method for rebooting Windows 2000 is as follows:

1. Press Ctrl+Alt+Del.
2. Click Shut Down.
3. Choose the Restart option from the What Do You Want The Computer To Do? drop-down list.
4. Click OK.

Using Remote Shutdown to Shut Down a Local System

To use remote shutdown to shut down a local system, perform the following steps:

1. Run the shutdown.exe application (see Figure 9.7).

2. Enter the name of the local server or browse to it.

3. Clear the Kill Applications Without Saving Data checkbox.

4. Clear the Reboot After Shutdown checkbox.

5. Enter a message in the Message Text box.

6. Enter an amount of time (in seconds) that the application should wait before initiating the shutdown.

7. Click OK.

NOTE: *The Remote Shutdown application (Shutdown.exe) is found on the Windows 2000 Resource Kit in the drive:\Program Files\Resource Kit\ folder.*

Using Remote Shutdown to Reboot a Local System

To use remote shutdown to reboot a local system, perform the following steps:

1. Run the shutdown.exe application.

2. Enter the name of the local server or browse to it.

3. Clear the Kill Applications Without Saving Data checkbox.

4. Check the Reboot After Shutdown checkbox.

5. Enter a message in the Message Text box.

6. Enter an amount of time (in seconds) that the application should wait before initiating the shutdown.

7. Click OK.

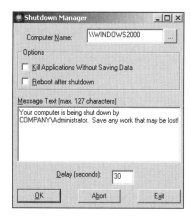

Figure 9.7   The Shutdown Manager.

Forcing a Shutdown for a Local System

To force a shutdown of a local system, perform the following steps:

1. Run the shutdown.exe application.
2. Enter the name of the local server or browse to it.
3. Check the Kill Applications Without Saving Data checkbox.
4. Clear the Reboot After Shutdown checkbox.
5. Enter a message in the Message Text box.
6. Enter an amount of time (in seconds) that the application should wait before initiating the shutdown.
7. Click OK.

WARNING!   *This method kills all services and applications without saving the data. Use caution with this method because it can corrupt your system. Only use this as a last resort.*

Forcing a Reboot for a Local System

To force a reboot of a local system, perform the following steps:

1. Run the shutdown.exe application.
2. Enter the name of the local server or browse to it.
3. Check the Kill Applications Without Saving Data checkbox.
4. Check the Reboot After Shutdown checkbox.
5. Enter a message in the Message Text box.
6. Enter an amount of time (in seconds) that the application should wait before initiating the shutdown.
7. Click OK.

WARNING!   *This method kills all services and applications without saving the data. Use caution with this method because it can corrupt your system. Only use this as a last resort.*

Using Remote Shutdown to Shut Down a Remote System

To use remote shutdown to shut down a remote system, perform the following steps:

1. Run the shutdown.exe application.
2. Enter the name of the remote server or browse to it.
3. Clear the Kill Applications Without Saving Data checkbox.
4. Clear the Reboot After Shutdown checkbox.

9. The Windows 2000 Boot Process

5. Enter a message in the Message Text box.

6. Enter an amount of time (in seconds) that the application should wait before initiating the shutdown.

7. Click OK.

Using Remote Shutdown to Reboot a Remote System

To use remote shutdown to reboot a remote system, perform the following steps:

1. Run the shutdown.exe application.

2. Enter the name of the remote server or browse to it.

3. Clear the Kill Applications Without Saving Data checkbox.

4. Check the Reboot After Shutdown checkbox.

5. Enter a message in the Message Text box.

6. Enter an amount of time (in seconds) that the application should wait before initiating the shutdown.

7. Click OK.

Forcing a Shutdown for a Remote System

To force a shut down of a remote system, perform the following steps:

1. Run the shutdown.exe application.

2. Enter the name of the local server or browse to it.

3. Check the Kill Applications Without Saving Data checkbox.

4. Uncheck the Reboot After Shutdown checkbox.

5. Enter a message in the Message Text box.

6. Enter an amount of time (in seconds) that the application should wait before initiating the shutdown.

7. Click OK.

WARNING!   *This method kills all services and applications without saving the data. Use caution with this method because it can corrupt your system. Only use this as a last resort.*

Forcing a Reboot for a Remote System

To force a reboot of a remote system, perform the following steps:

1. Run the shutdown.exe application.

2. Enter the name of the local server or browse to it.

3. Check the Kill Applications Without Saving Data checkbox.

4. Check the Reboot After Shutdown checkbox.

5. Enter a message in the Message Text box.

6. Enter an amount of time (in seconds) that the application should wait before initiating the shutdown.

7. Click OK.

WARNING! *This method kills all services and applications without saving the data. Use caution with this method because it can corrupt your system. Only use this as a last resort.*

Chapter 10

Windows 2000
Administration Tools

In Depth

This chapter explores the Windows 2000 Administrative Tools and the Control Panel. Nearly every administration, control, management, configuration, or monitoring task performed on a Windows 2000 system starts with using the tools found in these two areas. You'll recognize many of the tools in the Control Panel from Windows NT or Windows 98, and a few of the Administrative Tools may remind you of utilities from Windows NT. In any case, familiarity with these tools is essential to managing a Windows 2000 installation.

Microsoft Management Console

Windows 2000 is the first operating system from Microsoft to employ the Microsoft Management Console (MMC) interface for most of its administration and management functions. The MMC is a standardized graphical interface that hosts management tools called *snap-ins*. The MMC itself is nothing more than a structured architecture environment; it can perform no administration or management on its own. It is through the loading of snap-ins into the MMC that control over a computer system is gained. The MMC was designed to provide a versatile, customizable interface mechanism that allows administrators to create tool sets that match their regular activities.

The MMC is a shell into which consoles (similar to documents) are loaded. Within each console, one or more snap-ins can be loaded. Each snap-in can then be expanded with add-ons called *extensions*. Each snap-in's capabilities focus on a single object type within the Windows 2000 environment, such as storage, networking, users, and so on. The extensions expand the capabilities of a snap-in through the inclusion of additional functions. This multilevel modular design offers you the flexibility to build a tool set that is right for you. Plus, most of the tools based on snap-ins can manage objects locally or remotely.

The MMC was previously introduced to the Windows NT 4.0 environment via the Windows NT 4.0 Option Pack. It was required to manage the 4.0 version of Internet Information Server (IIS).

In addition to the snap-in tools and utilities included with Windows 2000, administrators can write or create their own snap-ins. MMC is a fully ISV (Independent Software Vendor) extensible control framework, which means that it complies with basic programming standards to allow third parties to create tools that will function within its predefined versatile environment.

The MMC can be launched without loading any snap-ins. This is done by typing "MMC" from a command prompt or the Run command. The empty MMC window, shown in Figure 10.1, displays the main menu, containing the Console, Window, and Help drop-down menus and a movable mini-icon bar with New, Open, Save, and New Window buttons. The display area can support multiple console windows that can be cascaded, tiled, or minimized as icons.

Each console window has a console menu bar, a console tree, and a details pane. The console menu bar contains the Action and View pull-down menus and another mini-icon bar containing Back, Forward, Up One Level, Show/Hide Console Tree/Favorites, and Help buttons. The console tree section is the area to the left that has a Tree tab and a Favorites tab. The console tree shows the organization of loaded plug-ins and extensions, along with context selections. A context selection depends on the plug-in's management object, such as domain, computer, organizational unit, user, folder, or service. The details pane is the area to the right; items displayed in the details pane are determined by the selection in the console tree. The contents of the console menu bar change based on the selected element within the console tree or details pane.

Starting from a blank MMC interface and an empty console window, you can load and customize your own administration tools using any or all of the snap-ins included with Windows 2000. The set of predefined snap-ins are:

- Active Directory Schema
- ActiveX Control
- ADSI Edit
- Certificates

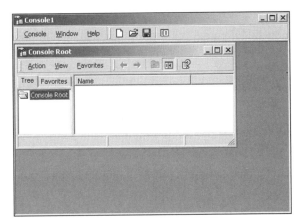

Figure 10.1   The Microsoft Management Console (empty).

- Component Services
- Computer Management
- Device Manager
- Disk Defragmenter
- Disk Management
- Event Viewer
- Fax Service Management
- Folder
- Group Policy
- Indexing Service
- IP Security Policy Management
- Link to Web Address
- Local Users and Groups
- Performance Logs and Alerts
- Removable Storage Management
- Resource Kits
- Security Configuration and Analysis
- Security Templates
- Services
- Shared Folders
- SIDWalker Security Manager
- System Information
- WinMgmt Control

NOTE: *The snap-ins may vary, depending on the various utilities you have loaded.*

These snap-ins are the same elements used to create the utilities found in Administrative Tools. By using one or more of the snap-ins, you can create a custom console. To add snap-ins to a console, just follow these steps:

1. Issue the Add/Remove Snap-In command from the Console menu.
2. Click the Add button on the Add/Remove Snap-In dialog box's Standalone tab.
3. Select a snap-in from the presented list.

4. Click Add. In some cases, additional configuration, such as source context, will be required. The Add Wizard will prompt you for this.

5. Repeat steps 3 and 4 until all desired snap-ins are added.

6. Click Close.

7. Click OK.

8. Your console will now contain the added snap-ins in the console tree.

Once your console is configured, you can save the console for later use using one of four formats:

- *Author Mode*—Enables users to add and remove snap-ins, create new windows, view the entire console tree, and save new versions of the console.

- *User Mode: Full Access*—Allows users to create new windows and view the entire console tree but prevents the adding or removing of snap-ins or the resaving of console files.

- *User Mode: Delegated Access, Multiple Windows*—Allows users to create new windows but restricts access to portions of the console tree, the adding or removing of snap-ins, or the resaving of console files.

- *User Mode: Delegated Access, Single Window*—Restricts users from creating new windows, accessing portions of the console tree, adding or removing snap-ins, or resaving console files.

To set the mode of the console, use the Options command in the Console menu. Then, use the Save or Save As command to save the console to a file. MMC console settings are stored in MSC files. Once you've created an MSC file, it can be distributed and used on any system with MMC.

Windows 2000 uses the MMC for many of its administration and management utilities. All the MMC snap-in predefined utilities (that is, preconfigured consoles) are found in Administrative Tools (see Figure 10.2). Administrative Tools can be accessed either from the Control Panel or from the Start menu.

NOTE: *The Administrative Tools section of the Start menu is disabled by default on Windows 2000 Professional systems.*

The utilities found in the Administrative Tools area are:

- *Active Directory Domains And Trusts*—Used to create and manage domains and trusts. This includes operations such as setting the domain names operation manager, changing a domain's mode, creating trusts between domains, and defining a managing user account. This tool is discussed in Chapter 3.

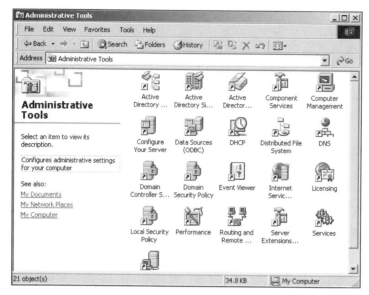

Figure 10.2   The Administrative Tools window.

- *Active Directory Sites And Services*—Used to configure server settings, site settings, and replication. This tool is discussed in Chapter 3.

- *Active Directory Users And Computers*—Used to create and manage users, groups, and computers within a domain. This tool is discussed in Chapter 3.

- *Component Services*—The renamed Microsoft Transaction Server, Component Services is used to deploy and control COM+, automate tasks using scripting or programming languages, manage transactions between processes, and create scalable component-based applications. For more details see the *Windows 2000 Server Resource Kit* (Microsoft Press, ISBN: 1-57231-805-8) or the Windows 2000 and IIS 5.0 SDKs.

- *Computer Management*—Offers single-interface access to several commonly used local computer management utilities, such as Event Viewer, Disk Management, and the Services applet (discussed later in this chapter).

- *Data Sources (ODBC)*—Used to define Data Source Names (DSNs) employed by applications and services to access database-management systems in the domain. See the *Windows 2000 Server Resource Kit* for details.

- *DHCP*—Used to configure the dynamic client configuration service for a domain. DHCP stands for Dynamic Host Configuration Protocol. See Chapter 9 for details.

- *Distributed File System*—Used to create and manage Dfs for a domain. See Chapter 8 for details.

- *DNS*—Used to configure the domain name-to-IP address resolution service for a domain. See Chapter 9 for details.

- *Domain Controller Security Policy*—Used to configure and define the security policy for all domain controllers. See Chapter 19 for details.

- *Domain Security Policy*—Used to configure and define the security policy for a domain. See Chapter 19 for details.

- *Event Viewer*—Used to view and manage the logs of Windows 2000.

- *Internet Services Manager*—Used to manage Internet information services, such as Web and FTP. See the *Windows 2000 Resource Kit* or the *IIS 5.0 Documentation* (Microsoft Press, ISBN: 0-7356-0652-8) for details.

- *Licensing*—Used to configure and manage the licenses of Windows 2000 and installed applications.

- *Local Security Policy*—Used to configure and define the security policy for the local system. See Chapter 19 for details.

- *Performance*—Used to monitor and record the performance levels of the system. See Chapter 16 for details.

- *Routing And Remote Access*—Used to configure and manage routing and remote access for a system. See Chapter 20 for details.

- *Server Extensions Administrator*—Used to manage FrontPage server extensions. See the *Windows 2000 Server Resource Kit, IIS 5.0 Documentation,* or the *Official Microsoft FrontPage 2000 Book* (Microsoft Press, ISBN: 0-57231-992-5) for details.

NOTE: *The Configure Your Server element of Administrative Tools is not an MMC snap-in tool; instead, it's a wizard with multiple menus for configuring a server. See Chapter 3 for details. The Services element is not an MMC snap-in; it's an applet. See the "Control Panel Tools" section later in this chapter. Finally, the Telnet Server element is not an MMC snap-in; it's a text-based menu system used to configure and manage the Telnet server service. See Chapter 20 for details.*

This is not an exhaustive list of the possible tools that can be found in Administrative Tools. Other tools may be added or some of these tools might not be present, based on the services installed on your Windows 2000 system. Many of these tools are found only on Windows 2000 Server (that is, those used to manage network services for a domain).

Computer Management

The Computer Management tool, shown in Figure 10.3, is an MMC console configured to grant quick access to many commonly used administration tools. This tool is divided into three sections: System Tools, Storage, and Services And Applications.

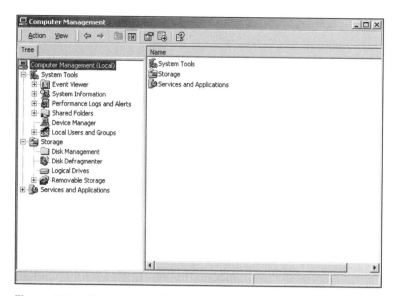

Figure 10.3   The Computer Management administrative tool.

The System Tools section contains six tools:

- *Event Viewer*—Used to view and manage the logs of Windows 2000.

- *System Information*—Used to view configuration, status, and setting information about the system. The multileveled information hierarchy, shown in Figure 10.4, displays the current data regarding the system, hardware resources, installed components and devices, software environment, and native Microsoft applications such as Internet Explorer 5. This tool is extremely handy in discovering system model numbers, free IRQs, resource conflicts, and component configurations.

- *Performance Logs And Alerts*—Used to create and manage counter logs, trace logs, and alerts. See Chapter 16 for details.

- *Shared Folders*—Used to create and manage shared folders on the local system. This tool displays both standard and hidden shares (see Figure 10.5), current sessions, and open files.

- *Device Manager*—Used to display and configure the settings of installed hardware devices. System resources can be altered, new drives installed, and device conflicts resolved.

- *Local Users And Groups*—Used to configure and manage local users and groups. This tool is disabled when Active Directory is present.

The Storage section of Computer Management has four tools:

- *Disk Management*—Used to manage partitions and volumes on hard drives. Its capabilities include converting from basic to dynamic storage, deleting,

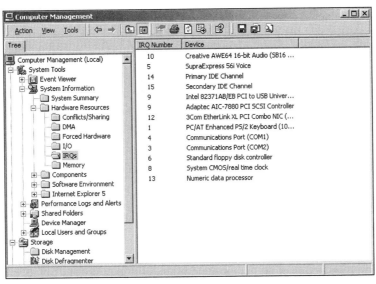

Figure 10.4   The System Information tool via the Computer Management window.

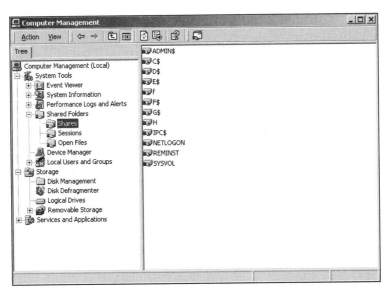

Figure 10.5   The Shared Folders tool via the Computer Management window.

formatting, assigning drive letters, and creating RAID drive configurations.
See Chapter 13 for details.

- *Disk Defragmenter*—Used to analyze the fragmentation level and defragment
  a volume. See Chapter 13 for details.

- *Logical Drives*—Used to view data about logical drives (formatted volumes and partitions). This is the same information shown by opening the Properties dialog box on a drive via My Computer or Windows Explorer. See Chapter 13 for details.

- *Removable Storage*—Used to track and manage definable libraries or media pools of removable media, including floppies, tapes, CDs, CDRs, CDRWs, and more (see Figure 10.6). See Chapter 13 for details.

The Services And Applications section of Computer Management has a variable number tools that depend upon installed services and applications. Possible tools include:

- *DHCP*—This is another access point for the DHCP configuration and management interface. See Chapter 9 for details.

- *Telephony*—Used to configure the installed communication providers (same as the Advanced tab of the Phone And Modem applet) and to define user access for each provider. See Chapter 20 for details.

- *Windows Management Instrumentation (WIM)*—Used to enable system management through a consistent interface.

- *Services*—Used to start and stop services and define their initialization and security credentials (discussed later in this chapter).

- *Indexing Service*—Used to define the folders that will be included in the Indexing Service's index, as distinguished between system and Web. See Chapter 6 for details.

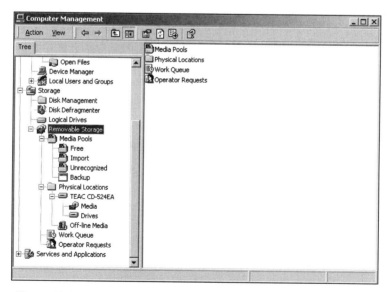

Figure 10.6   The Removable Storage tool via the Computer Management window.

- *Internet Information Services*—Used to configure and manage the Web, FTP, and Simple Mail Transport Protocol (SMTP) services of IIS 5.0. See Chapter 6 for details.

- *DNS*—Used to configure and manage the DNS service. See Chapter 9 for details.

Event Viewer

The Event Viewer is used to view the log files created by Windows 2000. There are three main log files—System, Application, and Security—plus log files specific to installed applications or services, such as Directory Service, DNS Server, and File Replication Service (see Figure 10.7). The Event Viewer can be used to view logs locally or from remote systems. The Event Viewer is accessed through Administrative Tools in the Start menu or Control Panel and through the Computer Management window.

The Windows 2000 log files record event details. An *event detail* is a report containing information specific to a condition, situation, or occurrence (that is, an event). Events can range from access denials, to driver failures, to service initialization announcements.

Information, warning, and error event details are recorded in the System and Application logs. Audit success and failure event details are recorded in the Security log. An event detail includes time and date, source, category, user account, computer account, and more.

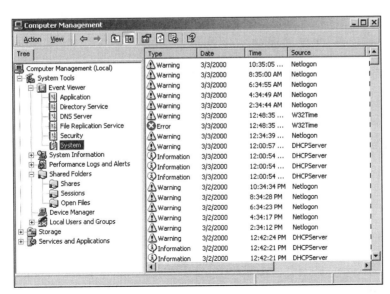

Figure 10.7   The Event Viewer tool via the Computer Management window.

NOTE: *For audit events to be recorded, auditing must be enabled and configured. See Chapter 19 for details.*

Logs can be customized as to their displayed name, the maximum size of the log, and how to manage a full log. Full logs can have the oldest events overwritten by new events, have only events more than a specific number of days old overwritten by new events, or new events can be discarded until the log is manually cleared. These configuration options are defined via the Properties dialog box for each log.

You can also define a display filter (through the **filter** command of the View menu) that reduces the number of event details shown. The Find command in the View menu is used to perform a keyword search in the selected log. Both of these tools will prove invaluable when you have to locate a single event in a log of thousands.

Licensing

The Licensing MMC snap-in is accessed through Administrative Tools. This utility, shown in Figure 10.8, is used to manage the use license for Windows 2000 and for distributed applications hosted on the system as well.

Windows 2000 licensing is available in two types: Per Server and Per Seat. Per Server licensing grants client-access licenses to a server. One client computer is able to establish a connection with the server for each installed client license. The client licenses can only be used on the server that holds the licenses. Per Seat licensing grants client access licenses to the client. The client can use that license to connect to any server on the network. Per Server licensing makes the most sense in smaller networks with fewer servers. Per Seat licensing makes the most sense in larger networks with lots of servers. You have the ability to

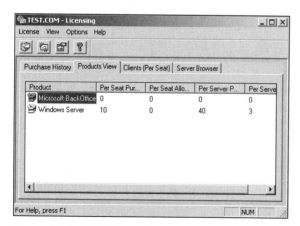

Figure 10.8   The Licensing tool.

convert your license mode from Per Server to Per Seat once, but the conversion cannot be reversed.

If a product, such as Microsoft BackOffice, is installed, it will automatically be added to the list of products that the Licensing tool can manage client access of. The Purchase History tab is used to add newly purchased licenses to a product. The Products View tab shows the number of Per Seat and Per Server licenses available and used for each product. The Clients (Per Seat) tab lists details about users employing licenses to access products. The Server Browser tab is used to view the license settings on other systems on the network.

Through the Advanced submenu of the Options menu, you can create or edit license groups. A *license group* is used to properly manage the use of licenses when the number of users, computers, and licenses are not identical. For example, if you have 100 users and 10 computers, you only need 10 licenses and a single user group with access to those licenses.

Services

The Services utility, shown in Figure 10.9, within Computer Management is used to start and stop services and define the initialization credentials of services. All installed services are listed along with a description, current status, startup type, and "log on as" credential. The status will either be started or paused. A blank here indicates the service is stopped. The startup type indicates how the system will handle the service; the options are Automatic (starts when the OS starts), Manual (starts by a user or a dependant service), and Disabled (prevents a service from being launched). The Log On As option lists the user account whose access credentials the service will use. A value of LocalSystem indicates the service is launched with system-level privileges. Any defined user account can be employed by a service.

Each service has a Properties dialog box consisting of four tabs. The General tab, shown in Figure 10.10, is used to define the displayed name, description, startup type, and start parameters as well as to start/stop/pause/resume the service. The Log On tab is used to define the privilege level of the service as either system level or a user account. This tab is also used to enable or disable a service within a hardware profile. The Recovery tab is used to define how the system will react to the first, second, and later failures of the service. The options are Take No Action, Restart The Service, Run A File, and Reboot The Computer. The Dependencies tab lists the services on which this service is dependant and the services that are dependant on this service.

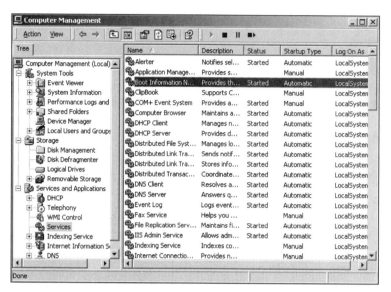

Figure 10.9   The Services utility.

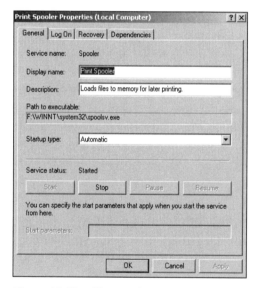

Figure 10.10   The services Properties dialog box.

Control Panel Tools

The Control Panel is a collection of configuration applets used to manage the installation of new hardware and software. The Control Panel is accessed either through the Start menu (by clicking the Start menu and selecting Settings|Services) or as an element in both My Computer and Windows Explorer. The Control Panel is basically an access window you can use to launch applets by double-clicking them. The set of applets that appears depends on the computer system (for example, if it is a notebook computer, the PC Card applet will be present) and installed applications and services (QuickTime, RealPlayer, Norton AntiVirus, TweakUI, and so on). The common Control Panel applets are described in the following sections.

Accessibility Options

The Accessibility Options applet is used to configure special keyboard, sound, display, mouse, and other features that improve interaction for the seeing-, hearing-, or movement-impaired user. Some of the features accessible through this applet are StickyKeys (pressing Ctrl, Shift, or Alt once instead of holding down the key), SoundSentry (a visual clue, such as a flashing title bar, that's assigned to all sounds), high-contrast color schemes, and the use of the numeric keypad to control mouse movements. If you need more information about the accessibility options, consult the *Windows 2000 Server Resource Kit*.

Add/Remove Hardware

The Add/Remove Hardware applet is used to perform several tasks, such as adding a new device, troubleshooting a device, and uninstalling or removing a device. The applet is actually a wizard, shown in Figure 10.11, that walks you through the selected activity. Adding and troubleshooting hardware tasks are grouped into the first selection, whereas tasks related to uninstalling and removing a device are grouped as the second selection.

To add a new device, select the Add/Troubleshoot radio button and click Next. The system will search for new hardware first; then it will prompt you with a list

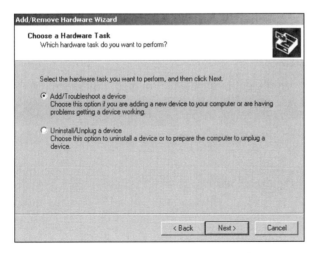

Figure 10.11   The Add/Remove Hardware Wizard.

of located devices. If you want to troubleshoot a listed device, select it. Devices with problems will have a yellow exclamation point or a stop sign over their device icon. If you want to install a new device, select the Add A New Device item. The rest of the wizard walks you through the process of either troubleshooting or installing the device.

To remove a device, select the Uninstall/Remove option. You then must decide whether to just unplug or eject the device (the driver stays installed) or to uninstall the device (remove the driver from the system). The former process will allow you to reattach the device at a later time without reinstalling the driver, and it will retain its original configuration (such as for a modem or network interface card). The latter process should only be used when a device is being permanently removed or a corrupt driver is present.

Add/Remove Programs

The Add/Remove Programs applet is used to perform three types of software management:

- *Change Or Remove Programs*—Change or remove installed third-party applications (that is, applications not natively included with Windows 2000 or on its distribution CD).

- *Add New Programs*—Install new applications from a vendor-supplied floppy or CD.

- *Add/Remove Windows Components*—It can add or remove Windows 2000 components.

The applet launches by default in the Change Or Remove Programs mode. This mode lists all installed applications along with details such as size (total amount of drive space consumed by files), used status (often, seldom, rarely), and last used date. There's also a Change/Remove button, which will either launch the selected application's own Configure/Remove tool or launch Windows 2000's removal tool.

The Add New Programs mode can pull software from a CD or floppy, from the Microsoft Update Web site, or from a network distribution site. It's used to initiate the setup procedure and ensure the process is recorded by the Windows 2000 removal tool for later management via the Change Or Remove Programs mode.

The Add/Remove Windows Components mode displays a list of all available components of Windows 2000 found on the distribution CD that are still available to be installed on the current system. This interface can also be used to remove already installed components. Simply mark the items you want installed and then clear the checkmarks for the items you no longer want present on your system. The tool manages adding and removing components based on your checkbox markings.

Administrative Tools

Administrative Tools is a link to another Control Panel-like window that hosts all the MMC snap-in tools used to manage and configure the operating system environment. These tools were discussed in the "Microsoft Management Console," section earlier in this chapter.

Date/Time

The Date/Time applet is used to set the calendar, date, and clock time for the local system. This interface is used to set the day, month, year, and time (to the second) as well as the time zone. Once you make a time/date change via this applet, it is immediately recorded onto the system's CMOS.

Display

The Display applet is used to control a wide range of desktop interface settings. The settings on each of the tabs of this applet dialog box are:

- *Background*—Used to define the desktop wallpaper.

- *Screen Saver*—Used to set the screen saver and idle time, enable password protection, and access the power-saving features of the monitor.

- *Appearance*—Used to define the color scheme. Can be selected from predefined sets or custom configured.

- *Web*—Used to configure the Active Desktop components.

- *Effects*—Used to define desktop icons and enable or disable several visual effects (such as menu transitions, smooth screen fonts, use all colors for icons, and so on).

- *Settings*—Used to set the display area and color depth and to change adapter- or monitor-specific settings.

Windows 2000 supports multiple displays. If multiple video adapters are installed (that is, their drivers have been installed via the Add/Remove Hardware applet), the Settings tab will display a monitor icon for each installed video adapter. You can drag these icons into the arrangement of your choice and then associate an adapter with each of the numbered monitor icons. The color depth and resolution can be set for each adapter/display. Using multiple displays requires compliance with the following rules:

- All video adapters must be Accelerated Graphics Port (AGP) and/or Peripheral Component Interconnect (PCI).

- Video adapters built into the motherboard can be used, but they can only be used as secondary adapters (that is, they cannot be assigned to the first numbered monitor icon), assuming the motherboard's BIOS will allow the onboard video adapter to function if an expansion card adapter is installed.

- Windows 2000 should be installed with only a single adapter. Additional adapters can be installed after installation has completed.

Fax

The Fax applet is used to manage faxing. Windows 2000 includes native support for basic fax capabilities, such as sending faxes, receiving faxes, and managing cover pages. Faxing requires a fax-capable modem (the modem must be installed via the Phone And Modem Options applet). See Chapter 6 for a discussion on using faxing.

Folder Options

The Folder Options applet is the interface accessed when you issue the Folder Options command from the Tools menu in Windows Explorer or My Computer. The following list explains the features of each tab in this applet:

- *General*—Used to enable/disable the Active Desktop, Web, or classic view of folders, open folders in the same or a different window, or select single or double clicks to open an item.

- *View*—Used to configure the advanced settings of displayed information, such as hidden files, known extensions, and so on, as well as hide protected files.

- *File Types*—Used to configure registered associations between file extensions and applications.

- *Offline Files*—Used to enable/disable caching of network files locally for use offline. This process is described in detail in Chapter 6.

Fonts

The Fonts folder contains a list of all installed fonts. New fonts can be added and existing fonts can be removed through this interface.

Game Controllers

The Game Controllers applet is used to manage gaming controls, such as joysticks and steering wheels. New devices can be installed and existing devices can be removed or configured.

Internet Options

The Internet Options applet controls how Internet Explorer functions. The tabs in this applet are used to configure the following settings:

- *General*—Used to define the home page, the path for temporary Internet files, site visit history, colors, fonts, languages, and accessibility options—all specific to Web surfing.
- *Security*—Used to define the security level of four Web zones. The security controls govern within that zone whether software will be automatically downloaded and installed, whether form data will be submitted, and whether cookies will be used.
- *Content*—Used to configure the Content Advisor (site-blocking control), manage certificates, configure AutoComplete, and define your online identity.
- *Connections*—Used to configure how an Internet connection is established if one is not already present.
- *Programs*—Used to associate applications with types of Internet services encountered on Web sites (email, newsgroups, and so on).
- *Advanced*—Used to configure advanced features, such as HTTP 1.1 Microsoft virtual machine, multimedia, printing, searching, security, and accessibility.

Keyboard and Mouse

The Keyboard applet is used to manage the keyboard and configure settings such as repeat delay and cursor blink rate. The Mouse applet is used to manage the mouse and configure settings such as double click speed and tracking acceleration.

Licensing

The Licensing applet is used to change licensing options. From within this applet, you can change from Per Server licensing to Per Seat, and add or remove licenses.

Network And Dial-Up Connections

The Network And Dial-Up Connections applet controls all network interfaces, including LAN, RAS, direct cable, and VPN connections. This applet is discussed in Chapters 9 and 20.

Phone And Modem Options

The Phone And Modem Options applet manages dialing locations, modem installation and configuration, as well as Remote Access Service (RAS) and Telephony Application Programming Interface (TAPI) drivers and services. This applet is discussed in Chapter 20.

Power Options

The Power Options applet manages a system's power-saving capabilities. For desktop systems, this includes powering down the monitor and hard drives. For portable systems, this can include hibernation and other device-specific controls. Predefined power schemes can be used, or you can customize your own. Simply select a scheme or create your own by configuring devices to power down after a defined time interval.

Printers

The Printers folder manages printers, including installation, sharing, configuration, and queue control. This applet manages both plain-paper printers as well as specialty printers and fax devices. This applet is discussed in Chapter 18.

Regional Settings

The Regional Settings applet manages geographic location-specific conventions for numbers, currency, time, dates, and more. You can select from a predefined scheme for a language and country or define your own.

Scanners And Cameras

The Scanners And Cameras applet manages the installation and configuration of digital cameras and scanners. Use this applet to install vendor-supplied drivers (if Windows 2000 does not automatically detect the device upon system boot); then use this applet to access vendor/device-specific property control interfaces.

Scheduled Tasks

The Scheduled Tasks folder manages task scheduling. With this tool, programs or batch files can be configured to launch automatically at a specific time or when an event occurs. Tasks can be launched with specific user credentials and allowed to run only when the system is idle or only when the system is not running on batteries. An Add Scheduled Task Wizard is used to create tasks. Then advanced options can be set by opening the Properties dialog box of a defined task. In spite of all the capabilities offered by this tool, it's amazingly simple to operate.

Sounds And Multimedia

The Sounds And Multimedia applet manages the association between system events and sounds, the creation and use of sound schemes, the setting of preferred playback and recording devices, and the troubleshooting and configuration of multimedia hardware.

System

The System applet manages many system and core functions of Windows 2000. The General tab of this applet displays the system version, registration information, and basic computer platform details. The Network Identification tab is used to change the name of the computer and to join a domain or workgroup. The Hardware tab has links to the Add/Remove Hardware applet, the Driver Signing Options dialog box, the Device Manager, and the Hardware Profiles dialog box. The User Profiles tab is used to create roaming profiles (see Chapter 6). The Advanced tab has links to performance options, environmental variables, and startup and recovery settings.

NOTE: *The options available on these tabs may vary depending on the software you have installed.*

Driver Signing Options

The Driver Signing Options dialog box defines how the system will handle nonsigned drivers when you're installing new hardware. A signed driver is a device driver digitally signed by Microsoft to validate its authenticity. The system can be configured to ignore signing, warn when nonsigned drivers are being used, or block all but signed drivers from being installed.

Device Manager

The Device Manager is a tool that displays all installed hardware. From this list, you can access the Properties dialog box for each device to change settings, update drivers, or troubleshoot problems. In the list of devices, the device icon may be enhanced with a yellow exclamation point or a red stop sign. These icons indicate problems or conflicts with the device or its driver. The list of devices can be displayed by type or connection. You can also view a list of system resources (DMA, I/O address, IRQ, and memory) by type or connection.

Hardware Profiles

A *hardware profile* is used to define a set of device drivers for a specific configuration of hardware. Hardware profiles make the most sense when used on portable computers that have changing hardware components, such as a docking bar, removable storage devices, or a PCMCIA/PC Card slot. Every Windows 2000 system has a single default hardware profile. When secondary and additional hardware profiles are defined, the system attempts to match the current state of hardware with a hardware profile upon bootup. If a match cannot be made, you'll be prompted to select a profile to use. One hardware profile is defined as the default. Through the Hardware Profiles interface, you can configure the system to automatically use the default profile after waiting a specified length of time for you to select an alternate profile in the event the system cannot automatically determine the hardware profile to use.

A hardware profile is created by copying an existing hardware profile and then booting using the copy. Once booted, devices can be enabled and disabled through the Device Manager by changing the Device Usage pull-down list on a device's Properties dialog box to Use This Device (Enable) or Do Not Use This Device In The Current Hardware Profile (Disable).

Performance Options

The Performance Options dialog box is used to configure the system optimization and virtual memory. The system can be optimized for applications or background services. By default, Windows 2000 Professional is optimized for applications. By default, Windows 2000 Server is optimized for background services.

Virtual memory is the memory scheme used by Windows 2000; it combines physical RAM with a paging file on a storage device to increase the amount of available memory to the system and hosted processes. Windows 2000 creates a paging file by default of one and a half times the amount of physical RAM installed, for example, if you have 128MB of RAM, the paging file will be 192MB. This initial paging file is placed on the boot partition.

To alter the paging file settings, click the Change button on the Performance Options dialog box. The Virtual Memory dialog box, shown in Figure 10.12, displays the current paging file configuration and is used to alter the paging file settings. The system automatically calculates an optimum size for the paging file and displays this value under the Total Paging File Size For All Drives section (labeled as Recommended). You should configure one or more paging files as large or larger than this value.

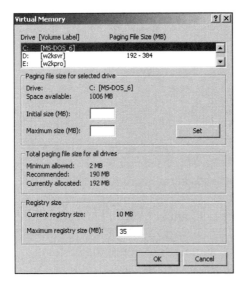

Figure 10.12   The Virtual Memory dialog box.

New paging files are created by selecting a host volume, defining the initial and maximum size values, and then clicking Set. The initial size is the amount of drive space exclusively allocated to the paging file. The maximum size is how large the paging file can grow, but that space is not allocated. In most cases, setting these numbers to the same value is recommended. Existing paging files are altered by selecting them and changing their initial and maximum values. Settings the values to 0 removes the paging file from that volume.

Environment Variables

The Environment Variables dialog box, shown in Figure 10.13, displays the variables and definitions or values defined for the currently logged on user and the system. These values can be edited when necessary. In most cases, the default values are sufficient. Installed applications will often alter or add environmental variables as necessary.

Startup And Recovery

The Startup And Recovery dialog box, shown in Figure 10.14, controls some aspects of the boot menu and how the system manages STOP errors. The System Startup section sets the default OS and the display timeout for the boot menu. The System Failure section configures whether an administrative alert, an automatic reboot, and/or a memory dump file is performed when a STOP error occurs. The Send An Administrative Alert and Automatically Reboot options are useful, but the memory dump can only be interpreted by a Microsoft technical specialist with specific debugging tools. Therefore, you can opt out from creating a memory dump file (debugging information file). If you do enable debugging,

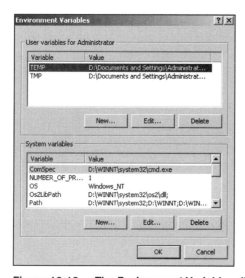

Figure 10.13   The Environment Variables dialog box.

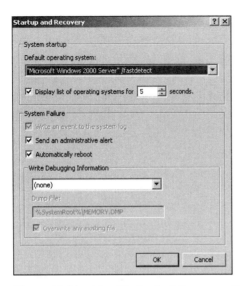

Figure 10.14   The StartupAnd Recovery dialog box.

you must have a paging file on the boot partition as large or larger than the amount of physical RAM present in the system. The default file name and path for the dump file is %systemroot%\memory.dmp.

Users And Passwords

The Users And Passwords applet is used to manage local user accounts and group memberships. This applet also manages certificates and whether Ctrl+Alt+Del is required for logging on. This applet is not present on Windows 2000 Server systems.

Immediate Solutions

Creating a Custom MMC Console

As an administrator, you want to create your own set of tools to facilitate your common management tasks. Therefore, you should create your own MMC console. Here are the steps to follow:

1. Click the Start menu and then click Run. The Run dialog box opens.

2. Type in "mmc" and then click OK. An empty MMC window opens (refer to Figure 10.1).

3. Click the Console menu and then select Add/Remove Snap-In. The Add/Remove Snap-In dialog box opens.

4. Click the Add button. The Add Standalone Snap-In dialog box opens.

5. Locate and select Device Manager (see Figure 10.15). Click Add.

6. Select the local computer and then click Finish.

7. Locate and select System Information. Click Add.

8. Select the local computer and then click Finish.

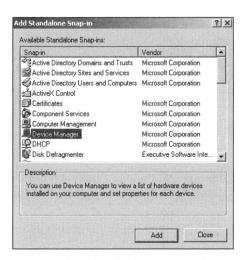

Figure 10.15   The Add Standalone Snap-In dialog box with Device Manager selected.

9. Click Close. You are returned to the Add/Remove Snap-In dialog box.

10. Click OK. You are returned to the MMC window.

11. Click the Console menu and then select Options. The Options dialog box opens.

12. Change the Console mode pull-down list to User Mode - Limited Access, Single Window.

13. Click OK.

14. Click the Console menu and select Save As.

15. Provide a file name, such as "devices". The default storage location should be within the Administrative Tools folder of the currently logged on user's Start menu. Click Save.

16. Click the Console menu and then select Exit to close the MMC window.

17. Click the Start menu, select Programs, select Administrative Tools, and then click Devices.msc. Your newly created MMC console is launched.

18. Click the Console menu and select Exit to close the MMC window.

Viewing System Information

When you need to install a new device, you want to make sure you have free system resources, such as IRQs and I/O addresses. Checking the resource status before adding new devices is always a good first step. Here's how:

NOTE: On Windows 2000 Professional systems, the Administrative Tools section of the Start menu is disabled by default. You can also access Administrative Tools via the Control Panel.

---

1. Click the Start menu, select Programs, select Administrative Tools, and then click Computer Management. The Computer Management window opens.

2. Select the System Information tool under the System Tools section.

3. Expand the System Information tool by clicking the boxed plus sign.

4. Select the System Summary item. Notice the amount of available physical memory. If this is less than 10MB, add more physical RAM.

5. Expand the Hardware Resources item.

6. Select the Conflicts/Sharing item. Take note of whether the resources are shared or in contention.

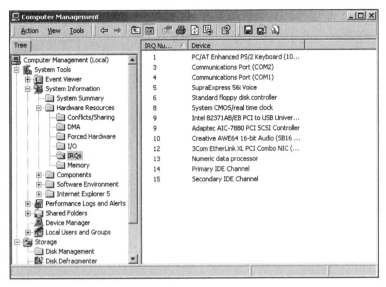

Figure 10.16 The IRQ item selected in the System Information utility in the Computer Management interface.

7. Select the IRQ item (see Figure 10.16). Take note of whether IRQs are still available. (Note that the IRQs are not always shown in numeric order. Click the IRQ Number button to put them in order.)

8. Explore the other areas of this tool for items or issues specific to the device you want to install.

9. Close the Computer Management window by clicking the close button (the X button) in the title bar.

Viewing and Managing Local Shares

You'll periodically want to verify that the correct drives are shared and whether users are accessing those drives. This is done through the Shared Folders tool of Computer Management. Follow these steps:

NOTE: *On Windows 2000 Professional systems, the Administrative Tools section of the Start menu is disabled by default. You can also access Administrative Tools via the Control Panel.*

---

1. Click the Start menu, select Programs, select Administrative Tools, and then click Computer Management. The Computer Management window opens.

2. Select the Shared Folders utility.

3. Expand the Shared Folders utility by clicking its boxed plus sign.

4. Select the Shares item. Notice that it lists all normal, hidden, and system shares of the local system.

5. Click the Action menu and select New File Share. The Create Shared Folder Wizard appears.

6. Click the Browse button. Locate and select a drive or folder to share. Then click OK.

7. Provide a share name and a share description. Then click Next.

8. Select the permission level for this share. Your options are All Users Have Full Control, Administrators Have Full Control and Other Users Have Read-Only Access, Administrators Have Full Control And Other Users Have No Access, and Custom Settings.

9. Click Finish to create the share.

10. You'll be prompted to indicate whether you want to create another share. Click No.

11. Notice that your new share now appears in the list of shares for this system.

12. Select the Sessions item. A list of all users and computers currently accessing resources from shares off this system are displayed.

13. By selecting an entry in this list and issuing the Close Session command from the Action menu, you can terminate an active session.

14. Select the Open Files item. A list of all open files and folders is displayed.

15. Close the Computer Management window by clicking the close button (the X button) in the title bar.

Using the Event Viewer

When system problems occur, you'll want to investigate the details as recorded in the Event Viewer. Here are the steps:

NOTE: *On Windows 2000 Professional systems, the Administrative Tools section of the Start menu is disabled by default. You can also access Administrative Tools via the Control Panel.*

1. Click the Start menu, select Programs, select Administrative Tools, and then select Event Viewer. The Event Viewer opens.

2. Select the System log. A list of events should be displayed in the right pane.

3. Double-click any listed Information event (its icon is a blue "i" inside a thought bubble).

4. View the data captured for this event.

5. Click OK to close this event detail.

6. Double-click any listed Warning event (its icon is a yellow triangle with a black exclamation point.)

7. View the data captured for this event.

8. Click OK to close this event detail.

9. Double-click any listed Error event (its icon is a red circle with a white X).

10. View the data captured for this event.

11. Click OK to close this event detail.

12. Click the Action menu and then click Properties. The System Log Properties dialog box opens.

13. Change the maximum log size from its 512KB default to 1,024KB.

14. Select the Overwrite Events As Needed radio button.

15. Click OK.

16. Click the View menu and then click Filter. The System Log Properties dialog box opens with the Filter tab selected.

17. Deselect all event types but Warning.

18. Change the From and To pull-down lists to Events On; then change the dates to yesterday's and today's dates, respectively. Click OK.

19. The Event Viewer should be displaying only Warning events that occurred yesterday or today.

20. Close the Event Viewer window by clicking the close button (the X button) in the title bar.

Managing Licensing

This solution should only be performed if you are actually purchasing real licenses. Knowing how many licenses are being used on your server can help you determine whether you need to purchase more. Here are the steps:

NOTE: *On Windows 2000 Professional systems, the Administrative Tools section of the Start menu is disabled by default. You can also access Administrative Tools via the Control Panel.*

1. Click the Start menu, select Programs, select Administrative Tools, and then click Licensing. The Licensing window opens.

2. Select the Products View tab.

3. Take note of the values for the Windows Server product.

4. If the Per Seat Allocated value is close to or more than the Per Seat Purchased value, you need to purchase more Per Seat licenses. If the Per Server Reached value is close to or more than the Per Server Purchased value, you need to purchase more Per Server licenses. Contact your license reseller before continuing with this solution.

5. Click the Purchase History tab.

6. Click the License menu and then click New License. The New Client Access License dialog box appears.

7. Select Windows Server in the Product window.

8. Change the quantity to the number of additional licenses you've purchased.

9. Select the Per Seat or Per Server mode (if applicable).

10. Provide a comment about the set of added licenses. Click OK.

11. Check the I Agree checkbox and then click OK.

12. Notice that the newly added licenses appear on the Purchase History tab.

13. Select the Products View tab. Notice that the number of Per Seat Purchased or Per Server Purchased licenses values has incremented.

14. Click the License menu and then click Exit.

Working with Services

From time to time, you may need to stop, restart, or reconfigure a service. This is done through the Services tool. Here's how:

NOTE: *On Windows 2000 Professional systems, the Administrative Tools section of the Start menu is disabled by default. You can also access Administrative Tools via the Control Panel.*

1. Click the Start menu, select Programs, select Administrative Tools, and then click Services. The Services window opens.

2. Notice that the right pane contains a list of all services installed in Windows 2000, along with description, status, startup type, and "log on as" information.

3. Select the Alerter service.

4. Click the Action menu and then click Properties. The Properties dialog box for the selected service opens.

5. Click the Stop button. The service is stopped.

6. Click the Start button. The service is restarted.

7. Select the Log On tab.

8. Select the This Account radio button.

9. Click Browse. Locate and select the Administrator user account. Click OK.

10. Type in the password and a confirmation for this user account.

11. Select the Recovery tab.

12. Change the Second Failure setting to Restart The Service.

13. Change the Subsequent Failure setting to Reboot The Computer.

14. Set the Reset Fail Count setting to 3 Days.

15. Select the Dependencies tab. Notice the services this service depends on.

16. Click Cancel to discard all settings and return the service to its original state.

17. Close the Services window by clicking the close button (the X button) in the title bar.

Enabling Accessibility Options

If a user is seeing, hearing, or movement impaired, several features of Windows 2000 can be turned on or altered to improve interaction and control. Here are the steps to follow:

NOTE: *To return your system to normal activity, simply reopen the Accessibility Options applet and deselect all enabled functions.*

---

1. Click the Start menu, select Settings, and then click Control Panel. The Control Panel opens.

2. Double-click the Accessibility Options applet. The Accessibility Options applet opens.

3. Enable StickyKeys by selecting its checkbox.

4. Click Settings under StickyKeys. The Settings for StickyKeys dialog box opens.

5. Make sure all setting checkboxes are marked. Click OK.

6. Enable ToggleKeys by selecting its checkbox.

7. Click Settings under ToggleKeys. The Settings For ToggleKeys dialog box opens.

8. Make sure the setting checkbox is marked. Click OK.

9. Select the Sound tab.

10. Enable SoundSentry by selecting its checkbox.

11. Click Settings under SoundSentry. The Settings For SoundSentry dialog box opens.

12. Set the warning to Flash Active Caption Bar.

13. Select the General tab.

14. Select the Turn Off Accessibility Features After Idle For checkbox.

15. Set the minutes to 5.

16. Click OK to close the Accessibility Options dialog box.

17. Close the Control Panel by clicking the File menu and selecting Close.

Troubleshooting a Device

When a hardware device does not function, you can use the Add/Remove Hardware applet to perform basic troubleshooting. To do so, follow these steps:

1. Click the Start menu, select Settings, and then click Control Panel. The Control Panel opens.

2. Double-click the Add/Remove Hardware applet. The Add/Remove Hardware applet opens (see Figure 10.11).

3. Select the Add/Troubleshoot radio button. Click Next.

4. From the list, select the device that's having difficulties that you want to troubleshoot. It will most likely have a yellow triangle or red stop sign added to its device icon. Click Next.

5. The final screen of the Add/Remove Hardware Wizard shows the current status of the device and indicates that the Troubleshooter will launch after this wizard is closed. Click Finish. The Troubleshooter opens.

6. The Troubleshooter is a Q&A Wizard that helps determine the problem and offers you possible solutions. Answer the questions and follow the instructions.

7. When this is completed, close the Troubleshooter by clicking the close button (the X button) in the title bar.

8. Close the Control Panel by clicking the File menu and selecting Close.

Adding New Hardware

If you've installed a new hardware device but Windows 2000 did not automatically detect it, you'll need to use the Add/Remove Hardware applet. Here's how:

1. Click the Start menu, select Settings, and then click Control Panel. The Control Panel opens.

2. Double-click the Add/Remove Hardware applet. The Add/Remove Hardware applet opens.

3. Select the Add/Troubleshoot radio button. Click Next.

4. Select the Add New Device item. Click Next.

5. Select the Yes, Search For New Hardware option and then click Next. The system will attempt to locate any new hardware.

6. If the hardware is located, a Found New Hardware window will be displayed with the name of the detected hardware. Windows 2000 will attempt to locate the driver(s) for the detected device(s). If necessary, you'll be prompted for the distribution CD or a driver diskette. A list of found devices will be displayed. Review this list and then click Next. A completed message is displayed. Click Finish. The drivers are installed. You may be asked to reboot your system.

7. If the new device is not detected, a message will be displayed stating this. Click Next.

8. Select the type of device from the list provided.

9. Select the manufacturer and model from the list provided or click the Have Disk button to install nonlisted devices or new drivers for listed devices.

10. A screen listing the name of the device to be installed is shown. Click Next to install the driver.

11. After the driver is installed, a completed message is displayed. Click Finish. The drivers are installed. You may be asked to reboot your system.

12. Close the Control Panel by clicking the File menu and selecting Close.

Removing a Device Permanently

If you remove a device from a computer and that device will never be reinstalled, you should remove the driver associated with that device as well. This is done through the Add/Remove Hardware applet. Follow these steps:

1. Click the Start menu, select Settings, and then click Control Panel. The Control Panel opens.

2. Double-click the Add/Remove Hardware applet. The Add/Remove Hardware applet opens.

3. Select the Uninstall/Unplug radio button. Click Next.

4. Select Uninstall a Device. Click Next.

5. From the list of devices, select the device to install. If the device is not listed, check the Show Hidden Devices checkboxes and look again. Once the device is selected, click Next.

6. Select the Yes, I Want To Uninstall This Device option and click Next.

7. A Completing message is displayed. Click Finish. The driver (or drivers) is removed. You may be asked to reboot your system.

8. Close the Control Panel by clicking the File menu and selecting Close.

Rejecting or Unplugging a Device Temporarily

If you need to remove or unplug a device temporarily, you don't need to remove the driver. Instead, you can just have the system disable the driver until the device is returned to the system. This is done through the Add/Remove Hardware applet. Here are the steps:

1. Click the Start menu, select Settings, and then click Control Panel. The Control Panel opens.

2. Double-click the Add/Remove Hardware applet. The Add/Remove Hardware applet opens.

3. Select the Uninstall/Unplug radio button. Click Next.

4. Select Unplug/Eject A Device. Click Next.

5. Select the device you want to unplug or eject. Click Next.

6. A Completing message is displayed. Click Finish. The driver (or drivers) is removed. You may be asked to reboot your system.

7. Close the Control Panel by clicking the File menu and selecting Close.

Installing New Applications

If you need to install a new software application, use the Add/Remove Programs applet. Follow these steps:

1. Click the Start menu, select Settings, and then click Control Panel. The Control Panel opens.

2. Double-click the Add/Remove Programs applet. The Add/Remove Programs applet opens.

3. Click the Add New Programs button.

4. Place the installation CD or floppy in the drive of the computer.

5. Click the CD or Floppy button and then click Next.

6. If an installation launch tool is found, its path will be displayed. If not, or if the displayed path and file name are incorrect, use the Browse button to find and select the installation routine for the application. Click Finish.

7. The installation routine for the application is launched. Follow its prompts as necessary. When completed, you may be asked to reboot your system.

8. Close the Add/Remove Programs applet by clicking the Close button.

9. Close the Control Panel by clicking the File menu and selecting Close.

Removing an Installed Application

If you want to remove an installed application, use the Add/Remove Programs applet. Here are the steps:

1. Click the Start menu, select Settings, and then click Control Panel. The Control Panel opens.

2. Double-click the Add/Remove Programs applet. The Add/Remove Programs applet opens.

3. Click the Change Or Remove Programs button.

4. Select the program you want to remove.

5. Click the Change/Remove button.

6. Follow the application-specific prompts for removing or changing the product.

7. Once this is completed, you may be asked to reboot your system.

8. Close the Add/Remove Programs applet by clicking the Close button.

9. Close the Control Panel by clicking the File menu and selecting Close.

Changing Installed Windows Components

If you want to add or remove Windows 2000 components from the original distribution, use the Add/Remove Programs applet. Here's how:

1. Click the Start menu, select Settings, and then click Control Panel. The Control Panel opens.

2. Double-click the Add/Remove Programs applet. The Add/Remove Programs applet opens.

3. Click the Add/Remove Windows Components button. The Windows Components Wizard opens.

4. Use this interface to select or deselect Windows components. Selecting a component and clicking Details will display the subcomponents. When all the subcomponents are selected, the checkbox will be marked with a white background. When at least one subcomponent but not all are selected, the checkbox will be marked with a gray background. Once you have made your selections, click Next.

5. The Windows Components Wizard will install or remove files based on your selections. When the Completing message is displayed, click Finish.

6. Close the Add/Remove Programs applet by clicking the Close button.

7. Close the Control Panel by clicking the File menu and selecting Close.

Changing Display and Desktop Settings

To alter the appearance of your desktop environment, use the Display applet. Here are the steps:

NOTE: *The Display applet can be reached by right-clicking an area of the desktop without an icon and selecting Properties from the pop-up menu.*

1. Click the Start menu, select Settings, and then click Control Panel. The Control Panel opens.

2. Double-click the Display applet. The Display applet opens.

3. On the Background tab, select a graphics file for your desktop wallpaper. If necessary, select the tile the image. You may be prompted to enable Active Desktop. Click Yes.

4. Select the Screen Saver tab.

5. Select a screen saver from the pull-down list. Set the wait interval to 10 minutes.

6. Select the Appearance tab.

7. Select a scheme from the pull-down list.

8. Select the Web tab.

9. Select the Smooth Edges Of Screen Fonts and Show Window Contents While Dragging checkboxes.

10. Select the Settings tab.

11. Set your screen resolution to 800 x 600 and the color to 16-bit High Color.

12. Click OK.

13. Close the Control Panel by clicking the File menu and selecting Close.

Configuring Regional Settings

If your computer is based in a country other than the United States, you are using a language other than English, or you want to change the conventions of your computer, you can do so via the Regional Settings applet. Here are the steps to follow:

1. Click the Start menu, select Settings, and then click Control Panel. The Control Panel opens.

2. Double-click the Regional Settings applet. The Regional Settings applet opens (with a title of Regional Options).

3. On the General tab, select the location of your computer.

4. Check any additional languages you want to install on this system.

5. Select the Numbers tab.

6. The default conventions for the language/location of your computer are shown. To alter any settings, use the pull-down list.

7. Select the Currency tab.

8. The default conventions for the language/location of your computer are shown. To alter any settings, use the pull-down list.

9. Select the Time tab.

10. The default conventions for the language/location of your computer are shown. To alter any settings, use the pull-down list.

11. Select the Date tab.

12. The default conventions for the language/location of your computer are shown. To alter any settings, use the pull-down list.

10. Windows 2000
Administration Tools

13. Select the Input Locales. This tab is where the hotkeys to switch to an alternate location are defined. Take note of the defaults or define your own.

14. Click OK to close the Regional Settings applet.

15. Close the Control Panel by clicking the File menu and selecting Close.

Scheduling a Task

If you want to automatically perform a task without user input, use the Task Scheduler. Here's how:

1. Click the Start menu, select Settings, and then click Control Panel. The Control Panel opens.

2. Double-click the Scheduled Tasks applet. The Scheduled Tasks applet opens into the same window as Control Panel.

3. Double-click the Add Scheduled Task Wizard. The wizard opens.

4. Click Next.

5. Select an application to launch or click the Browse button to select programs or batch files not listed. Click Next.

6. Set the frequency of this task. Click Next.

7. Set the start time, repeat intervals, start date, or other frequency-specific details, as prompted. Click Next.

8. Provide the user name and password for the user account this task will be executed under. Click Next.

9. Select the Open Advanced Properties For This Task When I Click Finish checkbox. Click Finish. The Properties dialog box for the scheduled task opens.

10. Select the Settings tab.

11. Select the Delete The Task If It Is Not Scheduled To Run Again checkbox.

12. Set the Stop The Task If It Runs For option to 8 Hours.

13. Select the Only Start The Task If The Computer Has Been Idle For At Least checkbox and set the idle time to 5 Minutes.

14. Click OK. Notice that the scheduled task now appears in the Scheduled Task window.

15. Click the Back button to return to the Control Panel.

16. Close the Control Panel by clicking the File menu and selecting Close.

Configuring a Sound Scheme

If you have a multimedia-capable system, you can customize the sounds your system makes based on application and interface events through the Sounds And Multimedia applet. Follow these steps:

1. Click the Start menu, select Settings, and then click Control Panel. The Control Panel opens.

2. Double-click the Sounds And Multimedia applet. The Sounds And Multimedia applet opens.

3. Select a scheme from the pull-down list.

4. To customize a sound for an event, select the event from the Sound Events list. Then, use the Name pull-down list, shown in Figure 10.17, or the Browse button to select a sound. Click the play button (the triangle pointing to the right, like a play button on a tape recorder) to hear the selected sound.

5. Once you've customized all desired sound events, click the Save As button. Provide a name for your new sound scheme. Click OK.

6. Click OK to close the Sounds And Multimedia applet.

7. Close the Control Panel by clicking the File menu and selecting Close.

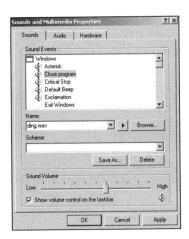

Figure 10.17   The Name pull-down list in the Sounds And Multimedia Properties dialog box.

Setting Driver Signing Options

If you're concerned about corrupted drivers being installed onto your system, use the driver signing options to protect yourself. Here are the steps:

1. Click the Start menu, select Settings, and then click Control Panel. The Control Panel opens.

2. Double-click the System applet. The System applet opens.

3. Select the Hardware tab.

4. Click the Driver Signing button. The Driver Signing Options dialog box opens, as shown in Figure 10.18.

5. Select the Block radio button to prevent nonsigned drivers from being installed.

6. Click OK to close the Driver Signing Options dialog box.

7. Click OK to close the System applet.

8. Close the Control Panel by clicking the File menu and selecting Close.

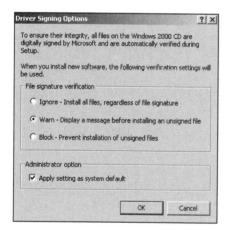

Figure 10.18   The Driver Signing Options dialog box.

Creating Hardware Profiles

If you have a computer with hardware devices that change periodically, you can use hardware profiles to define a set of drivers for each unique hardware configuration. Here are the steps to follow:

1. Click the Start menu, select Settings, and then click Control Panel. The Control Panel opens.

2. Double-click the System applet. The System applet opens.

3. Select the Hardware tab.

4. Click the Hardware Profiles button. The Hardware Profiles dialog box opens.

5. Select the Profile 1 hardware profile. Click Copy.

6. Type a name for the new profile. Click OK.

7. Click the Start menu and then click Shutdown. Select Reboot and then click OK.

8. When prompted during the booting process, use the arrow keys to select the new hardware profile you named in Step 6. Once you've made your selection, press Enter.

9. After the computer has booted, log on using Ctrl+Alt+Del.

10. If the Control Panel is not open, click the Start menu, select Settings, and then click Control Panel. The Control Panel opens.

11. Double-click the System applet. The System applet opens.

12. Select the Hardware tab.

13. Click the Device Manager button. The Device Manager opens.

14. Expand the list of devices. Select a device that will not be present when this hardware profile is used.

15. Click the Action menu and then click Properties.

16. Change the Device Usage pull-down list from Use This Device (Enable) to Do Not Use This Device In The Current Hardware Profile (Disable), as shown in Figure 10.19. Click OK.

NOTE: *If you want to add a device back into a hardware profile, change the Device Usage setting from Do Not Use This Device In The Current Hardware Profile (Disable) to Use This Device (Enable).*

---

17. Repeat Steps 14 through 16 for each device to be removed from this hardware profile.

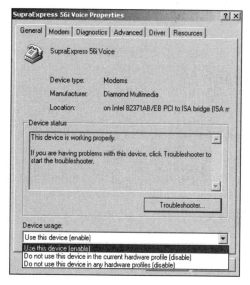

Figure 10.19   A device's Properties dialog box from the Device Manager.

18. When this is completed, shut down the system. Click the Start menu and then click Shutdown. Select Shutdown and then click OK.

19. Once the power is off, change the hardware configuration of the system to match the newly created hardware profile.

20. Power on the system. The hardware profile should be automatically selected.

21. After the computer has booted, log on using Ctrl+Alt+Del.

22. Repeat this solution to create other hardware profiles.

Chapter 11

Windows 2000 Registry: Structure, Editing, and Important Keys

In Depth

Although many people think that Windows 95 and NT were the first operating systems to have a Registry, that's not the case. In fact, Windows 3.x and NT 3.1 had a Registry of sorts. It was just stored and modified differently.

Anyone who worked with Windows 3.x will recall having to edit INI files. These initialization files get their name from the .ini extension that's most commonly assigned to the files. The INI files were simple text files. You could edit them from DOS (using the Edit command) or through Notepad in Windows. Having these configuration files stored as text files was great because they were very easy to edit. However, because they were easy to edit, they were corrupted easily. Any user or application could go into these files and modify them.

Windows NT 3.1 introduced a new way of storing configuration information—using the Registry. The Registry introduced in Windows NT 3.1 has not changed much in its format and structure and is very similar to the one you find in Windows 2000.

The Registry stores all configuration information about the system. This includes networking components, security, applications, desktop settings, and the actual appearance of the user interface.

Hives, Files, and Structures

The Windows 2000 Registry is designed much like a file system. Each component in the file system has a corresponding component in the Registry. The Registry is stored in binary databases on the local hard drive.

You have a couple ways to access the information stored in the Registry databases. The first is using either built-in or third-party Registry tools. The other is through a Win32 application programming interface (API).

As stated, the Registry can be compared to a file system. A file system consists of three main components: the disk, the folders, and the files. The root of the file system is the disk. It's most commonly assigned a letter (for example, C:). Underneath the root exist folders and files. Folders are containers that can hold other folders and/or files. Finally, the lowest part of the structure is the files. Files cannot contain other folders or files (archive files such as ZIP files are a special case).

With the Registry, the structure is similar—only the names have changed. At the root of the Registry are the root keys. There are five root keys (also known as *hives*): HKEY_CLASSES_ROOT (HKCR), HKEY_CURRENT_USER (HKCU), HKEY_LOCAL_MACHINE (HKLM), HKEY_USERS (HKU), and HKEY_CURRENT_CONFIG (HKCC). These root keys are listed in Table 11.1 with their descriptions.

Below the root keys are the keys. Several of the main keys are referred to *subkeys*. Table 11.2 deals with some of the most commonly used (and most important) subkeys.

Table 11.1   The root keys.

Root Key	Description
HKEY_CLASSES_ROOT (HKCR)	Creates the links between file extensions and old class system components. These links tell the system which application to launch for a specific extension (for example, launch Microsoft Word when a DOC file is opened).
HKEY_CURRENT_USER (HKCU)	Specifies the configuration properties of the currently logged on user. When the user logs on, the user's profile is written to this root key. When the user logs off, information from this root key is written into the user's profile.
HKEY_LOCAL_MACHINE (HKLM)	Stores all configuration information about the current system. This includes hardware, software, and operating system information.
HKEY_USERS (HKU)	Stores a copy of the profile of each user who has logged into this system before.
HKEY_CURRENT_CONFIG (HKCC)	Stores information about the current system configuration.

Table 11.2   The main subkeys.

Subkey	Description
HKLM\HARDWARE	Stores all hardware configurations currently known about the system. This subkey is created when the system is first started.
HKLM\SAM	Stores all the information about the user databases. In Windows 2000, this is stored in the Active Directory. The Security Accounts Manager (SAM) is no longer used as it was in Windows NT. The subkey is named SAM for backward compatibility.
HKLM\SECURITY	This subkey stores the security information for the system—information such as the currently logged on user's credentials and policy information. You cannot modify this subkey.

(continued)

Table 11.2   The main subkeys (continued).

Subkey	Description
HKLM\SOFTWARE	This subkey stores information about the different software packages installed on the system. The Windows 2000 operating system is defined as one of these applications, so you'll find many of the configuration properties for Windows 2000 within this subkey.
HKLM\SYSTEM	Stores all information about the currently loaded session (including services). This subkey also stores the configuration for the Last Known Good Configuration boot option.

Manipulating the Windows 2000 Registry

Because of the way the Registry is stored on the system, you need specialized tools to control all the changes in the Registry. Many of the day-to-day changes to the Registry are performed through the Control Panel applets. Sometimes, however, a manual Registry edit is required. Some of the tools available to perform these tasks are covered in this section.

WARNING!   Incorrectly editing the Registry can render your system unusable. Many of the tools discussed here will make the changes immediately and can crash your system if not used properly. Only edit the Registry directory as a last resort, if you have a current backup, and are absolutely certain you know what you're editing.

Registry Access Tools and Editors

Windows 2000 ships with two Registry editing tools: regedit.exe, shown in Figure 11.1, and regedt32.exe, shown in Figure 11.2. The differences between the two will become apparent later in this chapter. Both perform the same basic tasks, but as you'll see, one is considerably more powerful for editing the Registry.

These two editors have different backgrounds. When Microsoft shipped Windows NT 3.1, it included a tool to modify the Registry known as *regedt32.exe*. This tool could be used to view and modify the Registry, set permissions on the Registry, and search keys within the Registry. When Windows 95 was developed, Microsoft quickly realized that although Windows 95 needed a Registry—and therefore a Registry editor—the format of regedt32.exe did not fit. Therefore, the Windows 95 Registry editor, *regedit.exe*, was developed. This editor had all the basic capabilities of regedt32.exe but did not have the option of modifying Registry permissions. The reason for this is simple: There is no way in Windows 9x to control permissions by users. However, regedit.exe provided a more flexible search component (you could now search for keys, values, and data rather than only keys, as with regedt32.exe), better importing/exporting tools, the ability to rename keys, and the ability to copy key names.

11. Windows 2000 Registry: Structure, Editing, and Important Keys

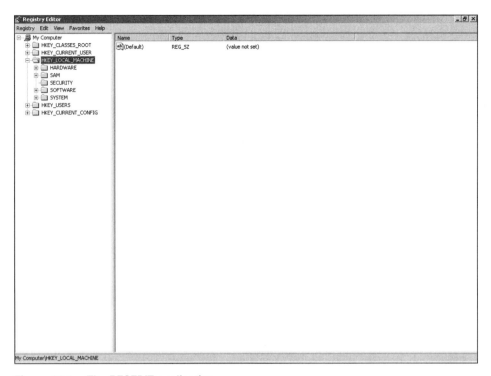

Figure 11.1   The REGEDIT application.

When Windows 2000 shipped, Microsoft decided to include both editors in the operating system. Although this might seem redundant, it is, in fact, not. Although it would be nice to have a single tool that does everything, Microsoft kept the two tools that administrators are used to.

Windows 2000 Resource Kit Registry Tools

The *Windows 2000 Server Resource Kit* (RK), (Microsoft Press, ISBN: 1-57231-805-8) is a must for all Windows 2000 administrators. Although Windows 2000 has most of the tools an administrator needs, the *Windows 2000 Server RK* has more advanced tools (but not always pretty) to help with everyday tasks. This is especially true with the Registry. Several Registry tools and help files ship with the RK, and this chapter looks at the following six:

- Regback.exe
- Regrest.exe
- Regdmp.exe
- Regfind.exe
- Scanreg.exe
- Dureg.exe

11. Windows 2000 Registry: Structure, Editing, and Important Keys

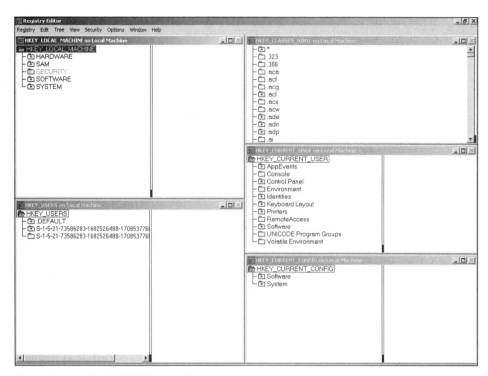

Figure 11.2   The REGEDT32 application.

Regback.exe

The *Windows 2000 Server Resource Kit* ships with a program that can be used to back up the Registry. This file, regback.exe, is found in the %root%\Program Files\Resource Kit folder and is executed using the following format:

```
REGBACK [-m \\servername] directoryPath [-u | -U outputFile]
```

The regback.exe application can be used to back up the Registry on the local machine or on a remote machine. It can also be used to back up the user profile. This is useful if you've created a profile you would like to easily back up and use with other users.

Regrest.exe

The flip side of regback.exe is regrest.exe. It can take the files backed up with regback.exe and restore them to the Registry. One nice feature of the regrest.exe application is that it will automatically back up the information in the Registry before restoring the new information. The format for running this application is as follows:

```
regrest <newfilename> <savefilename> <hivetype> <hivename>
```

WARNING! *The regrest.exe file does not actually overwrite any files. Instead, it moves the current Registry file to the location specified in the <savefilename> switch and then moves the new Registry file, as specified in the <newfilename> switch. For this reason, all files must reside on the same volume. For example, if the new files are on the D: drive and the current files are on the C: drive, you'll need to move the files from the D: drive to the C: drive.*

Regdmp.exe

This application allows you to dump the contents of the Registry to the screen, a file, or a printer. The regdmp.exe application uses the following format:

```
REGDMP [-m \\servername | -h hivefile hiveroot |
-w Win95 Directory][-i n][-o outputWidth][-s]
[-o outputWidth] RegistryPath
```

Regfind.exe

Although regedit.exe gives you some fairly good Registry search capabilities, its searching capabilities pale in comparison to those of regfind.exe. This tool not only allows you to search the Registry for a string, it also allows you to automatically replace those found strings. Its format is as follows:

```
REGFIND [-m \\machinename | -h hivefile hiveroot | -w Win95 Directory][-i n]
[-o outputWidth][-p RegistryKeyPath][-z | -t DataType][-b | -B][-y]
[-n][searchString [-r ReplacementString]]
```

Scanreg.exe

Scanreg.exe has been called the "grep" of the Registry. *Grep* is a Unix command-line tool for performing very complex searches on directories, files, and data. Scanreg.exe allows you to search the Registry for a specific string. You can have only keys, values, or data searched, or you can search all three. It also displays the output with different colors assigned to each type it finds. Scanreg.exe uses the following structure:

```
scanreg <[-s] string> < [-k][-v][-d] > [[-r] key][-c][-e][-n]
```

Dureg.exe

Dureg.exe is a tool that can be used to find the size of the Registry, a root key, or any key within the local Registry. Its format is as follows:

```
DuReg [/a | /cr | /cu | /u | /lm][/s | /d]
["Registry path"]["string to search"]
```

Popular Registry Tools

Many different Registry tools exist on the market today. As you can imagine, an entire chapter could be devoted to these tools. For this reason, this chapter only outlines some of the most popular Registry tools available today. These include:

- Registrar and Registry Search
- Registry Studio
- Registry Editor Extensions

These tools are introduced in the following sections.

Registrar and Registry Search

Both these tools are available from Resplendent Software Projects (**www.resplendence.com**). They're two independent tools that work together to make a fairly powerful suite of editing tools. The Registrar is an advanced Registry-editing utility as shown in Figure 11.3. This utility allows you to monitor the Registry for changes and create favorite bookmarks to commonly accessed sections of the Registry.

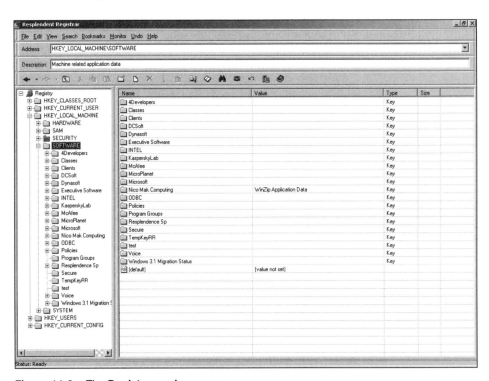

Figure 11.3   The Registrar main screen.

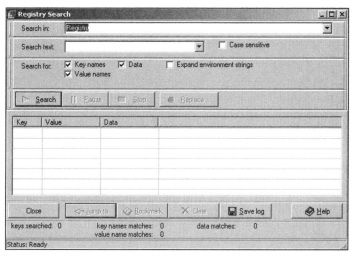

Figure 11.4   The Registry Search application's main screen.

Registry Search, shown in Figure 11.4, gives you full search capability of the Registry. Using this tool, you can search for keys, values, and data as well as limit your searches to specific root keys and subkeys.

Registry Studio

This utility, although very similar to regedit.exe, gives you some extra features. These include the ability to create bookmarks of favorite Registry keys, a button bar for accessing commonly used tools, and the ability to send a Registry key to a user. Figure 11.5 displays the Registry Studio screen.

Registry Editor Extensions

Registry Editor Extensions does just what its name suggests—it uses the current Registry editor and extends its capabilities (see Figure 11.6). It gives you the ability to add favorites to your commonly accessed keys and gives you a drop-down menu to access them.

11. Windows 2000
Registry: Structure, Editing,
and Important Keys

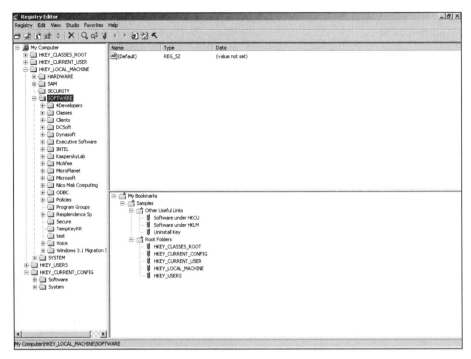

Figure 11.5   The Registry Studio screen.

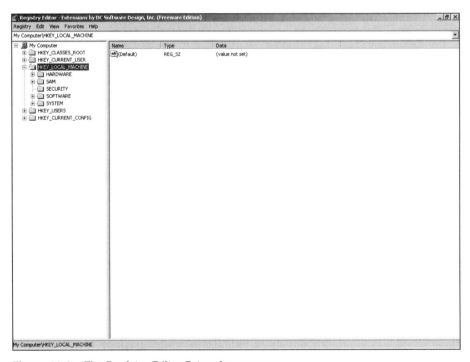

Figure 11.6   The Registry Editor Extensions screen.

Immediate Solutions

Working with Registry Keys and Values

The following sections explore the tasks involved with managing Registry keys and values.

Making a Shortcut to Regedt32.exe or Regedit.exe

By default, the Registry Editors do not have a shortcut assigned to it on the Start menu. The following steps create a shortcut for the Registry Editor of your choice:

1. Select Start|Settings|Taskbar & Start Menu.

2. Click the Advanced tab (see Figure 11.7).

3. Click Add.

4. When the Create Shortcut Wizard appears, enter the location of regedt32.exe or regedit.exe (by default, they're located in the %systemroot%\system32\ folder) or use the Browse button to locate it, select the file, and click Next.

5. Navigate to the location in the Start menu where you would like the shortcut created and click Next.

Figure 11.7   Modifying the Start menu.

6. Enter a display name for the Registry editor (for example, "Registry Editor 32" or "Regedit") and click Finish.

7. Click OK to close the Taskbar & Start Menu applet.

Finding a Registry Key

The two Registry editors search for keys somewhat differently. For this reason, both methods are presented.

Finding a Key Using Regedt32.exe

To find a key using regedt32.exe, perform the following steps:

1. Select Start|Run.

2. Enter "regedt32.exe" in the Open field and click OK.

3. Choose the Find Key option from the View menu.

4. The Find window will appear, as shown in Figure 11.8. Enter the name of the key in the Find What field and click Find Next.

5. To find subsequent keys with the same name, press F3.

Finding a Key Using Regedit.exe

To find a key using regedit.exe, perform the following steps:

1. Select Start|Run.

2. Enter "regedit.exe" in the Open field and click OK.

3. Choose the Find option from the Edit menu.

4. The Find window will appear, as shown in Figure 11.9. Enter the name of the key in the Find What field, ensure that the Keys checkbox is checked, and click Find Next.

5. To find subsequent keys with the same name, press F3.

Finding a Registry Value

Whereas regedt32.exe will only search for keys, regedit.exe will search for keys, values, and data:

1. Select Start|Run.

2. Enter "regedit.exe" in the Open field and click OK.

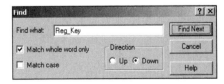

Figure 11.8   Finding a Registry key in regedt32.exe.

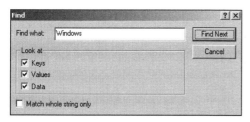

Figure 11.9   Finding a Registry key in regedit.exe.

3. Choose the Find option from the Edit menu.

4. The Find window will appear. Enter the name of the value in the Find What field, ensure that the Values checkbox is checked, and click Find Next.

5. To find subsequent values with the same name, press F3.

Running the Registry Editor in Read-Only Mode

When you modify the Registry using regedt32.exe, changes are made immediately. Because a simple mistake can make your system inoperative, regedt32.exe has the option to set the Registry Editor to Read Only:

1. Select Start|Run.

2. Enter "regedt32.exe" in the Open field and click OK.

3. Choose the Read Only Mode option from the Options menu.

Saving a Registry Key

You can save a Registry key as a backup or to duplicate a configuration from one system to another:

1. Select Start|Run.

2. Enter "regedt32.exe" in the Open field and click OK.

3. Select the key you would like to save.

4. Choose the Save Key option from the Registry menu.

5. Specify a location and a name for the saved key file and click OK.

Saving a Registry Subtree

To save a Registry subtree, perform the following steps:

1. Select Start|Run.

2. Enter "regedt32.exe" in the Open field and click OK.

3. Select the key you would like to save.

4. Choose the Save Subtree As option from the Registry menu.

5. Specify a location and a name for the saved subtree file and click OK.

Creating a New Key

The method for creating new keys varies between regedit.exe and regedt32.exe. Therefore, both methods are listed here.

Creating a New Key Using Regedt32.exe

1. Select Start|Run.
2. Enter "regedt32.exe" in the Open field and click OK.
3. Navigate to where you would like the new key created.
4. Choose the Add Key option from the Edit menu.
5. Enter a name for the new key in the Key Name field, enter a class for the key in the Class field, and click OK.

Creating a New Key Using Regedit.exe

To create a new key using regedit.exe, perform the following steps:

1. Select Start|Run.
2. Enter "regedit.exe" in the Open field and click OK.
3. Navigate to where you would like the new key created.
4. Choose the New|Key option from the Edit menu.
5. A new key will appear with a temporary name of New Key # n. Enter the name for the key and press Enter.

Creating a New Key on a Remote System

The two Registry editors create keys somewhat differently. For this reason, both methods are presented.

Creating a Key on a Remote System Using Regedt32.exe

To create a key on a remote system using regedt32.exe, perform the following steps:

1. Select Start|Run.
2. Enter "regedt32.exe" in the Open field and click OK.
3. Select the Select Computer option from the Registry menu.
4. Either enter the name of the computer to which you would like to connect or use the Browse button to locate it.
5. Click OK.
6. Choose the Add Key option from the Edit menu.
7. Enter a name for the new key and click OK.

Creating a Key on a Remote System Using Regedit.exe

To create a key on a remote system using regedit.exe, perform the following steps:

1. Select Start|Run.
2. Enter "regedit.exe" in the Open field and click OK.
3. Select Connect Network Registry from the Registry menu.
4. Enter the name of the computer or use the Browse button to locate it.
5. Click OK.
6. Navigate to where the value is to be created.
7. Select the New_Key option from the Edit menu.
8. Enter the name of the new key and press Enter.

Creating a New Value

The two Registry editors create values somewhat differently. For this reason, both methods are presented.

Creating a New Value Using Regedt32.exe

To create a new value using regedt32.exe, perform the following steps:

1. Select Start|Run.
2. Enter "regedt32.exe" in the Open field and click OK.
3. Navigate to where you would like the new value created.
4. Choose the Add Value option from the Edit menu.
5. Enter a name for the new value in the Value Name field, select the data type from the Data Type menu, and click OK.
6. Enter the data for the value and click OK.

Creating a New Value Using Regedit.exe

To create a new value using regedit.exe, perform the following steps:

1. Select Start|Run.
2. Enter "regedit.exe" in the Open field and click OK.
3. Navigate to where you would like the new value created.
4. Choose the New|String Value option from the Edit menu.

NOTE: *You can also use this method to create a binary or DWORD value by selecting the New|Binary Value or New|DWORD Value option from the Edit menu.*

---

5. A new value will appear with a temporary name of New Value # *n*. Enter the name for the value and press Enter.

6. Double-click the newly created value, enter its data, and click OK.

Creating a New Value on a Remote System

The two Registry editors create new values remotely somewhat differently. For this reason, both methods are presented.

Creating a Value on a Remote System Using Regedt32.exe

To create a value on a remote system using regedt32.exe, perform the following steps:

1. Select Start|Run.

2. Enter "regedt32.exe" in the Open field and click OK.

3. Select the Select Computer option from the Registry menu.

4. Either enter the name of the computer to which you would like to connect or use the Browse button to locate it.

5. Click OK.

6. Choose the Add Value option from the Edit menu.

7. A new value will appear with a temporary name of New Value # *n*. Enter the name for the value and press Enter.

8. Double-click the newly created value, enter its data, and click OK.

Creating a Value on a Remote System Using Regedit.exe

To create a value on a remote system using regedit.exe, perform the following steps:

1. Select Start|Run.

2. Enter "regedit.exe" in the Open field and click OK.

3. Select the Connect Network Registry option.

4. Enter the name of the computer or use the Browse button to locate it.

5. Click OK.

6. Navigate to where the value is to be created.

7. Select the New|String option from the Edit menu.

8. Enter the name of the new value and press Enter.

9. Select the value and choose the Modify option from the Edit menu.

10. Enter the data for the value and click OK.

Copying a Key Name

To copy a key name, perform the following steps:

1. Select Start|Run.

2. Enter "regedit.exe" in the Open field and click OK.

3. Navigate to the location of the key you would like to copy the name of.

4. Choose the Copy Key Name option from the Edit menu.

NOTE: *You can only copy a key using regedit.exe.*

Renaming a Key

To rename a key, perform the following steps:

1. Select Start|Run.

2. Enter "regedit.exe" in the Open field and click OK.

3. Navigate to the location of the key you would like to rename.

4. Choose the Rename option from the Edit menu.

5. Enter the new name for the key and press Enter.

NOTE: *Only regedit.exe can be used to rename a key.*

Renaming a Value

To rename a value, perform the following steps:

1. Select Start|Run.

2. Enter "regedit.exe" in the Open field and click OK.

3. Navigate to the location of the value you would like to rename.

4. Choose the Rename option from the Edit menu.

5. Enter the new name for the value and press Enter.

NOTE: *Only regedit.exe can be used to rename a value.*

Editing an Existing Value

The two Registry editors edit values somewhat differently. For this reason, both methods are presented.

Editing a Key Using Regedt32.exe

To edit a key using regedt32.exe, perform the following steps:

1. Select Start|Run.

2. Enter "regedt32.exe" in the Open field and click OK.

3. Navigate to the value to be edited.

4. Select the value and choose the Binary, String, DWORD, or Multi String option from the Edit menu, depending on the value data type.

5. Modify the value as desired and click OK when done.

Editing a Key Using Regedit.exe

To edit a key using regedit.exe, perform the following steps:

1. Select Start|Run.

2. Enter "regedit.exe" in the Open field and click OK.

3. Navigate to the value to be edited.

4. Select the value and choose the Modify option from the Edit menu.

5. Edit the value as desired and click OK when done.

Editing an Existing Value on a Remote System

The two Registry editors edit values remotely somewhat differently. For this reason, both methods are presented.

Editing a Value on a Remote System Using Regedt32.exe

To edit a value on a remote system using regedt32.exe, perform the following steps:

1. Select Start|Run.

2. Enter "regedt32.exe" in the Open field and click OK.

3. Select the Select Computer option from the Registry menu.

4. Either enter the name of the computer to which you would like to connect or use the Browse button to locate it.

5. Click OK.

6. Navigate to the value to be edited.

7. Select the value and choose the Binary, String, DWORD, or Multi String option from the Edit menu, depending on the value data type.

8. Modify the value as desired and click OK when done.

Editing a Value on a Remote System Using Regedit.exe

To edit a value on a remote system using regedit.exe, perform the following steps:

1. Select Start|Run.

2. Enter "regedit.exe" in the Open field and click OK.

3. Select the Connect Network Registry option.

4. Enter the name of the computer or use the Browse button to locate it.

5. Click OK.

6. Navigate to the value to be edited.

7. Select the value and choose the Binary, String, DWORD, or Multi String option from the Edit menu, depending on the value data type.

8. Modify the value as desired and click OK when done.

Deleting a Registry Key

To delete a key, perform the following steps:

1. Select Start|Run.

2. Enter "regedt32.exe" or "regedit.exe" in the Open field and click OK.

3. Navigate to the key to be deleted.

4. Select the key and choose the Delete option from the Edit menu.

5. Click Yes to confirm the deletion.

Deleting a Registry Key on a Remote System

The two Registry editors delete keys remotely somewhat differently. For this reason, both methods are presented.

Deleting a Key on a Remote System Using Regedt32.exe

To delete a key on a remote system using regedt32.exe, perform the following steps:

1. Select Start|Run.

2. Enter "regedt32.exe" in the Open field and click OK.

3. Select the Select Computer option from the Registry menu.

4. Either enter the name of the computer to which you would like to connect or use the Browse button to locate it.

5. Click OK.

6. Navigate to the key to be deleted.

7. Select the Delete option from the Edit menu.

8. Click Yes to confirm the deletion.

Deleting a Key on a Remote System Using Regedit.exe

To delete a key on a remote system using regedit.exe, perform the following steps:

1. Select Start|Run.
2. Enter "regedit.exe" in the Open field and click OK.
3. Select the Connect Network Registry option.
4. Enter the name of the computer or use the Browse button to locate it.
5. Click OK.
6. Navigate to the key to be deleted.
7. Select the Delete option from the Edit menu.
8. Click Yes to confirm the deletion.

Deleting a Registry Value

To delete a value, perform the following steps:

1. Select Start|Run.
2. Enter "regedt32.exe" or "regedit.exe" in the Open field and click OK.
3. Navigate to the value to be deleted.
4. Select the value and choose the Delete option from the Edit menu.
5. Click Yes to confirm the deletion.

Deleting a Registry Value on a Remote System

The two Registry editors delete values remotely somewhat differently. For this reason, both methods are presented.

Deleting a Value on a Remote System Using Regedt32.exe

To delete value on a remote system using regedt32.exe, perform the following steps:

1. Select Start|Run.
2. Enter "regedt32.exe" in the Open field and click OK.
3. Select the Select Computer option from the Registry menu.
4. Either enter the name of the computer to which you would like to connect or use the Browse button to locate it.
5. Click OK.
6. Navigate to the value to be deleted.
7. Select the Delete option from the Edit menu.
8. Click Yes to confirm the deletion.

Deleting a Value on a Remote System Using Regedit.exe

To delete value on a remote system using regedit.exe, perform the following steps:

1. Select Start|Run.

2. Enter "regedit.exe" in the Open field and click OK.

3. Select the Connect Network Registry option.

4. Enter the name of the computer or use the Browse button to locate it.

5. Click OK.

6. Navigate to the value to be deleted.

7. Select the Delete option from the Edit menu.

8. Click Yes to confirm the deletion.

Importing Registry Settings

To import a Registry, perform the following steps:

1. Select Start|Run.

2. Enter "regedit.exe" in the Open field and click OK.

3. Select the Import Registry File option from the Registry menu.

4. Navigate to the Registry file you would like imported and click OK (see Figure 11.10).

5. You'll be notified when the information has been successfully imported into the Registry.

Figure 11.10   Importing the Registry.

Manually Importing Registry Information

To import Registry information, perform the following steps:

1. Find the file you created (either manually or through the Export process).

Tip: The Registry file will have a .reg extension.

---

2. Right-click the file and choose the Merge option from the pop-up menu.
3. Click Yes to confirm the Registry merge.
4. Click OK when you are notified that the merge has completed.

Exporting the Entire Registry

To export a Registry, perform the following steps:

1. Select Start|Run.
2. Enter "regedit.exe" in the Open field and click OK.
3. Select the Export Registry File option from the Registry menu.
4. Select the All radio button in the Export Range section of the Export Registry File window, as shown in Figure 11.11.
5. Navigate to a location to save the file, enter a name for the file, and click OK.

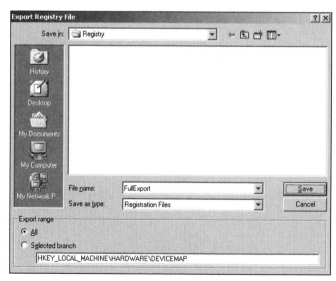

Figure 11.11   Exporting the entire Registry.

Exporting a Registry Branch

To export a Registry branch, perform the following steps:

1. Select Start|Run.

2. Enter "regedit.exe" in the Open field and click OK.

3. Navigate to the key or subkey from where you would like to export Registry information.

4. Select the Export Registry File option from the Registry menu.

5. Select the Selected Branch radio button in the Export Range section of the Export Registry File window (see Figure 11.12).

6. Navigate to a location to save the file, enter a name for the file, and click OK.

Creating Your Own REG File

You can use a REG file to very quickly apply several Registry modifications to multiple computers. You may want to create a REG file with your default configurations:

1. Select Start|Programs|Accessories|Notepad.

2. Type "Windows Registry Editor Version 5.00".

3. Leave a blank line. This line is required.

4. Enter the full path to the key in square brackets. Here's an example:

```
[HKEY_LOCAL_MACHINE\SOFTWARE\Microsoft\Windows NT\CurrentVersion]
```

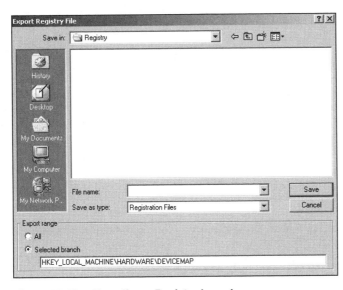

Figure 11.12   Exporting a Registry branch.

5. Enter values using the notation "Value"="Data". (The double quotes are required.)

6. For any values that have a DWORD data type, you can use the following notation:

```
"Value"=dword:000001
```

7. Save the file with a .reg extension.

Backing Up the Registry

To back up the Registry, perform the following steps:

1. Select Start|Programs|Accessories|System Tools|Backup.

2. Select the Backup tab.

3. Select the System State checkbox (see Figure 11.13).

4. Select the Backup Destination option from the drop-down menu (File, miniQIC, or Travan).

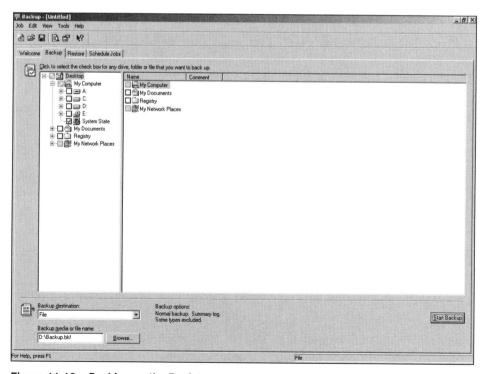

Figure 11.13 Backing up the Registry.

5. Enter any media-specific information.

6. Click Start Backup.

7. If you would like to verify the files after the backup, click Advanced, check the Verify Data After Backup option, and click OK.

8. If you want to schedule the backup, click Schedule. Otherwise, click Start Backup.

9. When the backup is completed, click Close.

Restoring the Registry

To restore the Registry, perform the following steps:

1. Select Start|Programs|Accessories|System Tools|Backup.

2. Select the Restore tab.

3. Navigate to the backup set you would like to recover and check the System State check box (see Figure 11.14).

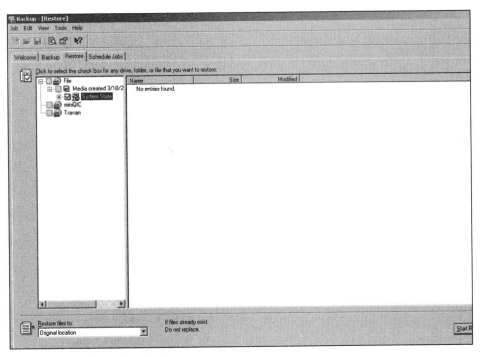

Figure 11.14   Restoring the Registry.

> **WARNING!**   *If the system for which you're trying to restore the Registry is also running Active Directory, you'll need to reboot the server and choose Directory Services Restore Mode from the Troubleshooting menu. Otherwise, your restore will fail.*

4. Click Start Restore.

5. Click Close.

Finding Registry Information

The following sections explore how to find information in the Registry.

Finding the Installed BIOS Date

BIOS updates are common tasks. The BIOS date can be found through the Registry rather than through a system reboot. Here's how:

1. Select Start|Run.

2. Enter "regedt32.exe" in the Open field and click OK.

3. Select the HKEY_LOCAL_MACHINE On Local Machine window.

4. Navigate to HARDWARE\DESCRIPTION\System.

5. Find the SystemBiosDate value in the right pane. This is the date associated with your system's BIOS.

Finding the Installed BIOS Version

BIOS updates are common tasks. The BIOS version number can be found through the Registry rather than through a system reboot. Here's how:

1. Select Start|Run.

2. Enter "regedt32.exe" in the Open field and click OK.

3. Select the HKEY_LOCAL_MACHINE On Local Machine window.

4. Navigate to HARDWARE\DESCRIPTION\System.

5. Find the SystemBiosVersion value in the right pane. This is the BIOS version.

Finding the Processor Type

1. Select Start|Run.

2. Enter "regedt32.exe" in the Open field and click OK.

3. Select the HKEY_LOCAL_MACHINE On Local Machine window.

4. Navigate to HARDWARE\DESCRIPTION\System\CentralProcessor.

5. Expand this key. You'll notice at least one key below CentralProcessor. Each processor has its own key. For example, on a single-processor system, you'll have a 0 key. With a dual-processor system, you'll have a 0 and a 1 key.

6. In the right pane, find the Identifier value. This is the processor type.

Finding the Processor Speed

To find the processor speed, perform the following steps:

1. Select Start|Run.

2. Enter "regedt32.exe" in the Open field and click OK.

3. Select the HKEY_LOCAL_MACHINE On Local Machine window.

4. Navigate to HARDWARE\DESCRIPTION\System\CentralProcessor.

5. Expand this key. You'll notice at least one key below CentralProcessor. Each processor has its own key. For example, on a single-processor system, you'll have a 0 key. With a dual-processor system, you'll have a 0 and a 1 key.

6. In the right pane, find the ~MHz value. This is the processor speed in hexadecimal.

7. To view the processor speed in decimal notation, double-click the ~MHz value and select the Decimal radio button.

Finding the Current Windows 2000 Build

To find the current Windows 2000 build, perform the following steps:

1. Select Start|Run.

2. Enter "regedt32.exe" in the Open field and click OK.

3. Select the HKEY_LOCAL_MACHINE On Local Machine window.

4. Navigate to SOFTWARE\Microsoft\Windows NT\CurrentVersion.

5. Find the CurrentBuildNumber value. This is the currently installed Windows 2000 build.

Modifying the Registry

You can make numerous changes to the Registry. The remainder of this chapter is dedicated to some of the most common Registry changes.

Modifying the Registered Owner

Sometimes, systems move from one person to another. By modifying the registered owner, you can customize the owner settings to fit the person using the system. Here are the steps to follow:

1. Select Start|Run.

2. Enter "regedt32.exe" in the Open field and click OK.

3. Select the HKEY_LOCAL_MACHINE On Local Machine window.

4. Navigate to SOFTWARE\Microsoft\Windows NT\CurrentVersion.

5. Double-click the RegisteredOwner value.

6. In the String field, enter the new name for the owner and click OK.

Modifying the Registered Organization

If your organization changes its name or merges with another organization, it may be necessary to modify the name used to install the system. Here are the steps to follow:

1. Select Start|Run.

2. Enter "regedt32.exe" in the Open field and click OK.

3. Select the HKEY_LOCAL_MACHINE On Local Machine window.

4. Navigate to SOFTWARE\Microsoft\Windows NT\CurrentVersion.

5. Double-click the RegisteredOrganization value.

6. In the String field, enter a new name for the organization and click OK.

Changing the Path for the Windows 2000 Source Files

When Windows 2000 is installed, it logs the initial location of the installation files. These locations, however, may change. Unfortunately, Windows 2000 will search for any additional files in this original location. You can use the following method to modify this location:

1. Select Start|Run.

2. Enter "regedt32.exe" in the Open field and click OK.

3. Select the HKEY_LOCAL_MACHINE On Local Machine window.

4. Navigate to SOFTWARE\Microsoft\Windows NT\CurrentVersion.

5. Double-click the SourcePath value.

6. In the String Field, enter the new path where the Windows 2000 source files are stored, including the drive letter, and click OK.

Adding a Font through the Registry

To add a font through the Registry, perform the following steps:

1. Select Start|Run.

2. Enter "regedt32.exe" in the Open field and click OK.

3. Select the HKEY_LOCAL_MACHINE On Local Machine window.

4. Navigate to SOFTWARE\Microsoft\Windows NT\CurrentVersion\Fonts.

5. Select the Add Value option from the Edit menu.

6. In the Value Name field, enter the name of the new font.

7. Select the REG_SZ option from the Data Type drop-down menu.

8. Click OK.

9. In the String field, enter the file name for the font (for example, font.ttf).

10. Click OK.

Modifying a Font File through the Registry

To modify a file font through the Registry, perform the following steps:

1. Select Start|Run.

2. Enter "regedt32.exe" in the Open field and click OK.

3. Select the HKEY_LOCAL_MACHINE On Local Machine window.

4. Navigate to SOFTWARE\Microsoft\Windows NT\CurrentVersion\Fonts.

5. Find the desired font in the right pane of the Registry Editor tools and double-click it.

6. In the String field, enter a new font file and click OK.

Deleting a Font through the Registry

To delete font through the Registry, perform the following steps:

1. Select Start|Run.

2. Enter "regedt32.exe" in the Open field and click OK.

3. Select the HKEY_LOCAL_MACHINE On Local Machine window.

4. Navigate to SOFTWARE\Microsoft\Windows NT\CurrentVersion\Fonts.

5. Select the font you would like to delete.

6. Select the Delete option from the Edit menu.

7. Click Yes to confirm the deletion.

Viewing Installed Hot Fixes in the Registry

To view hot fixes in the Registry, perform the following steps:

1. Select Start|Run.

2. Enter "regedt32.exe" in the Open field and click OK.

3. Select the HKEY_LOCAL_MACHINE On Local Machine window.

4. Navigate to SOFTWARE\Microsoft\Windows NT\CurrentVersion\HotFix.

5. Expand the HotFix key.

6. All installed hot fixes are listed below this key. Their names appear as Q*xxxxxx* (for example, Q147222).

Viewing the Installed Network Interface Cards

To view installed network adapters, perform the following steps:

1. Select Start|Run.

2. Enter "regedt32.exe" in the Open field and click OK.

3. Select the HKEY_LOCAL_MACHINE On Local Machine window.

4. Navigate to SOFTWARE\Microsoft\Windows NT\CurrentVersion\NetworkCards.

5. Expand the NetworkCards key.

6. All installed network cards are listed below this key and begin with 1 (other entries begin with 0). Select the desired network card.

7. The name of the network card will be displayed in the Description value in the right pane.

Modifying a Communication Port's Parameters

To modify a communication port's parameters, perform the following steps:

1. Select Start|Run.

2. Enter "regedt32.exe" in the Open field and click OK.

3. Select the HKEY_LOCAL_MACHINE On Local Machine window.

4. Navigate to SOFTWARE\Microsoft\Windows NT\CurrentVersion\Ports.

5. In the right pane, double-click the port to modify (usually COM1 through COM4).

6. Select the String option from the Edit menu.

NOTE: *The communication properties take on the format* Baudrate,Parity,Databits,Stopbits *(for example, 9600,n,8,1).*

---

7. Enter the new properties for the communication port and click OK.

Modifying the Print Spool Directory for a Local Computer

If your system is running out of disk space on the drive where the printer spool directory is located, print jobs may fail. You can modify this folder's location through the Registry:

1. Select Start|Run.

2. Enter "regedt32.exe" in the Open field and click OK.

3. Select the HKEY_LOCAL_MACHINE On Local Machine window.

4. Navigate to SOFTWARE\Microsoft\Windows NT\CurrentVersion\Print\Printers.

5. Select the DefaultSpoolDirectory value.

6. Choose the String option from the Edit menu.

7. Enter a new path for the default spool directory and click OK.

Modifying the Print Spool Directory for a Network Printer

To modify the print spool directory for a network printer, perform the following steps:

1. Select Start|Run.

2. Enter "regedt32.exe" in the Open field and click OK.

3. Select the HKEY_LOCAL_MACHINE On Local Machine window.

4. Navigate to SOFTWARE\Microsoft\Windows NT\CurrentVersion\Print\Providers.

5. Find the Printers key. Its exact location will vary depending on the provider and the network location. The location takes on the format HKEY_LOCAL_MACHINE\SOFTWARE\Microsoft\Windows NT\CurrentVersion\Print\Providers*PrintServices*\Servers*Servername*\Printers.

6. Select the DefaultSpoolDirectory value.

7. Choose the String option from the Edit menu.

8. Enter a new path for the default spool directory and click OK.

Modifying the Default User Profile

To modify the all default user profile, perform the following steps:

1. Select Start|Run.

2. Enter "regedt32.exe" in the Open field and click OK.

3. Select the HKEY_LOCAL_MACHINE On Local Machine window.

4. Navigate to SOFTWARE\Microsoft\Windows NT\CurrentVersion\ProfileList.

5. Select the DefaultUserProfile value.

6. Choose the String option from the Edit menu.

7. Enter a new name for the policy. This policy must exist in the location specified in the ProfilesDirectory value.

8. Click OK.

11. Windows 2000
Registry: Structure, Editing,
and Important Keys

Modifying the Profiles Directory

To modify the profiles directory, perform the following steps:

1. Select Start|Run.

2. Enter "regedt32.exe" in the Open field and click OK.

3. Select the HKEY_LOCAL_MACHINE On Local Machine window.

4. Navigate to SOFTWARE\Microsoft\Windows NT\CurrentVersion\ProfileList.

5. Select the ProfilesDirectory value.

6. Choose the String option from the Edit menu.

7. Enter a new path for user profiles. All new profiles will be created in this folder.

Modifying a User's Profile Directory Location

To modify a user's profile directory location, perform the following steps:

1. Select Start|Run.

2. Enter "regedt32.exe" in the Open field and click OK.

3. Select the HKEY_LOCAL_MACHINE On Local Machine window.

4. Navigate to SOFTWARE\Microsoft\Windows NT\CurrentVersion\ProfileList.

5. Select the SID of the desired user below the ProfileList key (you can ascertain which SID belongs to which users through the ProfileImagePath entry).

NOTE: *The user SID is a unique identifier assigned to each user. An example of a SID would be S-1-5-21-73586283-1682526488-1708537768-500.*

---

6. Select the ProfileImagePath option from the right pane.

7. Select the String option from the Edit menu.

8. Modify the path to the profile and click OK.

Modifying the Time Zone

To modify the time zone, perform the following steps:

1. Select Start|Run.

2. Enter "regedt32.exe" in the Open field and click OK.

3. Select the HKEY_LOCAL_MACHINE On Local Machine window.

4. Navigate to SOFTWARE\Microsoft\Windows NT\CurrentVersion\Time Zones.

5. Select a time zone on which to base the new time zone.

6. Select the Display value and choose the String option from the Edit menu.

7. Enter a new display name for the time zone and click OK.

8. Select the Dlt value and choose the String option from the Edit menu.

9. Enter a new daylight saving time description for the time zone and click OK.

10. Select the Std value and choose the String option from the Edit menu.

11. Enter a new standard time description for the time zone and click OK.

Controlling the Ctrl+Alt+Del Logon Screen

To control the Ctrl+Alt+Del logon screen, perform the following steps:

1. Select Start|Run.

2. Enter "regedt32.exe" in the Open field and click OK.

3. Select the HKEY_LOCAL_MACHINE On Local Machine window.

4. Navigate to SOFTWARE\Microsoft\Windows NT\CurrentVersion\Winlogon.

5. Choose the Add Value option from the Edit menu.

6. In the Value Name field, enter "DisableCAD".

7. Select the REG_DWORD option from the Data Type drop-down menu.

8. Click OK.

9. Enter a value of 0 to enable the Ctrl+Alt+Del logon screen or a value of 1 to disable the Ctrl+Alt+Del logon screen.

10. Click OK.

Hiding the Last Logged On Username

For security reasons, you might want to hide the name of the previously logged on user. Here are the steps to follow:

1. Select Start|Run.

2. Enter "regedt32.exe" in the Open field and click OK.

3. Select the HKEY_LOCAL_MACHINE On Local Machine window.

4. Navigate to SOFTWARE\Microsoft\Windows\CurrentVersion\Policies\system.

5. Choose the Add Value option from the Edit menu.

6. In the Value Name field, enter "dontdisplaylastusername".

7. Select the REG_DWORD option from the Data Type drop-down menu.

8. Click OK.

9. Enter a value of 0 to display the last logged on user or a value of 1 to hide the last logged on user.

10. Click OK.

Displaying a Warning Screen before Logon

Some organizations require a warning screen to appear before the user is presented with the logon screen. This information is stored in the Registry. Here are the steps to follow:

1. Select Start|Run.

2. Enter "regedt32.exe" in the Open field and click OK.

3. Select the HKEY_LOCAL_MACHINE On Local Machine window.

4. Navigate to SOFTWARE\Microsoft\Windows\CurrentVersion\ Policies\system.

5. Choose the Add Value option from the Edit menu.

6. In the Value Name field, enter "legalnoticecaption".

7. Select the REG_SZ option from the Data Type drop-down menu.

8. Click OK.

9. Enter the text that is to appear on the top of the caption window.

10. Click OK.

11. In the Value Name field, enter "legalnoticetext".

12. Select the REG_SZ option from the Data Type drop-down menu.

13. Click OK.

14. Enter the text that is to appear in the caption window.

15. Click OK.

Controlling the Shutdown Button on the Logon Screen

A shutdown button exists on the logon screen. In Windows 2000 Professional systems, this button is enabled by default. In Windows 2000 Server systems, the button is disabled by default. The shutdown button allows you to shut down or reboot the system without logging onto the system. For security purposes, you may want to modify this button. Here's how:

1. Select Start|Run.

2. Enter "regedt32.exe" in the Open field and click OK.

3. Select the HKEY_LOCAL_MACHINE On Local Machine window.

4. Navigate to SOFTWARE\Microsoft\Windows\CurrentVersion\Policies\system.

5. Choose the Add Value option from the Edit menu.

6. In the Value Name field, enter "shutdownwithoutlogon".

7. Select the REG_DWORD option from the Data Type drop-down menu.

8. Click OK.

9. Enter a value of 0 to disable the Shutdown button or a value of 1 to enable the Shutdown button.

10. Click OK.

Modifying the Default Logon Domain Name

To modify the default logon domain name, perform the following steps:

1. Select Start|Run.

2. Enter "regedt32.exe" in the Open field and click OK.

3. Select the HKEY_LOCAL_MACHINE On Local Machine window.

4. Navigate to SOFTWARE\Microsoft\Windows NT\CurrentVersion\Winlogon.

5. In the right pane, select the DefaultDomainName value.

6. Choose the String option from the Edit menu.

7. Enter the new name for the domain.

8. Click OK.

Modifying the Number of Cached Logons

To modify the number of cached logons, perform the following steps:

1. Select Start|Run.

2. Enter "regedt32.exe" in the Open field and click OK.

3. Select the HKEY_LOCAL_MACHINE On Local Machine window.

4. Navigate to SOFTWARE\Microsoft\Windows NT\CurrentVersion\Winlogon.

5. In the right pane, select the cachedlogoncount value.

6. Choose the String option from the Edit menu.

7. Enter the number of logons that should be cached.

8. Click OK.

Changing the Default Shell

To change the default shell, perform the following steps:

1. Select Start|Run.

2. Enter "regedt32.exe" in the Open field and click OK.

3. Select the HKEY_LOCAL_MACHINE On Local Machine window.

4. Navigate to SOFTWARE\Microsoft\Windows NT\CurrentVersion\Winlogon.

5. In the right pane, select the Shell value.

6. Choose the String option from the Edit menu.

7. Enter the name of the executable for the new shell (for example, try Progman.exe).

8. Click OK.

Adding a Windows Scripting Host Extension

To add a Windows Scripting Host extension, perform the following steps:

1. Select Start|Run.

2. Enter "regedt32.exe" in the Open field and click OK.

3. Select the HKEY_LOCAL_MACHINE On Local Machine window.

4. Navigate to SOFTWARE\Microsoft\Windows Scripting Host\Script Extensions.

5. Choose the New Key option from the Edit menu.

6. In the Key Name field, enter the name of the scripting engine extension, beginning with a period (for example, .SCR).

7. Click OK.

8. Select the newly created key.

9. Choose the New Value option from the Edit menu.

10. Leave the Value Name field blank, select the REG_SZ option from the Data Type drop-down menu, and click OK.

11. In the String field, enter a description for the extension (for example, SCRScript Script File) and click OK.

12. Choose the New Value option from the Edit menu.

13. In the Value Name field, enter "DefaultIcon", select the REG_SZ option from the Data Type drop-down menu, and click OK.

14. In the String field, enter "%SystemRoot%\System32\wscript.exe,n", where n is the nth icon in the wscript.exe file. There are only four icons in the wscript.exe files; therefore, only the values 1 to 4 may be used.

15. Click OK.

16. Choose the New Value option from the Edit menu.

17. In the Value Name field, enter "EngineID", select the REG_SZ option from the Data Type drop-down menu, and click OK.

18. In the String field, enter the engine ID (for example, SCRScript).

19. Click OK.

20. Choose the New Value option from the Edit menu.

21. In the Value Name field, enter "ScriptID", select the REG_SZ option from the Data Type drop-down menu, and click OK.

22. In the String field, enter the script ID (for example, SCRFile).

23. Click OK.

Hiding the File Menu

To hide the File menu, perform the following steps:

1. Select Start|Run.

2. Enter "regedt32.exe" in the Open field and click OK.

3. Select the HKEY_LOCAL_MACHINE On Local Machine window.

4. Navigate to SOFTWARE\Microsoft\Windows\CurrentVersion\Policies\Explorer.

5. Choose the New Value option from the Edit menu.

6. In the Value Name field, enter "NoFileMenu".

7. Choose the REG_DWORD option from the Data Type drop-down menu.

8. Click OK.

9. In the String field, enter a value of 0 to disable the Registry value or a value of 1 to enable the Registry value.

10. Click OK.

Hiding the Run Option from the Start Menu

To hide the Run option from the Start menu, perform the following steps:

1. Select Start|Run.

2. Enter "regedt32.exe" in the Open field and click OK.

3. Select the HKEY_LOCAL_MACHINE On Local Machine window.

4. Navigate to SOFTWARE\Microsoft\Windows\CurrentVersion\Policies\Explorer.

5. Choose the New Value option from the Edit menu.

6. In the Value Name field, enter "NoRun".

7. Choose the REG_DWORD option from the Data Type drop-down menu.

8. Click OK.

9. In the String field, enter a value of 0 to disable the Registry value or a value of 1 to enable the Registry value.

10. Click OK.

Hiding the Search Option from the Start Menu

To hide the Search option from the Start menu, perform the following steps:

1. Select Start|Run.

2. Enter "regedt32.exe" in the Open field and click OK.

3. Select the HKEY_LOCAL_MACHINE On Local Machine window.

4. Navigate to SOFTWARE\Microsoft\Windows\CurrentVersion\
   Policies\Explorer.

5. Choose the New Value option from the Edit menu.

6. In the Value Name field, enter "NoFind".

7. Choose the REG_DWORD option from the Data Type drop-down menu.

8. Click OK.

9. In the String field, enter a value of 0 to disable the Registry value or a value
   of 1 to enable the Registry value.

10. Click OK.

Hiding the Desktop Icons

To hide the desktop icons, perform the following steps:

1. Select Start|Run.

2. Enter "regedt32.exe" in the Open field and click OK.

3. Select the HKEY_LOCAL_MACHINE On Local Machine window.

4. Navigate to SOFTWARE\Microsoft\Windows\CurrentVersion\
   Policies\Explorer.

5. Choose the New Value option from the Edit menu.

6. In the Value Name field, enter "NoDesktop".

7. Choose the REG_DWORD option from the Data Type drop-down menu.

8. Click OK.

9. In the String field, enter a value of 0 to disable the Registry value or a value
   of 1 to enable the Registry value.

10. Click OK.

Hiding Individual Hard Drives

To hide a hard drive, perform the following steps:

1. Select Start|Run.

2. Enter "regedt32.exe" in the Open field and click OK.

3. Select the HKEY_LOCAL_MACHINE On Local Machine window.

4. Navigate to SOFTWARE\Microsoft\Windows\CurrentVersion\ Policies\Explorer.

5. Choose the New Value option from the Edit menu.

6. In the Value Name field, enter "NoDrives".

7. Choose the REG_DWORD option from the Data Type drop-down menu.

8. Click OK.

9. Each drive letter has a binary bit assigned to it. For example, the A: drive has a value of 1, the B: drive has a value of 2, the C: drive has a value of 4, and the D: drive has a value of 8. The Z: drive has a value of 33554432. To select all the drives, enter a value of 67108863.

10. Click OK.

Hiding the Control Panel on the Start Menu and Windows Explorer

To hide the Control Panel on the Start menu and Windows Explorer, perform the following steps:

1. Select Start|Run.

2. Enter "regedt32.exe" in the Open field and click OK.

3. Select the HKEY_LOCAL_MACHINE On Local Machine window.

4. Navigate to SOFTWARE\Microsoft\Windows\CurrentVersion\ Policies\Explorer.

5. Choose the New Value option from the Edit menu.

6. In the Value Name field, enter "NoSetFolders".

7. Choose the REG_DWORD option from the Data Type drop-down menu.

8. Click OK.

9. In the String field, enter a value of 0 to disable the Registry value or a value of 1 to enable the Registry value.

10. Click OK.

Hiding Printers on the Start Menu and Windows Explorer

To hide Printers on the Start menu and Windows Explorer, perform the following steps:

1. Select Start|Run.

2. Enter "regedt32.exe" in the Open field and click OK.

3. Select the HKEY_LOCAL_MACHINE On Local Machine window.

4. Navigate to SOFTWARE\Microsoft\Windows\CurrentVersion\ Policies\Explorer.

5. Choose the New Value option from the Edit menu.

6. In the Value Name field, enter "NoSetFolders".

7. Choose the REG_DWORD option from the Data Type drop-down menu.

8. Click OK.

9. In the String field, enter a value of 0 to display the printer's folder or a value of 1 to hide the printer's folder.

10. Click OK.

Hiding My Computer on the Start Menu and Windows Explorer

To hide My Computer on the Start menu and Windows Explorer, perform the following steps:

1. Select Start|Run.

2. Enter "regedt32.exe" in the Open field and click OK.

3. Select the HKEY_LOCAL_MACHINE On Local Machine window.

4. Navigate to SOFTWARE\Microsoft\Windows\CurrentVersion\ Policies\Explorer.

5. Choose the New Value option from the Edit menu.

6. In the Value Name field, enter "NoSetFolders".

7. Choose the REG_DWORD option from the Data Type drop-down menu.

8. Click OK.

9. In the String field, enter a value of 0 to hide My Computer or a value of 1 to display My Computer.

10. Click OK.

Hiding My Network Places on the Desktop

To hide My Network Placed on the desktop, perform the following steps:

1. Select Start|Run.

2. Enter "regedt32.exe" in the Open field and click OK.

3. Select the HKEY_LOCAL_MACHINE On Local Machine window.

4. Navigate to SOFTWARE\Microsoft\Windows\CurrentVersion\ Policies\Explorer.

5. Choose the New Value option from the Edit menu.

6. In the Value Name field, enter "NoNetHood".

7. Choose the REG_DWORD option from the Data Type drop-down menu.

8. Click OK.

9. In the String field, enter a value of 0 to display Network Neighborhood or a value of 1 to hide Network Neighborhood.

10. Click OK.

Locking the Desktop

To lock the desktop, perform the following steps:

1. Select Start|Run.

2. Enter "regedt32.exe" in the Open field and click OK.

3. Select the HKEY_LOCAL_MACHINE On Local Machine window.

4. Navigate to SOFTWARE\Microsoft\Windows\CurrentVersion\ Policies\Explorer.

5. Choose the New Value option from the Edit menu.

6. In the Value Name field, enter "NoSetTaskbar".

7. Choose the REG_DWORD option from the Data Type drop-down menu.

8. Click OK.

9. In the String field, enter a value of 0 to disable the Registry value or a value of 1 to enable the Registry value.

10. Click OK.

Removing the Shutdown Option from the Start Menu

To remove the Shutdown option from the Start menu, perform the following steps:

1. Select Start|Run.

2. Enter "regedt32.exe" in the Open field and click OK.

3. Select the HKEY_LOCAL_MACHINE On Local Machine window.

4. Navigate to SOFTWARE\Microsoft\Windows\CurrentVersion\ Policies\Explorer.

5. Choose the New Value option from the Edit menu.

6. In the Value Name field, enter "NoClose".

7. Choose the REG_DWORD option from the Data Type drop-down menu.

8. Click OK.

9. In the String field, enter a value of 0 to disable the Registry value or a value of 1 to enable the Registry value.

10. Click OK.

Changing the Boot or System Drive Letter

To change the boot or system drive letter, perform the following steps:

1. Select Start|Run.
2. Enter "regedt32.exe" in the Open field and click OK.
3. Select the HKEY_LOCAL_MACHINE On Local Machine window.
4. Navigate to SYSTEM\MountedDevices.
5. Select the Permissions option from the Security menu.
6. Ensure that the Administrator's group is assigned the Full Control permission.
7. Close regedt32.exe.
8. Select Start|Run.
9. Enter "regedit.exe" in the Open field and click OK.
10. Select the HKEY_LOCAL_MACHINE On Local Machine window.
11. Navigate to SYSTEM\MountedDevices.
12. Select the drive you would like to change the drive letter for. The values take on the form \DosDevices*driveletter:*.
13. Choose the Rename option from the Edit menu.
14. Enter the new drive letter in the format outlined in Step 12.
15. Press Enter.
16. Reboot the System.

Disabling Logon Using the Dial-Up Networking Checkbox

To disable logon using the Dial-Up Networking checkbox, perform the following steps:

1. Select Start|Run.
2. Enter "regedt32.exe" in the Open field and click OK.
3. Select the HKEY_LOCAL_MACHINE On Local Machine window.
4. Navigate to SOFTWARE\Microsoft\Windows NT\CurrentVersion\Winlogon.
5. Choose the New Value option from the Edit menu.
6. In the Value Name field, enter "RASDisable".
7. Choose the REG_SZ option from the Data Type drop-down menu.
8. Click OK.
9. In the String field, enter a value of 0 to disable the Registry value or a value of 1 to enable the Registry value.
10. Click OK.

Forcing Windows 2000 to Perform a Memory Dump with a Keystroke

To enable a keystroke memory dump, perform the following steps:

1. Select Start|Run.
2. Enter "regedt32.exe" in the Open field and click OK.
3. Select the HKEY_LOCAL_MACHINE On Local Machine window.
4. Navigate to \SYSTEM\CurrentControlSet\Services\i8042prt\Parameters.
5. Choose the New Value option from the Edit menu.
6. In the Value Name field, enter "CrashOnCtrlScroll".
7. Choose the REG_DWORD option from the Data Type drop-down menu.
8. Click OK.
9. In the String field, enter a value of 0 to disable the Registry value or a value of 1 to enable the Registry value.
10. Click OK.
11. Reboot the system. When you press the Ctrl+Scroll Lock key combination, the system performs a memory dump.

Modifying a Service Startup Type to Boot

To modify a service startup type to boot, perform the following steps:

1. Select Start|Run.
2. Enter "regedt32.exe" in the Open field and click OK.
3. Select the HKEY_LOCAL_MACHINE On Local Machine window.
4. Navigate to \SYSTEM\CurrentControlSet\Services*service*.
5. Select the Type value.
6. Choose the Edit DWORD option from the Edit menu.
7. Change the data to 0.
8. Click OK.

Modifying a Service Startup Type to System

To modify a service startup type to system, perform the following steps:

1. Select Start|Run.
2. Enter "regedt32.exe" in the Open field and click OK.
3. Select the HKEY_LOCAL_MACHINE On Local Machine window.
4. Navigate to \SYSTEM\CurrentControlSet\Services*service*.
5. Select the Type value.

6. Choose the Edit DWORD option from the Edit menu.

7. Change the data to 1.

8. Click OK.

Modifying a Service Startup Type to Automatic

To modify a service startup type to automatic, perform the following steps:

1. Select Start|Run.

2. Enter "regedt32.exe" in the Open field and click OK.

3. Select the HKEY_LOCAL_MACHINE On Local Machine window.

4. Navigate to \SYSTEM\CurrentControlSet\Services*service*.

5. Select the Type value.

6. Choose the Edit DWORD option from the Edit menu.

7. Change the data to 2.

8. Click OK.

Modifying a Service Startup Type to Manual

To modify a service startup type to manual, perform the following steps:

1. Select Start|Run.

2. Enter "regedt32.exe" in the Open field and click OK.

3. Select the HKEY_LOCAL_MACHINE On Local Machine window.

4. Navigate to \SYSTEM\CurrentControlSet\Services*service*.

5. Select the Type value.

6. Choose the Edit DWORD option from the Edit menu.

7. Change the data to 3.

8. Click OK.

Modifying a Service Startup Type to Disabled

To modify a service startup type to disabled, perform the following steps:

1. Select Start|Run.

2. Enter "regedt32.exe" in the Open field and click OK.

3. Select the HKEY_LOCAL_MACHINE On Local Machine window.

4. Navigate to \SYSTEM\CurrentControlSet\Services*service*.

5. Select the Type value.

6. Choose the Edit DWORD option from the Edit menu.

7. Change the data to 4.

8. Click OK.

Changing Your System's NetBIOS Name

To change your system's NetBIOS name, perform the following steps:

1. Select Start|Run.

2. Enter "regedt32.exe" in the Open field and click OK.

3. Select the HKEY_LOCAL_MACHINE On Local Machine window.

4. Navigate to \SYSTEM\CurrentControlSet\Control\ComputerName\ ActiveComputerName.

5. Select the ComputerName value.

6. Choose the String option from the Edit menu.

7. Enter the new name for the system.

8. Click OK.

9. Navigate to \SYSTEM\CurrentControlSet\Control\ComputerName\ ComputerName.

10. Select the ComputerName value.

11. Choose the String option from the Edit menu.

12. Enter the new name for the system.

13. Click OK.

Modifying Your System's Hostname

To modify your system's hostname, perform the following steps:

1. Select Start|Run.

2. Enter "regedt32.exe" in the Open field and click OK.

3. Select the HKEY_LOCAL_MACHINE On Local Machine window.

4. Navigate to \SYSTEM\CurrentControlSet\Services\Tcpip\Parameters.

5. Select the Hostname value.

6. Choose the String option from the Edit menu.

7. Enter the new hostname for the system.

8. Click OK.

9. Navigate to \SYSTEM\CurrentControlSet\Services\Tcpip\Parameters.

10. Select the NV Hostname value.

11. Choose the String option from the Edit menu.

12. Enter the new hostname for the system.

13. Click OK.

Modifying Your System's Domain Name

To modify your system's domain name, perform the following steps:

1. Select Start|Run.

2. Enter "regedt32.exe" in the Open field and click OK.

3. Select the HKEY_LOCAL_MACHINE On Local Machine window.

4. Navigate to \SYSTEM\CurrentControlSet\Services\Tcpip\Parameters.

5. Select the Domain value.

6. Choose the String option from the Edit menu.

7. Enter the new domain for the system.

8. Click OK.

9. Navigate to \SYSTEM\CurrentControlSet\Services\Tcpip\Parameters.

10. Select the NV Domain value.

11. Choose the String option from the Edit menu.

12. Enter the new domain for the system.

13. Click OK.

Disabling 8.3 File Name Creation on NTFS

To disable 8.3 file names on NTFS partitions, perform the following steps:

1. Select Start|Run.

2. Enter "regedt32.exe" in the Open field and click OK.

3. Select the HKEY_LOCAL_MACHINE On Local Machine window.

4. Navigate to \SYSTEM\CurrentControlSet\Control\FileSystem.

5. Select the NtfsDisable8dot3NameCreation value.

6. Choose the DWORD option from the Edit menu.

7. In the String field, enter a value of 0 to disable the Registry value or a value of 1 to enable the Registry value.

8. Click OK.

Configuring the System to Reboot Automatically on System Failure

To configure the system to reboot automatically on system failure, perform the following steps:

1. Select Start|Run.
2. Enter "regedt32.exe" in the Open field and click OK.
3. Select the HKEY_LOCAL_MACHINE On Local Machine window.
4. Navigate to \SYSTEM\CurrentControlSet\Control\CrashControl.
5. Select the AutoReboot value.
6. Choose the DWORD option from the Edit menu.
7. In the String field, enter a value of 0 to disable the Registry value or a value of 1 to enable the Registry value.
8. Click OK.

Enabling Crash Dump on Your System

To enable crash dump, perform the following steps:

1. Select Start|Run.
2. Enter "regedt32.exe" in the Open field and click OK.
3. Select the HKEY_LOCAL_MACHINE On Local Machine window.
4. Navigate to \SYSTEM\CurrentControlSet\Control\CrashControl.
5. Select the CrashDumpEnabled value.
6. Choose the DWORD option from the Edit menu.
7. In the String field, enter a value of 0 to disable the Registry value or a value of 1 to enable the Registry value.
8. Click OK.

Specifying the Dump File Name and Location

To specify the dump file name and location, perform the following steps:

1. Select Start|Run.
2. Enter "regedt32.exe" in the Open field and click OK.
3. Select the HKEY_LOCAL_MACHINE On Local Machine window.
4. Navigate to \SYSTEM\CurrentControlSet\Control\CrashControl.
5. Select the DumpFile value.
6. Choose the String option from the Edit menu.

11. Windows 2000 Registry: Structure, Editing, and Important Keys

7. Enter the new path and name for the dump file to be created. The destination folder must exist.

8. Click OK.

Configuring the System to Log an Event on System Failure

To configure the system to log an event on system failure, perform the following steps:

1. Select Start|Run.

2. Enter "regedt32.exe" in the Open field and click OK.

3. Select the HKEY_LOCAL_MACHINE On Local Machine window.

4. Navigate to \SYSTEM\CurrentControlSet\Control\CrashControl.

5. Select the LogEvent value.

6. Choose the DWORD option from the Edit menu.

7. In the String field, enter a value of 0 to disable the Registry value or a value of 1 to enable the Registry value.

8. Click OK.

Configuring the System to Overwrite an Old Dump File on System Failure

To configure the system to overwrite an old dump file on system failure, perform the following steps:

1. Select Start|Run.

2. Enter "regedt32.exe" in the Open field and click OK.

3. Select the HKEY_LOCAL_MACHINE On Local Machine window.

4. Navigate to \SYSTEM\CurrentControlSet\Control\CrashControl.

5. Select the Overwrite value.

6. Choose the DWORD option from the Edit menu.

7. In the String field, enter a value of 0 to disable the Registry value or a value of 1 to enable the Registry value.

8. Click OK.

Configuring the System to Send an Alert on System Failure

To configure the system to send an alert on system failure, perform the following steps:

1. Select Start|Run.

2. Enter "regedt32.exe" in the Open field and click OK.

3. Select the HKEY_LOCAL_MACHINE On Local Machine window.

4. Navigate to \SYSTEM\CurrentControlSet\Control\CrashControl.

5. Select the SendAlert value.

6. Choose the DWORD option from the Edit menu.

7. In the String field, enter a value of 0 to disable the Registry value or a value of 1 to enable the Registry value.

8. Click OK.

Specifying Files and Folders That Should Not Be Backed Up

To specify files and folders not to back up, perform the following steps:

1. Select Start|Run.

2. Enter "regedt32.exe" in the Open field and click OK.

3. Select the HKEY_LOCAL_MACHINE On Local Machine window.

4. Navigate to \SYSTEM\CurrentControlSet\Control\BackupRestore\ FilesNotToBackup.

5. Choose the Multi String option from the Edit menu.

6. Enter a description for the value in the Value Name field.

7. Choose the REG_MULTI_SZ option from the Data Type drop-down menu and click OK.

8. Enter the full path to the folder (and file if necessary) that's not to be backed up and then click OK.

TIP: *If you want all the files within a folder to be excluded, use the wildcard (*) character (for example, **c:\folder*** will exclude all the files within the C:\folder folder). If you would like to exclude subfolders within a folder, use the **/s** switch (for example, **c:\folder* /s** will exclude all files and subfolders in the C:\folder folder).*

Working with Welcome Tips

When users first log into the system, they are presented with a "Welcome to Windows" screen. This screen gives users different tips for getting the most out of their desktop experience. This Registry manipulation shows you how to modify these tips:

1. Select Start|Run.

2. Enter "regedt32.exe" in the Open field and click OK.

3. Select the HKEY_LOCAL_MACHINE On Local Machine window.

4. Navigate to \SOFTWARE\Microsoft\Windows\CurrentVersion\Explorer\Tips.

5. To delete a tip, select the value associated with that tip, choose the Delete option from the Edit menu, and click Yes to confirm the deletion.

11. Windows 2000 Registry: Structure, Editing, and Important Keys

6. To modify a tip, select the value of the tip that you would like to modify, choose the String option from the Edit menu, enter a new tip, and click OK.

7. To add a tip, find the next subsequent value number (there are 50 by default, starting 0 and ending with 49) and choose the Add Value option from the Edit menu.

8. Enter the tip number in the Value Name field, choose the REG_SZ option from the Data Type drop-down menu, and click OK.

9. Enter the tip and click OK.

Displaying/Hiding the Welcome Screen

To display or hide the Welcome screen, perform the following steps:

1. Select Start|Run.

2. Enter "regedt32.exe" in the Open field and click OK.

3. Select the HKEY_USERS On Local Machine window.

4. Navigate to *SID*\Software\Microsoft\Windows\CurrentVersion\Explorer\tips.

5. Select the Show value.

6. Choose the String option from the Edit menu.

7. In the String field, enter a value of 0 to disable the Registry value or a value of 1 to enable the Registry value.

8. Click OK.

Controlling the Cascading of the Control Panel Menu

To control the cascading of the Control Panel menu, perform the following steps:

1. Select Start|Run.

2. Enter "regedt32.exe" in the Open field and click OK.

3. Select the HKEY_USERS On Local Machine window.

4. Navigate to *SID*\Software\Microsoft\Windows\CurrentVersion\Explorer\Advanced.

5. Select the CascadeControlPanel value.

6. Choose the String option from the Edit menu.

7. To enable the cascading menu, enter "YES" and click OK.

8. To disable the cascading menu, enter "NO" and click OK.

Controlling the Cascading of the My Documents Menu

To control the cascading of the My Documents menu, perform the following steps:

1. Select Start|Run.
2. Enter "regedt32.exe" in the Open field and click OK.
3. Select the HKEY_USERS On Local Machine window.
4. Navigate to *SID*\Software\Microsoft\Windows\CurrentVersion\ Explorer\Advanced.
5. Select the CascadeMyDocuments value.
6. Choose the String option from the Edit menu.
7. To enable the cascading menu, enter "YES" and click OK.
8. To disable the cascading menu, enter "NO" and click OK.

Controlling the Cascading of the Network Connections Menu

To control the cascading of the Network Connections menu, perform the following steps:

1. Select Start|Run.
2. Enter "regedt32.exe" in the Open field and click OK.
3. Select the HKEY_USERS On Local Machine window.
4. Navigate to *SID*\Software\Microsoft\Windows\CurrentVersion\ Explorer\Advanced.
5. Select the CascadeNetworkConnections value.
6. Choose the String option from the Edit menu.
7. To enable the cascading menu, enter "YES" and click OK.
8. To disable the cascading menu, enter "NO" and click OK.

Controlling the Cascading of the Printers Menu

To control the cascading of the Printers menu, perform the following steps:

1. Select Start|Run.
2. Enter "regedt32.exe" in the Open field and click OK.
3. Select the HKEY_USERS On Local Machine window.
4. Navigate to *SID*\Software\Microsoft\Windows\CurrentVersion\ Explorer\Advanced.
5. Select the CascadePrinters value.

11. Windows 2000 Registry: Structure, Editing, and Important Keys

6. Choose the String option from the Edit menu.

7. To enable the cascading menu, enter "YES" and click OK.

8. To disable the cascading menu, enter "NO" and click OK.

Controlling the Administrative Tools Menu

To control Administrative Tools menu, perform the following steps:

1. Select Start|Run.

2. Enter "regedt32.exe" in the Open field and click OK.

3. Select the HKEY_USERS On Local Machine window.

4. Navigate to *SID*\Software\Microsoft\Windows\CurrentVersion\
Explorer\Advanced.

5. Select the StartMenuAdminTools value.

6. Choose the String option from the Edit menu.

7. To enable the Administrative Tools menu, enter "YES" and click OK.

8. To disable the Administrative Tools menu, enter "NO" and click OK.

Enabling the Windows 2000 IntelliMenu

You can configure the Start menu to track your most commonly used applications. Any applications that are not used are hidden until you request them. To control this behavior, follow these steps:

1. Select Start|Run.

2. Enter "regedt32.exe" in the Open field and click OK.

3. Select the HKEY_USERS On Local Machine window.

4. Navigate to *SID*\Software\Microsoft\Windows\CurrentVersion\
Explorer\Advanced.

5. Select the IntelliMenus value.

6. Choose the String option from the Edit menu.

7. To enable IntelliMenu, enter "YES" and click OK.

8. To disable IntelliMenu, enter "NO" and click OK.

Controlling How Hidden Files Are Displayed

To control how hidden files are displayed, perform the following steps:

1. Select Start|Run.

2. Enter "regedt32.exe" in the Open field and click OK.

3. Select the HKEY_USERS On Local Machine window.

4. Navigate to *SID*\Software\Microsoft\Windows\CurrentVersion\
   Explorer\Advanced.

5. Select the Hidden value.

6. Choose the String option from the Edit menu.

7. In the String field, enter a value of 0 to disable the Registry value or a value
   of 1 to enable the Registry value.

8. Click OK.

Controlling the Display Characteristics of Known Extensions

To control the display characteristics of known extensions, perform the following steps:

1. Select Start|Run.

2. Enter "regedt32.exe" in the Open field and click OK.

3. Select the HKEY_USERS On Local Machine window.

4. Navigate to *SID*\Software\Microsoft\Windows\CurrentVersion\
   Explorer\Advanced.

5. Select the HideFileExt value.

6. Choose the String option from the Edit menu.

7. In the String field, enter a value of 0 to hide known extensions or a value of
   1 to display known extensions.

8. Click OK.

Adding/Removing the Map Network Drive Button from Explorer and My Computer

To add or remove the Map Network Drive button from Explorer and My Computer, perform the following steps:

1. Select Start|Run.

2. Enter "regedt32.exe" in the Open field and click OK.

3. Select the HKEY_USERS On Local Machine window.

4. Navigate to *SID*\Software\Microsoft\Windows\CurrentVersion\
   Explorer\Advanced.

5. Select the MapNetDrvBtn value.

6. Choose the String option from the Edit menu.

7. In the String field, enter a value of 0 to hide the button or a value of 1 to
   display the button.

8. Click OK.

Controlling How Compressed Files and Folders Are Displayed

To control how compressed files and folders are displayed, perform the following steps:

1. Select Start|Run.
2. Enter "regedt32.exe" in the Open field and click OK.
3. Select the HKEY_USERS On Local Machine window.
4. Navigate to *SID*\Software\Microsoft\Windows\CurrentVersion\ Explorer\Advanced.
5. Select the ShowCompColor value.
6. Choose the String option from the Edit menu.
7. In the String field, enter a value of 0 to disable the Registry value or a value of 1 to enable the Registry value.
8. Click OK.

Showing/Hiding the Favorites Menu

To show or hide the Favorites menu, perform the following steps:

1. Select Start|Run.
2. Enter "regedt32.exe" in the Open field and click OK.
3. Select the HKEY_USERS On Local Machine window.
4. Navigate to *SID*\Software\Microsoft\Windows\CurrentVersion\ Explorer\Advanced.
5. Select the StartMenuFavorites value.
6. Choose the String option from the Edit menu.
7. In the String field, enter a value of 0 to disable the Registry value or a value of 1 to enable the Registry value.
8. Click OK.

Showing/Hiding the Logoff Option on the Start Menu

To show or hide the Logoff option in the Start menu, perform the following steps:

1. Select Start|Run.
2. Enter "regedt32.exe" in the Open field and click OK.
3. Select the HKEY_USERS On Local Machine window.
4. Navigate to *SID*\Software\Microsoft\Windows\CurrentVersion\ Explorer\Advanced.
5. Select the StartMenuLogoff value.

6. Choose the String option from the Edit menu.

7. In the String field, enter a value of 0 to disable the Registry value or a value of 1 to enable the Registry value.

8. Click OK.

Displaying the Full Path in the Menu Bar

To display the full path in the menu bar, perform the following steps:

1. Select Start|Run.

2. Enter "regedt32.exe" in the Open field and click OK.

3. Select the HKEY_USERS On Local Machine window.

4. Navigate to *SID*\Software\Microsoft\Windows\CurrentVersion\ Explorer\CabinetState.

5. Select the FullPath value.

6. Choose the String option from the Edit menu.

7. In the String field, enter a value of 0 to disable the Registry value or a value of 1 to enable the Registry value.

8. Click OK.

Displaying the Full Path in the Address Bar

To display the full path in the address bar, perform the following steps:

1. Select Start|Run.

2. Enter "regedt32.exe" in the Open field and click OK.

3. Select the HKEY_USERS On Local Machine window.

4. Navigate to *SID*\Software\Microsoft\Windows\CurrentVersion\ Explorer\CabinetState.

5. Select the FullPathAddress value.

6. Choose the String option from the Edit menu.

7. In the String field, enter a value of 0 to disable the Registry value or a value of 1 to enable the Registry value.

8. Click OK.

Enabling Account Lockout

To enable account lockout, perform the following steps:

1. Select Start|Run.

2. Enter "regedt32.exe" in the Open field and click OK.

3. Select the HKEY_LOCAL_MACHINE On Local Machine window.

4. Navigate to \SYSTEM\CurrentControlSet\Services\RemoteAccess\ Parameters\AccountLockout.

5. Select the MaxDenials value.

6. Choose the String option from the Edit menu.

7. Change the data to 1 to enable account lockout or to 0 to disable account lockout.

8. Click OK.

Modifying the Account Lockout Timeout

To modify the account lockout timeout, perform the following steps:

1. Select Start|Run.

2. Enter "regedt32.exe" in the Open field and click OK.

3. Select the HKEY_LOCAL_MACHINE On Local Machine window.

4. Navigate to \SYSTEM\CurrentControlSet\Services\RemoteAccess\ Parameters\AccountLockout.

5. Select the ResetTime (mins) value.

6. Choose the String option from the Edit menu.

7. Change the data to the number of minutes you would like the account locked out for.

8. Click OK.

Resetting a Locked Account

To reset a locked account, perform the following steps:

1. Select Start|Run.

2. Enter "regedt32.exe" in the Open field and click OK.

3. Select the HKEY_LOCAL_MACHINE On Local Machine window.

4. Navigate to \SYSTEM\CurrentControlSet\Services\RemoteAccess\ Parameters\AccountLockout*name:user name*.

5. Choose the Delete option from the Edit menu.

6. Click Yes to confirm the deletion.

Disabling Auto Address Configuration

To disable auto address configuration, perform the following steps:

1. Select Start|Run.

2. Enter "regedt32.exe" in the Open field and click OK.

3. Select the HKEY_LOCAL_MACHINE On Local Machine window.

4. Navigate to \SYSTEM\CurrentControlSet\Services\Tcpip\Parameters\ Interfaces*adapter_name*.

5. Choose the Add Value option from the Edit menu.

6. Enter "IPAutoconfigurationEnabled" in the Value Name field, choose the REG_DWORD option from the Data Type drop-down menu, and click OK.

7. Enter a value of 0 to disable auto configuration of IP addresses or a value of 1 to enable auto configuration of IP addresses.

8. Click OK.

Enabling IP Forwarding

To enable IP forwarding, perform the following steps:

1. Select Start|Run.

2. Enter "regedt32.exe" in the Open field and click OK.

3. Select the HKEY_LOCAL_MACHINE On Local Machine window.

4. Navigate to \SYSTEM\CurrentControlSet\Services\Tcpip\Parameters.

5. Select the IPEnableRouter value.

6. Click String from the Edit menu.

7. Enter a value of 0 to disable IP routing or a value of 1 to enable IP routing.

8. Click OK.

Halting a System When the Security Log Is Full

To halt a system when the Security log is full, perform the following steps:

1. Select Start|Run.

2. Enter "regedt32.exe" in the Open field and click OK.

3. Select the HKEY_LOCAL_MACHINE On Local Machine window.

4. Navigate to \SYSTEM\CurrentControlSet\Control\Lsa.

5. Select the CrashOnAuditFail value.

6. Click String from the Edit menu.

7. Enter a value of 1 to halt the system when the security log is full. Enter a value of 0 to disable this feature.

8. Click OK.

Chapter 12

Fault Tolerance and Recovery

In Depth

This chapter deals with disk management in Windows 2000. This discussion includes working with disks, partitions, and volumes. In addition, some of the recovery tools that ship with Windows 2000 are discussed.

Basic Disks Versus Dynamic Disks

Windows 2000 has introduced a new way of dealing with disks. These new disks can be modified and moved from one system to another without partition loss, and eliminate most disk configuration reboots. These new disks are known as *dynamic disks*.

Windows 2000 still fully supports disks that were formatted under Windows 95/98 and NT. In the Windows 2000 world, these legacy disks are known as *basic disks*. Windows 2000 can still manage, format, and modify these disks, but some of the more advanced disk-manipulation methods now require dynamic disks.

It is important to realize that dynamic disks are no different than basic disks in a physical sense. Only the way in which the disk is formatted and written to is changed. To differentiate between partitions created on a basic disk, Windows 2000 has new naming conventions for the different types of disks it can support. Instead of dealing with partitions, Windows 2000 deals with *volumes*. Table 12.1 shows the differences between the Windows NT basic disk naming conventions and Windows 2000 dynamic disks.

Basic disks are also limited in the number of partitions that can be created on them. With Windows 95/98/NT, a disk can have up to four partitions—either four

Table 12.1   Basic vs. dynamic disks.

Windows NT/Basic	Windows 2000/Dynamic
Partition	Simple volume
Volume set	Spanned volume
Mirror set	Mirrored volume
Stripe set	Striped volume
Stripe set with parity	RAID 5 volume

primary partitions or three primary partitions and one extended partition. This limitation no longer exists with dynamic disks in Windows 2000.

Disk Mirroring and Disk Duplexing

It is important to understand the differences between disk mirroring and disk duplexing. Both fault-tolerant methods maintain identical copies of the data on two physically separate disks. Where they differ is in the disk controller hardware.

Disk mirroring saves all data to two different disks that are connected to a single controller. Should one of the disks fail, the second disk has an identical copy. However, should the controller fail, neither disk will be available to the system (although the data on them might be intact).

With disk duplexing, on the other hand, each of the two mirrored disks are connected to a different controller. Should a single disk fail, the second disk will have an exact copy of the data. However, should one of the controllers fail, the second controller will continue to maintain the disk—and therefore its data—online.

RAID: Software Versus Hardware

One of the most common methods of designing fault-tolerant disk systems is by using Redundant Array of Independent Disks (RAID). Each RAID configuration is given a level (most commonly from Level 0 to 10). Windows 2000 supports three of the levels—Level 0, 1, and 5.

NOTE: *RAID also stands for* Redundant Array of Inexpensive Disks. *Although workstation-grade hard drives have dropped in price, high-speed, high-throughput SCSI drives are still very expensive. This is why* Independent *has replaced the word* Inexpensive.

RAID Level 0 is known in the Windows 2000 world as a *striped volume*. Although Level 0 does not give the disks any fault tolerance, it does increase performance on the disks by reading from multiple disks at the same time. RAID Level 1 is disk mirroring/disk duplexing, as outlined previously. These methods protect the data from a single disk failure. RAID Level 5 is the most commonly used RAID configuration on the market today. With Windows 2000, it is simply referred to as a *RAID 5 volume*. With RAID 5, one of the disks is used to store parity information that can completely recover the data should any *single* disk fail.

There are two different ways of dealing with RAID. The first is *software RAID*, as done with Windows 2000, and the second is *hardware RAID*. Although hardware RAID is much more expensive than software RAID (no special hardware is required with the software implementation of RAID), it is far superior in its performance.

As you may imagine, calculating the parity information and writing to multiple disks by the operating system uses valuable CPU cycles. With a high-end server, these cycles are needed to support the users and applications. With hardware RAID, a dedicated interface card does all the calculations. The controller then presents the operating system with a single logical disk. Although the RAID array may consist of three or more (up to 32) disks, Windows 2000 "sees" the disk as a single disk.

Windows 2000 Repair and Recovery Techniques

Windows 2000 includes tools that are far superior to the ones found in Windows NT. This chapter looks at the Windows 2000 Backup program, the Emergency Repair Disk (ERD), and a new feature called Recovery Console.

Windows 2000 Backup

Windows NT has always included a backup program. Many would argue that the backup program that ships with Windows NT is not very functional. The most common complaint about that iteration of the program is that data can only be backed up to tape. If data needs to be backed up to removable media (such as a CD-ROM, Zip, or Jaz drive), third-party programs are needed, which are too expensive for some smaller organizations.

The Windows 2000 Backup program fixes some of these complaints. It now has the ability to back up to tape or to a file. This file can reside on the floppy drive, on any local hard drive, on a network share, or on a removable device. It can also be transferred to a CD (for this method, a backup file must be created, which is then burned onto the CD).

NOTE: This built-in backup application is written by Veritas Software, one of the largest vendors of backup solutions for Windows NT/2000.

Emergency Repair Disk

Much like Windows NT, Windows 2000 supports an Emergency Repair Disk (ERD). The ERD contains information about the specific system that enables an administrator to recover some of the system settings in case of a failure. The information stored on the ERD includes the boot sector and the startup configuration.

Although Windows NT's ERD maintained copies of the some of the main Registry keys, this is no longer done in Windows 2000. Instead, the MS-DOS subsystem files (autoexec.nt and config.nt) and the setup.log file are copied to the disk. The setup.log file points the recovery process to the location on your disk for the recovery files.

WARNING! *Many administrators believe that an ERD is an ERD. This is not the case. Each ERD is unique to the server on which it was created. Using an ERD from one server on another server can have disastrous consequences. If an organization has 1,000 servers, it should maintain an ERD for each server.*

Every time a major change is made to the system, such as disk, security, or hardware changes, the ERD should be updated. In the past, the ERD was created using the RDISK utility. In Windows 2000, the Backup program performs this task.

NOTE: *The ERD is not bootable; you must use it in conjunction with a boot disk.*

Recovery Console

One of the coolest tools introduced with Windows 2000 for recovery is the Recovery Console. The Recovery Console allows an administrator to boot Windows 2000 into a DOS-like interface, which allows him or her to reset parts of the Registry, repair corrupted files, and modify files (such as the boot.ini file).

The Recovery Console is not installed by default, but it ships on the Windows 2000 installation CD. The process of installing and using the Recovery Console is described in the "Immediate Solutions" section of this chapter.

Immediate Solutions

Managing Disks

A number of issues are involved with disk management in Windows 2000. The following sections explore these tasks.

Formatting a Disk

To format a disk, follow these steps:

1. Select Start|Programs|Administrative Tools|Computer Management.
2. In the left pane, select Disk Management.
3. Select the disk that is to be formatted.
4. Choose All Tasks|Format from the Action menu.
5. Select the desired formatting parameters and click OK.
6. Click Yes to confirm the format.

Marking a Disk Active

To mark a disk active, follow these steps:

1. Select Start|Programs|Administrative Tools|Computer Management.
2. In the left pane, select Disk Management.
3. Select the disk that is to be marked as active.
4. Choose All Tasks|Mark Partition Active from the Action menu.

Assigning Drive Letters

To assign a drive letter to a disk, follow these steps:

1. Select Start|Programs|Administrative Tools|Computer Management.
2. In the left pane, select Disk Management.
3. Select the disk for which the drive letter is to be changed.
4. Choose All Tasks|Change Drive Letter And Path from the Action menu.
5. Click Edit.
6. From the Assign A Drive Letter list, select the letter to assign to this disk.
7. Click OK.
8. Click Yes to confirm the drive letter change.

Upgrading from a Basic Disk to a Dynamic Disk

To upgrade from a basic disk to a dynamic disk, follow these steps:

1. Select Start|Programs|Administrative Tools|Computer Management.
2. In the left pane, select Disk Management.
3. Select the basic disk that is to be upgraded to a dynamic disk.
4. Choose All Tasks|Upgrade To Dynamic Disk from the Action menu.
5. Select the desired disk and click OK.

Converting from a Dynamic Disk to a Basic Disk

To convert from a dynamic disk to a basic disk, follow these steps:

1. Select Start|Programs|Administrative Tools|Computer Management.
2. In the left pane, select Disk Management.
3. Select the dynamic disk that is to be converted to a basic disk.
4. Choose All Tasks|Revert To Basic Disk from the Action menu.

NOTE: *You need to be sure you want to perform this task because converting a dynamic disk back to a basic disk may result in the loss of other features. For example, after completing this process, you can only create partitions and logical drives on the basic disk; you can't create volumes.*

Managing Partitions

A number of issues are involved with partition management in Windows 2000. The following sections explore these tasks.

Creating a Primary Partition

To create a primary partition, follow these steps:

1. Select Start|Programs|Administrative Tools|Computer Management.
2. In the left pane, select Disk Management.
3. Select the disk where a primary partition is to be created.
4. Choose All Tasks|Create Partition from the Action menu. The Create Partition Wizard will appear, as shown in Figure 12.1.
5. Click Next.
6. Ensure that the Primary Partition radio button is selected and click Next.
7. Enter the amount of disk space that is to be allocated to this partition and click Next.

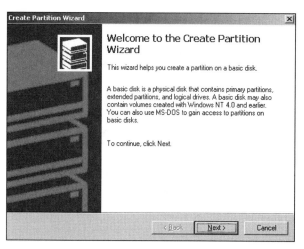

Figure 12.1   The Create Partition Wizard.

8. Decide whether to assign the partition a drive letter, mount it as a folder, or to not assign it a drive letter on this screen. Click Next.

9. If this partition is to be formatted, select Format This Partition With The Following Settings, choose the desired settings, and click Next. Otherwise, select Do Not Format This Partition and click Next.

10. Click Finish.

Deleting a Primary Partition

To delete a primary partition, follow these steps:

1. Select Start|Programs|Administrative Tools|Computer Management.

2. In the left pane, select Disk Management.

3. Select the primary partition that is to be deleted.

4. Choose All Tasks|Delete Partition.

5. Click Yes to confirm the deletion.

Creating an Extended Partition

To create an extended partition, follow these steps:

1. Select Start|Programs|Administrative Tools|Computer Management.

2. In the left pane, select Disk Management.

3. Select the disk where a primary partition is to be created.

4. Choose All Tasks|Create Partition from the Action menu.

5. Click Next.

6. Ensure that the Extended Partition radio button is selected and click Next.

7. Enter the amount of disk space that is to be allocated to this partition and click Next.

8. Click Finish.

Creating a Logical Partition

To create a logical partition, follow these steps:

1. Select Start|Programs|Administrative Tools|Computer Management.

2. In the left pane, select Disk Management.

3. Select the extended partition where a logical partition is to be created.

4. Choose All Tasks|Create Partition from the Action menu.

5. Click Next.

6. Click Next.

7. Enter the amount of disk space that is to be allocated to this partition and click Next.

8. Decide whether to assign the partition a drive letter, mount it as a folder, or to not assign it a drive letter on this screen. Click Next.

9. If this partition is to be formatted, select Format This Partition With The Following Settings, choose the desired settings, and click Next. Otherwise, select Do Not Format This Partition and click Next.

10. Click Finish.

Deleting a Logical Partition

To delete a logical partition, follow these steps:

1. Select Start|Programs|Administrative Tools|Computer Management.

2. In the left pane, select Disk Management.

3. Select the logical partition that is to be deleted.

4. Choose All Tasks|Delete Logical Partition from the Action menu.

5. Click Yes to confirm the deletion.

Deleting an Extended Partition

To delete an extended partition, follow these steps:

1. Select Start|Programs|Administrative Tools|Computer Management.

2. In the left pane, select Disk Management.

3. Select the extended partition that is to be deleted.

NOTE: *If the extended partition contains any logical partitions, they must be deleted before the Disk Management application will allow you to delete the extended partition.*

---

4. Choose All Tasks|Delete Partition from the Action menu.

5. Click Yes to confirm the deletion.

Managing Volumes

A number of issues are involved with volume management in Windows 2000. The following sections explore these tasks.

Creating a Simple Volume

To create a simple volume, follow these steps:

1. Select Start|Programs|Administrative Tools|Computer Management.

2. In the left pane, select Disk Management.

3. Select the dynamic disk on which the simple volume is to be created.

4. Choose All Tasks|Create Volume from the Action menu. The Create Volume Wizard will appear, as shown in Figure 12.2.

5. Click Next.

6. In the Select Volume Type window, shown in Figure 12.3, ensure that the Simple Volume radio button is selected and click Next.

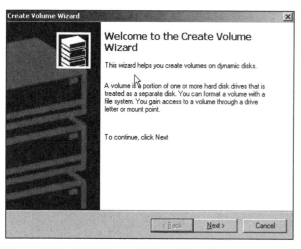

Figure 12.2   The Create Volume Wizard.

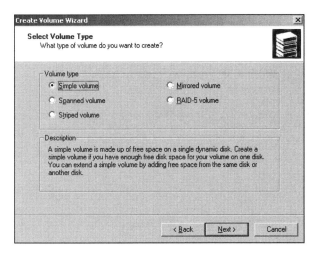

Figure 12.3   The Select Volume Type window.

7. Enter the amount of disk space that is to be allocated to this volume in the Size section and click Next.

8. Decide whether to assign the partition a drive letter, mount it as a folder, or to not assign it a drive letter on this screen. Click Next.

9. If this partition is to be formatted, select Format This Partition With The Following Settings, choose the desired settings, and click Next. Otherwise, select Do Not Format This Partition and click Next.

10. Click Finish.

Extending a Simple Volume

To extend a simple volume, follow these steps:

1. Select Start|Programs|Administrative Tools|Computer Management.

2. In the left pane, select Disk Management.

3. Select the simple volume that is to be extended.

4. Choose All Tasks|Extend Volume from the Action menu. The Extend Volume Wizard will appear.

5. Click Next.

6. To add a disk to the volume, select the disk in the All Available Dynamic Disks section and click Add.

TIP: *If the disk that the volume is created on has free space, you can use that disk to extend the partition. In this situation, an extra disk is not needed.*

---

7. Enter the amount of disk space that this volume is to be extended by in the Size section and click Next.

8. Click Finish.

Deleting a Volume

The method outlined here holds true for all types of volumes. To delete a volume, follow these steps:

1. Select Start|Programs|Administrative Tools|Computer Management.

2. In the left pane, select Disk Management.

3. Select the volume that is to be deleted.

4. Choose All Tasks|Delete Volume from the Action menu.

5. Click Yes to confirm the deletion.

Creating a Spanned Volume

To create a spanned volume, follow these steps:

1. Select Start|Programs|Administrative Tools|Computer Management.

2. In the left pane, select Disk Management.

3. Select the dynamic disk on which the spanned volume is to be created.

4. Choose All Tasks|Create Volume from the Action menu.

5. Click Next.

6. In the Select Volume Type window (refer to Figure 12.3), ensure that the Spanned Volume radio button is selected and click Next.

7. Select one or more dynamic disks from the All Available Dynamic Disks section and click Add.

8. Enter the amount of disk space that is to be allocated to this volume in the Size section and click Next. This can be configured on each dynamic disk independently.

9. Decide whether to assign the partition a drive letter, mount it as a folder, or to not assign it a drive letter on this screen. Click Next.

10. If this partition is to be formatted, select Format This Partition With The Following Settings, choose the desired settings, and click Next. Otherwise, select Do Not Format This Partition and click Next.

11. Click Finish.

Extending a Spanned Volume

To extend a spanned volume, follow these steps:

1. Select Start|Programs|Administrative Tools|Computer Management.

2. In the left pane, select Disk Management.

3. Select the spanned volume that is to be extended.

4. Choose All Tasks|Extend Volume from the Action menu. The Extend Volume Wizard will appear.

5. Click Next.

6. To add a disk to the volume, select the disk in the All Available Dynamic Disks section and click Add.

7. Enter the amount of disk space that this volume is to be extended by in the Size section and click Next.

8. Click Finish.

Creating a Striped Volume

To create a striped volume, follow these steps:

1. Select Start|Programs|Administrative Tools|Computer Management.

2. In the left pane, select Disk Management.

3. Select the dynamic disk on which the striped volume is to be created.

4. Choose All Tasks|Create Volume from the Action menu.

5. Click Next.

6. In the Select Volume Type window (refer to Figure 12.3), ensure that the Striped Volume radio button is selected and click Next.

7. Select one or more dynamic disks from the All Available Dynamic Disks section and click Add.

8. Enter the amount of disk space that is to be allocated to this volume in the Size section and click Next. This size is for the entire volume with equal amounts on each disk.

9. Decide whether to assign the partition a drive letter, mount it as a folder, or to not assign it a drive letter on this screen. Click Next.

10. If this partition is to be formatted, select Format This Partition With The Following Settings, choose the desired settings, and click Next. Otherwise, select Do Not Format This Partition and click Next.

11. Click Finish.

12. Fault Tolerance and Recovery

Creating a Mirrored Volume

To create a mirrored volume, follow these steps:

1. Select Start|Programs|Administrative Tools|Computer Management.
2. In the left pane, select Disk Management.
3. Select the dynamic disk that is to be used to create the mirrored volume.
4. Choose All Tasks|Create Volume from the Action menu.
5. Click Next.
6. In the Select Volume Type window (refer to Figure 12.3), ensure that the Mirrored Volume radio button is selected and click Next.
7. Select one dynamic disk from the All Available Dynamic Disks section and click Add.
8. Enter the amount of disk space that is to be allocated to this volume in the Size section and click Next.
9. Decide whether to assign the partition a drive letter, mount it as a folder, or to not assign it a drive letter on this screen. Click Next.
10. If this partition is to be formatted, select Format This Partition With The Following Settings, choose the desired settings, and click Next. Otherwise, select Do Not Format This Partition and click Next.
11. Click Finish.

Adding a Mirror to an Existing Simple Volume

To add a mirror to an existing simple volume, follow these steps:

1. Select Start|Programs|Administrative Tools|Computer Management.
2. In the left pane, select Disk Management.
3. Select the simple volume that is to be mirrored.
4. Choose All Tasks|Add Mirror from the Action menu.
5. Select the dynamic disk that this volume is to be mirrored with and click Add Mirror.

Breaking a Mirrored Volume

To break a mirrored volume, follow these steps:

1. Select Start|Programs|Administrative Tools|Computer Management.
2. In the left pane, select Disk Management.
3. Select the mirrored volume that is to be broken.
4. Choose All Tasks|Break Mirror from the Action menu.
5. Click Yes to confirm the breaking of the mirror.

Recovering from a Failed Mirror Volume

Should one of the volumes in the mirrored volume fail, the notification shown in Figure 12.4 will be displayed. To recover the mirror, follow these steps:

1. Shut down the system, replace the faulty disk, and boot up the system.

2. Select Start|Programs|Administrative Tools|Computer Management.

3. In the left pane, select Disk Management.

4. Select one of the disks in the mirrored volume.

5. Right-click the disk and choose Reactivate Disk from the pop-up menu.

Creating a RAID 5 Volume

To create a RAID 5 volume, follow these steps:

1. Select Start|Programs|Administrative Tools|Computer Management.

2. In the left pane, select Disk Management.

3. Select the dynamic disk on which the simple volume is to be created.

4. Choose All Tasks|Create Volume from the Action menu.

5. Click Next.

6. In the Select Volume Type window (refer to Figure 12.3), ensure that the RAID 5 Volume radio button is selected and click Next.

7. Select two or more dynamic disks from the All Available Dynamic Disks section and click Add.

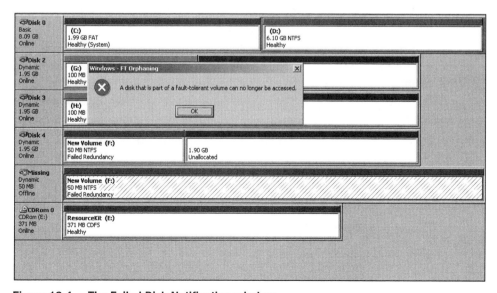

Figure 12.4   The Failed Disk Notification window.

NOTE: *At least three disks must be selected for a RAID 5 volume.*

---

8. Enter the amount of disk space that is to be allocated to this volume in the Size section and click Next. This can be configured on each dynamic disk independently.

9. Decide whether to assign the partition a drive letter, mount it as a folder, or to not assign it a drive letter on this screen. Click Next.

10. If this partition is to be formatted, select Format This Partition With The Following Settings, choose the desired settings, and click Next. Otherwise, select Do Not Format This Partition and click Next.

11. Click Finish.

Recovering from a Failed RAID 5 Volume

To recover from a failed RAID 5 volume, follow these steps:

1. Shut down the system, replace the faulty disk, and boot the system.

2. Select Start|Programs|Administrative Tools|Computer Management.

3. In the left pane, select Disk Management.

4. Select one of the disks in the RAID 5 volume.

5. Right-click the disk and choose Reactivate Disk from the pop-up menu.

Importing Disks from Another System

In some instances, the need will arise to remove a hard drive from one system and place it on another. With Windows 2000 and dynamic disks, the partition information is stored on the drives. For this reason, the drives will need to be imported. Figure 12.5 shows how foreign disks appear in the Disk Management applet. Here are the steps:

1. Select Start|Programs|Administrative Tools|Computer Management.

2. In the left pane, select Disk Management.

3. Select the disk that is to be imported and choose All Tasks|Import Foreign Disks from the Action menu.

4. Select the disk(s) to import and click OK.

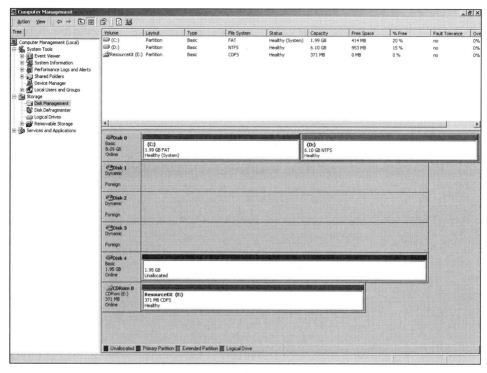

Figure 12.5   Importing disks in Disk Management.

Managing Backup and Recovery

A number of issues are involved with backing up and recovering a Windows 2000 system. The following sections explore these tasks.

Backing Up the System

To back up the system, follow these steps:

1. Select Start|Programs|Accessories|System Tools|Backup.

2. Click Backup Wizard. The Backup Wizard will appear.

3. Click Next.

4. Choose one of the three options: Backup Everything, Selected Files, or System State.

5. Click Next.

6. Select the backup media type and the corresponding media or file name and click Next.

7. Click Finish to start the backup or click Advanced to select the backup type, verify the backup, use hardware compression (if available), append or replace existing data, create a label for the backup set and media, and choose whether to schedule the backup.

8. Click Close.

Recovering the System

To recover the system, follow these steps:

1. Select Start|Programs|Accessories|System Tools|Backup.

2. Click Restore Wizard. The Restore Wizard will appear.

3. Click Next.

4. Select the backup set to restore and click Next.

5. Click Finish to start the restoration or click Advanced to select the restoration location and choose whether to replace files.

6. Click Close.

Creating an ERD

To create an ERD, follow these steps:

1. Select Start|Programs|Accessories|System Tools|Backup.

2. Click ERD.

3. Make sure you have a formatted, blank disk in your floppy drive.

4. If you would also like to back up the Registry information to the Repair folder on the hard drive, check the appropriate checkbox.

5. Click OK.

6. Click OK again.

Using an ERD

To use an ERD, follow these steps:

1. Start the Windows 2000 installation process.

2. On the Welcome to Setup screen, press R to repair the current Windows 2000 installation.

3. Press R to recover using the ERD.

4. Press M for manual selection of recovery options or F for fast recovery (fast recovery selects all the options).

5. If you have the ERD, press Enter.

6. Insert the disk and press Enter.

Installing the Recovery Console

To install the Recovery Console, follow these steps:

1. Insert the Windows 2000 CD-ROM.

2. Select Start|Run.

3. Type "*CD-ROMDrive*:\i386\winnt32\cmdcons", where *CD-ROMDrive* is the drive letter assigned to the CD-ROM drive, and click OK.

4. Click Yes to install the Recovery Console.

Using the Recovery Console

To use the Recovery Console, follow these steps:

1. Start the Windows 2000 installation process.

2. On the Welcome to Setup screen, press R to repair the current Windows 2000 installation.

3. Press C to recover using the Recover Console.

4. Choose the Windows 2000 installation to recover and press Enter.

Working with Clusters

Clustering is becoming more and more common. This section assumes that you have dedicated cluster hardware that is on the Windows 2000 Hardware Compatibility List. When preparing for the installation, install Windows 2000 Advanced Server as outlined in Chapter 5. The only difference is that you need to select Cluster Service from the Windows 2000 Components window.

Adding the First Node of the Cluster

To add the first node of the cluster, follow these steps:

1. Upon the final reboot of the server, the Configure Your Server window will appear. Click Finish.

2. In the Add/Remove Programs applet, click the Configure button to the right of Cluster Service (see Figure 12.6). The Cluster Service Configuration Wizard will appear.

3. Click Next.

4. Click I Understand and then click Next.

5. Select the First Node in the Cluster radio button and click Next, as shown in Figure 12.7.

6. Enter the name for the cluster and click Next.

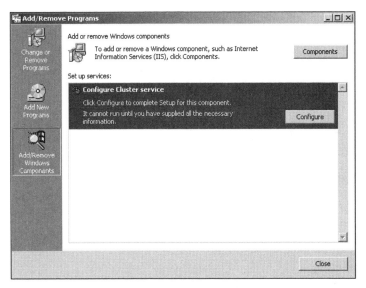

Figure 12.6   Configuring the Cluster service.

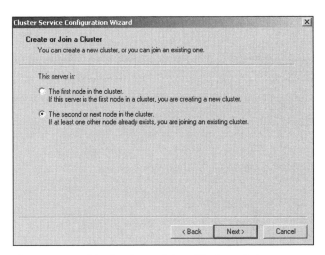

Figure 12.7   The Create or Join a Cluster window.

7. Enter the username, password, and domain for the cluster administrator. Click Next.

8. Click Next.

9. Select the cluster file storage volume and click Next.

10. Select the desired connections and click Next. Repeat this if more than one network adapter is installed in the system.

11. Click OK.

12. Assign a cluster IP address and click Next.

13. Click Finish.

Adding Subsequent Cluster Nodes

To add subsequent cluster nodes, follow these steps:

1. Upon final reboot of the server, the Configure Your Server window will appear. Click Finish.

2. In the Add/Remove Programs applet, click the Configure button to the right of Cluster Service. The Cluster Service Configuration Wizard will appear.

3. Click Next.

4. Click I Understand and then click Next.

5. Select the Second or Next Node in the Cluster radio button and click Next.

6. Enter the existing cluster information and click Next.

7. Click OK.

8. Select an account and password and then click Next.

9. Click Finish.

Evicting a Cluster Node Resource

To evict a cluster node, follow these steps:

1. Select Start|Programs|Administrative Tools|Cluster Administrator.

2. In the left pane, select the node that is to be evicted and choose the Stop Cluster Service from the File menu.

3. Select the Evict Node option from the File menu.

4. Uninstall the cluster service.

Adding a New Resource

To add a new resource to a cluster node, follow these steps:

1. Select Start|Programs|Administrative Tools|Cluster Administrator.

2. Double-click the Groups folder in the left pane.

3. In the right pane, select the group to which the new resource is to belong.

4. Right-click the group and choose New|Resource from the pop-up menu.

5. In the New Resource Wizard screen, enter the name and description of the new resource, select the resource type and group, and click Next.

6. Add any desired owner for the resource and click Next.

7. To add dependencies, select a resource under the Available Resources section and click Add.

8. Repeat Step 7 to add any other resource dependencies and click Finish when done.

Deleting a Resource

To delete a resource from a cluster node, follow these steps:

1. Select Start|Programs|Administrative Tools|Cluster Administrator.

2. Select the Resources folder in the left pane.

3. Right-click the resource that is to be deleted and select Delete from the pop-up menu.

Bringing a Resource Online

To bring a resource online, follow these steps:

1. Select Start|Programs|Administrative Tools|Cluster Administrator.

2. Select the Resources folder in the left pane.

3. Right-click the resource that is to be brought online and choose Bring Online from the File menu.

Taking a Resource Offline

To take a resource offline, follow these steps:

1. Select Start|Programs|Administrative Tools|Cluster Administrator.

2. Select the Resources folder in the left pane.

3. Right-click the resource that is to be taken offline and choose the Take Offline option from the File menu.

Adding a DHCP Server Resource

To add a DHCP server resource to a cluster node, follow these steps:

1. Select Start|Programs|Administrative Tools|Cluster Administrator.

2. Double-click the Groups folder in the left pane.

3. In the right pane, select the group for which the DHCP server resource is to belong.

4. Right-click the group and choose New|Resource from the pop-up menu.

5. In the New Resource Wizard screen, enter the name and description of the new resource, select the DHCP Service resource type and group, and click Next.

12. Fault Tolerance and Recovery

6. Add any desired owner for the resource and click Next.

7. To add dependencies, select a resource under the Available Resources section and click Add.

8. Repeat Step 7 to add any other resource dependencies and click Next.

9. Enter the appropriate database, audit file, and backup paths.

10. Click Finish.

Adding a File Share Resource

To add a file share resource to a cluster node, follow these steps:

1. Select Start|Programs|Administrative Tools|Cluster Administrator.

2. Double-click the Groups folder in the left pane.

3. In the right pane, select the group to which the File Share resource is to belong.

4. Right-click the group and choose New|Resource from the pop-up menu.

5. In the New Resource Wizard screen, enter the name and description of the new resource, select the File Share resource type and group, and click Next.

6. Add any desired owner for the resource and click Next.

7. To add dependencies, select a resource under the Available Resources section and click Add.

8. Repeat Step 7 to add any other resource dependencies and click Next.

9. Enter a share name, path, and comment.

10. If desired, enter a user limit and permissions.

11. Click Advanced.

12. Select the share type (Normal Share, DFS Root, or Share Subdirectories).

13. Click OK.

14. Click Finish.

Adding an IIS Server Resource

To add an IIS server resource to a cluster node, follow these steps:

1. Select Start|Programs|Administrative Tools|Cluster Administrator.

2. Double-click the Groups folder in the left pane.

3. In the right pane, select the group to which the IIS server resource is to belong.

4. Right-click the group and choose New|Resource from the pop-up menu.

5. In the New Resource Wizard screen, enter the name and description of the new resource, select the IIS server resource type and group, and click Next.

6. Add any desired owner for the resource and click Next.

7. To add dependencies, select a resource under the Available Resources section and click Add.

8. Repeat Step 7 to add any other resource dependencies and click Next.

9. Select whether this resource is for an FTP site or a WWW site, choose the desired site from the IIS server drop-down list, and click Finish.

Adding a Print Spooler Resource

To add a print spooler resource to a cluster node, follow these steps:

1. Select Start|Programs|Administrative Tools|Cluster Administrator.

2. Double-click the Groups folder in the left pane.

3. In the right pane, select the group to which the print spooler resource is to belong.

4. Right-click the group and choose New|Resource from the pop-up menu.

5. In the New Resource Wizard screen, enter the name and description of the new resource, select the Print Spooler resource type and group, and click Next.

6. Add any desired owner for the resource and click Next.

7. To add dependencies, select a resource under the Available Resources section and click Add.

8. Repeat Step 7 to add any other resource dependencies and click Next.

9. Enter the path to the spool folder.

10. Select a desired Job Completion Timeout setting.

11. Click Finish.

Adding an IP Address Resource

To add an IP address resource to a cluster node, follow these steps:

1. Select Start|Programs|Administrative Tools|Cluster Administrator.

2. Double-click the Groups folder in the left pane.

3. In the right pane, select the group to which the IP address resource is to belong.

4. Right-click the group and choose New|Resource from the pop-up menu.

5. In the New Resource Wizard screen, enter the name and description of the new resource, select the IP Address resource type and group, and click Next.

12. Fault Tolerance and Recovery

6. Add any desired owner for the resource and click Next.

7. To add dependencies, select a resource under the Available Resources section and click Add.

8. Repeat Step 7 to add any other resource dependencies and click Next.

9. Enter an IP address and subnet mask.

10. Select the appropriate network from the drop-down list.

11. If NetBIOS is to be enabled, check the Enable NetBIOS For This Address checkbox.

12. Click Finish.

Adding a WINS Server Resource

To add a WINS server resource to a cluster node, follow these steps:

1. Select Start|Programs|Administrative Tools|Cluster Administrator.

2. Double-click the Groups folder in the left pane.

3. In the right pane, select the group to which the WINS server resource is to belong.

4. Right-click the group and choose New|Resource from the pop-up menu.

5. In the New Resource Wizard screen, enter the name and description of the new resource, select the WINS Service resource type and group, and click Next.

6. Add any desired owner for the resource and click Next.

7. To add dependencies, select a resource under the Available Resources section and click Add.

8. Repeat Step 7 to add any other resource dependencies and click Next.

9. Enter the appropriate database and backup paths.

10. Click Finish.

Enabling Diagnostic Logging

To enable diagnostic logging on a cluster, follow these steps:

1. Select Start|Settings|Control Panel.

2. Double-click the System applet.

3. Select the Advanced Tab.

4. Click Environmental Variables.

5. Click New under the System Variables section.

6. In the Variable Name field, enter the name of the variable: clusterlog.

7. In the Variable Value field, enter the variable's value: c:\cluster\cluster.log.

8. Click OK.

9. Click OK.

10. Close Control Panel.

11. Select Start|Programs|Administrative Tools|Cluster Administrator.

12. In the left pane, select the node where diagnostic logging is to be enabled and choose the Stop Cluster Service command from the File menu.

13. In the left pane, select the node where diagnostic logging is to be enabled and choose the Start Cluster Service command from the File menu.

Disabling Diagnostic Logging

To disable diagnostic logging on a cluster, follow these steps:

1. Select Start|Settings|Control Panel.

2. Double-click the System applet.

3. Select the Advanced Tab.

4. Click Environmental Variables.

5. Select the Clusterlog variable in the System Variable section.

6. Click Delete.

7. Click OK.

8. Click OK.

9. Close Control Panel.

10. Select Start|Programs|Administrative Tools|Cluster Administrator.

11. In the left pane, select the node where diagnostic logging is to be enabled and choose the Stop Cluster Service command from the File menu.

12. In the left pane, select the node where diagnostic logging is to be enabled and choose the Start Cluster Service command from the File menu.

Chapter 13

IntelliMirror

In Depth

IntelliMirror is a collection of Windows 2000 services and applications that offer administrators control over desktops, user data, software installation, and more. IntelliMirror is not actually a standalone service or feature of Windows 2000; instead, it consists of the capabilities created through the interaction and integration of native Windows 2000 components. Through the use of Group Policies within an Active Directory environment, a user's desktop, software, and data can intelligently be available to him or her across a network and be available even when the user is offline.

IntelliMirror Overview

IntelliMirror and Remote Installation Services (RIS) make up change and configuration management within a Windows 2000 environment. IntelliMirror has three core features or capabilities:

- Management of user data
- Installation and maintenance of software
- Management of user settings and desktop environments

These capabilities can be used independently or combined into a total management solution. With all the IntelliMirror features in use in combination with RIS, it is possible to completely replace, rebuild, and restore a user's system. This grants administrators complete control over users' desktops and grants users the ability to focus on work tasks instead of system maintenance and data management.

The management of user data centers around maintaining the integrity and accessibility of data that's essential to users' work tasks. The User Data Management portion of IntelliMirror grants users reliable access to data no matter where they are located on the network, and even when they're offline. This portion of IntelliMirror takes advantage of the following Windows 2000 native services and capabilities:

- Active Directory
- Group Policy
- Offline Folders
- Synchronization Manager

13. IntelliMirror

- Enhancements to the Windows 2000 shell

- Folder Redirection

- Disk quotas

Installing and maintaining software ensures that users will always have the software necessary for accomplishing their work tasks. This portion of IntelliMirror can automatically install software on clients as needed by the users. Furthermore, IntelliMirror can update, repair, and remove software as well. This portion of IntelliMirror takes advantage of the following Windows 2000 native services and capabilities:

- Active Directory

- Group Policy

- Windows Installer

- Add/Remove Programs

- Enhancements to the Windows 2000 shell

Managing user settings and the desktop environment centers on maintaining a consistent user environment no matter where a user logs in. This includes retaining a user's customized desktop as well as enforcing environment restrictions. IntelliMirror ensures that the user's desktop settings are always present so the user can focus on work tasks instead of an unfamiliar layout and desktop scheme. This portion of IntelliMirror takes advantage of the following Windows 2000 native services and capabilities:

- Active Directory

- Group Policy

- Offline Folders

- Roaming User Profiles

- Enhancements to the Windows 2000 shell

Portions of IntelliMirror can be employed on a standalone system through the Local Computer Policy without Active Directory or Group Policy. Once a Group Policy has been applied to a system, those changes remain in effect even when the system is not connected to the network.

IntelliMirror eases the requirement and frequency of administrative intervention and simplifies a user's computing experience by performing all the necessary functions to maintain a consistent and functional computing environment for all network users, whether online or offline. IntelliMirror offers another level of disaster protection and data recovery from a client system perspective. Every element on a client system present at the moment of the most recent graceful network disconnection is available for restoration, reinstallation, or reapplication at the next logon. Even when a user deletes or destroys local data, software, configuration information, or even the entire OS, IntelliMirror can automatically restore and replace the damaged or lost elements, often without any need for administrative intervention.

In addition to the disaster protection it offers, IntelliMirror is also a control mechanism. Through the use of Group Policies on Windows 2000 organizational units (which includes domains, sites, and custom defined OUs), an administrator can retain control over the environment on all clients, even when they are disconnected from the network. This control ranges from implementing mandatory user profiles, to installing required software and removing unapproved software, to distributing patches, upgrades, and service packs (a.k.a. *service releases*), to granting or restricting access to native tools, Control Panel applets, the Registry, and more.

Management of User Data

Data management can be controlled on an OU basis through Group Policies or on an individual basis through manual configuration. IntelliMirror can maintain a copy of network resources on clients so when they are offline the data is still available to the user. In fact, the data is still accessed in the same manner from the user's perspective as if he or she were still connected to the network. This feature is primarily enabled through Offline Files.

Offline Files (discussed in Chapter 6) can be configured on a user-by-user basis or through a Group Policy in the Administrative Templates|Network|Offline Files section of either the Computer Configuration or User Configuration (see Figure 13.1) node. Once a file is managed by Offline Files, it can be restored when corrupted or deleted. Also, when multiple versions of the same file come into existence, you are prompted whether to keep both versions or overwrite one with the other. Offline Files offers administrators a network-wide intelligent document-management and version-control solution that operates over connected and transient clients.

Data management is also accomplished through intelligent positioning and mapping of user home and data directories (such as the My Documents folder). In most cases, the home directory and all user data directories should be stored on a network share. Then make these folders available offline (via Offline Files manually or through Group Policy). Additionally, use Group Policy to map common local folders to network share-stored versions of these folders as necessary—this is known as *Folder Redirection*. Once configured, users' data and folder hierarchies not only

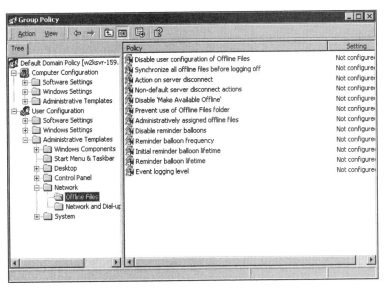

Figure 13.1   The Group Policy|Offline Folders section.

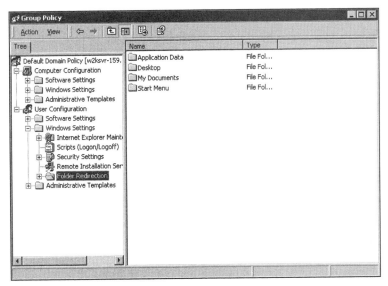

Figure 13.2   The Group Policy|Folder Redirection section.

are available no matter where they log in, they're also available on portable systems disconnected from the network. Folder Redirection (Figure 13.2) is defined in the User Configuration|Windows Settings|Folder Redirection area of Group Policy.

Installing and Maintaining Software

Software management is a key tool on many networks. It can be used to ensure that software is always available to users, that the latest version of the software is installed, and that no unapproved software is present. These control mechanisms are often essential to maintaining a virus- and corruption-free network and fostering a computing environment sufficient for all necessary work tasks to be accomplished.

Centralized automated software deployment is made possible through the Windows Installer tool. This tool creates deployable software images and installation scripts. The software distribution packages, known as *MSI* (*Microsoft Installer*) files, are added to a Group Policy (see Figure 13.3). Each time this policy is applied to a system, the software is validated. If the software is not present, it is installed. If the software is out of date or a new version or patch is present, it is upgraded. The software control adds desktop and Start menu icons for the distributed software. It is only installed when the user actually attempts to launch the software. Then any new applications, patches, or upgrades are installed or applied. This is known as *assigned software*. Once the installation process is complete, the application is launched.

In addition to mandatory software whose presence is automated, nonessential software can be included that users can selectively install as desired. This is known as *published software*. The Software portion of Group Policy can also

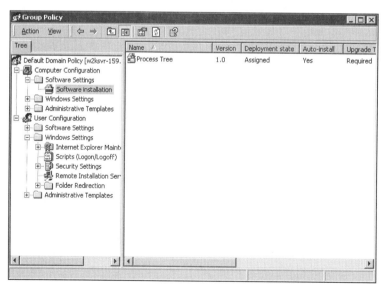

Figure 13.3   The Group Policy|Software Installation section.

be used to remove previously distributed software. This capability will restore damaged or corrupted software files so a reliable and functional system is always available for the users.

NOTE: *For information on the Microsoft Installer tool, see the Windows 2000 Server Resource Kit.*

Managing User Settings and the Desktop Environment

User profiles are nothing new to Windows networking administrators; however, under Windows 2000, roaming user profiles, when used in conjunction with Group Policies, offer users greater flexibility and administrators more control. User profiles and all related environmental settings, files, and controls can be protected from corruption or loss in the same manner as user data. Keep in mind that a roaming user profile is defined on the Profile tab of a user's Properties dialog box (see Figure 13.4).

The proper management of environmental data through IntelliMirror ensures that the user's personal desktop is always accessible, that administrative control is maintained, and that the least amount of data must be transferred to the client system each time the user logs on.

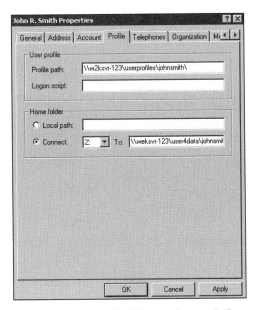

Figure 13.4   The Profile tab of a user's Properties dialog box.

Remote Installation Services

Remote Installation Services (RIS) is often used with IntelliMirror to create a complete disaster-recovery solution. In the event that a user's system is completely destroyed, a new computer can be reinstalled and reconfigured automatically to match that of the previous system. Such a recovery will restore the original user environment, including software, administrative control, and user data.

The Remote Installation Services of Windows 2000 Server can be used to automate the deployment of Windows 2000 Professional. This service relies on the following native components:

- Active Directory
- Group Policy
- DHCP
- DNS (Domain Name Service)

RIS can install Windows 2000 Professional onto new computer systems using two methods: first, using a DHCP PXE-based (Pre-Boot Execution Environment) remote boot ROM network interface card, or second, using an RIS boot disk. Alternatively, RIS can be used to overinstall any network-capable OS to Windows 2000 Professional. The biggest benefit of RIS is that after the power to boot the target system is turned on, all other elements of the remote deployment can be fully automated.

When RIS is used to deploy a client OS, the process occurs generally as follows:

NOTE: *All prompts contained in this general process can be automated so that no user interaction at the target is required.*

---

1. Boot the target system (either with a compliant PXE NIC or an RIS boot disk).
2. A DHCP server request is initiated by the target system.
3. The DHCP server responds with the address of the RIS server.
4. Unless otherwise automated, F12 must be pressed to initiate service from the RIS server.
5. The RIS server verifies that the target system is authorized for the remote installation process.
6. The Client Information Wizard (CIW) is copied to the target system.

7. A user must provide logon credentials for the network.

8. The installation options assigned to or available for the target are displayed on the target. If multiple selections are available, the user must select an option from the list. If only a single selection is available, it is initiated without prompting.

9. CIW issues a warning that the local hard drive will be formatted.

10. The OS installation is initiated. Any nonautomated element of the process will initiate a prompt requiring user interaction and input.

11. Once installation is complete, the system is rebooted into the new OS.

When combined with IntelliMirror, all relevant data, configuration, and software are transferred to the target upon bootup (Computer Configuration) and user logon (User Configuration). Once installed, RIS can be configured and managed from the Active Directory Users And Computers tool. The RIS controls are located on the Remote Install tab of the domain controller's Properties dialoe°box.

Target systems can employ a NIC with a PXE-based remote boot ROM or use an RIS boot floppy. The floppy generator tool, RBFG.EXE, must be launched manually. This tool is located in the %systemroot%\system32\reminst and \RemoteInstall\Admin\i386 folders. Once it's launched, just select the letter of the floppy drive, insert a formatted floppy, and click Create Disk (see Figure 13.5).

RIS does have some requirements for the target system, including:

- Hardware must meet the Windows 2000 Professional system requirements.

- All hardware must be HCL (Hardware Compatibility List) compliant.

- 1.2 GB of hard drive space is required.

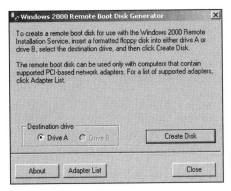

Figure 13.5   The RBFG floppy generator tool.

- An RIS-compatible PCI NIC must be present. As of June 2000, the only compatible devices are:
  - 3Com 3c900 (Combo and TP0), 3c900B (Combo, FL, TPC, TP0), 3c905 (T4 and TX), and 3c905B (Combo, TX, FX)
  - AMD PCNet and Fast PC Net
  - Compaq Netflex 100 (NetIntelligent II) and Netflex 110 (NetIntelligent III)
  - DEC DE 450 and DE 500
  - HP Deskdirect 10/100 TX
  - Intel Pro 10+, Pro 100+, and Pro 100B (including the E100 series)
  - SMC 8432, SMC 9332, and SMC 9432

NOTE: *Before booting a target client with a PXE NIC or a boot disk, be sure to create a DHCP scope for RIS clients.*

The displayed startup options on a target system can be controlled through Group Policy. The Remote Installation Services section offers control over automatic setup, custom setup, restart setup, and tool access (see Figure 13.6). RIS Group Policies are created and defined in the same manner as all other Group Policies.

Installation images used by RIS can be restricted to specific groups or users simply by setting the access permission on the image's templates subfolder. For users to have proper access to an installation image, they must have Read & Execute, List Folder Contents, and Read permissions to an image's folder and contents.

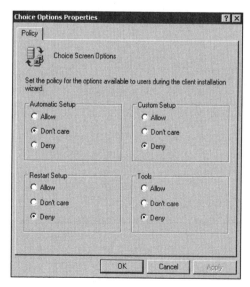

Figure 13.6   The Choice Options Properties dialog box for RIS via Group Policy.

The template directory is found in a path such as \RemoteInstall\Setup\ English\Images\<<image name>>\i386\templates.

Unattended answer files can be associated with RIS installation images to customize the install process. Answer files can be linked with installation images through the Advanced Settings button on the Remote Install tab of a domain controller's Properties dialog box. If two or more answer files are associated with a single RIS image, the target system will be required to select one of the options. If only a single answer file is linked to an RIS image, it will be launched without user input on the target system.

Fully customized RIS images can be created using the RIPrep tool. Custom images are extracted from installed and configured systems. In order to use RIPrep, Windows 2000 Professional must be installed onto drive C and all installed applications must be installed onto drive C as well. Furthermore, all target systems must have similar core hardware components—that is, be able to use the same HAL (Hardware Abstraction Layer) as the original system.

IntelliMirror Scenarios

The benefits of IntelliMirror are most easily recognized when the power and capabilities afforded a network administrator are discussed in the realm of possible common network situations. In the following sections, uses of IntelliMirror are exemplified.

Scenario: New Employee

The time-consuming task of configuring a new computer system for a new employee is virtually eliminated with IntelliMirror. With the use of RIS, a new system can be automatically installed and configured. When the new employee logs on the for the first time, he or she will discover all the necessary software, network mappings, and desktop and Start menu shortcuts required by his or her work tasks. Important company documents, procedural manuals, HR materials, and intranet Web page URLs can be added to the desktop and Favorites list so getting acquainted with the company's policies and procedures is simplified. Through the use of multimedia, companies may even offer network broadcasts of orientation and how-to videos right to the new desktop the first time the new user logs in.

Scenario: Software Distribution

Whether you're needing to distribute a new software application, a recent patch, or an upgrade, or are even needing to add older software to a new system, IntelliMirror offers centralized management of client software. Through the use of Windows Installer and Group Policy, new applications can be installed on a user's system as needed and existing applications can be upgraded.

Scenario: Mobile System Management

Managing the software and user data on a notebook is difficult enough. But add in security controls, access restrictions, software patches and upgrades, and access to network resources when offline, and the task becomes a nightmare. Fortunately, IntelliMirror was design to eliminate this specific horror. Notebook systems are fully controllable via Group Policies and all user data and network data can be made available to roaming users even when they're not connected to the network. IntelliMirror automatically manages version conflicts, alterations of folder hierarchies, and damaged or deleted files.

Scenario: System Replacement

In the event of a complete system failure—caused either by a hard drive crash or physical destruction—IntelliMirror offers the ability to duplicate the previous environment on a replacement system. In much the same way a new computer is installed and configured, a replacement system can be brought back up to standard client parameters. When users log in, their data and desktop settings are restored. The only data that cannot be restored is anything added or altered on the client since the last network logon.

Total Cost of Ownership

One of the most significant benefits of IntelliMirror is its ability to reduce the cost in actual dollars and man hours to sustain a growing network. IntelliMirror can be used to reduce the cost of client management for small and large networks alike. Obviously, the more desktops that are automatically managed, the larger the time and monetary savings. These cost of ownership benefits are afforded you via IntelliMirror due to the following components:

- *Group Policy*—This element of IntelliMirror is able to control both users and computers through a single centralized collection of settings.

- *Windows Installer*—This element of IntelliMirror is affectionately known as a *smart technology*. Windows Installer completely eliminates the need for an administrator to manually install software on every desktop. An installation package is added to the Group Policy and it is instantly available to every client on the network. In addition to reducing installation costs, it also reduces ongoing support, upgrading, and removal costs.

- *Data Redirection*—This element is a combination of Folder Redirection and Offline Files, which make user and network data available at all times from any client on or off the network. By centrally managing data and storing data on network servers, it decreases the cost of data management and reduces the risk

13. IntelliMirror

of data loss, primarily through the fact that data stored in a single location is easier to backup and will most likely be stored on a fault-tolerant drive system.

- *Remote Installation Services*—This component, when combined with IntelliMirror, reduces the cost of deploying new clients or restoring damaged clients.

Enhancement through Systems Management Server

IntelliMirror and Remote Installation Services can be further enhanced through the addition of Systems Management Server (SMS). The primary benefit of adding SMS to Windows 2000's IntelliMirror is the added support for non-Windows 2000 systems. This is especially helpful in environments that are not or will not fully migrate to Windows 2000 Professional on the desktop. SMS provides client management support for all Microsoft operating systems from Windows 3.x through Windows 2000. Table 13.1 shows a comparison between SMS and IntelliMirror and what their combined features can offer.

SMS offers several management facilities:

- *Hardware and software inventory*—Through Windows Management Instrumentation (WMI) and various software scanners, SMS is able to maintain a detailed inventory of the hardware and software present on individual systems and ultimately the entire network. This data is stored in a SQL Server-based system that can be used for budgeting, growth projection, and trending. The inventory is maintained automatically by SMS so that a current and accurate complete inventory is available with a click of the mouse. Additionally, the inventory gathered from systems can be processed by the compliance comparative database tool to determine which systems require hardware upgrades to properly support operating system upgrades or software deployments.

Table 13.1   The features of SMS and IntelliMirror.

Feature	SMS	IntelliMirror	Combined
Distribution	Yes	No	Yes
Targeting	Collection	Active Directory	Collection or group
Platform	All platforms	Windows 2000 only	All platforms
Installation	SMS or Windows Installer	Windows Installer	SMS or Windows Installer
Additional management support	Yes	No	Yes

- *Software distribution and installation*—Software can be distributed on a computer, user, or group basis. Rules-based deployment techniques can be employed to target application deployment on an even more detailed or controlled basis. SMS includes immediate deployment as well as rollback capabilities. This allows administrators to fully control the application environment of users, including situations where a user moves from one department to another, where a user's job description is drastically changed, or when a project requires a specific application.

- *Software metering*—Managing how much an application package is used is often important, especially when license restrictions limit the number of simultaneous users. SMS offers complete software usage tracking by user, group, client, time, and license. Reports can be generated to outline the usage scenarios based on real activity. These reports can be used for growth planning and budgeting for new hardware and software acquisitions. In addition to tracking and logging, SMS can control software use through the issuing of alerts and warnings as well as by preventing applications from launching when specific triggers are tripped.

- *Diagnostics and troubleshooting*—Overseeing an entire network can be quite a time-consuming task. SMS offers automated oversight through numerous advanced diagnostic tools, ranging from network traffic monitors to performance monitors. SMS is able to track activity and even offer troubleshooting and improvement advice for all Microsoft operating systems and most Microsoft software products, including the Microsoft BackOffice and Office suites.

Immediate Solutions

Installing Remote Installation Services

To add the ability to remotely install Windows 2000 Professional from a Windows 2000 Server system, perform the following steps:

NOTE: *To complete this exercise, RIS must be installed on a domain controller or have access to a domain controller. Plus, DHCP must already be present on the network.*

---

1. Log in as Administrator.

2. Launch the Add/Remove Programs applet from the Control Panel.

3. Click the Add/Remove Windows Components button. The Windows Components Wizard launches.

4. Locate and select the Remote Installation Services checkbox.

5. Click Next.

6. The installer may prompt for the Windows 2000 Server distribution CD during the installation process. If so, provide the correct path to the CD or a network-shared copy of the CD.

7. Once the installer completes and a completed message is displayed, click Finish.

8. Reboot your system as prompted.

9. After rebooting, log back into the system as Administrator.

10. Launch the Configure Your Server applet from Administrative Tools.

11. Click the Finish Setup link. The Add/Remove Programs applet will be launched.

12. Click the Configure button on the Configure Remote Installation Services area (it will be highlighted). This launches the Remote Installation Services Setup Wizard (see Figure 13.7).

13. Click Next.

14. When prompted, provide a path to store the remote installation images folder (see Figure 13.8). The path must point to a non-system drive formatted with NTFS, with plenty of free space (2GB is a reasonable minimum).

15. Click Next.

Figure 13.7   The Remote Installation Services Setup Wizard.

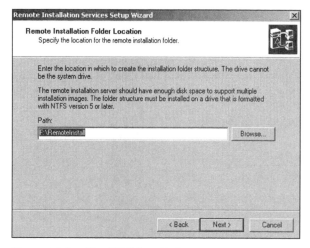

Figure 13.8   The RIS Wizard's Remote Installation Folder Location page.

16. Select whether to allow the RIS server to respond to targets immediately after installation of RIS is complete or whether to keep RIS offline until manually enabled at a later time (see Figure 13.9). In most cases, mark the Respond To Client Computers Requesting Service checkbox.

17. Click Next.

18. Provide the path to the Windows 2000 Professional distribution files from either a CD or a network shared copy.

19. Click Next.

20. Provide a name for the folder to host the installation images.

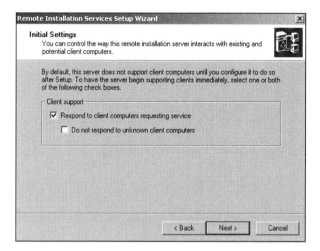

Figure 13.9   The RIS Wizard's Initial Settings page.

21. Click Next.

22. Provide a description of the installation image currently being created, as shown in Figure 13.10.

23. Click Next.

24. Review the outline of the defined settings.

25. Click Finish to accept and apply the settings.

26. RIS will be configured and an installation image will be created. A progress page displays the activity of the installation (see Figure 13.11).

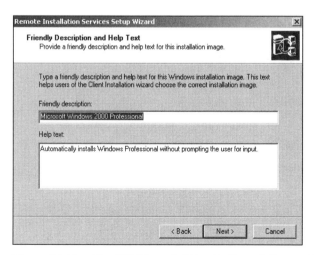

Figure 13.10   The RIS Wizard's Friendly Description and Help Text page.

Figure 13.11   The RIS Wizard's progress page.

27. When the process is complete, click Done.

28. Close the Add/Remove Programs applet (and Control Panel if open).

29. Close the Configure Your Server dialog box.

Configuring RIS

To configure RIS through the Active Directory Users And Computers utility, perform the following steps:

1. Launch the Active Directory Users And Computers utility from Administrative Tools.

2. Expand the left pane's list to reveal the Domain Controller section of the domain.

3. Select the Domain Controller section.

4. Locate and select the name of the domain controller hosting RIS.

5. Open the Properties dialog box for the domain controller.

6. Select the Remote Install tab (see Figure 13.12).

7. On this tab you can configure the following settings:

   • Respond To Clients Requesting Service

   • Do Not Respond To Unknown Client Computers

   • Verify the server configuration (via the Verify Server button)

   • Show the currently active RIS clients (via the Show Clients button)

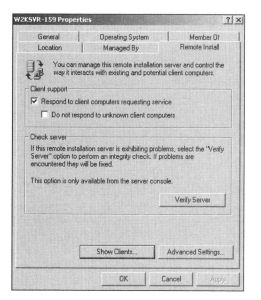

Figure 13.12   The Remote Install tab of an RIS-hosting domain controller's Properties dialog box.

8. Clicking the Advanced Setting button reveals another dialog box, shown in Figure 13.13, with three tabs. The New Clients tab offers the following settings:

- Generate client computer names using a selected naming convention (predefined or custom conventions can be used).

- Create the client computer account in the following directory service location: the default, the same as the user performing the installation, or a defined location (a Browse button is provided).

9. The Images tab is used to create new RIS images or associate unattend.txt files with existing RIS images.

10. The Tools tab is used by independent software vendors (ISVs) or original equipment manufacturers (OEMs) to provide software through RIS. See the *Windows 2000 Server Resource Kit* on how to add tools to the \RemoteInstall directory tree so they can be managed on this tab.

11. Click OK to close the Advanced Settings dialog box.

12. Click OK to close the domain controller's Properties dialog box.

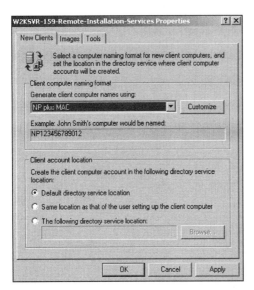

Figure 13.13   An RIS server's advanced settings Properties dialog box.

Using RIPrep to Create a Custom Installation Image

To use RIPrep to create an installation image to distribute installations with preinstalled software onto similar computer systems, perform the following steps:

1. Install Windows 2000 Professional onto a target system using RIS. This system will be known as the *base system*.

2. Manually install and configure additional components, other Microsoft products, or third-party software.

3. On the base system, launch the RIPrep wizard using a UNC similar to "\\<RISservername>\Reminst\Admin\I386\RIPrep" from the **run** command or a command prompt.

4. Click Next.

5. Provide the name of the Windows 2000 Server system hosting RIS.

6. Click Next.

7. Provide a name for the image folder.

8. Click Next.

9. Provide a description and help text for the image.

10. Click Next.

11. A list of any running applications or services is displayed. Stop any listed service before continuing.

12. Click Next.

13. Review the settings.

14. Click Next.

15. Click Next again.

16. The RIS image will be built and stored on the RIS host system. Then the workstation will be shut down.

Configuring Folder Redirection

To use Folder Redirection to ensure that a user's data will follow him or her around the network and be available (even when he or she is offline) via a network share, perform the following steps:

1. Open Active Directory Users And Computers. To manage the Group Policy for a site instead of a domain or OU, launch Active Directory Sites And Services.

2. Locate and select the domain or OU to configure Folder Redirection.

3. Open the Properties dialog box for the container.

4. Select the Group Policy tab.

5. Select a listed Group Policy for this container.

6. Click Edit.

NOTE: *If you want to add a new Group Policy instead of editing an existing Group Policy, click New.*

---

7. Expand the User Configuration section.

8. Expand the Windows Settings section under User Configuration.

9. Expand the Folder Redirection section.

10. Select the Application Data item in the right pane.

11. Open the Properties dialog box for this item.

12. On the Target tab, select whether to redirect all users' folders to the same location or specify different locations for users and groups.

13. If One Location For All (Basic) is selected, provide the UNC for the network share location for this folder.

14. If unique locations will be defined for user and groups, add each unique user/group along with the UNC for the network share location for this folder.

15. Select the Settings tab.

16. Select whether to grant exclusive access rights to the Application Data folder to each user.

17. Select whether to move the contents of the local location of the folder to its newly defined location.

18. Select whether to leave the contents of the folder in the new location or return the contents to the local original location in the event of this policy being removed.

19. Close the Application Data Properties dialog box by clicking OK.

20. Repeat Steps 11 through 19 for the Desktop, My Documents, and Start Menu items.

21. Close the Group Policy editor.

22. Click OK in the container's Properties dialog box.

23. Close Active Directory Users And Computers.

Defining a Network Share-Hosted Home Folder

To encourage users to store data in folder hierarchies that are protected by IntelliMirror, use a home folder designation to orient the user in the proper location each time a new file save is attempted by performing the following steps:

1. Open Active Directory Users And Computers.

2. Select the Users section.

3. Locate and select a user account for which to define a home folder.

4. Open the Properties dialog box for the selected user.

5. Select the Profile tab.

6. Select the Connect radio button under the Home Folder heading.

7. Select an unused drive letter in the pull-down list.

8. Type in the UNC name of the folder in a network share to be used as this user's home folder.

9. Click OK to save.

10. Repeat this procedure for all users. Be sure to define a unique folder for each user.

11. Close Active Directory Users And Computers.

Creating a Roaming User Profile

To create a roaming user profile, perform the following steps:

1. On a network server, create a share with sufficient drive space.

2. Open Active Directory Users And Computers.

3. Select the Users section.

4. Locate and select a user account for which to define a home folder.

5. Open the Properties dialog box for the selected user.

6. Select the Profile tab.

7. In the Profile Path field, type in the UNC of the network share location where the user profile should be stored. This should be in the form of *\\servername\sharename\username*. The username subfolder will be created by Windows 2000 automatically.

8. Click OK to save these changes.

9. Close Active Directory Users And Computers.

10. From a client system, log in with the user account and then log out. Until the user account logs on then logs off of the network, the roaming profile is not actually created.

Adding a Software Package to Group Policy

To add a software installation package to Group Policy, perform the following steps:

NOTE: *A Windows Installer software distribution package (MSI file) must be available.*

1. Open Active Directory Users And Computers. To manage the Group Policy for a site instead of a domain or OU, launch Active Directory Sites And Services.

2. Locate and select the domain or OU to configure software distribution.

3. Open the Properties dialog box for the container.

4. Select the Group Policy tab.

5. Select a listed Group Policy for this container.

6. Click Edit.

NOTE: *If you want to add a new Group Policy instead of editing an existing Group Policy, click New.*

---

7. Expand the Computer Configuration section.

8. Expand the Software Settings section under Computer Configuration.

9. Select the Software Installation section.

10. Issue the New|Package command from the Action menu.

11. Use the Open dialog box to locate and select the MSI file (the software distribution package). Be sure to select the file through a network path (that is, use My Network Places) instead of a local path.

12. Click Open.

NOTE: *If you select a local path, a warning dialog box will be displayed asking whether to go ahead and use the local path known. Most network users will be unable to access the installation files or to abort the configuration procedure. If this message appears, click No to abort and start over; then be sure to select the MSI file using a network path.*

---

13. Select what method of deployment to configure this software for. The options are Published, Assigned, and Advanced Published or Assigned. Keep in mind that a published package will only be installed when a user manually initiates the installation from the Add/Remove Programs applet and that an assigned package will be installed automatically when a user selects the application's preexisting Start menu shortcut icon.

14. Click OK.

15. If you selected Published or Assigned, the new installation package will appear in the list of packages in the right pane of the Group Policy MMC snap-in display. At this point, the basic configuration of the software package is complete. To fine-tune or customize the settings, select the listed package and issue the Properties command from the Action menu; then continue from Step 17.

16. If you selected Advanced Published or Assigned, the Properties dialog box for the installation package will open.

17. The General tab shows the displayed name of the process that can be customized along with details about the package itself, including version, publisher, language, platform, and support contact information.

18. Review this data; alter the displayed name if desired.

19. Select the Deployment tab.

20. This tab can be used to configure several options:

   • *Deployment type*—Used to set the installation package deployment type to Published or Assigned.

13. IntelliMirror

- *Deployment options*—Used to enable or disable various deployment options: Auto-Install This application By File Extension Activation, Uninstall This Application When It Falls Out Of The Scope Of Management, and Do Not Display This Package In The Add/Remove Programs Control Panel.

- *Installation user interface options*—Used to specify whether only basic minimal displays are shown to the user or complete messages, screens, and installation data is shown to the user.

21. Select the Upgrades tab.

22. Use this tab to specify whether this installation package is an upgrade to another installation package. When making this specification, you can also select whether to uninstall the existing package before installing the upgrade or to use this package to upgrade the existing installation.

23. Select the Categories tab.

24. Use this tab to place the installation package under a category displayed through the Add/Remove Programs applet.

25. Select the Modifications tab.

26. This tab is used to define modification scripts or install routines that should be used against this package once it is installed. These modification elements are MST files. Multiple MST files can be applied in a specified order.

27. Select the Security tab.

28. This tab is used to define which users have access to this installation package. Users who will be installing this package need Read access only.

29. Click OK to return to the container's Properties dialog box.

30. Click OK to return to the Group Policy MMC snap-in window.

31. Close the MMC window.

Chapter 14

Scripting and Automation

In Depth

Talk to any Unix administrator about why Unix is better than Windows NT and you'll start a war. When the smoke settles, one of the strengths of Unix is its ability to easily script administrative tasks. Before Windows Scripting Host (WSH), the only way to create administrative scripts in Windows NT was by using MS-DOS batch files. Although batch files are great for simple scripts and are easy to create, they fall apart when you try to accomplish any complex tasks.

All that changed when Microsoft released WSH. WSH gives administrators the ability to create very complex scripts using common scripting languages to perform complex tasks easily.

WSH is automatically installed with Windows 2000. It also installs two scripting engines: VBScript and JScript. These two scripting languages are Visual Basic Script and JavaScript, respectively. Any scripts written with these languages will be executed properly in Windows 2000.

Another nice feature of WSH is its ability to host any scripting language, including PerlScript, Python, Tool Command Language (TCL), and Rexx. These third-party scripting languages, however, need to be installed separately.

Two different scripting engines exist with WSH: WScript and CScript.

WScript

WScript is the 32-bit Windows-based scripting engine. This is the engine that's used to execute a script when you double-click the script file. You can, however, use it to run scripts from the command prompt and configure how scripts are run.

When executing WScript from the command prompt, the following format must be used:

```
WScript scriptname.extension [//B | //I][//D][//E:Engine][//H:scripthost][//
Job:nnn] [//Logo | //Nologo][//S][//T:nn][//X]
```

Table 14.1 lists all the command-line switches that can be used with WScript to configure the script execution.

Table 14.1   The WScript.exe command-line switches.

Switch	Description
//B	Specifies that the script should run in batch mode. Batch mode stops the script errors and prompts from displaying.
//D	Turns on active debugging.
//E:engine	Uses the specified engine.
//H:CScript	Specifies that Cscript.exe should be used as the default script host.
//H:WScript	Specifies that Wscript.exe should be used as the default script host. This is the default setting.
//I	Specifies that the script should run in Interactive mode. All script errors and prompts are displayed. This is the default setting.
//Job:*xxxx*	Executes the specified WScript job.
//Logo	Displays the logo. This is the default setting.
//Nologo	Hides the logo.
//S	Saves current command-line options for the user.
//T:*nn*	Specifies the maximum amount of time the script is allowed to execute. The time out is in seconds.
//X	Executes the script in debugger.

CScript

CScript.exe is the command line-based scripting engine. This engine will only be used if the script is configured to use it by default (the default is to run the script using WScript) or when a CScript command is issued, as follows:

```
CScript scriptname.extension [//B | //I][//D][//E:Engine][//H:scripthost][//
Job:nnn][//Logo | //Nologo][//S][//T:nn][//X][//U]
```

The command-line switches that are used with CScript to configure script execution are the same as the ones listed in Table 14.1 for WScript. There's only one additional one for CScript: **//U,** which you use to use Unicode for redirected I/O from the console.

Microsoft has supplied many different sample scripts to work with. Some sample scripts are found at **http://msdn.microsoft.com/scripting**. These are listed in Table 14.2. These scripts may not work properly without modification on your Windows 2000 system because they were released before Windows 2000. More up-to-date scripts are found in the *Windows 2000 Server Resource Kit* (Microsoft Press, ISBN: 1-57231-805-8) under the "Remote Administration Scripts" section. These are listed in Table 14.3.

Table 14.2   Microsoft-supplied sample scripts.

Script File	Description
Addusers.vbs	A VBScript to add users to Active Directory
DelUsers.vbs	A VBScript to delete users from Active Directory
Chart.vbs	A VBScript to create a chart in Microsoft Excel and rotate it
Chart.js	A JScript to create a chart in Microsoft Excel and rotate it
Excel.vbs	A VBScript to write application properties into a Microsoft Excel spreadsheet
Excel.js	A JScript to write application properties into a Microsoft Excel spreadsheet
Showvar.vbs	A VBScript to display variables configured on the system
Network.vbs	A VBScript to display network properties
Network.js	A JScript to display network properties
Registry.vbs	A VBScript to display/change Registry information
Registry.js	A JScript to display/change Registry information
Shortcut.vbs	A VBScript to create a shortcut
Shortcut.js	A JScript to create a shortcut

Table 14.3   Windows 2000 Resource Kit-supplied sample scripts.

Script File	Description
Bootconfig.vbs	Displays the boot configuration
Bus.vbs	Displays the bus information
Cacheinfo.vbs	Displays the cache information
Cdromdrives.vbs	Displays the CD-ROM configuration
CheckBios.vbs	Displays the BIOS configuration
Chkusers.vbs	Checks a domain for users
CodecFile.vbs	Displays codec information
CompSys.vbs	Displays the system properties
CreateUsers.vbs	Creates users in Active Directory
Desktop.vbs	Displays the desktop properties
Device.vbs	Controls a device
Devicemem.vbs	Displays device memory information
DiskPartition.vbs	Displays disk partition information

(continued)

14. Scripting and Automation

***Table 14.3   Windows 2000 Resource Kit-supplied sample scripts** (continued).*

Script File	Description
Dmachan.vbs	Displays the DMA channel information
Drives.vbs	Displays physical disk information
EnableDhcp.vbs	Enables DHCP on the system
Eventlogmon.vbs	Monitors event log commands
Exec.vbs	Executes a command
Fileman.vbs	Manages a file
Group.vbs	Displays a list of groups in a domain
Groupdescription.vbs	Displays the description for a group
IrqRes.vbs	Displays the IRQ resources
Keyboard.vbs	Displays the keyboard configuration
Ldordergrp.vbs	Displays service dependency groups
ListAdapters.vbs	Displays network adapters
Listdcs.vbs	Displays all domain controllers
ListDisplayConfig.vbs	Displays the display configuration
Listdomains.vbs	Displays all domains in a specified namespace
ListFreeSpace.vbs	Displays free space on all drives
Listmembers.vbs	Displays the members of a group
ListOs.vbs	Displays the OS properties
ListPrinters.vbs	Displays the installed printers
ListSpace.vbs	Displays the size of the physical drives
Logmeminfo.vbs	Displays logical memory configuration
Llstdpconinfo.vbs	Displays the display controller configuration
Modifyusers.vbs	Modifies user account properties
Motherboard.vbs	Displays motherboard information
NetConnections.vbs	Displays network connections
NetworkProtocol.vbs	Displays network protocols
OsReconfig.vbs	Displays and change OS Recover mode
PageFile.vbs	Displays the pagefile information
Parallelport.vbs	Displays parallel port configuration
PointDev.vbs	Displays mouse configuration
Processor.vbs	Displays processor information

14. Scripting and Automation

(continued)

Table 14.3   Windows 2000 Resource Kit-supplied sample scripts (continued).

Script File	Description
ProtocolBinding.vbs	Displays protocol binding configuration
Ps.vbs	Displays all processes running on the system
Regconfig.vbs	Displays Registry configuration
Restart.vbs	Restarts a local or remote computer
Schemadiff.vbs	Compares schema from two different forests
ScsiController.vbs	Displays SCSI controller information
SerialPort.vbs	Displays serial port configuration
Service.vbs	Controls a service
Share.vbs	Modifies shares on the system
Sounddevice.vbs	Displays sound card configuration
Startup.vbs	Displays the startup programs on the system
SystemAccount.vbs	Displays the system account information
TapeDrive.vbs	Displays tape drive configuration
Thread.vbs	Displays all threads on the system
UserAccount.vbs	Displays user account information
Usergroup.vbs	Adds or deletes multiple users from a group

AT and WinAT

The AT and WinAT applications from Microsoft can be used to schedule tasks. The first, at.exe, is built into the operating system and is found in the %windir%\system32 folder. The second utility is available on the *Windows NT Server 4 Resource Kit* using the winat.exe filename. Both of these applications rely on the Microsoft Task Scheduler service to run.

> **WARNING!**   *For some reason, winat.exe does not ship with the* Windows NT Server Resource Kit. *It is, however, included in the* Windows NT Server 4 Resource Kit *and runs properly under Windows 2000.*

These two applications are the same except for the user interface. At.exe is strictly a text-based application, which means that you have to run a command prompt to control it, whereas winat.exe is a graphical version of at.exe.

Because of at.exe's command-line execution mode, the following format must be used before at.exe will operate properly:

```
AT [\\Systemname][[id][/delete] | /delete [/yes]] time [/interactive][/
every:date][/next:date] "Command"
```

Table 14.4   The AT command-line switches.

Switch	Description
\\systemname	Specifies a remote computer. Commands are scheduled on the local computer if this parameter is omitted.
Id	An identification number assigned to a scheduled command.
/delete	Cancels a scheduled command. If **Id** is omitted, all the scheduled commands on the computer are canceled.
/yes	Used with the **cancel all jobs** command when no further confirmation is desired.
time	Specifies the time when the command is to run.
/interactive	Allows the job to interact with the desktop of the user who is logged on at the time the job runs.
/every:date[,...]	Runs the command on each specified day of the week or month. If **date** is omitted, the current day of the month is assumed.
/next:date[,...]	Runs the specified command on the next occurrence of the day (for example, next Thursday). If **date** is omitted, the current day of the month is assumed.
"command"	The Windows NT command or batch program to be run.

Table 14.4 lists the command-line switches that may be used with the at.exe command along with their descriptions. (Note that you can retrieve the information in Table 14.4 by typing **at /?** at the command line.)

Task Scheduler

Windows 2000 also comes with a built-in Task Scheduler. The Task Scheduler is accessed through the Control Panel. This is a simple graphical wizard that can be run to automate many administrative tasks without scripting.

14. Scripting and Automation

Immediate Solutions

Working with Scripts

Creating the actual Visual Basic Script (VBScript) and JavaScript (JScript) is beyond the scope of this book. For this reason, you'll look at ready-made scripts that Microsoft has made available as demo scripts. These scripts are found in a couple places: The sample files can be found at **http://msdn.microsoft.com/scripting** and in the *Windows 2000 Server Resource Kit*. Each time one of these scripts is used, the script's name and location will be supplied.

Executing a Script Using CScript

To execute a script using CScript, follow these steps:

1. Select Start|Programs|Accessories|Command Prompt.

2. Type "CScript *scriptname*" and press Enter.

3. Add the **//b** switch to run the script in batch mode or the **//I** switch to run the script in interactive mode. With interactive mode, all messages will be sent to the console, whereas with batch mode, these messages are suppressed.

4. Add the **//d** switch to turn active debugging on or **//x** to run the script in the debugger.

5. Add the **//e:*engine*** switch to run the script in a specific engine.

6. Add the **//h:CScript** switch to set the default script engine to CScript or the **//h:WScript** switch to set the default script engine to WScript.

7. Add the **//job:*nnn*** switch to run a specific WScript job.

8. Add the **//logo** switch to display a logo during execution or the **//nologo** switch to suppress the logo.

9. Add the **//s** switch to save the configuration for the currently logged on user. This is used when setting the script execution defaults for the user.

10. Add the **//t:*nn*** switch to control the amount of time the specified script has to execute before it is terminated by the scripting engine.

11. Add the **//u** switch to use Unicode for all redirected I/O for non-English operating systems.

14. Scripting and Automation

Executing a Script Using WScript

Because WScript is the default scripting engine, there are two ways to execute a script using WScript.

Method 1:

1. Navigate to the script you would like to execute.

2. Double-click the script.

NOTE: *When using this method, the script will be executed using any default settings defined for the scripting engine. For example, if you have not modified the scripting engine, the script will execute in interactive mode, with the logo being displayed, and in the WScript engine.*

Method 2:

1. Select Start|Programs|Accessories|Command Prompt.

2. Type "WScript *scriptname*" and press Enter.

3. Add the **//b** switch to run the script in batch mode or the **//I** switch to run the script in interactive mode. With interactive mode, all messages will be sent to the console, whereas with batch mode, these messages are suppressed.

4. Add the **//d** switch to turn active debugging on or **//x** to run the script in the debugger.

5. Add the **//e:***engine* switch to run the script in a specific engine.

6. Add the **//h:CScript** switch to set the default script engine to CScript or the **//h:WScript** to set the default script engine to WScript.

7. Add the **//job:***nnn* switch to run a specific WS job.

8. Add the **//logo** switch to display a logo during execution or the **//nologo** switch to suppress the logo.

9. Add the **//s** switch to save the configuration for the currently logged on user. This is used when setting the script execution defaults for the user.

10. Add the **//t:***nn* switch to control the amount of time the specified script has to execute before it is terminated by the scripting engine.

Setting Script Properties

To set script properties, follow these steps:

1. Navigate to the script for which you would like to modify the properties.

2. Right-click the script and choose Properties from the pop-up menu.

3. Select the Script tab.

14. Scripting and Automation

4. To set the timeout on the script, check the Stop Script After A Specified Number Of Seconds checkbox and enter an amount of time in the Seconds field.

5. To keep the logo from being displayed, clear the Display Logo When Script Executed In Command Console checkbox.

6. Click OK.

Setting Script Properties Using WSH Files

To set script properties using WSH files, follow these steps:

1. Create a text file with the same name as the desired script but with the .WSH extension.

2. Use the following format in the file:

```
[ScriptFile]
Path=%Systemroot%\folder\script.vbs
[Options]
Timeout=0
DisplayLogo=1
BatchMode=0
```

3. The **Path** property is the location of the script file to be executed. This can be a VBS file, a JS file, or any other supported scripting language file.

4. Specify a timeout (if any) in the **Timeout** property.

5. To display a logo, set the **DisplayLogo** property to 1. To suppress the logo, set the property to 0.

6. To run the script in interactive mode, set the **BatchMode** property to 0. To run the script in batch mode, set it to 1.

Running a Simple VBScript

To run a simple VBScript, follow these steps:

NOTE: *Externally, the only difference between a VBScript file and a JScript file is the extension. VBScript files use the .VBS extension, whereas JScript files use the .JS extension.*

---

1. Navigate to the script that you would like to execute.

2. Double-click the script to run it.

3. To set properties on the script, follow the instructions on running the script using CScript/WScript. Also see the Setting Script Properties or Setting Script Properties Using WSH Files solution.

Running a Simple JScript

To run a simple JScript, follow these steps:

NOTE: *Externally, the only difference between a VBScript file and a JScript file is the extension. VBScript files use the .VBS extension, whereas JScript files use the .JS extension.*

---

1. Navigate to the script that you would like to execute.

2. Double-click the script to run it.

3. To set properties on the script, follow the instructions on running the script using CScript/WScript. Also see the Setting Script Properties or Setting Script Properties Using WSH Files solution.

Adding a Scripting Language

To add a scripting language to the system, follow these steps:

1. Select Start|Run.

2. Enter "regedt32.exe" in Open field and click OK.

3. Select the HKEY_LOCAL_MACHINE on Local Machine window.

4. Navigate to SOFTWARE\Microsoft\Windows Scripting Host\Script Extensions.

5. Choose New Key from the Edit menu.

6. In the Key Name field, enter the name of the scripting engine extension beginning with a period (for example, .SCR).

7. Click OK.

8. Select the newly created key.

9. Choose New Value from the Edit menu.

10. Leave the Value Name field blank, select REG_SZ from the Data Type drop-down menu, and click OK.

11. In the String field, enter a description for the extension (for example, SCRScript Script File) and click OK.

12. Choose New Value from the Edit menu.

13. In the Value Name field, enter "DefaultIcon", select REG_SZ from the Data Type drop-down menu, and click OK.

14. In the String field, enter "%SystemRoot%\System32\wscript.exe,n", where n is the nth icon in the wscript.exe file. There are only four icons in the wscript.exe files; therefore, only a value from 1 to 4 may be used.

15. Click OK.

14. Scripting and Automation

16. Choose New Value from the Edit menu.

17. In the Value Name field, enter "EngineID", select REG_SZ from the Data Type drop-down menu, and click OK.

18. In the String field, enter the engine ID (for example, SCRScript).

19. Click OK.

20. Choose New Value from the Edit menu.

21. In the Value Name field, enter "ScriptID", select REG_SZ from the Data Type drop-down menu, and click OK.

22. In the String field, enter the script ID (for example, SCRFile).

23. Click OK.

Working with the Task Scheduler Service

The Windows 2000 **AT** and **WinAT** commands rely on a service called the *Task Scheduler* service. If this service is not running, no AT and WinAT events can be scheduled. This section deals with controlling this service:

TIP: *This service is the same as the Windows NT Scheduler Service. Only the name has changed.*

Starting the Task Scheduler Service

To start the Task Scheduler service, follow these steps:

1. Select Start|Programs|Administrative Tools|Services.

2. Select Task Scheduler.

3. Right-click the service and choose Start from the pop-up menu.

Stopping the Task Scheduler Service

To stop the Task Scheduler service, follow these steps:

1. Select Start|Programs|Administrative Tools|Services.

2. Select Task Scheduler.

3. Right-click the service and choose Stop from the pop-up menu.

14. Scripting and Automation

Using the **AT** Command

The text-based task-scheduling application is at.exe. This section illustrates some of the most common tasks for this application:

Adding an **AT** Command

To add an **AT** command, follow these steps:

1. Select Start|Programs|Accessories|Command Prompt.

2. Type **AT** *hh:mm Command* and press Enter. The time is entered in 24-hour notation, and the command can be a batch file, a script, or any executable.

3. The **AT** command will return an ID for the command using a format similar to what's shown in Figure 14.1.

Adding an Interactive **AT** Command

To add an interactive **AT** command, follow these steps:

1. Select Start|Programs|Accessories|Command Prompt.

2. Type **AT** *hh:mm Command* **/Interactive** and press Enter. The time is entered in 24-hour notation, and the command can be a batch file, a script, or any executable.

3. The **AT** command will assign the next available ID.

Viewing the Configured **AT** Commands

To view the configured **AT** commands, follow these steps:

1. Select Start|Programs|Accessories|Command Prompt.

```
D:\>at 08:00 c:\scripts\script.vbs
Added a new job with job ID = 1

D:\>
```

Figure 14.1   Creating a new **AT** command.

2. Type "AT" and press Enter.

3. All currently scheduled tasks will be listed.

Deleting an **AT** Command

To delete an **AT** command, follow these steps:

1. Select Start|Programs|Accessories|Command Prompt.

2. To delete a single command, type "AT *id* /delete" and press Enter. Note that *id* is the ID for the task to be deleted.

3. To delete all scheduled tasks, type "AT /delete", press Enter, and press Y to confirm the deletion.

Creating a Recurring **AT** Command

To create a recurring **AT** command, follow these steps:

1. Select Start|Programs|Accessories|Command Prompt.

2. Type "AT *hh:mm /every:{Su,m,t,w,th,f,sa} Command*" and press Enter. You can pick and choose the days of the week to run the task.

3. Alternatively, type "AT *hh:mm /next:{Su,m,t,w,th,f,sa} Command*" and press Enter. You can pick and choose the days of the week to run the task.

Using the **WinAT** Command

The graphical version of the **AT** command is the WinAT application. The *Windows 2000 Server Resource Kit* does not include winat.exe; the *Windows NT Server Resource Kit*, however, does. After you copy the WinAT files to your system, you can execute the WinAT application, shown in Figure 14.2. Notice that any tasks scheduled with the **AT** command appear here because they share the same database.

Adding a **WinAT** Command

To add a **WinAT** command, follow these steps:

1. Run the winat.exe application.

2. Select Add from the Edit menu. The window shown in Figure 14.3 appears.

3. Type the command to be executed in the Command field.

4. Select a day (or days) from the Days section.

5. Select the execution time.

6. Click OK.

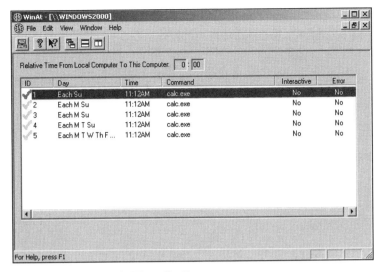

Figure 14.2   The WinAT application.

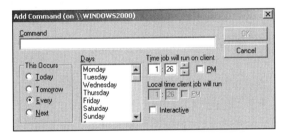

Figure 14.3   The WinAT Add Task window.

Adding an Interactive **WinAT** Command

To add an interactive **WinAT** command, follow these steps:

1. Run the winat.exe application.

2. Select Add from the Edit menu.

3. Type the command to be executed in the Command field.

4. Select a day (or days) from the Days section.

5. Select the execution time.

6. Check the Interactive checkbox.

7. Click OK.

Deleting a **WinAT** Command

To delete a **WinAT** command, follow these steps:

1. Run the winat.exe application.
2. Select the command you would like to delete.
3. Choose Remove from the Edit menu.
4. Click Yes to confirm the deletion.

Creating a Recurring **WinAT** Command

To create a recurring **WinAT** command, follow these steps:

1. Run the winat.exe application.
2. Select Add from the Edit menu.
3. Type the command to be executed in the Command field.
4. Select the Recurrence property from the This Occurs section of the window.
5. Select a day (or days) from the Days section.
6. Select the execution time.
7. If desired, check the Interactive checkbox.
8. Click OK.

Using the Windows 2000 Task Scheduler

To use the built-in task scheduler, perform the following steps:

1. Select Start|Settings|Control Panel.
2. Double-click the Scheduled Tasks icon.
3. Double-click Add Scheduled Task.
4. The Scheduled Task Wizard appears. Click Next.
5. Select a task to be automated (for this example, we'll select Disk Cleanup).

NOTE: *The steps that follow may vary depending on the task selected. Follow the on-screen prompts to complete automation settings for particular tasks.*

---

6. Enter a name for the task in the field provided and select how often the task is to be performed (see Figure 14.4). Click Next.
7. Enter the start time for the task and the day on which the task is to be performed (see Figure 14.5). Click Next.

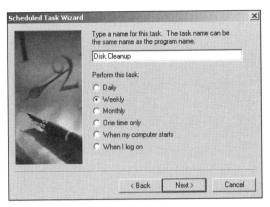

Figure 14.4   Entering a name and setting the frequency for a scheduled task.

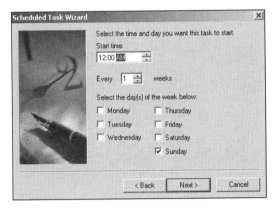

Figure 14.5   Setting the time and day for a scheduled task.

TIP: *Depending on the task, it's best to select a time and day when server activity and usage is at a minimum.*

---

8. Enter the username and password (and confirm password) under which the scheduled task will be run. Click Next.

9. If desired, check the Open Advanced Properties For This Task When I Click Finish checkbox if advanced settings are needed.

10. Click Finish.

11. Close the Scheduled Tasks applet.

Chapter 15

Tuning and Optimization

In Depth

One of the most difficult tasks a Windows 2000 administrator (or any systems administrator for that matter) encounters is answering client complaints on system slowness. One question that you should ask yourself when a user notifies you of a slow system is, what is slow? What is slow on one system might not be slow on another. To truly know when a system is slowing down, a baseline should be created and used. The next section deals with just that.

Building and Using Baselines

A *baseline* is simply an average of how a system performs during normal operation. What this means to a system is that users should be logged in and operating normally during the baseline calculation. Creating a baseline on a production system during regular operations involves taking a "snapshot" of the systems performance. Down the road (say, a few months), a second measurement can be taken and compared to the first. This comparison shows the growth of the system, thus allowing an administrator to predict when a system upgrade should be scheduled.

When creating a baseline, you should log the information about your system (memory, processor, disks, and network) for a prolonged time period with an interval that is longer than the default (say, every 30 seconds or 1 minute). This will decrease the log file size, while giving you a good snapshot. Also, make sure that the baseline runs through at least 24 hours. Extra baselines should be created for especially heavy days, such as the first or fifteenth of the month.

Resource Kit Tools

The *Windows 2000 Server Resource Kit* (ISBN 1-57231-805-8) contains tools that may be used for monitoring performance on your system. These include several CPU monitors, variations of the Performance application, and counter utilities. Three of these tools are covered in the following sections: Trace Dump, Trace Log, and Counter list.

NOTE: *The management and performance tools in the Windows 2000 Server Resource Kit are found in the Computer Management Tools and Performance Tools folders.*

TIP: *The Windows NT version of Performance Monitor is found in the Resource Kit as Perfmon5.exe.*

Trace Dump

The Trace Dump utility (tracedmp.exe) gathers information in a Trace Log file (or a real time trace) and outputs it into a CSV file. A CSV file then allows for the data to be imported into an Excel spreadsheet and manipulated.

Trace Log

The Trace Log utility (tracelog.exe) allows an administrator to start, stop, or enable trace logs from the command prompt. This allows for trace logs to be included in startup or login scripts.

Counter List

The Counter List utility (ctrlist.exe) outputs a list of all the counters installed on a system to a file. This data can be very useful in ensuring that specified logs run on all systems in the network by comparing the counters installed on those systems.

Network Monitor

Much like their predecessor Windows NT, Windows 2000 Server and Advanced Server ship with a Network Monitor utility. By default, the network card installed on a system will only accept packets of information addressed to it. Any packets addressed to another system are ignored. The Network Monitor utility places the network card in what is known as *promiscuous mode* (the card must support this). In this mode, the network card accepts all packets of information. The Network Monitor utility can then be used to view—and therefore troubleshoot—these packets.

Two different versions of this particular utility exist. One ships with Windows 2000, whereas the other ships with Microsoft Systems Management Server (SMS). The difference between the two is simple. The SMS version is more advanced in that it allows for packet captures to occur between any two systems on the network. The Windows 2000 version will only capture information between the local system and another system.

Many different types of packets exist on the network. Network Monitor uses what are known as *protocol parsers* to define what these packets are. This is done with the use of a separate DLL file for each of the protocols. Table 15.1 lists the protocols recognized by Network Monitor, their descriptions, and their associated DLL file, as listed by the Network Monitor manual.

15. Tuning and Optimization

Table 15.1   Recognized Network Monitor protocols.

Protocol	Description	DLL File
AARP	AppleTalk Address Resolution Protocol	atalk.dll
ADSP	AppleTalk Data Stream Protocol	atalk.dll
AFP	AppleTalk File Protocol	atalk.dll
AH	IP Authentication Header	tcpip.dll
ARP_RARP	Internet Address Resolution Protocol/Reverse Address Resolution Protocol	tcpip.dll
ASP	AppleTalk Session Protocol	atalk.dll
ATMARP	ATM Address Resolution Protocol	atmarp.dll
ATP	AppleTalk Transaction Protocol	atalk.dll
BONE	Bloodhound-Oriented Network Entity protocol	bone.dll
BOOKMARK	Network Monitor BOOKMARK protocol	trail.dll
BPDU	Bridge Protocol Data Unit	llc.dll
BROWSER	Microsoft Browser	browser.dll
CBCP	Callback Control Protocol	ppp.dll
CCP	Compression Control Protocol	ppp.dll
COMMENT	Network Monitor COMMENT protocol	trail.dll
DDP	AppleTalk Datagram Delivery Protocol	atalk.dll
DHCP	Dynamic Host Configuration Protocol	tcpip.dll
DNS	Domain Name System	tcpip.dll
EAP	PPP Extensible Authentication Protocol	ppp.dll
ESP	IP Encapsulating Security Payload	tcpip.dll
ETHERNET	Ethernet 802.3 topology	mac.dll
FDDI	FDDI topology	mac.dll
FINGER	Internet Finger protocol	tcpip.dll
FRAME	Base frame properties	frame.dll
FTP	File Transfer Protocol	tcpip.dll
GENERIC	Network Monitor GENERIC protocol	trail.dll
GRE	Generic Routing Encapsulation protocol	ppp.dll
ICMP	Internet Control Message Protocol	tcpip.dll
IGMP	Internet Group Management Protocol	tcpip.dll
IP	Internet Protocol	tcpip.dll

(continued)

Table 15.1   *Recognized Network Monitor protocols* (continued).

Protocol	Description	DLL File
IPCP	Internet IP Control Protocol	ppp.dll
IPX	NetWare Internetwork Packet Exchange protocol	ipx.dll
IPXCP	NetWare Internetwork Packet Exchange Control Protocol	ppp.dll
IPXWAN	NetWare Internetwork Packet Exchange Protocol for Wide Area Networks	ppp.dll
ISAKMP	Internet Security Association and Key Management Protocol	ppp.dll
L2TP	Layer 2 Tunneling Protocol	l2tp.dll
LAP	AppleTalk Link Access Protocol	atalk.dll
LCP	Link Control Protocol	ppp.dll
LLC	Logical Link Control 802.2 protocol	llc.dll
LPR	BSD printer	ppp.dll
MESSAGE	Network Monitor MESSAGE protocol	trail.dll
MSRPC	Microsoft Remote Procedure Call protocol	msrpc.dll
NBFCP	NetBIOS Frames Control Protocol	ppp.dll
NBIPX	NetBIOS on IPX	ipx.dll
NBP	AppleTalk Name Binding Protocol	atalk.dll
NBT	Internet NetBIOS over TCP/IP	tcpip.dll
NCP	NetWare Core Protocol	ncp.dll
NDR	NetWare Diagnostic Redirector	ipx.dll
NetBIOS	Network Basic Input/Output System protocol	netbios.dll
NETLOGON	Microsoft Netlogon broadcasts	netlogon.dll
NFS	Network File System	tcpip.dll
NMPI	Microsoft Name Management Protocol on IPX	ipx.dll
NSP	NetWare Serialization Protocol	ipx.dll
NWDP	NetWare WatchDog Protocol	ipx.dll
ODBC	Network Monitor ODBC protocol	trail.dll
OSPF	Open Shortest Path First	tcpip.dll
PAP	AppleTalk Printer Access Protocol	atalk.dll
PPP	Point-to-Point Protocol	ppp.dll

(continued)

15. Tuning and Optimization

Table 15.1   *Recognized Network Monitor protocols* (continued).

Protocol	Description	DLL File
PPPCHAP	PPP Challenge Handshake Authentication Protocol	ppp.dll
PPPML	Point-to-Point Multilink protocol	ppp.dll
PPPPAP	PPP Password Authentication Protocol	ppp.dll
PPTP	Point-to-Point Tunneling Protocol	ppp.dll
R_LOGON	Generated RPC for interface logon	logon.dll
R_LSARPC	Generated RPC for interface Lsarpc	lsarpc.dll
R_WINSPOOL	Generated RPC for interface Winspool	winspl.dll
RADIUS	Remote Authentication Dial-In User Service protocol	ppp.dll
RIP	Internet Routing Information Protocol	tcpip.dll
RIPX	NetWare Routing Information Protocol	ipx.dll
RPC	Remote Procedure Call	tcpip.dll
RPL	Remote Program Load	llc.dll
RSVP	RSVP Protocol	rsvp.dll
RTMP	AppleTalk Routing Table Maintenance Protocol	atalk.dll
SAP	NetWare Service Advertising Protocol	ipx.dll
SMB	Server Message Block protocol	smb.dll
SMT	FDDI MAC station management	mac.dll
SNAP	Sub-Network Access Protocol	llc.dll
SNMP	Simple Network Management Protocol	snmp.dll
SPX	NetWare Sequenced Packet Exchange protocol	ipx.dll
SSP	Security Support Provider protocol	msrpc.dll
STATS	Network Monitor Capture Statistics protocol	trail.dll
TCP	Transmission Control Protocol	tcpip.dll
TMAC	Token ring MAC layer	mac.dll
TOKENRING	Token ring 802.5 topology	mac.dll
TPCTL	Test Protocol Control Language	tpctl.dll
TRAIL	Network Monitor TRAIL protocol	trail.dll
UDP	User Datagram Protocol	tcpip.dll
VINES_FRAG	Banyan Vines Fragmentation protocol	vines.dll
VINES_IP	Banyan Vines Internet Protocol	vines.dll
VINES_TL	Banyan Vines Transport Layer protocol	vines.dll
XNS	Xerox Network System	xns.dll

Immediate Solutions

Working with Network Monitor

All the tasks covered in this section are available in the second version of Network Monitor. Any features not available in the Network Monitor application that ships with Windows 2000 Server are marked as such.

Installing Network Monitor

To install Network Monitor, follow these steps:

1. Select Start|Settings|Control Panel.
2. Double-click the Add/Remove Programs applet.
3. Click Add/Remove Windows Components. If the Add/Remove Windows Components Wizard appears, go to Step 4. Otherwise, click Components to start the Add/Remove Windows Components Wizard.
4. Select Management And Monitoring Tools and click Details.
5. Check the Network Monitor Tools checkbox and click OK.
6. Click Next.
7. Click Finish. Then click Close.

Installing the Network Monitor Driver

To install Network Monitor driver, follow these steps:

1. Right-click My Network Places and choose Properties from the pop-up menu.
2. Select Local Area Connection.
3. Choose Properties from the File menu.
4. Click Install.
5. Select Protocol and click Add.
6. Select the Network Monitor driver and click OK.
7. Click OK.

Starting Network Monitor

To start Network Monitor, follow these steps:

1. Select Start|Programs|Administrative Tools|Network Monitor.

15. Tuning and Optimization

2. If prompted for the network selection, click OK.

3. From the window in Figure 15.1, select the network to capture data on and click OK.

Starting a Network Capture

To start a network capture, follow these steps:

1. Select Start|Programs|Administrative Tools|Network Monitor.

2. Choose Start from the Capture menu. Network Monitor will begin the network capture, as shown in Figure 15.2.

Stopping a Network Capture

To stop a network capture, follow these steps:

1. Select Start|Programs|Administrative Tools|Network Monitor.

2. Choose Stop from the Capture menu.

Pausing a Network Capture

To pause a network capture, follow these steps:

1. Select Start|Programs|Administrative Tools|Network Monitor.

2. Choose Start from the Capture menu.

3. When the capture is to be paused, choose Pause from the Capture menu.

Starting a Paused Network Capture

To start a paused network capture, follow these steps:

1. Select Start|Programs|Administrative Tools|Network Monitor.

2. Choose Start from the Capture menu.

3. When the capture is to be paused, choose Pause from the Capture menu.

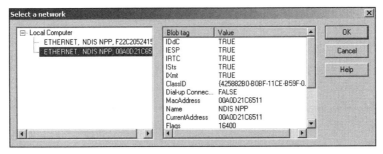

Figure 15.1   Making the network selection.

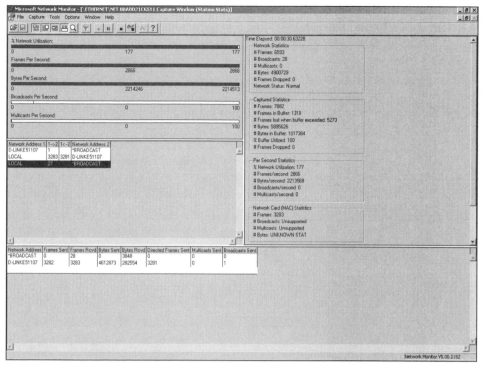

Figure 15.2   A network capture.

4. To continue the paused network capture, choose Continue from the Capture menu.

Viewing Captured Packet Information

To view captured packet information, follow these steps:

1. Select Start|Programs|Administrative Tools|Network Monitor.

2. Choose Start from the Capture menu.

3. To view the captured information, choose Stop And View from the Capture menu.

4. The captured information will be displayed as shown in Figure 15.3.

Identifying Network Monitor Users

To identify Network Monitor users, follow these steps:

1. Select Start|Programs|Administrative Tools|Network Monitor.

2. Choose Identify Network Monitor Users from the Tools menu.

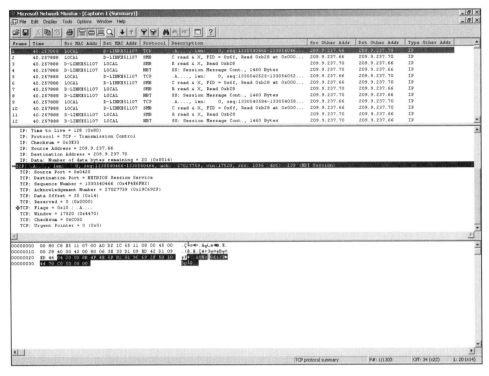

Figure 15.3   Network capture data.

Viewing Captured Addresses

To view captured addresses, follow these steps:

1. Select Start|Programs|Administrative Tools|Network Monitor.

2. Choose Addresses from the Capture menu. A list of the captured addresses appears, as shown in Figure 15.4.

Applying a Capture Filter

To apply a capture filter, follow these steps:

1. Select Start|Programs|Administrative Tools|Network Monitor.

2. Choose Filter from the Capture menu.

3. If the built-in version of Network Monitor is the one running, a warning message will be displayed specifying that this version only captures packets to or from the local system. Click OK.

4. Define your filter as desired (see Figure 15.5) and click OK.

15. Tuning and Optimization

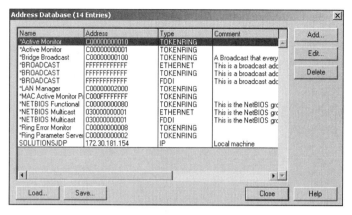

Figure 15.4   Viewing captured addresses.

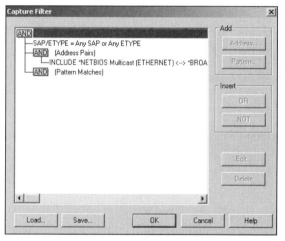

Figure 15.5   Filtering a network capture.

Working with the Performance Application

A number of issues are involved with running the Performance application. These tasks are covered in the following sections.

Starting the Performance Application

To start the Performance application, follow these steps:

1. Select Start|Programs|Administrative Tools|Performance.

2. The Performance application, as shown in Figure 15.6, appears.

15. Tuning and Optimization

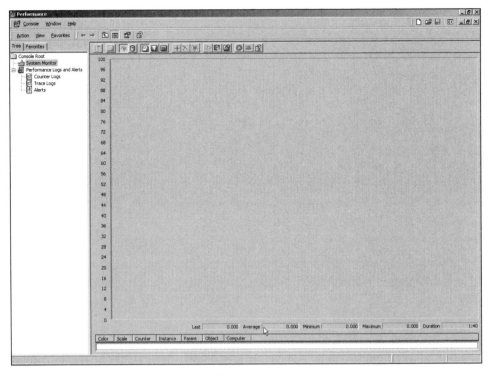

Figure 15.6   The Performance application.

Adding Counters

To add a counter, follow these steps:

1. Select Start|Programs|Administrative Tools|Performance.

2. Right-click in the right pane and choose Add Counters from the pop-up menu.

3. From the Add Counters window, shown in Figure 15.7, select to monitor either the current system by choosing Use Local Computer Counters or a remote system by entering a computer name in Select Counters From Computer.

NOTE: *When entering a name for a remote computer, use the Universal Naming Convention (UNC)—for example, \\server\share.*

---

4. Choose a performance object from the Performance Object drop-down list.

5. Select the counters to monitor. Shift+click (to select a range) and Ctrl+click (to select individual counters) can be used for the selection.

6. If multiple instances exist, choose the desired instance.

15. Tuning and Optimization

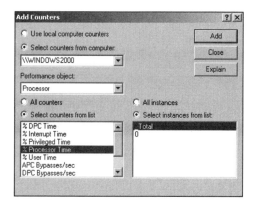

Figure 15.7   Adding a counter.

7. For extra information on a specific counter, select the counter and click Explain.

8. Click Add to add the counter.

9. Repeat Steps 3 to 8 for any other desired performance objects and counters.

10. Click Close.

Removing Counters

To remove a counter, follow these steps:

1. Select Start|Programs|Administrative Tools|Performance.

2. Choose the counter to be deleted in the bottom-right counter pane and either click the Delete button or press the Delete key.

3. Repeat Step 2 for any additional counters.

Controlling Disk Counters

Windows 2000 allows for much more flexibility than Windows NT did in how disk counters are controlled. By default, all disk counters are started during the boot process. This solution deals with all the different options available for disk counters:

1. Select Start|Programs|Accessories|Command Prompt.

2. To turn on all disk performance counters at boot time, type "diskperf -y" and press Enter. Restart the system for the setting to take effect.

3. To turn on disk performance counters for physical disks, type "diskperf -yd" and press Enter. Restart the system for the setting to take effect.

4. To turn on disk performance counters for logical disks, type "diskperf -yv" and press Enter. Restart the system for the setting to take effect.

15. Tuning and Optimization

5. To disable disk performance counters, type "diskperf -n" and press Enter. Restart the system for the setting to take effect.

6. To disable disk performance counters for physical disks, type "diskperf -nd" and press Enter.

7. To disable disk performance counters for logical disks, type "diskperf -nv" and press Enter.

TIP: *A \\system switch can be added to the options in Steps 2 through 7 to control disk performance counters on a remote system.*

Creating a Counter Log

To create a counter log, follow these steps:

1. Select Start|Programs|Administrative Tools|Performance.

2. In the left pane, select the Performance Logs And Alerts|Counter Logs container.

3. Right-click Counter Logs and choose New Log Settings from the pop-up menu.

4. Enter a name for the new counter log and click OK.

5. To add a counter, click Add and choose the counter or counters to be added to the log.

6. To remove a counter, select the counter and click Remove.

7. Specify the logging interval by entering in the number in the Interval field and the units for the interval (seconds, minutes, hours, or days) in the Units field.

8. Click the Log Files tab. Enter the log file information, including name, location, size, and type.

9. Click Schedule and enter the start and/or stop information for the counter log.

10. Click OK.

Starting a Counter Log

To start a counter log, follow these steps:

1. Select Start|Programs|Administrative Tools|Performance.

2. In the left pane, select the Performance Logs And Alerts|Counter Logs container.

3. Right-click the counter log in the right pane and choose Start from the pop-up menu.

15. Tuning and Optimization

Stopping a Counter Log

To stop a counter log, follow these steps:

1. Select Start|Programs|Administrative Tools|Performance.

2. In the left pane, select the Performance Logs And Alerts|Counter Logs container.

3. Right-click the counter log in the right pane and choose Stop from the pop-up menu.

Scheduling a Counter Log

To schedule a counter log, follow these steps:

1. Select Start|Programs|Administrative Tools|Performance.

2. In the left pane, select the Performance Logs And Alerts|Counter Logs container.

3. Right-click the counter log in the right pane and choose Properties from the pop-up menu.

4. Click the Schedule tab.

5. In the Start Log section, select the At radio button.

6. Enter a time and date on which this counter is to be started.

7. To specify a counter log with no scheduled end time, choose Manually (using the shortcut menu).

8. To stop the counter log after a set number of seconds, minutes, hours, or days, choose the After radio button and enter the number of units the system is to wait before stopping the counter log.

9. To stop the counter log on a specific date and time, choose At and enter the desired date and time.

10. If a command is to be executed after the log file closes, check the Run This Command checkbox and enter the command path, name, and desired switches.

11. Click OK.

Modifying the Counter Log Logging Rate

To modify the counter log logging rate, follow these steps:

1. Select Start|Programs|Administrative Tools|Performance.

2. In the left pane, select the Performance Logs And Alerts|Counter Logs container.

15. Tuning and Optimization

3. Right-click the counter log in the right pane and choose Properties from the pop-up menu.

4. In the General tab, modify the interval and interval unit and click OK.

Creating a Trace Log

To create a trace log, follow these steps:

1. Select Start|Programs|Administrative Tools|Performance.

2. In the left pane, select the Performance Logs And Alerts|Trace Logs container.

3. Right-click Trace Logs and choose New Log Settings from the pop-up menu.

4. Enter a name for the new trace log and click OK.

5. To log system provider events, select the Events Logged By System Provider radio button and select the desired providers from which to create the trace log.

6. To log nonsystem providers, select the Nonsystem Providers radio button.

7. Click Add (assuming that Step 5 was not performed).

8. Select the nonsystem providers to log and click OK.

9. Click the Log Files tab. Enter the log file information, including name, location, size, and type.

10. Click Schedule and enter the start and/or stop information for the counter log.

11. Click OK.

Starting a Trace Log

To start a trace log, follow these steps:

1. Select Start|Programs|Administrative Tools|Performance.

2. In the left pane, select the Performance Logs And Alerts|Trace Logs container.

3. Right-click the trace log in the right pane and choose Start from the pop-up menu.

Stopping a Trace Log

To stop a trace log, follow these steps:

1. Select Start|Programs|Administrative Tools|Performance.

2. In the left pane, select the Performance Logs And Alerts|Trace Logs container.

3. Right-click the trace log in the right pane and choose Stop from the pop-up menu.

Scheduling a Trace Log

To schedule a trace log, follow these steps:

1. Select Start|Programs|Administrative Tools|Performance.

2. In the left pane, select the Performance Logs And Alerts|Trace Logs container.

3. Right-click the trace log in the right pane and choose Properties from the pop-up menu.

4. Click the Schedule tab.

5. In the Start Log section, select the At radio button.

6. Enter a time and date on which this trace log is to be started.

7. To specify a trace log with no scheduled end time, choose Manually (using the shortcut menu).

8. To stop the trace log after a set number of seconds, minutes, hours, or days, choose the After radio button and enter the number of units the system is to wait before stopping the trace log.

9. To stop the trace log on a specific date and time, choose At and enter the desired date and time.

10. If a command is to be executed after the log file closes, check the Run This Command checkbox and enter the command path, name, and desired switches.

11. Click OK.

Creating an Alert

To create an alert, follow these steps:

1. Select Start|Programs|Administrative Tools|Performance.

2. In the left pane, select the Performance Logs and Alerts|Alerts container.

3. Right-click in the right pane and choose New Alert Settings from the pop-up menu.

4. Enter a name and an optional description for the alert.

5. To add a counter, click Add, select the desired counter, click Add, and click Close.

6. Ensure that the counter is selected. Choose to cause an alert when the counter is either over or under the limit by selecting Over/Under from the Value drop-down list and the limit in the Limit field.

7. To remove a counter, highlight the counter and click Remove.

8. Specify the logging interval by entering in the number in the Interval field and the units for the interval (seconds, minutes, hours, or days) in the Units field.

9. Select the Action tab.

10. To log an entry, check the Log An Entry In The Application Event Log checkbox.

11. To send an alert, check the Send A Network Message To checkbox and enter the username(s) or group name(s) in the field.

12. To start a performance log, check the Start Performance Data Log checkbox and choose the appropriate log type from the drop-down list.

13. To run an external program, check the Run This Program checkbox and enter the path and name of the program. To assign it command-line switches, click Command Line Arguments, choose the desired switches, and click OK.

14. To automatically start the alert, choose the At radio button and enter a date and time.

15. To specify an alert with no scheduled end time, choose Manually (using the shortcut menu).

16. To stop the alert after a set number of seconds, minutes, hours, or days, choose the After radio button and enter the number of units the system is to wait before stopping the counter log.

17. To stop the alert on a specific date and time, choose At and enter the desired date and time.

18. Click OK.

Configuring Alert Thresholds

To configure the alert thresholds, follow these steps:

1. Select Start|Programs|Administrative Tools|Performance.

2. In the left pane, select the Performance Logs And Alerts|Trace Logs container.

3. Double-click the desired alert.

4. Select the counter for which the threshold is to be set.

5. Choose either the Over or Under option from the drop-down list.

15. Tuning and Optimization

6. Enter a value for the threshold.

7. Click OK.

Configuring Alert Actions

To configure the alert actions, follow these steps:

1. Select Start|Programs|Administrative Tools|Performance.

2. In the left pane, select the Performance Logs And Alerts|Trace Logs container.

3. Double-click the desired alert.

4. Click the Action tab in the Alert dialog box (see Figure 15.8).

5. To log an entry, check the Log An Entry In The Application Event Log checkbox.

6. To send an alert, check the Send A Network Message To checkbox and enter the username(s) or group name(s) in the field.

7. To start a performance log, check the Start Performance Data Log checkbox and choose the appropriate log type from the drop-down list.

8. To run an external program, check the Run This Program checkbox and enter the path and name of the program. To assign it command-line switches, click Command Line Arguments, choose the desired switches (see Figure 15.9), and click OK.

9. Click OK.

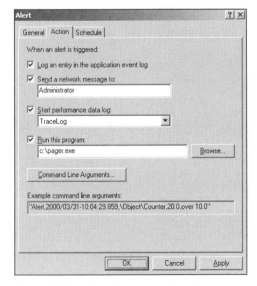

Figure 15.8   Configuring alert actions.

15. Tuning and Optimization

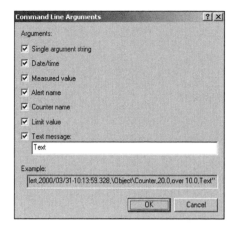

Figure 15.9   Configuring command-line switches.

Starting an Alert

To start a configured alert, follow these steps:

1. Select Start|Programs|Administrative Tools|Performance.

2. In the left pane, select the Performance Logs And Alerts|Alerts container.

3. Right-click the alert in the right pane and choose Start from the pop-up menu.

Stopping an Alert

To stop an alert, follow these steps:

1. Select Start|Programs|Administrative Tools|Performance.

2. In the left pane, select the Performance Logs And Alerts|Alerts container.

3. Right-click the alert in the right pane and choose Stop from the pop-up menu.

Highlighting a Desired Counter

To highlight a desired counter, follow these steps:

1. Select Start|Programs|Administrative Tools|Performance.

2. Right-click in the right pane and choose Add Counters from the pop-up menu.

3. From the Add Counters window, select to monitor either the current system by choosing Use Local Computer Counters or a remote system by entering a computer name in Select Counters From Computer.

4. Choose a performance object from the Performance Object drop-down list.

5. Select the counters to monitor. Shift+click and Ctrl+click can be used for multiple selections.

6. If multiple instances exist, choose the desired instance.

7. For extra information on a specific counter, select the counter and click Explain.

8. Click Add to add the counter.

9. Repeat Steps 3 to 8 for any other desired performance objects and counters.

10. Select the counter to be highlighted in the bottom-right counter pane.

11. Press Ctrl+H. The counter is now highlighted (see Figure 15.10).

12. To change the highlighted counter, select a different counter.

Exporting Data to an HTML File

To export data to an HMTL file, follow these steps:

1. Select Start|Programs|Administrative Tools|Performance.

2. Right-click in the right pane and choose Add Counters from the pop-up menu.

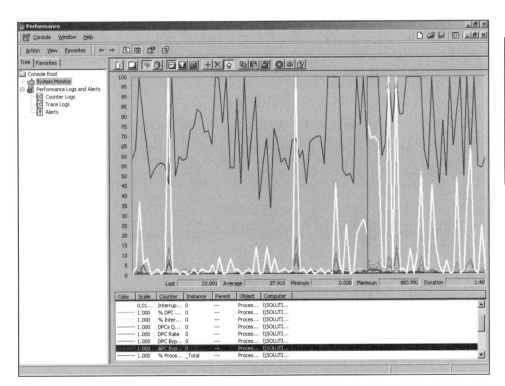

Figure 15.10   Highlighting a counter.

3. From the Add Counters window, select to monitor either the current system by choosing Use Local Computer Counters or a remote system by entering a computer name in Select Counters From Computer.

4. Choose a performance object from the Performance Object drop-down list.

5. Select the counters to monitor. Shift+click (to select a range of counters) and Ctrl+click (to select individual counters) can be used for the selection.

6. If multiple instances exist, choose the desired instance.

7. For extra information on a specific counter, select the counter and click Explain.

8. Click Add to add the counter.

9. Repeat for any other desired performance objects and counters.

10. Right-click the counter graph and choose Save As from the pop-up menu.

11. Enter a name for the HTML page and click Save.

Working with Events

A number of issues exist when working with Event Viewer. The following sections deal this these issues.

Viewing Event Details

To view event details, follow these steps:

1. Select Start|Programs|Administrative Tools|Event Viewer.

2. Choose the desired log in the console tree (the left pane).

3. Right-click the event to be viewed and choose Properties from the pop-up menu.

4. To skip to the next event, click the down-arrow button.

5. To move to the previous event, click the up-arrow button.

6. Click OK when finished.

Creating a New Log View

To create a new log view, follow these steps:

1. Select Start|Programs|Administrative Tools|Event Viewer.

2. Choose the log for which you would like a new view created in the left pane.

3. Right-click the log and choose New Log View from the pop-up menu.

15. Tuning and Optimization

4. Right-click the newly created log and choose Rename from the pop-up menu.

5. Enter a new name for the log and press Enter.

6. Right-click the log and choose Properties from the pop-up menu.

7. Choose the Filter tab.

8. Check the checkboxes for the event types that are to be displayed in this log view.

9. Choose more advanced filters if required.

10. Click OK when finished.

Saving the Log to a File

To save the logs to a file, follow these steps:

1. Select Start|Programs|Administrative Tools|Event Viewer.

2. In the right pane, right-click the event log that is to be saved and choose Save Log File As from the pop-up menu.

3. Enter a name for the log file in the File Name field.

4. Ensure that Event Log (*.evt) is selected in the Save As Type list.

5. Click Save.

Saving the Log to a Tab-Delimited File

To save the log to a tab-delimited file, follow these steps:

1. Select Start|Programs|Administrative Tools|Event Viewer.

2. In the right pane, right-click the event log that is to be saved and choose Save Log File As from the pop-up menu.

3. Enter a name for the log file in the File Name field.

4. Ensure that Text (Tab Delimited) (*.txt) is selected in the Save As Type pop-up list.

5. Click Save.

Saving the Log to a Comma-Delimited File

To save the log to a comma-delimited file, follow these steps:

1. Select Start|Programs|Administrative Tools|Event Viewer.

2. In the right pane, right-click the event log that is to be saved and choose Save Log File As from the pop-up menu.

3. Enter a name for the log file in the File Name field.

15. Tuning and Optimization

4. Ensure that CSV (Comma Delimited) (*.csv) is selected in the Save As Type list.

5. Click Save.

Viewing a Log File

To view a saved log file, follow these steps:

1. Select Start|Programs|Administrative Tools|Event Viewer.

2. Right-click the Event View container and click Open Log File in the pop-up menu.

3. Enter the name of the saved log file in the File Name field.

4. Specify the log type in the Log Type list.

5. Enter a display name in the Display Name field.

6. Click OK.

Connecting to a Remote System

To connect to a remote system, follow these steps:

1. Select Start|Programs|Administrative Tools|Event Viewer.

2. Right-click the Event Viewer container and choose Connect To Another Computer from the pop-up menu.

3. Enter the name of the remote computer in the Another Computer field (or click Browse to search for it).

4. Click OK.

Displaying Event Logs from Multiple Computers

To display the event logs of multiple computers, follow these steps:

1. Select Start|Run.

2. Type "MMC" and click OK.

3. Choose the Add/Remove snap-in from the Console menu.

4. Click Add.

5. Select Event Viewer and click Add.

6. Select the Another Computer radio button.

7. Enter the path to the remote computer and click Finish.

8. Repeat Steps 5 through 7 for any additional computers to be connected to.

9. Click Close.

10. Click OK.

Searching for Events

To search for events, follow these steps:

1. Select Start|Programs|Administrative Tools|Event Viewer.

2. Right-click the log to be searched and choose View|Find from the pop-up menu.

3. Select the types of events to search for.

4. Specify additional information about the events to be searched for in the Event Source, Category, Event ID, User, Computer, and Description sections.

5. Click Find Next.

Configuring the Log

To configure the event log, follow these steps:

1. Select Start|Programs|Administrative Tools|Event Viewer.

2. Right-click the log to be configured and choose Properties from the pop-up menu.

3. In the Log Size section, specify the maximum size for the log.

4. Choose the task to be performed should the maximum log size be reached.

5. Click OK.

Clearing the Log

To clear the event log, follow these steps:

1. Select Start|Programs|Administrative Tools|Event Viewer.

2. Right-click the log to be cleared and choose Clear All Events from the pop-up menu.

3. If you would like the log saved before it is cleared, click Yes, enter a file name, and click Save. Otherwise, click No.

15. Tuning and Optimization

Chapter 16
Managing Applications

In Depth

Windows 2000 supports several types of applications. These include Windows 32 bit, Windows 16-bit, MS-DOS, OS/2 character mode, and POSIX.1. This chapter examines the level and type of support for each of these application types.

Environment Subsystems

The Windows 2000 environment subsystems are the runtime mechanisms that support various types of applications. Windows 2000 supports five different types of applications: Win32, Win16, DOS, OS/2 version 1.x, and POSIX.1. These supported application types represent the most commonly used types of applications. Win32 is the native application type of Windows 2000. Most Win32 applications created for Windows 95, Windows 98, and Windows NT will function properly on Windows 2000. For best performance, you should attempt to use Win32 applications exclusively. Win16 and DOS are retained for backward compatibility with legacy applications. Win16 applications were originally designed for Windows 3.x, then for Windows for Workgroups. A limited number of 16-bit applications were created specifically for Windows 95. Most Win16 applications will function on Windows 2000. DOS applications, whether written specifically for MS-DOS or another vendor's DOS, will usually function on Windows 2000 as long as they don't attempt direct hardware access. OS/2 and POSIX are not fully supported; instead, only the minimum support required by government purchasing requirements is present.

The primary environment subsystem of Windows 2000 is Win32. All user mode graphical and user I/O passes through the Win32 subsystem. If this one subsystem fails, the operating system also fails. Fortunately, this subsystem is very robust and can handle most errors or problems without causing system failure. The secondary subsystems are OS/2 and POSIX. These subsystems launch independently, but they each rely on the Win32 subsystem to function as an API and to provide management of the graphical display and I/O from user devices (such as the keyboard and mouse). The dependent subsystems are Win16 and DOS. The DOS subsystem is created by the execution of NTVDM, which is a Win32 process. The Win16 subsystem is created by the execution of WOWEXEC, which is a DOS process. Therefore, the Win16 subsystem is dependent on the DOS subsystem, which is itself dependant on the Win32 subsystem. See Figure 16.1 for a graphical depiction of these associations.

16. Managing
Applications

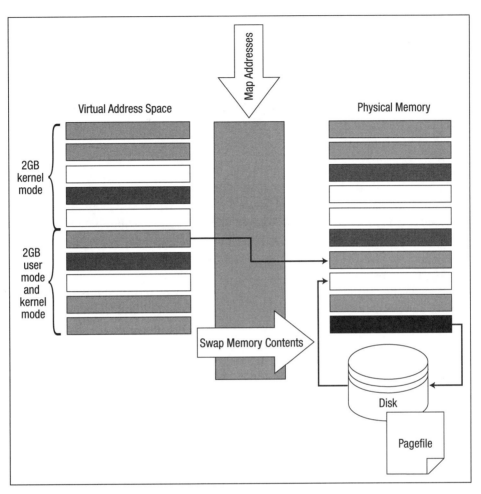

Figure 16.1 The Windows 2000 system architecture.

The environments created by each of these subsystems is managed automatically by Windows 2000. You have some control over startup initialization parameters for executables, but, by and large, the control of the runtime environment is retained by the system.

When an application, program, software, or executable (all nearly interchangeable terms) is launched, it is placed into its own virtual machine. A *virtual machine* is a software construct of a computer that fools its contained processes into thinking they have exclusive access to the computer. A virtual machine is assigned a 4GB address space that is divided into a 2GB portion available to the hosted process and the kernel and a 2GB portion that can be used only by the kernel. All resources requested by the enclosed process are redirected by the virtual machine to the Windows 2000 Executive for processing. The use of virtual machines (VMs) grants Windows 2000 the ability to isolate processes and carry out high-performance multitasking. Even though all Win32 applications are launched into distinct VMs, they are able to communicate and exchange data without difficulty. Additionally, if a Win32 application fails, hangs, or attempts to perform an illegal operation, it does not necessarily cause all Win32 applications to fail. Microsoft documentation claims that the failure of one Win32 application does not interfere with others. However, in reality there are some Win32 failures that will cause other applications to fail, if not the entire system. Fortunately, this is quite rare.

When an application is launched under Windows 2000, it is granted the access token of its parent process. When you log into Windows 2000, an access token consisting of your group memberships and user right assignments is created. That access token is used by the system to launch your shell (that is, your desktop environment). Therefore, your shell is assigned your access token so it can only perform operations permitted by your level of access permissions. The shell also serves as the parent process for all other processes initiated during a session. In general, it is not possible for a launched process to obtain a higher access permission than the user, shell, or process that initiated its execution. The only exceptions are possible for administrators: configuring services to launch with a system level context or a specified user account, and launching an application with system level privileges through the **AT** command with the **/interactive** switch (see Chapter 6 for an example).

Shortcuts are configuration and launch files that point to separate executable files (actually they can point to any type of file). Multiple shortcuts can be defined for a single program. A shortcut is created by selecting any file and issuing the Create Shortcut command from either the File menu or the right-click pop-up menu. A shortcut's properties can be configured to launch an application with different parameters or controls or into a different executable environment. Each type of application has unique shortcut controls. As discussed in Chapter 6, shortcuts can be used to define a target path using the **start** command to launch applications at execution priorities other than normal. You can also customize the launch string to include command-line parameters. Check the documentation of your applications to see what command-line parameters are supported. Often these can be used to preopen empty documents, preload documents or resources, change save directories, and more.

In the following sections, each of the five environment subsystems is discussed in greater detail.

Windows 32 Bit

The Windows 32-bit subsystem, or *Win32*, is the only environment subsystem required by Windows 2000. It is also the only subsystem started by default each time Windows 2000 boots. All other subsystems are only initiated when a process requiring them is launched. Win32 supports many essential functions, including maintaining the user's desktop environment and providing a standard interface for graphical and user device I/O. Without Win32, Windows 2000 could not function.

The Win32 subsystem supports multithreaded applications. This allows for more flexible programming techniques and usually results in more efficient and more powerful applications. All Win32 applications are launched into separate and distinct VMs. However, data can be shared via Dynamic Data Exchange (DDE) or Object Linking and Embedding (OLE) and information can be cut and pasted between Win32 applications. The Properties dialog box of a Win32 application offers no control over the application's execution or its virtual machine. However, a shortcut to a Win32 application does offer the following controls via the Shortcut tab, shown in Figure 16.2, of its Properties dialog box:

NOTE: *Run In Separate Memory Space is a Win16 control; it does not apply to Win32. Therefore, it is grayed out for Win32 applications.*

- *Launch As A Different User*—Used to run the program with the access token of a different user. Once this shortcut is initiated, you'll be prompted for the username, password, and domain of the alternate user account to serve as the program's security context.

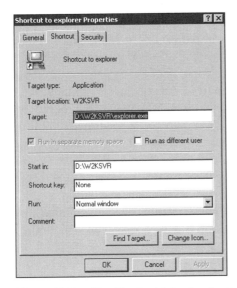

Figure 16.2   The Shortcut tab of a shortcut's Properties dialog box.

- *Start In*—Used to define the directory or folder that the program will use by default.

- *Shortcut Key*—Used to define a keyboard sequence that will automatically launch this shortcut.

- *Run*—Used to set the window size to normal, maximized, or minimized.

- *Comment*—Used to provide a comment for the program.

- *Find Target*—Used to locate or change the target program.

- *Change Icon*—Used to alter the program's displayed icon.

MS-DOS

The MS-DOS environment subsystem supports many DOS programs, but it has a significant limitation. No application, including DOS applications, can access hardware directly. Any DOS applications that attempt to access hardware directly will be terminated. This serves as a security measure to protect the system from failure due to poorly written hardware-interaction routines. A significant portion of DOS applications use direct hardware access.

DOS applications are launched within a *virtual DOS machine* (VDM). Under Windows 2000, the executable process that creates this environment is ntvdm.exe. Therefore, you'll often see VDM and NTVDM used interchangeably. NTVDM is a Win32 process that creates a DOS-emulation environment. Nearly 99 percent of all DOS applications that do not require direct hardware access function within the NTVDM environment.

The DOS environment is created by Windows 2000 when a DOS application is launched. The DOS environment is terminated by Windows 2000 when the DOS application within it exits, closes, or is terminated. If you look on the Processes tab of the Task Manager, you'll see the NTVDM process. However, the actual DOS process does not appear in the list of processes because it does not function as any other normal process but rather executes as a parameter or data block for the NTVDM process instead. A unique instance of NTVDM is launched for each DOS application launched. In other words, each DOS application executes independently of all other DOS applications. You can evaluate a DOS application's amount of CPU time and consumed memory by watching the NTVDM's statistics. Be sure to watch based on process IDs so you can distinguish between applications and instances. DOS applications cannot share data, and cut-and-paste operations between DOS applications is not supported natively. In some cases, it is possible to copy displayed NTVDM data into the Windows 2000 Clipboard and then paste that data into a different NTVDM window.

The Properties dialog box for a DOS executable and a shortcut to a DOS executable offer the same controls over the DOS environment. These controls are placed

16. Managing
Applications

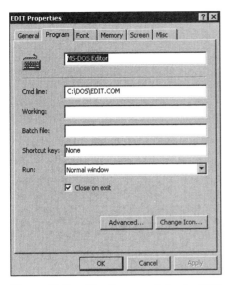

Figure 16.3 The Program tab of a DOS application's Properties dialog box.

on the Program, Font, Memory, Screen, and Misc tabs. The Program tab offers the following controls (see Figure 16.3):

- *Cmd Line*—The executable command line used to launch the application. It can be edited to contain command-line parameter syntax switches.

- *Working*—Used to define the directory or folder that the program uses by default.

- *Batch File*—Used to define a batch or script file that executes within the NTVDM before the application itself is launched.

- *Shortcut Key*—Used to define a keyboard sequence that automatically launches this shortcut.

- *Run*—Used to set the window size to normal, maximized, or minimized.

- *Close On Exit*—A checkbox that is either selected or deselected.

- *Advanced*—Used to define the path to custom autoexec.nt and config.nt files.

- *Change Icon*—Used to alter the program's displayed icon.

If you recall from the days of DOS, autoexec.bat and config.sys were the two startup and initialization files that controlled memory configuration, TSRs, preloaded drivers, and other settings for the DOS environment. Windows 2000 itself does not need or use these files, but it retains the functionality of these DOS startup files via autoexec.nt and config.nt, used in customized NTVDMs.

Autoexec.nt is used to load CD-ROM drivers and network redirectors and to enable DOS Protected Mode Interface (DPMI) support (allows applications to access more than 1MB of memory). Config.nt is used to load drivers into the upper memory area and to manage upper memory via himem.sys. Default examples of these files are found in the *%systemroot%*\System32\ subdirectory. You can modify these default files to modify the environments of all DOS applications, or you can create customized copies (with unique file names or stored in alternate directories) to alter the environment of only specific DOS applications via their shortcuts.

The Font tab, shown in Figure 16.4, offers controls for the following:

- Enabling the use of bitmap fonts or TrueType fonts, or both

- Setting font size

The Memory tab, shown in Figure 16.5, offers controls to customize the memory architecture of the NTVDM environment, as described in the following list:

- *Conventional Memory*—Defines the amount of conventional memory, up to 640K, to be used by the application. The default is Auto. Defines the amount of memory reserved for command.com, up to 4,096K; default is Auto. Enables/disables protection of system memory (that is, command.com) from this program.

- *Expanded (EMS) Memory*—Defines the amount of expanded memory (EMS), up to 16,384K, to be used by the application. The default is None.

- *Extended (XMS) Memory*—Defines the amount of extended memory (XMS), up to 16,384K, to be used by the application. The default is None. Enables/disables the use of HMA (high memory area).

- *Protected-mode (DPMI) Memory*—Defines the amount of conventional memory, up to 16,384K, to be used by the application. The default is Auto.

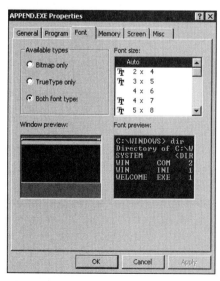

Figure 16.4   The Font tab of a DOS application's Properties dialog box.

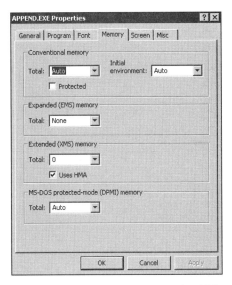

Figure 16.5   The Memory tab of a DOS application's Properties dialog box.

For more information on configuring memory for DOS applications, consult the *Windows 2000 Server Resource Kit*.

The Screen tab, shown in Figure 16.6, offers controls for:

- Setting screen usage to Full or Window
- Restoring the window settings (size, position, and font) to the last saved settings
- Improving performance through the use of Fast ROM emulation and/or dynamic memory allocation

The Misc tab, shown in Figure 16.7, offers controls for:

- Allowing the Windows 2000 screen saver to function over a DOS application
- Consigning the mouse to exclusive use by the DOS application
- Suspending the DOS application when it is not in the foreground
- Issuing a warning if the DOS application is still active when you attempt to terminate the NTVDM process
- Setting how long the program will remain idle waiting for input from the keyboard. Once this time limit has expired, system resources for this application are reduced to allow other applications to continue functioning normally. A low setting defines a long timeout period, whereas a high setting defines a short timeout period.
- Enabling/disabling fast pasting
- Setting whether common shortcut keys are noticed by the DOS application or Windows 2000

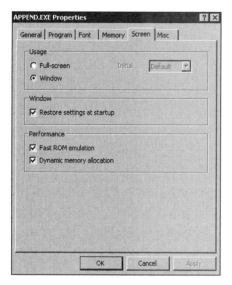

Figure 16.6   The Screen tab of a DOS application's Properties dialog box.

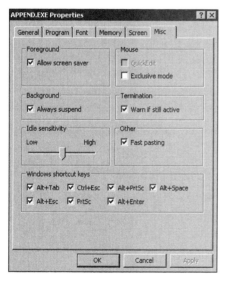

Figure 16.7   The Misc tab of a DOS application's Properties dialog box.

Windows 16 Bit

The Windows 16-bit environment subsystem, or *Win16*, is designed to support Windows 3.x, Windows for Workgroups 3.11, and Win16 Windows 95 applications in a simulated Windows 3.x environment. The runtime environment for Win16 applications is created by launching the wowexec.exe process within an NTVDM processthat is hosted by a Win32 VM. WOWEXEC (Windows on

Windows executable) creates and maintains the cooperative multitasking environment used by Windows 3.x processes.

Windows 2000 is a preemptive multitasking environment. This means the kernel retains control of the CPU and can interrupt any executing process. In a cooperative multitasking environment, the process currently using the CPU has full control and will only release control of the CPU when its execution is completed. Windows 2000 simulates this type of multitasking environment within a single WOW VM. The WOW VM is multitasked along with all other VMs present on the system, but the WOW VM's assigned CPU execution cycles are managed via cooperative multitasking rules among the processes hosted within it.

NOTE: *All Win16 applications are launched by default in the same VM. This allows Win16 applications to share data and system resources.*

Resource and system calls made by Win16 applications within a WOW VM are thunked to the associated 32-bit interface or driver. Likewise, if the resource needs to communicate with the Win16 application, its 32-bit message must be thunked back to 16-bit form for the Win16 application to accept it. *Thunking* is the programmatic process of converting a 16-bit call into a 32-bit call, and vice versa. This additional overhead of bit-level changes for all I/O causes processes with the WOW VM to function slower than similar processes on Windows 95/98 or Windows 3.x systems, where thunking does not occur.

Once a WOW VM is created, it is retained by Windows 2000 even after the Win16 process it contained has been terminated. This also means that the NTVDM hosting the WOW VM process is retained as well. On systems where many Win16 applications are used, this ultimately saves system resources and improves performance. However, on systems where Win16 applications are used infrequently, you may want terminate the WOW VM manually. Viewing the Processes tab, shown in Figure 16.8, of the Task Manager reveals that the WOWEXEC process acts as a subelement of the NTVDM process. Selecting either the WOWEXEC or NTVDM process and clicking the End Process button will terminate the WOW VM. Unless manually terminated, all WOW VMs will be retained by the system until a reboot occurs. A WOW VM is not created until the first Win16 application is launched or a Win16 application is launched into its own memory space (in other words, it's a unique, separate, and distinct WOW VM).

All Win16 applications launch into the same WOW VM by default. You can see this by viewing the Processes tab of the Task Manager when two or more Win16 applications are active. With a shared memory space, message queue, and set of system resources, if a single Win16 application fails, all Win16 applications within the WOW VM can fail as well. To isolate a Win16 application from other Win16

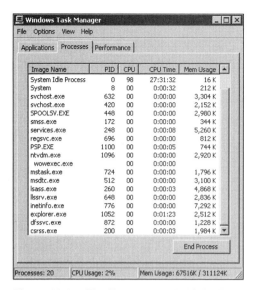

Figure 16.8   The Processes tab of the Task Manager.

applications, it must be launched into its own memory space. This is done by creating a shortcut to the Win16 executable and then selecting the Run In Separate Memory Space checkbox on the Shortcut tab of the shortcut's Properties dialog box (see Figure 16.9). Win16 applications launched in separate memory spaces cannot share data with other Win16 applications.

OS/2 Version 1.x

Windows 2000 includes only basic support for the OS/2 operating system environment. In fact, only OS/2 version 1.x character mode programs can be launched without third-party modifications to the Windows 2000 environment. This level of support is essentially useless, but it is included to qualify under government purchasing regulations. Similar to the WOWEXEC process, the OS/2 process (OS2SS) will remain active using system resources until it's terminated or the system is restarted. The OS/2 environment is not initiated until an actual OS/2 application is launched.

POSIX.1

Windows 2000 includes only basic support for the POSIX (Portable Operating System Interface for Computing Environments based on Unix) operating system environment. In fact, only POSIX.1 text-only applications can be launched without third-party modifications to the Windows 2000 environment. This level of support is essentially useless, but it is included to qualify under government purchasing

16. Managing Applications

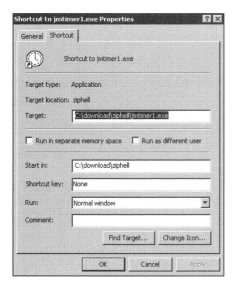

Figure 16.9   The Shortcut tab of a shortcut's Properties dialog box.

regulations. Similar to the WOWEXEC process, the POSIX process (POSIX) will remain active using system resources until it's terminated or the system is restarted. The POSIX environment is not initiated until an actual POSIX application is launched.

POSIX support requires that an NTFS-formatted volume be present. POSIX applications cannot function on volumes formatted with FAT or FAT32. POSIX files have extended attributes and differentiate between uppercase and lowercase file names.

For more information on POSIX support and its extension under Windows 2000, consult the *Windows 2000 Server Resource Kit* or visit the Microsoft Interix Web site at **www.microsoft.com/windows2000/guide/server/solutions/interix.asp**.

Execution Priorities

All processes launched within user mode are assigned an execution priority between 0 and 15. These are the lower 16 priority levels used by Windows 2000. The 16 higher priority levels are used by processes in kernel mode. Normally, a program launched by a user is assigned the normal priority of 8. However, you can launch applications with a priority of Low (4), BelowNormal (6), AboveNormal (10), High (13), or Realtime (24). Because Realtime assigns a kernel mode priority level, only administrators are granted the ability to launch applications with or set executing applications to this priority.

To alter the priority of an already executing application, use the Task Manager. The Task Manager can be launched by one of the following means:

- Pressing Ctrl+Shift+Esc

- Pressing Ctrl+Alt+Delete and then clicking the Task Manager button on the WinLogon Security dialog box

- Right-clicking over an empty area of the Taskbar and then selecting Task Manager from the pop-up menu

Once Task Manager is loaded, changing a process's priority is performed on the Processes tab by selecting a priority level from the Set Priority fly-open menu of the selected process's right-click pop-up menu. As a normal user or even an administrator, you can only alter the priority of user mode processes.

A process's priority can also be set at the time the application is launched using the **start** command. For complete syntax details, enter **start /?** from a command prompt. The basic command is **start /<priority-level> <program>**, where the priority level can be Low, BelowNormal, Normal, AboveNormal, High, or Realtime.

Troubleshooting Application Problems

Resolving problems with applications is not always an easy task. In most cases, the problem lies within the programming code of the application, thus offering you no real solutions. However, when a program hangs, you can terminate it using the Application tab or Processes tab of the Task Manager. Just select the problematic process/application and click End Process or End Task, respectively.

When an application experiences an internal error, it may terminate on its own or Windows 2000 will terminate the application. When this occurs, Dr. Watson attempts to record information about the system and the error. By default, Dr. Watson dumps the contents of the application's VM's memory to a file. But this data is not often useful because it requires special deciphering tools that are not generally available. Therefore, you'll want to reconfigure Dr. Watson. To access the Dr. Watson dialog box, shown in Figure 16.10, execute "drwtsn32" from the **run** command. The configurable options are:

- *Log File Path*—The default is %systemroot%\Documents\DrWatson.

- *Crash Dump*—This is the path where memory dumps will be stored; its default is \Documents and Settings\All Users\Documents\DrWatson\user.dmp.

- *Wave File*—The path to the wave file to play each time Dr. Watson performs an error capture for a failed application.

- *Number Of Instructions*—Defines the number of application instructions to include in the crash dump.

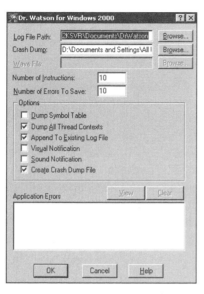

Figure 16.10   The Dr. Watson configuration dialog box.

- *Number Of Errors To Save*—Sets the number of application errors to retain in the crash dump.

- *Dump Symbol Table*—Sets Dr. Watson to include the symbol table in each crash dump.

- *Dump All Thread Contexts*—Sets Dr. Watson to include all data for all threads of the failed application in the crash dump.

- *Append To Existing Log File*—Sets Dr. Watson to add the current crash dump to the existing crash dump file; otherwise, a new file is created.

- *Visual Notification*—Dr. Watson displays a dialog box when an application fails.

- *Sound Notification*—Dr. Watson plays a sound (defined in Wave File) when an application fails.

- *Create Crash Dump File*—Instructs Dr. Watson to create a crash dump file.

- *Application Errors*—Lists all errors currently recorded in the Dr. Watson log file.

You can also troubleshoot application-related problems with some of the following actions:

- Verify that the operating user has sufficient privileges and access for all the data and essential files for the application in question.

- Verify that the current drivers for all hardware devices are present, especially for devices used by the application.

16. Managing Applications

- Verify the path defined in the shortcut's Start In field.

- If the application is a DOS application, verify its memory settings and requirements.

Software Installation

Windows 2000 includes numerous utilities and tools used to configure and manage its own environment, but it offers little in the area of productivity software. *Productivity software* is anything that can be used to perform an assigned work task. A *work task* is anything a network or computer user must do to fulfill his or her job description or accomplish a personal task. Microsoft produces and distributes numerous software products that can be added to standalone or networked Windows 2000 systems, including Office 2000, SQL Server, and Visual Basic Studio. Windows 2000 does include Internet Explorer (a Web browser), Outlook Express (an email client), Notepad (a text editor), WordPad (an RTF document editor), and Paint (a basic graphic tool). However, to be able to perform most computer-based job-related activities, you'll need other applications. In other words, you'll need to install software.

Installation of software can occur through several avenues. The most obvious is manual installation from a CD or floppies. However, this is not the only avenue available on Windows 2000. In addition to manual installation, you can employ IntelliMirror and Remote Installation Services to automatically deploy applications throughout a network (see Chapter 13). You can also use the Windows Installer tool to create distribution packages to create network distributable application packages. Microsoft even offers numerous tools and applications via the Windows Update Web site. Through some creating planning, you can also include applications in the initial installation of Windows 2000 through the use of SYSPREP, SYSDIFF, and SYSPART (see Chapter 5).

The primary means by which software can be installed, managed, and removed is the Add/Remove Programs applet in the Control Panel. The Add/Remove Programs applet is used to perform three types of software management. It can change or remove installed third-party applications (that is, not natively included with Windows 2000 or on its distribution CD) via Change or Remove Programs. It can install new applications from a vendor-supplied floppy or CD via Add New Programs. Finally, it can add or remove Windows 2000 components via Add/Remove Windows Components.

The applet launches by default in the Change or Remove Programs mode (see Figure 16.11). This mode lists all installed applications along with details such as size (total amount of drive space consumed by their files), used status (often,

16. Managing Applications

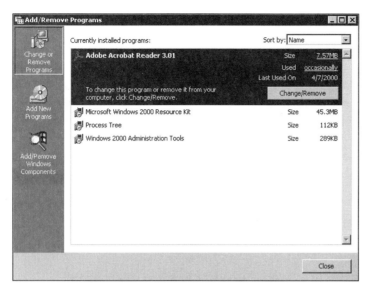

Figure 16.11   The Change Or Remove Programs mode of Add/Remove Programs.

seldom, rarely), and last used date. There's also a Change/Remove button. The Change/Remove button either launches the selected application's own configuration/removal tool or it launches Windows 2000's removal tool.

The Add New Programs mode, shown in Figure 16.12, can pull software from a CD or floppy, from the Microsoft Update Web site, or from a network distribution

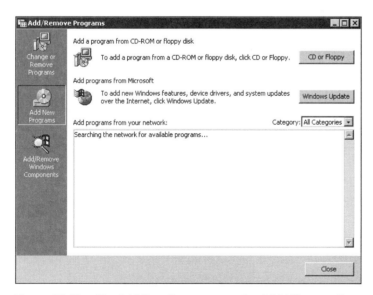

Figure 16.12   The Add New Programs mode of Add/Remove Programs.

site. It's basically used to initiate the setup procedure and ensure the process is recorded by the Windows 2000 removal tool for later management via the Change Or Remove Programs mode.

The Add/Remove Windows Components mode, shown in Figure 16.13, displays a list of all available components of Windows 2000 found on the distribution CD that are still available to be installed on the current system. This interface can also be used to remove already installed components. Simply mark the items you want installed with a checkmark. Then, clear the checkmarks from the items you no longer want on your system. The tool manages the addition and removal of components based on your checkbox markings.

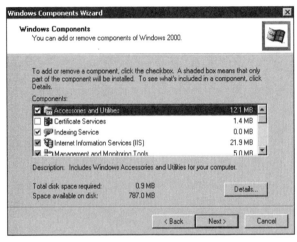

Figure 16.13   The Add/Remove Windows Components mode of Add/Remove Programs (also the Windows Components Wizard dialog box).

Immediate Solutions

Terminating an Active Application

If an application stops responding, behaves improperly, or fails to close when instructed, you many need to manually terminate it. This is done through the Task Manager. Here are the steps to follow:

NOTE: *This solution launches Notepad as the application to be terminated.*

---

1. Launch Notepad to use as an application to terminate. Click Start|Programs|Accessories and then click Notepad.

2. Press Ctrl+Shift+Esc to launch the Task Manager.

3. Select the Application or Processes tab.

4. Locate and select Notepad from the list of applications or processes.

5. Click the End Task or End Process button.

6. Click Yes to confirm the termination. The application is terminated.

7. Click the File menu and select Exit Task Manager to close the Task Manager.

Altering the Security Context for an Application

If you need to launch an application under a security context other than your own current user account's context, use the Run As Different User feature of an application's shortcut. Here are the steps:

1. Open Windows Explorer.

2. Locate and select the application's main executable or launch file.

3. Click the File menu and then select Create Shortcut. A shortcut for the selected file is created within the current folder.

4. Select the newly created shortcut.

5. Click the File menu and then select Properties.

6. Select the Shortcut tab.

7. Select the Run As Different User checkbox and click OK.

8. Move or copy the shortcut to your desired location, such as the desktop or the Start menu.

9. When the new altered shortcut is used, a logon credentials dialog box appears, prompting you for a username, password, and domain name to be used to establish the security context for the application.

Watching Win16 Applications as They Are Launched into the Same WOW VM

To watch as Win16 applications are launched into the same WOW VM via the Task Manager, follow these steps:

NOTE: *This solution requires a Win16 application. Win16 applications are not included with Windows 2000.*

1. Press Ctrl+Shift+Esc to launch the Task Manager.

2. Select the Processes tab.

3. Launch a Win16 application using the original executable or a shortcut that does not have the Run In Separate Memory Space checkbox marked.

4. Through the Processes tab of Task Manager, locate the NTVDM hosting WOWEXEC and the Win16 process.

5. Launch the Win16 application a second time.

6. Watch the Processes tab of Task Manager to see the second instance of the Win16 process appear within the existing VM.

7. Launch the Win16 application a third and fourth time.

8. Watch the Processes tab of Task Manager to see these instances of the Win16 process appear within the existing VM.

9. Close all Win16 applications.

10. Terminate the WOW VM. See the solution titled "Terminating an Active WOW Process" for details.

11. Close Task Manager by selecting Exit Task Manager from the File menu.

Terminating an Active WOW Process

Windows 2000 retains all WOW VMs just in case they are needed again by another Win16 application. You must manually terminate all unused WOW VMs to regain system resources. Here are the steps:

NOTE: *This solution should be performed after any Win16 application has been launched and terminated, leaving an active WOW VM.*

1. Press Ctrl+Shift+Esc to launch the Task Manager.
2. Select the Processes tab.
3. Locate and select the NTVDM with a subprocess of WOWEXEC.
4. Make sure that no Win16 processes are currently listed as subprocesses of this NTVDM. If any are present, terminating this VM will cause these applications to terminate as well.
5. Click the End Process button and click Yes to confirm the termination.
6. Notice that the NTVDM and the WOWEXEC processes are no longer listed on the Processes tab of the Task Manager.
7. Close Task Manager by selecting Exit Task Manager from the File menu.

Launching Win16 Applications in Distinct Memory Spaces

To protect or isolate Win16 applications, they must be launched into separate memory spaces. This is done using a shortcut. Here are the steps to follow:

NOTE: *This solution requires a Win16 application. Win16 applications are not included with Windows 2000.*

1. Open Windows Explorer.
2. Locate and select the application's main executable or launch file.
3. Click the File menu and then select Create Shortcut. A shortcut for the selected file is created within the current folder.
4. Select the newly created shortcut.
5. Click the File menu and then select Properties.
6. Select the Shortcut tab.
7. Select the Run In Separate Memory Space checkbox and click OK.

8. Move or copy the shortcut to the desired location, such as the desktop or the Start menu.

9. When the new altered shortcut is used, the application will be launched in a new and separate WOW VM from all other Win16 applications.

Verifying Win16 Applications Are Launched into Distinct WOW VMs

To verify that Win16 applications are actually launched into distinct WOW VMs, use the Task Manager. Follow these steps:

NOTE: *This solution requires a Win16 application. Win16 applications are not included with Windows 2000.*

1. Create a shortcut to a Win16 application. Configure it to launch the Win16 application into a separate memory space. See the previous solution "Launching Win16 Applications in Distinct Memory Spaces" for details.

2. Locate and launch your Win16 application using the original execution file, not the new shortcut.

3. Press Ctrl+Shift+Esc to launch the Task Manager.

4. Select the Processes tab.

5. Locate the NTVDM that hosts the WOWEXEC process. Notice that the application is listed as a subprocess of the NTVDM process.

6. Locate and launch the Win16 application a second time.

7. View the Task Manager's Processes tab. Notice that the second instance of the application appears as another subprocess of the NTVDM process.

8. Locate and launch the Win16 application using the configured shortcut from Step 1.

9. View the Task Manager's Processes tab. Notice that a new instance of the NTVDM process, along with the WOWEXEC subprocess, has been launched to accommodate the Win16 application launched into a separate memory space.

10. Close Task Manager by selecting Exit Task Manager from the File menu.

11. Close all Win16 applications.

12. Terminate the two WOW VMs. See the solution titled "Terminating an Active WOW Process" for details.

16. Managing Applications

Creating and Using Custom DOS VM Startup Files

If you need a DOS VM environment other than that created by the default autoexec.nt and config.nt files, follow these steps:

NOTE: *This solution requires a DOS application. DOS applications are not included with Windows 2000.*

---

1. Open Windows Explorer.

2. Locate the %systemroot%\System32 folder.

3. Locate and select autoexec.nt.

4. Click the File menu and then select Copy.

5. Click the File menu and then select Paste.

6. Select the pasted copy of autoexec.nt.

7. Click the File menu and then select Rename.

8. Type in a new file name, such as autoexe2.nt, and then press Enter.

9. Repeat Steps 3 through 8 for config.nt.

10. Launch Notepad by clicking the Start menu, selecting Programs|
    Accessories, and then clicking Notepad. Notepad will open.

11. Click the File menu and select Open.

12. Use the Open dialog box to browse to %systemroot%\System32.

13. Locate and select the new autoexe2.nt file.

14. Add or edit the contents of this file to meet your new DOS VM environment
    requirements.

15. Click the File menu and select Save.

16. Click the File menu and select Open.

17. Use the Open dialog box to browse to %systemroot%\System32.

18. Locate and select the new config2.nt file.

19. Add or edit the contents of this file to meet your new DOS VM environment
    requirements.

20. Click the File menu and select Save.

21. Click the File menu and then select Exit to close Notepad.

22. Locate and select the DOS application's main executable or launch file.

23. Click the File menu and then select Create Shortcut. A shortcut for the
    selected file is created within the current folder.

24. Select the newly created shortcut.

16. Managing Applications

25. Click the File menu and then select Properties.

26. Select the Program tab.

27. Click the Advanced button.

28. Change the path file names to point to the new autoexe2.nt and config2.nt files.

29. Click OK.

30. Click OK.

31. When this shortcut is used to launch the DOS application, the custom autoexe2.nt and config2.nt files will be used to create the DOS VM environment.

Customizing the Memory Configuration of a DOS VM

If the default memory configuration for DOS VMs is not sufficient for a specific DOS application, it can be customized through a shortcut. Here's how:

NOTE: *This solution requires a DOS application. DOS applications are not included with Windows 2000.*

1. Open Windows Explorer.

2. Locate and select the DOS application's main executable or launch file.

3. Click the File menu and then select Create Shortcut. A shortcut for the selected file is created within the current folder.

4. Select the newly created shortcut.

5. Click the File menu and then select Properties.

6. Select the Memory tab.

7. Alter the configuration for conventional memory, EMS, XMS, and/or DPMI to meet the needs of your DOS application.

8. Click OK.

9. When this shortcut is used to launch the DOS application, the new memory configuration settings will be used to create the memory structure of the DOS VM.

16. Managing Applications

Changing the Priority of an Active Process

After an application is launched, you can still leverage some minor control over its execution priority. Here are the steps to follow:

1. Select Start|Programs|Applications|Command Prompt. The Command Prompt window opens.

2. At the command prompt, type **start /low notepad**, and then press Enter. The Notepad application opens.

3. Press Ctrl+Alt+Esc to launch the Task Manager.

4. Select the Processes tab.

5. Locate and select the notepad.exe process.

6. Right-click the notepad.exe process and select Set Priority from the pop-up menu. Notice the selected priority is currently Low.

7. Click the High setting from the list of priorities in the pop-up menu.

8. A warning message may appear stating that changing the priority might cause system instability. Click Yes.

9. Right-click the notepad.exe process and select Set Priority from the pop-up menu. Notice the selected priority is now High.

10. Click the Notepad button in the Taskbar.

11. Select File|Exit to close Notepad.

12. Click the Task Manager button in the Taskbar.

13. Close the Task Manager by selecting File|Exit Task Manager.

14. Click the Command Prompt button in the Taskbar.

15. Close the command prompt by typing **exit** and pressing Enter.

Changing the Priority of an Active Kernel Mode Process

Even as an administrator, you only have control over user mode process priorities. You can see evidence of this with the following steps:

1. Press Ctrl+Alt+Esc to launch the Task Manager.

2. Select the Processes tab.

3. Locate and select a kernel mode process, such as System or lsass.exe.

4. Right-click the process and select Set Priority from the pop-up menu.

5. Click the High setting from the list of priorities in the pop-up menu.

16. Managing Applications

6. A warning message may appear stating that changing the priority might cause system instability. Click Yes to confirm the change.

7. An error message appears stating that the operation could not be completed and access is denied. This is evidence that you, even as administrator, do not have sufficient privileges to manage kernel mode processes.

8. Close the Task Manager by selecting File|Exit Task Manager.

Launching an Application with a Non-Normal Priority

The default execution priority for user mode applications (that is, anything a user can launch) is 13 (or normal). Using the **START** command, you can launch applications at other priority levels. Here are the steps to follow:

1. Select Start|Programs|Applications|Command Prompt. The Command Prompt window opens.

2. At the command prompt, type **start /low notepad** and then press Enter. The Notepad application will launch.

3. Press Ctrl+Alt+Esc to launch the Task Manager.

4. Select the Processes tab.

5. Locate and select the notepad.exe process.

6. Right-click the notepad.exe process and select Set Priority from the pop-up menu. Notice the selected priority is currently Low.

7. Click the Notepad button in the Taskbar.

8. Click the File menu and then click Exit to close this instance of Notepad.

9. Click the Command Prompt button in the Taskbar.

10. At the command prompt, type **start /high notepad** and then press Enter. The Notepad application will launch.

11. Click the Task Manager button in the Taskbar.

12. Locate and select the notepad.exe process.

13. Right-click the notepad.exe process and select Set Priority from the pop-up menu. Notice the selected priority is currently High.

14. Click the Notepad button in the Taskbar.

15. Click the File menu and click Exit to close this instance of Notepad.

16. Repeat steps 9 through 15 for BelowNormal, AboveNormal, and Realtime (note that Realtime can only be set by administrators).

17. Click the Task Manager button in the Taskbar.

18. Close the Task Manager by selecting File|Exit Task Manager.

19. Click the Command Prompt button in the Taskbar.

20. Close the command prompt by typing **exit** and pressing Enter.

Installing Software via Add/Remove Programs

If you need to install a new application, you can use the Add/Remove Programs applet to initiate the install. Follow these steps to learn how:

1. Open the Control Panel.

2. Launch the Add/Remove Programs applet by double-clicking its icon.

3. Click Add New Programs.

4. Insert the floppy or CD used to install your new application.

5. Click the CD or Floppy button.

6. Click Next.

7. The system will attempt to locate the setup launch file automatically. If one is not found, use the Browse button to select it manually.

8. Click Finish.

9. Follow any prompts required by the software's installation routine.

10. When installation is complete, close the Add/Remove Programs applet.

Uninstalling Applications

When an application is consuming space you need to recover, is no longer used, or is being replaced by a new version that won't upgrade, you'll need to uninstall that application. Follow these steps to do just that:

1. Open the Control Panel.

2. Launch the Add/Remove Programs applet by double-clicking its icon.

3. Change Or Remove Programs should be selected by default.

4. Click the name of the application you want to remove.

5. Click the Remove button within the highlighted application area.

6. Click Yes when prompted for confirmation.

7. If any prompts appear during the uninstallation, respond appropriately.

8. Once the uninstall is complete, the application's information will be removed from the Add/Remove Programs applet.

9. Close the Add/Remove Programs applet.

Chapter 17

Providing Print Services

(continued)

In Depth

The terms used by Windows 2000 for printing must be defined for printers to be fully understood. The whole subject of printers with Windows operating systems has been extremely confusing in the past.

With Windows NT, the actual physical printer was referred to as the *print device* and the software was known as the *printer*. This has been extremely confusing. To make matters worse, these terms have changed yet again with Windows 2000. The physical printer is now known as the *printer*, whereas the software component is the *logical printer*.

This chapter will use this new Windows 2000 naming convention. However, you should choose one that works for you and stick with it.

If you understand the process Windows 2000 follows when printing, troubleshooting printer problems will become easier. The following section describes the process that Windows 2000 follows when sending a print job through the server, finally arriving at the printer.

When the print option is selected in a Windows application, the application sends the data to the Graphical Device Interface (GDI). The GDI is the component that makes the applications independent of the printers.

In the old DOS world, it was the application's job to print the actual print job. If a word processor was running on a system and a printer of type X was installed, the driver for printer type X for the application had to be installed. This was true for each application installed on the system. Each one of these applications required a dedicated driver.

GDI changed all that. Now, the application needs to know only how to communicate with GDI, whereas GDI needs to know how to communicate with the printer. The application now sends the print job to the GDI, which formats it using the printer driver, thus using the mini-driver/unidriver model, and sends it to the spooler.

The spooler passes the print job to the Remote Print Provider (RPP), which then sends it over the network to the print router on the server. The print router is part of the Print Spooler service on the server. It is this service that's responsible for passing the print job to the print monitor.

17. Providing Print Services

The print monitor manages all the printers and print jobs on the server. It is the print monitor that controls scheduling and priority. When the printer is ready, the print monitor will send the print job to the printer.

Printers and Networks

There are two main methods for connecting printers to the physical network: by using print servers and by using network printers. Each of these technologies are presented and explained in the following sections.

Working with Print Servers

Print servers come in two different flavors—either a network device or a computer. The network device, known simply as a *print server*, or computer with the appropriate software installed simply acts as the communication link between the clients attempting to print to the printer and the physical printer.

Generally speaking, the print server device has a network connection and a printer connection. The printer is connected to the printer port and the print server; the print server is connected to the network and is then configured so that it can operate on the network (for example, it is assigned an IP address). The print server is very similar to a network printer in its operation, but it's normally used on older printers that do not have network capabilities.

> **WARNING!**   All versions of Windows 2000 will operate as print servers; however, be aware that a limitation has been set on Windows 2000 Professional. Although Windows 2000 Server and Advanced Server have no limitations on the number of users supported on a single printer, Windows 2000 Professional only allows 10 concurrent users to connect.

There are really two approaches to how computer-based print servers operate. Microsoft has taken the "intelligent" approach, whereas most Unix systems have taken the "dumb" approach. It is important that these two approaches not be taken as "good" and "bad," respectively. Instead, just remember that they are different but perform the same task. With the "intelligent" approach, the print server performs all the tasks necessary for printing to occur. This includes providing the necessary printer drivers to the clients when they connect to the printer and handling the actual communication between the client and the printer. All spooling tasks occur at the print server, not at the client. That is to say, it is the print server that controls all the print jobs when multiple jobs are sent to the printer at the same time.

With the "dumb" approach, the print server is just an interface between the network and the printer. It is up to each client to maintain the printer driver and the

17. Providing Print Services

printer queue when multiple print jobs are sent to the printer at the same time (this task is sometimes performed by the printer as well). The most popular implementation of this method is known as the *Line Printer Daemon* (LPD). The clients must then connect to the print server using the Line Printer Remote (LPR) service to send the print jobs to the printer.

NOTE: *Windows 2000 can operate as both an LPD server and an LPR client. Both these services are optional and are not installed by default.*

TIP: *A third service exists, known as Line Printer Queue (LPQ). This service is used to control print jobs already at the print server. LPQ can be used to display information about the currently queued print jobs as well as to modify or delete jobs.*

Working with Network Printers

Network printers are simply regular printers that have additional networking hardware installed. These printers can usually support multiple protocols (such as TCP/IP, IPX, and AppleTalk). Once they are connected to the network and are configured, they simply become another device on the network.

These network printers are normally used in conjunction with print servers (such as a Windows 2000 Server). Although most printers have client software available to allow the clients to connect directly to the printer, this method is not always the desired approach for a couple of reasons. The first is security: If clients have the appropriate software installed to connect to the network printer, it becomes extremely difficult to control who has rights to print to the printer. The second is scalability: If, for example, a network printer supports 100 clients and breaks down or cannot handle the volume, it needs to be either repaired or replaced. If each client is connected directly to the printer, each of those clients will have to be reconfigured. However, if all the clients connect through a Windows 2000 print server, only the server needs to be modified. The clients will automatically get the new printer drivers installed the next time they connect to the print server.

Fixing Printer Problems

For the most part, printing problems are one of the biggest problems that an administrator has to live with. Luckily, these are fairly easy to fix. The two troubleshooting fixes listed in this section should fix about 90 percent of printer problems (excluding physical problems).

The first problem deals with print jobs coming out garbled with foreign characters on the printer. The problem is most commonly caused by corrupted printer drivers (either on the server or on the client). When this occurs, simply reinstall the printer driver. If the problem is occurring on a single system, reinstall the client's driver. If, however, the problem is occurring from all the systems, the driver must be reinstalled on the server.

The second problem is caused when the Spooler service gets corrupted and ceases to respond to requests. Fixing this problem is easy: Simply stop and restart the service on the system controlling the printer or printers. At times, the spooler is using so much of the system's CPU cycles that it's easier to restart the service from a remote system.

Immediate Solutions

Creating a Parallel Port Printer

To create a parallel port printer, perform the following steps:

1. Select Start|Settings|Printers.

2. Double-click Add Printer. The Add Printer Wizard appears.

3. Click Next.

4. Ensure that the Local Printer radio button is selected, as shown in Figure 17.1, and click Next.

5. Select a parallel (LPT) port and click Next, as shown in Figure 17.2.

6. Select the printer manufacturer and the model, as shown in Figure 17.3, and click Next.

7. Enter a printer name and click Next.

8. To share the printer, choose the Share As radio button, enter a share name, and click Next. To not share the printer, choose the Do Not Share This Printer radio button and click Next.

9. If the printer is to be shared, enter a location and a printer description and click Next.

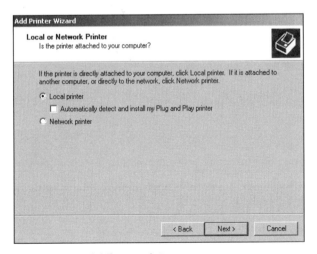

Figure 17.1   Adding a printer.

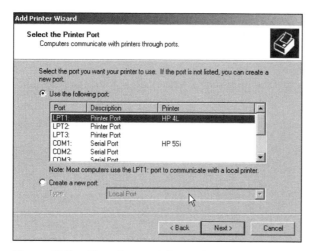

Figure 17.2   Choosing a printer port.

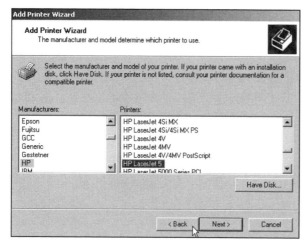

Figure 17.3   Selecting the printer manufacturer and model.

10. If desired, select to print a test page and click Next.

11. Click Finish.

Creating a Serial Port Printer

To create a serial port printer, perform the following steps:

1. Select Start|Settings|Printers.

2. Double-click Add Printer. The Add Printer Wizard appears.

17. Providing Print Services

3. Click Next.

4. Ensure that the Local Printer radio button selected and click Next.

5. Select a serial (COM) port and click Next.

6. Select the printer manufacturer and the model and click Next.

7. Enter a printer name and click Next.

8. To share the printer, choose the Share As radio button, enter a share name, and click Next. To not share the printer, choose the Do Not Share This Printer radio button and click Next.

9. If the printer is to be shared, enter a location and a printer description and click Next.

10. If desired, select to print a test page and click Next.

11. Click Finish.

Creating a Server Shared Printer

To create a shared printer, perform the following steps:

1. Select Start|Settings|Printers.

2. Double-click Add Printer. The Add Printer Wizard appears.

3. Click Next.

4. Ensure that the Network Printer radio button selected and click Next.

5. If the printer name is known, enter it in the Name field and click Next. Otherwise, click Next to browse for the printer.

6. If the printer name was left blank in the previous step, navigate to the desired printer, select it, and click Next.

7. Click Finish.

Creating a TCP/IP Port Printer

To create a TCP/IP port printer, perform the following steps:

1. Select Start|Settings|Printers.

2. Double-click Add Printer. The Add Printer Wizard appears.

3. Click Next.

4. Ensure that the Local Printer radio button selected and click Next.

17. Providing Print Services

5. Select the Create New Port radio button and click Next.

6. Choose the standard TCP/IP port from the Type drop-down list and click Next. The Add Standard TCP/IP Printer Port Wizard appears.

7. Click Next.

8. Enter the TCP/IP address for the printer and click Next.

9. Select the device type and click Next.

10. Click Finish.

11. Continue with the standard printer installation.

Creating a Network-Attached Printer

To create a network-attached printer, perform the following steps:

1. Select Start|Settings|Printers.

2. Double-click Add Printer. The Add Printer Wizard appears.

3. Click Next.

4. Ensure that the Local Printer radio button selected and click Next.

5. Select the Create New Port radio button and click Next.

6. Choose the standard TCP/IP port from the Type drop-down list and click Next. The Add Standard TCP/IP Printer Port Wizard appears.

7. Click Next.

8. Enter the TCP/IP address for the printer and click Next.

9. Select the device type and click Next.

10. Click Finish.

11. Select the printer manufacturer and the model and click Next.

12. Enter a printer name and click Next.

13. To share the printer, choose the Share As radio button, enter a share name, and click Next. To not share the printer, choose the Do Not Share This Printer radio button and click Next.

14. If the printer is to be shared, enter a location and a printer description and click Next.

15. If desired, select to print a test page and click Next.

16. Click Finish.

Publishing a Printer in Active Directory

To publish a printer in Active Directory, perform the following steps:

1. Select Start|Settings|Printers.

2. Right-click the printer that is to be published in Active Directory and choose Sharing from the pop-up list.

3. If the printer is not shared, select the Shared As radio button and enter a share name for the printer.

4. Check the List In The Directory checkbox.

NOTE: *Active Directory must be installed on the system for this checkbox to be visible.*

---

5. Click OK.

Pausing a Printer

To pause a printer, perform the following steps:

1. Select Start|Settings|Printers.

2. Highlight the printer to be paused.

3. Right-click the printer and choose Pause Printing from the pop-up menu.

Selecting the Default Printer

To modify the default printer, perform the following steps:

1. Select Start|Settings|Printers.

2. Highlight the printer to be set as the default printer.

3. Right-click the printer and choose Set As Default Printer from the pop-up menu.

17. Providing Print Services

Sharing a Printer

To share a printer, perform the following steps:

1. Select Start|Settings|Printers.
2. Highlight the printer to be shared.
3. Right-click the printer and choose Sharing from the pop-up menu.
4. Select the Shared As radio button.
5. Enter a share name for the printer and click OK.

Setting a Printer to Work Offline

To set a printer to work offline, perform the following steps:

1. Select Start|Settings|Printers.
2. Highlight the printer to be set to work offline.
3. Right-click the printer and choose Use Printer Offline from the pop-up menu.

Setting Printing Security

To modify printer security, perform the following steps:

1. Select Start|Settings|Printers.
2. Highlight the printer for which security is to be set.
3. Right-click the printer and choose Properties from the pop-up menu.
4. Select the Security tab.
5. To add a user or group, click the Add button, select the user or group, and click OK.
6. Assign any desired permissions to the selected user or group.
7. For more advanced features, click the Advanced button.
8. Click OK when done.

Auditing Printers

To audit printer use, perform the following steps:

1. Select Start|Settings|Printers.

2. Highlight the printer to be audited.

3. Right-click the printer and choose Properties from the pop-up menu.

4. Select the Security tab.

5. Click Advanced.

6. Select the Auditing tab.

7. Click Add.

8. Choose the user for which auditing on the printer is to be enabled and click OK.

9. Select the access types to audit (Print, Manage Printers, Manage Documents, Read Permissions, Change Permissions, and Take Ownership) and whether to audit success and failure. Click OK.

10. Click OK.

11. Click OK.

Deleting a Printer

To delete a printer, perform the following steps:

1. Select Start|Settings|Printers.

2. Highlight the printer to delete.

3. Right-click the printer and choose Delete from the pop-up menu.

4. Click Yes to confirm the deletion.

Restarting a Stalled Print Job

To restart a stalled print job, perform the following steps:

1. Select Start|Settings|Printers.

2. Highlight the printer where the stalled print job exists.

3. Right-click the printer and choose Open from the pop-up menu.

4. Highlight the stalled print job.

5. Select the Resume option from the Document menu.

Pausing a Print Job

To pause a print job, perform the following steps:

1. Select Start|Settings|Printers.

2. Highlight the printer where the print job to be paused exists.

3. Right-click the printer and choose Open from the pop-up menu.

4. Highlight the print job.

5. Select the Pause option from the Document menu.

Removing a Print Job

To remove a print job, perform the following steps:

1. Select Start|Settings|Printers.

2. Highlight the printer where the print job is to be removed.

3. Right-click the printer and choose Open from the pop-up menu.

4. Highlight the print job to be removed.

5. Select Cancel from the Document menu.

Deleting All Print Jobs

To delete pending print jobs, perform the following steps:

1. Select Start|Settings|Printers.

2. Highlight the printer where the print jobs to be deleted reside.

3. Right-click the printer and choose Open from the pop-up menu.

4. Select Cancel All Documents from the Printer menu.

Taking Ownership of a Printer

To take ownership of a printer, perform the following steps:

1. Select Start|Settings|Printers.

2. Highlight the printer of which you want to take ownership.

3. Right-click the printer and choose Properties from the pop-up menu.

4. Select the Security tab.

5. Click Advanced.

6. Select the Ownership tab.

7. Choose the user or group that is to take ownership and click OK.

8. Click OK.

9. Click OK.

Creating a Printing Pool

To create printing pool, perform the following steps:

1. Create all the printers that will participate in the pool.

TIP: Microsoft recommends that only printers of the same make and model be used when creating a printing pool. In practice, however, as long as all the printers can use the same driver, they may be pooled.

2. Select Start|Settings|Printers.

3. Highlight the first printer in the printing pool.

4. Right-click the printer and choose Properties from the pop-up menu.

5. Choose the Ports tab.

6. Check the Enable Printer Pooling checkbox.

7. Select one or more extra ports and click OK (see Figure 17.4).

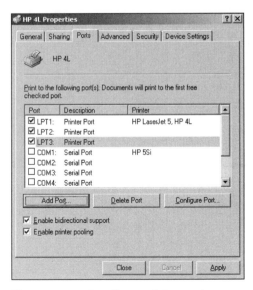

Figure 17.4   Creating a printer pool.

Configuring Multiple Printers for a Single Device

Sometimes, it's desired to create printers with different configuration properties assigned to them. For example, if only a single printer exists, the administrator might want to schedule the printer differently for managers and users. For this, the administrator can create multiple printers for a single device. Here's how:

1. Select Start|Settings|Printers.

2. Create the first printer as outlined in this chapter.

3. Create the second printer and assign it to the same port.

4. Repeat if desired.

Scheduling Printing

To set up scheduled printing, perform the following steps:

1. Select Start|Settings|Printers.

2. Highlight the printer to be scheduled.

3. Right-click the printer and choose Properties from the pop-up menu.

4. Select the Advanced tab.

5. Choose the Available From radio button (see Figure 17.5).

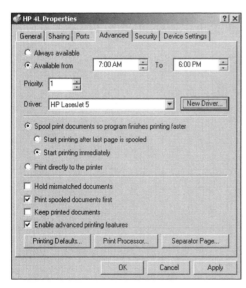

Figure 17.5   Scheduling a printer.

17. Providing Print Services

6. Enter the start and end times this printer is to be available.

7. Click OK.

Configuring Printer Priorities

To configure printer priorities, perform the following steps:

1. Select Start|Settings|Printers.

2. Highlight the printer for which the priority is to be set.

3. Right-click the printer and choose Properties from the pop-up menu.

4. Select the Advanced tab.

5. Choose the priority from the Priority section.

6. Click OK.

Using Separator Pages

To set up the use of separator pages between print jobs, perform the following steps:

1. Select Start|Settings|Printers.

2. Highlight the printer on which to use separator pages.

3. Right-click the printer and choose Properties from the pop-up menu.

4. Select the Advanced tab.

5. Click Separator Page.

6. Enter the name of the separator page (or browse to it).

NOTE: *Separator pages are used to separate print jobs when the printer switches modes—for example, changing from Postscript to PCL. Several separator pages ship with Windows 2000 that end with the .sep extension.*

---

7. Click OK.

8. Click OK.

Installing Multiple OS-Specific Drivers

To install multiple OS print drivers, perform the following steps:

1. Select Start|Settings|Printers.

2. Highlight the printer for which multiple OS drivers need to be added.

3. Right-click the printer and choose Properties from the pop-up menu.

4. Select the Sharing tab.

5. Click Additional Drivers. The Additional Drivers page is displayed, see Figure 17.6.

6. Select the operating system or systems for which drivers need to be installed.

7. Click OK.

8. Insert the requested CD-ROM.

9. Click Close.

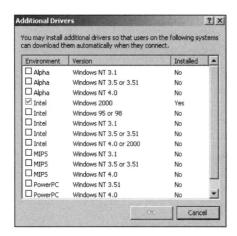

Figure 17.6   The Additional Drivers window.

Updating the Printer Driver

To update a printer driver, perform the following steps:

1. Select Start|Settings|Printers.

2. Highlight the printer that needs the updated driver.

3. Right-click the printer and choose Properties from the pop-up menu.

4. Select the Advanced tab.

17. Providing Print Services

5. Click New Driver. The New Driver Wizard appears.

6. Click Next.

7. Select the manufacturer and printer or click Have Disk to install a new driver.

8. Click Next.

9. Click Finish.

10. Click OK.

Printing to a Printer from a Command Line

To use a printer from the command line, perform the following steps:

1. Select Start|Programs|Accessories|Command Prompt.

2. Type "net use lpt2: \\server\printername" and press Enter.

3. To print the boot.ini file, type "print c:\boot.ini > lpt2:".

Managing Printers

A few issues are involved in managing existing printers. These are discussed in the following sections.

Managing Printers from Windows 2000

To manage an existing printer, perform the following steps:

1. Select Start|Settings|Printers.

2. Highlight the printer to manage.

3. Right-click the printer and choose Open from the pop-up menu.

4. Make any management changes needed and click OK.

Managing Printers through a Browser

To manage a printer through Internet Explorer, perform the following steps:

1. Select Start|Programs|Internet Explorer.

NOTE: *Internet Information Services must be installed for this feature to be functional.*

2. In the address field, enter **http://*Servername*/Printers** and click OK.

3. The printer list appears, as shown in Figure 17.7.

17. Providing Print Services

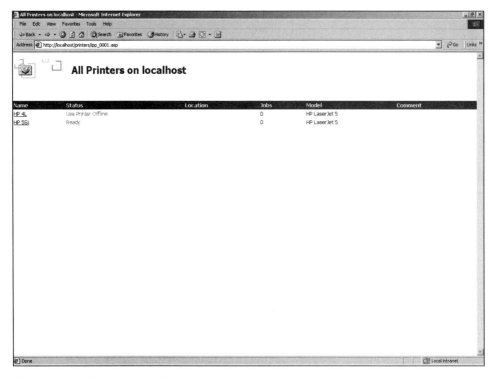

Figure 17.7   The Internet printer list.

4. Select the printer that's to be managed. The printer's properties window appears, as shown in Figure 17.8.

5. To pause the printer, click the Pause option under the Printer Actions section.

6. To resume the printer, click the Resume option under the Printer Actions section.

7. To cancel all documents, click the Cancel All Documents option under the Printer Actions section.

8. To pause a document, select the document and click the Pause option under the Document Actions section.

9. To resume a document, select the document and click the Resume option under the Document Actions section.

10. To delete a print job, select the document and click the Cancel option under the Document Actions section.

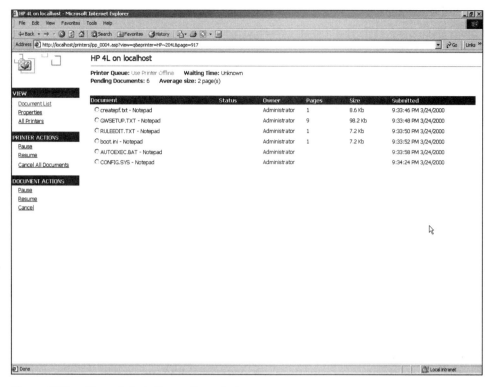

Figure 17.8   The printer's Properties window.

Stopping the Spooler Service

To stop the Spooler service, perform the following steps:

1. Select Start|Programs|Administrative Tools|Services.

2. Highlight the Spooler service.

3. Right-click the service and choose Stop from the pop-up menu.

Starting the Spooler Service

To start the Spooler service, perform the following steps:

1. Select Start|Programs|Administrative Tools|Services.

2. Highlight the Spooler service.

3. Right-click the service and choose Start from the pop-up menu.

Setting Printing Preferences

Many different printing options can be set in Windows 2000. The available options depend on the type of printer installed and on the printer driver. The following solutions deal with some of the common preferences set on printers.

Setting Paper Size

To set the paper size, perform the following steps:

1. Select Start|Settings|Printers.
2. Right-click the printer that is to be configured and choose Printing Preferences from the pop-up menu.
3. Click Advanced.
4. Under the Paper/Output section, click Paper Size.
5. Select the desired paper size.
6. Click OK.
7. Click OK.

Modifying Page Orientation

To modify the page orientation, perform the following steps:

1. Select Start|Settings|Printers.
2. Right-click the printer for which the page orientation is to be configured and choose Printing Preferences from the pop-up menu.
3. Choose the Layout tab.
4. Select the desired orientation from the Orientation section.

NOTE: *Three different page orientations are available: portrait, landscape, and rotated landscape. Portrait prints the print job vertically on the page, landscape prints the print job horizontally on the page, and rotated landscape prints the print job rotated 90 degrees counterclockwise on the page.*

5. Click OK.

Setting Print Resolution

To set the print resolution, perform the following steps:

1. Select Start|Settings|Printers.
2. Right-click the printer for which the print resolution is to be set and choose Printing Preferences from the pop-up menu.
3. Click Advanced.
4. Select Graphic|Print Quality.

5. Choose the desired resolution from the pop-up menu.

6. Click OK.

7. Click OK.

Configuring Paper Trays

To configure the paper trays' configuration, perform the following steps:

1. Select Start|Settings|Printers.

2. Right-click the printer for which the paper trays are to be configured and choose Properties from the pop-up menu.

3. Choose the Device Settings tab.

4. Select the desired paper tray under the Form To Tray Assignment section.

5. Choose the appropriate paper size.

6. Repeat Steps 4 and 5 for each paper tray.

7. Click OK.

Monitoring Printer Queue Performance

To monitor printer queue performance, perform the following steps:

1. Select Start|Programs|Administrative Tools|Performance.

2. Click the + button.

3. Choose the print server computer to be monitored from the Select Counters From Computer list box.

4. Select Print Queue from the Performance object list box.

5. Choose the counter to be monitored and click Add.

6. Repeat Step 5 for each additional counter.

7. Click Close when finished.

Tracking Printer Usage

To track printer usage, perform the following steps:

1. Select Start|Settings|Printers.

2. Right-click the printer for which usage is to be tracked and choose Properties from the pop-up menu.

3. Choose the Security tab.

4. Click Advanced.

5. Choose the Auditing tab.

6. Click Add.

7. Select the user or group for which to track usage and click OK.

8. Choose the successful and failed printing events to be audited and click OK.

9. Click OK.

10. Click OK.

Keeping a Copy of Print Jobs

To keep a copy of all print jobs, perform the following steps:

1. Select Start|Settings|Printers.

2. Right-click the printer for which this feature is to be enabled and choose Properties from the pop-up menu.

3. Choose the Advanced tab.

4. Check the Keep Printed Documents checkbox.

TIP: *To delete all kept printed documents from the spool, clear the Keep Printed Documents checkbox, click Apply, check the Keep Printed Documents checkbox, and click OK.*

---

5. Click OK.

Modifying the Print Spool Folder Location

To modify the print spool folder location, perform the following steps:

1. Select Start|Settings|Printers.

2. Select File|Server Properties.

3. Choose the Advanced tab.

4. Enter a new path for the spool folder in the Spool Folder field.

5. Stop and restart the Spooler service.

6. Click OK.

Enabling Completed Print Job Notification

To enable completed print job notification, perform the following steps:

1. Select Start|Settings|Printers.

2. Select File|Server Properties.

3. Choose the Advanced tab.

4. Check the Notify When Remote Documents Are Printed checkbox.

5. Click OK.

Disabling Completed Print Job Notification

To disable completed print job notification, perform the following steps:

1. Select Start|Settings|Printers.

2. Select File|Server Properties.

3. Choose the Advanced tab.

4. Clear the Notify When Remote Documents Are Printed checkbox.

5. Click OK.

Viewing Printer Driver Files

To view the printer driver files, perform the following steps:

1. Select Start|Settings|Printers.

2. Select File|Server Properties.

3. Choose the Drivers tab.

4. Select the driver for which the files are to be viewed.

5. Click Properties.

6. The files are now displayed. To get more information about a particular file, click Properties.

7. Click Close.

8. Click OK.

Setting Printer Priorities

To set printer priority, perform the following steps:

1. Select Start|Settings|Printers.

2. Highlight the printer for which the priority is to be set.

3. Right-click the printer and choose Properties from the pop-up menu.

4. Choose the Advanced tab.

5. Set the desired priority by entering a value in the Priority field or by clicking the up or down arrow.

NOTE: With printer priorities, 1 is the lowest priority level and 99 is the highest.

---

6. Choose the Security tab.

7. Ensure that only the users or groups that are to be given this priority have permissions to connect and print to this printer.

8. Click OK.

9. Double-click Add Printer to add another logical printer for the same physical printer (see the "Creating a Parallel Port Printer" section in this chapter for a step-by-step description).

10. Right-click the newly created printer and choose Properties from the pop-up menu.

11. Choose the Advanced tab.

12. Set the desired priority by entering a value in the Priority field or by clicking the up or down arrow.

13. Choose the Security tab.

14. Ensure that only the users or groups that are to be given this priority have permissions to connect and print to this printer.

15. Click OK.

Chapter 18

Security

587

In Depth

It is the administrator's job to make sure that a network and all its data is secure. Windows 2000 provides a number of features to assist in this quest. Basically, an administrator must prevent unauthorized access to information and damage (either unintentional or malicious) to data and systems. However, security restrictions should not prevent authorized users from getting access to the data they require. The following Windows 2000 features help secure various components of a server:

- Extensible Authentication Protocol (EAP)
- Kerberos version 5
- Microsoft Challenge Handshake Authentication Protocol version 2 (MS-CHAP v2)
- Password Authentication Protocol (PAP)
- Secure Sockets Layer/Transport Layer Security (SSL/TLS)
- Windows NT LAN Manager (NTLM)

Kerberos Version 5

Windows 2000 uses Kerberos (version 5) as its default security and network authentication protocol. It is important to understand that Kerberos security is not a new concept or protocol; it has been used for years in the Unix world. This gives credibility to the protocol. Kerberos is currently at version 5 and has been tested in the industry for several years.

First, here are some definitions. Kerberos security has three components to it: the client, the server, and the Key Distribution Center (KDC). The term *principal* is assigned to any system on the network. Each principal has a secret key, known as a *long-term key*, that it shares only with the KDC. This is what gives the Kerberos protocol its strength. When a principal wants to communicate with another principal, another key is used, which is known as the *session key*. For example, suppose a client computer, shown in Figure 18.1, wants to communicate with the server named Products.

The first thing the client does is to request a ticket to communicate with the Products server. The KDC returns an encrypted message back to the client. This message contains two different session keys: the client's session key and the Product server's session key (see Figure 18.2). Although the client has both of these session keys, it cannot decrypt the Product server's session key. Recall

18. Security

Figure 18.1   A Kerberos example.

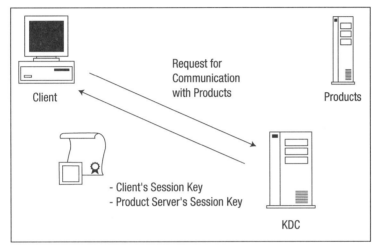

Figure 18.2   Key-encrypted communication.

that each principal shares a secret key. Because only the KDC and the Product server have access to the Product server's secret key, only the Product server can decrypt the message.

Finally, the client sends a message to the Product server. This message contains the session ticket (both the client's and the server's session keys) and an authenticator that has been encrypted with the client's session key, as shown in Figure 18.3.

Once the server receives this information, it decrypts the session ticket using the session key it shares with the KDC. Finally, the Product server uses the session key to decrypt the authenticator. If this is successful, the Product server now trusts the client and can communicate with it.

TIP: *The session key has a limited life span and may only be used for a single logon session. After it expires, a new session key must be generated.*

This process is a bit complicated, but it also creates a very secure method of authentication, which makes Windows 2000 the most secure Microsoft operating system ever.

18. Security

- Client's Session Key
- Product Server's Session Key

Client   Products

Figure 18.3   Session communication.

Working with Hot Fixes and Service Packs

One of the inevitable tasks of administering an operating system as large and complex as Windows 2000 is installing updates. Microsoft provides two different types of updates: hot fixes and service packs (SPs). As one may expect, with an operating system as complex as Windows 2000 (or any other operating system for that matter), flaws, security holes, and bugs will exist. These are fixed using hot fixes and service packs.

Hot fixes are usually used to fix any major bugs or security holes. These are applied individually, but they usually must be applied in a specific order. A list of the currently available hot fixes can be found on the Microsoft Web site.

Service packs are a collection of hot fixes and add-ons. Any time a hot fix is released, it is automatically added to the service pack that will be released next. Service packs also include product enhancements. Some of the utilities and applications that Microsoft was working on for Windows 2000 were either not finished or not stable enough to release with the operating system in February 2000. These utilities and applications are therefore included in the service packs. Many administrators install the service packs to keep ahead of hackers in protecting their operating system from intrusion. What many do not realize is that the service packs are much more than that; they enhance the operating system as well. Service packs can be downloaded from the Microsoft Web site.

The normal steps involved in applying hot fixes and service packs is to install the most recent service pack and then install the hot fixes released after that service pack (known as the *post-SP hot fixes*).

One of the major drawbacks with service packs in the past (with Windows NT) is that a service pack had to be reapplied every time a new application was installed on the system. The reason for this is simple. Suppose the file required.dll, which ships on the Windows 2000 CD, has a security hole in it. The administrator therefore applies a service pack (or hot fix) that replaces required.dll with a fixed version. Next, an application that relies on required.dll is installed. As with many applications, the required.dll file that was used in the creation of the application is also copied to the system. If this required.dll file is the one with the security hole, the fix applied by the service pack or hot fix has been reversed. The service pack or hot fix must therefore be reapplied.

With Windows 2000, Microsoft has come up with a new method of installing service packs to fix this issue. This method is known as *slipstreaming*. Slipstreaming assumes that the Windows 2000 installation files (the i386 directory) exist either on the system or on a network share. An administrator can then apply the service pack to this directory. The service pack will then fix any issues with the original files. Any time files (such as required.dll) are needed, the updated ones will be used from this folder. This effectively means that service packs need only be applied once.

Several command-line switches are available to the administrator when installing service packs. These switches, along with their descriptions, are shown in Table 18.1.

Auditing for Security

Much like in Windows NT, Windows 2000 enables the administrator to control what access is audited by the system. Windows 2000, however, does provide some extra auditing features not found in Windows NT.

Table 18.1   The service pack command-line switches.

Switch	Description
/f	Forces all running applications to shut down before the system is restarted.
/n	Does not back up the current information before installing the service pack. This does not allow the administrator to uninstall the service pack.
/o	Overwrites all original equipment manufacturer (OEM) files without asking the operator for permission.
/q	Runs the service pack installation in quiet mode. No user intervention is required.
/s	Slipstreams the installation.
/u	Runs an unattended service pack installation.
/z	Does not restart the system when the installation of the service pack is completed.

18. Security

Here's a list of the available audit policies:

- Audit account logon events
- Audit account management
- Audit directory service access
- Audit logon events
- Audit object access
- Audit policy change
- Audit privilege use
- Audit process tracking
- Audit system events

It is important to note that enabling some of these policies starts auditing immediately, whereas others are just an intermediary step (as with object access). For example, when an administrator enables the audit policy, an event will be logged in the Security section of the Event Viewer immediately specifying that the audit policy has been modified. On the other hand, no events will be logged when the administrator enables the audit object Access Audit Policy (unless, of course, the audit policy change policy is enabled). Once the audit object access audit policy is enabled, the administrator must selectively specify which users (and/or groups) the policy is to be applied to and which objects should be audited for access.

Auditing is logged as one of two events: a success or a failure. These audit log entries are viewed in the Security Log section of the Event Viewer (see Figure 18.4). Successful audits are displayed with a key icon, whereas failed audits uses a lock icon.

It is important to control what is audited rather than turning all success and failure events on for all audit policies. Even on a rarely used server, turning everything on will overload both the system logs and the administrator who's attempting to go through the log files. Only turn on the audit policies that make sense for your organization. For example, failed logon attempts are much more useful than successful logon events. Also, unauthorized access to your company's confidential information (such as payroll) is more important than unauthorized access to nonsensitive information (such as what is being served for lunch on Thursday). In situations such as this, both the successful and failed attempts should be logged on the sensitive information and no auditing should be logged on the nonsensitive information. This is another reason why object access is audited on a per-object basis rather than an all-or-none basis.

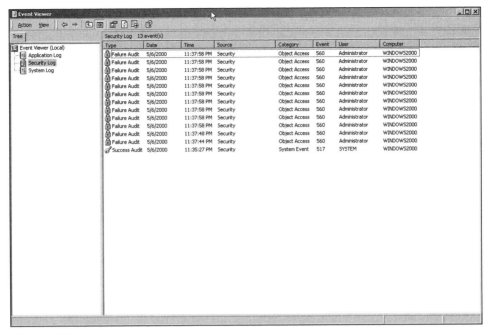

Figure 18.4   Viewing audited events in the Event Viewer.

About Organizational Security Policies

Two tools allow an administrator to control security policies: Local Security Policy and Domain Security Policy. The one used depends on the configuration. Their names are self-explanatory; the first is used to apply security to the local machine, whereas the latter is used to apply security policies to the domain.

Local Security Policy is divided into four sections: account policies (which include password and account lockout policies), local policies (which include audit policies, user rights assignment, and security options), public key policies (which include encrypted data-recovery agents), and IP security policies. Table 18.2 lists all the local policies and their containers.

The second tool, Domain Security Policy, is used to configure the system policies for the entire domain. These policies override the ones set at the local level. Table 18.3 lists all the domain policies and the containers in which they are located.

Table 18.2   Local security policies.

Policy	Location
Enforce password history	Account Policies/password policy
Maximum password age	Account Policies/password policy
Minimum password age	Account Policies/password policy
Minimum password length	Account Policies/password policy
Passwords must meet complexity requirements	Account Policies/password policy
Store passwords using reversible encryption for all users	Account Policies/password policy
Account lockout duration	Account Policies/account lockout policy
Account lockout threshold	Account Policies/account lockout policy
Reset account lockout counter after	Account Policies/account lockout policy
Audit account logon events	Local Policies/audit policy
Audit account management	Local Policies/audit policy
Audit directory service access	Local Policies/audit policy
Audit logon events	Local Policies/audit policy
Audit object access	Local Policies/audit policy
Audit policy change	Local Policies/audit policy
Audit privileged use	Local Policies/audit policy
Audit process tracking	Local Policies/audit policy
Audit system events	Local Policies/audit policy
Access this computer from the network	Local Policies/user rights assignment
Act as part of the operating system	Local Policies/user rights assignment
Add workstations to domain	Local Policies/user rights assignment
Back up files and directories	Local Policies/user rights assignment
Bypass traverse checking	Local Policies/user rights assignment
Change the system time	Local Policies/user rights assignment
Create a pagefile	Local Policies/user rights assignment
Create a token object	Local Policies/user rights assignment
Create permanent shared objects	Local Policies/user rights assignment
Debug programs	Local Policies/user rights assignment
Deny access to this computer from the network	Local Policies/user rights assignment
Deny logon as a batch job	Local Policies/user rights assignment

(continued)

18. Security

Table 18.2   *Local security policies* (continued).

Policy	Location
Deny logon as a service	Local Policies/user rights assignment
Deny logon locally	Local Policies/user rights assignment
Enable computer and user accounts to be trusted	Local Policies/user rights assignment
Force shutdown from a remote system	Local Policies/user rights assignment
Generate security audits	Local Policies/user rights assignment
Increase quotas	Local Policies/user rights assignment
Increase scheduling priority	Local Policies/user rights assignment
Load and unload device drivers	Local Policies/user rights assignment
Lock pages in memory	Local Policies/user rights assignment
Log on as a batch job	Local Policies/user rights assignment
Log on as a service	Local Policies/user rights assignment
Log on locally	Local Policies/user rights assignment
Manage auditing and security log	Local Policies/user rights assignment
Modify firmware environment values	Local Policies/user rights assignment
Profile single process	Local Policies/user rights assignment
Profile system performance	Local Policies/user rights assignment
Remove computer from docking station	Local Policies/user rights assignment
Replace a process level token	Local Policies/user rights assignment
Restore files and directories	Local Policies/user rights assignment
Shut down the system	Local Policies/user rights assignment
Synchronize directory service data	Local Policies/user rights assignment
Take ownership of files or other objects	Local Policies/user rights assignment
Additional restrictions for anonymous connections	Local Policies/security options
Allow server operators to schedule tasks	Local Policies/security options
Allow system to be shut down without having to log on	Local Policies/security options
Allowed to eject removable NTFS media	Local Policies/security options
Amount of idle time required before disconnecting session	Local Policies/security options
Audit the access of global system objects	Local Policies/security options
Audit use of Backup and Restore privilege	Local Policies/security options
Automatically log off users when logon time expires	Local Policies/security options

(continued)

18. Security

***Table 18.2   Local security policies** (continued).*

Policy	Location
Clear virtual memory pagefile when system shuts down	Local Policies/security options
Digitally sign client communication (always)	Local Policies/security options
Digitally sign client communication (when possible)	Local Policies/security options
Digitally sign server communication (always)	Local Policies/security options
Digitally sign server communication (when possible)	Local Policies/security options
Disable Ctrl+Alt+Del requirement for logon	Local Policies/security options
Do not display last username in logon screen	Local Policies/security options
LAN Manager Authentication Level	Local Policies/security options
Message text for users attempting to log on	Local Policies/security options
Message title for users attempting to log on	Local Policies/security options
Number of previous logons to cache	Local Policies/security options
Prevent system maintenance of computer account pwd	Local Policies/security options
Prevent users from installing printer drivers	Local Policies/security options
Prompt user to change password before expiration	Local Policies/security options
Recovery console: Allow automatic administrative logon	Local Policies/security options
Recovery console: Allow floppy copy	Local Policies/security options
Rename administrator account	Local Policies/security options
Rename guest account	Local Policies/security options
Restrict CD-ROM access to locally logged-on user only	Local Policies/security options
Restrict floppy access to locally logged-on user only	Local Policies/security options
Send unencrypted password to connect to 3rd part SMB	Local Policies/security options
Shut down system immediately if unable to log security	Local Policies/security options
Smart card removal behavior	Local Policies/security options
Strengthen default permissions	Local Policies/security options
Unsigned driver installation behavior	Local Policies/security options
Unsigned non-driver installation behavior	Local Policies/security options

18. Security

Table 18.3   *Domain security policies.*

Policy	Location
Enforce password history	Account Policies/password policy
Maximum password age	Account Policies/password policy
Minimum password age	Account Policies/password policy
Minimum password length	Account Policies/password policy
Passwords must meet complexity requirements	Account Policies/password policy
Store passwords using reversible encryption for all users	Account Policies/password policy
Account lockout duration	Account Policies/account lockout policy
Account lockout threshold	Account Policies/account lockout policy
Reset account lockout counter after	Account Policies/account lockout policy
Enforce user logon restrictions	Account Policies/Kerberos policy
Maximum lifetime for service ticket	Account Policies/Kerberos policy
Maximum lifetime for user ticket	Account Policies/Kerberos policy
Maximum lifetime for user ticket renewal	Account Policies/Kerberos policy
Maximum tolerance for computer clock synchronization	Account Policies/Kerberos policy
Audit account logon events	Local Policies/audit policy
Audit account management	Local Policies/audit policy
Audit directory service access	Local Policies/audit policy
Audit logon events	Local Policies/audit policy
Audit object access	Local Policies/audit policy
Audit policy change	Local Policies/audit policy
Audit privileged use	Local Policies/audit policy
Audit process tracking	Local Policies/audit policy
Audit system events	Local Policies/audit policy
Access this computer from the network	Local Policies/user rights assignment
Act as part of the operating system	Local Policies/user rights assignment
Add workstations to domain	Local Policies/user rights assignment
Back up files and directories	Local Policies/user rights assignment
Bypass traverse checking	Local Policies/user rights assignment
Change the system time	Local Policies/user rights assignment
Create a pagefile	Local Policies/user rights assignment
Create a token object	Local Policies/user rights assignment

(continued)

18. Security

Table 18.3   Domain security policies (continued).

Policy	Location
Create permanent shared objects	Local Policies/user rights assignment
Debug programs	Local Policies/user rights assignment
Deny access to this computer from the network	Local Policies/user rights assignment
Deny logon as a batch job	Local Policies/user rights assignment
Deny logon as a service	Local Policies/user rights assignment
Deny logon locally	Local Policies/user rights assignment
Enable computer and user accounts to be trusted	Local Policies/user rights assignment
Force shutdown from a remote system	Local Policies/user rights assignment
Generate security audits	Local Policies/user rights assignment
Increase quotas	Local Policies/user rights assignment
Increase scheduling priority	Local Policies/user rights assignment
Load and unload device drivers	Local Policies/user rights assignment
Lock pages in memory	Local Policies/user rights assignment
Log on as a batch job	Local Policies/user rights assignment
Log on as a service	Local Policies/user rights assignment
Log on locally	Local Policies/user rights assignment
Manage auditing and security log	Local Policies/user rights assignment
Modify firmware environment values	Local Policies/user rights assignment
Profile single process	Local Policies/user rights assignment
Profile system performance	Local Policies/user rights assignment
Remove computer from docking station	Local Policies/user rights assignment
Replace a process-level token	Local Policies/user rights assignment
Restore files and directories	Local Policies/user rights assignment
Shut down the system	Local Policies/user rights assignment
Synchronize directory service data	Local Policies/user rights assignment
Take ownership of files or other objects	Local Policies/user rights assignment
Additional restrictions for anonymous connections	Local Policies/security options
Allow server operators to schedule tasks	Local Policies/security options
Allow system to be shut down without having to log on	Local Policies/security options

(continued)

Table 18.3   ***Domain security policies*** (continued).

Policy	Location
Allowed to eject removable NTFS media	Local Policies/security options
Amount of idle time required before disconnecting session	Local Policies/security options
Audit the access of global system objects	Local Policies/security options
Audit use of Backup and Restore privilege	Local Policies/security options
Automatically log off users when logon time expires	Local Policies/security options
Clear virtual memory pagefile when system shuts down	Local Policies/security options
Digitally sign client communication (always)	Local Policies/security options
Digitally sign client communication (when possible)	Local Policies/security options
Digitally sign server communication (always)	Local Policies/security options
Digitally sign server communication (when possible)	Local Policies/security options
Disable Ctrl+Alt+Del requirement for logon	Local Policies/security options
Do not display last username in logon screen	Local Policies/security options
LAN Manager Authentication Level	Local Policies/security options
Message text for users attempting to log on	Local Policies/security options
Message title for users attempting to log on	Local Policies/security options
Number of previous logons to cache	Local Policies/security options
Prevent system maintenance of computer account pwd	Local Policies/security options
Prevent users from installing printer drivers	Local Policies/security options
Prompt user to change password before expiration	Local Policies/security options
Recovery console: Allow automatic administrative logon	Local Policies/security options
Recovery console: Allow floppy copy	Local Policies/security options
Rename administrator account	Local Policies/security options
Rename guest account	Local Policies/security options
Restrict CD-ROM access to locally logged-on user only	Local Policies/security options
Restrict floppy access to locally logged-on user only	Local Policies/security options
Send unencrypted password to connect to 3rd part SMB	Local Policies/security options
Shut down system immediately if unable to log security	Local Policies/security options
Smart card removal behavior	Local Policies/security options
Strengthen default permissions	Local Policies/security options

(continued)

18. Security

Table 18.3   Domain security policies **(continued).**

Policy	Location
Unsigned driver installation behavior	Local Policies/security options
Unsigned non-driver installation behavior	Local Policies/security options
Maximum application log size	Event Log/Settings for Event Logs
Maximum security log size	Event Log/Settings for Event Logs
Maximum system log size	Event Log/Settings for Event Logs
Restrict guest access to log	Event Log/Settings for Event Logs
Retain application log	Event Log/Settings for Event Logs
Retain security log	Event Log/Settings for Event Logs
Retain system log	Event Log/Settings for Event Logs
Retention method for application log	Event Log/Settings for Event Logs
Retention method for security log	Event Log/Settings for Event Logs
Retention method for system log	Event Log/Settings for Event Logs
Shut down the computer when the security audit log is full	Event Log/Settings for Event Logs

Encrypting File System (EFS)

Encrypting File System (EFS) is a new feature in Windows 2000 that allows users to encrypt their files and directories. This allows users to protect their data without worrying about unauthorized users accessing the data. EFS can only be used on disks formatted as NTFS. This gives Windows 2000 an added level of protection on shared systems.

> **NOTE:**   *With Windows NT, administrators could usually view all files even if they did not have permissions. With EFS, however, these documents are secure from all prying eyes.*

Encrypting and decrypting files is a simple task. In Windows Explorer, simply right-click the object, choose Properties, click Advanced, and check the Encrypt Contents To Secure Data checkbox. Windows 2000 also ships with a command-line utility (cipher.exe) that performs the same task. This tool, however, gives the user more control over what is encrypted/decrypted. The format for the **cipher** command (as shown in the Windows 2000 Help) is as follows:

```
Cipher [/E|/D][/S:dir][/A][/I][/F][/Q][H][/K][path]
```

Table 18.4 lists the command-line switches and their tasks.

Table 18.4   The Cipher command-line switches.

Switch	Description
/A	Encrypts or decrypts files and directories.
/D	Decrypts the specified directory. All files added to the directory will not be encrypted.
/E	Encrypts the specified directory. All files added to the directory will be encrypted.
/F	Forces encryption of all objects, regardless as to whether they have been encrypted before.
/H	Displays all files (including hidden and system files).
/I	Ignores any errors encountered.
/K	Creates a new encryption key for the user.
/Q	Reports only essential information.
/S	Encrypts or decrypts all subdirectories.

Immediate Solutions

Controlling Objects

One of the most common lapses in security involves locking down objects (files, folders, and printers). This section deals with how this is done.

Managing Drive Permissions

To manage drive permissions, perform the following steps:

1. Right-click the desired disk and choose Properties from the pop-up menu.

2. Select the Security tab.

WARNING!   The Security tab will only appear on the drive's Properties dialog box if the disk is formatted with NTFS.

3. To add a user or group, click the Add button, choose the user/group, and assign the desired Allow or Deny permissions (see Figure 18.5).

4. To remove a user or group, select the object to be removed and click Remove.

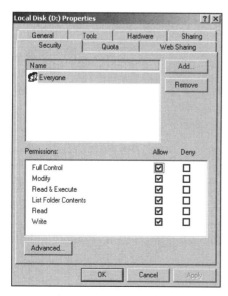

Figure 18.5   Setting disk permissions.

18. Security

5. To view all the permissions individually, enable auditing, or set the disk owner, click Advanced.

6. Click OK to set the permissions.

Managing File Permissions

To manage file permissions, perform the following steps:

1. Right-click the desired file and choose Properties from the pop-up menu.

2. Select the Security tab.

3. To add a user or group, click Add, choose the user/group, and assign the desired Allow or Deny permissions.

4. To remove a user or group, select the object to be removed and click Remove.

5. To view all the permissions individually, enable auditing, or set the file owner, click Advanced.

6. Click OK to set the permissions.

Managing Folder Permissions

To manage folder permissions, perform the following steps:

1. Right-click the desired folder and choose Properties from the pop-up menu.

2. Select the Security tab.

3. To add a user or group, click Add, choose the user/group, and assign the desired Allow or Deny permissions.

4. To remove a user or group, select the object to be removed and click Remove.

5. To view all the permissions individually, enable auditing, or set the folder owner, click Advanced.

6. Click OK to set the permissions.

Managing Shared Folder Permissions

To manage shared folder permissions, perform the following steps:

1. Right-click the desired shared folder and choose Properties from the pop-up menu.

2. Select the Sharing tab.

3. Click Permissions.

4. To add a user or group, click Add, choose the user/group, and assign the desired Allow or Deny permissions.

18. Security

5. To remove a user or group, select the object to be removed and click Remove.

6. Click OK to set the permissions.

7. Click OK to close the folder's Properties dialog box.

NOTE: *If the shared folder resides on an NTFS drive, both share permissions and NTFS permissions apply.*

Managing Printer Permissions

To manage printer permissions, perform the following steps:

1. Right-click the desired printer and choose Properties from the pop-up menu.

2. Select the Security tab.

3. To add a user or group, click Add, choose the users/groups, and assign the desired Allow or Deny permissions.

4. To remove a user or group, select the object to be removed and click Remove.

5. To view all the permissions individually, enable auditing, or set the printer owner, click Advanced.

6. Click OK to set the permissions.

Taking Ownership

To take ownership of an object, perform the following steps:

1. Right-click the desired object and choose Properties from the pop-up menu.

2. Select the Security tab.

3. Click Advanced.

4. Select the Owner tab.

5. Select the user or group that is to become the new owner and click OK.

6. Click OK twice.

Granting Domain Controller Logon Permission

By default, all users are not allowed to log onto the domain controller locally (that is to say, by physically sitting in front of the domain controller). To grant a user the right to log onto a domain controller, perform the following steps:

1. Select Start|Programs|Administrative Tools|Domain Security Policy.

2. Double-click Security Settings in the left pane, expand Local Policies, and select User Rights Assignment.

3. Double-click the Log On Locally policy in the right pane; the Log On Locally Policy window will appear (see Figure 18.6).

4. Mark the Define These Policy Settings checkbox and click Add to add a user or a group.

5. Assign the right to the desired users or groups.

6. Click OK.

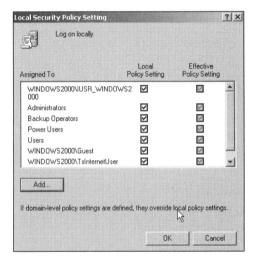

Figure 18.6   The Log On Locally policy.

Using Audit Policies

There are a few issues involved with audit policies. These tasks are discussed in the following sections.

Setting an Audit Policy

To establish an audit policy, perform the following steps:

1. Select Start|Programs|Administrative Tools|Domain Security Policy (or Local Security Policy).

2. Double-click the audit policy to be enforced.

3. Select whether to audit successes, failures, or both (see Figure 18.7). Click OK.

18. Security

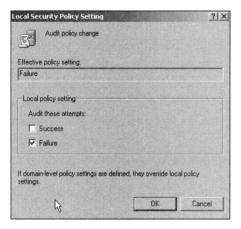

Figure 18.7   Enabling an auditing policy.

Enabling Auditing on Objects

To enable object auditing, perform the following steps:

1. Right-click the object that is to be audited and choose Properties from the pop-up menu.

2. Select the Security tab.

3. Click Advanced (see Figure 18.8).

4. Select the Auditing tab.

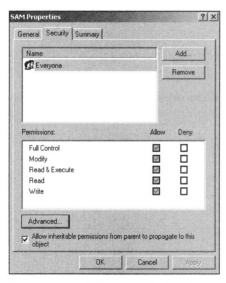

Figure 18.8   Setting permissions to audit an object.

5. To add a user or group, click Add, select the user/group, and select the access to audit. Click OK.

6. To remove a user or group, highlight the user/group and click Remove.

7. Click OK twice.

Viewing the Security Log

To view the security log, perform the following steps:

1. Select Start|Programs|Administrative Tools|Event Viewer.

2. Select the security log to view.

Working with Encryption

A new feature of Windows 2000's NTFS allows users to encrypt their files and folders. The following sections illustrates how this is done.

Encrypting Files and Folders

To encrypt files and folders, perform the following steps:

1. Right-click the file or folder to be encrypted and choose Properties from the pop-up menu.

2. Click Advanced.

3. Check the Encrypt Contents To Secure Data checkbox.

4. Click OK twice.

Encrypting Files from the Command Prompt

To encrypt files from the command prompt, perform the following steps:

1. Select Start|Programs|Accessories|Command Prompt.

2. Navigate to the folder where the files to be encrypted are located.

3. Type "cipher /e *filename*" and press Enter.

Encrypting Folders from the Command Prompt

To encrypt folders from the command prompt, perform the following steps:

1. Select Start|Programs|Accessories|Command Prompt.

2. Navigate to the folder where the files to be encrypted are located.

3. Type "cipher /e *folder*" and press Enter.

Decrypting Files and Folders

To decrypt files and folders, perform the following steps:

1. Right-click the file or folder to be decrypted and choose Properties from the pop-up menu.

2. Click Advanced.

3. Clear the Encrypt Contents To Secure Data checkbox.

4. Click OK twice.

Encrypting Remote Files and Folders

To encrypt remote files and folders, perform the following steps:

1. Map a drive to the location of a remote file or folder.

2. Right-click the file or folder to be encrypted and choose Properties from the pop-up menu.

3. Click Advanced.

4. Check the Encrypt Contents To Secure Data checkbox.

5. Click OK twice.

Decrypting Files from the Command Prompt

To decrypt files from the command prompt, perform the following steps:

1. Select Start|Programs|Accessories|Command Prompt.

2. Navigate to the folder where the files to be decrypted are located.

3. Type "cipher /d *filename*" and press Enter.

Decrypting Folders from the Command Prompt

To decrypt folders from the command prompt, perform the following steps:

1. Select Start|Programs|Accessories|Command Prompt.

2. Navigate to the folder where the folders to be decrypted are located.

3. Type "cipher /d *folder*" and press Enter.

Displaying Encryption/Decryption Information from the Command Prompt

To display encryption/decryption information from the command prompt, perform the following steps:

1. Select Start|Programs|Accessories|Command Prompt.

2. Navigate to the folder where the folders to be decrypted are located.

3. Type **cipher** and press Enter.

NOTE: *Any encrypted object will show the letter* E *in the left column, whereas unencrypted files will show the letter* U.

Decrypting Remote Files and Folders

To decrypt remote files and folders, perform the following steps:

1. Map a drive to the location of a remote file or folder.

2. Right-click the file or folder to be decrypted and choose Properties from the pop-up menu.

3. Click Advanced.

4. Clear the Encrypt Contents to Secure Data checkbox.

5. Click OK twice.

Using Group Policy to Delegate Recovery

To use Group Policy to delegate recovery, perform the following steps:

1. Select Start|Programs|Administrative Tools|Group Policy.

2. Navigate to Computer Configuration|Windows Settings|Security Settings|Public Key Policies.

3. Right-click Encrypted Data Recovery Agents and choose Add from the pop-up menu.

4. When the Add Recovery Agent Wizard window appears, click Next.

5. If the recovery certificates are located on the file system, click Browse Folders, navigate to the location, and click OK.

6. If the recovery certificates are located in Active Directory, click Browse Directory, navigate to the container, and click OK.

7. Repeat Step 5 or 6 for any additional recovery agents.

8. Click Next.

9. Click Finish.

Adding a Recovery Agent for the Local Computer

To add a recovery agent for the local computer, perform the following steps:

1. Select Start|Run.

2. Type "MMC" and click OK.

3. Choose Console|Add/Remove Snap-In.

18. Security

4. Click Add.

5. Select Group Policy.

6. Click Add.

7. Click Browse.

8. Ensure that the This Computer radio button is selected and click OK.

9. Click Finish.

10. Click Close.

11. Click OK.

12. Expand Local Computer Policy.

13. Expand Computer Configuration.

14. Expand Windows Settings.

15. Expand Security Settings.

16. Expand Public Key Policies.

17. Right-click Encrypted Data Recovery Agents and select Add from the pop-up menu.

18. Click Add.

19. When the Add Recovery Agent Wizard appears, click Next.

20. Click Browse Folders.

21. Navigate to the CER file and click OK.

22. Click Next.

23. Click Finish.

Changing the Recovery Policy for the Local Computer

To change the recovery policy for the local computer, perform the following steps:

1. Select Start|Run.

2. Type "MMC" and click OK.

3. Choose Console|Add/Remove Snap-In.

4. Click Add.

5. Select Group Policy.

6. Click Add.

7. Click Browse.

8. Ensure that the This Computer radio button is selected and click OK.

9. Click Finish.

10. Click Close.

11. Click OK.

12. Expand Local Computer Policy.

13. Expand Computer Configuration.

14. Expand Windows Settings.

15. Expand Security Settings.

16. Expand Public Key Policies.

17. Right-click Encrypted Data Recovery Agents and select Delete Policy from the pop-up menu.

18. Click Yes.

Adding an Encrypted Data Recovery Agent for a Group Policy Object.

To add an encrypted data recovery agent for a Group Policy object, perform the following steps:

1. Select Start|Programs|Administrative Tools|Group Policy.

2. Expand Local Computer Policy.

3. Expand Computer Configuration.

4. Expand Windows Settings.

5. Expand Security Settings.

6. Expand Public Key Policies.

7. Right-click Encrypted Data Recovery Agents and select Add from the pop-up menu.

8. Click Add.

9. When the Add Recovery Agent Wizard appears, click Next.

10. Click Browse Folders.

11. Navigate to the CER file and click OK.

12. Click Next.

13. Click Finish.

Working with Security Templates

Windows 2000 has some MMC snap-ins available to the administrator for setting security policies. These tools must be configured the first time (as shown in the first solution). The following solutions all assume that this MMC snap-in is created.

Starting the Security Templates Snap-In

To enable the Security Templates snap-in, perform the following steps:

1. Select Start|Run.
2. Enter "MMC" in the Open field and click OK.
3. Select Console|Add/Remove Snap-In.
4. Click Add.
5. Select Security Templates and click Add.
6. Select Security Configuration And Analysis.
6. Click Close.
7. Click OK.
8. Select Console|Save.
9. Enter a desired name and click Save.

Modifying an Existing Security Template

To modify a security template, perform the following steps:

1. Select the Security Templates snap-in configured previously.
2. Double-click the default path folder.
3. Right-click the security template to be modified and choose Save As from the pop-up menu.
4. Enter a name for the template and click Save.
5. Double-click the newly created template.
6. Make the desired modifications.

Creating a New Security Template

To create a security template, perform the following steps:

1. Select the Security Templates snap-in configured previously.
2. Right-click the default path folder and choose New Template from the pop-up menu.

3. Enter a name and description for the new security template and click OK.

4. Double-click the newly created security template.

5. Make any desired modifications.

Deleting a Security Template

To delete a security template, perform the following steps:

1. Select the Security Templates snap-in configured previously.

2. Right-click the security template to be deleted and choose Delete.

3. Click Yes to confirm the deletion.

Applying a Security Template

To apply a security template, perform the following steps:

1. Select the Security Templates snap-in configured previously.

2. Right-click Security Configuration And Analysis and choose Open Database from the pop-up menu.

3. Enter a name for the database and click Open.

4. Select Import Template.

5. Right-click Security Configuration And Analysis and choose Configure System Now.

Working with Service Packs

There are a few issues involved in the management of service packs. The following sections discuss these tasks.

Installing a Service Pack

To install a service pack, perform the following steps:

1. Select Start|Run.

2. Enter the path to the service pack (either a CD or the network) and click OK.

3. The Windows 2000 Service Pack Setup screen will appear (see Figure 18.9). Accept the license agreement by checking the Accept The License Agreement checkbox and then click Install.

4. If the Uninstall feature of the service pack is required, check the Backup Files Necessary To Uninstall This Service Pack At A Later Time checkbox and click Install.

18. Security

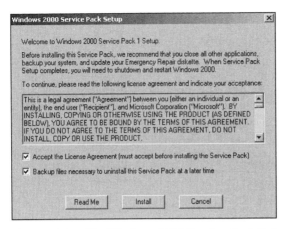

Figure 18.9   The Windows 2000 Service Pack Setup window.

NOTE: *If enough space exists on your hard drive, the setup program will automatically back up the required information.*

---

5. Click Restart to restart the system.

Installing a Service Pack Using Slipstreaming

To install a service pack using slipstreaming, perform the following steps:

1. Select Start|Run.

2. Enter "*drive:\i386\update\update.exe /s:installfolder*" (where *drive* is the CD drive where the service pack exists and *installfolder* is the location of the Windows 2000 installation files).

3. Click OK. Figure 18.10 illustrates the slipstream process.

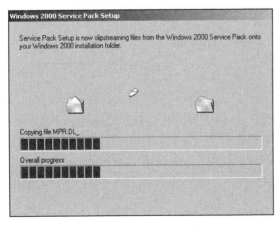

Figure 18.10   Slipstreaming a service pack.

Uninstalling a Service Pack

To uninstall a service pack, perform the following steps:

1. Select Start|Settings|Control Panel.

2. Double-click Add/Remove Programs.

3. Select the service pack to be removed and click Change/Remove.

4. Click Yes to uninstall the service pack.

Chapter 19

Remote Access and
Windows 2000

In Depth

Windows 2000 offers a wide range of remote access options, including dial-up, dial-out, VPN (virtual private networking), and Terminal Services. These options and abilities expand the type of clients that can be used in a Windows 2000 environment as well as the physical range of clients that can connect to a Windows 2000 network.

Remote Control versus Remote Access

Remote control and remote access are two technologies that are often confused or improperly used interchangeably. *Remote control* is the function of taking over control of a remote system using a keyboard, monitor, and mouse. *Remote access* is the function of establishing a network connection between two systems so normal network activities can take place.

Using remote control, the local system's functions are all sent to the remote system where they actually control the system. The local system is often called a *dumb terminal* because it does no actual processing but instead just relays the I/O from keyboard, mouse, and monitor to and from the remote system.

Using remote access, the local system's functions control the local system and network resources can be requested over the remote access link. The local system retains all its normal capabilities and still performs all local processing. Remote access grants a true network connection with distant clients. Remote control gives distant clients control over a system. Remote access clients can establish network connections over WAN links (phone, Integrated Services Digital Network [ISDN], cable modem, Asymmetric Digital Subscriber Line [ADSL], and so on). Remote control clients must use an existing network connection (either direct cable connection or preestablished remote access connection).

Terminal Services

Terminal Services is a Windows 2000 service that's more like remote control than it is remote access. Terminal Services enables thin clients (or computers with low capabilities) to make a remote control-like connection with a server. The terminal clients don't actually take over control of the server but are logged into the server and presented with their own desktop environment. Terminal Services allows thin clients to take advantage of the powerful features and applications of

Windows 2000 without having Windows 2000 installed locally. Terminal clients can employ either a direct cable connection to the network or a preestablished remote access connection to the network to gain communication with the Terminal Services server.

Terminal Services is an add-on component for Windows 2000 Server that's used to support terminal clients. Terminal clients are network devices that perform little or no processing locally but rather simply exchange I/O from keyboard, mouse, and monitor with the Terminal Services server. This allows the power of Windows 2000 and applications to be accessed from devices without having Windows 2000 installed locally (see Figure 19.1). Terminal Services supports all the Microsoft Windows operating systems as clients, plus many non-Windows platforms, such as the Apple Macintosh, MS-DOS, and Unix, when running a third-party client product. Therefore, as a Terminal Services client, even a Macintosh system can exploit the power of Windows 2000.

The types of systems that can be used as Terminal Service clients are:

• Windows CE-based terminals and handheld professional devices (H/PC Pro).

• 32-bit Windows-based computers supporting Windows 95, Windows 98, Windows NT 3.51 Server, Windows NT 3.51 Workstation, Windows NT 4.0 Server, Windows NT 4.0 Workstation, or Windows 2000 Professional.

• 16-bit Windows-based computers supporting Windows for Workgroups 3.11 with MS TCP/IP-32.

• Any non-Windows platforms, including Apple Macintosh, MS-DOS, Linux, and Unix, supporting a third-party terminal client product, such as that available from Citrix (**www.citrix.com**).

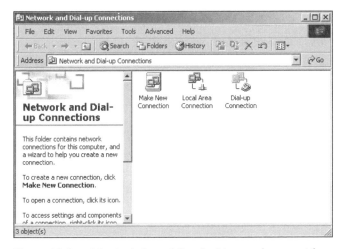

Figure 19.1   A typical view of the desktop environment from a Terminal Services client.

Terminal Services can be deployed for numerous specific purposes, including remote administration, remote access, line-of-business applications, and centralized desktop management. Each of these purposes requires different features or capabilities from Windows 2000 Server and the licensing manager (see Table 19.1).

NOTE: *This table is extracted from the Windows 2000 Server Resource Kit.*

Terminal Services can be used in one of two ways: in remote administration mode or application server mode. System management and administration tasks can be performed from any terminal client when remote administration mode is employed. This is the only mode currently supported by cluster servers. Central access to applications and resources from any terminal client is supported by the application server mode. Unfortunately, these modes are mutually exclusive. Terminal Services is managed through four tools added to the Administrative Tools: Terminal Services Client Creator, Terminal Services Configuration, Terminal Services Licensing, and Terminal Services Manager.

The basic process of deploying Terminal Services is as follows:

1. Install Terminal Services on a Windows 2000 Server. This can be performed at the same time the main OS is being installed or at any point after the main OS has been installed.

2. To configure Terminal Services clients, you must install the client software on those systems. This can be performed in at least two ways: You can use the Terminal Services Client Creator to create client software installation disks, or you can create a network distribution point where the client installation software is stored and accessible from all network clients.

3. Create client-based connection profiles.

Table 19.1   *Terminal Server functions and feature requirements.*

Feature	Remote Administration	Remote Access Application	Line of Business	Centralized Desktop Deployment
Domain structure	Yes	No	Yes	Yes
License server	No	Yes	Yes	Yes
Licensing	No	Yes	Yes	Yes
Load balancing	No	Yes	Yes	Yes
Local printing	Yes	Yes	Yes	Yes
Roaming profiles	No	Yes	No	No
Security	Yes	Yes	Yes	Yes

4. Configure the Terminal Services server.

5. Establish a terminal session.

The Terminal Services Client Creator utility, shown in Figure 19.2, is very straight-forward. Select whether to build client installation disks for 16-bit Windows or for 32-bit Windows, indicate the destination floppy drive, select whether to format the disks, and click OK to initiate the creation. Keep in mind that 16-bit Windows client installation software requires four floppies, whereas 32-bit Windows client installation software requires only two floppies.

Installing the client software from either floppies or a network distribution point requires that the setup.exe file be launched. You'll need to agree to the license agreement and then answer a few system-specific prompts. Once these tasks are completed, the computer will be able to connect to Terminal Services.

Terminal Services server configuration is performed using the Terminal Services Configuration utility (see Figure 19.3). There is only a single native connection type, namely Microsoft RDP (Remote Desktop Protocol) 5.0. This tool is used to configure each connection type's settings and server-related properties. Connection type settings include control over encryption level, session timeouts, program launch on session initialization, remote control options, client drive and printer mappings, network adapter controls, session permissions, and logon credential management. Server-related property controls include deleting temporary folders on session termination, allowing Internet access from sessions, supporting Active Desktop within sessions, and whether permissions are compatible with just Windows 2000 or all possible terminal clients.

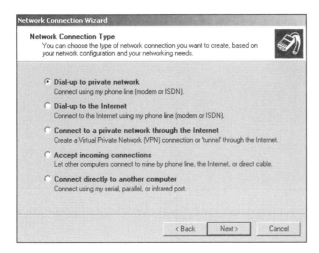

Figure 19.2   The Terminal Server Client Creator utility.

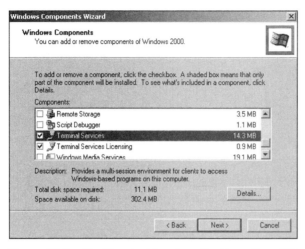

Figure 19.3   The Terminal Services Configuration utility.

Connection-specific configuration settings are accessed through the Connections node of the Terminal Services Configuration tool. Select the connection and issue the Properties command from the Action menu to view the Properties dialog box for that connection. This eight-tabbed configuration dialog box, shown in Figure 19.4, offers the following configuration controls:

- *Encryption Level*—Used to configure the level of encryption used by the client and server. Settings are Low, Medium, and High.

- *Logon Credentials*—Used to configure how client sessions are authenticated. Options include unique credentials for each user or to authenticate all sessions

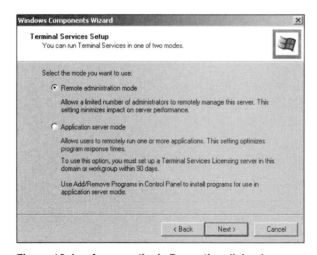

Figure 19.4   A connection's Properties dialog box.

through a single user account. Also configure if a password is required to grant access even when a shared user account is employed for authentication.

- *Session Timeouts*—Used to configure the length of time a session can continue. Timeout values for inactive and active sessions can be determined from either the client or the server side of the connection.

- *Launch Program*—Used to configure whether a program or batch file is launched at the start of each session and whether to allow desktop wallpaper.

- *Remote Control*—Used to configure the ability to control or observe a connected session. Also used to configure whether the user of a session must approve before administrative control or observation can occur.

- *Client Settings*—Used to configure whether to retain and use a client's settings for network drive mappings and printers. Also used to configure whether to disable network drive, printer, LPT port, COM port, Clipboard, and audio mappings.

- *Network Adapter*—Used to configure which network interfaces can be used by Terminal Services and the number of sessions that can occur over that NIC.

- *Permissions*—Used to configure which users and groups can establish Terminal Services sessions and what level of access these sessions will be assigned: Full Control, User Access, or Guest Access.

Server-specific configuration settings are listed under the Server Settings node. These elements are:

- *Terminal Server Mode*—Displays the mode of the Terminal Services server; it will display either remote administration or application server. This cannot be changed without removing and reinstalling Terminal Services.

- *Delete Temporary Folders On Exit*—Used to configure whether to remove temporary files and folders on Terminal Services shutdown. The default is Yes.

- *Use Temporary Folders Per Session*—Used to configure whether to remove temporary files and folders each time a session is terminated. The default is Yes.

- *Internet Connector Licensing*—Used to configure the sharing of Windows-based software with up to 200 Internet-connected users. This feature requires specific-use licenses and is set to Disable by default.

- *Active Desktop*—Used to configure whether to allow Active Desktop during Terminal Services sessions. This is set to Enable by default. To conserve server resources, set it to Disable.

- *Permission Compatibility*—Used to configure whether to use permissions that are specific to Windows 2000 only or that are compatible with any possible Terminal Services client. This is configured to the latter option by default.

User licensing and license management is required to deploy Terminal Services in Application Server mode. The Terminal Services Licensing utility, shown in Figure 19.5, is used to perform this function. You'll need to contact a Microsoft license distributor with this tool to activate your user licenses. Windows 2000 includes the Terminal Services software, but it does not include any actual use licenses. You are granted a 90-day grace period to obtain your licenses before you'll be operating in violation of the purchase and license agreement from Microsoft. If you'll be using Terminal Services in remote administration mode, there is a limit of two users, but licenses are not required. However, if you'll be using Terminal Services in application server mode, you can have an unlimited number of users, and licenses are required for each user.

The Terminal Services Manager, shown in Figure 19.6, is used to manage active terminal client sessions. This tool is also used to initiate remote control of other terminal sessions when it is launched by an administrator from a terminal session. You can quickly view details about sessions, users, servers, and session processes, and you can send messages to sessions, terminate active sessions, terminate processes within sessions, and reset connection protocols.

When Terminal Services is installed, several of the native Windows 2000 management utilities are enhanced to control Terminal Services-specific capabilities and features:

- *Active Directory Users And Computers (Windows 2000 Server) and Local Users And Groups (Windows 2000 Professional)*—These tools are enhanced to offer user account controls specific to Terminal Services sessions. These

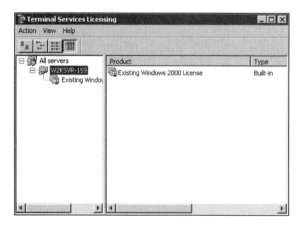

Figure 19.5   The Terminal Services License utility.

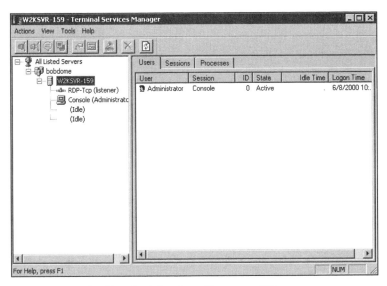

Figure 19.6   The Terminal Services Manager utility.

new controls include Terminal Services user profiles, logon enablement, session timeouts, reconnection procedures, remote control capability, application launch at session startup, and retaining of mapped drives and printers.

- *System Monitor*—The User object and Session object are added to this performance-monitoring tool so that Terminal Service session-specific activities can be monitored. Also, the Process and System objects are enhanced with several Terminal Server-specific counters.

- *Task Manager*—Two new process information optional columns are added to the Processes tab, namely Session ID and User Name. Plus, the ability to terminate all processes associated with all Terminal Services sessions is added.

- *Add/Remove Programs*—This application-installation tool has been enhanced to support the installation of software used on multisession environments.

Most of the functions of Terminal Services can be performed using command-line tools.

Terminal Services can share applications specifically designed for multiuser environments as well as those that are not. However, if Terminal Services is ever disabled and then reenabled, some programs will need to be reinstalled to function properly. Also, keep the use of Win16 applications within Terminal Services sessions to a minimum because the overhead required to support Win16 applications reduces the capabilities of a server to support multiple sessions by 40 percent and the amount of memory used by each session increases by 50 percent.

Troubleshooting Terminal Services involves employing one or more of the following tactics:

- Double-check configuration settings on the Terminal Services server and all terminal clients.

- Reboot the Terminal Services server system.

- Check the Properties dialog boxes of user accounts that use Terminal Services. The last four tabs configure session details.

- Check that users have proper permissions to establish terminal sessions and access resources.

- Automatic logon will not function for Windows NT clients; therefore, manual logon is required.

- If an application fails to operate correctly, after rebooting the Terminal Server, remove then reinstall the application.

- You cannot use both Offline Files and Terminal Services at the same time; these services are mutually exclusive.

More information on Terminal Services and its use in a Windows 2000 network are discussed in the *Windows 2000 Server Resource Kit* and the original manuals.

Remote Access

Remote access allows Windows 2000 to serve as a network router, Internet connection proxy, a VPN sever, or a dial-in/dial-out server. Some of the features of the Remote Access Service (RAS) are:

- A wide range of clients, including Windows 2000, Windows NT, Windows 95/98, Windows for Workgroups, MS-DOS (with Microsoft network client software installed), and LAN Manager. Plus, any client that supports PPP.

- Supports PPP for inbound connections. Can employ PPP or SLIP for outbound connections. PPP can tunnel TCP/IP, NWLink, and NetBEUI. ARAP (AppleTalk Remote Access Protocol) is also supported for inbound connections from Macintosh clients.

- VPN is supported through PPTP or L2TP.

- Supports most WAN connectivity technologies, including phone line, ISDN, T-carrier lines, ASDL, and more. Also supports X.25, ATM, and RS-232C null modem connections.

- Supports channel aggregation through Multilink PPP.

- Integrated with Windows 2000 logon, domain, and file-level security.

- Dial-up connections can be protected with callback security.

- Supports restartable file copy for failed transfers caused by disconnection.

- Supports idle disconnect.

- Supports autodial, log-on dial, and dial-on-demand.

Remote access is a default component of Windows 2000 that's integrated into the networking capabilities and is therefore a required component even if you do not employ its special remote access capabilities. Remote access connections are managed through the Network And Dial-Up Connections utility (see Figure 19.7). See Chapter 8 for general (non-RAS-specific) interface information on this tool.

All RAS connection objects must be created manually. This is done by double-clicking the Make New Connection icon in the Network And Dial-Up Connections applet (see Figure 19.8).

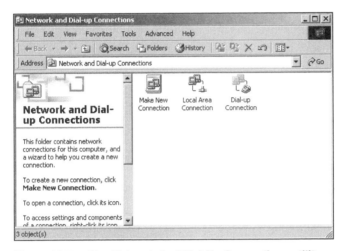

Figure 19.7   The Network And Dial-Up Connections utility.

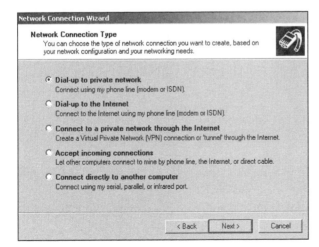

Figure 19.8   The Network Connection Wizard.

This tool is used to create the following types of remote connections:

- *Dial-Up To Private Network*—Creates a connection object to link with a Windows 2000 or Windows NT RAS server

- *Dial-Up To The Internet*—Creates a connection object to link with an Internet Service Provider (ISP) for Internet access

- *Connect To A Private Network Through The Internet*—Creates a connection object to establish a virtual private network (VPN) link using Point-to-Point Tunneling Protocol (PPTP) or Layer 2 Tunneling Protocol (L2TP)

- *Accept Incoming Connections*—Creates a connection object to configure the system to accept inbound connections

- *Connect Directly To Another Computer*—Creates a connection object to establish a communications link over a serial cable, parallel cable, or infrared port

The Network Connection Wizard is very easy to use. However, it only prompts for minimal unique information. To alter the defaults and customize a connection object, you'll need to open that object's Properties dialog box. The properties for each object type are discussed in the following sections.

Dial-Up To Private Network

The Dial-Up To Private Network connection object is used to dial up to a Windows 2000 or Windows NT RAS server to establish a network connection. Once connected, you can participate in any normal network activity (access files and printers, gain proxied Internet access, and so on) with only the speed of your connection to be concerned about. Also, when this connection object is in use, an icon of two overlapping monitors will appear in the icon tray. Double-clicking this icon opens the connection's status page, where you can see information about the link.

The Properties dialog box for a Dial-Up To Private Network connection object has five tabs: General, Options, Security, Networking, and Sharing. The General tab, shown in Figure 19.9, is used to configure the following:

- Connect using one or more select devices

NOTE: *Multilink is enabled simply by selecting two or more devices and providing the necessary phone numbers.*

- A checkbox to set all devices to dial the same phone number

- A Configure button to access the Properties dialog box for the selected device

- Provide the area code, phone number, and country/region codes for dialing

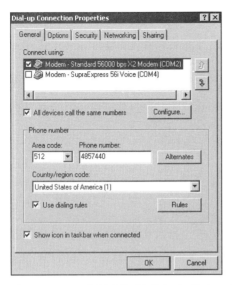

Figure 19.9   A Dial-Up To Private Network connection object's General tab.

- Define alternate phone numbers in case of busy signals or failure to connect
- Enable and define dialing rules
- A checkbox to enable the Connection icon in the Taskbar

The Options tab, shown in Figure 19.10, is used to configure the following:

- Enable/Disable The Display Progress While Connecting checkbox
- Enable/Disable The Prompt For Name And Password, Certificate, Etc. checkbox
- Enable/Disable The Include Windows Logon Domain checkbox
- Enable/Disable The Prompt For Phone Number checkbox
- Number Of Redial Attempts
- Time Between Redial Attempts
- Idle Time Before Hanging Up
- A Checkbox To Redial If Line Is Dropped
- Multiple-device dialing preferences, where the selections are Dial Only First Available Device, Dial All Devices, and Dial Devices Only As Needed Based On Custom Levels Of Bandwidth Usage (see Figure 19.11).
- Access X.25 controls

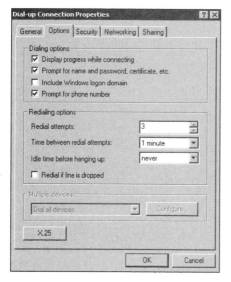

Figure 19.10   A Dial-Up To Private Network connection object's Options tab.

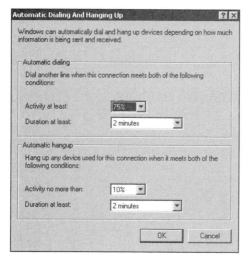

Figure 19.11   The Automatic Dialing And Hanging Up dialog box.

The Security tab, shown in Figure 19.12, is used to configure the following:

- Select whether to use typical (recommended) settings or advanced (custom) settings for security.

- Typical settings include: allow unsecured password, require secured password, and use smart card.

- When secured passwords are required, automatic use of the local/network logon name and password can be enabled.

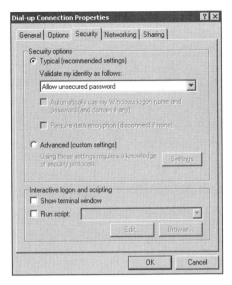

Figure 19.12   A Dial-Up To Private Network connection object's Security tab.

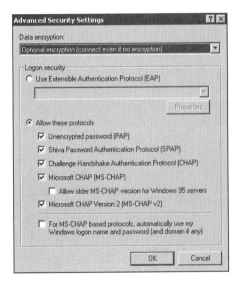

Figure 19.13   The Advanced Security Settings dialog box.

- When either secured passwords or smart cards are required, the requirement for data encryption can be enabled.

- Custom settings, shown in Figure 19.13, can employ custom or native authentication encryption schemes and can require data encryption.

- A checkbox to display a terminal window upon connection.

- Configure an automated logon script. Sample scripts are included with Windows 2000 in the %systemroot%\System32\RAS\ folder. These sample scripts can be customized for your own needs using any text editor.

The Networking tab, shown in Figure 19.14, is used to configure the following:

- Set the server type being connected to: PPP or SLIP.
- Via the Settings button, enable LCP extensions, software compression, and negotiate multilink as needed by the remote server.
- Bind network components to this connection object as needed.
- Install or uninstall networking components (applies to all networking objects).
- Click the Properties button to configure the selected network component.

The Sharing tab, shown in Figure 19.15, is used to configure the following:

- Whether to enable Internet Connection Sharing for this connection object
- Whether to enable on-demand dialing for this connection object when shared

Dial-Up To The Internet

The Dial-Up To The Internet connection object is used to establish a link with an ISP to obtain Internet access. This object can be configured to create a new MSN account, transfer an existing MSN account to this system, connect to the Internet via a modem, or connect to the Internet over a LAN. The Properties dialog box for this type of connection object is the same as a Dial-Up To Private Network connection object.

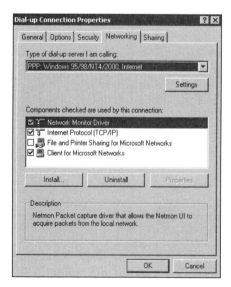

Figure 19.14   A Dial-Up To Private Network connection object's Networking tab.

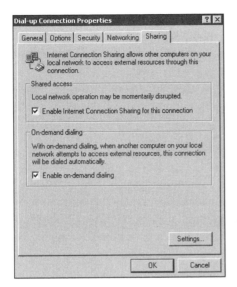

Figure 19.15   A Dial-Up To Private Network connection object's Sharing tab.

See Chapter 6 for more information about Internet access, utilities, and services related to Windows 2000.

Connect To A Private Network Through The Internet

The Connect To A Private Network Through The Internet connection object is used to establish a VPN connection over the Internet using PPTP or L2TP. VPN connections encrypt all data transferred between the client and server as well as enable long-distance connections without the associated long-distance charges. The RAS server you are connecting to must have an Accept Incoming Connections connection object properly defined to accept your connection.

The Properties dialog box for this connection object type is similar to the previous two objects. The General tab sets the domain name or IP address of the VPN server and whether to connect to the Internet via an alternate connection object first. The Options tab sets dialing options and redial (reattempt) parameters. The Security tab sets the security requirements for the connection. The Networking tab sets the VPN server type to automatic, PPTP, or L2TP, and it binds available network components to this object. The Sharing tab enables Internet Connection Sharing and on-demand dialing for this connection.

Accept Incoming Connections

The Accept Incoming Connections connection object is used to transform a system into a RAS server that accepts inbound connections from VPN, ISDN, X.25, telephone lines, or direct cable mediums.

The Properties dialog box for this type of connection has three tabs: General, Users, and Networking. The General tab sets the devices or connection types that can accept inbound calls and whether to allow VPN connections. The Users tab sets which users have permission to connect to this RAS server, as well as configures user-specific security settings (such as callback). The Networking tab sets the binding for networking components to this object.

Connect Directly To Another Computer

The Connect Directly To Another Computer connection object is used to create a link between two systems without using network interface cards (NICs). This type of connection can take place over a serial cable, a parallel cable, or infrared (IR) ports. Before creating this link, go ahead and attach the cable or orient the IR ports. You'll need to create one of these objects on each system, selecting one to be the host (server) and the other to be the guest (client).

The Properties dialog box for the host connection object is the same as an Accept Incoming Connections connection object. The Properties dialog box for the guest connection object is the same as a Dial-Up To Private Network connection object.

Phone And Modem Options

The Phone And Modem Options applet in the Control Panel is used to manage location-based dialing rules, configure modems, and add/remove/configure the Telephony Application Programming Interface (TAPI) service providers. Location-based dialing rules are profiles used by dial-out connection objects to define how to establish a communication link over standard telephone lines. These profiles include settings such as area code, open line prefix, disable call-waiting, and make credit card calls. The ability to manage modem configurations is the same as that found in the Device Manager. Managing TAPI services is usually unnecessary because they offer few user settings and are installed automatically based on connection types.

Immediate Solutions

Installing Terminal Services

To support terminal clients, Terminal Services must be installed on a Windows 2000 Server system. This can be performed during initial installation of the OS, through the Configure Your Server Wizard, or via the Control Panel (as described here):

NOTE: *Windows 2000 Server is required for this solution.*

1. Log into the system as Administrator.
2. Open the Control Panel and double-click the Add/Remove Programs applet.
3. Click the Add/Remove Windows Components button.
4. Click Next.
5. Locate and select Terminal Services from the list of components.
6. If you will be using Terminal Services in Applications Server mode, you should also select Terminal Services Licensing (see Figure 19.16).
7. Click Next.

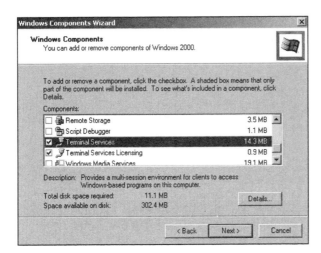

Figure 19.16   Installing Terminal Services and Terminal Services Licensing.

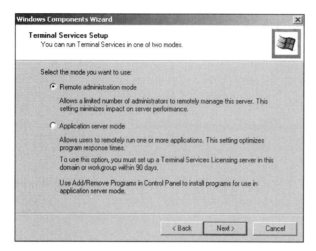

Figure 19.17   Selecting the Terminal Services mode.

8. Select whether to use Terminal Services in Remote administration mode or Application server mode (see Figure 19.17).

9. Click Next.

10. Select whether Terminal Services will use permissions exclusive to Windows 2000 or employ permissions compatible with any Terminal Services-compatible client (see Figure 19.18).

11. Click Next.

12. The wizard displays a list of possible problematic applications (see Figure 19.19). Review this list.

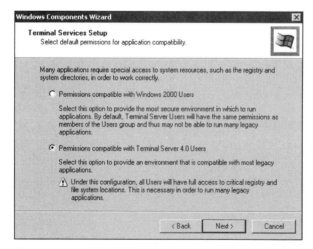

Figure 19.18   Selecting the Terminal Services user permissions.

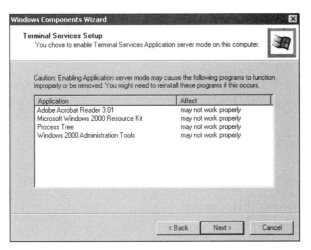

Figure 19.19   Identifying applications that may cause problems with Terminal Services.

13. Click Next.

14. Select whether to make the license server available only to this domain or workgroup or to the entire enterprise (see Figure 19.20). (This item only appears if Terminal Services Licensing was selected.)

15. Click Next.

16. Provide the Windows 2000 Server CD-ROM when/if prompted.

17. When prompted, click Finish.

18. When prompted, reboot the system.

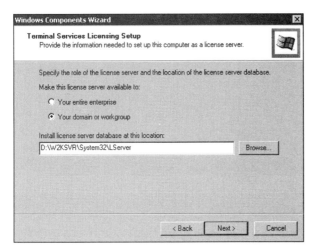

Figure 19.20   Selecting the Terminal Services licensing setup.

Creating a Network Distribution Point for Terminal Services

A *network distribution* point is a shared folder where the client software installation files reside. To create a network distribution point, perform the following steps:

1. Launch Windows Explorer or My Computer.

2. Locate and select the %systemroot%\system32\clients\tsclient\net folder. This was created automatically by the Terminal Services installation.

3. Click the File menu and select Sharing.

4. Select the Share This Folder radio button and define a share name, such as "TSClients".

5. Click the Permissions button. Change the Everyone group's permissions to Read Only (that is, deselect the Full Control and Modify permissions). Click OK.

6. Click OK.

Creating Terminal Services Installation Disk Sets

If a terminal client-to-be device is not already connected to the network or is unable to access the network distribution point, you can create a set of installation floppies. To create Terminal Services installation disks, perform the following steps:

1. Gather floppies. Four disks are required for the 16-bit client. Two disks are required for the 32-bit client.

2. Launch the Terminal Services Client Creator tool from Administrative Tools.

3. Select either the 16-bit client or the 32-bit client.

4. Select the correct letter for the floppy drive.

5. Select whether to format the disks.

6. Click OK.

7. Follow the prompts to insert the disks.

8. As you remove the disks, be sure to label them properly (for example, Terminal Services client 16-bit disk 1/4).

Installing the Terminal Services Client Software

To install the client software for Terminal Services, perform the following steps:

NOTE: *This solution can only be performed for Windows 95/98/NT/2000 clients. Special instructions are included in the Windows 2000 Resource Kit and the Windows 2000 manuals for installing the client software on Windows CE clients.*

1. If you want to install from a floppy set, place the first disk in the floppy drive.

2. Open the **run** command by clicking the Start menu and selecting Run.

3. Click the Browse button.

4. Locate the setup.exe file from either the local floppy or the network distribution point (this is the share named TSClients from an earlier solution).

5. Agree to the license agreement.

6. Select to install the software for all users.

Connecting to a Terminal Services Server from a Terminal Services Client

The whole purpose of the Terminal Services client software is to establish communication sessions with the Terminal Services server. This can be accomplished in two ways: Either use the Terminal Services client from Administrative Tools to connect immediately or create a connection profile with unique settings and then employ that profile to connect. Here are the steps to follow:

1. Launch the Client Connection Manager.

2. Click the File menu and select New Connection.

3. Click Next.

4. Define a name for the connection profile and then provide the server name or IP address of the terminal server.

5. Click Next.

6. Select whether to enable automatic logon for this connection profile. If this is enabled, provide the user account logon credentials.

7. Click Next.

8. Select a screen resolution and whether to display the connection full screen. Click Next.

9. Select whether to enable data compression and/or caching of bitmaps. Click Next.

10. Select if a program or batch file should be launched upon logging in. If this option is selected, provide the path to the executable or batch file and the startup directory. Click Next.

11. Select an icon to associate with this connection profile and then select a program group in the Start menu where this connection profile will be placed. Click Next.

12. Click Finish.

13. Double-click the connection profile object from within the Client Connection Manager or select it from its location in the Start menu to connect to the terminal server.

Creating a Dial-Up To Private Network Connection Object

To establish a network link with a remote network (a Dial-Up To Private Network connection object is required), perform the following steps:

1. Double-click the Make New Connection icon in the Network And Dial-Up Connections utility. The Network Connection Wizard launches. Click Next.

2. Select the Dial-Up To Private Network radio button. Click Next.

3. Select one or more communication devices for this object by marking their checkboxes.

4. Provide the dial-up phone number to the remote network's RAS server.

5. If this system is a portable computer, select the Use Dialing Rules checkbox and provide the area code and select the country/region code. Click Next.

6. Select whether to allow all users of this computer to use this connection object or restrict access to just your user account. Click Next.

7. Provide a name for this connection object.

8. Select whether to add a shortcut for this connection object to the desktop by marking the appropriate checkbox.

9. Click Finish.

Creating a Dial-Up To The Internet Connection Object

To establish a link to the Internet (a Dial-Up To The Internet connection object is required), perform the following steps:

1. Double-click the Make New Connection icon in the Network And Dial-Up Connections utility. The Network Connection Wizard launches. Click Next.

2. Select the Dial-Up To The Internet radio button. Click Next.

3. Select one of the following options (for this solution, select to Configure The Internet Connection Manually.

   - Create a new Internet account (creates a new MSN account)

   - Transfer an existing Internet account to this computer (transfers an existing MSN account)

   - Configure Internet connection manually or connect through a LAN (allows you to dial any ISP or use LAN Internet access)

4. Click Next.

5. Select whether to create a connection object that uses a modem or the LAN to obtain Internet access.

6. Click Next. If you selected LAN, skip to Step 14.

7. Select the communication device. Click Next.

8. Provide the telephone number for the ISP. Verify the settings for area code and country/region. Click Next.

9. Enter the username and password used to log into the ISP. Click Next.

10. Type in a name for the connection object. Click Next.

11. If you need to configure Outlook Express for Internet email, select Yes. Otherwise, select No. Click Next.

12. If you selected Yes to configure Outlook Express, provide the requested information for profile name, email address, email server addresses, and email server logon credentials. Click Next.

13. Deselect the To Connect To The Internet Immediately, Select This Box Then Click Finish checkbox. Click Finish.

14. By selecting a LAN connection, you must provide the details to obtain Internet access on the LAN. This may be via automatic detection, a configuration script at a URL, a manually configured proxy server, or direct routing (clear all checkboxes). Click Next.

15. If your LAN uses a proxy server, you may be presented with further proxy-specific configuration settings. Usually the defaults are correct. Click Next to continue.

16. If your LAN uses a proxy server, you may be presented with the option to provide addresses that will bypass the proxy when accessed. Configure as necessary and then click Next.

17. If you need to configure Outlook Express for Internet email, select Yes. Otherwise, select No. Click Next.

18. If you selected Yes to configure Outlook Express, provide the requested information for profile name, email address, email server addresses, and email server logon credentials.

19. Click Next.

20. Deselect the To Connect To The Internet Immediately, Select This Box Then Click Finish checkbox.

Creating a Connect To A Private Network Through The Internet Connection Object

To establish a VPN link over the Internet (a Connect To A Private Network Through The Internet connection object is required), perform the following steps:

1. Double-click the Make New Connection icon in the Network And Dial-Up Connections utility. The Network Connection Wizard launches. Click Next.

2. Select the Connect To A Private Network Through The Internet radio button. Click Next.

3. Select whether to dial an Internet connection object. If this option is selected, also select which defined connection object should be used to establish Internet connection before the VPN link is attempted. Click Next.

4. Supply the domain name or IP address of the Windows 2000 or Windows NT RAS server you will establish a VPN connection with over the Internet. Click Next.

5. Select whether this link will be used by all users or just your user account. Click Next.

6. Type in a name for the connection object. Click Finish.

Creating an Accept Incoming Connections Connection Object

To answer inbound calls to your system (an Accept Incoming Connections connection object is required), perform the following steps:

1. Double-click the Make New Connection icon in the Network And Dial-Up Connections utility. The Network Connection Wizard launches. Click Next.

2. Select the Accept Incoming Connections radio button. Click Next.

3. Select one or more devices over which inbound connections will be answered. Click Next.

4. Select whether to allow VPN connections over inbound links. Click Next.

5. Select which users to grant permission to connect to this system via this connection object. Click Next.

6. Alter any bindings and change any network component configurations for this connection object. Click Next.

7. Type in a name for the connection object. Click Finish.

Creating a Connect Directly To Another Computer Connection Object

To establish a direct link to another computer over a serial, parallel, or infrared (IR) port (a Connect Directly To Another Computer connection object is required), perform the following steps:

NOTE: *Two Connect Directly To Another Computer connection objects must be created, one on each computer (that is, one configured as the host and the other configured as the guest).*

1. On the system to serve as the host (server), double-click the Make New Connection icon in the Network And Dial-Up Connections utility. The Network Connection Wizard launches. Click Next.

2. Select the Connect Directly To Another Computer radio button. Click Next.

3. Select the Host radio button. Click Next.

4. Select the device type for the link. Click Next.

5. Select the users to grant permission to use this connection object. Click Next.

6. Type in a name for this connection object. Click Finish.

7. On the system to serve as the guest (client), double-click the Make New Connection icon in the Network And Dial-Up Connections utility. The Network Connection Wizard launches.

8. Click Next.

9. Select the Connect Directly To Another Computer radio button. Click Next.

10. Select the Guest radio button. Click Next.

11. Select the device type for the link (it must be the same as the host's). Click Next.

12. Select the users to grant permission to use this connection object. Click Next.

13. Type in a name for this connection object. Click Finish.

14. In the Connect Direct Connection dialog box, provide your username and password.

15. Click Connect to establish the connection.

Chapter 20

Troubleshooting Windows 2000

In Depth

Even though Windows 2000 is a very robust operating system, problems can and do occur. This chapter takes a look at some of the troubleshooting tools and techniques you can use to restore a system to full working order.

Troubleshooting 101

Before diving into any troubleshooting endeavor, take a moment, step back, breath, and then analyze the problem with a calm mind. Attempting to force a solution or performing operations and alterations hurriedly or with an angry and frustrated disposition will often just cause you more stress without resolving the issue. In many cases, problems occur at the most inopportune times, such as when you are against a deadline, all your users are online, or you are on vacation. If you can take the time to relax and examine the situation, you'll often find your troubleshooting efforts will consume less time than when they are attempted in a less positive mood.

To help you overcome the stress of the situation and obtain satisfactory results, keep the following common-sense rules and procedures about troubleshooting in mind:

- *Try to be patient*—Being rushed, hostile, angry, or frantic will often exacerbate the problem rather than helping you remedy it.

- *Know your system's hardware and software*—Nothing can substitute for thorough and intimate knowledge of your system and network. If you don't know what is normal or how a system is configured, you'll have more difficulty resolving problems.

- *Use a process of elimination to isolate the problem*—Systematically testing and removing from suspicion segments of a system or a network will help locate and isolate the problem.

- *Undo any recent alterations*—In many cases, the most recent change to a system is the cause of the current problem. A common first step is to repeal the last changes. Keep in mind this may include configuration changes, software upgrades, or adding or removing hardware devices.

- *Review previous points of failure*—If you have experienced repeated problems on the same system or network, always double-check those areas where problems occurred before. In many cases, the weak link in your system is acting up again.

- *Attempt the quick fixes first*—Although they're not always the most obvious, in the long run, attempting to resolve the problem with the simplest solutions first will save time. Trying system reboots, replacing cables, and using different user accounts may result in a cheaper, faster, easier resolution than the more involved and tedious solutions such as Registry hacking, software reinstallation, and hardware replacement.

- *One change at a time*—Always only make a single significant alteration to a system at a time. Then reboot (if applicable) and test the alteration. This process may reveal that your resolution is incorrect or that changes are not taking proper effect. This process will also reveal the exact alteration that resolves the issue, an important data item in the event of a future reoccurrence.

- *Cause the failure to reoccur*—In some cases, only repeating the failure and monitoring various aspects of your system with human eyes as well as automated monitoring tools is the only way to locate the exact problem. If you are unable to repeat a failure on demand, you'll need to implement an automated monitoring system to watch for the next occurrence.

- *Maintain a problem and solution log*—Documenting the process of troubleshooting can provide invaluable information for resolving future issues. Keep track of what the problem was, its symptoms, the attempted solutions that failed, and the solution that succeeded.

Although there's probably very little new to you in this list of basic troubleshooting procedures, it never hurts to review the obvious, especially because you may forget the important basics in a crisis.

Event Viewer

The Event Viewer, shown in Figure 20.1, is used to access the Windows 2000 system logs. There are three default or common logs as well as numerous service- and application-specific logs that may be present in the Event Viewer.

The common Event Viewer logs are:

- *System log*—Records details about hardware and software issues related to Windows 2000 itself and installed drivers

- *Security log*—Records details about security occurrences and audit events

- *Application log*—Records various application-specific details

The logs record event details. An event detail contains information relevant to the event that caused the log record to be created (see Figure 20.2). These details include date, time, source, category, event, user ID, computer name, and some

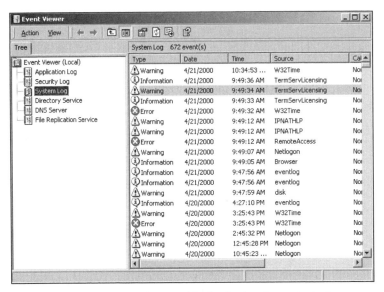

Figure 20.1   The Event Viewer with the System log selected.

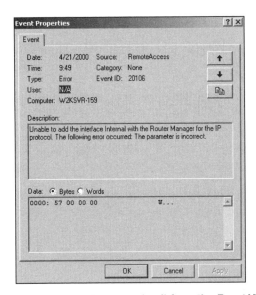

Figure 20.2   An event detail from the Event Viewer's System log.

level of detail about the error, such as an error code number or a detailed description with a memory hexadecimal buffer capture. Through the details captured in a log, you can discover where problems have occurred and often what steps are necessary to resolve them.

Troubleshooting

The following sections explore troubleshooting specific problems that can occur with Windows 2000 Server.

Installation

Windows 2000 is a very robust operating system. This robustness extends even into the installation process. In most cases, with hardware that is Hardware Compatibility List (HCL) compatible, Windows 2000 will install without a hitch. However, even in the perfect world according to Microsoft, problems can and do occur. Generally, installation problems are related to one of the following four issues:

- *Media errors*—These occur either with a damaged distribution CD or when a corrupted or missing file is present in the copied version of the files from the distribution CD. Media errors can also occur between the storage location of the files and the system reading the files due to network link interruptions or damaged hardware. When a media error occurs, you must either change CDs, recopy the material to the distribution point, or use a different pathway to get to the distribution files.

- *Domain controller communications*—When attempting to join a domain or installing a second domain controller, you must be able to communicate with an existing domain controller on the network. Human errors in typing in the name, password, and domain name can cause problems. Also, network communication interruptions can cause problems. Make sure the domain controller is online and that other systems can communicate with it.

- *Hardware/driver problems*—Using the wrong driver or a device not listed on the HCL (**www.microsoft.com/windows2000/upgrade/compat/search/ devices.asp**) can prevent the installation from completing successfully. Both these can cause STOP errors. The only solution is to use the correct driver and replace all non-HCL-compliant devices.

- *Dependency issues*—When one service or driver fails, other services or drivers that depend upon that service or driver can also fail. This is known as a *dependency failure*. If your network interface card (NIC) driver fails, the networking components of Windows 2000 will fail, which will prevent you from communicating with the domain controller. If Windows 2000 boots, check the Event Viewer's System log for details on what element of the system failed. In most cases, the issue will be a bad or corrupted driver or a non-HCL-compliant device. If Windows 2000 will not boot, try to view the %systemroot%\ntbtlog.txt file created using the Enable Boot Logging option of the Advanced Boot Options menu. In fact, during the actual installation, Windows 2000 creates six log files at various stages along the way. All six logs are created within the %systemroot% or %systemroot%\Debug folders (C:\WINNT and C:\WINNT\DEBUG, by default). You can use these six logs to troubleshoot installations.

No matter which of these situations is the actual cause of an installation failure, you must always restart the installation from the beginning after the issue has been resolved. Don't assume that a partially completed installation will function properly.

Booting

When problems occur that cause Windows 2000 to no longer boot properly, you need to use special boot troubleshooting techniques and tools. In many cases, you'll be able to restore a system with minimum effort, but having a full system backup is always an important insurance policy against total catastrophe. Restoring a system to bootable capability can require additional elements or components, such as the following:

- The four setup boot disks for your version of Windows 2000. These disks can be built using the files from the \bootdisk folder on the CD.

- The original Windows 2000 distribution CD and any applied service packs.

- An Emergency Repair Disk (ERD) built via the Backup utility.

- A recent full backup of your entire system.

With these tools, you can attempt to repair the boot problem.

Advanced Startup Options

Your first course of action should be to employ one or more of the advanced startup options. In some cases, just booting into Safe Mode and then rebooting normally will restore a system. To access these alternate boot settings, you must press F8 when the boot menu is displayed before the timer expires (the default setting for the timer is 30 seconds). Fortunately, there's a message that prompts you to press F8 when this menu is displayed so you'll know exactly when to enter the keystroke. The Advanced Options menu that appears due to this keystroke looks like this:

```
OS Loader v5.0
Windows 2000 Advanced Options Menu
Please select an option:
Safe Mode
Safe Mode with Networking
Safe Mode with Command Prompt
```

```
Enable Boot logging
Enable VGA Mode
Last Known Good Configuration
Directory Services Restore Mode (Windows 2000 domain controllers only)
Debugging Mode

Use [up] and [down] to move the highlight to your choice.
Press Enter to chose.
```

The selections in this menu offer the following controls over booting and system activities:

- *Safe Mode*—Boots Windows 2000 using only the required minimal drivers and system files. The components required for networking are not loaded.

- *Safe Mode With Networking*—Boots Windows 2000 using only the required minimal drivers and system files plus the components required for networking. However, the drivers for PC card services are not loaded, so PC card network connections are not enabled.

- *Safe Mode With Command Prompt*—Boots Windows 2000 using only the required minimal drivers and system files. Boots to a text-only command prompt instead of the GUI desktop.

- *Enable Boot Logging*—Turns on the logging process to record the names of loaded drivers and services in the %systemroot%\ntbtlog.txt file.

- *Enable VGA Mode*—Boots Windows 2000 with only standard VGA video drivers and a desktop resolution of 640 by 480 at 256 or 16 colors.

- *Last Known Good Configuration*—Boots Windows 2000 using the Registry configuration stored at the point of the last successful logon.

- *Directory Service Restore Mode*—Boots Windows 2000 and rebuilds or restores the Active Directory. This option is only used on Windows 2000 domain controllers.

- *Debugging Mode*—Boots Windows 2000 and transmits debugging data over the serial port to be captured by a second system. See the *Windows 2000 Server Resource Kit* for more information.

See Chapter 9 for detailed information on the Windows 2000 boot process.

Startup File Repair

If the advanced startup options don't enable your system to boot, you may have problems with the boot files or some of the basic system files. Windows 2000 includes a repair process that can often rebuild or restore these essential files. The process involves the four setup boot floppies.

If neither the advanced startup options or the startup file repair process returns your system to a functioning state, your only remaining options are to restore the system from backup and perform an upgrade or fresh installation.

Printers

Resolving printer problems typically involves one or more of the following actions:

- Verify that all physical aspects of the printer are addressed. This includes parallel cable, power, network connection (if applicable), paper, toner, and so on. Also be sure that the printer is online.
- Verify that a logical printer has been created on the system to act as the print server.
- Verify that the printer is shared with the network (if applicable).
- Verify that a logical printer has been created on the client that connects to the correct network printer share.
- See whether any stalled print jobs are present in the print queue. Delete and resend any stalled jobs.
- Reinstall the printer drivers.
- Test the printer by printing from a different application and a different client.
- Verify that the user has proper permissions to print.
- Stop and restart the spooler service.
- Verify that there is enough free space—usually 100MB is sufficient, but heavier printer loads (i.e., more printing users, larger print jobs, and types of data being printed) will require more. If necessary, change the spooler destination folder (see Figure 20.3).

See Chapter 17 for detailed information on printing in Windows 2000.

Remote Access

Remote access is an area that can experience several problems. Here are some recommended resolution actions that may help eliminate problems:

- Verify that all physical connections are tightly seated and that all cables and connections are undamaged.
- Verify that the communication media (phone line, cable, ISDN, and so on) itself is working properly. This can involve calling your service company.
- Verify that the communication device (that is, modem) is installed properly and that the correct drivers are present. Update the drivers if necessary.
- Verify the settings of the communication device. The settings should match that of the answering system.

20. Troubleshooting Windows 2000

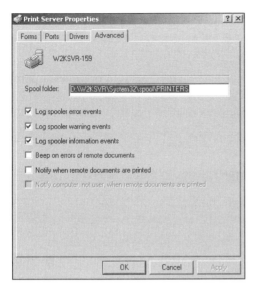

Figure 20.3   The Printer Server Properties dialog box, where the spooler folder is defined.

- Verify that both the client and the server systems are attempting to use the same protocol, connection medium, security settings, and other configurations related to your remote access connection.

- Verify that the user account has dial-out privileges.

- View the contents of the device.log and modemlog.txt file for information on where problems are occurring.

- Verify that you are not attempting to use multilink and callback on the same connection. They are mutually exclusive.

- Verify that a common authentication protocol and encryption level is present on both the server and the client. Mismatched authentication protocols will prevent user logon and system communication.

See Chapter 19 for detailed information on remote access in Windows 2000.

Networking

Network problems are related most often to misconfiguration or damage to the physical connections. Therefore, here are some actions you can take to help eliminate problems:

- Verify that all physical connections are secure.

- Verify that all media cables and connectors are undamaged.

- Ensure that all standalone network devices are powered and online (when applicable).

- Verify the protocol settings on each system. When working with TCP/IP, make sure no IP addresses are repeated, that all subnet masks are appropriate, and that the correct gateway is defined.

- Verify that a common authentication protocol and encryption level is present on both the server and the client. Mismatched authentication protocols will prevent user logon and system communication.

- Verify that the NIC is functioning. Update the driver if necessary. Resolve all hardware conflicts.

- Verify that the user account has proper access to connect to the system and/ or network.

- Verify that all Windows NT/2000 systems have a computer account in the domain.

See Chapter 8 for detailed information on networking Windows 2000.

The Registry

The Registry is the central storage location for all configuration information about the Windows 2000 environment. This hierarchical database should be protected. Unfortunately, it's fairly easy to damage or overwrite portions of the Registry. Nearly every installed application, driver, and service makes a change to the Registry. When you discover the need to edit the Registry, first attempt to locate a Control Panel applet, Administrative Tool, or MMC snap-in that will provide you with a GUI interface to make setting changes. If you must edit the Registry directly, use extreme caution.

The Registry is not an exhaustive collection of the settings that control how Windows 2000 operates. Instead, it is only a collection of exceptions to the defaults. This means that many components of Windows 2000, including drivers, services, and applications, will operate based on their own internally defined default values when an alternate value is not found in the Registry. This makes locating and altering the operation of Windows 2000 very difficult. If you do not know the exact syntax, spelling, location, and valid values required to alter a default behavior, your alterations may result in a DOA system. The *Windows 2000 Server Resource Kit* includes a help file that contains all the native Registry entries and valid values, namely regentry.chm. We highly encourage you to employ this tool when working with the Registry.

The Registry is divided into five keys, as shown in Figure 20.4. Each key has several subdivisions of subkeys, each of which can contain further subkeys and/or value entries. A *value entry* is a named parameter placeholder that contains a value. The value is the setting change that modifies the default behavior of a component. A value entry can contain a single binary digit, a decimal value, a string of ASCII characters, or a hexadecimal number.

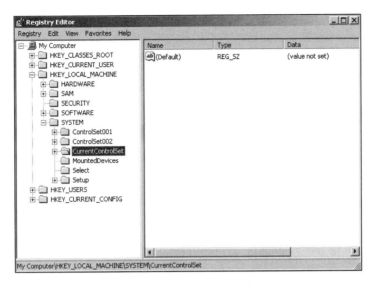

Figure 20.4   REGEDIT showing the five Registry keys.

The five Registry keys are:

- *HKEY_LOCAL_MACHINE*—Contains the value entries specific to the local computer hardware. The contents of this key are not dependant on a user account or any applications, services, or processes in use.

- *HKEY_CLASSES_ROOT*—Contains the value entries that define the relationships between file extensions (that is, file formats) and applications. This key is actually just a redirector to the HKEY_LOCAL_MACHINE\Software\Classes subkey.

- *HKEY_CURRENT_CONFIG*—Contains the value entries used to control the currently active hardware profile. This key is built each time the system boots by duplicating the contents of the HKEY_LOCAL_MACHINE\System\ CurrentControlSet\HardwareProfiles\### subkey relative to the active hardware profile.

- *HKEY_CURRENT_USER*—Contains the value entries specific to the currently logged on user. This key is built each time a user logs on by duplicating the user-specific subkey from the HKEY_USERS key and the ntuser.dat or ntuser.man file from the user's profile.

- *HKEY_USERS*—Contains the value entries for all users who have ever logged onto this system, plus a default user profile for new users who do not already have a user profile.

NOTE: *A sixth key may appear when Windows 95 applications are installed onto a Windows 2000 system. The HKEY_DYN_DATA key acts as a redirector to HKEY_CLASSES_ROOT key, where the data required by the application actually resides under Windows 2000.*

The Registry is stored in files on the hard drive. Each time Windows 2000 boots, these files are loaded into memory. While active, Windows 2000 interacts with only the in-memory version of the Registry. The Registry is saved back to disk when a flush occurs. A flush occurs only when the system is shut down, when an application forces one (such as Backup), or immediately after an alteration.

Chapter 11 provides detailed information about the Windows 20000 Registry.

Value Entries

A value entry is defined by three elements: its name, its data type, and the value or data it contains. The name of a value entry is usually a multiword phrase without spaces and often with intercap or title capitalization—for example, WinLogon and LastLoggedOnUserAccount. The data type specifies how the value is stored. The value or data stored within a value is limited (in length and content) by its value type. The supported value types under Windows 2000 are:

- *REG_BINARY*—Binary format
- *REG_DWORD*—Binary, hex, or decimal format
- *REG_SZ*—Text-string format
- *REG_MULTI_SZ*—Text-string format that contains multiple human-readable values separated by null characters
- *REG_EXPAND_SZ*—Expandable text-string format that contains a variable that's replaced by an application when it is used (for example, %Systemroot%\file.exe)

Once a value entry is created, its data type cannot be changed without deleting and re-creating the value entry.

Registry Storage Files

The files used to store the Registry are located in the %systemroot%\system32\config folder on the boot partition. Only the HKEY_LOCAL_MACHINE and HKEY_USERS keys are actually stored in files because all the others are either copies or redirectors or are rebuilt each time they are needed. The files used to store and protect the integrity of the Registry are shown in Table 20.1.

Registry Editors: REGEDIT and REGEDT32

Two Registry editors are included with Windows 2000. REGEDIT, shown in Figure 20.5, is a 16-bit application that can be used to search the entire Registry at once and to edit/add those portions that the current user has access rights to. REGEDT32, is a 32-bit application that can be used to edit the security of keys and subkeys, search on a key-by-key basis, configure auditing, and enable a read-only mode to prevent accidental changes. Both tools must be manually launched from the **run** command or a command prompt.

Table 20.1   Files used to store the Registry.

Registry Hive	Filenames
HKEY_LOCAL_MACHINE\SAM	Sam, Sam.log, and Sam.sav
HKEY_LOCAL_MACHINE\Security	Security, Security.log, and Security.sav
HKEY_LOCAL_MACHINE\Software	Software, Software.log, and Software.sav
HKEY_LOCAL_MACHINE\System	System, System.alt, System.log, and System.sav
HKEY_USERS\.DEFAULT	Default, Default.log, and Default.sav
HKEY_USERS\<user_SID>	\Documents and Settings\<username>\NTUSER.DAT or NTUSER.MAN
HKEY_CURRENT_USER	Ntuser.dat and Ntuser.dat.log
(Not associated with a hive)	Userdiff and Userdiff.log

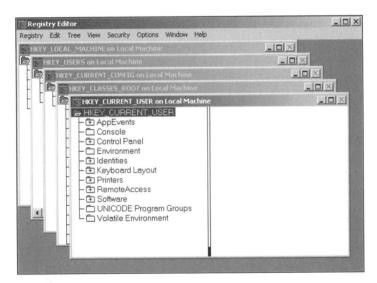

Figure 20.5   REGEDIT.

WARNING!   When using either of these tools to modify the Registry, be sure to perform the following tasks:

- *Back up the system.*
- *Use these tools to create a backup of the Registry.*
- *Reboot the system.*
- *Alter only a single value entry at a time. Test each change before proceeding to the next alteration.*
- *Reboot after all modifications are complete, even if not prompted by the system.*
- *Always test Registry alterations on a nonessential system first.*

Registry Tools from the Windows 2000 Resource Kits

The Windows 2000 Server and Professional Resource Kits include many tools that offer functionality in addition to those offered by REGEDIT and REGEDT32 or those that can be used in command line/batch format. Using these tools effectively will require thorough familiarity with a scripting or batch file system. The Resource Kit itself discusses scripting and batching as well as includes numerous other tools not specific to the Registry that you may want to employ as troubleshooting or administrative shortcuts.

Some of the tools from the Resource Kit that are used on the Registry are:

- *REG.EXE*—A command-line tool used to perform manipulations and alterations within the Registry. It can perform numerous operations, such as adding value entries, changing the value of existing value entries, searching for keywords, copying keys, backing up and restoring keys, and more.

- *REGDUMP.EXE*—A command-line tool used to dump all or part of the Registry to the STDOUT. The resultant output from this tool can be used by the REGINI.EXE tool.

- *REGFIND.EXE*—A command-line tool used to search for items in the Registry using a keyword or a text string.

- *COMPREG.EXE*—A graphical interface tool used to compare two Registry keys. The comparison can occur between local and remote systems. All differences will be highlighted in the display.

- *REGINI.EXE*—A command-line tool used to add keys to the Registry.

- *REGBACK.EXE*—A command-line tool used to back up all or part of the Registry.

- *REGREST.EXE*—A command-line tool used to restore all or part of the Registry from saved key files.

- *SCANREG.EXE*—A graphical interface tool used to search for items in the Registry using a keyword or a text string.

Permissions

When a user is unable to access a resource, you may have permission problems. These can often be resolved through the following tasks:

- Check for multigroup memberships with conflicting permissions.

- Using the same client, access the same resource using an Administrator account.

- Using the same client, access a different resource.
- Using a different client, access the same resource.
- Verify that network connectivity is functioning.
- Verify that the user is authenticated to the domain.
- Check for Deny settings for this user and any group memberships.
- Verify that the resource has permissions granted to the user either directly or via groups.
- After changing group memberships, force the user to log on again so a new access token is generated.

The Recovery Console

The Recovery Console is a tool that grants administrators command-line access to system files when the graphical interface will not boot. This tool often affords a method to restore key driver and system files, replace Registry items, change service startup settings, repair the master boot record (MBR), format drives, copy files, and more. The Recovery Console is documented thoroughly in the Resource Kit, so before delving into this complex tool, be sure to review the documentation.

The Recovery Console can either be launched from the Windows 2000 setup floppies or installed onto the system. To launch the Recovery Console from the setup floppies, select the Recovery Console option when the menu appears. To install the Recovery Console onto your system, execute \i386\winnt32.exe /cmdcons from the Windows 2000 distribution CD. After rebooting, the Recovery Console will now appear as an additional option on the boot menu.

When the Recovery Console is started, you must log on as the administrator for that system. Once logged on, you are presented with a command prompt from which all your troubleshooting and repair activities will occur. For a complete list of the commands supported by the Recovery Console and details on their use, issue the **help** command (see Table 20.1).

Troubleshooting Documentation

Microsoft has several publications that include invaluable troubleshooting documentation you should obtain or have access to. When you are in a crunch, nothing can substitute for knowledge—whether it is already in your head or available at your fingertips. Here are four resources you need:

- *Microsoft's Web site*—An overall useful resource on Microsoft's products with numerous technical documents, how-to's, and white papers (**www.microsoft.com/windows/**).

- *The Knowledge Base*—The online and CD collection of technical documents created by Microsoft's support team. It is available online at **http:// support.microsoft.com/** or offline on the TechNet CD.

- *TechNet*—A monthly subscription service that includes complete documentation and technical resources for all of Microsoft's documentation. It includes all the Resource Kits, numerous utilities and tools unavailable elsewhere, plus CD versions of patches, upgrades, and service packs. For subscription information and online content, visit **www.microsoft.com/technet/**.

- *Resource Kits*—The *Windows 2000 Server Resource Kit* and *Windows 2000 Professional Resource Kit* include wonderful information on subjects such as advanced configuration, administration, and troubleshooting. These kits also include additional documentation not included in the manuals and other tools and utilities you'll find extremely useful. The Resource Kits are available both as a separate product and as part of TechNet.

Immediate Solutions

Creating the Four Setup Boot Floppies

To create a new set of setup boot floppies, perform the following steps:

NOTE: *You must obtain four floppies for this solution. These floppies should be preformatted.*

---

1. Insert the Windows 2000 distribution CD into the CD-ROM drive.

2. From the **run** command or a command prompt, execute the **makeboot** (for 16-bit operating systems) or **makebt32** (for 32-bit operating systems) command from the \bootdisk folder on the distribution CD.

3. Type the letter of the floppy driver (most likely this will be "a").

4. Insert the first floppy and then press any key.

5. Repeat Step 4 for all remaining floppies as prompted.

6. When completed, the disk-building tool will exit. Label each disk clearly as to its number (1/4, 2/4, and so on) and which OS it is used for (for example, Windows 2000 Professional or Windows 2000 Server).

Creating an Emergency Repair Disk

The Emergency Repair Disk is used by the Windows 2000 repair process to restore a system to a functioning state.

NOTE: *This solution requires a blank floppy.*

To build an ERD for a system, perform the following steps:

1. Launch the Backup utility for Windows 2000 by selecting Start|Programs|Accessories|System Tools|Backup.

2. Click the Emergency Repair Disk button.

3. Select the Also Back up the Registry to the Repair Directory checkbox.

4. Insert a floppy into the drive.

5. Click OK.

6. When prompted, remove the floppy, label it as the ERD, and click OK.

7. Close the Backup utility.

Using Startup File Repair

If the essential files on the system partition or key files on the boot partition are damaged or missing, the startup file repair process may return your system to working order. Here are the steps to follow:

NOTE: *This solution requires a set of setup boot floppies for the respective version of Windows 2000. It also requires an ERD for this system.*

1. Place the first boot floppy in the drive of the damaged system.

2. Boot the system from the floppy.

3. Insert each subsequent floppy when prompted.

4. When prompted for a startup option after the fourth disk, press R for Repair to begin the repair process.

5. You'll be prompted whether to repair using the Recovery Console or the Emergency Repair Disk. Press R to select the Emergency Repair Process.

6. Select whether to perform a manual or fast repair. A manual repair requires user response to prompts between repairs; a fast repair suppresses these prompts. Select Fast.

7. When the repair process prompts you, provide the Windows 2000 distribution CD and/or the ERD.

8. Other prompts may appear, depending on the repairs performed and the problems encountered. Respond as necessary to further prompts.

9. Once the repair is complete, your system will be rebooted. Be sure to remove any floppies before the reboot occurs.

Searching the Registry Using REGEDIT

To use the 16-bit Registry editor for searching through the Registry, perform the following steps:

WARNING!   *This solution should be used with caution to prevent accidental changes to the Registry. Always make sure you have a current, reliable backup of the Registry before launching a Registry editor.*

1. Launch the editor by executing **regedit** from the **run** command.

2. Select Edit|Find.

3. Type **DefaultUserName**.

4. Click Find Next.

5. The first element that matches this string will be highlighted. The first occurrence found will typically be AltDefaultUserName, which appears in HKLM\...\Winlogon.

6. Issue the **find next** command from the Edit menu.

7. The next element that matches this string is highlighted.

8. Repeat Step 6 until no more matches are discovered.

9. Close the editor by issuing the **exit** command from the Registry menu.

Saving a Registry Key

To store keys into files, perform the following steps:

1. Launch the editor by executing **regedit** from the **run** command.

2. Select the HKEY_LOCAL_MACHINE key.

3. Issue the Export Registry File command from the Registry menu.

4. Select a destination folder and provide a name for the file.

5. Select the Selected Branch radio button to save only the contents of the selected key.

6. Click Save.

7. Close the editor by issuing the **exit** command from the Registry menu.

Restoring a Registry Key

To restore a damaged portion of the Registry by importing a saved version of a key, perform the following steps:

WARNING!   This solution should be used with caution because the existing Registry will be overwritten with the contents of the saved file.

1. Launch the editor by executing **regedit** from the **run** command.

2. Issue the **Import Registry File** command from the Registry menu.

3. Locate and select the Registry file containing the portion of the Registry you want to restore.

4. Click Open

5. Wait for the "import completed" message and then click OK.

6. Close the editor by issuing the **exit** command from the Registry menu.

Viewing the Security Settings on Registry Keys

To use REGEDT32 to work with Registry key security, perform the following steps:

1. Launch the editor by executing **regedt32** from the **run** command.

2. Select the HKEY_USERS key.

3. Issue the **permissions** command from the Security menu.

4. A message may appear that states that you only have view permissions for this key. If so, click OK.

5. The familiar security dialog box appears. View the settings.

6. Click Cancel.

7. Close the editor by issuing the **exit** command from the Registry menu.

Using the Event Viewer

To use the Event Viewer to view the contents of the log files, perform the following steps:

1. Launch the Event Viewer. It is located in the Start menu under Programs|Administrative Tools|Event Viewer.

2. Select the System log.

3. Double-click an event in the right pane.

4. View the contents of this event detail.

5. Click OK.

6. Select a different log.

7. Open an event detail.

8. Close the event detail by clicking OK.

9. Close the Event Viewer by clicking the X button in the upper-right corner of the title bar.

Booting Windows 2000 into Safe Mode

When a driver or a configuration setting renders your system unusable, booting into Safe Mode may resolve the issue. To boot into Safe Mode, perform the following steps:

1. Power on the system.

2. When the boot menu is displayed, press F8.

3. On the Advanced Options menu, use the up- and down-arrow keys to select Safe Mode.

4. Press Enter.

5. The system will boot into Windows 2000 Safe Mode.

6. Once the system has booted, use the **start|shut down** command to restart the system. This will cause the system to reboot back into normal mode.

Booting Using the Last Known Good Configuration

If you've installed a driver or changed a configuration that causes the system to malfunction or prevent logon, use the Last Known Good Configuration (LKGC) to restore the state of the Registry stored by the system at the last successful logon.

NOTE: *Any changes made to the Registry since the LKGC was saved will be lost with this procedure.*

To boot a system using the Last Known Good Configuration, perform the following steps:

1. Power on the system.

2. When the boot menu is displayed, press F8.

3. On the Advanced Options menu, use the up- and down-arrow keys to select Last Known Good Configuration.

4. Press Enter.

5. The system will boot into Windows 2000 using the LKGC.

Installing the Recovery Console

The Recovery Console can be used to repair damaged systems. Here's how:

NOTE: *The Recovery Console is an advanced tool. Consult the Windows 2000 Server Resource Kit for instructions on using this tool*

---

1. Using the **run** command, launch "winnt32 /cmdcons" from the Windows 2000 distribution CD.

2. When prompted, click Yes to install the Recovery Console.

3. When the "Finished" message appears, click OK.

4. Restart the system using the **shut down** command from the Start menu.

5. When the boot menu appears, select Windows 2000 Recovery Console and press Enter.

6. Type in the number of the operating system from the provided list; then press Enter.

7. Provide the administrative account password and press Enter.

8. Type "help" and press Enter to see a list of commands.

9. Type "exit" to reboot the system into normal mode.

Appendix A

Windows 2000 Resources

Many excellent resources are available for Windows 2000 on the Internet. This appendix lists some of the most popular ones. This list, however, is nowhere near complete:

- WinFiles.com Shareware: **www.winfiles.com**. This site provides a great collection of Windows-based drivers, utilities, and fixes.

- Ask the Experts: **www.allexperts.com**. Allexperts allows for the exchange of questions and answers between people. This is a great place to post those hard to find an answer for questions.

- BHS Software: **www.bhs.com**. This is a good Windows NT/2000 resource center. Lists many FAQs, as well as downloads and tech support.

- C|Net's Download.com: **www.download.com**. This is one of the best places on the Internet to find and download demo versions of different software packages. Ratings and prices are usually included.

- C|Net's Shareware.com: **www.shareware.com**. This is a good place to search for and download shareware programs for Windows 2000.

- *ComputerWorld*: **www.computerworld.com**. *ComputerWorld* is one of the most popular magazines available today. The site takes over where the magazine ends with resource centers and job postings.

- *ENT Magazine*: **www.entmag.com**. This is a great place to find the newest Windows NT/2000 news.

- Jim Buyens Web Resources: **www.interlacken.com**. This site has a great Windows NT/2000 resource site.

- L0pht: **www.l0pht.com**. L0pht is a site that lists many of the Windows NT/2000 security holes and how to fix them. It also has tools available to test the security of your network and passwords.

- *Microsoft Certified Professional Magazine*: **www.mcpmag.com**. This is the online version of the popular *Microsoft Certified Professional Magazine*.

- Microsoft MSDN: **msdn.microsoft.com**. This site is the Microsoft Developer Network online. It has full search capability on the Web and links to demo code and applications.

- Microsoft TechNet: **www.microsoft.com/technet**. This is the online version of TechNet, and is usually more up to date than the TechNet CD-ROMS.

- Microsoft's Windows 2000 Portal: **www.microsoft.com/windows2000**. This is the main Microsoft Windows 2000 site. It contains all released security fixes, hot fixes, and service packs.

- Net Admin Tools: **www.netadmintools.com**. This site contains a very comprehensive list of Windows NT/2000 admin tools. It also has a "Tricks of the Trade" section.

- Netmation's Index of Windows Resources: **www.netmation.com/listnt.htm**. This site contains a huge list of Windows NT/2000-based links. This is a good starting place when looking for Windows resources.

- NT Bugtraq: **www.ntbugtraq.com**. This site maintains a complete list of Windows NT/2000 security holes and bugs. The fixes are usually listed as well.

- *NT Explorer Magazine*: **www.explorermag.com**. This is an online Windows 2000 magazine created by the folks at *Windows 2000 Magazine*. Included are news stories, product reviews, and certification information.

- NTSecrets.com: **www.ntsecrets.com**. This site provides a good list of Windows NT/2000 secrets that an administrator should use on a daily basis.

- PC Webopedia: **www.pcwebopedia.com**. This is an online dictionary for computer terms. Not only are most terms defined, links to more complete definitions are usually included.

- *PCWatch*: **www.pcwatch.com**. This is another online news magazine. This one focuses on the entire PC market, not just Windows NT.

- Slaughterhouse Download: **www.slaughterhouse.com**. Don't let the name fool you, this is a great site for downloading utilities and applications for Windows 2000.

- Sunbelt Software: **www.sunbelt-software.com**. This is a leading software reseller of some of the most powerful software packages for Windows NT/2000.

- System Internals: **www.sysinternals.com**. This is the freeware version of **www.winternals.com**. It contains Windows NT/2000 utilities that should be in every administrator's tool kit.

- TechWeb: **www.techweb.com**. Check out the IT Tech Centers for information on anything from security to careers and training to system management.

- Tek Tips: **www.tek-tips.com**. This site contains a long list of discussion forums. It is a great place to find information on the latest hardware and software and what experiences other admins have had with them.

- TISC: **tisc.corecom.com**. The Internet Security Conference's site deals with all flavors of Internet security. A must for anyone concerned about securing their networks from the Internet (read: everyone).

- Tucows Download: **www.tucows.com**. This is one of the largest download sites on the Internet with hundreds of mirror sites located all over the world.

- Windows 2000 Hot Fixes and Service Packs: **ftp.microsoft.com/bussys/ winnt-public/fixes/usa**. This is the place to find the latest hot fixes and service packs for Windows NT

- *Windows 2000 Magazine*: **www.win2000mag.com**. This is the online version of the popular *Windows 2000 Magazine* (formerly *Windows NT Magazine*). Many of the articles are available online in a searchable format.

- Windows Fax FAQ: **www.ntfaxfaq.com**. Looking for a Windows 2000 fax solution? This is the site for you. Many of the major fax solution products are showcased and evaluated.

- Windows Internals: **www.winternals.com**. This is the retail side of **www.sysinternals.com**. Once the demo runs out, purchase the full version here.

- Windows NT FAQ: **www.Windows2000faq.com**. This is the place to find answers to your Windows 2000 questions.

- Windows NT Links: **www.windows2000security.com**. This is a great site for securing Windows 2000. The site reviews some of the security products available for Windows 2000.

- Windows NT Resource Page: **www.chancellor.com/ntmain.html**. This is an excellent collection of Windows NT/2000 resources.

- Windows NT Tips: **www.chami.com/tips/windows**. This site contains a long list of Windows NT/2000 tips that every administrator should know.

- WinPlanet: **www.winplanet.com**. This is a Windows NT/2000 site that offers discussions, opinions, reviews, tutorials, and downloads.

Appendix B

CD Contents

Utilities and applications that have passed the criteria to be certified for Windows 2000 operating systems deliver advanced features by utilizing the improvements in reliability and manageability in Windows 2000. You can be sure you have well-behaved applications that require less administration and cause less downtime.

Certified Windows 2000 Applications

To be certified, applications must comply with the Application Specification for Windows 2000. The Application Specification for Windows 2000 was put together by Microsoft in cooperation with customers and third-party developers. The idea is to provide clear, concise guidelines to help developers create reliable and manageable applications. The specification for Windows 2000 has two flavors: a core spec for desktop applications and a more comprehensive one for distributed applications.

Certified applications for Windows 2000 Professional must:

- Provide a robust, self-repairing installation that helps minimize dynamic link library (DLL) conflicts
- Have improved software deployment and management
- Maintain user settings, enabling roaming users and multiple users per machine
- Run in a secure Windows environment
- Use OnNow device power management for mobile computing
- Provide a consistent user experience and support accessibility standards to reduce support and training costs
- Have the ability to upgrade from previous versions of Windows $9x$ to Windows 2000 Professional

Certified applications for Windows 2000 Server must provide the same benefits of a desktop (client) application, plus:

- Support a globally available management infrastructure using Active Directory services

- Provide secure access to system-wide resources and security, such as Single Sign-On (SSO) for user and administrator interactions

- Improve management of power transitions, including pending shutdown scenarios when running on battery backup

- Reduce service downtime caused by system failures or planned server maintenance and upgrades by exploiting cluster services (for applications that comply with Windows 2000 Advanced Server requirements)

What Are the Benefits of Using Windows 2000 Certified Applications?

Certified applications provide the following features:

- *Better application performance*—Certified applications are designed to be more reliable and available, virtually eliminating reboots and providing superior speed and performance.

- *Roaming and multiple-user support*—Certified applications separate the settings for user and machine for roaming and multiple-user experiences. This becomes more important for environments in which your users may roam, environments in which many users share machines, or situations in which a single user logs on to several different machines. Windows 2000 certified applications allow your users to be more productive by sharing multiple machines and by providing access to shared resources quickly and easily.

- *Adherence to Group Policy*—Certified applications check and adhere to Group Policy when taking actions that change the desktop makeup. For example, reconfiguring your network settings can be controlled by a policy.

- *Integrated security*—Certified applications have security settings that are easy to manage and provide a simplified authentication process. Both clients and services use Windows 2000 integrated security.

- *Easier management*—Certified applications use Active Directory as a data source for (among other things) security, policies, and addresses for machines, users, and other objects. This provides simplified user and computer settings and higher automation of system administration tasks so that time spent on configuring and managing systems will be reduced.

- *Clean installation and uninstallation*—Certified applications install in a simple and predictable fashion, without damaging any of your existing desktop configurations.

By using certified applications, you can maximize your Windows 2000 investment (and save time) by taking advantage of Windows 2000 technologies such as the Windows Installer, IntelliMirror management technologies, and Active Directory.

For more information on the continuing list of applications that are certified, consult these sites:

- **www.veritest.com/mslogos/windows2000/certification/**
- **www.microsoft.com/windows2000/guide/server/solutions/certified.asp**

What's on the CD?

The following Windows 2000 utilities are included on the CD that accompanies this book.

AutoProf.com's Profile Maker V4.0

Profile Maker is a network administration utility for automating the configuration of Windows applications and includes support for messaging applications. Profile Maker can configure all computers and users on a network with no workstation setup required. It can help control messaging client migrations, rollouts services, and walk-up and login profile configurations. For more information, visit **www.autoprof.com**.

Executive Software's Diskeeper 5.0 Server

Diskeeper is a disk defragmenter utility that defragments files on FAT, FAT32, and NTFS volumes. It can be run interactively or can be scheduled to run at regularly scheduled times. The user can configure Diskeeper to run at lower CPU priorities and to exclude certain files and folders from defragmentation, among other things. Diskeeper Server allows the user to connect to remote computers (that already have Diskeeper installed) and perform online defragmentation and configuration. For more information, visit **www.execsoft.com**.

Executive Software's Undelete Server V2.0

Undelete is a unique file-recovery solution for Windows NT and Windows 2000. Undelete allows you to recover files that have been deleted—even after you've really deleted them by emptying your Recycle Bin or have deleted them from Windows Explorer or other applications or even from the Windows command prompt. For more information, visit **www.execsoft.com**.

Sunbelt Software's UltraAdmin V2.0

As a network administrator, you often have to shift between multiple utilities and learn difficult user interfaces to get the job done. Soon you'll be migrating to

Windows 2000, whose many new features only compound those problems. UltraAdmin is a centralized domain-administration tool that remains fully interoperable as you manage both NT4 and Windows 2000 computers, user, and groups. For more information, visit **www.sunbelt-software.com**.

Sunbelt Software's UltraBac V5.5

UltraBac is able to perform live backups of open databases with optional agents for SQL and Exchange. UltraBac's unique features include backup to disk or tape, backup of open shared files, SMTP messaging, and the fastest Windows NT backup available—up to 19GB per hour. For more information, visit **www.sunbelt-software.com**.

Sunbelt Software's DirectoryAnalyzer V1.04

You can't afford to take chances with Active Directory. You need to proactively manage the availability and performance of your directory with the only tool built specifically for that purpose: DirectoryAnalyzer, manufactured by NetPro Computing, Inc. and distributed by Sunbelt Software. Active Directory is logically distributed across your network, and it can only be managed with a tool that sees the service as a whole, not just one server at a time. For more information, visit **www.sunbelt-software.com**.

TIDAL Software's Sys*Admiral V2.3

This tool is an enterprise job-scheduling and workload-management solution designed to manage complex, dynamic, and geographically dispersed organizations. It can control a complex mix of batch jobs and other repetitive tasks across heterogeneous networks. For more information, visit **www.tidalsoft.com**.

Trend Micro's PC-cillin 2000

PC-cillin 2000 provides antivirus features for Windows 2000. For more information, visit **www.trend.com**.

VERITAS Software Corp.'s Backup Exec 8.0 (SL)

Backup Exec 8.0 provides 100-percent compatibility for the total Windows NT and Windows 2000 environments while offering reliable backup and recovery of Windows 2000 Active Directory, Distributed File System, and the System State components. For more information, visit **www.veritas.com**.

Appendix B:
CD Contents

Glossary

Active Directory—A centralized resource and security management, administration, and control mechanism in Windows 2000 that is used to support and maintain a Windows 2000 domain. The Active Directory is hosted by domain controllers.

Active Directory Domains And Trusts—A Windows 2000 utility used to create and manage domains and trusts. This includes operations such as setting the domain name's operation manager, changing a domain's mode, creating trusts between domains, and defining a managing user account.

Active Directory Sites And Services—A Windows 2000 utility used to configure server settings, site settings, and replication.

Active Directory Users And Computers—A Windows 2000 utility used to create and manage users, groups, and computers within a domain.

answer file—A file that contains a complete set of instructions for installing Windows 2000 without sitting at the keyboard to answer queries from the setup program.

Application log—Records various application-specific details.

AT (*automated task*)—A utility that provides a way of programming an operating system to perform management functions automatically.

auditing—The process of recording the occurrence of a defined event or action.

baseline—A measurement of normal system operation.

basic disks—Standard hard disks.

boot.ini—The text file that tells a computer how to load an operating system and creates the Windows 2000 boot loader's menu.

cluster—A group of Windows 2000 computers that act as a single server.

Component Services—The renamed Microsoft Transaction Server, Component Services are used to deploy and control COM+, automate tasks using scripting or programming languages, manage transactions between processes, and create scalable component-based applications.

compression—The process of compacting data to save disk space.

Computer Management—A Windows 2000 utility that offers single-interface access to several commonly used local computer-management utilities, such as Event Viewer, Disk Management, and the Services applet.

Control Panel—A collection of tools, called *applets*, within Windows 2000, where most system and hardware configuration takes place.

Counter list—A Resource Kit utility that outputs a list of all the counters installed on a system to a file. This data can be very useful in ensuring that specified logs run on all systems in the network by comparing the counters installed on those systems.

CryptoAPI version 2—An application programming interface that enables applications to encrypt or digitally sign data.

CScript—A command-line scripting engine that comes with Windows 2000.

Data Link Control (DLC)—A low-level network protocol designed for IBM connectivity, remote booting, and network printing.

Data Sources (ODBC)—A Windows 2000 utility used to define DSNs (Data Source Names) employed by applications and services to access database management systems in the domain.

defragmentation—The process of reorganizing files so they are stored contiguously on the hard drive.

delegation—A new feature in Windows 2000 that enables an administrator to specifically assign certain administrative tasks to another user or group.

Device Manager—A Windows 2000 administrative tool used to install, configure, and manage hardware devices.

Disk Cleanup—A tool used to regain access to hard drive space through deleting temporary, orphaned, or downloaded files, emptying the Recycle Bin, compressing little-used files, and condensing index catalog files.

distinguished name (DN)—A unique name that identifies an object and its location on a network.

Glossary

domain controller (DC)—A computer that maintains a Windows 2000 domain's Active Directory, which stores all information and relationships about users, groups, policies, computers, and resources.

Domain Name Service (DNS)—A naming system used to locate resources on a TCP/IP-based network.

Domain Security Policy—A Windows 2000 utility used to configure and define the security policy for a domain.

domains—The main structure of Active Directory. By placing objects within one or more domains in an organization, you can duplicate the organization's physical structure.

driver signing—All drivers from Microsoft and approved vendors are signed. You can configure Windows 2000 to refuse to install any drivers that aren't signed.

dynamic disks—Hard disks that can only house dynamic volumes created through the Disk Management administrative tool. These disks do not include partitions or logical drives, and they cannot be accessed by DOS.

Dynamic DNS—Automates the addition and removal of systems in DNS.

Dynamic Host Configuration Protocol (DHCP)—A protocol that automates the dynamic assignment of IP addresses to clients.

Emergency Repair Disk (ERD)—A disk that can be used to repair a failed system. It's created through the Backup utility.

Encrypting File System (EFS)—A file system supported by Windows 2000 that provides encryption of data stored on NTFS volumes.

encryption—A method of scrambling data to protect it from anyone who doesn't have a decryption key.

Event Viewer—Used to view and manage the logs of Windows 2000.

Executive Services—The collection of kernel mode components for operating system management.

Extensible Authentication Protocol (EAP)—A protocol that provides remote user authentication.

fault tolerance—An operating system's capability to guarantee data integrity after a hardware failure.

file allocation table (FAT)—The file system originally introduced with DOS, FAT does not provide file system security features.

Glossary

forest—A collection of one or more trees.

fragmentation—The division of data into two or more parts, where each part is stored in a different location on the hard drive. As the level of fragmentation on a drive increases, disk performance decreases.

Fully Qualified Domain Name (FQDN)—A friendly name, such as microsoft.com, that's linked to an IP address, such as 207.46.130.45.

global catalog—A replica of every domain and object in an Active Directory.

Graphical Device Interface (GDI)—The software component that interacts with the Windows 2000 printing system on behalf of applications.

graphics device drivers—These components manage the graphical rendering of the desktop environment.

Group Policy—An MMC snap-in that manages the appearance of user desktop settings.

Hardware Abstraction Layer (HAL)—A loadable kernel-level DLL (called Hal.dll; stored in the *%systemroot%*\system32 folder on a Windows 2000 computer) that provides the low-level interface to the hardware of the computer on which Windows 2000 is installed.

Hardware Compatibility List (HCL)—A list of hardware devices supported by Windows 2000. A version of the HCL appears on the Windows 2000 Server distribution CD, but the version at **www.microsoft.com/hwtest/hcl/** is updated regularly.

HKEY_CLASSES_ROOT—A Registry key that contains the value entries that define the relationships between file extensions (that is, file formats) and applications. This key is actually just a redirector to the HKEY_LOCAL_MACHINE\ Software\Classes subkey.

HKEY_CURRENT_CONFIG—A Registry key that contains the value entries used to control the currently active hardware profile. This key is built each time the system boots by duplicating the contents of the HKEY_LOCAL_MACHINE\ System\CurrentControlSet\HardwareProfiles\### subkey relative to the active hardware profile.

HKEY_CURRENT_USER—A Registry key that contains the value entries specific to the currently logged on user. This key is built each time a user logs on by duplicating the user-specific subkey from the HKEY_USERS key and the ntuser.dat or ntuser.man file from the user's profile.

HKEY_LOCAL_MACHINE—A Registry key that contains the value entries specific to the local computer hardware. The contents of this key are not dependant on a user account or any applications, services, or processes in use.

HKEY_USERS—A Registry key that contains the value entries for all users who have ever logged onto this system plus a default user profile for new users that do not already have a user profile.

hot fixes—Software releases that are used to fix any major bugs or security holes in an operating system.

I/O Manager—A Windows 2000 software component that manages all I/O channels, including file systems and devices.

IntelliMirror—A network desktop-management system that allows administrators to retain control over systems not permanently connected to the network. Each time a portable computer logs back onto the network, the domain's Group Policies are reinforced, software is added or removed, and user data files are updated.

Internet connection sharing—Built into Windows 2000's routing support is a basic proxy server. This tool can be used to grant Internet access to a small network without requiring additional hardware or applications. Plus, the network clients are automatically configured to use the shared connection.

Internet Information Services (IIS) 5.0—The latest generation of Microsoft Internet Information Server, version 5, is included with Windows 2000. IIS offers a solid platform for building personal Web pages through true distributed, dynamic e-commerce Web sites. IIS integrates with the Windows 2000 system, seamlessly granting Web administrators access to networked resources, security, and management controls.

Internet Protocol Security (IPSec)—A secure, industry-standard implementation of the popular TCP/IP protocol.

Internet Services Manager—A Windows 2000 utility used to manage Internet information services, such as Web and FTP.

Internetwork Packet Exchange/Sequenced Packet Exchange (IPX/SPX)—The protocol used on Novel NetWare networks.

IPC (Interprocess Communication) Manager—A Windows 2000 software component that manages all transactions between server and client processes, both within the local computer and with remote computers.

Kerberos version 5—An encryption-authentication protocol employed by Windows 2000 to verify the identity of a server and a client before data is transferred.

Glossary

Glossary

kernel mode—The level of Windows 2000 where objects can only be manipulated by a thread directly from an application subsystem.

Key Distribution Center (KDC)—A Kerberos service that issues ticket-granting tickets and service tickets for domain authentication.

Layer 2 Tunneling Protocol (L2TP)—A protocol that creates a secure connection, relying on other encryption methods (such as IPSec) for communication.

lease—A measurement of time that an IP addressed assigned by DHCP is assigned to a client.

Licensing—A Windows 2000 utility used to configure and manage the license settings for Windows 2000 and installed applications.

Lightweight Directory Access Protocol (LDAP)—An access protocol for Active Directory protocol.

Local Security Policy—The Windows 2000 control mechanism used to configure and define the security policy for a local system, including password restrictions, account lockout, auditing, user rights, security options, public keys, and IP security.

logical printer—The software component that provides print services in Windows 2000.

Master Boot Record (MBR)—The first sector on a disk that contains executable code and a partition table, which stores information about the disk's primary and extended partitions.

Media Access Control (MAC) address—A unique address assigned to a network interface card.

Memory Manager—A Windows 2000 software component that manages virtual memory.

Microsoft Challenge Handshake Authentication Protocol Version 2 (MS-CHAP v2)—An authentication protocol developed by Microsoft for remote user authentication via remote access or dial-up connections.

Microsoft Management Console (MMC)—A new standardized Web-capable management interface. Most of the Windows 2000 administration tasks are accessible through an MMC snap-in.

mixed mode—A domain setting that enables communication between Active Directory and Windows NT domain controllers.

mount point—A directory on an NTFS volume that's used as an access point to a volume that does not have an assigned drive letter.

MS-DOS subsystem—An environmental subsystem provided to support DOS applications.

multicast scopes—A range of IP addresses that can be assigned to clients by DHCP.

native mode—A domain setting signifying that all domain controllers on a network are using Active Directory.

NetBIOS Enhanced User Interface (NetBEUI)—A native Microsoft networking protocol that's being phased out with Windows 2000.

NetWare Directory Services (NDS)—A distributed database on NetWare servers that maintains network resource information.

Network Address Translation (NAT)—An Internet standard that enables a local area network (LAN) to use one set of IP addresses for internal traffic and a second set of addresses for external traffic.

Network Monitor—A Windows 2000 utility used to view and troubleshoot data packets.

New Technology File System (NTFS)—The preferred file system of Windows 2000. It supports file-level security, encryption, compression, auditing, and more.

NWLink—The Microsoft implementation of IPX/SPX.

Object Manager—This component manages all resource objects within the system.

Offline Files—A Windows 2000 feature that allows mobile Windows 2000 users to access copies of shared files and folders even when they are not connected to the network.

Open Shortest Path First (OSPF)—A routing protocol that propagates routing information.

organizational unit—A container that's used to organize objects into logical administration groups. Organizational units can contain objects such as users, groups, printers, computers, applications, file shares, and even other organizational units.

OS/2 subsystem—An environmental subsystem provided to support OS/2 character-mode applications.

paging file—A file, called pagefile.sys, used by the Virtual Memory Manager as a temporary storage container for inactive memory pages.

Password Authentication Protocol (PAP)—A connection-negotiation protocol that passes authentication information in clear text, which is not very secure.

PDC emulator—A Windows 2000 domain controller that acts as though it were an NT Server to systems that do not support Active Directory.

Plug and Play—A technology that allows an operating system to recognize a device, install the correct driver, and enable the device automatically.

Plug and Play Manager—This component manages all Plug and Play-compliant devices and their associated drivers.

Point-to-Point Tunneling Protocol (PPTP)—A protocol used in virtual private networking that allows remote users to access a network over the Internet securely.

POSIX.1 subsystem—An environmental subsystem provided to support POSIX.1 text-only applications.

Power Manager—This component manages the power-conservation capabilities of Windows 2000.

Print Monitor—The printing component that manages printers and print jobs on the server as well as print job scheduling and priority.

Process Manager—This component manages the creation, disassembling, and maintenance of processes.

Public Key Infrastructure (PKI)—The settings involved in the management of digital certificates and public and private cryptography keys.

quotas—An assignment in Windows 2000 that limits the amount of disk space available to individual users.

Recovery Console—A command-line control system used in system recovery in the event of a failure of a core system component or driver. Through the Recovery Console, simple commands can be used to restore the operating system to a functional state.

Redundant Array of Independent Disks (RAID)—A drive configuration of three or more drives in which data is written to all drives in equal amounts to spread the workload. For fault tolerance, parity information is added to the written data to allow for drive failure recovery.

REGEDIT—The Registry-editing program intended for use on 16-bit operating systems.

REGEDT32—The 32-bit Registry-editing program that only works with Windows NT and 2000, it also shows five variable types versus the three in Regedit.

Glossary

Registry—The hierarchical database that stores the majority of Windows 2000 system information.

Remote Installation Services—A service that allows for clients to be easily installed across the network by booting from a preboot execution environment (PXE) ROM (read-only memory) NIC(network interface card) or a boot floppy. The installation routine can be fully automated once the destination computer is turned on, or a full or partial user interaction-required installation can be customized.

reverse lookup zone—A query process in which the IP address of a computer is translated to its DNS name.

RIPrep—A type of installation used with remote OS installation where an administrator can take an entire image of one Windows 2000 Professional machine and install that image onto other workstations.

ScanDisk—A native tool used to discover and correct problems on hard drives. Both physical and logical errors can be detected by ScanDisk.

schema—The objects and classes, and their attributes, in Active Directory.

scopes—The range of IP addresses that can be leased to clients by DHCP.

Security Accounts Manager (SAM)—A Windows 2000 service that maintains user account information.

security identifier (SID)—The unique identification number assigned to Windows 2000 client computers.

Security log—Records details about security occurrences and audit events.

Security Reference Monitor—A Windows component that manages the security services, including authentication, resource access, and group memberships.

service packs (SPs)—A collection of hot fixes and add-ons to fix bugs in an operating system.

slipstreaming—A new way of applying service packs. Slipstreaming ensures that updated files will be used so that service packs need only be applied once.

snap-ins—The consoles that can be added to the Microsoft Management Console to manage Windows 2000 features.

Spooler Service—The service responsible for passing a print job to the print monitor.

superscopes—A feature that allows DHCP to use separate scopes of IP addresses for client assignment.

SYSDIFF—The Windows 2000 utility used to take a snapshot of a basic installation and, after changes have been made, record the changes and then apply them to another installation.

SYSPREP—A tool used to duplicate an entire hard drive. This tool is useful when installing Windows 2000 onto multiple identical systems that require identical configurations.

System log—Records details about hardware and software issues related to Windows 2000 itself and installed drivers.

Task Scheduler—A Windows 2000 component that automates the execution or launch of programs and batch files based on time and system conditions.

Terminal Services—Windows 2000 includes native Terminal Services (previously available to Windows NT only as an add-on), which allows thin clients to be employed as network clients. Terminal Services grants remote access to applications and offers limitation controls over application access.

Time-to-Live—The amount of time that a packet is held before being discarded.

Trace Dump—A Resource Kit utility that gathers information in a trace log file (or a realtime trace) and outputs it into a CSV file. A CSV file then allows for the data to be imported into an Excel spreadsheet and manipulated.

Trace Log—A Resource Kit utility that allows an administrator to start, stop, or enable trace logs from the command prompt. This allows for trace logs to be included in startup or login scripts.

Transmission Control Protocol/Internet Protocol (TCP/IP)—The most popular protocol suite in use today, TCP/IP was originally based on the network protocols developed by the Department of Defense. TCP/IP is the protocol used on the Internet.

unattended installation—A Windows 2000 installation that uses a previously made script to install the OS without user interaction.

uniqueness database file (UDF)—A text file that contains a partial set of instructions for installing Windows 2000 to specify settings for individual users. Used to supplement an answer file when only minor changes are needed that don't require a new answer file.

tree—A collection or group of one or more Windows 2000 domains.

virtual memory—A Windows 2000 service that stores memory pages not currently in use by the system. This frees up memory for other uses. Virtual memory also hides the swapping of memory from applications and higher-level services.

virtual private network (VPN)—An extension of a network that can be accessed securely through a public network, such as the Internet.

Web-Based Enterprise Management (WBEM)—This Distributed Management Task Force (DMTF) initiative, included in Windows 2000 via Windows Management Instrumentation (WMI), grants you the ability to remotely manage, configure, and control nearly every aspect of your systems and networks—from software to hardware.

Win16 subsystem—An environmental subsystem designed to support Windows 3.x, Windows for Workgroups 3.11, and Win16 Windows 95 applications in a simulated Windows 3.x environment.

Win32 subsystem—An environment subsystem required by Windows 2000. Win32 supports many essential functions, including maintaining the user's desktop environment and providing a standard interface for graphical and user device I/O.

Window Manager—This component manages the input (mouse and keyboard) and display of windowing and dialog boxes.

Windows 2000 Backup—The built-in backup program in Windows 2000.

Windows 2000 Executive—The collection high-level system services in Windows 2000.

Windows file protection—An automated protection measure that prevents in-use system files, such as SYS, DDL, OCX, TTF, and EXE files, from being overwritten by other programs or installation routines.

Windows Internet Naming Service (WINS)—A service that maps IP addresses to NetBIOS computer names used by Microsoft operating systems other than Windows 2000.

Windows Scripting Host (WSH)—Native scripting capabilities of Windows 2000 grant administrators a wider set of automation options. Most tasks can be accomplished through command-line utilities. Using WSH, an administrator can automate many redundant tasks.

Wscript—The 32-bit, Windows-based scripting engine included with Windows 2000.

zone—A subtree of a DNS database.

Index

C

U

Windows® 2000 Titles from Coriolis

Windows® 2000 Server Architecture and Planning, 2E

By Morten Strunge Nielsen
ISBN: 1-57610-607-1
$59.99 U.S. • $89.99 CAN

Discover the latest capabilities of Windows 2000 Server, as well as Professional, and the fine points of the new Active Directory features. In-depth discussions on how to migrate or interoperate Windows 2000 from NT, NetWare, Unix, and various host systems are provided.

Windows® 2000 Systems Programming Black Book

By Al Williams
ISBN: 1-57610-280-7
$49.99 U.S. • $74.99 CAN

Discusses crucial and little-understood aspects of Windows 2000, such as multitasking, threading, alertable timers, APCs, and fibers. Also covers Active Directory Services, Microsoft Message Queue, overlapped I/O, advanced memory management, networking, and security.

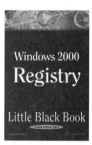

Windows® 2000 Registry Little Black Book

By Nathan Wallace
ISBN: 1-57610-348-X
$24.99 U.S. • $37.99 CAN

Serves as a complete reference for any problem or change needed to Windows 2000 that requires manipulating the Registry. Covers Active Desktop, Asynchronous Transfer Mode, backup, encrypted file system, Internet printing, and more.

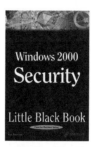

Windows® 2000 Security Little Black Book

By Ian McLean
ISBN: 1-57610-387-0
$24.99 U.S. • $37.99 CAN

Discusses potential security holes in the Windows 2000 system and how to prevent them. Covers desktop security, as well as server security. Emphasizes security issues raised by high-bandwidth connections to the Internet with and without firewalls.

Windows® 2000 Reducing TCO Little Black Book

By Robert E. Simanski
ISBN: 1-57610-315-3
$24.99 U.S. • $37.99 CAN

Teaches how to use each feature of TCO, which will result in reduction of operating costs in any organization. Explains how to detect, gather, and analyze hardware and software inventory remotely. Provides over 250 immediate solutions.

Windows® 2000 Mac Support Little Black Book

By Gene Steinberg and Pieter Paulson
ISBN: 1-57610-388-9
$24.99 U.S. • $37.99 CAN

Focuses on difficult Mac/Windows 2000 and Mac/NT integration issues. Covers migration of Mac systems to Windows 2000, as well as migrating data back from Windows 2000 to Mac. Gives special emphasis to networking addresses.

Black Books. Solutions. Now.™

The Coriolis Group, LLC

Telephone: 480.483.0192 • Toll-free: 800.410.0192 • **www.coriolis.com**

Coriolis books are also available at bookstores and computer stores nationwide.

What's On The CD-ROM

The *Windows 2000 System Administrator's Black Book* companion CD-ROM contains elements specifically selected to enhance the usefulness of this book, including:

- *AutoProf.com's Profile Maker V4.0*—Profile Maker is a network administration utility for automating the configuration of Windows applications and includes support for messaging applications.

- *Executive Software's Diskeeper 5.0 Server*—Diskeeper is a disk defragmenter utility that defragments files on FAT, FAT32, and NTFS volumes. Diskeeper Server allows the user to connect to remote computers (that already have Diskeeper installed) and perform online defragmentation and configuration.

- *Executive Software's Undelete Server V2.0*—Undelete allows you to recover files that have been deleted.

- *Sunbelt Software's UltraAdmin V2.0*—UltraAdmin is a centralized domain-administration tool that remains fully interoperable as you manage both NT4 and Windows 2000 computers, users, and groups.

- *Sunbelt Software's UltraBac V5.5*—UltraBac is able to perform live backups of open databases with optional agents for SQL and Exchange.

- *Sunbelt Software's DirectoryAnalyzer V1.04*—This tool manages Active Directory.

- *TIDAL Software's Sys*Admiral V2.3*—This tool is an enterprise job-scheduling and workload-management solution designed to manage complex, dynamic, and geographically dispersed organizations.

- *Trend Micro's PC-cillin 2000*—PC-cillin 2000 provides antivirus features for Windows 2000.

- *VERITAS Software Corp.'s Backup Exec 8.0 (SL)*—Backup Exec 8.0 provides 100-percent compatibility for the total Windows NT and Windows 2000 environments while offering reliable backup and recovery.

For more information, please see Appendix B of this book.

System Requirements

Software

- Your operating system must be Windows 95, 98, NT4 or higher.

Hardware

- An Intel (or equivalent) Pentium 100MHz processor is the minimum platform required; an Intel (or equivalent) Pentium 133MHz processor is recommended.

- 32MB of RAM is the minimum requirement.

- A color monitor (256 colors) is recommended.